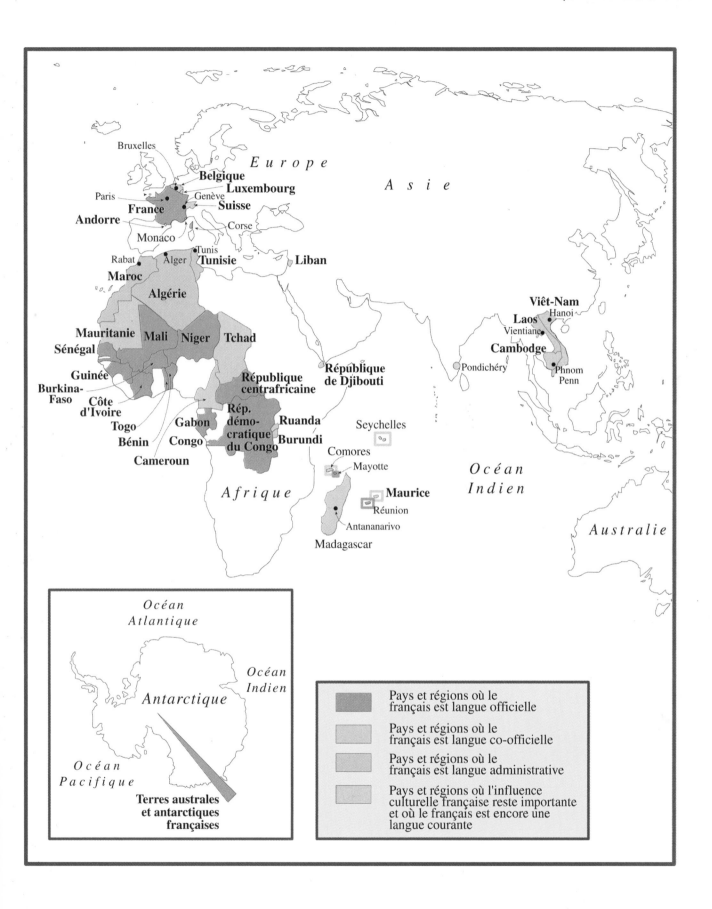

Europe

Asie

Bruxelles

Belgique

Luxembourg

Paris

Genève

France **Suisse**

Andorre

Monaco

Corse

Tunis

Rabat Alger **Tunisie** **Liban**

Maroc

Algérie

Viêt-Nam
Hanoi

Laos
Vientiane

Mauritanie **Mali** **Niger** **Tchad**

Sénégal

Cambodge

Guinée

Burkina-
Faso

Côte
d'Ivoire

Togo

Bénin

Gabon

Cameroun

Congo

Rép.
démo-
cratique
du Congo

République
centrafricaine

Ruanda

Burundi

République
de Djibouti

Pondichéry

Phnom
Penn

Seychelles

Océan
Indien

Comores
Mayotte

Maurice
Réunion

Australie

Afrique

Antananarivo

Madagascar

Océan
Atlantique

Océan
Indien

Antarctique

Océan
Pacifique

Terres australes
et antarctiques
françaises

Pays et régions où le
français est langue officielle

Pays et régions où le
français est langue co-officielle

Pays et régions où le
français est langue administrative

Pays et régions où l'influence
culturelle française reste importante
et où le français est encore une
langue courante

Horizons

SECOND EDITION

Joan H. Manley
University of Texas—El Paso

Stuart Smith
Austin Community College

John T. McMinn
Austin Community College

Marc A. Prévost
Austin Community College

HEINLE & HEINLE
™
THOMSON LEARNING

Australia ♦ Canada ♦ Mexico ♦ Singapore ♦ Spain ♦ United Kingdom ♦ United States

HEINLE & HEINLE

TM

THOMSON LEARNING

Horizons
Second Edition
Instructor's Annotated Edition
Manley ♦ Smith ♦ McMinn ♦ Prévost

Publisher: Wendy Nelson
Senior Production & Developmental Editor Supervisor: Esther Marshall
Developmental Editors: Anne Besco & Lara Semones
Marketing Manager: Jill Garrett
Associate Marketing Manager: Kristen Murphy-LoJacono
Production/Editorial Assistant: Diana Baczynskyj
Production Assistant: Matthew Drapeau
Manufacturing Manager: Marcia Locke
Project Manager: Patricia Menard
Compositor: Clarinda
Text Designer: Sue Gerould, Perspectives
Cover Designer: Diane Lévy
Cover Photo: © Roger Antrobus/CORBIS
Printer: R. R. Donnelley

Printed in the United States of America
1 2 3 4 5 6 7 8 9 10   06 05 04 03 02 01

For more information contact Heinle & Heinle, 25 Thomson Place, Boston, Massachusetts 02210 USA, or you can visit our Internet site at http://www.heinle.com

For permission to use material from this text or product contact us:
Tel   1-800-730-2214
Fax   1-800-730-2215
Web   www.thomsonrights.com

Library of Congress Cataloging-in-Publication Data

Horizons / Joan H. Manley . . . et al.].—2nd ed.
     p. cm.
   Includes index.
   ISBN 0-8384-1370-6 (student ed.)—ISBN 0-8384-1373-0 (instructor's annotated ed.)
     1. French language—Textbooks for foreign speakers—English.   I. Manley, Joan H.

PC2129.E5 H67 2001
448.2′421–dc21
                                                        2001051612

INSTRUCTOR'S GUIDE CONTENTS

Horizons

...offering the flexibility to create the richest possible course for your students

Whether your French class meets three times a week or five, *Horizons* offers you the flexibility to create a rich course for first-year students. *Horizons'* unique modular design makes it easy to navigate through the chapter. Reflecting the guidelines of the National Standards, *Horizons* pairs acquisition of language skills with exploration of French and francophone cultures.

What do your students need… in textbook organization?

Horizons was designed with today's class in mind. Ten main chapters can be comfortably completed in one year. A preliminary chapter moves quickly through basic material, while a final chapter (*Chapitre de révision*) offers rewarding, global review in the context of a mystery story that students solve using the language they have learned.

The well-organized design of *Horizons* makes lesson planning easy and less time-consuming. Chapters are divided into four color-coded *Compétences* presenting grammar, vocabulary, pronunciation, and strategies for listening and reading. Each two-chapter unit is set in a different part of the francophone world (Côte d'Azur; North America—including Quebec and Louisiana; Paris; Normandy; Côte d'Ivoire) to facilitate the integration of culture into the language syllabus.

NEW TO THIS EDITION: *A chapter set in Louisiana exposes students to the rich French culture right here in the U.S.*

Designed to support both experienced and first-time instructors, *Horizons'* unparalleled wealth of instructional annotations facilitates expansion of any topic, theme, or activity that interests you . . . or your students!

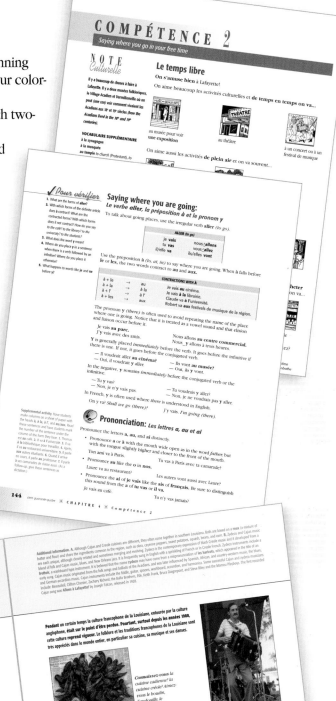

What do your students need…in language presentation?

Whether it is grammar or vocabulary, *Horizons* presents material functionally, in context, and with constant recycling. Active vocabulary is carefully controlled, while marginal annotations provide supplementary words and phrases to encourage students to personalize their vocabulary acquisition. Vocabulary is introduced at the beginning of each of the four *Compétences* per chapter.

Presentation of vocabulary through illustrations encourages students to avoid using English-French translation to learn new vocabulary, while offering an effective learning modality for visual learners.

Grammar is presented through concise charts and clear explanations, and appears in every *Compétence*. Convenient *Pour vérifier* notes act as brief self-checks to build students' confidence and check their comprehension of the most important grammar rules.

All activities engage students in meaningful communication; even the simplest are designed so students must demonstrate an understanding of both form and meaning. The new edition includes even more communicative activities that lead to smoother communication in French.

What do your students need...in listening and speaking?

Your students need input and plenty of opportunities for meaningful practice. Input is provided through the *Text Audio CDs* that accompany the *Horizons* textbook, through the *Lab Audio CDs* that accompany the *Workbook/Lab Manual,* and through the text-specific *Video,* available upon adoption. Students then use the language in a variety of activities and tasks. To sustain conversation, students need to learn strategies, and *Horizons* has an abundance of listening and speaking strategies to help develop more extended discourse.

But what do you need? A communicative classroom is not always an easy classroom to manage, especially for new instructors. *Horizons'* thoughtful instructor annotations can guide you from the warm-up at the start of class through alternative activities involving pairs and groups of students, complete with sample scripts and scene-setting hints.

NEW TO THIS EDITION: *Online Quia Workbook/Lab Manual makes it even easier to develop listening comprehension skills through on-line delivery of audio content linked to specific activities.*

What do your students need...in reading?

Recent research indicates that students benefit from both literary and non-literary selections. From surprisingly in-depth explanations of topics (for example, the history of the Acadians in **Chapitre 4**) to surveys, menus, poetry, and prose, *Horizons* exposes students to written French at an appropriate level and builds their skills through a sequence of reading strategies.

NEW TO THIS EDITION: *A web page from Laval University on Les résidences and lyrics to the song Cœur des Cajuns*

LECTURE ET composition

Note. The vocabulary in this section does not appear in the end-of-chapter vocabulary lists and is meant for recognition only. You may wish to let students know in advance whether you intend to test them on this vocabulary.

Suggestions. Point out: **1.** Since Cajun French was not primarily a written language and was preserved in oral tradition, one sees a variety of spellings for some words. **2.** In Cajun French, using *après* before a verb is the equivalent of **être en train de...** (*to be . . . ing*). For example, *aprévaser = après valser = être en train de valser.*

LECTURE: Cœur des Cajuns

Music is an integral part of life on the bayou. You are going to read the lyrics to the song **Cœur des Cajuns** (*Heart of the Cajuns*) by Bruce Daigrepont, in which he sees Cajun music as the expression of both the **joie de vivre** (*joy of living*) and the **chagrin de cœur** (*heartache*) of the Cajun people. Before reading the lyrics, do this exercise to make your reading easier.

Familles de mots. Servez-vous des mots donnés pour déterminer le sens des mots en caractères gras.

danser: *to dance* → une danse: *a _____*
chanter: *to sing* → une chanson: *a _____*
prier: *to pray* → une prière: *a _____*
valser: *to waltz* → une valse: *a _____*
vivre: *to live* → une vie: *a _____*

CŒUR DES CAJUNS

La joie de vivre, c'est dans l'accordéon,
La joie de vivre, c'est dans les belles chansons.
La musique c'est une tradition
Et c'est dans les cœurs de tous les Cajuns.

Chagrin de cœur, c'est dans l'accordéon,
Chagrin de cœur, c'est dans les belles chansons.
La musique c'est une tradition
Et c'est dans les cœurs de tous les Cajuns.

Dansez ensemble les vieux et les jeunes.
Priez ensemble les vieux et les jeunes.
La tradition c'est **pour tout quelques-uns**
Et c'est dans les cœurs de tous les Cajuns.

Un **'tit** bébé dans **les bras** de sa maman,
Aprévalser dans les bras de sa maman.
Il va apprendre la tradition
Et c'est dans les cœurs de tous les Cajuns.

La joie de vivre, c'est dans l'accordéon,
La joie de vivre, c'est dans les belles chansons.
La musique c'est une tradition
Et c'est dans les cœurs de tous les Cajuns.

Chagrin de cœur, c'est dans l'accordéon,
Chagrin de cœur, c'est dans les belles chansons.
La musique c'est une tradition
Et c'est dans les cœurs de tous les Cajuns.

by Bruce Daigrepont
(Bayou Pon Pon, ASCAP-Happy Valley Music, BMI)
from *Cœur Des Cajuns* on Rounder Records (#6026)

pour tout quelques-uns *for everyone (regional)* **'tit = petit** **les bras** *the arms* **Aprévalser** *Waltzing (regional)*

What do your students need...in culture?

Students increasingly feel themselves part of a global community, and students of French are particularly interested by the many cultures of the French-speaking world. From *Notes culturelles* (the kind of insights that students used to learn only if they traveled abroad) to end of chapter readings, and the provocative *Comparaisons culturelles*, *Horizons* goes far beyond the simple culture factoid. *Horizons'* web site offers up-to-the-minute cultural activities based on authentic web sites.

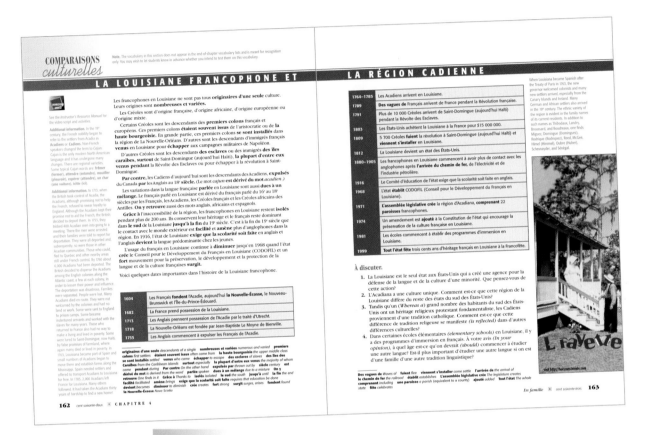

NEW TO THIS EDITION: *Embedded culture—Horizons incorporates culture into activities.*

What do your students need...in pronunciation?

Research indicates that pronunciation instruction divorced from content is frustrating for students. *Horizons* integrates pronunciation into the explanation of structures. For example, the vowel sounds of **a**, **au**, and **ai** are taught in the context of studying the present tense of the verb **aller** and the forms of the preposition **à**.

What do your students need...in writing instruction?

Horizons offers writing development that emphasizes both the "process" and the "product". Every chapter ends with an integrative *Lecture et composition* that helps students learn new composition modes. In addition, each of the four *Compétences* sections of the Workbook ends with a *Journal* entry where students use what they learned to communicate in French. Each writing task is broken down into clear steps that encourage students to exploit the French they have learned, rather than depend on a English-French dictionary to translate their thoughts from English. And, all writing activities are correlated to the latest release of *Système-D* Writing Assistant for French.

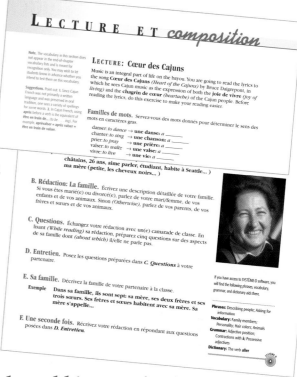

What do your students need...in real-world integration?

Profiles of real people who have studied French and put it to rewarding use in their personal lives and careers are a feature of *Horizons*. *Branchez-vous sur le français* occurs after every other chapter and includes interviews with a wide range of people who have put their French to real use.

What do your students need…in new technology?

The authors of *Horizons* don't believe in "technology for technology's sake." Rather, the technology developed for *Horizons* second edition is both varied and unique in the exposure it offers to French and francophone culture and language:

● *Quia Online Workbook/Lab Manual:* Offering the convenience of an on-line gradebook for instructors and the instant feedback of an interactive environment for students, the *Quia Online Workbook/Lab Manual* contains all the activities from the print *Workbook/Lab Manual*. It also has all the audio from the *Lab Audio CDs* embedded in the program, so that students can easily access particular audio tracks and do the activities that accompany them.

COMPÉTENCE 3   *Asking about someone's day*

A. Prononciation: Les lettres *qu*. Pause the recording and review the *Prononciation* section on page 80 of the textbook. Then turn on the recording and repeat these questions after the speaker. When you have finished, turn off the recording and match the questions to their logical responses by writing the number of the question in the blank next to the corresponding answer.

À l'université.

1. Est-ce que tu travailles?

2. Où

3. Qua

4. Ave

5. Qu'

6. Pou

B. C'e est-ce

Exempl

1. tou

2. ave

3. un

4. à la

5. le s

6. tou

7. en

8. en

C. Pro ciatio in the those repeat

1. Vou

2. Yve

Nom _____   Date _____

COMPÉTENCE 4   *Communicating in class*

By the time you write the journal entry at the end of this *Compétence*, you should be able to spell words aloud, follow instructions in class, and ask your professor for clarification.

A. Les instructions en classe. What did the professor say to these students? Write the appropriate phrase from the list in the blank corresponding to the matching illustration.

Allez au tab
Écoutez la c
Répondez à
Écrivez la ré

1.

1. _____
2. _____
3. _____
4. _____

5

5. _____
6. _____
7. _____
8. _____

G. Une conversation. Here is a conversation between two students on the first day of classes. Rewrite it in more formal French, such as between two business associates. You may use any last names you wish.

— Bonjour, je m'appelle Alice. Et toi, tu t'appelles comment?
— Salut! Je suis Alain. Comment ça va?
— Ça va bien. Et toi?
— Ça va assez bien.
— Au revoir! À demain!
— Au revoir!

_____
_____
_____
_____

Journal. Write both roles of a logical conversation in which you do the following. Be sure to use informal greetings.

• greet a classmate from your French class
• introduce yourself and ask his/her name
• ask how he/she is
• answer his/her questions about how you are
• say good-bye

VOUS: _____
L'ÉTUDIANT(E) (*THE STUDENT*): _____
VOUS: _____
L'ÉTUDIANT(E): _____
VOUS: _____
L'ÉTUDIANT(E): _____
VOUS: _____
L'ÉTUDIANT(E): _____

QUIA

- Text-specific web site: The ***Horizons*** web site contains two components for students: carefully-guided culture activities that explore authentic francophone web sites and recycle the themes and locales of the particular chapter; and, new to the second edition, vocabulary and grammar drill exercises linked to each ***Compétence*** in the chapter. This organization makes it easy to assign the web site activities as homework, and results can be e-mailed directly to you.

- Text-specific Video (filmed on location in France, Guadeloupe, and Québec) builds both listening comprehension and cultural awareness.

- *Système-D* Writing Assistant for French develops writing skills and vocabulary.

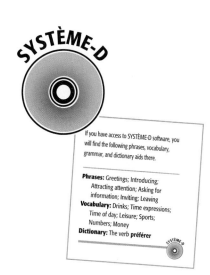

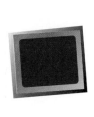

What do you need...in instructor support?

A book that is clearly-organized and easy to teach from would be an important start. *Horizons*' color-coded *Compétences* assure you (and your students) of never getting lost in an endless string of exercises. Varied, creative, and timely instructor annotations support all the activities and content in each chapter. The *Instructor's Resource Manual* provides additional teaching guidance. *Horizons* offers a complete array of ancillaries to facilitate whatever goals you have established for your curriculum.

Horizons... offering the flexibility to create the richest possible course for your students

PREFACE

Horizons **is a complete first-year French program for today's college students. The focus is on communication, skill-building, and culture. A truly innovative approach to culture prepares students for global communication in the 21st century, and process-writing sections and learning strategy annotations enable students to function successfully in French.**

This is the kind of textbook we always wanted to use: a communication-based program with a truly francophone focus that provides a clear presentation of vocabulary, grammar, and pronunciation, along with multiple opportunities for students to function in the language. *Horizons* presents structures students are likely to need in everyday conversations, recycles each one in a variety of contexts, and promotes increased practice of these structures through a variety of listening, speaking, reading, and writing activities. All four skills are actively practiced in realistic communicative situations.

Experience has shown that students must use new structures and vocabulary repeatedly and in a variety of contexts before they learn to control them consistently. Students also have to be willing to participate in communicative activities. To encourage students—and to avoid frustration—presentations must be organized so that students constantly build their communication skills without being asked to perform tasks for which they are not ready. In *Horizons*, material is presented so that it increases students' confidence as their skills develop. New material is first presented in context, followed by recognition activities to familiarize students with it. After the recognition activities, new structures are explained and students work with them in numerous, varied activities. Production activities build from simple exercises where students answer with a word or a phrase, to realistic role plays. All activities create meaningful communication; even the simplest have been designed so that students must understand what they are saying. Listening, speaking, reading, and writing strategies allow students to read authentic texts as well as to perform everyday tasks. Personalized exercises encourage students to express their own thoughts in French.

A unique feature of *Horizons* is its presentation of pronunciation, which is integrated into explanations of structures. For example, the vowel sounds of **le** and **les** are taught with the definite article in the context of distinguishing singular and plural nouns.

Writing *Horizons* gave us the opportunity to achieve our own teaching goals and to resolve issues that still concern most introductory French instructors. With the emergence of the ACTFL National Standards for Foreign Language Learning, we, of course, wanted to be sure our book helped teachers address the "five C's"—communication, culture, comparisons, connections, community—in the classroom. We also wanted to help speak to the problem of declining French enrollments by showing students the practical applications of French in real life. Finally, we wanted a book with ample material for students in classes meeting four or five hours a week, giving them a variety of opportunities to practice their skills in reading, writing, listening, speaking, and cultural awareness, which was also accessible to students in a course that meets three times a week.

The Features

With these thoughts in mind, we have included the following elements in our program.

A modular design. *Horizons* has a clear, easy-to-follow structure. Each new vocabulary and grammar section is laid out across two pages, so that presentation of vocabulary or grammar always appears on the left-hand page and exercises on the right. This format enhances teaching flexibility and enables students to find the new information they need to study more easily. When topics require more practice, a section is expanded to four pages or the topic is recycled across several sections.

A manageable scope and sequence. *Horizons* emphasizes the structures needed for common communication situations. The large number of activities and suggestions in the marginal annotations of the IAE and the *Lecture et composition* and *Comparaisons culturelles* sections provide instructors flexibility in creating a syllabus for a variety of student needs.

Process-writing activities. The *Lecture et composition* section at the end of each chapter contains a series of writing tasks, going from simple to more complex, that guide the students through the writing process as they make notes, exchange compositions with classmates, and finally produce short pieces of written work that can become part of a portfolio.

Activity-based culture sections. Each chapter opens with two pages of photos and information on the francophone region on which the chapter is based. Each ends with a ***Comparaisons culturelles*** section that gives students information about various aspects of francophone culture and encourages them to make cross-cultural comparisons. Shorter ***Notes culturelles*** are interspersed in the margin of the text to catch the student's eye and to provide interesting bits of information.

Internet activities. Supplemental activities related to each chapter's ***Comparaisons culturelles*** prompt students to use French to negotiate authentic materials on the World Wide Web and investigate different aspects of francophone cultures. Self-correcting grammar and vocabulary activities provide students additional practice with the structures in each chapter.

Branchez–vous sur le français. This two-page spread appears every two chapters and consists of interviews with Americans who have used French to realize professional and personal goals, such as studying in another country, conducting business, traveling, and working for an international organization. This section also provides pertinent contact information and shows students that French is a viable and useful tool in the modern world.

Bearing in mind our original goal of emphasizing culture in a communicative setting, *Horizons* also includes:

A focus on the francophone world. Each regional unit (two chapters) of *Horizons* revolves around a story of visitors to a different part of the francophone world (**Côte d'Azur, Québec, Louisiane, Paris, Normandie, Côte-d'Ivoire**). Each chapter opens with a photo exposé of the region with geographical information to set the scene and give students a visual representation of the area. As students follow the characters through the region, they learn about a particular culture: the customs, perspectives, and daily life of the people.

Visual and contextualized presentation of new vocabulary and structures. All new material is presented in context, making learning easier and leading more easily to true communication. Grammar explanations are concise and clear and students are given self-check questions so they can verify their own comprehension of new rules and forms.

Functional dialogues. Dialogues illustrate new structures in context and also supply students with models of how to fulfill certain functions in specific contexts.

Interesting and realistic exercises that progress from recognition to production and from more structured to increasingly open ended. This allows time for acquisition to take place and lowers students' affective filters. All exercises in *Horizons* encourage students to communicate. They are meaningful, so that students use grammar, vocabulary, and pronunciation as the tools of communication, not as ends in themselves.

Explicitly explained and practiced learning strategies. Students develop their reading, writing, listening, and speaking skills more quickly when taught strategies.

Video program. An up-to-date and exciting video made especially for *Horizons* contains footage from Paris, Guadeloupe, and Québec.

Plentiful teacher notes. On-page teacher notes make *Horizons* user-friendly for instructors with varying levels of experience. These notes help teachers create lesson plans, suggest additional activities, and provide further cultural and linguistic information to share with students.

Chapter Structure

Horizons contains ten regular chapters plus a preliminary chapter and a review chapter. A chapter is made up of four ***Compétences,*** each based on a specific language function. The four ***Compétences*** in the preliminary chapter have two vocabulary sections each. This chapter is designed to get students speaking in French as soon as possible and covers basic functions such as greeting people, spelling and counting, and getting acquainted in class. The review chapter is a mystery story. Students work through a series of review exercises to discover "whodunit."

The four ***Compétences*** of the ten principal chapters each contain three parts. The first ***Compétence*** is composed of a vocabulary section followed by one structure section and a ***Lecture/Compréhension auditive*** section, which consists of either pre-reading and reading practice or pre-listening and listening practice. The next two ***Compétences*** each consists of a vocabulary section followed by two structure sections. The last ***Compétence*** is composed of a vocabulary section followed by one structure section and a general review section. ***Lecture et composition*** and ***Comparaisons culturelles*** wrap up each chapter and are followed by the end-of-chapter ***Vocabulaire,*** which contains the active vocabulary from each ***Compétence.*** At the end of each two-chapter regional unit is the ***Branchez-vous sur le français*** feature.

Components of the *Horizons* package

For the Instructor

The *Instructor's Annotated Edition* includes instructor's notes in the margins with creative tips for presenting material, suggestions for supplemental classroom activities, and helpful background information on francophone history, geography, and culture. New instructors will find these an invaluable source of guidance, and experienced instructors will appreciate their excellent quality.

The *Instructor's Resource Manual* is an all-in-one guide that contains detailed lesson planning information, the script for the *Lab Audio CDs,* the *Video Guide* (including a script and classroom activities), and the *Transparency Masters.* Sample lesson plans for courses that meet three, four, and five times per week show instructors how easy it is to use the *Horizons* program to meet the needs of different student groups.

The *Lab Audio CDs* contain the activities for the lab manual. Students will hear the same voices of the recurring characters as in the *Text Audio.*

The *Answer Key* contains answers to the workbook and lab manual activities, so that instructors may provide students with a means of checking their own work.

The *Test Bank on Dual Platform CD-ROM* contains testing material for each chapter. Designed for maximum flexibility, it enables instructors to create customized tests that are appropriate for specific student groups.

The *Horizons Video,* produced especially for *Horizons,* features authentic footage coordinated in theme with each chapter. The accompanying *Video Guide,* found in the *Instructor's Resource Manual,* provides a script and classroom activities.

For the Student

The *Student Text* is colorful and up-to-date, with a user-friendly design that makes it easy for students to find what they need. Ideal for two-semester courses, *Horizons* contains ten basic chapters, plus the preliminary and review chapters. Chapters are divided into clearly marked modules on appealing two-page spreads. Self-check questions in the margins next to grammar explanations guide students during home study.

The *Cahier d'activités écrites et orales* is a workbook/lab manual that contains a wide variety of written and oral activities that guide students from simple to more complex and open-ended tasks. Each **Compétence** of the workbook ends with a journal activity. The lab manual portion includes excellent pronunciation activities and drills, as well as real-life listening tasks. The *Cahier d'activités écrites et orales* is also available in an on-line version.

The *Text CD* includes the **Prononciation** sections of the **Compétences,** listening comprehension tasks for the **Lecture/Compréhension auditive** sections, and all model dialogues in the chapters.

World Wide Web activities augment the *Horizons* program with student activities related to the **Comparaisons culturelles.** Students use the Internet to explore the virtual francophone world and investigate aspects of francophone and American culture related to each chapter's theme. New to the second edition, Web-based grammar and vocabulary activities provide additional practice and allow students to self-correct.

Additional Resources to Enhance the *Horizons* Program

Système-D Writing Assistant for French is a software program that can be used with both the student text and the workbook. It consists of a bilingual dictionary, a phrase bank, and a handy reference grammar.

Parle-moi un peu! This collection of information gap activities for beginning French classes provides instructors with the guidance they want to facilitate fun and meaningful use of the target language in the classroom.

Horizons has been designed to appeal to students with diverse reasons for studying French: practical, intellectual, communicative. In accordance with the ACTFL national standards, *Horizons* will help them make comparisons and connections in the world around them and to understand and communicate with other communities and cultures in our rapidly shrinking world. We hope you enjoy teaching with *Horizons*.

Joan H. Manley, University of Texas—El Paso
Stuart Smith, Austin Community College
John T. McMinn, Austin Community College
Marc Prévost, Austin Community College

Horizons

SECOND EDITION

Joan H. Manley
University of Texas—El Paso

Stuart Smith
Austin Community College

John T. McMinn
Austin Community College

Marc A. Prévost
Austin Community College

HEINLE & HEINLE ™

THOMSON LEARNING

Australia ◆ Canada ◆ Mexico ◆ Singapore ◆ Spain ◆ United Kingdom ◆ United States

Horizons
Second Edition
Manley ♦ Smith ♦ McMinn ♦ Prévost

Publisher: Wendy Nelson
Senior Production & Developmental Editor Supervisor: Esther Marshall
Developmental Editors: Anne Besco & Lara Semones
Marketing Manager: Jill Garrett
Associate Marketing Manager: Kristen Murphy-LoJacono
Production/Editorial Assistant: Diana Baczynskyj
Production Assistant: Matthew Drapeau
Manufacturing Manager: Marcia Locke
Project Manager: Patricia Menard
Compositor: Clarinda
Text Designer: Sue Gerould, Perspectives
Cover Designer: Diane Lévy
Cover Photo: © Roger Antrobus/CORBIS
Printer: R. R. Donnelley

Printed in the United States of America
1 2 3 4 5 6 7 8 9 10   06 05 04 03 02 01

For more information contact Heinle & Heinle, 25 Thomson Place, Boston, Massachusetts 02210 USA, or you can visit our Internet site at http://www.heinle.com

For permission to use material from this text or product contact us:
Tel   1-800-730-2214
Fax   1-800-730-2215
Web   www.thomsonrights.com

Library of Congress Cataloging-in-Publication Data

Horizons / Joan H. Manley . . . et al.].—2nd ed.
        p. cm.
    Includes index.
    ISBN 0-8384-1370-6 (student ed.)—ISBN 0-8384-1373-0 (instructor's annotated ed.)
    1. French language—Textbooks for foreign speakers—English.   I. Manley, Joan H.

    PC2129.E5 H67 2001
    448.2′421–dc21

                                2001051612

DEDICATION

To our parents, our first and our best teachers.

*À nos parents, dont la sagesse et le dévouement
nous ont servi d'exemple.*

TABLE DES MATIÈRES

STUDENT PREFACE

Do you have a gift for languages?

Have you ever heard people say that they know someone who has a gift for languages? What does that mean? Are some people born with a special ability to learn languages? How do you know if you have a gift for languages? If you understood the sentence you just read, then you have a gift for languages. After all, you have already learned to speak and understand at least one language well—English. Everybody is born with a natural ability to learn languages, but some individuals seem to learn languages more quickly than others do. This is because, over time, we develop different learning styles.

The process individuals use to learn languages depends a great deal on their personality. As with any other process, such as learning a new computer program or writing a composition for English class, individuals can attain similar results, although they approach the task differently. Some language learners like to plan each step before beginning. Others prefer to jump in as soon as they know enough to get started, and continue from there using a hit-or-miss method. Some language learners like to understand in detail why a language works the way it does before they try to use it, whereas others are ready to try speaking as soon as they know only the most basic rules, making educated guesses about how to express themselves.

Both methods have advantages and disadvantages. Some people become so bogged down in details that they lose sight of their main purpose—communication. Others pay so little attention to details that what they say is unintelligible. No matter what sort of learner you are, the most important part of the language-learning process is to constantly try to use the language to express yourself. Always alternate study of vocabulary and structures with attempts to communicate.

Since you now know that you have a gift for languages, you might think of the following pages as a user's manual that suggests how to use your language-learning capacity to learn French efficiently. Some of the learning techniques will work for you, others may not fit your learning style. Read through the following three sections before beginning your French studies, and refer to them later to develop the language-learning process that works best for you.

- **Goals and expectations:** How much French should you expect to learn in your first year of study and how much time and effort will be required of you?
- **Motivation:** How do you motivate yourself to study and practice the language?
- **Learning techniques:** What are some study tips that will facilitate learning French?

Goals and Expectations

Who can learn a language?

Many people believe that, as an adult, you cannot learn a language as well as you might have when you were a child. It is true that children are good language learners, but there is no reason why adults cannot learn to speak a language with near-native fluency. Children learn languages well because they can adapt very easily and they do it willingly. Being able to adapt is very important in language learning. Children are not afraid to try something new, and they are not easily embarrassed if things do not turn out as they expect. Adults, on the other hand, are often afraid of doing something wrong or looking ridiculous. Don't be afraid to experiment, using what you already know to guess at how to express yourself in French. It does no harm if you try to say something and you do not get the expected response. Just try again.

By the time people become adults, they generally learn by analyzing, rather than by doing. They have also grown so accustomed to their own way of doing things that they are reluctant to change. Similarly, adult language learners often feel that the way English works is the natural way. They try to force the language they are learning into the same mold. In fact, languages work in variety of ways, all equally natural. Learn to accept that the French way of doing things is just as natural and valid as the English way.

Another difference in the way that children and adults learn languages is that children spend a lot more time focused on what they are doing. When children learn languages, they spend almost every hour they are awake for several years doing nothing but learning the language. Learning to communicate is their principal objective in life. Most adults, on the other hand, spend just a few hours a week studying a new language, and during this time they are often distracted by many other aspects of their lives. In a classroom setting where small children have contact with a foreign language for just a few hours per week, children do not learn better than adults. In fact, adults have several advantages over children, such as their ability to organize and their longer attention spans. Your ability to develop fluency in French depends mainly on three things: the amount of time you spend with the language, how focused you are, and how willing you are to try to communicate using it.

How well will you speak after a year?

Those of you who are new to foreign language study probably have a variety of ideas about what you will be doing in this course. People who become frustrated in foreign language study generally do so because they start off with the wrong expectations. Some people begin a foreign language course with a negative attitude, thinking that it is impossible to really learn a language without going to a country where it is spoken. Although it is indeed usually easier to learn French in a French-speaking region, you can learn to speak French very fluently here as well. Once again, it is a question of spending time with the language, while focusing on how to communicate with it.

There are also some students who begin foreign language classes with expectations that are too high, thinking that they will begin speaking French with complete fluency nearly overnight. Learning a language takes time. Even after two years of concentrated study, it is reasonable to have achieved only basic fluency. If you set a goal for yourself to have everyday conversation skills after your second year of study, and if you work hard toward this goal, you will be able to function in most everyday conversation settings; however, you will still frequently have to look for words, you will probably still speak in short simple sentences, and you will often have to use circumlocution to get your meaning across. In *Horizons,* you will learn how to function in the most common situations in which you are likely to find yourself in a francophone region. To illustrate how much you will learn during the first few weeks of study, take out a sheet of paper, and list, in English, the first eight questions you would probably ask in the following situation: Before the first day of class, you sit down next to a student you have never seen before and you begin to chat.

In this situation, students generally ask questions like the following:
- How are you doing?
- What's your name?
- What are you studying?
- Where are you from?
- Where do you live?/ Do you live on campus?
- Do you like it there?
- Do you work? Where?
- When are you graduating?

This is the extent of the conversation that you have with many people you will meet, and you will be able to do this in French after only a few weeks.

How much time and effort must you invest to be a successful language learner?

There are three P's involved in learning a language: patience, practice, and persistence. We have already said that success in learning a foreign language depends on how much time you spend studying and practicing it. You might wonder how time-consuming French class will be. The amount of time required depends on your study skills and attention span. However, nobody can be successful without devoting many hours to studying and using the language. Generally, to make steady progress at the rate that material is presented in most college or university classes, you should expect to spend two to three hours on the language outside of class, for every hour that you are in class.

What is involved in learning to express yourself in another language?

Students studying a foreign language for the first time may have false expectations about what is involved in learning to speak another language. Many people think that you just substitute a French word for the equivalent word in English. Most of the time, you cannot translate word for word from one language to another. For example, if a French speaker substituted the equivalent English word for each French word in the following sentence, it would create a very unusual sentence.

Nous ne l'avons pas encore fait.
We not it have not still done.

You might be able to figure out that this sentence means, "We haven't done it yet," but sometimes translating word for word can give a completely wrong meaning. For example, if you translate the following sentence word for word, you would think that it has the first meaning that follows it, whereas it really has the second. This is because the indirect object pronoun **vous** *(to) you* precedes the verb in French.

Je voudrais vous parler demain, s'il vous plaît.
I would like you to speak tomorrow, if it you pleases.
I would like to speak to you tomorrow, please.

You probably noticed in this last example that one word in English may be translated by several words in French and vice versa **(voudrais** = *would like*, **vous** = *to you*, **parler** = *to speak*, **s'il vous plaît** = *please).*

Differences in languages are not due simply to a lack of one-to-one correspondence between words and structures. Cultural differences also strongly affect how we communicate. Culture and language are so interrelated that it is impossible to learn a language fluently without becoming familiar with the culture(s) where it is spoken. For example, in French, a cultural difference that affects the spoken language is that French society is not as informal as ours. Adults generally do not call each other by their first names, and the words for *sir* and *madame* are used much more frequently than in English. For example, it is normal to say **Bonjour, monsieur** *(Hello, sir),* whereas English speakers say, "Hello."

Cultural differences affect the spoken language and also nonverbal communication. For instance, when the French speak to each other, they generally stand closer than we do. When we are talking to a French-speaker, we may feel that our space is invaded and back away. The French interpret this as standoffishness. As you can see, learning to communicate in French entails a lot more than substituting French words for English words in a sentence.

Does practice make perfect?

Your goal in learning French should not be to say everything perfectly. If you set this goal for yourself, you will probably be afraid to open your mouth, fearing mistakes. Your goal should be to communicate clearly, but you should expect to make mistakes when speaking. If you make a mistake that impedes communication, those you are speaking to will ask for clarification or repeat what you have said to be sure of what you mean. Listen carefully to how they express themselves, and make adjustments the next time you need to convey a similar message.

Although perfection is not the goal of language learners, practice is vital to success. (Remember the three P's of language learning: patience, practice, and persistence.) You can learn every vocabulary word and rule in the book, but unless you practice regularly, listening to French and attempting to speak it, you will not learn the language. Practicing a language is just as necessary for success as practicing a sport or a musical instrument. Imagine that you are a football player or pianist. You might know every play in the book, or you might understand music theory completely, but unless you practice, you will never be able to perform. It is important to learn the rules of French, but you must also practice it regularly.

What do you do if foreign languages make you panic?

Most individuals feel nervous when they have to speak to strangers. This is true when you speak your own language, and it's even truer when speaking a foreign language. There is no reason to be nervous, yet fear of looking ridiculous is often difficult to control. It is normal to experience some anxiety in class. If you suffer extreme anxiety in language class—to such a degree that it impedes your ability to concentrate—it is best to recognize that you fear having to perform in class. Go see your instructor and discuss your anxiety. In order to conquer it, you must acknowledge it.

Motivation

How can learning a foreign language help you?

Learning a foreign language should be fun. After all, you will spend a lot of class time chatting with classmates, which most of us find enjoyable. However, learning French takes time and effort. No matter how much you enjoy it, there will be times when you need to motivate yourself to study or practice. You can use motivation techniques for practicing a language similar to those musicians or athletes use to practice an instrument or a sport.

Many musicians and athletes have a personal goal. They imagine themselves playing a great concert at Carnegie Hall or winning a big game, receiving applause and praise. Simi-

larly, each time you start to practice French, imagine yourself speaking French fluently with a beautiful accent. In this mental image, you might be a diplomat, or you might be talking to the waiter at a French restaurant, impressing your friends.

Some people who practice an instrument or a sport do so for personal growth. Many people feel that learning a new language helps them discover a new side of their personality. By learning to appreciate another culture, you learn to understand your own better. You come to know yourself better and you broaden your horizons.

Of course, a lot of people are motivated to practice an instrument or a sport because they make their living from it. This is good motivation for learning a language too. In today's international economy, the best jobs are going more and more to those who speak more than one language, and who have an understanding of other cultures. Many jobs in the travel industry, in communications, in government, and in companies dealing in international trade and business require proficiency in another language.

How can you learn to enjoy studying?

As with any accomplishment, learning a foreign language requires a lot of work. You will enjoy it more if you think of it as a hobby or a pastime and as an opportunity to develop a skill. Here are some training techniques that can help you learn a new language.

- Get into a routine. Devote a particular time of day to studying French. It is best to find a time when you are fresh and free of distractions, so you can concentrate on what you are doing. If you study at the same time every day, getting started will become habitual, and you will have won half the battle. Once you are settled working and learning, it becomes fun.
- Make sure that the place where you study is inviting and that you enjoy being there.
- Study frequently for short periods of time, rather than having marathon sessions. After about two hours of study, the ability of the brain to retain information is greatly reduced. You tend to remember what you learn at the beginning of each study session and at the end. What you study in the middle tends to become blurred. To illustrate this, read the following words one time, then turn the page and see how many you remember.

dog, house, sofa, cat, rooster, room, telephone, mouse, book, pencil, television

Most people can remember the first word and the last. The longer the list, the harder it is to remember the words in the middle. The same is true with studying. Study smaller "chunks" of material more frequently. Set reasonable goals for yourself. Don't try to learn it all at once.

- Study with a classmate or a friend. It is much easier to practice talking with someone else, and it is easier to spend more time working with the language if you are interacting with another person. Also, by studying with classmates, you will feel more comfortable speaking in front of them, which eliminates some of the embarrassment some adults feel when trying to pronounce foreign words in front of the whole class.
- Play games with the language. It is fun to learn how to say things in a new language. For instance, ask yourself how you would say things you hear on the radio or television in French. If you do know how to say something in French that you hear, your knowledge will become more certain. If you don't know how to say something in French, that's normal if you are a beginner. When you finally learn the word or expression you were wondering about, you will remember it more easily, because you have already thought about it.
- Surround yourself by French. Rent French videos, listen to French music, and read French comic books and magazines. Magazines with a lot of pictures are the best, because the pictures give you clues to the meaning of unfamiliar words. You probably will not understand very much at first in movies and songs, but they will motivate you to learn more. They teach you about cultural differences, and they help give you a sense of good pronunciation.
- Don't let yourself get frustrated. If you are frustrated each time you sit down to study, ask yourself why. First of all, make sure that you are not studying when you are too tired or hungry. Also, make sure that you clearly understand your assignment and its purpose. Learn to distinguish a language-learning problem from a problem understanding instructions. If you are confused about what you are to do or why, see your instructor during office hours or contact another student. (This is another reason to study with a classmate!)

Learning Techniques

How can you spend your study time most efficiently?

Individuals organize material differently as they learn it. Some people learn better by seeing something; others learn better by hearing it. The following are some study tips for how to go about learning French. You may find that some of these methods work for you and others do not. Be creative in practicing your French, using a variety of study techniques.

General study tips

- Learn not to translate word for word. Learn to read and listen to whole sentences at a time.
- Keep a log of your study time in a small spiral notebook. This will help you learn to study more efficiently. Each time you sit down to study new material, write down the time you begin. When you finish, write down the time you stop, and two or three sentences summarizing what you studied. Students often feel frustrated that they spend a lot of time studying, but they do not retain much. By keeping a log, you will know exactly how much time you spend on French. Writing one or two sentences summarizing what you studied helps you check your retention.
- Alternate speaking, listening, reading, and writing activities. By changing tasks frequently, you will be able to study longer without losing your concentration.

Vocabulary-learning techniques

- Use your senses. Pronounce words aloud as you study them. Close your eyes as you pronounce the word and picture the thing or activity represented by nouns or verbs.
- Use flashcards, working from English to French. When possible, draw a simple picture instead of the English word. Also, write a sentence using the word on the card, trying to remember it each time you look at the card. Use different colored inks to help you visualize the meaning of words. For example, when studying colors, write them on the flashcard in that color. When learning food items, write the words for red foods, such as strawberries and tomatoes, in red, the words for green foods in green, etc. Write words that can be associated with shapes, such as tall, short, big, small, round, or square, with letters having similar shapes.
- Learn useful common phrases such as "What time is it?" or "How are you?" as a whole.
- Label household items in French on masking tape.
- Tape lists of vocabulary in places where you spend time doing routine tasks.
- Study vocabulary in manageable "chunks". Each morning, write out a list of 20 new words and carry it in your pocket. A few times during the day, spend two minutes trying to remember the words on the list. Take out the list and review the words you forgot for two minutes. By the end of the day, you will have spent just a few minutes and you will have learned the 20 words.
- Learn 10 useful phrases every day.
- If you know a French speaker, ask him or her to record the vocabulary words you want to learn on a cassette so you can play them at home, while you jog, or in your car.
- Make tests for yourself. At the end of a study session, write the English words or phrases on a sheet of paper. Put the sheet of paper away for a few hours. Later, take it out and see how many of the French equivalents of these words or phrases you remember.
- Group words in logical categories. For example, learn words for fruits together, words for animals together, sports-related vocabulary together, etc.

- Make flashcards with antonyms on each side such as hot/cold, near/far, to go to sleep/to wake up, etc.
- Use related English words to help you remember the French. For example, the French word for *to begin* is **commencer.** Associate it with *to commence.* Be creative in finding associations. For example, the word for *open* is **ouvert.** You can associate it with *overture,* which is the opening part of a musical piece, or an *overt* action, which is one that is done in the open. Write related English words on flashcards.
- Learn to say **"Comment dit-on... ?"** (*"How do you say . . . ?"*) when you do not know a word or phrase.
- Remember we cannot say everything even in our own language. If you do not know a word, try to think of another way to say what you want. Use circumlocution. For example, if you do not know how to say "to drive," say "to take the car" instead.

Grammar-learning techniques

- Play teacher. Try to guess what your instructor would ask you to do if he or she were giving a quiz the next day.
- Do the ***Pour vérifier*** self-checks in the margins next to explanations of structures.
- Use color coding to help you remember grammatical information. For example, all nouns in French are categorized either as masculine or feminine, and you must memorize in which category each noun belongs. When you make the flashcards, write feminine nouns on pink cards or with pink ink and use blue for masculine nouns. Use an eye-catching color on flashcards to indicate points you want to remember, such as irregular plurals or verbs that take **être** in the **passé composé.**
- If you like to use lists to study, organize them so that they help you remember information about words. For example, to remember noun gender, write masculine words in a column on the left and feminine words in a column on the right. If you can visualize where the word is on the list, you can remember its gender.
- Learn to accept ambiguity. Sometimes, as soon as you learn a new rule, you find out that it doesn't always work the way you expect it to.

Pronunciation-learning techniques

- Repeat everything you hear in French under your breath or in your head, even if you have no idea what it means. This will not only help your pronunciation, it will help your listening comprehension and your ability to learn vocabulary. For instance, if you keep repeating an unfamiliar word you hear in your head, when you finally find out what it means, you will remember it very easily.
- Read French words aloud as you study.
- Listen to the CDs that go with the book and the *Cahier d'activités orales* (Lab Manual) several times. It is impossi-

ble to concentrate both on meaning and pronunciation the first time you listen to them. Listen to them at least once focusing on pronunciation only.
- Make tapes of yourself and compare them to those of native speakers.
- Exaggerate as you practice at home. Any pronunciation that is not English will seem like exaggeration. Psychologically, it is very difficult to listen to yourself speaking another language. Pretend you are a French actor playing a role as you practice pronunciation.

Using the *Text Audio CDs* and the *Lab Audio CDs*

There are two distinct CDs that go with each chapter of the *Horizons* program: the *Text Audio CD* and the *Lab Audio CD.* The activities on the *Text Audio CDs* correspond to the listening sections marked with an earphone symbol in the textbook. These CDs are provided so that you can review material covered in class on your own, or prepare for the next day's class. The activities corresponding to the *Lab Audio CDs* are found in the *Cahier d'activités orales.* These activities give you extra practice listening to and pronouncing French. When you are preparing to do a listening activity in the textbook or the *Cahier d'activités orales,* it is important to make sure that you have the right CD.

In order to get maximum benefit from the CDs, approach listening activities with the right attitude. It takes time, patience, and practice to understand French spoken at a normal conversational speed. Do not be surprised if you find it difficult at first. Relax and listen to passages more than once. You will understand a little more each time. Remember that you will not understand everything and that, for some exercises, you are only expected to understand enough to answer specific questions. Read through exercises prior to starting the CD, so that you know what to listen for.

If you find you do not have enough time to process and respond to a question before the next one, take advantage of the pause or stop button on your CD player to give yourself more time. Most importantly, be patient and remember that you can always listen again.

Be willing to listen to the CDs several times. It is important to listen to them at least one separate time focusing solely on pronunciation. Practice, patience, and persistence pay!

We hope that the preceding suggestions on how to go about learning French will serve you well, helping you to become a successful language learner. We are always anxious to hear from students what works for them. If you have any study tips or ideas that you would like to share with us, please write to us in care of Heinle & Heinle Publishers, 25 Thomson Place, Boston, Massachusetts 02210. Good luck with your French studies, and most of all, enjoy yourself!

ACKNOWLEDGMENTS

We are grateful to a great many people for helping us transform our collective classroom experience into this text.

Principal among these are:
— Wendy Nelson for the opportunity to work with Heinle & Heinle and for her editorial guidance.
— Production and Developmental Editing Supervisor Esther Marshall and Project Manager and copyeditor Patricia Ménard for their support and hard work down the home stretch.
— Diana Baczynskyj and Matthew Drapeau for photo research.
— May Waggoner, from the University of Louisiana at Lafayette, for her invaluable assistance on the culture of Louisiana.
— Edgard Sankara, from the University of Texas at Austin, for his expertise on the culture of Côte-d'Ivoire.

We would particularly like to thank our reviewers of the previous edition and the new edition:

Patricia Brand, *University of Colorado, Boulder*
Lawrence Busenbark, *University of Oregon*
Glenda Carl, *Southwestern University*
Brigette Cross, *Marquette University*
Nadine DeVito, *University of Chicago*
Beatrice Dupuy, *Louisiana State University*
Diane Fagin Adler, *North Carolina State University*
Al Ford, *California State University, Northridge*
Carol Hofmann, *University of Southern California*
Andrea Javel, *Boston College*
Catherine Jolivet, *University of Louisiana*
Denise Jones, *Southwestern Louisiana University*
Alice Kornovich, *Loyola University, New Orleans*
June Legge, *Clayton State University*
Marie Léticée, *University of Central Florida*
Jane Lindebaugh, *York College*
Kathy Lorenz, *University of Cincinnati*
Roy Luna, *Miami Dade Community College, Wolfson*
Marie-Laure Marecaux, *University of Northern Colorado*
Chantal Marechal, *Virginia Commonwealth University*
Heather MacLean, *Kent State University*
Mari O'Brien, *Wright State University*
Jean-Louis Picherit, *University of Wyoming*
Jocelyn Rapinac, *Tufts University*
Kittye Robbins-Herring, *Mississippi State University*
Dianne Sears, *University of Massachusetts*
Larry Schehr, *North Carolina State University*
Michael Schwartz, *East Carolina University*
Leslie Sconduto, *Armstrong State College*
Alex Silverman, *School for International Training*
Katheryn Stewart, *Oakland Community College*
Robert M. Terry, *University of Richmond*
Louise Wills, *Harvard University*
C.W. Vance, *University of North Carolina, Charlotte*
May Waggoner, *University of Louisiana at Lafayette*

Special thanks go to the following: Sev Champeny for her editorial help; Josiane Pelltier, native reader; Sue Gerould, interior designer; Digital Stock and Dave Sullivan, illustrators; Jackie Rebisz, Susan Lake, and Kristina Baer, proofreaders.

Last, but obviously not least, we thank each other for the tolerance, mutual encouragement, and strengthened bonds of friendship such an endeavor requires.

Merci mille fois!

Text Audio CDs: Tracking Information

CD #1

Chapitre préliminaire
[Track 2] Conversation, p. 6
[Track 3] Prononciation: Les consonnes muettes et la liaison, p. 7
[Track 4] Conversation, p. 8
[Track 5] Prononciation: Les voyelles *a, e, i, o, u*, p. 8
[Track 6] Prononciation: Les chiffres et les voyelles nasales, p. 10
[Track 7] Conversation, p. 16
[Track 8] Conversation, p. 18
[Track 9] Prononciation: Les voyelles groupées, p. 21

Chapitre 1
[Track 10] Conversation, p. 31
[Track 11] Prononciation: *Il est + adjectif / Elle est + adjectif*, p. 33
[Track 12] Qui est-ce?, pp. 34-35
[Track 13] Conversation, p. 36
[Track 14] Conversation, p. 43
[Track 15] Prononciation: L'article indéfini, p. 44
[Track 16] Conversation, p. 48
[Track 17] Prononciation: La voyelle *e* et l'article défini, p. 50

Chapitre 2
[Track 18] Conversation, p. 65
[Track 19] Prononciation: La consonne *r* et l'infinitif, p. 66
[Track 20] Script for A. Quand?: Scène A, Scène B, Scène C, p. 68
[Track 21] Script for B. Qu'est-ce qu'elles font?: Scène A, Scène B, Scène C, p. 68
[Track 22] Script for On sort ensemble, pp. 68-69
[Track 23] Conversation, p. 71
[Track 24] Prononciation: Les verbes en *-er*, p. 73
[Track 25] Prononciation: Les verbes à changements orthographiques, p. 76
[Track 26] Conversation, p. 78
[Track 27] Prononciation: Les lettres *qu*, p. 80
[Track 28] Prononciation: L'inversion et la liaison, p. 82
[Track 29] Conversation, p. 84
[Track 30] Prononciation: Les chiffres, p. 86

Chapitre 3
[Track 31] Conversation, p. 103
[Track 32] Un nouvel appartement, pp. 106-107
[Track 33] Conversation, p. 109
[Track 34] Prononciation: *avoir* et *être*, p. 110
[Track 35] Prononciation: *de, du, des*, p. 112
[Track 36] Conversation, p. 115
[Track 37] Prononciation: La voyelle *o* de *notre/votre* et de *nos/vos*, p. 118
[Track 38] Conversation, p. 120
[Track 39] Prononciation: La voyelle *e* de *ce/cet/cette/ces*, p. 122

Chapitre 4
[Track 40] Conversation, p. 137
[Track 41] Script for A. Je ne comprends pas: Scène A, Scène B, Scène C, p. 140
[Track 42] Script for B. Comment?: Scène A, Scène B, Scène C, p. 140
[Track 43] Script for La famille de Robert, p. 141
[Track 44] Conversation, p. 143
[Track 45] Prononciation: Les lettres *a, au* et *ai*, p. 144
[Track 46] Conversation, p. 148
[Track 47] Conversation, p. 154
[Track 48] Prononciation: Le verbe *prendre*, p. 156

Chapitre 5
[Track 49] Conversation, p. 173
[Track 50] Qu'est-ce qu'elle fait?, p. 177

[Track 51] Conversation, p. 178
[Track 52] Conversation, p. 185
[Track 53] Conversation, p. 192
[Track 54] Prononciation: Les verbes auxiliaires *avoir* et *être*, p. 194

CD # 2

Chapitre 6
[Track 2] Conversation, p. 208
[Track 3] Script for A. Prenez des notes: Invitation A, Invitation B, Invitation C, p. 212
[Track 4] Script for On va au cinéma, p. 213
[Track 5] Conversation, p. 214
[Track 6] Prononciation: Les verbes *sortir, partir* et *dormir*, p. 216
[Track 7] Prononciation: Les terminaisons de l'imparfait, p. 218
[Track 8] Conversation, p. 221
[Track 9] Prononciation: Le passé composé et l'imparfait, p. 225
[Track 10] Conversation, p. 228

Chapitre 7
[Track 11] Conversation, p. 247
[Track 12] Il n'est jamais trop tard!, pp. 252-253
[Track 13] Conversation, p. 254
[Track 14] Conversation, p. 263
[Track 15] Conversation, p. 268

Chapitre 8
[Track 16] Prononciation: Le *h* aspiré, p. 285
[Track 17] Conversation, p. 286
[Track 18] Script for A. Pendant le repas, p. 292
[Track 19] Script for Au restaurant, p. 292
[Track 20] Conversation, p. 296
[Track 21] Conversation, p. 303
[Track 22] Prononciation: La lettre *s* et les verbes en *-ir*, p. 306
[Track 23] Conversation, p. 308
[Track 24] Prononciation: La consonne *r* et le conditionnel, p. 311

Chapitre 9
[Track 25] Conversation, p. 328
[Track 26] Une lettre de Côte-d'Ivoire, p. 333
[Track 27] Conversation, p. 334
[Track 28] Prononciation: Le *e* caduc, p. 338
[Track 29] Conversation, p. 341
[Track 30] Conversation, p. 347

Chapitre 10
[Track 31] Conversation, p. 364
[Track 32] Script for A. Dans le guide, p. 368
[Track 33] Script for B. Le ton de la voix, p. 369
[Track 34] Script for À la réception, p. 369
[Track 35] Conversation, p. 370
[Track 36] Conversation, p. 377
[Track 37] Conversation, p. 383

Chapitre de Révision
[Track 38] Un mystère dans les Ardennes, pp. 404-405
[Track 39] Script pour E. Vous êtes le détective, p. 406
[Track 40] Script for G. Dans quelle chambre?, p. 408
[Track 41] Script for H. Relations (part 1), p. 408
[Track 42] Script for H. Relations (part 2), p. 408
[Track 43] Script for S. Deux billets pour Tahiti, p. 415
[Track 44] Script for X. Que faisait le domestique?, p. 417
[Track 45] Épilogue, p. 419

Le monde francophone

On commence!

Le monde francophone

NOTE
Boldfaced words are glossed at the bottom of the page. Try to guess their meaning from the context before looking at the glosses.

TRANSPARENCIES: MAP 1-A, MAP 1-B

Note. Each chapter of *Horizons* opens with a francophone culture section. Vocabulary used in this section is not treated as active vocabulary.

Suggestions. A. Using a transparency of the francophone world or the map inside the front cover, discuss the role of French in different regions where it is the native language of most of the population; in bilingual and multilingual nations, such as Belgium, Switzerland, and Canada; in countries where it is one of the official languages used in business, government, and education, but not necessarily the most commonly spoken language of the population at home; and in countries where French is rarely used, but that share some aspects of French culture and heritage. **B.** You may wish to point out the **Départements d'outre-mer** (**Martinique, Guyane, Guadeloupe, Réunion**), the **Territoires d'outre-mer** (**Nouvelle-Calédonie, Polynésie-Française, Wallis-et-Futuna, Terres australes et antarctiques françaises**), and the **Collectivités territoriales** (**Mayotte, Saint-Pierre-et-Miquelon**). **C.** You may also wish to discuss: **1.** the historical reasons for the dissemination of French in the world; **2.** the concept of **francophonie** as a cultural identity; **3.** the pride and protective stance of some French speakers in a changing world.

Bienvenue dans le monde francophone!
Spoken in 44 countries, French plays an important role in international business and diplomacy. It is one of the official languages of the United Nations.

Connaissez-vous...

la cuisine et le vin français: le pâté, la quiche, le champagne, le beaujolais, le cognac?

la mode française: Hubert de Givenchy, Coco Chanel, Yves Saint Laurent?

la littérature francophone: Jean-Paul Sartre, George Sand, Léopold Senghor, Albert Camus, Victor Hugo, Molière?

les cinéastes, les acteurs, les actrices: Louis Malle, François Truffaut, Euzhan Palcy, Catherine Deneuve, Gérard Depardieu?

Bienvenue dans le monde francophone! *Welcome to the French-speaking world!* **Connaissez-vous... ?** *Are you familiar with . . . ?*

les peintres et les sculpteurs: Pierre Auguste Renoir, Camille Claudel, Auguste Rodin?

*la musique de Claude Debussy, d'Édith Piaf, de Jacques Brel? la musique **cadienne?** la musique zouk?*

Supplemental activity. Have students use the map inside the front cover to answer questions like: In how many South American countries is French spoken? In what parts of the United States is French spoken? Can you name some cities in the United States with French names? Where in Canada is French spoken? On what tropical islands could you practice your French? In what wars would French have been useful for U.S. soldiers? Name three African countries north of the Sahara Desert where French is spoken.

la technologie française: Ariane, le TGV?

les produits français: Bic, Danone, Yoplait, Michelin, Thomson, Lancôme, Perrier, Renault?

Suggestion. Divide the class into teams and use the questions below for a trivia game. You may wish to add additional questions of your own.

Quick-reference answers.
1. about 40 2. Louisiana, New England, Canada, Haiti, Martinique, Guadeloupe, Dominica, French Guiana, St. Martin, St. Pierre and Miquelon 3. Haiti, Guadeloupe, Martinique 4. False. It is spoken in French Polynesia (Tahiti) and New Caledonia. 5. True 6. True 7. Belgium, Switzerland, Luxembourg, Monaco, Andorra 8. the north and west 9. the Norman Conquest 10. French Guiana

Test your knowledge of the francophone world. Before you look at the map inside the front cover, see how many of these questions you can answer.

❶ In how many countries is French spoken: about 5, about 25, about 40, or about 100?
❷ There are several places in the Americas where French is spoken. Name two.
❸ In which three of these places in the Caribbean is French an important language: the Dominican Republic, Haiti, Guadeloupe, the Virgin Islands, the Bahamas, Martinique, the Cayman Islands?
❹ True or false? French is not spoken in any areas of the South Pacific.
❺ True or false? Some people in Laos, Cambodia, and Vietnam speak French.
❻ True or false? The existence of French-speaking people in the Americas, Africa, Asia, and the Pacific is largely due to the history of French colonialism.
❼ French is spoken in several other countries of Europe, besides France. Name two.
❽ French is spoken in many countries in Africa. Are most of them found in the north, west, east, or south?
❾ French developed from a Latin base, whereas English developed from a Germanic base. However, English was greatly influenced by French largely due to what historical event?
❿ In what country in South America is French spoken?

cadien(ne) *Cajun*

COMPÉTENCE 1

Greeting people

NOTE Culturelle

Traditionally, French first names often have religious, historical, or legendary origins. Hyphenated names, such as **Jean-Marc** and **Marie-Laure**, are also popular. Many French names have both masculine and feminine forms. Do you see any patterns?

Adrien / Adrienne
André / Andrée
Christian / Christiane
Claude / Claude
Daniel / Danièle, Danielle
Denis / Denise
Dominique / Dominique
Fabien / Fabienne
François / Françoise
Gabriel / Gabrielle
Jean / Jeanne
Martin / Martine
Michel / Michèle, Michelle
Pascal / Pascale
René / Renée
Simon / Simone
Yves / Yvette

NOTE

Items accompanied by this symbol are recorded on the *Text Audio CD*.

NOTES DE VOCABULAIRE

1. Use **mademoiselle** instead of **madame** with younger unmarried women.
2. Bonjour can be used to say *hello* at any time of day, but **bonsoir** can only be used to say *good evening*.
3. Generally, you do not just say **bonjour** in French. Instead, include the word **monsieur, madame,** or **mademoiselle,** or the person's name.
4. People in France generally shake hands when they meet.

Les formules de politesse

Use these expressions to greet adult strangers and those to whom you show respect.

TRANSPARENCIES: CP-1A, CP-1B

— Bonjour, madame (mademoiselle).
— Bonjour, monsieur. Je suis Hélène Cauvin. Et vous, comment vous appelez-vous?
— Je m'appelle Jean-Marc Bertin.

Use these expressions to ask how other people are and to tell how you are doing.

Bonsoir, monsieur. Comment allez-vous?

Je vais très bien, merci.
Et vous?

Assez bien. / Pas mal.

Pas très bien.

Prononciation: *Les consonnes muettes et la liaison*

In French, consonants at the end of words are often silent, and **h** is always silent. As you hear these greetings, note which consonants are not pronounced.

—Bonjour, monsieur. Je m'appelle Paul Richard. Et vous, comment vous appelez-vous?
—Je m'appelle Henri Dulac.
—Comment allez-vous?
—Très bien, et vous, monsieur?
—Très bien.

With a few exceptions, the consonants **c, r, f,** and **l** (CaReFuL) are the only consonants that are generally pronounced at the end of a word. The final **r** of **monsieur,** however, is not pronounced.

    Marc   bonjour   actif   Chantal

If a consonant at the end of a word is followed by a word beginning with a vowel sound (**a, e, i, o, u, y**) or mute **h,** the final consonant sound often links to the beginning of the next word. This linking is called **liaison.** In liaison, a single **s** is pronounced like a **z.**

    Comment vous‿appelez-vous?

    Comment‿allez-vous?

A. Prononcez bien.
Copy these sentences, crossing out the consonants that should not be pronounced and marking where liaison would occur (‿). Then listen to your instructor read each one and check your work. Finally, go back and reorder the four sentences to create a logical conversation to read with a partner.

Exemple   Comment‿allez-vous, monsieur?

1. Je suis Chantal Hubert.
2. Bonjour, madame. Comment allez-vous?
3. Très bien, monsieur. Comment vous appelez-vous?
4. Je m'appelle Henri Dufour. Et vous?

B. Que dit-on?
Complétez les conversations.

1.
2.
3.

C. Bonsoir!
Imagine that you are at a formal reception. Greet three people, exchange names, and find out how they are doing. Be sure to shake hands.

Script for *A. Prononcez bien.* Read the sentences from the textbook aloud.

Supplemental activities. A. Have three students stand in line, as if at a reception. Each of the other students will go down the line, greeting them and exchanging names. As they finish, they will join the end of the reception line and become part of it. **B.** Put names of celebrities on slips of paper. Try to pick some who have had good or bad things happen to them recently. Distribute the slips of paper to students, telling them not to show them to anyone. Ask two students to greet each other as if they were the celebrities on their papers. They should shake hands, ask each other's name, and ask how each other is doing. **C.** To check the roll the first day of class, have students stand up and introduce themselves to the class in French. As they introduce themselves, students should form a line along the front wall of the classroom, placing themselves in alphabetical order by last name. When the line is complete, check it against the class roll.

TRANSPARENCY: CP-2

Suggestions. Briefly mention the difference between the uses of **tu** and **vous**. This is explained in detail in *Chapitre 1.* Point out that using **à tout à l'heure** implies that you will see someone later the same day.

VOCABULAIRE SUPPLÉMENTAIRE

Comment t'appelles-tu? *What's your name?* (informal)

Comment vas-tu? *How are you?* (informal)

Ciao! *Bye!* (informal)

Salut! *Bye! Hi!* (informal)

Bon week-end! *Have a good weekend!*

Bonne journée! *Have a good day!*

Note. The *Vocabulaire supplémentaire* provides options for personalized communication, but it is not tested in the testing program.

Les salutations familières

To greet and exchange names with classmates, friends, family members, and children, say:

— Bonjour, je m'appelle Anne-Marie. Et toi, tu t'appelles comment?
— Moi, je m'appelle Robert.

— Salut, Jean-Pierre. Ça va?
— Salut, Micheline. Ça va. Et toi, comment ça va?
— Pas mal.

Here are several ways to say good-bye in both formal and informal situations.

Au revoir.	*Good-bye.*
À tout à l'heure.	*See you in a little while.*
À bientôt.	*See you soon.*
À demain.	*See you tomorrow.*

Prononciation: *Les voyelles a, e, i, o, u*

When you pronounce vowels in English, your tongue or lips move as you say them, so that your mouth's position is not the same at the end of a vowel as at the beginning. In French, you hold your tongue and mouth firmly in one place while pronouncing vowels. This gives vowels a tenser sound. Practice saying these letters: **a, e, i, o, u.**

a [a]: *à, ça, va, madame, mal, assez, appelle*

e [ə]: *je, ne, que, de, me, demain*

i [i]: *quiche, idéal, Paris, Micheline, six*

o [ɔ]: *comment, octobre, novembre, espagnol*

u [y]: *tu, salut, Luc, super*

The vowel **e** can have three distinct pronunciations in French [ə], [e], [ɛ]. You will learn more about this later. Final unaccented **e** is not generally pronounced, unless it is the only vowel in a word, as in **je.**

France, madame, appelle, une, Anne

A. Dans quelle situation? Would you be more likely to hear these phrases in situation **A** or **B**?

A

B

1. Bonsoir, madame.
2. Salut, Thomas.
3. Très bien, merci. Et vous?
4. Tu t'appelles comment?

5. Ça va?
6. Comment allez-vous?
7. Ça va. Et toi?
8. Comment vous appelez-vous?

Now, go back and indicate how one might respond to the phrases above.

Supplemental activities. **A.** Read the following and have students repeat the expression that implies you will see them soonest: **1.** À tout à l'heure. / À demain. **2.** À tout à l'heure. / Au revoir. **3.** À bientôt. / À tout à l'heure. **4.** À demain. / Au revoir. **B.** What might you say in the following situations? **1.** You are meeting a new professor for the first time. **2.** You are meeting another student for the first time. **3.** You run into your French professor at the library in the evening. **4.** You run into a new acquaintance who calls you by the wrong name. **5.** You are saying good-bye to a friend with whom you plan to study later. **6.** You are saying good-bye to friends whom you will see tomorrow.

B. Conversations. Act out the following conversations with a partner. Then act them out again, making the suggested changes.

1. — Comment ça va, Jean-Marc?
   — Pas mal. Et toi, Martine?
   — Ça va.
   — Bon, à demain!
   — À demain!

   a. Jean-Marc is not having a very good day.
   b. The two friends plan to see each other later today.
   c. The conversation is between two business associates, **Edgard Sankara . . .** and **Véronique Dupont . . .**

2. — Bonjour, monsieur. Je suis Cécile Pastini. Et vous, comment vous appelez-vous?
   — Bonjour, madame. Je m'appelle André Cardin.

   a. The woman is young and unmarried.
   b. The conversation is between two students, Philippe and Christine.

C. Que disent-ils? Imagine what these people are saying. Prepare brief exchanges with a partner.

1.

2.

3.

COMPÉTENCE 2

Counting and telling time

The French manner of counting on one's fingers differs from ours. One counts with palms facing in and starting with the thumb instead of the index finger.

TRANSPARENCY: CP-3

Note. The teacher notes in each *Compétence* begin with a warm-up activity reviewing material from an earlier *Compétence*.

Warm-up. What could you respond if someone said the following to you? (Some have more than one possibility.) **1.** Bonjour, monsieur / madame / mademoiselle. **2.** Bonsoir, monsieur / madame / mademoiselle. **3.** Salut. **4.** Comment vous appelez-vous? **5.** Tu t'appelles comment? **6.** Ça va? **7.** Comment allez-vous? **8.** À demain. **9.** À tout à l'heure.

Suggestion for practicing numbers. Have students write the numbers 0–30 in order on a piece of paper. Call out twenty numbers in random order, having students cross them out as you say them. Then have a student read aloud the ten numbers that remain.

Suggestions for *Prononciation*. Point out: **A.** Some speakers pronounce un / um as [œ̃]. **B.** The on in monsieur is an exception. **C.** The nasal sound of the diphthong -ien sounds like [ɛ̃] (bien, combien). **D.** Give students the phrase un bon vin blanc to practice all the nasal sounds.

Supplemental activity. Read the following words and have students say whether they hear the nasal vowel sound **a.** [ɛ̃] as in **vingt**, **b.** [ɑ̃] as in **trente**, or **c.** [ɔ̃] as in **onze**. EXEMPLE font → c **1.** on **2.** Henri **3.** quinze **4.** bonjour **5.** demain **6.** Alain **7.** cinq **8.** France **9.** Simon **10.** Martin **11.** Jean **12.** Christian

Les chiffres de zéro à trente

Comptez de zéro **à** trente, **s'il vous plaît!**

0	zéro				
1	un	**11**	onze	**21**	vingt et un
2	deux	**12**	douze	**22**	vingt-deux
3	trois	**13**	treize	**23**	vingt-trois
4	quatre	**14**	quatorze	**24**	vingt-quatre
5	cinq	**15**	quinze	**25**	vingt-cinq
6	six	**16**	seize	**26**	vingt-six
7	sept	**17**	dix-sept	**27**	vingt-sept
8	huit	**18**	dix-huit	**28**	vingt-huit
9	neuf	**19**	dix-neuf	**29**	vingt-neuf
10	dix	**20**	vingt	**30**	trente

$2 + 2 = 4$ **Combien** font deux et deux?
Deux et deux font quatre.

$10 - 3 = 7$ Combien font dix moins trois?
Dix moins trois font sept.

Prononciation: *Les chiffres et les voyelles nasales*

Although final consonants are generally silent in French, they are pronounced in the following numbers when counting. In **sept**, the **p** is silent, but the final **t** is pronounced. The final **x** in **six** and **dix** is pronounced like the *s* in *so*.

cinq   six   sep̸t   huit   neuf   dix

Many numbers also contain nasal vowels. In French, when a vowel is followed by the letter **m** or **n** in the same syllable, the **m** or **n** is silent and the vowel is nasal. Use the words below as models of how to pronounce each of the three nasal sounds. The letter combinations that are grouped together are all pronounced alike.

[ɛ̃]: un / um / in / im / ain / aim	**un**	**cinq**	**quinze**	**vingt**
[ɑ̃]: en / em / an / am	**trente**	**Henri**	**Jean**	**comment**
[ɔ̃]: on / om	**onze**	**bonjour**	**bonsoir**	**Simon**

A. C'est logique! Complétez avec les chiffres logiques.

1. 1, 3, 5, ?, 9, 11, ?, 15, 17, ?
2. 2, 4, ?, 8, 10, ?, 14, ?, 18, 20
3. 0, 5, 10, ?, 20, ?, 30
4. 3, 6, 9, ?, 15, 18, ?

5. 20, 19, 18, ?, 16, 15, ?
6. 10, 11, 12, ?, 14, 15, ?
7. 11, 13, 15, ?, 19, 21, 23, 25, ?
8. 0, 10, 20, ?

Comptez *Count*   **de** *from*   **à** *to*   **s'il vous plaît** *please*   **Combien** *How much, How many*

B. Messages secrets. You will hear a series of numbers. Write the letter corresponding to each number and you will discover a secret message. When you hear **zéro**, you should start another word **(un autre mot)**.

Exemple   VOUS ENTENDEZ *(YOU HEAR)*: 8, 30, 29, 9, 30, 6, 10, 0, 12, 18, 0, 15, 18
VOUS ÉCRIVEZ *(YOU WRITE)*: **Bonjour, ça va?**

0	un autre mot	8	b	16	ô	24	m
1	é	9	j	17	t	25	e
2	q	10	r	18	a	26	p
3	c	11	f	19	s	27	y
4	i	12	ç	20	h	28	è
5	d	13	g	21	l	29	n
6	u	14	x	22	w	30	o
7	z	15	v	23	à		

Script for B. Messages secrets. Answers are given in parentheses. EXEMPLE 8, 30, 29, 9, 30, 6, 10, 0, 12, 18, 0, 15, 18 (Bonjour, ça va?) **1.** 23, 0, 5, 25, 24, 18, 4, 29 (À demain.) **2.** 3, 30, 24, 26, 17, 25, 7, 0, 5, 25, 0, 7, 1, 10, 30, 0, 23, 0, 17, 10, 25, 29, 17, 25 (Comptez de zéro à trente.) **3.** 18, 6, 0, 10, 25, 15, 30, 4, 10 (Au revoir.)

Suggestion for B. Messages secrets. First have students listen to these secret messages. Then have them prepare one themselves for the class.

C. Combien font... ?

1. 2 + 3 =	**4.** 14 + 16 =	**7.** 18 − 12 =
2. 1 + 6 =	**5.** 10 + 9 =	**8.** 13 − 5 =
3. 9 + 4 =	**6.** 28 − 17 =	**9.** 16 − 1 =

D. Loto. Write down any five numbers between 1 and 30 on a sheet of paper. Another student will randomly call out numbers. The first person to have all five numbers called out wins.

E. Populations. The population of France is about 60 million. Can you guess the population of these other French-speaking countries, using the populations listed in the right column? Populations are rounded to the nearest million. If you guess wrong, your instructor will give you cues, by saying **plus que ça** *(more than that)* or **moins que ça** *(less than that)*, until you guess the correct number. The first one is done as an example.

Exemple   la Suisse
— **Seize millions.**
— **Moins que ça.**
— **Cinq millions.**
— **Plus que ça.**
— **Sept millions.**
— **Oui, c'est sept millions.**

1.	la Suisse	3 millions
2.	le Tchad	15 millions
3.	la Côte-d'Ivoire	16 millions
4.	la Belgique	7 millions
5.	la République centrafricaine	5 millions
6.	le Canada	10 millions
7.	le Maroc	30 millions
8.	Madagascar	31 millions
9.	le Togo	8 millions
10.	le Burkina Faso	12 millions

Suggestion for C. Combien font... ? Point out the examples of math problems on the facing page.

Supplemental activities. A. Read pairs of numbers aloud and have students repeat the one that is larger. **2/12, 9/5, 6/7, 11/1, 20/15, 3/9, 4/14, 18/15, 19/17, 20/30. B.** Have students write a number between 1 and 30 on a sheet of paper. Class members take turns trying to guess a student's number. That student responds **plus** or **moins** until the class narrows it down to the correct number. (Tell students that **plus** and **moins** mean *more* and *less*.)

Note for E. Populations. This exercise and several others throughout the Preliminary Chapter are intended to familiarize students with the countries of the francophone world. You may wish to have students look at the map inside the front cover as they do these activities. It is not intended that students learn these populations but simply become familiar with the names of some francophone countries.

Suggestion for E. Populations. Model the pronunciation of **million** before beginning.

Quick reference answers for E. Populations. 1. la Suisse, 7 millions **2.** le Tchad, 8 millions **3.** la Côte-d'Ivoire, 16 millions **4.** la Belgique, 10 millions **5.** la République centrafricaine, 3 millions **6.** le Canada, 31 millions **7.** le Maroc, 30 millions **8.** Madagascar, 15 millions **9.** le Togo, 5 millions **10.** le Burkina Faso, 12 millions

NOTE DE VOCABULAIRE

There is an **e** on the end of **demi(e)** when it is used with the word **heure**, but not with **midi** and **minuit**.

Suggestions. Point out that: **A. Heures** has an **-s** except with **une heure; B. À** is always used in French, even when it is omitted in English (**À quelle heure?** = *(At) What time?*); **C.** The pronunciation of some numbers changes in liaison with **heures:**

deux → deux ᶻheures,
trois → trois ᶻheures,
six → six ᶻheures,
neuf → neuf ⱽheures,
dix → dix ᶻheures

Suggestions for presenting the time. First present the question **Quelle heure est-il maintenant?** and demonstrate telling time on the hour only. Give students paper-plate clocks with moveable hands and, as you say what time it is, have them show the time on their clocks. Next present telling time between the hour and half-hour only and repeat the same activity. Then, do the same for telling time after the half-hour. Finally, have students tell time in five-minute intervals for one hour.

L'heure

Quelle heure est-il **maintenant?**

Il est une heure.

Il est une heure dix.

Il est une heure et quart.

Il est une heure et demie.

Il est deux heures moins vingt-cinq.

Il est deux heures moins le quart.

Il est deux heures moins cinq.

Il est deux heures.

Il est midi.

Il est midi et demi.

Il est minuit.

Il est minuit et demi.

The French do not use A.M. and P.M. to distinguish morning from afternoon and evening. Instead, they use:

du matin *(from after midnight until noon)*   Il est huit heures **du matin.**
de l'après-midi *(from after noon until 6:00 P.M.)*   Il est cinq heures de **l'après-midi.**
du soir *(from 6:00 P.M. until midnight)*   Il est neuf heures **du soir.**

Do not use these expressions with **midi** or **minuit.**

*Use **à** to ask or tell **at** what time something takes place.*

— À quelle heure **ouvre la bibliothèque?**
— À huit heures du matin.
— À quelle heure **ferme** la bibliothèque?
— À dix heures du soir.

Le cours de français **commence** à une heure.

Le cours de français **finit** à deux heures moins dix.

---

maintenant *now* **ouvre** *opens* **la bibliothèque** *the library* **ferme** *closes* **le cours de français** *the French class* **commence** *begins* **finit** *finishes, ends*

*To say that you do something **from** a certain time **to** another, use **de... à**. Use **avant** to say **before** and **après** to say **after**.*

Avant dix heures, **je suis à la maison.**

Après dix heures, **je ne suis pas** à la maison. Je suis **en cours** de dix heures à deux heures.

Je travaille de deux heures à sept heures.

Après sept heures, **je ne travaille pas.**

In official schedules and sometimes in conversations, the French use the 24-hour clock. With the 24-hour clock, you continue counting 13 to 24, instead of beginning with 1 to 12 o'clock again during the P.M. hours. Also state the number of minutes after the hour with a number, instead of using **et quart, et demie,** or **moins.** To convert from the 24-hour clock, just subtract twelve hours:

13h15 (treize heures quinze) = 1h15 (une heure et quart)
18h30 (dix-huit heures trente) = 6h30 (six heures et demie)

To use the 24-hour clock, you will need the numbers **quarante** *(forty),* and **cinquante** *(fifty).*

22h45 (vingt-deux heures quarante-cinq) = 10h45 (onze heures moins le quart)

A. En français! To get accustomed to the expressions used in telling time, complete these expressions to tell the time in French.

Exemple   *4:30 A.M.*
             Il est quatre heures **et demie du matin.**

1. *5:10 A.M.* Il est cinq heures...
2. *5:15 A.M.* Il est cinq heures...
3. *3:20 P.M.* Il est trois heures...
4. *3:30 P.M.* Il est trois heures...
5. *7:35 P.M.* Il est huit heures...
6. *7:45 P.M*   Il est huit heures...
7. *7:50 P.M.* Il est huit heures...
8. *8:00 P.M.* Il est...
9. *12:00 A.M.* Il est...
10. *12:00 P.M.* Il est...

---

je suis à la maison *I'm at home*   **je ne suis pas** *I'm not*   **en cours** *in class*   **Je travaille** *I work*   **je ne travaille pas** *I do not work*

B. Quelle heure est-il?

Exemple  — **Quelle heure est-il?**
— **Il est une heure de l'après-midi.**

1.   2.   3.

4.   5.

6.   7.

C. Quand? Complete these sentences so that they are true for you the first day of the week you have your French class.

Exemple   La bibliothèque ouvre <u>**à**</u>   <u>**sept heures et demie.**</u>
                                    at   [time]

1. Je suis à la maison ____ _____.
                             before   [time]
2. Le cours de français commence ____ _____.
                                        at   [time]
3. Le cours de français finit ____ _____.
                             at   [time]
4. Je suis en cours ____ _____ ____ _____.
                  from   [time]   to   [time]
5. Je travaille ____ _____ ____ _____. [Je ne travaille pas.]
             from   [time]   to   [time]
6. La bibliothèque ferme ____ _____.
                        at   [time]
7. Je suis à la maison ____ _____.
                     after   [time]

Script for *D. Il est quelle heure?*
EXEMPLE Il est dix heures et quart. **1.** Il est une heure cinq. **2.** Il est midi vingt. **3.** Il est quatre heures moins dix. **4.** Il est minuit et demi. **5.** Il est dix heures moins le quart. **6.** Il est neuf heures et quart.

Follow-up for *D. Il est quelle heure?*
Have students draw six clock faces with no hands on a sheet of paper. Tell them to fill in the first three by drawing in hands to indicate any time they choose. Assign partners, but tell students not to show their clocks to their partners. Students tell their partners the time on each of their clocks and the partners draw in the time on their blank clocks.

D. Il est quelle heure? Write the times you hear dictated. Notice how the word **heure(s)** is abbreviated in French.

Exemple   VOUS ENTENDEZ *(YOU HEAR):* Il est dix heures et quart.
                VOUS ÉCRIVEZ *(YOU WRITE):* **10h15**

E. Fuseaux horaires.
You are working for an international corporation in Louisiana, and you have to telephone clients in other French-speaking places around the globe. Using the time zone comparison chart, tell what time it is in each place.

Tahiti	Louisiane	Québec	Guyane française	Côte-d'Ivoire / République centrafricaine	France / Belgique / Suisse	Madagascar
MATIN—————APRÈS-MIDI————————————————————SOIR						
8h00	12h00	1h00	3h00	6h00	7h00	9h00

Exemple   Il est 8h15 du matin en Louisiane. En France, il est...
Il est huit heures et quart du matin en Louisiane. En France, il est trois heures et quart de l'après-midi.

1. Il est 8h10 du matin en Louisiane. À Madagascar, il est...
2. Il est 9h15 du matin en Louisiane. En République centrafricaine, il est...
3. Il est 10h25 du matin en Louisiane. En Côte-d'Ivoire, il est...
4. Il est 11h30 du matin en Louisiane. En Belgique, il est...
5. Il est midi en Louisiane. En Suisse, il est...
6. Il est 1h05 de l'après-midi en Louisiane. En Guyane française, il est...
7. Il est 1h45 de l'après-midi en Louisiane. À Montréal, il est...
8. Il est 7h40 du soir en Louisiane. À Tahiti, il est...

F. L'heure officielle.
Convert these official times to conversational time, as in the example.

Exemple   13h20   **Il est treize heures vingt. / Il est une heure vingt.**

1. 16h15	3. 12h10	5. 19h45	7. 23h40
2. 10h30	4. 17h25	6. 21h55	8. 24h

G. Au restaurant.
From what time to what time are these restaurants open?

Exemple   **L'Européen est ouvert** *(is open)* **de onze heures à une heure du matin.**

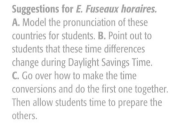

COMPÉTENCE 3

Talking about yourself and your schedule

NOTE Culturelle

What would the average French person say about himself/herself? Around 75% of the French live in urban areas. About 20% of the total population live in the Paris area.

All students finishing secondary school have studied several years of a foreign language. Many have studied more than one language. How does this compare with the typical American? What about French-speaking Canadians?

NOTES GRAMMATICALES

1. The words **je** *(I),* **ne,** and **de** *(from, of)* change to **j'**, **n'**, and **d'** before vowels or a mute **h.** Similarly, **parce que** *(because)* changes to **parce qu'. 2.** Many adjectives in French add an extra **-e** when describing females. You will learn more about this in *Chapitre 1.*

TRANSPARENCY: CP-5

Warm-ups. A. Ask students simple addition and subtraction problems. **B.** Say various times and have students say whether they are usually home at that time.

Note. These expressions are presented as lexical items only. Grammar explanations for verb forms, negation, elision, and adjective agreement are discussed in *Chapitre 1.* Students are expected to produce only the forms with **je. Vous** forms and questions are taught here for recognition only.

Suggestions. A. Model the difference in pronunciation between the masculine and feminine forms of **étudiant(e)**, **américain(e), canadien(ne),** and **un(e).** These are explained in *Chapitre 1.* **B.** Explain that **camarades de chambre** *(roommates)* share a room, as in a dorm. **Colocataires** *(Housemates)* share an apartment or house, but not a room.

Un autoportrait

Use these expressions to talk about yourself. Include the ending in parentheses if you are female.

Je suis... Je ne suis pas...	étudiant(e). professeur. américain(e). canadien(ne). **de** Chicago. d'**ici.**

Je suis étudiante à l'université de Montpellier.

J'habite... Je n'habite pas...	à Toronto. avec **un ami.** avec **une amie.** avec deux ami(e)s. avec **un camarade de chambre.** avec **une camarade de chambre.** **seul(e).** avec ma famille.

Je parle français et anglais.

Je travaille... Je ne travaille pas...	**beaucoup.** à l'université. **pour** IBM.

Je parle... Je ne parle pas...	anglais. français. espagnol. beaucoup en cours.

Je suis de Guadeloupe, mais je suis étudiante à Paris maintenant.

Je pense que le français est...	assez **facile.** **un peu** difficile. intéressant. super!

 In the following conversation, two people meet at a Canadian-American cultural event in Montreal.

— **Vous êtes** canadien?
— Oui, je suis d'ici. Et vous, vous êtes canadienne **aussi?**
— Non, je suis de Cleveland.
— **Mais** vous parlez très bien français! Vous habitez ici maintenant?
— Oui, **parce que** je suis étudiante à l'université. Et vous, vous travaillez ici?
— Non, je suis étudiant aussi.

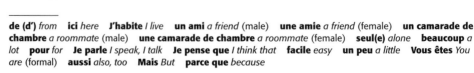

de (d') *from* **ici** *here* **J'habite** *I live* **un ami** *a friend* (male) **une amie** *a friend* (female) **un camarade de chambre** *a roommate* (male) **une camarade de chambre** *a roommate* (female) **seul(e)** *alone* **beaucoup** *a lot* **pour** *for* **Je parle** *I speak, I talk* **Je pense que** *I think that* **facile** *easy* **un peu** *a little* **Vous êtes** *You are* (formal) **aussi** *also, too* **Mais** *But* **parce que** *because*

A. Moi, je... Choose the words in parentheses so that each sentence describes you.

1. (Je suis / Je ne suis pas) étudiant(e).
2. (Je suis / Je ne suis pas) en cours maintenant.
3. (Je suis / Je ne suis pas) de Los Angeles.
4. (Je suis / Je ne suis pas) canadien(ne).
5. (J'habite / Je n'habite pas) à Minneapolis.
6. (J'habite / Je n'habite pas) avec ma famille maintenant.
7. (Je travaille / Je ne travaille pas) à l'université.
8. (Je parle / Je ne parle pas) très bien français.

B. Nationalités. Some international students from different French-speaking countries are talking about themselves. Can you find the sentences from each column that go together?

Exemple   **Je suis français(e). Je suis de France. J'habite à Paris.**

Je suis français(e).	Je suis de Belgique.	J'habite à Alger.
Je suis algérien(ne).	Je suis d'Haïti.	J'habite à Genève.
Je suis haïtien(ne).	Je suis d'Algérie.	J'habite à Paris.
Je suis belge.	Je suis de Côte-d'Ivoire.	J'habite à Port-au-Prince.
Je suis ivoirien(ne).	Je suis de Suisse.	J'habite à Abidjan.
Je suis suisse.	Je suis de France.	J'habite à Bruxelles.

C. Descriptions. Change the words in italics so that each statement is true for you. If a statement already is true, read it as it is.

1. Je m'appelle *Paul Jones.*
2. Je suis de *Raleigh.*
3. Maintenant, j'habite à *Chapel Hill.*
4. Je suis *canadien(ne).*
5. Je suis étudiant(e) à *l'université de Caroline du Nord.*
6. J'habite *avec un(e) camarade de chambre.*
7. Je parle *anglais et espagnol.*
8. Je parle *un peu* français.
9. Je pense que le français est *très facile.*

D. Et vous? Répondez aux questions suivantes.

1. Comment vous appelez-vous?
2. Comment allez-vous?
3. Vous êtes étudiant(e)?
4. Vous travaillez aussi?
5. Vous êtes américain(e)?
6. Vous êtes d'ici?
7. Vous habitez à Denver maintenant?
8. Vous parlez espagnol?

E. Conversations. Reread the conversation at the bottom of the previous page. Then act it out with a partner, making the following changes.

1. Both people work at the university rather than study there.
2. Both are from New York.
3. You and a partner meet at a Canadian-American cultural event in your city. Change the conversation to make it true for you.

Les jours de la semaine et votre emploi du temps

To ask and tell the day of the week, say:

— **C'est quel jour aujourd'hui?**
— C'est lundi.

lundi	mardi	mercredi	jeudi	vendredi	samedi	dimanche
(17)	18	19	20	21	22	23
24	25	26	27	28	29	30

Do not translate the word *on* to say that you do something on a certain day. To say that you do something every Monday (or another day), use **le** with the day of the week.

| Je suis en cours lundi. | *I'm in class on Monday.* (this Monday) |
| Je suis en cours le lundi. | *I'm in class on Mondays.* (every Monday) |

Notice how to say *from . . . to . . .* with days of the week.

| Je travaille de lundi à vendredi. | *I work from Monday to Friday.* (this week) |
| Je travaille du lundi au vendredi. | *I work Mondays to Fridays.* (every week) |

Use **le matin, l'après-midi,** and **le soir** to say you do something *in the morning, in the afternoon,* or *in the evening,* and **le week-end** to say *on the weekend.*

Le matin, je suis en cours.	*In the morning, I'm in class.*
L'après-midi, je travaille.	*In the afternoon, I work.*
Le soir et le week-end, je suis à la maison.	*In the evening and on the weekend, I'm at home.*

 Two friends are talking about their schedule this semester.

—**Tu es** en cours quels jours **ce semestre?**
—Je suis en cours le lundi, le mercredi et le vendredi.
—Tu travailles aussi?
—Oui, je travaille le mardi matin, le jeudi matin et le week-end.

A. Ciao! Say good-bye to a friend whom you will see again in two days.

Exemple   Aujourd'hui, c'est lundi.
Au revoir! À mercredi!

Aujourd'hui c'est...

1. dimanche   **2.** mercredi   **3.** samedi   **4.** jeudi   **5.** vendredi   **6.** mardi

---

Les jours de la semaine *The days of the week*   **votre emploi du temps** *your schedule*   **C'est quel jour aujourd'hui?** *It's what day today?*   **Tu es... ?** *You are . . . ?* (familiar)   **ce semestre** *this semester*

B. C'est quel jour?

1. Aujourd'hui, c'est...
2. Demain, c'est...
3. Après demain, c'est...
4. Après le week-end, c'est...
5. Avant le week-end, c'est...
6. Les jours du week-end sont...
7. Les jours du cours de français sont...
8. Je suis en cours...
9. Je travaille...
10. Je suis souvent *(often)* à la maison...

C. Quand?

Change the words in italics so that each statement is true. If a statement is already true, read it as it is.

1. Je suis à l'université *du lundi au vendredi.*
2. Je travaille *le mardi matin, le jeudi matin et le week-end. Le mardi,* je travaille de *huit heures* à midi. [Je ne travaille pas.]
3. Aujourd'hui, c'est *lundi* et maintenant il est *huit heures vingt.*
4. Aujourd'hui, je suis en cours de *dix heures et demie* à *quatre heures.*
5. Le lundi, la bibliothèque ouvre à *sept heures du matin.*
6. Le vendredi, la bibliothèque ferme à *onze heures du soir.*

D. Votre emploi du temps.

On a sheet of paper, copy the schedule below twice, changing it to describe your schedule on one copy and leaving the other one blank. You and your partner take turns describing your schedules to each other. On your second (blank) schedule, fill in your partner's schedule as he/she describes it to you.

Suggestion for *D. Votre emploi du temps.* You may prefer to distribute two photocopies of a blank schedule to each student to save class time.

Exemple   **Le lundi, je suis en cours de dix heures à une heure. Je travaille de deux heures à cinq heures. Je suis à la maison à cinq heures. Le mardi...**

lundi		mardi	
8:00		8:00	
9:00		9:00	
10:00	} en cours	10:00	
11:00		11:00	
12:00		12:00	
13:00		13:00	
14:00	} travail	14:00	
15:00		15:00	
16:00		16:00	
17:00	à la maison	17:00	

E. Conversations.

Reread the conversation at the bottom of the previous page. Then act it out with a partner, making the following changes.

1. The student is in class in the morning on Tuesdays and Thursdays and does not work.
2. The student is in class in the afternoon from Monday to Friday and works on Tuesday mornings and Saturday evenings.
3. Change the conversation so that it describes your schedule or your partner's. Then switch roles.

COMPÉTENCE 4

NOTE *Culturelle*

Generally, homework is less controlled at French universities than here, and course grades are mainly determined by a few tests. Students must be responsible for their own daily progress. Would you prefer to have this type of system?

Warm-up. Make statements like the following about yourself and elicit similar statements from students by saying **Et vous?** at the end of each one. **1.** Je m'appelle... Et vous? **2.** Je suis de... Et vous? **3.** Je suis *[your nationality]*. Et vous? **4.** J'habite *[with whom]*... Et vous? **5.** Je travaille pour l'université. Et vous? **6.** Je suis professeur. Et vous? **7.** Je travaille *[days]*. Et vous? **8.** Le lundi *[or another day]*, je travaille de... à... Et vous? **9.** Je suis en cours *[days]*. Et vous? **10.** Je parle français, anglais,... Et vous?

TRANSPARENCIES: CP-7A, CP-7B

Suggestions. A. Teach the expressions in the section **Le professeur dit...** for recognition only. These expressions may be presented and practiced using total physical response activities. **B.** Give one of the classroom commands and either act it out or do something else. Students say **oui,** if you are following the directions, **non,** if not. **C.** Perform an action and give students two statements to choose from to indicate which directions you are following.

En cours

Le professeur dit aux étudiants:

En cours.

Ouvrez votre livre à la page 23.

Fermez votre livre.

Écoutez la question.

Répondez à la question.

Allez au tableau.

Écrivez la réponse en phrases complètes.

Prenez une feuille de papier et un crayon ou un stylo.

Faites l'exercice A à la page 21.

Donnez-moi votre feuille de papier.

À la maison.

Lisez la page 17.

Apprenez les mots de vocabulaire et préparez l'examen pour le **prochain** cours.

Faites les devoirs dans le cahier et écoutez le CD / les cassettes.

Le professeur dit aux étudiants *The professor says to the students*   **prochain(e)** *next*   **Faites les devoirs** *Do the homework*

Prononciation: *Les voyelles groupées*

Note the pronunciation of the following vowel combinations:

ai [ɛ]:   français   je vais   je sais   vrai
oi [wa]:   moi   toi   trois   au revoir   devoirs
ui [ɥi]:   huit   fruit   aujourd'hui
au, eau [o]:   au   aussi   beaucoup   tableau
ou [u]:   vous   douze   ouvre   pour   jour   cours

The combination **eu** has two different sounds, depending on whether it is followed by a pronounced consonant in the same syllable.

MORE OPEN [œ]:   heure   neuf   professeur   seul(e)
MORE CLOSED [ø]:   deux   veut   jeudi   monsieur

A. Où? Is your professor telling you to do these things **en cours** or **à la maison?**

1. Fermez votre livre.
2. Apprenez les mots de vocabulaire.
3. Écoutez et répondez, s'il vous plaît.
4. Allez au tableau.
5. Prenez une feuille de papier.
6. Lisez les pages 12, 13 et 14.
7. Faites les devoirs dans le cahier.
8. Ouvrez votre livre à la page 23.

B. En cours. In groups, make up commands your instructor might give you by matching items from the two columns. Which group can come up with the most?

Fermez...   ... les devoirs.
Allez...   ... les mots de vocabulaire.
Lisez...   ... le CD.
Apprenez...   ... à la page 12.
Comptez...   ... de 0 à 30.
Écoutez...   ... au tableau.
Prenez...   ... une feuille de papier.
Écrivez...   ... la phrase.
Faites...   ... votre livre.

C. C'est logique? How many logical ways can you complete these commands?

1. Écrivez...
2. Lisez...
3. Apprenez...
4. Prenez...
5. Faites...
6. Écoutez...

Supplemental activities. **A.** Read these commands and have students point at the part of the body they would use to carry them out: **1.** Écoutez la question. **2.** Répondez à la question. **3.** Écrivez la question au tableau. **4.** Lisez la question au tableau. **5.** Répétez la réponse. **B.** Tell students to give you these things: **Donnez-moi votre livre (votre stylo, votre crayon, votre cahier, une feuille de papier). C.** Tell students to turn to various pages from 1 to 30. For example: **Ouvrez votre livre à la page 19.** Then ask someone to read something on the page. For example, **Lisez B, numéro 2. D.** Play **Jacques a dit** *(Simon says),* using classroom commands.

TRANSPARENCIES: CP-8A, CP-8B

Des expressions utiles et l'alphabet

When you hear new words, it may be helpful to see how they are spelled. You can ask:

Ça s'écrit comment?
How is that written?

Ça s'écrit avec un accent ou sans accent?
Is that written with an accent or without an accent?

Ça s'écrit avec un ou deux **s** en français / en anglais?
*Is that written with one **s** or two in French / in English?*

Ça s'écrit...

a	a	**i**	i	**q**	ku	**y**	i grec
b	bé	**j**	ji	**r**	erre	**z**	zède
c	cé	**k**	ka	**s**	esse		
d	dé	**l**	elle	**t**	té	**é** =	e accent aigu
e	e	**m**	emme	**u**	u	**è** =	e accent grave
f	effe	**n**	enne	**v**	vé	**â** =	a accent circonflexe
g	gé	**o**	o	**w**	double vé	**ï** =	i tréma
h	hache	**p**	pé	**x**	iks	**ç** =	c cédille

You may also need to use these expressions.

Comment? Répétez, s'il vous plaît.
What? Please repeat.

—Est-ce que vous comprenez?
—Do you understand?

—Oui, je comprends. /
Non, je ne comprends pas.
—Yes, I understand. /
No, I don't understand.

—Comment dit-on *a pen* en français?
*—How do you say **a pen** in French?*

—On dit **un stylo.**
*—You say **un stylo.***

—Qu'est-ce que ça veut dire **votre**?
*—What does **votre** mean?*

—Ça veut dire *your.*
*—It means **your.***

—Je ne sais pas.
—I don't know.

A. Dans l'ordre logique. Put the sentences of the following conversations in the logical order.

1. — Ça veut dire *pen.*
— Non, qu'est-ce que ça veut dire?
— Est-ce que vous comprenez le mot **stylo**?

2. — Je ne sais pas.
— Comment dit-on *hi* en français?
— On dit **salut.**

3. — Comment? Répétez s'il vous plaît.
— Qu'est-ce que ça veut dire **bientôt**?
— Je ne sais pas.
— Qu'est-ce que ça veut dire **bientôt**?

4. — Ça s'écrit B-E-A-U-C-O-U-P.
— Comment dit-on *a lot* en français?
— On dit **beaucoup.**
— Ça s'écrit comment?

B. Réponses.
How would you respond if your instructor said the following to you?

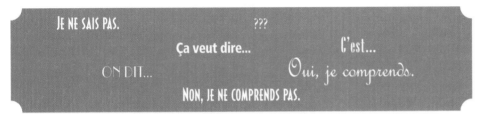

JE NE SAIS PAS. ???

Ça veut dire... C'est...

ON DIT... Oui, je comprends.

NON, JE NE COMPRENDS PAS.

1. **Stylo** veut dire *pen*. Est-ce que vous comprenez?
2. J'ai besoin de vous voir demain. Est-ce que vous comprenez?
3. C'est quel jour, aujourd'hui?
4. Qu'est-ce que ça veut dire **stylo?**
5. Comment dit-on *See you tomorrow* en français?
6. Comment dit-on *mild* en français?

C. La francophonie.
Say what letter is missing at the beginning of the following names of French-speaking places. Can you locate each place on the map inside the front cover of the book?

Exemple   __uébec
         Q

1. __rance
2. __lgérie
3. __ôte-d'Ivoire
4. __aïti
5. __ahiti
6. __uadeloupe
7. __artinique
8. __elgique
9. __énégal
10. __ouisiane
11. __uanda
12. __uinée

Ghardaia, Algérie

D. Ça s'écrit comment?
Here are some French words that are similar to English but spelled slightly differently. Explain to a French friend how to spell them in English. Your friend already knows not to use accents.

Exemples   indépendance   **En anglais, *independence,* ça s'écrit avec un *e.***
          appartement   **En anglais, *apartment,* ça s'écrit avec un *p* et sans *e.***

1. littérature
2. activité
3. chocolat
4. symptôme
5. criminel
6. dîner
7. environnement
8. moderne
9. hôpital

E. Présentations.
Introduce yourself to a classmate, who will ask you to spell your last name.

Exemple   — Bonjour, je suis Paul Wyndel.
             — Wyndel? Ça s'écrit comment?
             — W-Y-N-D-E-L. Et toi, tu t'appelles comment?
             — Je m'appelle Lynn Phan.
             — Phan? Ça s'écrit comment?
             — P-H-A-N.

COMPÉTENCE 1

Greeting people

À bientôt.	*See you soon.*
À demain.	*See you tomorrow.*
À tout à l'heure.	*See you in a little while.*
Au revoir.	*Good-bye.*
Bonjour.	*Hello., Good morning.*
Bonsoir.	*Good evening.*
Comment allez-vous?	*How are you? (formal)*
Je vais très / assez bien.	*I'm doing very / fairly well.*
Pas mal.	*Not badly.*
Pas très bien.	*Not very well.*
Comment ça va? / Ça va?	*How's it going? (familiar)*
Ça va.	*It's going fine.*
Comment vous appelez-vous?	*What's your name? (formal)*
Tu t'appelles comment?	*What's your name? (familiar)*
Je m'appelle...	*My name is . . .*
Je suis...	*I'm . . .*
et	*and*
Et toi?	*And you? (familiar)*
Et vous?	*And you? (formal)*
madame	*Mrs., madam*
mademoiselle	*Miss*
merci	*thank you*
moi	*me*
monsieur	*Mr., sir*
Salut!	*Hi!*

COMPÉTENCE 2

Counting and telling time

Combien font... et... ?	*How much is . . . plus . . . ?*
Combien font... moins... ?	*How much is . . . minus . . . ?*
... et... font...	*. . . plus . . . equals . . .*
... moins... font...	*. . . minus . . . equals . . .*
Comptez de... à...	*Count from . . . to . . .*
s'il vous plaît	*please (formal)*
Quelle heure est-il?	*What time is it?*
Maintenant...	*Now . . .*
Il est une heure / deux heures.	*It's one o'clock / two o'clock.*
et quart / et demi(e)	*a quarter past / half past*
moins le quart	*a quarter till*
midi	*noon*
minuit	*midnight*
À quelle heure?	*At what time?*
à... heure(s)	*at . . . o'clock*
du matin	*in the morning*
de l'après-midi	*in the afternoon*
du soir	*in the evening*
Je (ne) suis (pas) à la maison.	*I'm (not) at home.*
Je (ne) suis (pas) en cours.	*I'm (not) in class.*
Je (ne) travaille (pas)...	*I (don't) work . . .*
de... à...	*from . . . to . . .*
avant	*before*
après	*after*
La bibliothèque ouvre / ferme...	*The library opens / closes . . .*
Le cours de français commence / finit...	*The French class starts / finishes . . .*
quarante	*forty*
cinquante	*fifty*

Pour les chiffres de zéro à trente, voir la page 10.

C'est quel jour aujourd'hui?	*What day is today?*
C'est...	*It's . . .*
lundi	*Monday*
mardi	*Tuesday*
mercredi	*Wednesday*
jeudi	*Thursday*
vendredi	*Friday*
samedi	*Saturday*
dimanche	*Sunday*
les jours de la semaine	*the days of the week*
votre emploi du temps	*your schedule*
Je suis en cours /	*I am in class /*
à la maison...	*at home . . .*
le lundi, le mardi...	*on Mondays, on Tuesdays. . .*
le matin, l'après-midi,	*in the morning, in the afternoon,*
le soir	*in the evening*
le week-end	*weekends / on the weekend*
de lundi à vendredi	*from Monday to Friday*
	(this week)
du lundi au vendredi	*from Monday to Friday*
	(every week)
Tu es... ? / Vous êtes... ?	*Are you . . .?*
Je suis / Je ne suis pas...	*I am / I am not . . .*
américain(e)	*American*
canadien(ne)	*Canadian*
de (d')... (+ city)	*from . . . (+ city)*
d'ici	*from here*
étudiant(e)	*a student*
professeur	*a professor*
Vous habitez... ?	*Do you live . . . ?*
J'habite / Je n'habite pas...	*I live / I do not live . . .*
à (+ city)	*in (+ city)*
avec ma famille	*with my family*
avec un(e) ami(e)	*with a friend*
avec un(e) camarade de	*with a roommate*
chambre	
seul(e)	*alone*
Vous parlez... ?	*Do you speak . . . ?*
Je parle / Je ne parle pas...	*I speak / I do not speak . . .*
anglais	*English*
espagnol	*Spanish*
français	*French*
beaucoup en cours	*a lot in class*
très bien	*very well*
Je pense que...	*I think that . . .*
le français est...	*French is . . .*
un peu difficile	*a little difficult, hard*
assez facile	*fairly easy*
intéressant	*interesting*
super	*great*
Tu travailles... ? /	*Do you work . . . ?*
Vous travaillez... ?	
Je travaille /	*I work /*
Je ne travaille pas...	*I do not work . . .*
pour	*for*
à	*at*
à l'université	*at the university*
aussi	*also*
ce semestre	*this semester*
ici	*here*
mais	*but*
non	*no*
oui	*yes*
parce que	*because*
un peu	*a little*

Comment? Répétez, s'il vous plaît.	*What? Please repeat.*
Est-ce que vous comprenez?	*Do you understand?*
Oui, je comprends. / Non, je ne comprends pas.	*Yes I understand. / No, I don't understand.*
Comment dit-on...	*How do you say . . .*
en français / en anglais?	*in French / in English?*
On dit...	*You say . . .*
Qu'est-ce que ça veut dire?	*What does that mean?*
Ça veut dire...	*That means . . .*
Je ne sais pas.	*I don't know.*
Ça s'écrit comment?	*How is that written?*
Ça s'écrit...	*That's written . . .*
avec	*with*
ou	*or*
sans	*without*
un accent	*an accent*
Le professeur dit aux étudiants...	*The professor says to the students . . .*
en cours	*in class*
Ouvrez votre livre à la page 23.	*Open your book to page 23.*
Fermez votre livre.	*Close your book.*
Écoutez la question.	*Listen to the question.*
Répondez à la question.	*Answer the question.*
Allez au tableau.	*Go to the board.*
Écrivez la réponse en phrases complètes.	*Write the answer in complete sentences.*
Prenez une feuille de papier et un crayon ou un stylo.	*Take out a piece of paper and a pencil or a pen.*
Faites l'exercice A à la page 21.	*Do exercise A on page 21.*
Donnez-moi votre feuille de papier.	*Give me your piece of paper.*
à la maison	*at home*
Lisez la page 17.	*Read page 17.*
Apprenez les mots de vocabulaire et préparez l'examen pour le prochain cours.	*Learn the vocabulary words and prepare for the exam for the next class.*
Faites les devoirs dans le cahier et écoutez le CD / les cassettes.	*Do the homework in the workbook and listen to the CD / the cassettes.*

Pour l'alphabet, voir la page 22.

Baie de Cannes

Pablo Picasso (1881–1973)
1958
Paris, Musée Picasso
Giraudon/Art Resource, New York
© 1998 Estate of Pablo Picasso/Artists Rights Society (ARS), New York

This is a view of Cannes, a resort town on the **Côte d'Azur,** as seen from a window of Picasso's 19th-century villa, **La Californie.** The same view is the subject of many of Picasso's paintings from this period.

Suggestion. The first two chapters take place in Nice. Ask students what they know about Nice, Marseilles, Toulon, St-Tropez, and Cannes. Point out the popularity of the **Côte d'Azur** and surrounding areas with painters, such as Matisse, Cézanne, Van Gogh, and Picasso. You may also wish to show films that take place in southern France, such as *Jean de Florette, Manon des sources, La Gloire de mon père,* and *Le Château de ma mère.* The comedy *Les Compères* was filmed largely in Nice. You should preview films for appropriateness of content.

Sur la Côte d'Azur

LA FRANCE (LA RÉPUBLIQUE FRANÇAISE)

SUPERFICIE: 549 000 kilomètres carrés

POPULATION: 60 186 000 (les Français)

CAPITALE: Paris

INDUSTRIES PRINCIPALES: aéronautique, agriculture, industries manufacturières, secteur des services, technologie, tourisme

À l'université

La France et ses régions

Additional information. Côte d'Azur, Provence: The Greeks established Marseilles over 2000 years ago and Antibes, near Nice, in the fifth century B.C. Several parts of the area were occupied by the Romans and some remains are still visible. The medieval areas of several cities can still be visited. During the Middle Ages, eagle-nest villages, such as Èze, near Nice, were built on the mountain tops for protection against invasion and illnesses such as malaria. Still surrounded by ramparts and looking much as they did hundreds of years ago, they now often house artisans and craftsmen.

Quelles régions françaises **connaissez-vous?** Regardez les photos, lisez les descriptions et identifiez la région:

- **les Pays-de-la-Loire/le Centre**
- **la Côte d'Azur**
- **l'Alsace**
- **la Bretagne**

Pays-de-la-Loire: The popularity of this region for establishing castles began with Charles VII. Expelled from Paris by the English in the fifteenth century, he spent much of his exile in this region. Subsequent kings shared his enthusiasm for the area and the nobility followed the royal lead. The principal cities of the region are Orléans and Tours, which lies at the heart of the Vouvray wine region.

*Dans cette région au long de la Loire, **il y a** plus de 120 **châteaux. Parmi** les plus **connus** sont Chambord, Chenonceaux, Blois, Amboise, Cheverny et Sully-sur-Loire.*

__Nommée__ pour la couleur __de l'eau__ et __du ciel__, cette région __se trouve__ le long de la mer Méditerranée. C'est the Riviera __en__ anglais.

---

connaissez-vous? *do you know?* **il y a** *there is, there are* **châteaux** *castles* **Parmi** *Among* **connus** *known*
Nommée *Named* **de l'eau** *of the water* **du ciel** *of the sky* **se trouve** *is located*

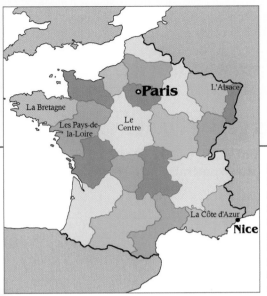

Bretagne: Some of the first permanent inhabitants of France, the Stone Age people who erected the **menhirs,** settled in Brittany. At Carnac, several thousand stones, **menhirs,** are found set in rows, similar to those at Stonehenge. The **menhirs** were probably connected with a sun cult, but were later adapted by Romans and early Christians to their own rites. Many ancient stone tombs, **dolmens,** are also found in the area. The later Celtic settlers from Wales and Cornwall in the fifth and sixth centuries brought with them their language and religion.

Alsace: In 843, Charlemagne's vast empire was split into three kingdoms. Alsace was traded to a German prince after the division of Charlemagne's empire and did not return to French rule for 800 years, when it was ceded to France in gratitude for French aid against Austria. Strasbourg, the region's principal city, was the site of numerous wars and invasions, including Roman and Hun occupations. It maintains, in its original condition, a medieval town and a Gothic cathedral with a famous astronomical clock adorned with a parade of mechanical figures.

Historiquement et géographiquement ***liée à la Grande-Bretagne,*** *cette région* ***maintient*** *l'esprit religieux et indépendant de ses* ***ancêtres*** *celtes. Les dolmens et les menhirs* ***reflètent*** *les traditions de ses anciens habitants.*

Jadis *une partie de* ***l'Allemagne,*** *cette région* ***montre*** *des influences allemandes et françaises dans sa culture.*

---

liée à la Grande-Bretagne *connected to Great Britain*   **maintient** *maintains*   **ancêtres** *ancestors*
reflètent *reflect*   **Jadis** *Formerly*   **l'Allemagne** *Germany*   **montre** *shows*

COMPÉTENCE 1

Identifying people and describing appearance

NOTE Culturelle

Les études *(studies)* universitaires sont très importantes en France. Il y a plus de *(There are more than)* 1,5 millions d'étudiants dans les universités en France. La majorité des universités sont des universités publiques, contrôlées par l'État *(government)*. Généralement, il y a une université publique dans toutes *(all)* les grandes villes *(cities)*. Les cinq villes universitaires les plus populaires sont: Paris, Lille, Versailles, Lyon et Toulouse.

Note. Each chapter of **Horizons** is divided into four **Compétences.** The first **Compétence** of each chapter consists of a vocabulary presentation followed by a structure explanation section and either a reading or listening comprehension section with learning strategies. The next two **Compétences** consist of a vocabulary presentation followed by two structure explanation sections. The final **Compétence** is composed of a vocabulary presentation followed by a structure explanation section and a review. Vocabulary in the opening sections of each **Compétence** is presented lexically and students are asked to use it only as such. Relevant grammatical structures are explained in the structure sections that follow, in which students are given the opportunity to manipulate the grammatical structures. If you wish, you may at any time proceed to a grammar explanation when presenting vocabulary.

NOTES DE VOCABULAIRE

Use **c'est** *(he / she / it / this is)* to identify people and things and **il est** *(he / it is)* or **elle est** *(she / it is)* when describing them. Notice that adjectives have a different form depending on whether a man or a woman is being described. You will learn more about this later in this chapter.

Les gens à l'université

Ce sont mes amis, David et Annette. Ils sont étudiants à l'université de Nice. Ils sont dans **le même** cours de littérature.

C'est David, **un jeune homme** français.
Il est étudiant.
Il est de Nice.

C'est Annette, **une jeune femme** américaine.
Elle est étudiante.
Elle est de Los Angeles.

C'est Jean, **le frère de** David.
Il n'est pas étudiant.
Il travaille.

C'est Yvette, **la sœur jumelle d'**Annette.
Elle n'est pas étudiante.
Elle travaille.

Yvette et Annette ne sont pas françaises. Elles sont américaines. Annette est à Nice pour **étudier.** Yvette est en France pour **voir sa** sœur et pour visiter la France.

Comment est David?

Il est petit.
Il n'est pas grand.
Il est mince.
Il n'est pas gros.

Il est jeune et beau.
Il n'est pas vieux ou laid.
Il est **célibataire.**
Il n'est pas marié, fiancé ou divorcé.

Comment est Annette?

Elle est petite.
Elle n'est pas grande.
Elle est mince.
Elle n'est pas grosse.

Elle est jeune et belle.
Elle n'est pas vieille ou laide.
Elle est célibataire.
Elle n'est pas mariée, fiancée ou divorcée.

Les gens *People* **Ce sont...** *They are . . .* **mes** *my* **le même** *the same* **C'est...** *He/She/It/This is . . .* **un jeune homme** *a young man* **une jeune femme** *a young woman* **le frère de** *the brother of* **la sœur de** *the sister of* **jumeau (jumelle)** *twin* **étudier** *to study* **voir** *to see* **sa** *his, her, its* **Comment est... ?** *What is . . . like?* **célibataire** *single*

David et Annette **font connaissance la première semaine des cours.**

DAVID: Salut! **Nous sommes** dans le même cours de littérature, non? Je suis David Cauvin.

ANNETTE: Bonjour. Moi, je m'appelle Annette Clark. Tu es d'ici?

DAVID: Oui, je suis de Nice. Et toi, tu es **d'où?**

ANNETTE: Je suis de Los Angeles, mais j'habite ici maintenant parce que je suis étudiante à l'université.

A. Identification. Qui est-ce? *(Who is it?)*

C'est...	David	Jean	Annette	Yvette
Ce sont...	David et Annette	Annette et Yvette	David et Jean	

1. Il n'est pas étudiant.
2. C'est le frère de David.
3. Elles sont de Los Angeles.
4. C'est la sœur jumelle d'Yvette.
5. Elle est à Nice pour voir la France.
6. Ce sont des jeunes femmes.
7. Ils sont français.
8. Ils sont dans le même cours de littérature.

B. C'est vrai? Regardez les illustrations de David et d'Annette à la page précédente. Décidez si ce que *(what)* vous entendez est vrai *(true)* ou faux *(false)*.

Exemples VOUS ENTENDEZ: Annette est très grande. David n'est pas laid.

VOUS DITES: **C'est faux.** **C'est vrai.**

C. Après les cours. Vous êtes dans un café et vous pensez reconnaître *(to recognize)* un(e) camarade de classe. Préparez une conversation avec les questions suivantes.

1. Tu es étudiant(e) à *(name of your college)*, non?
2. Tu es en cours de français *(days of your French course)* à *(time of your French course)*?
3. Le professeur, c'est un homme ou une femme?
4. Le professeur, c'est *(name of your professor)*?
5. Nous sommes dans le même cours, non?

D. Nous sommes dans le même cours! Avec un(e) partenaire, changez la conversation entre David et Annette comme indiqué *(as indicated)*.

1. David and Annette are in the same Spanish class.
2. David is from Paris and he is in Nice to study.
3. The conversation is between you and a classmate. Change it to make it true for you.

---

font connaissance (faire connaissance *to meet)* **la première semaine des cours** *the first week of classes*
Nous sommes *We are* **d'où** *from where*

Warm-up activities. A. Questions orales. 1. Comment allez-vous? **2.** Comment vous appelez-vous? **3.** Ça s'écrit comment? **4.** Vous êtes américain(e)? **5.** Vous habitez à... ? **6.** Vous parlez anglais? **7.** Vous parlez français aussi? **8.** Vous êtes étudiant(e)? **9.** Vous travaillez aussi? **10.** Quelle heure est-il maintenant? **11.** C'est quel jour, aujourd'hui? **B.** Have students write two or three true or false statements about themselves to read to the class. The other students should try to guess which are true and which are false.

Suggestion for the conversation. Set the scene and have students listen to the conversation twice with books closed. Put these partial statements on the board or on a transparency and have students listen for how to complete them. **1.** Annette est de... **2.** David est de... **3.** David et Annette sont dans le même cours de... Afterward, have them listen to the conversation again while reading along in the text.

Warm-up for A. Identification. C'est Annette ou David? **1.** C'est un jeune homme. **2.** C'est une jeune femme. **3.** Elle est étudiante. **4.** Elle est américaine. **5.** Il est français. **6.** Il est étudiant. **7.** Elle est belle. **8.** Il est petit. **9.** Il est beau aussi.

Suggestions for A. Identification. A. Before doing **A. Identification,** model the pronunciation of the sentences and have students read them aloud to practice pronunciation. **B.** Have students do **A. Identification** in pairs and alternate the giving of cues and responses.

Script for B. C'est vrai? EXEMPLES Annette est très grande. David n'est pas laid. **1.** Annette est vieille. **2.** David et Annette sont minces. **3.** David n'est pas vieux. **4.** David est grand. **5.** Annette est grosse. **6.** David et Annette sont jeunes. **7.** Annette est belle. **8.** David n'est pas gros. **9.** Annette n'est pas petite. **10.** David est beau.

Supplemental activities. A. Read the following names from French literature and have students respond **C'est un homme,** or **C'est une femme:** Colette, Molière, Simone de Beauvoir, Jean-Paul Sartre, Gabrielle Roy, Marguerite Duras, Voltaire, Victor Hugo, Jean de La Fontaine, George Sand, Alexandre Dumas. **B.** Bring pictures of celebrities and have students identify and describe them. EXEMPLE C'est Arnold Schwarzenegger. Il est...

1. What two expressions are used to identify who someone is? What are the negative forms of these expressions?

2. When describing someone, how do you say *he is? she is? they are* for a group of all females? *they are* for a group of all males or for a mixed group? What are the negative forms of these expressions?

3. What is the base form of an adjective? What do you usually do to make it feminine? masculine plural? feminine plural?

4. What is the feminine form of **gros? canadien? beau? vieux?**

5. Is there a difference in pronunciation between **petit** and **petite?**

Note. Here students are introduced to the concept of using **c'est/ce sont** and **il/elle est** and **ils/elles sont** to identify and describe people. The difference in use between **c'est** and **il/elle est** is presented in more detail and practiced on page 46, where the use of **il/elle est** and **ils/elles sont** to represent things is presented. The concept of grammatical gender is presented on page 44. Additional recycling and practice with adjectives is done throughout this chapter and again in later chapters.

Suggestions. Point out that the feminine form of adjectives such as **canadienne** and **américaine** loses its nasality. Point out that the consonant before the final **s** in masculine plural adjectives is still silent (**grands**).

Identifying and describing people:
C'est et il/elle est et les adjectifs

To *identify* people, use **c'est** and **ce sont.** Note their negative forms.

C'est (+ noun)	*He is* *She is* *It is* *This is*		**Ce n'est pas** (+ noun)	*He isn't* *She isn't* *It isn't* *This isn't*	
Ce sont (+ noun)	*They are*		**Ce ne sont pas** (+ noun)	*They aren't*	

To *describe* people with adjectives, use **il est, elle est, ils sont,** and **elles sont.** Use **ils** for a group of males or a mixed group and **elles** for a group of all females. Note their negative forms.

Il est **Elle est**	(+ adjective)	*He is* *She is*	**Il n'est pas** **Elle n'est pas**	(+ adjective)	*He isn't* *She isn't*
Ils sont **Elles sont**	(+ adjective)	*They are* *They are*	**Ils ne sont pas** **Elles ne sont pas**	(+ adjective)	*They aren't* *They aren't*

In French, adjective forms vary depending on whether they describe a male or a female, and whether they describe one person or more than one.

The masculine singular form of the adjective is used as the base form. To change the form to feminine, add an **-e** to the masculine form, unless it already ends in an *unaccented* **e.** If it ends in *accented* **é,** add another **-e** to form the feminine. Add **-s** to make an adjective plural, unless it already ends in **s** or **x.**

MASCULINE		FEMININE	
singular	*plural*	*singular*	*plural*
petit	petit**s**	petit**e**	petit**es**
jeune	jeune**s**	jeune	jeune**s**
marié	marié**s**	marié**e**	marié**es**
français	français	français**e**	français**es**

Some adjectives, such as **gros** and **canadien,** double their final consonant before adding **-e** for agreement with feminine nouns.

MASCULINE		FEMININE	
singular	*plural*	*singular*	*plural*
gros	gros	gros**se**	gros**ses**
canadien	canadien**s**	canadien**ne**	canadien**nes**

The adjectives **beau, jumeau,** and **vieux** are irregular. They follow a similar pattern.

MASCULINE		FEMININE	
singular	*plural*	*singular*	*plural*
beau	beaux	belle	belles
jumeau	jumeaux	jumelle	jumelles
vieux	vieux	vieille	vieilles

Warm-up for *A. Claude qui?* Écoutez les phrases et déterminez si elles décrivent *(describe)* David, Annette ou les deux. 1. Il est petit. 2. Il est beau. 3. Elle n'est pas grande. 4. Ils sont étudiants. 5. Il n'est pas américain. 6. Elle est américaine. 7. Elle est petite.

Script for *A. Claude qui?* 1. Claude est grande. 2. Claude n'est pas petit. 3. Claude est française. 4. Claude n'est pas canadienne. 5. Claude n'est pas gros.

Continuation for *A. Claude qui?* Claude n'est pas petite (grosse, américain, vieux, laide, vieille).

Follow-ups for *A. Claude qui?* A. Show students how to spell the masculine and feminine forms **Daniel** and **Danielle**. Tell them that David is describing two of his friends, **Daniel** and **Danielle**. They listen to what David says and write the name of the person he is describing on a sheet of paper. If they cannot tell, they write a question mark. 1. Danielle est canadienne. 2. Daniel (Danielle) est célibataire. 3. Daniel n'est pas petit. 4. Danielle est petite. 5. Danielle est belle. 6. Danielle est grosse. 7. Daniel est beau. 8. Danielle n'est pas américaine. B. Give similar sentences as dictation. C. Have students write sentences to describe Claude Bellon and Claude Lacoste. They then read one choice from each pair and the class says which Claude is being described. D. Have students describe the ideal partner. Remind them to use negatives such as **Il/Elle n'est pas laid(e)**.

Follow-up for *B. Comment sont-ils?* Répondez. EXEMPLE David est américain ou français? **Il est français. Il n'est pas américain.** 1. David est grand ou petit? 2. Jean et David sont français ou américains? 3. Annette est laide ou belle? 4. David et Annette sont dans le même cours d'espagnol ou de littérature? 5. Yvette est à Nice pour étudier ou pour voir sa sœur? 6. David et Annette sont étudiants ou professeurs? 7. Annette et Yvette sont américaines ou françaises? 8. Annette et Yvette sont de New York ou de Los Angeles?

Quick-reference answers for *C. Gens célèbres.* 1. Non, elle n'est pas mince. Elle est grosse. 2. Non, elle n'est pas grosse. Elle est mince. 3. Non, il n'est pas marié. Il est célibataire. 4. Non, il n'est pas beau. Il est laid. 5. Non, elle n'est pas laide. Elle est belle. 6. Non, il n'est pas petit. Il est grand. 7. Non, elle n'est pas vieille. Elle est jeune. 8. Non, il n'est pas vieux. Il est jeune.

Supplemental activities. A. Annette and David are alike. Describe Annette according to the description of David. EXEMPLE David est petit. → **Annette est petite.** David est jeune (mince, étudiant, beau, célibataire). B. Now describe David according to the description of Annette. Annette n'est pas canadienne (grande, grosse, mariée, vieille, laide).

Prononciation: *Il est + adjectif / Elle est + adjectif*

Since most final consonants are silent, you will not hear or say the final consonant of masculine adjective forms, unless they end in **c, r, f,** or **l.** When the **-e** is added to make the feminine form, the consonant is no longer final and is pronounced.

gran~~d~~ / grande
françai~~s~~ / française

The final **-s** of plurals is not pronounced.

Il~~s~~ sont peti~~ts~~.
Elle~~s~~ sont petite~~s~~.

Be careful to pronounce the vowels in **il/ils** and **elle/elles** distinctly. The letter **i** in French is pronounced similarly to the double *ee* in the English words *see* and *feed*, but it is said more quickly and the tongue is held more tensely. The letter **e** in **elle/elles** is pronounced somewhat like the *e* in the English word *bet*.

Il est grand.	Elle est grande.
Ils sont beaux.	Elles sont belles.

A. Claude qui?
Écoutez les phrases. C'est la phrase **a** pour Claude Bellon ou la phrase **b** pour Claude Lacoste?

1. **a.** Claude est grand.
   b. Claude est grande.
2. **a.** Claude n'est pas petit.
   b. Claude n'est pas petite.
3. **a.** Claude est français.
   b. Claude est française.
4. **a.** Claude n'est pas canadien.
   b. Claude n'est pas canadienne.
5. **a.** Claude n'est pas gros.
   b. Claude n'est pas grosse.

a. Claude Bellon
b. Claude Lacoste

B. Comment sont-ils?
Décrivez David et Annette comme dans l'exemple.

Exemple   David n'est pas marié.
   Il est célibataire.

1. David n'est pas gros.
2. David n'est pas vieux.
3. David n'est pas laid.
4. Annette n'est pas mariée.
5. Annette n'est pas laide.
6. Annette n'est pas vieille.

C. Gens célèbres.
Répondez logiquement.

Exemple   Tom Cruise est grand?
   Non, il n'est pas grand. Il est petit.

1. Rosie O'Donnell est mince?
2. Calista Flockhart est grosse?
3. Jude Law est marié?
4. Woody Allen est beau?
5. Julia Roberts est laide?
6. Dennis Rodman est petit?
7. Jennifer Lopez est vieille?
8. Will Smith est vieux?

Stratégies et lecture:
Using cognates and familiar words to read for the gist

Note. Vocabulary in this section is taught for recognition only. The prereading section is essential for student comprehension of the reading. Students may do it as a class, in groups, or they may prepare it at home.

Supplemental activity. Write the following cognates on the board and have students guess their meaning: **entièrement, activement, probablement, normalement, relativement, rarement, préoccupé, cultivé, intoxiqué, démoralisé, hôtesse, pâte, bête, rôti de porc, hâte.**

Cognates are words that look the same or similar in two languages and have the same meaning. Take advantage of cognates to help you read French more easily. There are some patterns in cognates. What three patterns do you see here? What do the last two words in each column mean?

soudainement	*suddenly*	obligé	*obliged*	hôpital	*hospital*
décidément	*decidedly*	décidé	*decided*	île	*isle, island*
complètement	*???*	compliqué	*???*	honnête	*???*
généralement	*???*	sauvé	*???*	forêt	*???*

Recognizing words you have already learned in different forms will also help you read. Use the phrases you already know on the left to guess the meaning of those on the right.

Comment dit-on *pen* en français? Qu'est-ce que tu dis?
Je ne sais pas la réponse. Yvette ne sait pas quoi répondre.

You will run across many unknown words in reading French, but this should not prevent you from understanding. Be flexible, changing forms of words or word order if necessary, and skip over little words that may not be needed to get the message.

Suggestion for *A. Avant de lire.* Encourage students to read the whole sentence before they respond. Remind them that they do not have to understand every word for general comprehension. Ask them to guess meaning from context.

A. Avant de lire.
Can you state the general idea of the following sentences? Do not try to read them word by word; rather, focus on the words that you can understand.

Yvette hésite un moment avant de répondre.
C'est juste à ce moment qu'Annette arrive.
Annette sauve la pauvre Yvette.
David voit Annette et Yvette et s'exclame: «Je vois double!»

B. Mots apparentés.
Before reading the following text, ***Qui est-ce?***, skim through it and list the cognates you see. You should find about twenty.

 Qui est-ce?

*Yvette Clark is visiting her twin sister, Annette, a student at the University of Nice. As she waits for her sister in front of the **musée des Beaux-Arts**, a young man approaches. Since she does not speak French very well, Yvette is unsure what to say when he speaks to her.*

— Salut, Annette! Ça va?

Yvette hésite un moment avant de répondre.

— Non, non... euh, ça va, mais... euh... je regrette... je ne suis pas Annette. Je suis Yvette.

— Qu'est-ce que tu dis, Annette?

Yvette pense en elle-même: *«He thinks I'm Annette. How do I tell him . . .?»*

— Non, non, répond Yvette. Vous ne comprenez pas. Je ne suis pas Annette.

— Comment ça, tu n'es pas Annette?

Décidément, ce jeune homme ne comprend rien! Yvette insiste encore une fois.

— Je ne suis pas Annette. Vous ne comprenez pas! Écoutez! Je ne suis pas Annette! Je ne suis pas étudiante.

— Mais qu'est-ce que tu dis? demande David. Tu es malade? C'est moi, David. Nous sommes dans le même cours de littérature.

Yvette pense: *«I'm never going to get this guy to understand. He's so sure I'm Annette.»*

C'est juste à ce moment qu'Annette arrive. La pauvre Yvette est sauvée.

— Salut, Yvette! Bonjour, David!

David, très surpris de voir les deux sœurs jumelles, s'exclame:

— Mais, ce n'est pas possible! Je vois double! Maintenant je comprends. C'est ta sœur jumelle, Annette.

— Pauvre David! Je te présente ma sœur, Yvette.

— Bonjour, Yvette. Désolé pour la confusion, mais quelle ressemblance!

Note. It is not intended that readings be read aloud by students. You may wish to have students follow along as you read aloud or play the CD. This will encourage them to read for the gist and not translate word for word. Remind students to read for general comprehension and not to worry about understanding every word. Point out the use of dashes indicating a change in speaker, as well as the use of **guillemets**.

A. Avez-vous compris? Qui parle: **David, Yvette** ou **Annette?**

1. Vous ne comprenez pas. Je ne suis pas Annette.
2. Mais nous sommes dans le même cours de littérature.
3. Je ne suis pas étudiante à l'université de Nice.
4. Je ne parle pas très bien français.
5. Je te présente ma sœur.

B. D'abord... Which happens first, **a** or **b?**

1. **a.** David dit bonjour à Yvette.
   b. Yvette arrive au musée des Beaux-Arts.

2. **a.** David dit: «Bonjour, Annette.»
   b. Yvette pense: «Il ne comprend pas.»

3. **a.** Yvette hésite à répondre parce qu'elle ne parle pas très bien français.
   b. Yvette répond: «Non, non, vous ne comprenez pas.»

4. **a.** David comprend qu'Annette et Yvette sont des sœurs jumelles.
   b. Annette arrive.

5. **a.** David dit: «Désolé *(Sorry)* pour la confusion.»
   b. David comprend la situation.

COMPÉTENCE 2

NOTE Culturelle

Voilà les étapes *(steps)* du système d'éducation en France. C'est très différent d'ici?

la crèche *(government-sponsored day care)*

l'école maternelle *(kindergarten)*

l'école *(school)* élémentaire

l'école secondaire (le collège et le lycée)

l'université ou une école spécialisée

TRANSPARENCIES: 1-2

Warm-up questions. Answer each question about your best friend. **1.** C'est un homme ou une femme? **2.** Il/Elle est jeune? **3.** Il/Elle est marié(e)? **4.** Il/Elle est canadien(ne)? français(e)? américain(e)? **5.** Il/Elle est d'ici? **6.** Il/Elle est grand(e) ou petit(e)? **7.** Il/Elle est étudiant(e)?

Suggestions. Point out the false cognates **sympathique, gentil,** and **dynamique.** Point out the difference between **mon meilleur ami** and **ma meilleure amie.**

Les personnalités

Je suis très… Je suis **plutôt**… Je suis assez… Je suis un peu… Je **ne** suis **pas (du tout)**…

optimiste, idéaliste / pessimiste / réaliste

timide / extraverti(e)

sympathique, gentil(le), agréable / méchant(e), désagréable

intelligent(e), intellectuel(le) / **bête**

amusant(e), intéressant(e) / ennuyeux (ennuyeuse)

dynamique, sportif (sportive) / paresseux (paresseuse)

What are you like, compared to your best friend?

Je suis **plus** dynamique **que mon meilleur ami (ma meilleure amie).**
Je suis **aussi** sportif (sportive) **que** mon meilleur ami (ma meilleure amie).
Je suis **moins** bête **que** mon meilleur ami (ma meilleure amie).

 Une **nouvelle** amie, Marie-Louise, parle avec David.

NOTE DE VOCABULAIRE
Le football veut dire *soccer*. On dit **le football américain** pour dire *football*.

MARIE-LOUISE: **Tes amis** et toi, vous êtes étudiants, non?
DAVID: Oui, nous sommes étudiants à l'université de Nice.
MARIE-LOUISE: Vous êtes intellectuels, **alors?**
DAVID: Moi, je ne suis pas très intellectuel, mais mes amis sont assez intellectuels. Et toi? Tu es étudiante?
MARIE-LOUISE: Non, **les études, ce n'est pas mon truc.**
DAVID: Et le sport? **Tu aimes** le sport?
MARIE-LOUISE: Oui, j'aime le sport. Je suis très sportive. J'aime beaucoup le tennis, mais je n'aime pas beaucoup le football.

Suggestion for the conversation. Set the scene and introduce the expressions **une nouvelle amie, j'aime,** and **je n'aime pas.** Put these statements on the board or on a transparency and have students listen to the conversation to determine if they are true or false. **1.** La nouvelle amie de David est étudiante. **2.** Elle est sportive. **3.** Elle aime beaucoup le tennis. Afterward, have them listen to the conversation again while reading along in the text.

---

plutôt *rather* **ne… pas du tout** *not at all* **sympathique** *nice* **gentil(le)** *nice* **bête** *stupid, dumb*
dynamique *active* **plus… que** *more . . . than* **mon meilleur ami (ma meilleure amie)** *my best friend*
aussi… que *as . . . as* **moins… que** *less . . . than* **nouveau (nouvelle)** *new* **Tes amis** *Your friends*
alors *so, then* **les études** *studies, going to school* **ce n'est pas mon truc** *it's not my thing* **Tu aimes** *You like*

A. Ils sont comment? Complétez les phrases.

Exemple   Arnold Schwarzenegger est (plus, moins, aussi) grand que Tom Cruise.
Arnold Schwarzenegger est plus grand que Tom Cruise.

1. Arnold Schwarzenegger est (plus, moins, aussi) beau que Tom Cruise.
2. Jay Leno est (plus, moins, aussi) amusant que David Letterman.
3. Tiger Woods est (plus, moins, aussi) sportif que Sammy Sosa.
4. Julia Roberts est (plus, moins, aussi) belle que Demi Moore.
5. Barbara Walters est (plus, moins, aussi) intelligente que Rosie O'Donnell.
6. Les Républicains sont (plus, moins, aussi) idéalistes que les Démocrates.

B. Comment sont-ils? Complétez les phrases.

1. Moi, *je suis / je ne suis pas* très extraverti(e).
2. *Je suis / Je ne suis pas* pessimiste.
3. Mon meilleur ami *est / n'est pas* bête.
4. *Il est / Il n'est pas* américain.
5. Mes amis *sont / ne sont pas* sportifs.
6. *Ils sont / Ils ne sont pas* paresseux.
7. Ma famille et moi, *nous sommes / nous ne sommes pas* très dynamiques.
8. *Nous sommes / Nous ne sommes pas* gentils.
9. Et vous, *(name your professor), vous êtes / vous n'êtes pas* très méchant(e)!

C. Et vous? Comment êtes-vous?

très	plutôt	assez	un peu	ne... pas du tout

Exemple   optimistic
Je suis très / plutôt / assez / un peu optimiste. /
Je ne suis pas (du tout) optimiste.

1. idealistic   3. lazy   5. shy   7. athletic
2. mean   4. intellectual 6. boring   8. married

D. Réponses. Quelle est la réponse logique?

1. Tu es étudiant(e)?
2. Tu aimes le sport?
3. Tes amis et toi, vous êtes sportifs?
4. Tes amis et toi, vous êtes intellectuels?
5. Tes amis sont extravertis?
6. Tes amis sont dynamiques?

a. Oui, nous sommes très sportifs.
b. Oui, nous sommes assez intellectuels.
c. Oui, je suis étudiant(e).
d. Non, ils sont plutôt paresseux.
e. Oui, j'aime beaucoup le football et le tennis.
f. Non, ils sont plutôt timides.

E. Faisons connaissance! Avec un(e) partenaire, changez la conversation entre David et Marie-Louise comme indiqué.

1. David is fairly intellectual, but his friends are not very intellectual. Marie-Louise likes soccer, but not tennis.
2. Marie-Louise is a student. She does not like sports and is not athletic.
3. The conversation is between you and a classmate. Change it to make it true for you.

Supplemental activities. A. Dans une classe idéale... **1.** Les étudiants sont optimistes ou pessimistes? **2.** Le professeur est timide ou extraverti? **3.** Les étudiants sont intelligents ou bêtes? **4.** Le livre est ennuyeux ou intéressant? **5.** Les devoirs sont intéressants ou ennuyeux? **6.** La classe est petite ou grande? **7.** Le professeur est méchant ou sympathique? **8.** Le professeur est intéressant ou ennuyeux? **B.** Donnez le contraire: **optimiste / extraverti / méchant / ennuyeux / dynamique / bête. C.** Have students pick the two adjectives that describe them best and the two adjectives that describe them least, using **Je suis (très)...** and **Je ne suis pas (du tout)...**

Suggestion for *C. Et vous?* Remind students to use the correct form of the adjectives and to pronounce them correctly. Students review adjective agreement and study the new patterns on pp. 38–39.

Follow-up for *C. Et vous?* Write adjectives on slips of paper, making sure that you have an antonym for each one (tall/short, optimistic/pessimistic, etc.) and distribute one to each student. Students pretend that this trait describes them. Have them go around the room and say **Je suis *(whatever is on their slip). Et toi?*** until they have found their opposite. Once they find their opposite, they have their partner for the next pair activity.

Suggestion for *D. Réponses.* Have students work in pairs, with one reading the question and the other giving the response. Have them take turns asking and answering.

1. What pronoun would you use to address a child? two children? a salesclerk?

2. How do you say *I* in French? *We? He? She? They?*

3. What is an infinitive? How do you say *to be?*

4. What form of **être** do you use with each of the subject pronouns?

5. What do you place before a conjugated verb to negate it? What do you place after it? What happens to **ne** when it is followed by a vowel sound?

6. What is elision?

7. What are five patterns of adjective agreement? What is the feminine form of **gros?** of **gentil?** of **beau?** of **nouveau?**

Describing people:

Les pronoms sujets, le verbe être, la négation et d'autres adjectifs

Below are the subject pronouns in French. Notice that there are two ways to say *you*. Use **tu** to talk to a friend, a family member, a classmate, or a child. Use **vous** when you are addressing an adult stranger or someone to whom you should show respect. Always use **vous** when talking to more than one person.

je	*I*		nous	*we*
tu	*you* (singular familiar)		vous	*you* (singular formal, all plurals)
il	*he, it* (masculine)		ils	*they* (masculine or a mixed group)
elle	*she, it* (feminine)		elles	*they* (feminine)

You have seen all of the forms of the verb **être** *(to be)*. The word **être** is the infinitive, the form of the verb you would find in a dictionary. The conjugation chart shows the forms you use with each subject pronoun.

ÊTRE *(to be)*					
je	**suis**	*I am*	nous	**sommes**	*we are*
tu	**es**	*you are*	vous	**êtes**	*you are*
il/elle	**est**	*he/she/it is*	ils/elles	**sont**	*they are*

With nouns, use the same form of the verb as for **il/elle** or **ils/elles.**

Le professeur **est** sympathique.   Mes amis **sont** intelligents.

To negate a conjugated verb, place **ne** before and **pas** after it. **Ne** changes to **n'** before a vowel or silent **h.** Generally, a final unaccented **e** in single-syllable words is dropped when the next word begins with a vowel or silent **h.** This is called **élision.**

Elles ne sont pas mariées.	*They aren't married.*
Il n'est pas grand.	*He's not tall.*
Je n'habite pas ici.	*I don't live here.*

Remember that adjectives agree in gender (masculine, feminine) and number (singular, plural) with what they describe. Review the forms of adjectives on page 32.

You have seen that some adjectives, such as **gros(se)** and **gentil(le),** double their final consonant before adding **-e** for agreement with feminine nouns. Adjectives ending in **-eux** and **-if** change their final consonant before adding **-e** for feminine agreement. Notice these patterns.

Notes. A. The subject pronoun **on** is introduced in *Chapitre 4.* **B.** Students learn the concept of grammatical gender on p. 44 and the use of **il, elle, ils,** and **elles** for things on p. 46.

Suggestions. A. Point out that, of the subject pronouns, only **je** elides, that **tu** and **elle** do not, and that elision is obligatory, not optional as it is in English. **B.** Remind students of the rules of adjective agreement they learned in *Compétence 1* (p. 32) and that **vieux** and **jumeau** follow a pattern similar to that of **beau** and **nouveau.**

Supplemental activity. Contradict what I say. EXEMPLE **Nous sommes optimistes.** → **Nous ne sommes pas optimistes. Nous sommes pessimistes.** 1. Annette est timide. 2. Yvette est bête. 3. Annette et David sont mariés. 4. Le professeur de littérature est sympathique. 5. Jean et David sont dynamiques. 6. Annette et David sont idéalistes.

MASCULINE	FEMININE	MASCULINE		FEMININE	
		singular	*plural*	*singular*	*plural*
-eux	-euse	paresseux	paresseux	paresseuse	paresseuses
-en	-enne	canadien	canadiens	canadienne	canadiennes
-if	-ive	sportif	sportifs	sportive	sportives
-el	-elle	intellectuel	intellectuels	intellectuelle	intellectuelles
-er	-ère	premier	premiers	première	premières

The adjective **nouveau** follows the same pattern as **beau.**

MASCULINE		FEMININE	
singular	*plural*	*singular*	*plural*
nouveau	nouveaux	nouvelle	nouvelles
beau	beaux	belle	belles

A. Tu ou vous? Demandez à ces personnes s'ils sont fatigués *(tired).*

Exemples   your sister: **Tu es fatiguée?**
your boss: **Vous êtes fatigué(e)?**

1. your roommate
2. your classmate
3. your parents
4. a salesclerk
5. two friends
6. an elderly neighbor

B. Au contraire! Complétez les descriptions avec le verbe **être.**

Exemple   Les étudiants du cours de français… (bêtes, dynamiques, intelligents)
Les étudiants du cours de français ne sont pas bêtes. Ils sont dynamiques. Ils sont intelligents.

1. Moi, en classe, je… (extraverti[e], dynamique, timide, un peu paresseux [paresseuse])
2. En général, mes professeurs… (intéressants, intellectuels, bêtes, ennuyeux, intelligents)
3. Les autres *(other)* étudiants du cours de français… (intéressants, extravertis, ennuyeux, désagréables, agréables)
4. Mes amis et moi, nous… (sportifs, intellectuels, paresseux, sympathiques)

C. Comment sont-ils? Dites si chaque adjectif donné décrit la personne indiquée. Faites attention à la forme de l'adjectif!

Exemple   Annette… beau, laid   **Annette est belle. Elle n'est pas laide.**

Annette…
intellectuel, dynamique,
paresseux, gros

Annette et Yvette…
américain, français,
gentil, méchant, beau

David et Jean…
laid, beau, vieux,
jeune

Moi, je…
dynamique, paresseux,
ennuyeux, sportif

D. Descriptions. Décrivez ces personnes. Faites attention à la forme de l'adjectif!

1. votre meilleur ami
2. votre meilleure amie
3. vos *(your)* amis et vous
4. vous
5. les étudiants du cours de français
6. les étudiantes du cours de français

elles nous il je elle ils	(ne / n')	suis est sommes sont	(pas)	sportif sympathique ennuyeux amusant marié timide extraverti ???

Follow-up for A. Tu ou vous? Tell students that Jean is asking Annette questions. Put his questions on the board or on a transparency. Students complete them with **tu es** or **vous êtes.** You may wish to have students do this activity in pairs, with stronger students answering the questions as if they were Annette. Tell them to make up any information they don't know about Annette. **1.** Toi, Annette, _____ étudiante? **2.** Yvette et toi, _____ intellectuelles? **3.** Et toi? _____ américaine? **4.** Ta famille et toi, _____ de Los Angeles? **5.** David et toi, _____ dans le même cours de littérature? **6.** Et toi? _____ sportive? **7.** Tes amis et toi, _____ intellectuels? **8.** Et toi, _____ en cours le lundi?

Warm-up for B. Au contraire! Tell students that David is talking about his friends and himself. Students make three columns on a sheet of paper: **David / David et ses** *(his)* **amis / Ses amis.** Tell them to write the number of each sentence they hear under the column that indicates about whom David is speaking. You may want to do the first sentence as an example. **1.** Ils ne sont pas très sportifs. **2.** Je suis assez intellectuel. **3.** Ils sont très intelligents. **4.** Nous sommes étudiants à l'université de Nice. **5.** Je suis célibataire. **6.** Ils sont plutôt extravertis. **7.** Nous sommes très dynamiques.

Supplemental activities. A. Qui parle: Annette, David ou Yvette? **1.** Je ne suis pas française mais je suis étudiante à l'université de Nice. **2.** Annette et moi, nous sommes dans le même cours de littérature. **3.** Je suis en France pour voir ma sœur. **4.** Je suis de Nice. **5.** Je ne suis pas étudiante. **B.** Cut photos of celebrities out of magazines for students to compare. **C.** Have students compare **les hommes** and **les femmes** for the following personality traits: **sportif, pessimiste, réaliste, intellectuel, bête. D.** Have students say whether these adjectives now describe them more or less than five years ago (**Je suis plus… maintenant. / Je suis moins… maintenant.**): **sportif (sportive), optimiste, idéaliste, intellectuel(le), grand(e), paresseux (paresseuse), timide.**

1. What are three ways of asking a question that can be answered **oui** or **non?** What happens to your intonation in each case?

2. What happens to **est-ce que** before a vowel sound?

Note. Inversion is presented in *Chapitre 2*.

Suggestion. You may wish to point out that the more traditional **n'est-ce pas?** is largely being replaced by **non?** in conversation.

Asking what someone is like: *Les questions*

There are several ways of asking a question that will be answered **oui** or **non**.

- You can ask a question with rising intonation, that is by raising the pitch of your voice at the end. A statement normally has falling intonation.

STATEMENT: Tu es extravertie.
You are outgoing.

QUESTION: Tu es extravertie?
Are you outgoing?

- You can also ask a question by adding **est-ce que** to the beginning of a statement and using rising intonation.

STATEMENT: Tu es sportif.
You are athletic.

QUESTION: Est-ce que tu es sportif?
Are you athletic?

- If you are presuming that someone will probably answer **oui** to a question, you can use either **n'est-ce pas?** *(isn't that right?)* or **non?** at the end of a question with rising intonation.

STATEMENT: Il est marié.
He's married.

QUESTION: Il est marié, n'est-ce pas?
Il est marié, non?
He's married, isn't he?

Due to elision, **est-ce que** becomes **est-ce qu'** before vowel sounds.

— Est-ce qu'il est d'ici?
— Non, il est d'Atlanta.

— Est-ce qu'elles sont canadiennes?
— Non, elles sont d'ici.

Script for A. C'est une question?
1. David est de Nice. 2. Annette est canadienne? 3. Annette est américaine? 4. Annette est de Los Angeles. 5. Est-ce qu'elle est mariée? 6. David est petit. 7. Ils sont amis, n'est-ce pas?

Suggestions for B. Et toi? A. You may wish to supply the expression **ne... ni... ni...** along with an example such as **Je ne suis ni intellectuel(le) ni sportif (sportive). B.** Before doing the second part of the exercise, remind students to use **c'est** to say who someone is and **il/elle est** and the correct form of the adjective to describe someone.

Follow-ups for B. Et toi? A. Have students say what they and their partner have in common and how they are different. EXEMPLE **Mario est plutôt intellectuel, mais je ne suis pas très intellectuel(le). Je suis plutôt sportif (sportive). Nous sommes idéalistes... B.** Have students write five sentences about themselves. Collect their papers and read them aloud. Students guess who it is, using questions with **n'est-ce pas? C.** Have students create one or two questions to ask classmates other than their partners.

A. C'est une question? Two classmates are talking about David and Annette. Listen to what they say. If they make a statement, write a period on your paper. If they ask a question, write a question mark.

B. Et toi? Demandez à un(e) camarade de classe comment il/elle est. Faites attention à la forme de l'adjectif!

Exemple sportif ou intellectuel
— **Est-ce que tu es sportif (sportive) ou intellectuel(le)?**
— **Je suis plutôt sportif (sportive) / plutôt intellectuel(le) / les deux *(both)*.**

1. idéaliste ou réaliste
2. timide ou extraverti
3. gentil ou méchant
4. intelligent ou bête
5. amusant ou ennuyeux
6. dynamique ou paresseux
7. optimiste ou pessimiste
8. marié, célibataire, fiancé ou divorcé

Maintenant, présentez votre partenaire à la classe en suivant l'exemple.

Exemple **C'est Mario.**
Il est intellectuel...

C. Et le professeur? Posez ces questions à votre professeur. Utilisez **est-ce que, n'est-ce pas** ou **non**.

Exemple   Vous êtes marié(e)?
                Est-ce que vous êtes marié(e)? /
                Vous êtes marié(e), n'est-ce pas / non?

1. Vous êtes américain(e)?
2. Le français est facile pour vous?
3. La bibliothèque ouvre à huit heures?
4. La bibliothèque ferme à minuit?
5. Vous êtes à l'université le lundi matin?
6. Vous êtes en cours à trois heures?

Suggestion for C. Et le professeur?
Have a student or students play the role of the professor and answer the questions.

D. Encore des questions! David pose des questions à Annette. Qu'est-ce qu'il dit? Formez des questions logiques avec le verbe **être**.

Exemple   **Est-ce que tu es plus jeune que moi?**

Est-ce que	tes amis... nous... tu... ta sœur...	américaine de Los Angeles étudiante d'ici dans le même cours plus extravertis que toi plus jeune que moi en cours à une heure aussi intelligente que toi

E. Entretien. Interviewez votre partenaire.

1. Est-ce que tu es américain(e)? Ta famille et toi, vous êtes d'ici? Est-ce que vous êtes plutôt idéalistes ou plutôt réalistes?
2. Est-ce que les études sont faciles ou difficiles pour toi? Est-ce que les professeurs ici sont intéressants ou ennuyeux? Ton meilleur ami (Ta meilleure amie) est étudiant(e) aussi? Tes amis et toi, est-ce que vous êtes intellectuels? Est-ce que tes amis sont intelligents ou bêtes? Ils sont amusants ou ennuyeux?
3. Est-ce que tu aimes le sport? Tu es plutôt sportif (sportive)? Est-ce que tu es dynamique ou plutôt paresseux (paresseuse)?

Supplemental activity. Write sets of the same three personality traits on two slips of paper of different colors. Have students place themselves in two rows facing one another. Distribute the slips of paper of one color to one row and the matching slips of the other color to the other row, mixing up the order. Tell students that they have a clone on the other side, and going down the row, have them ask somebody on the other side a yes/no question. They continue taking turns asking questions until they figure out who their clones are. Make several of the sets vary only by one trait and tell students that many of them are out of the same gene pool, but that they are not clones.

Le concept d'une université et d'un campus est très différent en France et aux USA. En France, l'université n'est pas un centre social. Il y a peu d'activités extra-scolaires ou de sport sur le campus. La majorité des étudiants vont *(go)* à l'université dans leurs propres villes *(their own cities)* et ils habitent avec leurs parents. Ils vont à l'université juste pour aller en cours. Dans une autre *(another)* partie de la ville, il y a un quartier où se trouvent *(are located)* des résidences universitaires. Ce quartier s'appelle la cité universitaire.

TRANSPARENCIES: 1-3A, 1-3B

Warm-up activities. A. Have students say whether each of these statements describes **David** or **Annette**. **1.** Elle est américaine. **2.** Il est étudiant à l'université de Nice. **3.** Il est français. **4.** Elle est étudiante à l'université de Nice. **5.** Elle n'est pas française. **6.** Il est de Nice. **B.** Have students complete these sentences logically: **1.** Je suis... **2.** Ma famille et moi, nous sommes... **3.** Mes amis sont...

VOCABULAIRE SUPPLÉMENTAIRE

un arrêt d'autobus *a bus stop*
un centre administratif *an administration building*
un centre d'étudiants *a student center*
une infirmerie *a health center*
un court de tennis *a tennis court*
une fontaine *a fountain*
un gymnase *a gym*
une piscine *a pool*

Le campus et le quartier

Qu'est-ce qu'il y a sur votre campus?

Sur le campus, **il y a...**

1. beaucoup de vieux bâtiments
2. **quelques** nouveaux bâtiments
3. **une librairie**
4. des résidences *(f)*
5. un stade (avec des matchs *[m]* de football américain)
6. une bibliothèque
7. des salles *(f)* de classe
8. des bureaux *(m)* de profs
9. un grand amphithéâtre
10. un bon / **mauvais** restaurant
11. un parking
12. un laboratoire de langues / d'informatique moderne

Dans le quartier universitaire, près de l'université, il y a...

1. un café
2. un fast-food
3. une boîte de nuit populaire
4. un club de gym
5. un **joli** parc
6. un théâtre
7. des concerts *(m)* de jazz *(m)* / de rock *(m)* / de musique *(f)* populaire / de musique classique
8. un cinéma (avec des films **étrangers** et des films américains)
9. des maisons *(f)*
10. des arbres *(m)*

Qu'est-ce qu'il y a *What is there* **sur** *on* **il y a** *there is, there are* **quelques** *some, a few* **une librairie** *a bookstore* **mauvais(e)** *bad* **Dans** *In* **le quartier** *the neighborhood* **universitaire** *university* (adj.) **près de** *near* **joli(e)** *pretty* **étranger (étrangère)** *foreign*

Annette et un ami parlent du campus et du quartier.

MICHEL: Comment est **ton** université? Tu aimes le campus?
ANNETTE: Oui, il est très agréable.
MICHEL: Qu'est-ce qu'il y a sur le campus?
ANNETTE: Il y a des bâtiments modernes, une grande bibliothèque et beaucoup d'arbres.
MICHEL: Qu'est-ce qu'il y a dans le quartier?
ANNETTE: Il y a de jolies maisons, des cafés et des restaurants. Mais **il n'y a pas assez de** parkings!

A. Chez nous. Décrivez votre université.

1. Le campus ici est *grand / petit / joli / laid / ???*.
2. Sur le campus il y a *plus de nouveaux bâtiments / plus de vieux bâtiments*.
3. La bibliothèque universitaire est *grande / petite / agréable / ???*.
4. *Il y a / Il n'y a pas* assez de résidences sur le campus.
5. *Il y a / Il n'y a pas* beaucoup d'arbres sur le campus.
6. Le restaurant universitaire, c'est un *bon / mauvais* restaurant. *(Il n'y a pas de restaurant sur le campus.)*
7. *Il y a / Il n'y a pas* assez de parkings.
8. Le week-end, il y a souvent *des matchs de football américain / des matchs de basket / des concerts / des films / ???*.
9. Dans le quartier près de l'université, il y a *des restaurants / des cafés / des fast-foods / un joli parc / ???*.
10. *Barnes & Noble / Bookstop / Bookpeople / ???* est une bonne librairie dans le quartier.

B. Qu'est-ce qu'il y a? Complétez ces phrases pour décrire votre quartier universitaire.

1. Sur le campus, il y a…
2. Dans le quartier universitaire, il y a…

C. À l'université. Avec un(e) partenaire, changez la conversation entre Michel et Annette comme indiqué.

1. Annette thinks the campus is pretty. There are modern classrooms and a good restaurant on campus, but there are not enough trees in the neighborhood.
2. The conversation is between you and a classmate. Change it to make it true for you.

---

ton (ta, tes) *your*   **il n'y a pas** *there isn't, there aren't*   **assez de** *enough*

L'université de Casablanca, Maroc

Suggestions. A. Point out the meaning of **il y a** and the use and pronunciation of **un, une,** and **des.** Ask students why there might be two different forms for the word *a.* The concept of grammatical gender and the use of the indefinite article is explained and practiced in the next section. **B.** Point out the difference between **un cinéma** and **un théâtre,** between **une bibliothèque** and **une librairie,** and between **l'université** and **universitaire. C.** Point out that some descriptive adjectives precede the noun being described and some follow it. This is explained and practiced later in this *Compétence.* **D.** Tell students that the combination **th** is usually pronounced /t/ **(théâtre).**

Suggestion for the conversation. Set the scene and have students listen to the conversation twice with books closed for the answers to these questions.
1. Annette aime le campus? **2.** Qu'est-ce qu'il y a sur le campus? **3.** Qu'est-ce qu'il y a dans le quartier? Afterward, have them listen to the conversation again while reading along in the text.

Suggestion for B. Qu'est-ce qu'il y a? Have students do this activity as a chain drill, where each student adds an item after listing all those already named, or as a team competition in which each team tries to list the most items. You may wish to have them do this with books closed.

1. What are the two forms of the word for *a*? When do you use each? How do you say *some*?

2. How do you say *there is*? *there are*? *there isn't*? *there aren't*?

3. In what three circumstances do you use **de (d')** instead of **un, une,** or **des**? What is an exception to replacing **un, une,** or **des** with **de (d')** in a negative sentence?

Saying what there is:

Le genre, l'article indéfini et l'expression il y a

All nouns in French have gender (masculine or feminine). The categorization of most nouns as masculine or feminine cannot be guessed, unless they represent people.

The short word **un** *(a, an),* **une** *(a, an),* or **des** *(some)* before a noun is called the indefinite article. Use **un** with masculine singular nouns, **une** with feminine singular nouns, and **des** with all plural nouns.

To make a noun plural, add an **-s** to the end of it. Do not add an **-s,** however, if the noun already ends in an **s, x,** or **z.** Nouns that end in **eau (bureau)** form their plural in -**x (bureaux).**

	SINGULAR	PLURAL
MASCULINE	un théâtre	des théâtres
FEMININE	une bibliothèque	des bibliothèques

Always learn a new noun as a unit with the article **(un, une)** in order to remember its gender!

To say *there is* or *there are* in French, use the expression **il y a (un, une, des…).** To say *there isn't* or *there aren't,* use **il n'y a pas (de…).**

Note the following:

- **Un, une,** and **des** nearly always change to **de (d')** after a negative.

Il y a **un** stade.	Il n'y a pas **de** stade.
Il y a **une** librairie.	Il n'y a pas **de** librairie.
Il y a **des** matchs de basket.	Il n'y a pas **de** matchs de basket.

This change does *not* occur, however, if the verb in the sentence is a form of **être.**

C'est **un** bon restaurant.	Ce n'est pas **un** bon restaurant.
C'est **une** bibliothèque.	Ce n'est pas **une** bibliothèque.
Ce sont **des** films américains.	Ce ne sont pas **des** films américains.

- **Un, une,** and **des** also change to **de (d')** after expressions of quantity, such as **beaucoup** and **assez.**

Il y a **des** cinémas.	Il y a **beaucoup de** cinémas.
Il y a **un** parking.	Il n'y a pas **assez de** parkings.

- Also use **de (d')** instead of **des** *directly* before a plural adjective.

Il y a **des** bâtiments **modernes.**	Il y a **de nouveaux** bâtiments.

Suggestions. A. Have students look up words whose gender seems illogical according to their meaning, for example *beard* or *purse.* **B.** Point out the use of the *(m)* and *(f)* to indicate gender when needed. **C.** Tell students to learn new nouns with their articles to remember the gender. Suggest that they use flashcards of different colors, putting feminine words on one color of card and masculine words on another, or that they write the words using different colors of ink. **D.** You may also wish to point out that **des** becomes **de** when it is followed directly by an adjective (**de beaux arbres**) in formal or written French, but that in spoken French this change commonly does not occur.

Prononciation: *L'article indéfini*

Be careful to pronounce **un** and **une** differently. Use the very tight sound **u** with lips rounded, as in **tu,** to say **une.** To pronounce the **u** sound, position your mouth to pronounce a French **i** with your tongue held high in your mouth. Then, round your lips. The vowel sound of **un** is nasal. Pronounce the **n** in **un** only when there is **liaison** with a following noun beginning with a vowel sound.

une résidence	**un** bâtiment
une amie	**un** ami

Suggestions. Tell students to position their lips as if to whistle when pronouncing the letter **u** /y/. Contrast the pronunciation of **des** and **de** as well as that of **un** and **une.**

Supplemental activity. You will hear a list of things found or not found at a certain university. You may hear words you don't recognize, but for each one, write just the article you hear: **un, une, des,** or **de (d').** 1. Il y a une fontaine. 2. Il n'y a pas de résidences. 3. Il y a un stade. 4. Il y a des amphithéâtres. 5. Il y a une piscine. 6. Il y a des courts de tennis. 7. Il n'y a pas de café. 8. Il y a un gymnase.

A. Scènes.
Complétez ces questions avec **un, une** ou **des.** Après, posez les questions à votre partenaire.

1. C'est _____ bibliothèque ou _____ restaurant?
   Ce sont _____ étudiants ou _____ professeurs?

3. C'est _____ concert ou _____ film?
   C'est _____ concert de jazz ou de musique classique?

2. C'est _____ cinéma ou _____ salle de classe?
   Ce sont _____ femmes ou _____ hommes?

4. C'est _____ librairie ou _____ boîte de nuit?
   Ce sont _____ gens timides ou _____ gens extravertis?

B. Qu'est-ce qu'il y a?
Est-ce qu'il y a les choses *(things)* indiquées entre parenthèses dans chaque endroit *(each place)?*

Exemple   à l'université (une bibliothèque, une boîte de nuit)
À l'université, il y a une bibliothèque. Il n'y a pas de boîte de nuit.

1. dans la salle de classe (un professeur, des matchs de basket, des étudiants, des livres, des arbres, un tableau)
2. dans le quartier universitaire (des maisons, un cinéma, des films étrangers, un théâtre, des concerts, un restaurant, des boîtes de nuit)

C. Qu'est-ce qu'il y a?
Relisez la *Note culturelle* à la page 42. Sur le campus d'une université française, est-ce qu'il y a probablement ces choses?

Exemples   un restaurant universitaire
Oui, il y a un restaurant universitaire.

des matchs de basket
Non, il n'y a pas de matchs de basket.

La cour de la Sorbonne

1. des amphithéâtres
2. un stade
3. des bureaux de profs
4. une bibliothèque
5. des résidences
6. des salles de classe
7. une boîte de nuit
8. des matchs de football américain

D. Est-ce qu'il y a... ?
Complétez ces questions avec **un, une, des** ou **de (d').** Après, posez-les à votre partenaire.

Exemple   — Ici à l'université, est-ce qu'il y a **des** concerts de rock?
   — **Oui, il y a des concerts de rock. /**
   Non, il n'y a pas de concerts de rock.

Ici à l'université, est-ce qu'il y a…

1. … beaucoup _____ vieux bâtiments?
2. … _____ grands amphithéâtres?
3. … _____ salles de classe modernes?
4. … _____ grande bibliothèque?
5. … assez _____ parkings?
6. … _____ grand stade?
7. … _____ théâtre?
8. … _____ librairie?
9. … _____ jolis arbres?
10. … _____ concerts de jazz?

Follow-up to D. *Est-ce qu'il y a… ?*
Complétez ces phrases. À l'université,…
1. il y a… **2.** il y a beaucoup de… **3.** il n'y a pas assez de… **4.** il n'y a pas de… (Repeat the same items for **Dans le quartier universitaire...** and for **Dans mon quartier, près de la maison...**)

Supplemental activities. A. Bring a map of your university, another university, or an area of town popular with students and have them say what is located there. **B.** Have students compare what there is at their university with what there is at a rival university.

1. Do you use **c'est** and **ce sont** or **il/elle est** and **ils/elles sont** to identify *who* or *what* someone or something is? to say *where* someone or something is? to say *what* someone or something *is like* using an adjective?

2. Are most adjectives placed before or after the noun they describe? Which adjectives are placed before the noun they describe?

3. What are the alternate masculine singular forms of **beau**, **nouveau**, and **vieux**? When are they used?

Suggestions. A. Remind students to use **elles sont** for groups of all feminine nouns and **ils sont** for groups of all masculine nouns or for mixed groups. **B.** Point out the feminine form of **bon** (**bonne**), that **moderne** ends in **-e** in the masculine form, and remind students of the **-er** to **-ère** pattern, as seen in **étranger** (**étrangère**). **C.** Give students the mnemonic device BAGS (beauty, age, goodness, and size) to help remember which adjectives precede the noun. **D.** To help students remember how to spell the alternate forms **bel**, **nouvel**, and **vieil**, point out that they are truncated versions of the feminine forms. Remind students to use these alternate forms only in the singular.

Identifying and describing people and things:
C'est ou il/elle est et la place de l'adjectif

Since all nouns in French are either masculine or feminine, there is no neuter *it.* Use **il est, elle est, ils sont,** and **elles sont** with *an adjective to describe* things, just as you do with people.

— Comment est Annette? — Comment sont les résidences?
— **Elle est** grande. — **Elles sont** grandes.

Note that you use **il/elle est** and **ils/elles sont** to state someone's profession, nationality, or religion. You do not use any equivalent for the English word *a* and you do not capitalize nationalities or religions.

Elle est étudiante. Elle est américaine. Il est catholique.

Also use **il est, elle est, ils sont,** and **elles sont** with *a preposition of place to say where* someone or something is.

Où est David? *Where's David?*
Il est dans un café. *He's in a café.*
Où est le café? *Where's the café?*
Il est près de l'université. *It's near the university.*

Use **c'est** and **ce sont** with *a noun to identify* or describe someone or something.

Ce n'est pas Annette. ***She's not*** Annette.
C'est Yvette. ***She's*** Yvette.
Ce n'est pas un parc. ***It's not*** a park.
C'est un grand campus. ***It's*** a big campus.
Ce ne sont pas mes amis. ***They're not*** my friends.
Ce sont mes frères. ***They're*** my brothers.

Remember to use **il y a** to say what *there is/are.*

Il y a un parc dans le quartier. ***There is*** *a park in the neighborhood.*

In French, unlike in English, most adjectives *follow* the nouns they describe.

Il y a **des résidences** *modernes* sur le campus.

Only a few adjectives go before the noun. They include:

beau (belle)	jeune	bon (bonne)	grand(e)	autre *(other)*
joli(e)	vieux (vieille)	mauvais(e)	petit(e)	même
	nouveau (nouvelle)	gentil(le)	gros(se)	

The adjectives **beau, nouveau,** and **vieux** have alternate masculine singular forms, **bel, nouvel,** and **vieil,** that are used before nouns beginning with a vowel sound.

MASCULINE SINGULAR (PLUS CONSONANT SOUND)	MASCULINE SINGULAR (PLUS VOWEL SOUND)	FEMININE
un beau quartier	un bel ami	une belle amie
un nouveau quartier	un nouvel ami	une nouvelle amie
un vieux quartier	un vieil ami	une vieille amie

A. Qu'est-ce ce que c'est?
Identifiez ces personnes ou ces choses. Après, décrivez-les.

Exemples

 café (grand / petit)
C'est un café.
Il est petit.

 étudiantes (sympa / méchant)
Ce sont des étudiantes.
Elles sont sympas (sympathiques).

1.

maisons (nouveau / vieux)

2.

amphithéâtre (grand / petit)

3.

maison (grand / petit)

4.

femme (sportif / paresseux)

5.

parc (joli / laid)

6.

salle de classe (moderne / vieux)

B. Descriptions.
Faites des phrases comme dans l'exemple.

Exemple **C'est un jeune homme. Il est dynamique.**
Il n'est pas paresseux. Il est sportif. Il est beau.

Exemple un jeune homme, dynamique, paresseux, sportif, beau

1. des hommes, étudiants, jeunes, sympathiques

2. Yvette, française, en France, étudiante, à l'université, à la maison

C. Compliments?
Faites des compliments. Écrivez la forme correcte de l'adjectif logique dans la phrase pour faire un compliment.

Exemple C'est une _____ femme _____. (intelligent / bête)
C'est une femme intelligente.

1. C'est un _____ restaurant _____. (bon / mauvais)
2. Ce sont des _____ étudiants _____. (sympa / méchant)
3. C'est un _____ campus _____. (beau / laid)
4. C'est un _____ professeur _____. (intéressant / ennuyeux)
5. C'est une _____ femme _____. (joli / laid)
6. C'est un _____ homme _____. (beau / laid)
7. Ce sont des _____ étudiantes _____. (dynamique / paresseux)
8. C'est un _____ laboratoire de langues _____. (nouveau / vieux)
9. C'est une _____ salle de classe _____. (agréable / désagréable)
10. C'est une _____ famille _____. (gentil / méchant)

Follow-up for C. Compliments? Have students go back and say the opposite for each item. EXEMPLE C'est une _____ femme _____. (intelligent / bête) **C'est une femme bête.**

NOTE Culturelle

Les universités françaises sont divisées en facultés. Les quatre facultés avec le plus grand nombre d'étudiants sont: la faculté des lettres *(Arts and Humanities)*, la faculté des sciences, la faculté de droit *(Law)* et la faculté de médecine. Les étudiants entrent directement à la faculté de droit ou de médecine après les études secondaires.

Suggestion for the *Note culturelle*. Ask students what courses one might study at each **faculté**. Point out that over twice as many students are enrolled at the **faculté des lettres** as at any other **faculté**.

TRANSPARENCIES: 1-4A, 1-4B

Warm-ups. A. Have students use **il y a** to name as many things as they can that are found **1.** in the classroom **2.** on campus **3.** in the university neighborhood. Then have them name one or more things that are not found in each of these places. You may wish to do these as chain activities. **B.** Have students introduce a classmate (**C'est…**) and say two things to describe him/her.

Suggestions. A. Point out the various forms of the word *the* in French and the pronunciation of each. Ask students why they think there are several forms. The definite article is presented on page 50. **B.** Point out the pronunciation of **ps** in **la psychologie** and that **les mathématiques** is plural.

Additional information. You may wish to tell students that students in France generally study two languages before going to college. Have students guess which are the most studied (**l'anglais 80%, l'allemand 18%, l'espagnol 4%, l'italien 3%, l'arabe 1,2%**).

L'université et les cours

Est-ce que vous aimez l'université?

J'aime beaucoup…	J'aime assez…	Je n'aime pas (du tout)…	Je préfère…
l'université	le campus	les cours	**les boums** *(f)*
les professeurs	la bibliothèque	les devoirs *(m)*	le sport
les étudiants	les salles de classe	les examens *(m)*	les matchs de football américain
			les matchs de basket

Qu'est-ce que vous étudiez?

J'étudie la philosophie.   Je n'étudie pas la littérature.

LES LANGUES *(f)*
l'allemand *(m)*
l'anglais *(m)*
l'espagnol *(m)*
le français

LES SCIENCES HUMAINES *(f)*
l'histoire *(f)*
la psychologie
les sciences politiques *(f)*

LES BEAUX-ARTS *(m)*
le théâtre
la musique

LES COURS DE COMMERCE
la comptabilité
le marketing

LES COURS TECHNIQUES
les mathématiques *(f)*
l'informatique *(f)*

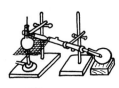

LES SCIENCES
la biologie
la chimie
la physique

J'aime beaucoup le cours de…
Il est facile / difficile / intéressant.

  David et Annette parlent de leurs études.

DAVID: Qu'est-ce que tu étudies ce semestre?
ANNETTE: J'étudie le français et la littérature classique. Et toi?
DAVID: J'étudie la philosophie et la littérature classique, **comme toi.**
ANNETTE: Comment sont tes cours?
DAVID: J'aime beaucoup le cours de philosophie. Il est très intéressant. Je n'aime pas du tout le cours de littérature parce que le prof est ennuyeux.

---

une boum *a party*   **l'allemand** *(m) German*   **les sciences politiques** *(f) government, political science*   **les beaux-arts** *fine arts*   **la comptabilité** *accounting*   **l'informatique** *(f) computer science*   **la chimie** *chemistry*   **comme toi** *like you*

A. Préférences. Qu'est-ce que vous préférez?

Exemple   le français / les mathématiques
   Je préfère le français.

1. la littérature / les sciences
2. les cours de commerce / les langues
3. les cours à huit heures du matin / les cours à deux heures de l'après-midi
4. les matchs de football américain / les matchs de basket
5. les cours dans les grands amphithéâtres / les cours dans les petites salles de classe
6. les examens / les boums

B. L'université. Write these four columns on a sheet of paper. Each time you hear a *positive* remark about the university, place a ✔ in the appropriate column. If the remark is *negative,* write ✗.

Exemple   VOUS ENTENDEZ: La bibliothèque est désagréable.

	LA BIBLIOTHÈQUE	LE CAMPUS	LES PROFESSEURS	LES COURS
EX.	✗			
1.				

C. Et vous? Changez les phrases pour parler de vous.

1. J'étudie *le français, la biologie et les mathématiques.*
2. À l'université, j'aime *les étudiants.*
3. À l'université, je n'aime pas *les matchs de football américain.*
4. Je préfère les cours à *dix heures du matin.*
5. J'aime *le cours de français.* Il est intéressant.
6. Je n'aime pas *le cours de marketing.* Il est ennuyeux.

D. Les cours. Avec un(e) partenaire, changez la conversation entre David et Annette comme indiqué.

1. David likes his literature class because the professor is nice, but he does not like his philosophy course because it is hard.
2. Annette is studying chemistry and math. David is studying physics and math. He likes the physics course because it is interesting, but he does not like the math course because the professor is mean.
3. The conversation is between you and a classmate. Change it to make it true for you.

Suggestion for the conversation on the preceding page. Set the scene and play the conversation twice with books closed. Have students listen for the answers to these questions. 1. Qu'est-ce que David étudie? Et Annette? 2. Quel cours *(Which course)* est-ce que David aime? Quel cours est-ce qu'il n'aime pas? Pourquoi *(Why)?* Afterward, have them listen again, while reading along in the text.

Continuation for A. Préférences.
1. les cours à huit heures du matin / les cours à sept heures du soir 2. le laboratoire de langues / la bibliothèque 3. la philosophie / l'informatique 4. la chimie / la physique 5. la chimie / la biologie 6. l'espagnol / l'allemand

Script for B. L'université. EXEMPLE **La bibliothèque est désagréable.** 1. Les cours sont intéressants. 2. J'aime beaucoup le campus. 3. Je n'aime pas les cours. 4. Les professeurs sont intéressants. 5. Le campus est beau. 6. La bibliothèque est grande. 7. Les professeurs sont sympathiques. 8. Le campus est agréable.

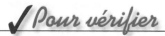
1. What are the four forms of the word for *the* in French? When do you use each?
2. Besides meaning *the,* what are two other uses of the definite article in French?
3. When is the **-s** of the plural form **les** pronounced?

Suggestion. Remind students to learn new nouns with their articles to remember the gender. Again suggest that they use flashcards of different colors, putting feminine words on one color and masculine words on another. You may also point out that the sciences given in this chapter are feminine, that all languages are masculine, and that words ending in **-té, -tion, -ique,** and **-ie** are usually feminine.

Supplemental activity. Dictate the following courses, then have students rank them from one to ten, numbering them from the least (1) to the most (10) interesting: **le français, l'informatique, les sciences politiques, l'histoire, la biologie, la philosophie, la comptabilité, la musique, les mathématiques, la chimie.** Also have them rank the same courses according to difficulty. Finally, have students tell which course they ranked as **le plus intéressant / le moins intéressant (le plus ennuyeux)** and **le plus difficile / le moins difficile (le plus facile).**

Identifying people and things: *L'article défini*

The short words **le, la, l', les** *(the)* before nouns are called definite articles.

le campus   la bibliothèque   l'université   les cours

The form of the definite article you use depends on the noun's gender, whether it starts with a consonant or vowel sound, and whether it is singular or plural.

	SINGULAR BEFORE CONSONANT SOUND	SINGULAR BEFORE VOWEL SOUND	PLURAL
MASCULINE	**le** livre	**l'**homme	**les** livres, **les** hommes
FEMININE	**la** librairie	**l'**étudiante	**les** librairies, **les** étudiantes

Use the definite article before nouns:

- To specify items, as when using *the* in English.
  Apprenez **les** mots de vocabulaire.   *Learn **the** vocabulary words.*

- To say what you like, dislike, or prefer.
  Je n'aime pas **les** devoirs.   *I don't like homework.*

- To talk about something as a general category or an abstract noun.
  Les langues sont faciles pour moi.   *Languages are easy for me.*

In the last two cases, there is no article in English.

 # Prononciation: *La voyelle e et l'article défini*

As you know, final unaccented **e** is usually not pronounced, unless it is the only vowel, as in **le.**

grand**e**   histoir**e**   langu**e**   bibliothèqu**e**   j'aim**e**

Otherwise, unaccented **e** has three different pronunciations, depending on what follows it.

- In short words like **le** or **je,** or when **e** is followed by a single consonant within a word, pronounce it as in:

  j**e**   n**e**   l**e**   r**e**garde   d**e**voirs

- When, as in **les,** e is followed by an unpronounced consonant at the end of a word, pronounce it as in:

  l**es**   m**es**   parl**ez**   aim**ez**   étudi**ez**

- In words like **elle,** where **e** is followed by two consonants within a word, or by a single pronounced consonant at the end of a word, pronounce it as in:

  int**e**ll**e**ctuel   b**e**lle   qu**e**l   **e**spagnol   bask**e**t

Since the final **-s** of plural nouns is not pronounced, you must pronounce the article correctly to differentiate singular and plural nouns. Listen carefully as you repeat each of the following nouns. Notice the **z** sound of final **-s** in liaison.

le livre	la science	l'étudiant	l'étudiante
les livres	les sciences	les ᶻétudiants	les ᶻétudiantes

A. Parlez bien.
Listen as David talks about university life. In each sentence, you will hear the singular or plural form of one of the following nouns. Indicate which form you hear by writing the article on your paper.

1. le professeur — les professeurs
2. le cours — les cours
3. l'étudiant — les étudiants
4. l'examen — les examens
5. le livre — les livres
6. le cours — les cours
7. le campus — les campus
8. la bibliothèque — les bibliothèques

B. Vos cours.
Est-ce que vous étudiez les matières suivantes *(following subjects)?*

Exemple Oui, j'étudie la chimie. / Non, je n'étudie pas la chimie.

1.

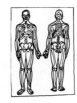

2.

3.

4.

5.

6.

7.

C. Et vous?
Complétez les phrases pour parler de vos cours et de votre université.

1. J'étudie...
2. J'aime beaucoup...
3. J'aime assez...
4. Je n'aime pas beaucoup...
5. Je n'aime pas du tout...
6. Je ne comprends pas...
7. Je comprends bien...
8. Je pense que le cours de... est...

D. Entretien.
Complétez les questions suivantes avec l'article défini (**le, la, l', les**) ou l'article indéfini (**un, une, des**). Après, posez ces questions à votre partenaire.

1. Est-ce que vous aimez _____ université?
2. Est-ce que vous aimez _____ cours de français?
3. Est-ce qu'il y a _____ étudiants étrangers dans _____ classe *(f)*?
4. Est-ce qu'il y a _____ examen aujourd'hui?
5. Est-ce que vous comprenez bien _____ français?
6. À quelle heure est-ce que _____ bibliothèque ferme aujourd'hui?
7. Est-ce que vous travaillez à _____ université?
8. Est-ce que vous travaillez dans _____ restaurant?

Reprise: *Talking about the university and your studies*

In *Chapitre 1,* you practiced talking about your classes and identifying and describing the people, places, and things found at and around a university. Now you have a chance to review what you have learned.

A. Qui est-ce? Complétez les descriptions de ces célébrités francophones avec **c'est** ou **il est.**

Zinedine Zidane (joueur de foot *[soccer player]*)

Michel Poucet (musicien)

_____ Zinedine Zidane.
_____ un homme.
_____ assez grand.
_____ joueur de foot.
_____ français.

_____ Michel Poucet
_____ un homme.
_____ intéressant.
_____ musicien.
_____ de Louisiane.

Maintenant, identifiez un(e) camarade de classe et parlez un peu de lui *(him)* ou d'elle.

B. Interview. Formez des questions logiques avec le verbe **être.** Interviewez votre partenaire avec les questions.

Exemple   Est-ce que tu / en cours le lundi?
— **Est-ce que tu es en cours le lundi?**
— **Oui, je suis en cours le lundi. /**
Non, je ne suis pas en cours le lundi.

1. Est-ce que le cours de français / très facile?
2. Est-ce que le prof / méchant?
3. Est-ce que tu / timide en cours?
4. Est-ce que les devoirs / intéressants?
5. Est-ce que les examens / difficiles?
6. Est-ce que tu / dynamique en classe?
7. Est-ce que les autres étudiants / intelligents?
8. Tes amis et toi, est-ce que vous / intellectuels?
9. Tes amis et toi, est-ce que vous / sportifs aussi?

C. Descriptions. Demandez à votre partenaire comment sont les éléments suivants dans votre université.

Exemple restaurant
— **Comment est le restaurant?**
— **Il est bon. / Il n'y a pas de restaurant à l'université.**

1. université
2. campus
3. cours
4. étudiants
5. bibliothèque
6. salles de classe

D. Préférences. Indiquez votre préférence. (Faites attention à la position de l'adjectif dans la phrase!)

Exemple les restaurants (petits, grands)
Je préfère les petits restaurants. /
Je préfère les grands restaurants.

1. les professeurs (ennuyeux, intéressants)
2. les cours (faciles mais ennuyeux, difficiles mais intéressants)
3. les hommes / femmes (sportifs [sportives], intellectuel[le]s)
4. les classes (grandes, petites)
5. les hommes / femmes (intelligent[e]s, beaux [belles])
6. la musique (moderne, classique)

E. Descriptions. Identifiez et décrivez les personnes et les objets suivants avec les adjectifs donnés.

Exemple maison (petit, laid)
C'est une petite maison laide.

1. femme (joli, sportif)
2. homme (sympa, vieux)
3. homme (beau, sportif)

4. restaurant (mauvais, désagréable)
5. femme (intelligent, jeune)
6. boîte de nuit (grand, populaire)

F. Vos cours. Avec un(e) partenaire, préparez la conversation suivante. Ensuite *(Then),* changez de rôles.

Ask your partner:

- what he/she is studying this semester
- what his/her course(s) is (are) like
- if he/she likes the university
- what the students and professors are like
- what the campus is like
- what there is on campus and in the neighborhood

Note. Vocabulary found in the **Lecture** and **Comparaisons culturelles** sections is meant for recognition only and does not appear in the end-of-chapter vocabulary lists. Since students could be intimidated by so many new words, you may wish to let students know in advance whether you intend to test them on this vocabulary.

LECTURE: **Deux écoles**

As anywhere, decisions about higher education in France are difficult, but there are many student-oriented magazines and books published to inform students about their options. You are going to read ads for the schools SPLEF and IPAG from the magazine *L'Étudiant.* Remember that although you will not be able to understand every word, you should comprehend much of what is written. First, before reading in depth, skim the ads and find as many cognates as you can.

From skimming the advertisements, can you tell what kind of schools these are? Now, read the ads in greater depth and answer the questions about each one.

LANGUES ÉTRANGÈRES
UN ATOUT SUPPLÉMENTAIRE

OBJECTIVES

LANGUES :
- Allemand • Anglais • Portugais
- Espagnol • Italien • Russe

NIVEAUX :
- Débutant
- Intermédiaire
- Perfectionnement
- Mise à niveau.

COURS :
- Du jour et du soir
- Annuels et semi-intensifs
- Généraux, conversation, spécialités ...
- Laboratoire, vidéo.

EXAMENS : Examen SPLEF à Paris et province :
- Langue générale
- Langue commerciale
- Accueil et tourisme
Chambres de commerce, Cambridge.

SPLEF
Promotion des Langues Étrangères

2, rue Gabriel Vicaire - 75003 Paris
Tél. : 01 48 87 62 26
M° Temple - République

DEPUIS 100 ANS NOUS VOUS AIDONS À COMMUNIQUER

ipag

ÉCOLE SUPÉRIEURE DE COMMERCE

4 ans d'études - Alternance École/Entreprise - Management International

Diplôme visé par le Ministère de l'Enseignement Supérieur

Depuis 1965, l'IPAG forme des généralistes de haut niveau en commerce et gestion, avec une forte dimension internationale.

1er cycle :
Tronc commun en 1ère et 2ème années.

- Formation généraliste.

- Étude des techniques de commerce et gestion.

- 2 stages en entreprises.

- Définition du projet professionnel personnel.

2ème cycle :
En 3ème et 4ème années, choix entre 5 cursus de spécialisation.
- **Professionnelle :** Finances d'entreprise, Comptabilité-Contrôle de gestion, Banque-Assurance, Marketing Opérationnel, Commerce International, Vente, Gestion des Ressources Humaines…
ou
- **À l'international :** 52 universités partenaires en Europe et aux USA, accès à des doubles-diplômes. Programmes soutenus par l'Union européenne.

Tous les diplômés de l'IPAG ont de 10 à 16 mois d'expérience en entreprise et 5 mois minimum d'expérience à l'étranger.

Concours ouvert aux bacheliers (VISA)
Clôture des inscriptions le 30 avril - Épreuves écrites les 14 et 15 mai
Admissions parallèles en 2ème et 3ème années sur concours

IPAG PARIS
184, bd Saint-Germain
75006 PARIS
Tél. : 01 42 22 08 55

IPAG NICE
4, bd Carabacel
06000 NICE
Tél. : 04 93 13 39 00

SPLEF

1. What languages can you study at this school?
2. Using the word **intermédiaire**, guess what **niveaux** means.
3. What types of courses are there? When are they offered?
4. What facilities does the school have to support instruction?

IPAG

1. How many cycles of study are there? Which years **(années)** of study are in the first? in the second?
2. During the first cycle there are **2 stages en entreprises.** What might you do at an **entreprise** while still a student? What do you think **stages** means?
3. How many schools abroad are associated with IPAG? Can you get a diploma from both schools at the same time?
4. How many months **(mois)** of experience do graduates have with businesses when they leave the school?

Composition

A. Organisez-vous. You will be writing a short description of yourself and your studies. When you write in French, use and combine what you know and avoid translating from English. It is very difficult to translate correctly. First organize your thoughts by completing these sentences in French.

1. Je m'appelle…
2. Je suis de (d')…
3. J'habite…
4. Du point de vue physique, je suis…
5. Du point de vue personnalité, je suis…
6. Je suis étudiant(e) à…
7. Sur le campus, il y a… mais il n'y a pas…
8. Dans le quartier universitaire, il y a… mais il n'y a pas…
9. En général, j'aime / je n'aime pas l'université parce que…
10. J'étudie…
11. J'aime / Je n'aime pas…

> If you have access to SYSTÈME-D software, you will find the following phrases, vocabulary, grammar, and dictionary aids there.
>
> **Phrases:** Introducing; Describing people
> **Vocabulary:** Studies, courses; Personality
> **Grammar:** Indefinite article; Nouns after **c'est, il est;** Comparison **que**
> **Dictionary:** The verb **être**

B. Rédaction: autoportrait. Write a short paragraph introducing yourself. Use the sentences you completed in **A. Organisez-vous!** to guide you. Link sentences with words like **et, mais,** or **parce que** to make your paragraph flow better.

Je m'appelle Daniel Reyna. Je suis de San Antonio mais maintenant j'habite à Austin…

C. Présentations. After you have completed **B. Rédaction: autoportrait,** exchange papers with a classmate. Read each other's composition, then go around the room and introduce your partner to several classmates, telling them a few things that you learned about him or her. You will need to use the following verb forms to describe him or her: **il (elle) s'appelle, il (elle) étudie, il (elle) aime, il (elle) habite.**

D. Comparaisons. Now that you know your partner from **C. Présentations** better, work together to prepare at least five sentences comparing yourselves to each other and take turns reading them to the class.

Exemple   ALEX: **Monique est plus sportive que moi.**
MONIQUE: **Alex est moins dynamique que moi.**

COMPARAISONS *culturelles*

LES ÉTUDES

How similar is the French education system to the education system in your area? Read these descriptions of secondary schools and universities in France and compare them to schools in your region, by saying one of the following.

C'est très semblable *(similar)* ici. / C'est assez semblable ici. / C'est très différent ici.

1. Students in high school **(le lycée)** already have a "major." They pursue their diploma, **le baccalauréat,** in a chosen field, such as **le bac littéraire, scientifique, économique, technologique,** or **professionnel.**
2. At the end of their secondary studies, French students must pass a series of difficult national exams covering all the material they have studied in order to receive the **baccalauréat.**
3. The failure rate of the **baccalauréat** in recent years has been a little over 25%. If students do not pass, they cannot go on to the university, unless they repeat the last year at the **lycée** and successfully retest.
4. University students enter directly into field-specific courses (including law and medical school).
5. Tuition is almost free at most French universities.
6. In France, most older universities do not have campuses. The **facultés** have a building or buildings in which they meet their classes, often older buildings in the center of town.
7. Different **facultés** may be in various areas of town.
8. Some more modern universities, however, do have a campus that is more similar to that found at universities in the United States and Canada.
9. Most French students live at home with their parents and attend the university in their region.
10. There are few student activities; extracurricular events and sports are not generally a part of the university.
11. Traditionally, most university classes in France took place in huge lecture halls in a lecture format. Grades were based almost entirely on one or two exams. Recently, there has been a movement toward smaller classes, working in groups, and more frequent assignments.
12. If you want to continue your education after high school, you have the following choices:

L'université:
Two-year degrees: **un DEUG (diplôme d'études universitaires générales); un DEUST (diplôme d'études universitaires scientifiques et techniques)**
Three-year degree: **une licence**
Four-year degree: **une maîtrise**
Seven-year degree: **un doctorat**
Five–seven year degrees: **un diplôme de médecine, de chirurgie dentaire ou de pharmacie**

Une école spécialisée:
Three-year degrees: **un diplôme de travail social ou de commerce**

Un institut universitaire de technologie (IUT):
Two-year degree: **un DUT (diplôme universitaire de technologie)**

Une grande école (GE):
Five-year degree: **un diplôme d'ingénieur, de sciences, d'économie, de commerce ou de lettres**

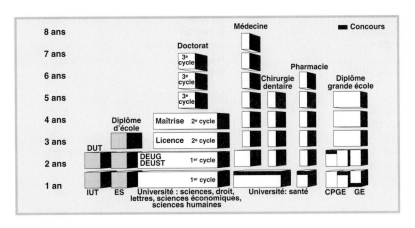

		Médecine	■ Concours

(Chart showing French higher education system by number of years)

8 ans
7 ans — Doctorat — 3e cycle
6 ans — 3e cycle — Chirurgie dentaire — Pharmacie — Diplôme grande école
5 ans — 3e cycle
4 ans — Diplôme d'école — Maîtrise 2e cycle
3 ans — DUT — Licence 2e cycle
2 ans — DEUG DEUST 1er cycle
1 an — IUT ES — 1er cycle — Université : sciences, droit, lettres, sciences économiques, sciences humaines — Université: santé — CPGE GE

A. Le baccalauréat.
Using the preceding information and the headlines about the **baccalauréat** exam below, answer the questions that follow.

JOUR J pour les aspirants-bacheliers

598 863 candidats à l'assaut du bac

Bac: l'heure de vérité

Ils seront cette année 598 863 à tenter de décrocher, toutes séries confondues, ce diplôme convoité.

L'épreuve de philosophie, c'est aujourd'hui

1. About how many students take the **baccalauréat** exam per year?
   a. 600,000   **b.** 300,000   **c.** 1 million
2. About how many students who take the exam will probably pass?
   a. 1 of 2   **b.** 1 of 10   **c.** 3 of 4
3. The results of the **bac** are so important that the bac is sometimes referred to as:
   a. l'examen final   **b.** le Jour J *(D-Day)*   **c.** bonjour ou au revoir

B. À discuter.

1. What would be the advantages and disadvantages of a system in which students must pass a cumulative exam in order to receive a secondary education diploma?
2. How do you think students feel about taking the **baccalauréat** exam? What percentage fail the test? Do you think this has a positive or a negative effect on secondary education in France? Why?
3. Should higher education be almost free in the United States as in France? What would be the advantages and disadvantages?

visit http://horizons.heinle.com

VOCABULAIRE

COMPÉTENCE 1

Identifying people and describing appearance

NOMS MASCULINS

mes amis	my friends
un cours de littérature	a literature class
un frère	a brother
les gens	people
un (jeune) homme	a (young) man

NOMS FÉMININS

mes amies	my friends
une (jeune) femme	a (young) woman
la France	France
une semaine	a week
une sœur	a sister
l'université	the university

ADJECTIFS

américain(e)	American
beau (belle)	handsome, pretty
célibataire	single
divorcé(e)	divorced
fiancé(e)	engaged
français(e)	French
grand(e)	tall, big
gros(se)	fat
jeune	young
jumeau (jumelle)	twin
laid(e)	ugly
marié(e)	married
même	same
mince	thin
petit(e)	short, small
premier (première)	first
vieux (vieille)	old

EXPRESSIONS VERBALES

C'est…	He/She/This/It is . . .
Ce sont…	They are . . .
Ce n'est pas…	He/She/It/This is not . . .
Ce ne sont pas…	They are not . . .
Comment est… ?	What is . . . like?
Il/Elle est…	He/She/It is . . .
Ils/Elles sont…	They are . . .
Il/Elle n'est pas…	He/She/It is not . . .
Ils/Elles ne sont pas…	They are not . . .
faire connaissance	to meet
Nous sommes…	We are . . .
(pour) étudier	(in order) to study
(pour) visiter	(in order) to visit
(pour) voir	(in order) to see
Tu es…	You are . . .

DIVERS

à	to, at, in
dans	in
de	of, from, about
d'où	from where
non?	right?
sa	his, her, its

COMPÉTENCE 2

Describing personality

NOMS MASCULINS

tes amis	your friends
le football	soccer
mon meilleur ami	my best friend
le sport	sports
le tennis	tennis

NOMS FÉMININS

tes amies	your friends
les études	studies, going to school
ma meilleure amie	my best friend
la personnalité	personality

ADJECTIFS

agréable	pleasant
amusant(e)	fun, amusing
bête	stupid, dumb
désagréable	unpleasant
dynamique	active
ennuyeux (ennuyeuse)	boring
extraverti(e)	extroverted, outgoing
gentil (gentille)	nice
idéaliste	idealistic
intellectuel(le)	intellectual
intelligent(e)	intelligent
intéressant(e)	interesting
méchant(e)	mean
nouveau (nouvelle)	new
optimiste	optimistic
paresseux (paresseuse)	lazy
pessimiste	pessimistic
réaliste	realistic
sportif (sportive)	athletic
sympathique	nice
timide	timid, shy

EXPRESSIONS VERBALES

être	to be
je suis…	I am . . .
tu es…	you are . . .
il est…	he/it is . . .
elle est…	she/it is . . .
nous sommes…	we are . . .
vous êtes…	you are . . .
ils/elles sont…	they are . . .
j'aime/je n'aime pas	I like/I don't like
tu aimes	you like

DIVERS

alors	so, then
assez	rather
aussi… que	as . . . as
Ce n'est pas mon truc.	That's not my thing.
Est-ce que…	(particle used in questions)
moins… que	less . . . than
ne… pas (du tout)	not (at all)
n'est-ce pas?	right?
plus… que	more . . . than
plutôt	rather
un peu	a little

COMPÉTENCE 3

NOMS MASCULINS

un amphithéâtre	a lecture hall
un arbre	a tree
un bâtiment	a building
un bureau	an office
un café	a café
un campus	a campus
un cinéma	a movie theater
un club de gym	a gym, a fitness club
un concert (de jazz, de rock, de musique populaire, de musique classique)	a (jazz, rock, pop music, classical music) concert
un fast-food	a fast-food restaurant
un film	a movie, a film
un laboratoire de langues/d'informatique	a language/computer lab
un match de football américain	a football game
un parc	a park
un parking	a parking lot
un quartier (universitaire)	a (university) neighborhood
un restaurant	a restaurant
un stade	a stadium
un théâtre	a theater (for live performances)

NOMS FÉMININS

une bibliothèque	a library
une boîte de nuit	a nightclub
une librairie	a bookstore
une maison	a house
une résidence	a dormitory
une salle de classe	a classroom

ADJECTIFS

autre	other
bon(ne)	good
étranger (étrangère)	foreign
joli(e)	pretty
mauvais(e)	bad
moderne	modern
populaire	popular
quelques	some, a few
universitaire	university

EXPRESSIONS VERBALES

Comment est... ?	What is . . . like ?
Comment sont... ?	What are . . . like ?
Il y a...	There is, There are . . .
Il n'y a pas (de)...	There isn't, There aren't . . .
Où est... ?	Where is . . . ?
Qu'est-ce qu'il y a... ?	What is there . . . ?

DIVERS

assez (de)	enough (of)
beaucoup (de)	a lot (of)
dans	in
des	some
près de	near
sur	on
ton	your
un(e)	a, an

COMPÉTENCE 4

NOMS MASCULINS

l'allemand	German
l'anglais	English
le basket	basketball
les beaux-arts	the fine arts
un cours de commerce	a business course
un cours technique	a technical course
les devoirs	homework
l'espagnol	Spanish
un examen	an exam
le français	French
le marketing	marketing
le théâtre	theater, drama

NOMS FÉMININS

la biologie	biology
une boum	a party
la chimie	chemistry
la comptabilité	accounting
l'histoire	history
l'informatique	computer science
une langue	a language
la littérature classique	classical literature
les mathématiques	mathematics
la musique	music
la philosophie	philosophy
la physique	physics
la psychologie	psychology
les sciences (humaines)	the (social) sciences
les sciences politiques	political science, government

EXPRESSIONS VERBALES

Est-ce que vous aimez... ?	Do you like . . . ?
J'aime beaucoup/assez...	I like a lot / somewhat . . .
Je n'aime pas (du tout)...	I don't like (at all) . . .
Je préfère...	I prefer . . .
Qu'est-ce que vous étudiez/tu étudies?	What are you studying?, What do you study?
J'étudie...	I study . . .
Je n'étudie pas...	I don't study . . .

DIVERS

ce semestre	this semester
comme toi	like you

Nature morte aux grenades
Henri Matisse (1869–1954)
1947
Nice, Musée Matisse
Giraudon/Art Resource, New York
© 1998 Succession H. Matisse/Artists Rights Society (ARS), New York

Nice was the subject of many of Matisse's paintings. He painted indoor scenes as well as outdoor scenes of the city he loved. This still life focuses on the contrast between the brilliant Mediterranean light and the shadowed interior of a room.

Santon
Nice, France
Photograph: Beryl Goldberg, 1993

Santon means *little saint*. **Santons** are placed in Christmas manger scenes in Provence.

Sur la Côte d'Azur

NICE

POPULATION: 345 800 (les Niçois)

DÉPARTEMENT: Alpes-Maritimes

RÉGION: Provence-Alpes-Côte d'Azur

INDUSTRIES PRINCIPALES: tourisme, agriculture [fruits, primeurs *(produce)*, fleurs *(flowers)*, riz *(rice)*, vin *(wine)*]

PLATS RÉGIONAUX: bouillabaisse, salade niçoise

Après les cours

Nice

I maginez que vous êtes touriste à Nice et faites une liste de ces activités dans l'ordre de vos préférences.

Voir la mer Méditerranée et la Baie des Anges.

Faire une promenade le long de la mer sur la Promenade des Anglais.

Visiter les ruines romaines à Nice-Cimiez.

Visiter le quartier médiéval du Vieux Nice.

Voir les peintures d'Henri Matisse au musée Matisse.

Additional information. You may wish to point out the importance of Nice as a commercial, university, cultural, and tourist area. Nice was first established by Greek settlers from Marseilles more than 2,000 years ago. It got its name from the Greek word for victory. It was subsequently occupied by Romans, Saracens, and Turks, and at various times was ruled by Provence, Savoy, and Sardinia-Piedmont. In 1860, it was ceded to France by Italy in gratitude for French aid in unifying Italy. Nice, with its colorful flower market, is the distribution center of the flowers produced in the region, and nearby **Grasse** is the heart of the French perfume industry.

Aller au Carnaval de Nice.

Aller dans les boutiques, les restaurants et les cafés de la rue Masséna.

Visiter l'université de Nice et parler avec des étudiants.

Saying what you like to do

NOTE Culturelle

Le passe-temps le plus populaire en France, c'est de regarder la télé. Près de 80% des Français regardent la télé tous les jours *(every day)*.

NOTE DE VOCABULAIRE

To say what you *like*, use **j'aime.** To say what you *would like,* or *want,* use **je voudrais.**

VOCABULAIRE SUPPLÉMENTAIRE

courir *to run*
faire du ski *to ski*
faire du shopping *to go shopping*
faire du vélo *to go bike-riding*
faire de l'exercice *to exercise*
jardiner *to garden*
louer une vidéo *to rent a video*
nager *to swim*

Warm-up activities. A. Write these choices on the board: **J'aime beaucoup... J'aime assez... Je n'aime pas...** Ask students how they feel about various aspects of university life **(les professeurs, les étudiants, le laboratoire de langues, le cours de français, les matchs de football américain / de base-ball / de basket / de volley, les examens, le prof de français).** Then ask students how they feel about various courses **(la biologie, la comptabilité, etc.).** **B.** Have students complete these sentences with an aspect of university life and explain their feelings using **parce que: J'aime beaucoup... J'aime assez... Je n'aime pas beaucoup... Je n'aime pas du tout...**

Suggestion. Point out the false cognate **rester.**

Supplemental activity. Have students say which of each pair of activities is better exercise: **1.** jouer au tennis ou dîner au restaurant **2.** faire du jogging ou regarder la télévision **3.** dormir ou faire du jogging **4.** prendre un verre ou jouer au basket **5.** écouter la radio ou jouer au tennis **6.** faire du jogging ou rester à la maison

Les passe-temps

— Qu'est-ce que vous aimez **faire** après les cours?
— J'aime... Je n'aime pas... Je préfère...

— Qu'est-ce que **vous voudriez** faire aujourd'hui après les cours?
— **Je voudrais...**

SORTIR AVEC DES AMIS

aller au cinéma
(aller) voir un film

aller au café
(aller) **prendre un verre**

aller en boîte
(aller) danser

dîner au restaurant

faire du sport
jouer au tennis / au basket /
au football / au volley

faire du jogging

RESTER À LA MAISON

dormir

travailler sur l'ordinateur
surfer le Net

lire

écouter la radio / la chaîne
stéréo / de la musique

regarder la télé(vision) /
une vidéo
jouer à des jeux vidéo

bricoler

---

faire *to do*   **vous voudriez** *you would like*   **Je voudrais** *I would like*   **sortir** *to go out*   **aller** *to go*   **prendre**
un verre *to have a drink*   **rester** *to stay, to remain*   **bricoler** *to do handiwork*

jouer de la guitare / **de la batterie** / du piano

parler au téléphone

inviter des amis à la maison

 David invite Annette à sortir.

DAVID: Tu es **libre ce soir?** Tu voudrais faire **quelque chose?**
ANNETTE: Je voudrais bien. Où est-ce que tu voudrais aller?
DAVID: Je ne sais pas. Tu voudrais aller en boîte?
ANNETTE: Non, je préfère aller au cinéma.
DAVID: Bon, **d'accord! On va** prendre un verre avant?
ANNETTE: **Pourquoi pas? Vers** quelle heure?
DAVID: Vers sept heures, sept heures et demie... au café La Martinique?
ANNETTE: D'accord. Alors, à tout à l'heure.
DAVID: Au revoir, Annette. À ce soir!

Suggestion for the conversation. Set the scene for the dialogue. Point out that you say **Je voudrais bien** to say *I'd like to.* Have students listen twice, with books closed, to determine what two things David and Annette decide to do. Verify comprehension; then have students read along as you play the conversation again.

Suggestion. Point out the difference between **ce soir, le soir,** and **du soir.**

A. Qu'est-ce que vous aimez faire? Complétez les phrases.

1. Après les cours, j'aime... mais je n'aime pas...
2. Aujourd'hui après les cours, je voudrais...
3. Le vendredi soir, je préfère...
4. Le samedi matin, j'aime...
5. Le samedi soir, j'aime...
6. Le dimanche, je préfère...
7. Ce week-end, je voudrais...
8. À la maison, j'aime...
9. J'aime... seul(e) et je préfère... avec des amis.
10. Je n'aime pas du tout...

B. Invitations. Invitez votre partenaire à faire les choses suivantes.

Exemple (demain) jouer au tennis
—**Tu es libre demain? Tu voudrais jouer au tennis avec moi?**
—**Oui, je voudrais bien. / Non, je préfère aller au cinéma.**
—**Vers quelle heure, alors?**
—**Vers deux heures.**
—**Bon, d'accord. Alors, à demain.**
—**À demain. Au revoir!**

1. (ce soir) dîner au restaurant
2. (vendredi soir) aller voir un film
3. (aujourd'hui après les cours) faire les devoirs
4. (demain après-midi) aller prendre un verre
5. (aujourd'hui après les cours) ???

Warm-ups for A. Qu'est-ce que vous aimez faire? A. Have students ask partners if they like each of the activities shown on the preceding page. EXEMPLE – **Est-ce que tu aimes aller au cinéma?** – **Oui, j'aime (beaucoup / assez) aller au cinéma. / Non, je n'aime pas aller au cinéma. B.** Again point out the difference between **je voudrais** and **j'aime** and between **le week-end** and **ce week-end.** Write these items on a transparency or on the board and have students complete them with **j'aime** or **je voudrais. 1.** ... aller au cinéma le samedi soir. **2.** Ce week-end... aller en boîte. **3.** En général, après les cours, ... rester à la maison. **4.** Aujourd'hui après les cours... aller au cinéma. **5.** Le matin... dormir. **6.** Demain matin... aller au café.

Suggestion for A. Qu'est-ce que vous aimez faire? Take a class survey of each item.

---

de la batterie *drums*   **libre** *free*   **ce soir** *this evening*   **quelque chose** *something*   **d'accord** *okay*   **On va... ?**
Shall we go . . . ?   **Pourquoi pas?** *Why not?*   **Vers** *About, Around, Toward*

1. What do you call the basic form of the verb that you find listed in the dictionary?
2. What are the three possible endings for infinitives in French?
3. When you have a sequence of more than one verb, which one is conjugated? Which ones are in the infinitive?

Suggestions. A. Have students scan a page of the glossary and pick out infinitives. **B.** Have students look up words for other sports and musical instruments they want to know. You may wish to point out that some sports and activities use **faire** rather than, or as well as, **jouer**.

Saying what you like to do: *L'infinitif*

To name an activity in French, use the verb in the infinitive. The infinitive is the basic form of the verb that you find listed in the dictionary. Some examples of infinitives in English are *to play, to sleep,* and *to be.* French infinitives are single words ending in **-er, -ir,** or **-re,** like **jouer, dormir,** or **être.** In French, whenever there are two or three verbs together in a clause, the first verb is conjugated, but the second and third verbs are in the infinitive.

— Qu'est-ce que tu **aimes faire?**   — Est-ce que tu **voudrais sortir?**
— J'**aime aller danser.**   — Je **préfère rester** à la maison.

Use **jouer au** to talk about playing most sports.

jouer au base-ball / au basket / au football / au football américain / au golf / au hockey / au tennis / au volley...

Je joue au base-ball.   Je ne joue pas au hockey.

Use **jouer du/de la** to talk about playing most musical instruments. The use of **du** or **de la** depends on the gender of the word that follows. You will learn the rules for these changes later. For now, learn these forms as part of the expressions that follow. As with **un, une,** and **des, du** and **de la** change to **de** in a negative sentence.

jouer du clavier *(keyboard)* / du piano / du saxophone / de la batterie / de la guitare / de la trompette...

Je joue du piano.   Je ne joue pas **de** trompette.

 Prononciation: *La consonne r et l'infinitif*

The consonant **r** is one of the few (CaReFuL) consonants that are often pronounced at the end of words. The final **r** of infinitives ending in **-er** is an important exception and is not pronounced. The **-er** ending is pronounced like the **é** in **café.**

parler	inviter	danser
regarder	jouer	écouter

The **r** in infinitives ending in **-ir** or **-re** is pronounced. To pronounce a French **r,** hold the back of your tongue firmly arched upward in the back of your mouth and pronounce a vocalized English *h* sound in your throat.

sortir	dormir	lire
faire	être	prendre

NOTE DE VOCABULAIRE

To say you don't like either activity, use **ne... ni... ni...** *(neither . . . nor . . .).* Je n'aime **ni** lire **ni** faire les devoirs.

Suggestion for A. Préférences. Go over the pronunciation of **tu préfères, je préfère,** and each infinitive, reminding students to focus on pronouncing the infinitive correctly.

Follow-up for A. Préférences. Have students list activities you do at home and those that you do when you go out.

A. Préférences. Demandez à votre partenaire quelle activité il/elle préfère.

Exemple   lire / faire les devoirs
                 — **Tu préfères lire ou faire les devoirs?**
                 — **Je préfère lire.**

1. faire du jogging / dormir
2. sortir avec des amis / inviter des amis à la maison
3. prendre un verre au café / dîner au restaurant
4. jouer au tennis / regarder un match de tennis à la télé

5. regarder la télé / aller au cinéma
6. dîner au restaurant / dîner à la maison
7. être à la maison / être en cours
8. parler à un ami au téléphone / inviter un ami à la maison

B. Chacun ses goûts. Est-ce que vous aimez ces activités?

Exemple **J'aime beaucoup bricoler. / J'aime assez bricoler. / Je n'aime pas bricoler.**

Suggestion for *B. Chacun ses goûts.* Have students move around the classroom trying to find two people who like each of the activities pictured by asking questions of classmates. EXEMPLE —John, tu aimes bricoler?

C. Entretien. Interviewez votre partenaire.

1. Qu'est-ce que tu aimes faire après les cours? Qu'est-ce que tu voudrais faire aujourd'hui après les cours?
2. Est-ce que tu aimes rester à la maison le week-end? Qu'est-ce que tu aimes faire le week-end? Qu'est-ce que tu voudrais faire ce week-end?
3. Est-ce que tu voudrais regarder la télévision ce soir? Quels jours est-ce que tu aimes regarder la télévision?
4. Est-ce que tu voudrais aller au cinéma ce week-end? Quel film est-ce que tu voudrais voir? Tu préfères aller voir un film au cinéma ou regarder une vidéo à la maison?
5. Quel sport est-ce que tu préfères, le tennis, le golf ou le basket? Est-ce que tu préfères faire du sport ou regarder des matchs à la télévision?

D. On fait quelque chose? Avec un(e) partenaire, préparez la conversation suivante. Ensuite, présentez la conversation à la classe.

You run into a classmate outside of class. Ask your classmate what he/she likes to do after class. Discuss several things that you do and do not like to do. Then, invite him/her to do something tomorrow after class. Decide what you will do, where, and when.

Suggestion for *D. On fait quelque chose?* Tell students to use questions like those in the preceding exercise (*C. Entretien*) to discuss what they like to do and refer back to *B. Invitations* on page 65 for a model on issuing an invitation.

Script for *A. Quand?*

SCÈNE A.

– Michèle, tu veux aller au cinéma avec moi? Il y a un vieux film de Truffaut au cinéclub.

– Je voudrais bien, mais je ne suis pas libre. Tu ne peux pas y aller lundi?

– Bon, d'accord. Lundi à six heures?

– D'accord!

SCÈNE B.

– Je voudrais t'inviter au restaurant ce soir.

– Ce n'est pas possible ce soir. J'ai un examen demain et je dois travailler.

– Eh bien, tu voudrais y aller jeudi soir?

– Oui, jeudi, ça va. Vers quelle heure?

– Vers huit heures et demie?

– D'accord.

SCÈNE C.

– Monique veut sortir ce soir mais je ne suis pas libre.

– Alors, pourquoi ne pas l'inviter à nous accompagner au cinéma mercredi?

– Bonne idée. Le film est à quelle heure?

– À trois heures et quart.

Script for *B. Qu'est-ce qu'elles font?*

SCÈNE A.

– Qu'est-ce qu'on fait ce soir? Tu veux sortir?

– Oui, pourquoi pas? Allons danser avec David.

– Moi, je préfère aller au cinéma.

SCÈNE B.

– David m'a invitée au restaurant. Tu veux nous accompagner?

– Non merci, je préfère rester à la maison ce soir.

SCÈNE C.

– Tu veux aller prendre un verre maintenant? J'ai un peu soif.

– Merci, mais je suis en route pour le club de gym.

Script for *On sort ensemble?*

THOMAS: Regarde, Gisèle... voilà David. Eh, salut, David!

GISÈLE: Bonjour, David. Ça va?

DAVID: Salut, Thomas. Salut, Gisèle. Ça va bien. Et vous?

GISÈLE: Pas mal.

THOMAS: Moi, ça va assez bien.

DAVID: Thomas, Gisèle, je voudrais vous présenter mes amies américaines, Annette et Yvette Clark. Annette, Yvette, voilà mes amis Thomas Dutoit et Gisèle Hardy.

ANNETTE ET YVETTE: Bonjour, Thomas. Bonjour, Gisèle.

THOMAS ET GISÈLE: Bonjour, Annette. Bonjour, Yvette.

GISÈLE: Alors, vous êtes d'où?

ANNETTE: Nous sommes de Los Angeles. Mais moi, j'habite ici maintenant parce que je suis étudiante à l'université.

Stratégies et compréhension auditive:
Listening for specific information

It takes time and practice to understand a foreign language when you hear it. However, you can use some strategies to help you learn to understand spoken French more quickly.

In everyday conversations, you usually do not need to comprehend everything you hear. Practice listening for specific details, such as times, places, or prices. Do not worry about understanding every word.

 A. Quand? Écoutez ces trois scènes. Indiquez le jour et l'heure choisis *(chosen)*.

SCÈNE A: LE JOUR _____

L'HEURE _____

SCÈNE B: LE JOUR _____

L'HEURE _____

SCÈNE C: LE JOUR _____

L'HEURE _____

Note. Alternating chapters introduce a story line in a reading. The following chapters present listening strategies and a recorded passage. To do this section in class, use the Text Audio CD or read the script. You may prefer to go over the strategies and have students do the pre-listening and listening exercises at home. Remind them to use the Text Audio CD. You can use the post-listening exercises as a comprehension check the following day.

 B. Qu'est-ce qu'elles font? Annette invite Yvette à sortir. Pour les trois scènes, indiquez ce qu'Yvette préfère faire.

SCÈNE A: _____

SCÈNE B: _____

SCÈNE C: _____

 # On sort ensemble?

David, Yvette, and Annette run into two of David's friends. Listen to their conversation. Do not try to understand every word. The first time, listen only for the leisure activities they mention. Each time you hear one mentioned, write it down.

A. Vous comprenez? Écoutez une seconde fois *(time)* la conversation entre David et ses amis et répondez à ces questions.

1. Est-ce que Thomas et Gisèle sont des amis d'Annette?
2. Faites une liste de trois choses que Thomas et Gisèle découvrent *(discover)* au sujet d'Annette et d'Yvette *(about Annette and Yvette)*.

B. Tu voudrais sortir? Invitez votre partenaire à faire les choses suivantes. Utilisez *B. Invitations* à la page 65 comme modèle.

voir un film

jouer au foot

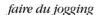

faire du vélo

faire du jogging

THOMAS: Et toi, Yvette, tu n'habites pas ici, alors?

YVETTE: Non, j'habite à Los Angeles. Je suis ici pour voir ma sœur.

THOMAS: Écoutez... justement nous allons voir le nouveau film de Steven Spielberg à l'Étoile. Vous voulez nous accompagner?

DAVID: Écoute, je regrette, mais j'ai déjà vu ce film. Annette, Yvette et moi pensions aller prendre un verre au café et ensuite aller dîner au restaurant. Venez donc prendre un verre avec nous avant d'aller voir le film!

GISÈLE: Quelle heure est-il?

ANNETTE: Cinq heures moins le quart.

GISÈLE: Bon, d'accord. Je veux bien.

THOMAS: Moi aussi!

Suggestion for *B. Tu voudrais sortir?*
First have students find out from their partners which activities they like (**Tu aimes... ?**). When they find one they both enjoy, have them make plans to do it together.

COMPÉTENCE 2

Saying how you spend your free time

NOTE Culturelle

En France, soixante-quinze pour cent (75%) des hommes et cinquante pour cent (50%) des femmes se livrent à *(participate in)* une activité sportive régulière. Un Français sur cinq est membre d'un club de sport. Le sport le plus populaire, c'est le football.

Warm-up activities. A. Have students say whether you normally do these activities **à la maison**, by saying **oui** or **non**: **1.** faire les devoirs **2.** dîner au restaurant **3.** danser **4.** aller voir un film au cinéma **5.** lire **6.** jouer au tennis **7.** dormir **8.** regarder la télé **9.** écouter la radio. **B.** Have students tell how well they like each of the preceding activities. **C.** Review **je voudrais** and have students say what they would like to do at these moments: **1.** après les cours aujourd'hui **2.** demain **3.** ce week-end **4.** ce soir **5.** demain soir.

Suggestions. A. Point out that these adverbs all follow immediately after the verb, except **comme ci comme ça**. Adverb position is discussed in the next section. **B.** Remind students of the difference in use between **samedi** et **le samedi**. **C.** Point out that the use of the English word *matinee* to mean *afternoon performance* does not correspond to the meaning of **matinée** in French. **D.** Point out that you use **étudier** to say at what school or what fields you study. To talk about studying as an activity, you use **travailler** or **préparer les cours/un examen**. Also tell students that you do not say **préparer** *pour* les cours. **E.** Remind students that they saw **je vais** in the *Chapitre préliminaire* in the expression **Je vais bien**.

Le week-end

Comment est-ce que vous aimez **passer le temps?** Qu'est-ce que **vous faites d'habitude** le samedi?

toujours	**souvent**	**quelquefois**	**rarement**	**ne… jamais**
always	*often*	*sometimes*	*rarely*	*never*

Le samedi matin, je passe **presque** toujours **la matinée** à la maison.

Je reste au lit **jusqu'à** 10 heures.

Je mange quelque chose.

Je regarde la télé.

Je prépare les cours.

L'après-midi, j'aime faire du sport.

Le samedi soir, je ne reste jamais à la maison... je préfère sortir avec des amis.

Je nage souvent.

Quelquefois je joue au foot(ball).

Je dîne souvent au restaurant.

Je vais presque toujours au cinéma.

Quels sont **vos** passe-temps **préférés?** Est-ce que vous aimez faire du sport? de la musique? Comment est-ce que vous jouez?

très bien	**assez bien**	**comme ci comme ça** *so-so*	**assez mal**	**très mal**
very well	*fairly well*		*fairly badly*	*very badly*

Je joue très bien au foot.

Je joue assez bien au hockey.

Je joue du piano comme ci comme ça.

Je chante assez mal.

Je danse très mal.

Je joue **mieux** au tennis **qu'**au hockey. **Quand** je joue au tennis, **je gagne** presque toujours!

---

passer le temps *to spend time*   **vous faites (faire** *to do, to make)*   **d'habitude** *usually, generally*   **presque** *almost*   **la matinée** *the morning*   **jusqu'à** *until*   **Je vais (aller** *to go)*   **vos** *your*   **préféré(e)** *favorite*   **mieux (que)** *better (than)*   **quand** *when*   **gagner** *to win*

Annette et David parlent de **leurs** activités *(f)* du week-end.

ANNETTE: Qu'est-ce que **tu fais** d'habitude le week-end?
DAVID: Le samedi matin je reste au lit, le samedi après-midi je joue au tennis et le soir j'aime sortir. Et toi?
ANNETTE: Le matin je prépare mes cours, l'après-midi j'aime **faire du shopping** et le soir, moi aussi, j'aime sortir.
DAVID: Alors, tu es libre samedi soir? Tu voudrais sortir? Il y a un bon film au cinéclub **à la fac.** C'est un vieux classique de Truffaut.
ANNETTE: Oui, oui, je voudrais bien.
DAVID: Le film commence à huit heures. Je **passe chez toi** vers sept heures?
ANNETTE: D'accord! À samedi, alors.

A. Passe-temps. Complétez ces phrases pour parler de vous.

1. Je danse *très bien / assez bien / comme ci comme ça / assez mal / très mal.*
2. Je chante *très bien / assez bien / comme ci comme ça / ???.*
3. Je chante *mieux / aussi bien / moins bien* que je danse.
4. Quand je joue *au tennis / au hockey / ???,* je gagne *toujours / souvent / rarement.*
5. Je joue *du piano / de la batterie / ???. (Je ne joue pas de musique.)*
6. Le samedi matin, je passe *presque toujours / souvent / rarement* la matinée à la maison. *(Je ne passe jamais la matinée à la maison.)*
7. Le samedi matin, je reste au lit jusqu'à *huit heures / dix heures / ???.*
8. D'habitude, le samedi matin, je mange quelque chose *à la maison / dans un fast-food / au café / ???. (Je ne mange pas le samedi matin.)*
9. D'habitude je prépare les cours *à la maison / à la bibliothèque / chez un(e) ami(e) / au café / ???.*
10. Comme *(For)* exercice, je préfère *faire du sport / faire du jogging / nager.*
11. Le samedi soir, le plus souvent *je reste à la maison / j'invite des amis à la maison / je préfère sortir.*
12. Je vais plus souvent au cinéma *seul(e) / avec des amis / avec mon meilleur ami / avec ma meilleure amie / avec ma famille / ???.*

B. Parlons du week-end! Avec un(e) partenaire, changez la conversation entre David et Annette comme indiqué.

1. David invites Annette to a restaurant instead of to the movies.
2. David works Saturday morning and studies Saturday afternoon. Annette plays tennis Saturday morning and goes to the movies Saturday afternoon, so David invites her to the movie in the afternoon.
3. The conversation is between you and a classmate. Change it to make it true for you. Make the invitation to do something you would like to do.

Suggestion for the conversation. Set the scene and have students listen to the conversation twice with books closed for the answers to these questions. 1. Qu'est-ce que David aime faire le samedi matin? le samedi après-midi? le samedi soir? 2. Qu'est-ce qu'Annette aime faire? 3. Qu'est-ce que David invite Annette à faire? À quelle heure? Afterward, have students listen to the conversation again while reading along in the text.

Suggestions. A. Explain the terms **cinéclub** and **la fac. B.** Briefly discuss Truffaut. **C.** Point out the expression **chez** and how it is used, giving various examples. Tell students that you never say **à** before **chez.**

Warm-up for *A. Passe-temps.* Have students repeat the sentence that indicates that someone does something more often: 1. Je bricole souvent. / Je bricole rarement. 2. Je travaille beaucoup sur l'ordinateur. / Je travaille peu sur l'ordinateur. 3. Nous n'invitons jamais d'amis à la maison. / Nous invitons souvent des amis à la maison. 4. Je joue quelquefois au tennis. / Je joue rarement au tennis. 5. Ma famille ne regarde jamais la télévision le week-end. / Ma famille regarde toujours la télévision le week-end. 6. Je travaille souvent le week-end. / Je travaille quelquefois le week-end.

Follow-ups for *A. Passe-temps.* **A.** Have students finish each of these statements with a logical word: 1. Shaquille O'Neal joue très bien au... 2. Les Dallas Cowboys jouent au... 3. Wynonna Judd chante... 4. Popeye chante... 5. Gloria Estefan chante... 6. Tim Allen bricole... 7. Moi, je chante (danse, travaille...). **B.** Introduce the words **notre équipe** and **la chorale** and ask: **Est-ce que notre équipe de football américain / basket / base-ball / volley joue bien ou mal? Est-ce que la chorale universitaire chante bien ou mal? Est-ce que l'orchestre joue bien ou mal? Est-ce que les étudiants travaillent souvent sur l'ordinateur? Est-ce que les professeurs travaillent beaucoup?**

---

leur(s) *their*   **tu fais (faire** *to do, to make)*   **faire du shopping** *to go shopping*   **à la fac** *at the university*
passer *to pass (by)*   **chez toi** *your house* **(chez...** = *to/at/in/by the house of . . .)*

1. How do you determine the stem of an **-er** verb? What endings do you add to it?
2. When do you drop the final **-e** of words like **je, ne,** and **le?**
3. Where do you generally place adverbs such as **bien?**
4. Which **-er** verb endings are silent?

Telling what you do, how often, and how well:
Les verbes en -er et les adverbes

Regular verbs are groups of verbs that follow a predictable pattern of conjugation. The largest group of regular verbs have infinitives ending in -er. All verbs ending in -er that you have learned, *except* **aller,** are conjugated in the present tense by dropping the -er and adding the following endings.

PARLER *(to speak, to talk)*			
je	parl**e**	nous	parl**ons**
tu	parl**es**	vous	parl**ez**
il/elle	parl**e**	ils/elles	parl**ent**

Note. Students learn about accent spelling change verbs and have further opportunities for practice with **-er** verbs in the next section.

The present tense can be expressed in three ways in English, depending on the context. Express all three of the following English structures by a single verb form in French.

I work.
I am working. } Je travaille.
I do work.

He speaks French.
He is speaking French. } Il parle français.
He does speak French.

Here are the regular -er verbs that you have seen so far.

aimer	*to like, to love*	jouer	*to play*
bricoler	*to do handiwork*	manger	*to eat*
chanter	*to sing*	nager	*to swim*
commencer	*to begin, to start*	parler	*to speak, to talk*
compter	*to count*	passer	*to pass (by), to spend (time)*
danser	*to dance*	penser	*to think*
dîner	*to have dinner*	préférer	*to prefer*
donner	*to give*	préparer	*to prepare*
écouter	*to listen (to)*	regarder	*to look (at), to watch*
étudier	*to study*	répéter	*to repeat*
fermer	*to close*	rester	*to stay, to remain*
habiter	*to live*	surfer	*to surf*
inviter	*to invite*	travailler	*to work, to study*

NOTE DE GRAMMAIRE

Verbs whose infinitives do not end in **-er,** and a few irregular verbs whose infinitives do, such as **aller,** do not follow the pattern of conjugation shown here. You will learn how to conjugate such verbs later. You may want to use these forms now to talk about your activities.

I go: **je vais**

I sleep: **je dors**

I do, I make: **je fais**

I read: **je lis**

I take: **je prends**

I go out: **je sors**

Suggestion. Go over the pronunciation of **je vais, je dors, je fais, je lis, je prends,** and **je sors.** Point out that all these forms end in **-s.**

Remember that with words such as **je, le, que,** and **ne,** you replace the e with an apostrophe before a vowel sound.

j'habite / je **n'**habite pas   **j'**aime / je **n'**aime pas

Adverbs such as **bien, souvent,** and **beaucoup** tell how well, how often, or how much you do something. In French, these adverbs generally follow directly after the conjugated verb. **Comme ci comme ça,** however, is placed at the end of a sentence or clause, and **quelquefois** can be placed after the conjugated verb or at the beginning of a sentence or clause.

Thomas regarde **souvent** la télévision.   *Thomas **often** watches television.*
Je joue au tennis **comme ci comme ça.**   *I play tennis **so-so.***
Quelquefois, je joue **assez bien.**   *Sometimes, I play **fairly well.***

To say *never,* place **ne** before the conjugated verb and **jamais** after it, as you do with **ne... pas.** Do not use **pas** with **jamais.**

Je **ne** joue **jamais** au golf.   *I **never** play golf.*

Prononciation: *Les verbes en -er*

All the present tense endings of **-er** verbs, except for the **nous (-ons)** and **vous (-ez)** forms, are silent.

je resté   tu restés   il resté   elle resté   ils restént   elles restént

Rely on context to distinguish between **il** and **ils,** or **elle** and **elles.** You will hear a difference only with verbs beginning with a vowel sound.

il travaillé — ils travaillént   il aimé — ils ᶻaimént

The **-ons** ending of the **nous** form rhymes with the **bon** of **bonjour,** and the **-ez** of the **vous** form rhymes with **les** and sounds like the **-er** ending of the infinitive. There is liaison between the **s** of **nous** and **vous** and verbs beginning with vowel sounds.

noús parlons   voús parlez   nous ᶻétudions   vous ᶻétudiez

A. Préférences. Est-ce que les personnes indiquées aiment faire ces choses?

Exemple   **Moi, j'aime jouer du piano. /**
                Moi, je n'aime pas jouer de piano.

Moi, je (j')...
Mes amis...
Ma famille et moi, nous...

Mes amis et moi, nous...
Mon meilleur ami (Ma meilleure amie)...
(to a classmate) Est-ce que tu... ?

Mon meilleur ami (Ma meilleure amie)...
Ma famille et moi, nous...
(to your professor) Est-ce que vous... ?

Moi, je (j')...
Mes amis...
(to a classmate) Est-ce que tu... ?

Mes amis...
Moi, je (j')...
(to your professor) Est-ce que vous... ?

Warm-up for *A. Préférences.* Write these two columns on the board or a transparency and have students match them. **COLUMN 1: 1.** Le samedi soir, j'... **2.** Toi, *[name of student in the class],* qu'est-ce que tu... **3.** Et vous, *[professor's name],* est-ce que vous... **4.** Mes amis et moi, nous... **5.** Les étudiants à *[name of university]...* **COLUMN 2: a.** invitez des amis à la maison? **b.** aimes faire? **c.** aime sortir avec des amis. **d.** préférons aller danser. **e.** aiment mieux sortir que travailler. To correct their work, have them read the sentences they have formed, paying particular attention to the pronunciation of the verbs.

Suggestion for *A. Préférences.* You may wish to have students prepare this exercise ahead, writing the correct form of the conjugated verb. Remind them that all the forms sound the same, except those for **nous** and **vous.** To correct their responses, have students spell out the conjugated verb as they do the activity.

Follow-up for *A. Préférences.* Have students say what the indicated people like to do and then what they do not like to do.

B. Et vous? Est-ce que vous faites toujours, souvent... ces choses le samedi?

Exemple   le samedi matin: passer la matinée à la maison
Le samedi matin, je passe toujours (souvent...) la matinée à la maison. / Je ne passe jamais la matinée à la maison.

1. le samedi matin:
rester à la maison
manger à la maison
travailler
préparer les cours

2. le samedi après-midi:
nager
jouer au foot
regarder la télé
surfer le Net

3. le samedi soir:
dîner au restaurant
manger dans un fast-food
inviter des amis à la maison
danser

Follow-up for *C. Opinions*. As a composition topic, have students write a short paragraph describing the ideal roommate.

C. Opinions.   Comment est le/la camarade de chambre idéal(e)?

Exemple   travailler beaucoup
**Il/Elle travaille beaucoup. /
Il/Elle ne travaille pas beaucoup.**

1. aimer beaucoup aller en boîte
2. parler beaucoup
3. parler souvent au téléphone
4. bricoler bien
5. passer beaucoup de temps à la maison
6. inviter souvent des amis à la maison
7. regarder toujours la télé le week-end
8. chanter beaucoup
9. écouter toujours de la musique rap

Follow-ups for *D. Et toi?* A. Have students write four sentences about their partners. Collect them and read them aloud, having students guess who is being described. **B.** Giving the students the following example as a model, have them work with their partner and say what they have in common and how they are different. **EXEMPLE** Nous (ne) sommes (pas) (très) différent(e)s. Il/Elle aime aller en boîte mais moi, je n'aime pas aller en boîte. Nous travaillons...

D. Et toi?   Interviewez un(e) partenaire avec les verbes de l'exercice précédent.

Exemple   **— Est-ce que tu travailles beaucoup?
— Oui, je travaille beaucoup. /
Non, je ne travaille pas beaucoup.**

Après, parlez de votre partenaire à la classe.

Exemple   **Il/Elle travaille beaucoup et...**

E. C'est vrai?   Formez des phrases pour décrire *(to describe)* votre classe.

Exemple   je / parler beaucoup en cours
**Je parle beaucoup en cours. /
Je ne parle pas beaucoup en cours.**

1. le professeur / parler quelquefois anglais en cours
2. les étudiants / commencer à parler très bien français
3. nous / travailler beaucoup en cours
4. je / aimer dormir en cours
5. nous / regarder souvent la télé en cours
6. les étudiants / travailler quelquefois ensemble
7. nous / aimer travailler ensemble
8. je / écouter toujours les CD
9. les étudiants / manger quelquefois en cours

F. Qu'est-ce qu'ils font? Qu'est-ce que ces personnes font *(are doing)?*

Exemple **Il écoute une cassette.**

1.

2.

3.

4.

5.

6.

7.

8.

Maintenant, dites si vous faites souvent (rarement, bien...) ces choses.

Exemple **J'écoute souvent des cassettes.**

très / assez bien	comme ci comme ça	très / assez mal
TOUJOURS	souvent QUELQUEFOIS	**rarement** ne... jamais

G. Entretien. Interviewez votre partenaire.

1. Tu es musicien(ne)? Est-ce que tu danses bien ou mal? Est-ce que tu chantes bien? Tu préfères écouter la radio ou regarder la télé? Est-ce que tu regardes la télé quand tu manges? Tu écoutes de la musique quand tu prépares les cours?

2. Est-ce que tu es sportif (sportive)? Est-ce que tu aimes le sport? Quel sport est-ce que tu préfères, le football américain, le basket, le golf ou le base-ball? Est-ce que tu joues au tennis? au golf? au volley? (Est-ce que tu gagnes souvent?)

3. Est-ce que tu restes souvent à la maison le week-end? Est-ce que tu bricoles quelquefois le week-end? Est-ce que tu prépares les cours à la maison? Est-ce que tu préfères bricoler ou préparer les cours?

Suggestion for *F. Qu'est-ce qu'ils font?* Before doing the second part of the exercise, remind students of the appropriate position of the adverbs and have them use **Je sais...** / **Je ne sais pas...** to say how well they know how to do these things: **jouer au tennis, travailler sur l'ordinateur, parler espagnol, lire l'allemand, danser, jouer au basket.** EXEMPLE **Je sais très bien jouer au tennis.**

Follow-up for *F. Qu'est-ce qu'ils font?* Use these words to describe what you and your friends do. EXEMPLE bien **Nous dansons bien. 1.** bien **2.** quelquefois **3.** ne... jamais **4.** assez mal **5.** comme ci comme ça

Suggestion for *G. Entretien.* Point out the word **musicien(ne)** and its pronunciation before beginning the exercise.

1. In verbs like **préférer**, which forms have a spelling change in the stem in the present tense? What is the change? Which forms have stems like the infinitive?

2. What is special about the **nous** form of a verb with an infinitive ending in **-ger**? in **-cer**?

Telling what you do:
Quelques verbes à changements orthographiques

A few **-er** verbs have spelling changes in their stems when they are conjugated in the present tense.

- When the next-to-last syllable of an infinitive has an **e** or **é**, this letter often changes to **è** in all forms except **nous** and **vous**. The stem for the **nous** and **vous** forms is like the infinitive.

PRÉFÉRER *(to prefer)*		RÉPÉTER *(to repeat)*	
je préfère	nous préférons	je répète	nous répétons
tu préfères	vous préférez	tu répètes	vous répétez
il/elle préfère	ils/elles préfèrent	il/elle répète	ils/elles répètent

- Verbs ending in **-cer** and **-ger** also have spelling changes. With verbs ending in **-ger**, like **manger, nager,** and **voyager** *(to travel),* you must insert an **-e-** before the **-ons** ending in the **nous** form. With verbs ending in **-cer**, like **commencer**, the **c** changes to a **ç** before the **-ons** ending in the **nous** form.

Suggestion. Point out the new verb **voyager**.

VOYAGER *(to travel)*		COMMENCER *(to start, to begin)*	
je voyage	nous voyageons	je commence	nous commençons
tu voyages	vous voyagez	tu commences	vous commencez
il/elle voyage	ils/elles voyagent	il/elle commence	ils/elles commencent

 # Prononciation:
Les verbes à changements orthographiques

Spelling changes occur in verbs like **préférer, manger,** and **commencer** to reflect pronunciation. Compare the **é** and **è** sounds in the conjugated forms of **préférer.** The letter **é (e accent aigu)** sounds like the vowel of **les.**

— Vous préférez passer la matinée à la maison?
— Non, nous préférons passer la matinée au café.

The letter **è (e accent grave),** which often occurs in the final syllable of words ending in **e (Michèle),** is a less tight sound. It is similar to the *e* in the English word *let.*

Je préfère aller à la bibliothèque avec Michèle.

Spelling changes occur in the **nous** form of **-cer** and **-ger** verbs due to the pronunciation of **c** and **g** before the **-ons** ending. In French, **c** and **g** are pronounced soft (the **c** like an **s** and the **g** like a French **j**) before an **e, i,** or **y.** They are pronounced hard (the **c** like a **k** and the **g** similar to the *g* in the English word *go*) before an **a, o, u,** or a consonant.

Suggestions. A. Have the class work together to list words they have seen with **ç. B.** Put the following words on the board, leaving off the cedillas. Pronounce the words and have students decide which word in each pair requires a **cédille: facile/façade; comme ci/comme ça, France/français; Provence/provençal, Nice/niçois.**

Hard **g:** Gabrielle, Hugo, Guillaume   Soft **g:** Georges, Gérard, Gilbert
Hard **c:** Catherine, Colette   Soft **c:** Cécile, Maurice

The letter **ç** is used to indicate that a **c** is soft before **a, o,** or **u.** In **-er** verb endings, an **e** is introduced to keep **g** soft before **o.**

commen**ç**ons   **ç**a va   fran**ç**ais   mang**e**ons   voyag**e**ons   nag**e**ons

A. Qui est-ce? Prononcez ces noms. Qui sont ces gens?

1. Gabrielle Roy
2. Hubert de Givenchy
3. Charles de Gaulle
4. Guillaume le Conquérant
5. George Sand

Warm-up for A. Qui est-ce? Put these words on the board for students to pronounce: **collège, collègue, gigot, gecko, bougie, dégoûté.**

Suggestion for A. Qui est-ce? Tell students that Gabrielle Roy is a writer originally from Manitoba. Have students identify the others.

B. Ça s'écrit comment? Écoutez ce message. Faites une liste de tous les mots dans lesquels *(in which)* c est prononcé /s/. Après, ajoutez *(add)* la cédille où c'est nécessaire.

Script for B. Ça s'écrit comment? Chère Cécile, Comment ça va? L'examen de maths est bientôt, n'est-ce pas? David et moi, nous commençons à préparer l'examen après le cours de commerce demain. Est-ce que tu voudrais travailler avec nous? Annette

Chère Cécile,

Comment ca va? L'examen de maths est bientôt, n'est-ce pas? David et moi, nous commencons à préparer l'examen après le cours de commerce demain. Est-ce que tu voudrais travailler avec nous?

Annette

C. Préférences. Complétez ces questions avec le verbe **préférer** et interviewez votre partenaire.

1. Avec qui *(With whom)* est-ce que tu _____ sortir?
2. Quel jour est-ce qu'il/elle _____ sortir?
3. Est-ce que vous _____ dîner ensemble à la maison ou au restaurant?
4. Vous _____ aller voir un film au cinéma ou regarder un film à la télévision?
5. En général, est-ce que les étudiants _____ aller voir un film ou préparer les cours?

D. Et vous? Demandez à un(e) camarade de classe s'il/si elle fait ces choses avec ses amis.

Suggestion for D. Et vous? Have students write the questions and answers on the board to verify correct spelling.

Supplemental activity. Have students write a paragraph describing how they typically spend their weekend. Then ask pairs of students to exchange papers and comment on what they do and do not do in common.

Exemple   manger souvent ensemble
— **Tes amis et toi, est-ce que vous mangez souvent ensemble?**
— **Oui, nous mangeons souvent ensemble. /**
  Non, nous ne mangeons pas souvent ensemble.

1. voyager souvent ensemble
2. manger plus souvent ensemble dans un fast-food ou à la maison
3. nager souvent
4. manger souvent au restaurant universitaire
5. préférer aller au théâtre ou au cinéma
6. préférer voir des films français ou des films américains

NOTE Culturelle

En France, il est considéré impoli de poser des questions personnelles. Les Français tiennent beaucoup à *(value highly)* la discrétion.

TRANSPARENCY: 2-3

Warm-up activity. Briefly review days and times. Then ask the following questions: **1.** C'est quel jour, aujourd'hui? **2.** Et demain? **3.** Nous sommes en cours quels jours? **4.** Quelle heure est-il maintenant? **5.** Le cours de français est à quelle heure? **6.** À quelle heure ouvre la bibliothèque? **7.** À quelle heure ferme la bibliothèque? **8.** À quelle heure est-ce que vous dînez d'habitude? **9.** Quels jours de la semaine est-ce que vous aimez sortir avec des amis?

Suggestions. A. Briefly go over the meaning and pronunciation of the various question words (**quand, qui, que, où, pourquoi**). The formation of questions with question words is presented in the next section. **B.** Remind students of the use of the definite article with days of the week to indicate habitual actions. Point out similar structures with **le week-end, le matin, l'après-midi, le soir.** Point out the difference between **tous les jours** and **toute la journée. C.** Point out the new regular **-er** verbs **déjeuner** (contrast this with **dîner** and **manger**), **rentrer**, and **aimer mieux**. Also point out that **demander** means *to ask* and not *to demand*.

Suggestion for the conversation. Set the scene and play the conversation twice with books closed. Have students pick out all the activities Annette mentions. Afterward, have them listen to the conversation again while reading along in the text.

La journée

— Quand est-ce que vous êtes à l'université?
— Je suis à l'université... le lundi, le mardi...
                le matin, l'après-midi, le soir
                de dix heures à quatre heures
                tous les jours, **sauf** le week-end
                toute la journée

— Où est-ce que vous **déjeunez** les jours **que** vous êtes en cours?
— Je déjeune... chez moi / chez des amis
           au restaurant universitaire
           au café Trianon / dans un fast-food
           ???

— Qu'est-ce que vous aimez faire après les cours?
— J'aime... aller au parc
          rentrer à la maison
          manger
          dormir
          ???

— **Avec qui** est-ce que vous **aimez mieux** sortir?
— J'aime mieux sortir... avec mon ami(e)...
           avec mon meilleur ami (ma meilleure amie)
           avec **mon petit ami (ma petite amie)**
           avec **mon mari (ma femme)**
           avec ma famille

— **Pourquoi** est-ce que vous préférez sortir avec... ?
— Parce qu'il/elle est amusant(e), sexy, riche, beau (belle)...
    Parce qu'ils/elles sont sympas, intéressant(e)s, dynamiques...

— Quand est-ce que vous préférez sortir **ensemble?**
— Nous préférons sortir... le vendredi soir
                ???

Jean **demande** à Annette comment elle passe la journée.

JEAN: Quand est-ce que tu es en cours ce semestre?
ANNETTE: Je suis en cours tous les jours, sauf le week-end.
JEAN: Et comment est-ce que tu passes la journée typiquement?
ANNETTE: Euh... eh bien, le lundi, par exemple, je suis en cours de midi à trois heures. Le matin, je prépare mes cours à la bibliothèque.
JEAN: Et après les cours, qu'est-ce que tu fais?
ANNETTE: Après les cours, je rentre à la maison. Je travaille ou **je dors** un peu.
JEAN: Et le soir?
ANNETTE: Le soir, je reste à la maison et je prépare les cours ou je regarde la télé.

---

sauf *except* **toute la journée** *all day* **déjeuner** *to eat lunch* **que** *that* **rentrer** *to return, to go back (home)*
Avec qui *With whom* **aimer mieux** *to like better, to prefer* **mon petit ami (ma petite amie)** *my boyfriend (my girlfriend)* **mon mari (ma femme)** *my husband (my wife)* **Pourquoi** *Why* **ensemble** *together* **demander** *to ask* **je dors (dormir** *to sleep)*

A. Précisions.
Demain David déjeune avec des amis au café Le Trapèze. Quelle est la réponse logique pour chaque question?

1. Quand est-ce que nous déjeunons ensemble?
2. À quelle heure?
3. Qui déjeune avec nous?
4. Pourquoi est-ce que tu n'invites pas Thomas?
5. Où est-ce que nous déjeunons?
6. Qu'est-ce que tu voudrais faire après?

a. Au café Le Trapèze.
b. Gisèle et Bruno.
c. Demain.
d. Aller jouer au tennis.
e. Parce qu'il travaille demain.
f. À midi.

LE TRAPEZE

SALON DE THÉ • SNACK • BAR • GLACIER
17, Bd Delfino 06000 NICE
☎ 04 93 26 48 38

PIZZAS
(Sauf le samedi)   euros

MARGUERITE: 5,00
Tomate, fromage.

NAPOLITAINE: 5,20
Tomate, fromage, anchois, olives.

POIVRONS: 5,80
Tomate, fromage, champignons, poivrons.

REINE: 5,80
Tomate, fromage, olives, champignons, jambon.

CALZONE: 6,00
Tomate, champignons, œuf, crème fraîche.

Service continu de midi à 2h du matin

B. C'est vrai?
C'est vrai ou **ce n'est pas vrai** pour vous et votre cours de français?

1. Je suis à l'université tous les jours, sauf le dimanche.
2. Nous sommes en cours le matin, tous les jours sauf le week-end.
3. Le cours de français est de dix heures à onze heures.
4. Les autres étudiants et moi passons beaucoup de temps ensemble après les cours.
5. Nous préparons toujours les examens ensemble et nous déjeunons souvent ensemble.
6. Le samedi, je travaille toute la journée pour préparer le cours de français.
7. J'aime mieux aller en cours de français que de sortir avec des amis.

Maintenant, corrigez les phrases qui ne sont pas vraies.

C. Entretien.
Interviewez votre partenaire.

1. Quels jours est-ce que tu es à l'université? De quelle heure à quelle heure est-ce que tu es en cours? Est-ce que tu restes à l'université toute la journée? À quelle heure est-ce que tu rentres?
2. Quand est-ce que tu prépares les cours? Où est-ce que tu aimes mieux faire les devoirs: à la maison ou à la bibliothèque? Avec qui est-ce que tu préfères préparer les cours?
3. Où est-ce que tu aimes mieux déjeuner? À quelle heure? Est-ce que tu déjeunes souvent chez toi? Où est-ce que tu préfères manger le soir? Est-ce que tu dînes plus souvent chez toi ou au restaurant? Est-ce que tu manges souvent dans un fast-food? Qu'est-ce que tu préfères: les hamburgers, la pizza ou les tacos?
4. Qu'est-ce que tu aimes faire le week-end? Où est-ce que tu aimes mieux aller avec des amis: au cinéma ou en boîte? Avec qui est-ce que tu préfères sortir?

D. La journée.
Avec un(e) partenaire, changez la conversation entre Jean et Annette comme indiqué.

1. Annette asks Jean about his day. He works in the morning. In the afternoon, he swims and plays tennis with David. David plays better and he often wins.
2. The conversation is between you and a classmate. Change it to make it true for you. Both of you should ask the other how he/she spends the day.

✓ *Pour vérifier*

1. How do you form an information question?
2. Which word becomes **qu'** before a vowel, **qui** or **que**?
3. When are the three times you do not use **est-ce que**?

Asking for information: *Les mots interrogatifs*

You have learned to ask questions with **est-ce que.** To ask for information such as *what, where, when,* or *why,* just add the appropriate question word before **est-ce que,** as in the following examples.

Est-ce que vous étudiez les maths?	*Are you studying / Do you study . . . ?*
Qu'est-ce que vous étudiez?	*What . . . ?*
Pourquoi est-ce que vous étudiez le français?	*Why . . . ?*
Où est-ce que vous étudiez le français?	*Where . . . ?*
À quelle heure est-ce que vous êtes en cours?	*At what time . . . ?*
Quand est-ce que vous préparez les cours?	*When . . . ?*
Avec qui est-ce que vous préparez les cours?	*With whom . . . ?*
Comment est-ce que vous aimez passer la journée?	*How . . . ?*

Do not use **est-ce que** with **qui** when it is the subject of the verb, or with **où** or **comment** when they are followed by **être.**

Qui mange?   Où est Thomas?   Comment est l'université?

Use **Qui est-ce?** to ask *who* someone is. Use **Qu'est-ce que c'est?** to ask *what* something is.

— Qui est-ce?   — Qu'est-ce que c'est?
— C'est Jean.   — C'est un livre.

Prononciation: *Les lettres qu*

In French, **qu** is usually pronounced like an English *k* sound, as in the word **quiche.** It is generally only pronounced with the *kw* sound heard in the English word *quite* when it is followed by **oi,** as in **pourquoi.**

qui	que	quand	quelle heure	pourquoi

A. Invitations. Des amis parlent du week-end. Complétez leurs conversations avec des mots de la liste. Suivez l'exemple à la page prochaine.

	qui	que	où	COMMENT
quand		POURQUOI	à quelle heure

1. —Tu voudrais déjeuner avec nous?
   — **Quand?**
   —Vers midi.
   —____ est-ce que vous mangez?
   —Au café.

2. —Tu voudrais dîner avec moi?
   —____ est-ce que tu dînes?
   —À la maison.
   —____ est-ce que tu prépares?
   —Une pizza.

3. —Tu voudrais jouer au volley?
   —Avec ____ est-ce que tu joues?
   —Avec des amis.
   —____ est-ce que vous jouez?
   —Maintenant.

4. —Est-ce que tu voudrais sortir ce soir?
   —____ est-ce que tu voudrais faire?
   —Aller en boîte.
   —____?
   —Vers neuf heures.

B. On sort? Invitez un(e) camarade de classe à sortir. Il/Elle va poser au moins deux questions logiques. Utilisez les conversations dans *A. Invitations* comme modèle.

C. Un jeu. In teams, think of an appropriate question to elicit the answer in each box, using a question word *(who, what . . .)* based on the boldfaced word(s). Teams take turns selecting an item. A correct response earns the team the indicated points.

	A	B	C	D
5 points	Ça va **bien**, merci.	Je m'appelle **Annette.**	Il est **5 heures.**	Aujourd'hui, c'est **lundi.**
10 points	C'est **Yvette.**	C'est **un stade.**	David est **sympa.**	Je travaille **du lundi au jeudi.**
15 points	Yvette aime **la musique.**	David travaille **le week-end.**	David prépare les cours **avec Thomas.**	Nous aimons **aller au cinéma.**
20 points	**Annette et David** étudient les maths.	Les étudiants du cours de français sont **sympas.**	**Parce que le prof est intéressant.**	Annette parle **très bien** français.

Warm-up for C. Un jeu. Give students these statements on a transparency or on the board and ask what questions elicit them. First, remind them of the difference between *yes/no* and information questions and of when not to use **est-ce que**. EXEMPLE Après les cours, j'aime *aller au cinéma.* **Qu'est-ce que vous aimez faire après les cours? 1.** J'étudie *à (name of your university).* **2.** J'aime étudier ici *parce que les étudiants sont sympas.* **3.** Je suis en cours *tous les jours.* **4.** J'habite *à (name of your town).* **5.** J'habite *avec ma famille.* **6.** Ce soir, je voudrais *aller au cinéma.*

Note. Students are introduced to the basic concept of inversion at this point. They will have multiple opportunities for practice in later chapters and may not exhibit mastery at this stage.

Suggestion. You may wish to point out that inversions such as **Marie est-elle intelligente?** are not commonly used in conversation.

Asking questions: *Les questions par inversion*

You already know how to ask a question in French using **est-ce que... ?**, **non?**, or vocal inflection. You can also form questions using inversion; that is, by inverting the subject and verb. Notice that you place a hyphen between the verb and the subject when you invert.

> Parlez-vous français? = Est-ce que vous parlez français?

Here are a few things to remember when you use inversion.

- Inversion is the equivalent of **est-ce que.** Never use both inversion and **est-ce que** in the same question.

  > Voudrais-tu sortir? *OR* Est-ce que tu voudrais sortir?

- You do not normally use inversion with **je.** Use another question-forming device instead.

  > Est-ce que je travaille aujourd'hui?   Je travaille aujourd'hui, non?

- Invert the *conjugated* verb and the subject pronoun, but not a following infinitive.

  > Aimes-tu aller au cinéma?   Voudriez-vous aller danser?

- If the subject of the question is a *noun*, rather than a *pronoun*, state the noun first, then supply a matching pronoun for inversion.

  > Le prof est-il français?   Marie est-elle intelligente?
  > Les cours sont-ils difficiles?   Danielle et Antoinette étudient-elles ici?

- When the inverted subject is **il** or **elle** and *the verb ends in a vowel*, place a **-t-** between the verb and the pronoun. Do not add **-t-** if the verb ends in a consonant.

  > Parle-**t**-il anglais?   Travaille-**t**-elle ici?   Est-il d'ici?   Est-elle d'ici?

- The inverted forms of **il y a** and **c'est** are **y a-t-il** and **est-ce.**

  > Y a-t-il un café dans le quartier?   Est-ce un bon café?

- To ask information questions, place the question word before the inverted verb. Use **que (qu')** instead of **qu'est-ce que** when using inversion.

  > **Où** voudrais-tu aller?   **Que** voudrais-tu faire?   **Qu'**aimes-tu faire?

Suggestion. Dictate statements similar to the examples in the *Prononciation* section for students to write.

 # Prononciation: *L'inversion et la liaison*

When the subject is **il, elle, ils,** or **elles,** there is liaison between the verb and its pronoun in inversion.

> Yvette est‿elle américaine?
> David et Thomas parlent‿ils anglais?

Suggestion for A. Questions logiques. Tell students that this exercise reviews inversion questions they already know. Point out to students that they have been using inversion since the first day of class (**Comment allez-vous?**). Point out that the **est-ce** in **Qui est-ce?** is the inversion of **c'est.**

A. Questions logiques. Quelle est la question logique?

1. — _____?
   — Je m'appelle Georges Dubœuf. Et vous?
2. — _____?
   — Très bien, merci. Et vous?

3. — _____?
— Il est trois heures.

4. — _____?
— On dit «un stylo».

5. — _____?
— C'est Marie.

Suggestion for _B. Invitations_. Review the question words _who, what_ . . . before doing this exercise.

Follow-up for _B. Invitations_. Have students rephrase each question, using **est-ce que.**

B. Invitations.
Un ami invite David à jouer au tennis et David pose des questions à cet ami. Complétez ses questions par des mots interrogatifs logiques.

1. — ____ joues-tu?
— Avec Florence et Micheline.

2. — ____ aimes-tu jouer avec elles?
— Parce qu'elles ne gagnent pas souvent.

3. — ____ jouent-elles?
— Assez bien.

4. — ____ commencez-vous le match?
— À trois heures.

5. — ____ jouez-vous?
— Au parc.

6. — ____ voudrais-tu faire après?
— Je voudrais bien aller prendre un verre.

Mary Pierce, célèbre joueuse franco-américaine

C. Notre classe.
Utilisez l'inversion pour poser ces questions à un(e) camarade de classe.

Follow-up for _C. Notre classe._ Have students prepare two additional questions about the class, using inversion.

Exemple Est-ce que le prof de français est intéressant?
— **Le prof de français est-il intéressant?**
— **Oui, il est très intéressant.**

1. Les étudiants aiment le cours?
2. Pourquoi est-ce qu'ils aiment le cours?
3. Le cours est facile?
4. Est-ce que les examens sont faciles?
5. Quand est-ce que tu écoutes les CD?
6. Tu voudrais préparer le cours avec moi?

D. Entretien.
Changez ces phrases pour parler de vous. Après, posez une question logique à un(e) camarade de classe. Utilisez l'inversion.

Exemple Je travaille _le matin._ Et toi?...
Je travaille le soir. Et toi? Quand travailles-tu?

1. Je suis en cours _le lundi, le mercredi et le jeudi._ Et toi?...
2. Je préfère faire les devoirs _chez moi._ Et toi?...
3. Je prépare les cours _avec des amis._ Et toi?...
4. Je préfère étudier _le français._ Et toi?...
5. Je préfère étudier _le français parce que c'est facile._ Et toi?...

E. On sort?
Avec votre partenaire, préparez une conversation basée sur cette situation. Après, présentez la conversation à la classe.

Invite your partner to do something. He/She will ask at least three questions about the outing, using inversion as in _**B. Invitations.**_

NOTE Culturelle

Au café et au restaurant, l'expression service compris *(tip included)* **indique que le service est inclus** *(included)* **dans les prix.**

TRANSPARENCY: **2-4**

Suggestion for *Note culturelle*. Ask students if the tip is included in the prices on the **L'heure du thé** menu on p. 89. Ask them how they know.

Warm-up. Review the numbers from 0 to 30. Explain the use of the euro. (See pages 85 and 86.) Dictate these prices for students to write down in numerals. To correct their answers, have them call back in French what they have written while you write the numbers on the board. 30 €, 21 €, 2 €, 5 €, 11 €, 14 €, 28 €, 13 €, 19 €, 23 €, 4 €, 16 €, 17 €, 12 €, 15 €.

Suggestion. Explain that a French sandwich is traditionally served on half of a **baguette** with butter as the only condiment. Tell students that the name **un demi** comes from **un demi-litre**, because it used to refer to *a half-liter* of draft beer. It is now only a quarter of a liter. Explain that an **Orangina** is a carbonated orange drink. It is now available in the United States, bottled by the Coca-Cola Company.

Au café

Vous êtes au café. Qu'est-ce que vous allez prendre?

— Je voudrais...   — Pour moi...

un express

un café au lait

un thé au citron

une eau minérale

un jus de fruit ou un jus d'orange

un coca

un Orangina

un verre de vin rouge ou un verre de vin blanc

une bière

un demi

un sandwich au jambon

un sandwich au fromage

des frites

NOTE DE VOCABULAIRE

To say *I'm hungry / I'm not hungry,* say **J'ai faim / Je n'ai pas faim** *(I have hunger / I don't have hunger).* To say *I'm thirsty / I'm not thirsty,* say **J'ai soif / Je n'ai pas soif** *(I have thirst / I don't have thirst).* **J'ai** rhymes with **je vais.** You will learn more about these expressions in a later chapter.

 David et Annette **commandent une boisson** au café.

DAVID: **Je n'ai pas faim,** mais **j'ai soif.** Je voudrais un demi. Et toi?
ANNETTE: Moi, je vais prendre un chocolat **chaud.**
DAVID: Monsieur, s'il vous plaît.
LE GARÇON: Bonjour, monsieur, mademoiselle. Vous désirez?
DAVID: Pour moi, un demi. Et pour mademoiselle, un chocolat chaud.
LE GARÇON: Très bien.

―――――――

un demi *a draft beer*   **commander** *to order*   **une boisson** *a drink, a beverage*   **Je n'ai pas faim** *I am not hungry* **(j'ai faim** *I'm hungry)*   **j'ai soif** *I'm thirsty*   **chaud(e)** *hot*   **un garçon** *a waiter*

Après, David et Annette **paient.**

DAVID: Ça fait combien, monsieur?
LE GARÇON: Ça fait sept euros cinquante.
DAVID: **Voilà** dix euros.
LE GARÇON: Et **voici** votre **monnaie.** Merci **messieurs-dames.**

A. À votre santé. Quelle boisson est meilleure pour la santé *(health)?*

1. un café au lait / un jus d'orange
2. un Orangina / une eau minérale
3. un jus de fruit / un express
4. un thé / une bière
5. une eau minérale / un demi
6. un chocolat chaud / un jus d'orange

B. Préférences. Offrez les choses suivantes à un(e) camarade de classe.

Exemple   — **Tu voudrais une eau minérale ou un coca?**
            — **Je voudrais une eau minérale / un coca.**

1.

2.

3.

4.

5.

C. J'aime... Est-ce que vous aimez les choses indiquées dans l'exercice précédent? Utilisez **le, la, l'** ou **les** pour indiquer ce que vous aimez ou ce que vous n'aimez pas.

Exemple   **J'aime bien l'eau minérale. / Je n'aime pas du tout le coca.**

D. S'il vous plaît. Avec un(e) partenaire, changez la conversation entre David et Annette comme indiqué. Un(e) autre camarade de classe va jouer le rôle du garçon / de la serveuse *(waitress).*

1. Annette wants a cheese sandwich, fries, and an Orangina. David wants a glass of red wine. The bill comes to 15,30 € (15 euros 30).
2. The conversation is between you and a classmate. Change it to order what you would like.

---

ils paient (payer *to pay)*   **Voilà** *There is, There are*   **voici** *here is, here are*   **la monnaie** *change*   **messieurs-dames** (term used to address a group of males and females)

1. When do you use **et** with numbers? Do you use **et** with 81 and 91?

2. How do you say *one hundred*? Do you translate the word *one*?

Suggestions. A. Point out that: **1. Et** is used with numbers ending in 1, except with 81 and 91. **2. Quatre-vingts** ends in **s**, but the other numbers in the eighties do not. **3.** You never say **un cent**. **B.** Explain the euro system, how prices are abbreviated, the use of the comma in prices, and how prices are read. Have students call a bank or check the paper to find out the current value of the euro. Discuss the difficulties of changing monetary systems.

Supplemental activities. A. Have students count by ones, twos, fives, and tens. **B.** Tell students they are at an auction and whatever you bid, they must bid 5 € higher: 5 €, 25 €, 40 €, 55 €, 10 €, 30 €, 15 €, 65 €, 85 €, 45 €, 60 €, 20 €, 35 €, 50 €, 44 €. **C.** Say these pairs of numbers and have students repeat the larger one: 2/12, 30/20, 14/40, 50/60, 34/38, 16/6, 21/41, 69/67, 52/32, 11/59, 55/66, 19/49, 50/5, 60/16, 30/13, 44/43, 10/17. **D.** Have a lottery in class. Each student writes ten numbers on a sheet of paper. Randomly call out numbers. The winner is the person who has the most numbers called out. To verify, he/she should read his/her winning numbers back to the class. **E.** Ask students simple addition and subtraction problems (**Combien font 60 et 10?**).

Suggestions. You may wish to explain to students that the final **q** of **cinq** is traditionally considered silent before nouns beginning with consonants, but is often pronounced in conversational French. Also point out the pronunciation of **neuf** in **neuf heures**.

Suggestion for *A. Prononcez bien.* Allow students time to decide how each number should be pronounced.

Follow-up for *A. Prononcez bien.* Have students look over the **L'heure du thé** menu on page 89 for cognates and identify as many things as they can. To review numbers, call out the name of one of the items from the menu and have students give the price. EXEMPLE **Un café express, c'est combien? – C'est un euro quatre-vingts.**

Paying the bill:
Les chiffres de trente à cent et l'argent français

— Un café au lait, c'est combien?
— 3,50 € (trois euros cinquante).

30 trente	**40** quarante	**50** cinquante	**60** soixante
31 trente et un	**41** quarante et un	**51** cinquante et un	**61** soixante et un
32 trente-deux	**42** quarante-deux	**52** cinquante-deux	**62** soixante-deux
33 trente-trois...	**43** quarante-trois...	**53** cinquante-trois...	**63** soixante-trois...

70 soixante-dix	**80** quatre-vingts	**90** quatre-vingt-dix	**100** cent
71 soixante et onze	**81** quatre-vingt-un	**91** quatre-vingt-onze	
72 soixante-douze	**82** quatre-vingt-deux	**92** quatre-vingt-douze	
73 soixante-treize...	**83** quatre-vingt-trois...	**93** quatre-vingt-treize...	

The French monetary system has gone through a period of transition, as France changed from the franc to the euro, the official currency of the European Union.

> January 2000: The euro replaces the franc as the currency used in official banking and money exchanges, while the franc remains in use for most personal transactions.
> January 2001: The euro becomes the official currency for all transactions, but the franc continues to be accepted during a transition period.
> January 2002: The euro becomes the single official currency.

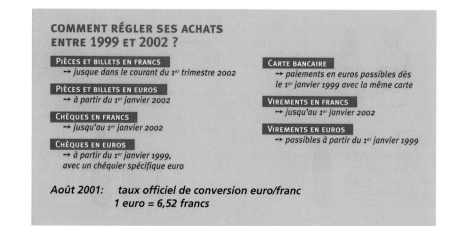

COMMENT RÉGLER SES ACHATS ENTRE 1999 ET 2002 ?

PIÈCES ET BILLETS EN FRANCS
→ *jusque dans le courant du 1er trimestre 2002*

PIÈCES ET BILLETS EN EUROS
→ *à partir du 1er janvier 2002*

CHÈQUES EN FRANCS
→ *jusqu'au 1er janvier 2002*

CHÈQUES EN EUROS
→ *à partir du 1er janvier 1999, avec un chéquier spécifique euro*

CARTE BANCAIRE
→ *paiements en euros possibles dès le 1er janvier 1999 avec la même carte*

VIREMENTS EN FRANCS
→ *jusqu'au 1er janvier 2002*

VIREMENTS EN EUROS
→ *possibles à partir du 1er janvier 1999*

Août 2001: taux officiel de conversion euro/franc
1 euro = 6,52 francs

 # Prononciation: *Les chiffres*

Some French numbers are pronounced differently, depending on what follows them.

deux	deux cafés	deux ᶻexpress	trois	trois cafés	trois ᶻexpress
six^s	six cafés	six ᶻexpress	dix^s	dix cafés	dix ᶻexpress
huit^t	huit cafés	huit ᵗexpress			

A. Prononcez bien. Commandez ces boissons.

Exemple	trois demis	**Trois demis, s'il vous plaît.**
	trois express	**Trois express, s'il vous plaît.**

deux demis	trois demis	six demis	huit demis	dix demis
deux express	trois express	six express	huit express	dix express

B. Numéros de téléphone. Lisez les numéros de téléphone comme dans l'exemple.

Exemple 02.43.29.12.32
C'est le zéro deux, quarante-trois, vingt-neuf, douze, trente-deux.

1. 04.42.72.95.59
2. 02.97.55.64.78
3. 05.49.27.91.62
4. 02.47.63.06.54
5. 01.94.13.30.83
6. 01.79.40.14.48

C. Transitions. Voici un article écrit par le gouvernement français pour aider les Français à faire la transition entre le franc et l'euro. Combien coûte chaque chose en francs et en euros?

Exemple une baguette **C'est 61 centimes d'euro ou 4 francs.**

Prix indicatifs*
pour vous familiariser avec l'euro

0,61 €	0,73 €	0,83 €	0,73 €	0,70 €	6,36 €	0,91 €
4 F	4,80 F	5,50 F	4,80 F	4,60 F	42 F	6 F
1.	2.	3.	4.	5.	6.

*Taux indicatif retenu : 1 euro = 6,60 francs. Sur la base de la valeur de l'Écu au 23 septembre 1998, le taux serait de 6,57947.
Le taux définitif sera fixé le 1ᵉʳ janvier 1999.

1. un journal
2. un express
3. un croissant
4. un litre de lait
5. un billet de cinéma
6. un litre d'essence

D. Ça fait combien? Écrivez les prix *(prices)* que vous entendez.

Exemple VOUS ENTENDEZ: C'est dix euros cinquante.
VOUS ÉCRIVEZ: **10,50 €**

E. Votre monnaie. Vous êtes au café et vous payez pour vos amis et vous. Suivez l'exemple.

Exemple 6,85 € (10 €)
— C'est combien, monsieur?
— Six euros quatre-vingt-cinq, mademoiselle.
— Voilà dix euros.
— Et voici votre monnaie.

1. 12,98 € (15 €)
2. 23,68 € (30 €)
3. 36,75 € (40 €)
4. 12,50 € (20 €)

F. Au café. Préparez une conversation basée sur cette situation. Après, présentez la conversation à la classe.

In groups of three, prepare a scene in which you meet a friend at a café. One classmate plays the waitperson and takes your orders. The two customers order, then decide what they would like to do after leaving the café. Finally, they call the waitperson back and pay the bill.

Warm-up for B. Numéros de téléphone. Divide students into teams. The first team thinks of a number between zero and one hundred. The other teams take turns asking questions to narrow the field until one guesses the right number. Teams take turns thinking of numbers. Tell students to use **entre** to say *between* and give them this example.
EXEMPLE — C'est entre 20 et 30?
— Non. — C'est entre 60 et 70? — Oui.
— C'est 65? — Oui, c'est ça.

Suggestion for B. Numéros de téléphone. Point out that French phone numbers are read in pairs.

Suggestion for C. Transitions. Model the pronunciation of each item by asking how much it is (**Une baguette, c'est combien?**).

Follow-up for C. Transitions. Give the current euro/dollar exchange rate and have students figure out how to convert prices. Then give them prices to convert from euros to dollars and from dollars to euros.

Script for D. Ça fait combien? EXEMPLE **C'est dix euros cinquante. 1.** C'est quarante euros cinquante. **2.** Ça fait cinquante-cinq euros. **3.** C'est trente-quatre euros. **4.** C'est cinq euros cinquante. **5.** Ça fait quatre-vingt-un euros soixante-quinze. **6.** C'est soixante-cinq euros quatre-vingt-dix. **7.** C'est quatre-vingt-deux euros soixante. **8.** Ça fait cent euros.

Reprise: *Talking about how you spend your time*

In *Chapitre 2,* you practiced saying what you like to do, asking about and telling how people spend their time, and ordering food and drink in a café. Now you have a chance to review what you learned.

Follow-up to *A. Passe-temps préférés.*
Have students make a list of five things they could invite a classmate to do. Then they take turns asking a classmate to do one of them. The classmate must respond by suggesting another activity. **EXEMPLE**
– Tu voudrais aller au cinéma ce soir?
– Non, je préfère aller danser.

A. Passe-temps préférés. Demandez à votre partenaire quelle activité il/elle préfère.

Exemple

— Est-ce que tu préfères inviter des amis à la maison ou parler au téléphone?
— Je préfère parler au téléphone. /
Je n'aime ni inviter des amis à la maison ni parler au téléphone.

1.

2.

3.

4.

5.

Warm-up for *B. Qu'est-ce qu'ils font?*
Put these sentences on the board or a transparency and have students complete them with the correct form of the verb **aimer** and the name of an activity. **EXEMPLE** Moi, j'… après les cours. **Moi, j'aime rentrer à la maison après les cours. 1.** Et toi, ____ (insert name of another student), est-ce que tu… après les cours? **2.** Le samedi matin, j'… **3.** Le week-end, j'… avec des amis. **4.** Mes amis… le samedi soir. **5.** Mon meilleur ami (Ma meilleure amie)… le week-end. **6.** Mes amis et moi… ensemble. **7.** Mes parents… le samedi. **8.** Et vous, ____ (insert professor's name), est-ce que vous… le samedi?

B. Qu'est-ce qu'ils font? Est-ce que ces personnes font les choses indiquées? Si oui *(If so),* est-ce qu'ils les font souvent, rarement, bien… ?

> TOUJOURS   souvent   **quelquefois**   rarement   NE… JAMAIS
> *beaucoup*   ASSEZ   (un) peu   **ne… pas du tout**
> *très bien*   ASSEZ BIEN   *comme ci comme ça*   ASSEZ MAL   très mal

Exemple   Mon meilleur ami (Ma meilleure amie) / jouer au tennis
Mon meilleur ami (Ma meilleure amie) joue assez bien au tennis. / Mon meilleur ami (Ma meilleure amie) ne joue jamais au tennis.

1. Moi, je / jouer au golf
2. Mon meilleur ami (Ma meilleure amie) / aimer le sport
3. Nous / jouer au volley
4. Je / manger à la maison
5. Ma famille et moi / dîner ensemble
6. Nous / manger ensemble
7. Mes amis / aimer voyager
8. Nous / voyager ensemble

C. Au café. Complétez les phrases.

1. Quand j'ai très soif, j'aime prendre…
2. Le matin, j'aime prendre…
3. Maintenant, je voudrais…
4. Avec un hamburger, j'aime prendre…
5. Quand je dîne au restaurant, j'aime prendre… comme *(as a)* boisson.

D. C'est combien? Demandez à votre partenaire les prix des choses indiquées.

Exemple un café express
— **Un café express, c'est combien?**
— **C'est un euro quatre-vingts.**

1. un lait chaud
2. un cappuccino
3. un café décaféiné
4. un double express
5. un vin chaud
6. un café au lait
7. un Irish Coffee
8. un chocolat
9. un croissant

L'heure du thé
Prix Service Compris [15%]

Café express	1,80	Thé à la menthe	3,00
Double express	3,50	Thé au fruit de la passion	3,00
Café au lait	3,00	Thé à la framboise	3,00
Infusion	3,00	Cappuccino	3,90
(Tilleul, verveine, menthe, tilleul-menthe,		Croissant	1,10
verveine-menthe, camomille)		Confiture pot	1,00
Lait chaud	2,80	Tartines beurrées	1,00
Café décaféiné	1,80	Viandox	1,80
Double express avec pot de lait	3,60	Viandox avec vin	2,10
Chocolat	3,00	Grog au rhum	3,50
Café ou chocolat viennois	3,50	Vin chaud	2,00
Thé (avec lait ou citron)	3,00	Irish Coffee	7,00

Note. Viandox is similar to bouillon.

E. Questions. Complétez la conversation comme indiqué. Utilisez **est-ce que** pour poser les questions.

— Je voudrais sortir ce soir.
— _____ ?
What would you like to do?
— Je voudrais aller voir le film *Star Time.*
— _____ ?
Why would you like to see Star Time?
— Parce qu'il y a beaucoup d'action. Et toi? _____ ?
Would you like to see Star Time *too?*

— Oui, beaucoup!
— _____ ? _____ ?
Are you free this evening?   *Would you like to go to the movies with me?*
— Bon, d'accord. _____ ?
What time does the movie start?
— Vers 9 heures. Je passe chez toi vers 8 heures?
— D'accord.

Maintenant, recommencez la conversation. Utilisez l'inversion pour poser les questions.

F. Invitations. Avec un(e) partenaire, préparez une conversation basée sur cette situation. Après, présentez la conversation à la classe.

Ask your partner what he/she likes to do on the weekend. Ask for some details such as when, where, with whom, and why. Make plans to do something together and decide on a place and time.

LECTURE: Aux Trois Obus

By using cognates and your ability to make intelligent guesses, you should be able to find several choices to order from this Parisian café menu. The following exercise will guide you.

Vous savez déjà... What you already know about cafés and restaurants will help you determine the following information.

1. Under **Buffet chaud,** what would **une omelette jambon** be? **une omelette fromage? une omelette nature?**

2. What you see at the bottom of the menu indicates that checks are accepted under one condition. What is usually the condition for accepting checks?

3. At the bottom of the menu, you see that the management claims it is not responsible for something. For what does management usually claim not to be responsible?

Note. The vocabulary in this section does not appear in the end-of-chapter vocabulary lists and is meant for recognition only. You may wish to let students know in advance whether you intend to test them on this vocabulary.

AUX TROIS OBUS
120, rue Michel-Ange
Paris

NOS SALADES

SALADE VERTE	2,60
SALADE NIÇOISE	7,00
(Tomate, œuf, thon, olives, salade, anchois, riz, poivron)	
SALADE 3 OBUS	7,00
(Salade, choux-fleur, foies de volaille, jambon, œuf dur)	
SALADE POULET	7,00
(Émincé de poulet, maïs, riz, tomates, poivron, salade)	

SALADE MIXTE	5,00
(Tomates, œuf dur, salade)	
SALADE CHEF	7,00
(Tomates, pommes à l'huile, jambon, gruyère, salade, œuf dur)	
SALADE DE CRUDITÉS	6,00
(Concombres, tomates, carottes, choux)	

BUFFET CHAUD

ŒUFS AU PLAT NATURE (3 œufs)	4,00
ŒUFS PLAT JAMBON (3 œufs)	4,50
OMELETTE NATURE	4,00
OMELETTE JAMBON	4,50
OMELETTE FROMAGE	4,50
OMELETTE MIXTE *(Jambon, fromage)*	6,50
OMELETTE PARMENTIER	4,50

CROQUE-MONSIEUR	4,00
CROQUE-MADAME	4,80
HOT-DOG	4,00
FRANCFORTS FRITES	5,00
ASSIETTE DE FRITES	2,60

MOULES MARINIERES	7,00 €
FRISEE AUX LARDONS	7,00 €
ROTI DE BOEUF PUREE	7,50 €
CASSOULET AU CONFIT	11,00 €
ST JACQUES PROVENCALE	14,00 €

NOS SANDWICHES

JAMBON DE PARIS	2,20
SAUCISSON SEC	2,20
SAUCISSON A L'AIL	2,20
RILLETTES	2,20
MIXTE *(Jambon, gruyère)*	3,50
SANDWICH CRUDITÉS	3,50

JAMBON DE PAYS	4,00
PÂTÉ	2,20
TERRINE DU CHEF	4,00
CLUB SANDWICH	6,00
(Pain de mie, poulet, jambon, tomates, œuf, laitue, mayonnaise)	
JAMBON A L'OS	4,00
GRUYÈRE, CAMEMBERT	2,20

Suppl. Pain mie 0,50   Campagne 0,80

FROMAGES

Camembert	2,60
Roquefort	3,00
Brie	3,00
Cantal	3,00
Chèvre	3,00

Gruyère	3,00
Assiette de fromages	5,00

PRIX SERVICE COMPRIS (15%)

Les chèques sont acceptés sur présentation d'une pièce d'identité.

La direction n'est pas responsable des objets oubliés dans l'établissement.

A. Mots apparentés. Lisez le menu. Utilisez les mots apparentés *(cognates)* pour identifier:

1. Two kinds of sandwiches.
2. Three or four items used in the salads.
3. Two or three items you could order from the **buffet chaud.**

Suggestion for *A. Mots apparentés.*
Identify the other food items on the menu for the students and have them say whether they like them.

Follow-up for *A. Mots apparentés.*
Have students practice prices with **euros**, using the menu items. Ask them about the price of various items (**Une omelette nature, c'est combien?**). Give them the current exchange rate and have them convert the prices to dollars.

B. Lisez bien. Lisez le menu et répondez à ces questions.

1. C'est combien pour une salade verte? pour une salade niçoise? pour une salade de crudités? pour une omelette jambon?
2. Le service est compris? Les chèques sont acceptés?

C. Bon appétit! Faites une liste de toutes les choses que vous pouvez *(can)* identifier sur ce menu. Après, commandez quelque chose.

Composition

A. Organisez-vous. You are going to prepare a scene in which two friends meet, talk, and order at a café. Before you begin, make sure you remember how to do these things in French.

- How do you greet a friend?
- How do you call the waitperson over and order a drink?
- How do you talk about what you do on the weekend?
- How do you ask what your companion likes to do and say what you like or do not like to do?
- How do you invite a friend to do something?
- How do you pay the bill?
- How do you say good-bye?

If you have access to SYSTÈME-D software, you will find the following phrases, vocabulary, grammar, and dictionary aids there.

Phrases: Greetings; Introducing; Attracting attention; Asking for information; Inviting; Leaving
Vocabulary: Drinks; Time expressions; Time of day; Leisure; Sports; Numbers; Money
Dictionary: The verb **préférer**

B. Rédaction. Using your answers from *A. Organisez-vous,* write a scene in which two college students meet at a café. They greet each other, order a drink, and start to chat about what they have in common. Remember to add details, such as when they like to do some things or why they do not like to do other things. They finally make plans to do something later, they get the bill, and they pay.

C. Scène: Au café. Compare the conversation you prepared in *B. Rédaction* with that of two classmates and prepare a scene together to act out for the class.

Suggestions for *C. Scène: Au café.*
Bring props for a café and videotape the scenes. Also ask follow-up questions: **Qu'est-ce qu'ils aiment faire? Qu'est-ce qu'ils voudraient faire aujourd'hui? À quelle heure?...**

COMPARAISONS *culturelles*

LE CAFÉ

et le

See the *Instructor's Resource Manual* for the video script and activities.

Note. The vocabulary in this section does not appear in the end-of-chapter vocabulary lists and is meant for recognition only. You may wish to let students know in advance whether you intend to test them on this vocabulary.

Suggestion. Tell students that **magot** means *a pile of money* or *a nest egg* as well as *Barbary ape*. In the main room of the café Les Deux Magots, there are two Chinese figurines of monkeys sitting on a chest.

Le café en France est presque une institution sociale. Il y a des cafés **partout.** Les gens aiment aller au café pour...

prendre un café

déjeuner

passer du temps avec des amis

passer une heure tranquille

Dans un café-tabac, **on peut aussi acheter** des cigarettes, des **timbres,** des cartes téléphoniques et des cartes postales.

Il y a une grande variété de cafés.

*Il y a des cafés élégants comme Les Deux Magots à Paris, fréquenté **autrefois** par des artistes et des écrivains tels que Cocteau et Hemingway.*

*Certains cafés servent une clientèle particulière: touristes, étudiants, travailleurs, **cadres.***

*Il y a aussi **le café du coin** ou du village.*

---

partout *everywhere*   **on peut aussi acheter** *one can also buy*   **un timbre** *a stamp*   **autrefois** *formerly*   **un cadre** *a business executive*   **un café du coin** *a neighborhood café*

Voilà **quelques renseignements utiles.**

Au bar, **les prix** *sont plus* **bas.**

Si vous préférez être à la terrasse, les prix sont souvent plus **élevés.** *Les chaises font face à la rue parce qu'un des plaisirs du café, c'est de regarder les* **passants.**

Bon appétit Bon Baguépi

Malgré la renommée *du café, il y a de moins en moins de cafés en France et de plus en plus de fast-foods comme McDonald's (Macdo) et Quick.*

À discuter.

1. Vous visitez la France. Préférez-vous déjeuner dans un fast-food ou dans un café? Pourquoi?
2. En France, il y a de plus en plus de fast-foods et de moins en moins de cafés. Pourquoi?
   a. Le service dans un fast-food est plus rapide.
   b. Les Français pensent que les hamburgers sont meilleurs que les sandwichs.
   c. Les choses américaines sont très à la mode *(in fashion)*.
3. En France, le service est presque toujours compris *(included)*. Aimez-vous cette idée? Pourquoi?
   a. Non, parce que c'est plus cher *(expensive)*.
   b. Oui, parce que c'est plus simple. (Je n'aime pas faire de calculs.)
   c. Non, ça influence la qualité du service.
4. Pourquoi est-ce que le café est plus populaire en France qu'ici? Qu'est-ce qu'on aime *(one likes)* faire au café? Est-ce que ces activités sont plus populaires en France qu'ici? Ici, où est-ce qu'on va *(one goes)* pour faire ces choses?

---

quelques renseignements utiles *some useful information*   **les prix** *prices*   **bas(se)** *low*   **élevé(e)** *high*   visit http://horizons.heinle.com
un(e) passant(e) *a passer-by*   **Malgré** *In spite of*   **la renommée** *the fame*

COMPÉTENCE 1

EXPRESSIONS VERBALES

J'aime...	I like . . .
Je préfère...	I prefer . . .
Je voudrais (bien)...	I would like . . .
aller en boîte / au café / au cinéma	to go to a club / to the café / to the movies
bricoler	to do handiwork
danser	to dance
dîner au restaurant	to have dinner in a restaurant
dormir	to sleep
écouter la radio / la chaîne stéréo / de la musique	to listen to the radio / the stereo / music
faire	to do, to make
faire du jogging	to jog, to go jogging
faire du sport	to play sports
faire quelque chose	to do something
inviter des amis à la maison	to invite friends to the house
jouer à des jeux vidéo	to play video games
jouer au base-ball / au basket / au football / au football américain / au golf / au hockey / au tennis / au volley	to play baseball / basketball / soccer / football / golf / hockey / tennis / volleyball
jouer du clavier / du piano / du saxophone / de la batterie / de la guitare / de la trompette	to play keyboard / piano / saxophone / drums / guitar / trumpet
lire	to read
parler au téléphone	to talk on the phone
prendre un verre	to have a drink
regarder une vidéo	to watch a video
regarder la télé(vision)	to watch TV
rester à la maison	to stay home
sortir avec des ami(e)s	to go out with friends
surfer le Net	to surf the Net
travailler sur l'ordinateur	to work on the computer
voir un film	to see a movie
On va... ?	Shall we go . . . ?
Qu'est-ce que vous aimez faire?	What do you like to do?
Qu'est-ce que vous voudriez faire?	What would you like to do?
Tu voudrais... ?	Would you like . . . ?

DIVERS

À ce soir!	See you tonight! / See you this evening!
après les cours	after class
D'accord!	Okay!
où	where
un passe-temps	a pastime
Pourquoi pas?	Why not?
quelque chose	something
Tu es libre ce soir?	Are you free this evening?
vers	about, around, toward

COMPÉTENCE 2

NOM MASCULIN

le cinéclub	the cinema club

NOMS FÉMININS

une activité	an activity
la fac	the university, the campus

EXPRESSIONS VERBALES

Qu'est-ce que vous faites?	What are you doing? / What do you do?
Qu'est-ce que tu fais?	What are you doing? / What do you do?
chanter	to sing
commencer	to begin, to start
faire de la musique	to play music
faire du shopping	to go shopping
gagner	to win
manger	to eat
nager	to swim
passer chez...	to go by . . . 's house
passer le temps / la matinée	to spend one's time / the morning
préférer	to prefer
préparer les cours	to prepare for class, to study
répéter	to repeat
rester au lit	to stay in bed
voyager	to travel
je vais	I am going, I go

ADVERBES

(très / assez) bien	(very / fairly) well
comme ci comme ça	so-so
d'habitude	usually
jusqu'à	until
(très / assez) mal	(very / fairly) badly
mieux (que)	better (than)
ne... jamais	never
presque	almost
quand	when
quelquefois	sometimes
rarement	rarely
souvent	often
toujours	always

DIVERS

chez...	to / at / in / by . . . 's house
classique	classic
leur(s)	their
préféré(e)	favorite
le samedi matin / après-midi / soir	(on) Saturday mornings / afternoons / evenings
vos	your
le week-end	the weekend, weekends, on the weekend

COMPÉTENCE 3

NOMS MASCULINS

l'après-midi	the afternoon
un fast-food	a fast-food restaurant
un jour	a day
mon mari	my husband
le matin	the morning
un parc	a park
mon petit ami	my boyfriend
le soir	the evening

NOMS FÉMININS

ma femme	my wife
ma petite amie	my girlfriend

EXPRESSIONS VERBALES

aimer mieux	to like better, to prefer
aller au parc	to go to the park
déjeuner	to have lunch, to eat lunch
demander	to ask (for)
je dors	I am sleeping, I sleep
manger dans un fast-food	to eat in a fast-food restaurant
rentrer	to return, to go back (home)

EXPRESSIONS ADVERBIALES

l'après-midi	in the afternoon, afternoons
ensemble	together
le matin	in the morning, mornings
le soir	in the evening, evenings
tous les jours	every day
toute la journée (de... à... heures)	all day (from . . . o'clock to . . . o'clock)
typiquement	typically

EXPRESSIONS INTERROGATIVES

à quelle heure	at what time
avec qui	with whom
comment	how
où	where
pourquoi (parce que)	why (because)
quand	when
que	what
qu'est-ce que	what
Qu'est-ce que c'est?	What is this / it?, What are they?
qui	who(m)
Qui est-ce?	Who is he / she / it / this?, Who are they?

DIVERS

par exemple	for example
que	that
riche	rich
sauf	except
sexy	sexy

COMPÉTENCE 4

NOMS MASCULINS

un café (au lait)	a coffee (with milk)
un centime	a centime, a cent
un chocolat (chaud)	a (hot) chocolate
un coca	a Coke, a cola
un demi	a draft beer
un euro	a euro
un express	an espresso
un franc	a franc
un garçon	a waiter
un jus de fruit / d'orange	a fruit / an orange juice
un Orangina	an Orangina
un sandwich au fromage / au jambon	a cheese / ham sandwich
un thé (au citron)	a tea (with lemon)
un verre de vin blanc / rouge	a glass of white / red wine

NOMS FÉMININS

une bière	a beer
une boisson	a drink, a beverage
une eau minérale	a mineral water
des frites	some fries
la monnaie	change

CHIFFRES

quarante, quarante et un...	forty, forty-one . . .
cinquante, cinquante et un...	fifty, fifty-one . . .
soixante, soixante et un...	sixty, sixty-one . . .
soixante-dix, soixante et onze...	seventy, seventy-one . . .
quatre-vingts, quatre-vingt-un...	eighty, eighty-one . . .
quatre-vingt-dix, quatre-vingt-onze...	ninety, ninety-one . . .
cent	one hundred

DIVERS

Ça fait combien?	How much is it?
Ça fait... euros.	That makes . . . euros.
C'est combien?	How much is it?
chaud(e)	hot
commander	to order (food and drink)
J'ai faim. / Je n'ai pas faim.	I'm hungry. / I'm not hungry.
J'ai soif. / Je n'ai pas soif.	I'm thirsty. / I'm not thirsty.
messieurs-dames	(term used to address a group of males and females)
payer	to pay
Pour moi... s'il vous plaît.	For me . . . please.
Qu'est-ce que vous allez prendre?	What are you going to have?
Je vais prendre...	I'm going to have . . .
voici	here is, here are
voilà	there is, there are
votre (vos)	your
Vous désirez?	What would you like?

Branchez-vous sur le français

Have you ever dreamed of studying abroad? Study abroad offers you experiences that will enrich your life forever, and knowing French opens doors to educational opportunities not only in France and several other European countries, but also in Canada and Africa.

L'université de Paris VIII, Saint-Denis

L'université Laval, Québec

There is a wealth of information about study abroad at the French Embassy website at www.info-france.org. You can also visit your school's international studies office or your local library and bookstores for books and useful addresses.

Living in another country for a year sounds exciting, but many students have questions about how to organize and finance a summer, semester, or year abroad. Do not let these questions keep your dreams from becoming reality. Study abroad is accessible to everyone, but you should start planning well in advance.

How much will it cost?

The cost of studying abroad varies, depending on the program, its location, and your length of stay. Many American universities organize study abroad programs in France, Quebec, and other francophone countries.

Federal financial aid and many state aid programs can be used for study abroad if your university agrees to transfer credit for your coursework. There are also many fellowships available for study abroad. Check with the financial aid officer or the international studies office at your campus for more information.

Will the credit count toward my degree?

Once you have chosen possible study abroad programs, check with your university to see if the courses will count toward your degree. If you enroll in a program sponsored by an American university, transfer credit is easier to determine, because that school will issue a transcript. If a foreign institution will be issuing the transcript, your registrar's office will need information such as the number of hours you will be in class and related labs and field work.

DOSSIER: **Eric Arcese**

Interviewer: *Où est-ce que vous étudiez et quelle est votre spécialisation?*

Eric: J'étudie à l'université du Massachusetts. Je fais des études de commerce.

Interviewer: *Où est-ce que vous avez étudié à l'étranger?*

Eric: J'ai étudié à l'étranger à Rouen, la capitale de la Haute-Normandie, où **j'ai eu l'occasion** d'étudier à la fac et à l'École Supérieure de Commerce. **J'ai fait la connaissance de** beaucoup d'étudiants français et internationaux aussi. J'ai visité beaucoup d'**endroits** magnifiques avec mes nouveaux amis: des abbayes, des cathédrales, des **musées**, des **plages...**

Interviewer: *Qu'est-ce que vous avez trouvé le plus intéressant dans cette expérience?*

Eric: La chose la plus intéressante de mon expérience à l'étranger, ce sont les voyages que j'ai faits. Le système de trains est très avancé en Europe. En **quelques** heures **on peut se trouver** dans un autre **pays** où **tout** est complètement différent: la langue, les gens et les **coutumes.**

Interviewer: *Quelles recommandations **pouvez-vous** faire à d'autres étudiants qui pensent étudier à l'étranger?*

Eric: La recommandation la plus importante pour les étudiants qui voudraient voyager à l'étranger, c'est de bien travailler et de bien apprendre pour profiter le plus possible de cette expérience.

---

vous avez étudié *did you study*   **à l'étranger** *abroad*   **j'ai eu l'occasion** *I had the opportunity*   **J'ai fait la connaissance de** *I met*   **un endroit** *a place*   **un musée** *a museum*   **une plage** *a beach*   **quelques** *a few*   **on peut se trouver** *one can find oneself*   **un pays** *a country*   **tout** *all, everything*   **une coutume** *a custom*   **pouvez-vous...?** *can you . . . ?*

Tadoussac

Charles F. Comfort (1900–1994)
1935
The National Gallery of Canada
Vincent Massey Bequest, 1968

The town of Tadoussac (from the Montagnais Indian word *Tatoushak*) is located at the confluence of the Saguenay and Saint Lawrence rivers, in the province of **Québec.** It was the first fur trading post in the province and has been a favorite vacation resort for many years.

Suggestions. *Chapitre 3* takes place in Quebec. Before beginning, have students locate Quebec on a map and discuss what they already know about it. Have them locate Montreal and Quebec City. Point out that in French the province is **le Québec** and the city, **Québec.**

En Amérique: Au Québec

LE QUÉBEC

SUPERFICIE: 1 450 680 kilomètres carrés

POPULATION: 7 139 000 (les Québécois)

CAPITALE: Québec

INDUSTRIES PRINCIPALES: agriculture, exploitation forestière, exploitation minière, hydroélectricité, technologie, tourisme

Un nouvel appartement

COMPÉTENCE

1 Talking about where you live

Le logement
Giving prices and other numerical information
Les chiffres au-dessus de 100 et les nombres ordinaux
Stratégies et lecture
Guessing meaning from context
    Un nouvel appartement

2 Talking about your possessions

Les effets personnels
Saying what you have
Le verbe **avoir**
Saying where something is
Quelques prépositions

3 Describing your room

Les meubles et les couleurs
Identifying your belongings
Les adjectifs possessifs **mon, ton** et **son**
Indicating to whom something belongs
Les adjectifs possessifs **notre, votre** et **leur**

4 Giving your address and phone number

Des renseignements
Telling which one
Les adjectifs **quel** et **ce**
Reprise
Saying where you live and what you have

Lecture et composition   **Les résidences de l'université Laval**

Comparaisons culturelles   **Le Québec et la Révolution tranquille**

En Amérique:
Le Canada et le Québec

En Amérique, **on** parle français!

En Amérique du Sud, la Guyane française est francophone.

Aux États-Unis, il y a des communautés francophones en Louisiane, **bien sûr**, et dans **plusieurs états** de la **Nouvelle-Angleterre**.

On parle français dans plusieurs îles caraïbes: la Martinique, la Guadeloupe, Saint-Martin et Haïti.

Tout le Canada est considéré officiellement bilingue (français / anglais) et plus de 83% de la population de la province de Québec parle français!

Sur le plan politique, le Canada est une confédération démocratique parlementaire composée de dix provinces et trois territoires.

Sur le plan social, c'est une mosaïque de populations de diverses origines ethniques et culturelles: **les Amérindiens**, les Britanniques, les Français et **bien d'autres**.

Le Québec est la province francophone la plus importante du Canada. **Grâce à** son histoire, à sa langue et à **ses coutumes**, le Québec est, à **bien des égards**, une société distincte à l'intérieur du Canada.

*Plus vaste que l'Alaska, le Québec est la plus grande des provinces canadiennes et **la deuxième** en population.*

---

on *one, people, they*   **bien sûr** *of course*   **plusieurs** *several*   **un état** *a state*   **la Nouvelle-Angleterre** *New England*   **Tout** *All*   **les Amérindiens** *Native Americans*   **bien d'autres** *many others*   **Grâce à** *Due to*   **ses coutumes** *its customs*   **à bien des égards** *in many regards*   **la deuxième** *the second*

*Le Québec est très riche et **produit** 25% du **revenu national brut** du Canada. Les forêts couvrent une grande partie du Québec et jouent un rôle important dans l'économie. L'exploitation forestière est une industrie importante.*

*La **ville** de Québec est la capitale de la province. Fondée en 1608, c'est la plus vieille ville du Canada et la seule ville fortifiée en Amérique du Nord.*

Montréal, grand centre culturel et commercial, est la plus grande ville du Québec et la deuxième ville francophone du monde, après Paris.

produit *produces*   **le revenu national brut (R.N.B.)** *the gross national product (GNP)*   **une ville** *a city*

Le logement

J'habite...

   dans un appartement
   dans une maison
   dans **une chambre** à la
     résidence universitaire

Il/Elle est...

   grand(e) / petit(e)
   moderne / vieux (vieille)
   joli(e) / laid(e)
   (trop) cher (chère)
   confortable

Il/Elle **se trouve...**

   sur le campus
   (tout) près de l'université
   (assez, très) **loin de** l'université

au centre-ville (dans un grand **immeuble)**   en ville   en banlieue *(f)*   à la campagne

Le loyer est de... **par mois.**

400$	650$	1200$
quatre cents dollars	six cent cinquante dollars	mille deux cents dollars

Je n'ai pas de loyer!

Chez moi, il y a six **pièces** *(f).*

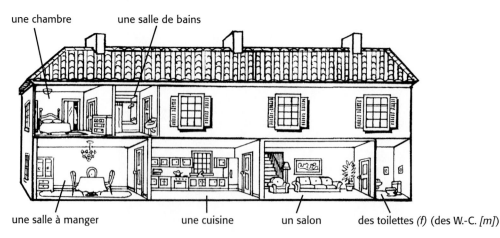

une chambre   une salle de bains

une salle à manger   une cuisine   un salon   des toilettes *(f)* (des W.-C. *[m]*)

---

le logement *lodging, housing*   **une chambre** *a bedroom*   **trop** *too*   **cher (chère)** *expensive*   **se trouver** *to be found, to be located*   **(tout) près (de)** *(very) near*   **loin (de)** *far (from)*   **un immeuble** *an apartment building*   **Le loyer** *The rent*   **par mois** *per month*   **Je n'ai pas** *I don't have*   **une pièce** *a room*

Robert, un jeune Américain, **va** étudier à l'université Laval, au Québec. Il parle au téléphone à son ami Thomas, avec qui il pense habiter.

l'appartement de Thomas

l'ascenseur *(m)*

une fenêtre

la porte

au troisième étage (3ᵉ)

au deuxième étage (2ᵉ)

au premier étage (1ᵉʳ) *on the second floor*

au rez-de-chaussée (R.d.C.) *on the first / ground floor*

au sous-sol / *in the basement*

l'escalier *(m)*

ROBERT: Où est-ce que tu habites?
THOMAS: J'habite dans un immeuble au centre-ville.
ROBERT: À quel étage?
THOMAS: Mon appartement est au deuxième étage.
ROBERT: Tu habites seul?
THOMAS: Non, j'habite avec Claude, **mon colocataire.**
ROBERT: L'université est loin de chez toi?
THOMAS: Non, pas très loin. Et il y a **un arrêt d'autobus** tout près. C'est très **commode.**
ROBERT: Et l'appartement est agréable?
THOMAS: J'aime beaucoup mon appartement. Il est assez grand et pas trop cher.

A. Et vous? Complétez les phrases avec les mots en italique qui vous décrivent le mieux.

1. J'habite dans *un appartement / une maison / une chambre.*
2. Il/Elle est *sur le campus / (tout) près de l'université / loin de l'université.*
3. Il/Elle se trouve *au centre-ville / en ville / en banlieue / à la campagne.*
4. Il/Elle est *joli(e) / grand(e) / moderne / confortable / ???.*
5. Il/Elle *est / n'est pas* trop cher (chère).
6. Le loyer est de *plus / moins* de cinq cents dollars par mois.
7. Chez moi, il y a *une / deux / trois / quatre / ???* chambre(s).
8. Je passe beaucoup de temps dans *la cuisine / le salon / ma chambre / ???.*
9. Ma chambre se trouve *au rez-de-chaussée / au premier étage / ???.*

B. Entretien. Interviewez votre partenaire.

1. Est-ce que tu habites dans une maison, dans un appartement ou dans une chambre à la résidence universitaire? Comment est la maison / la chambre / l'appartement? Est-ce qu'il est cher / elle est chère?
2. Tu habites près de l'université, loin de l'université ou sur le campus? Est-ce que c'est commode? Est-ce qu'il y a un arrêt d'autobus tout près?
3. Préfères-tu habiter au centre-ville, en ville, en banlieue ou à la campagne? Tu préfères habiter seul(e) ou avec un(e) camarade de chambre ou un(e) colocataire? Préfères-tu habiter au rez-de-chaussée ou au premier étage?
4. Quelles pièces y a-t-il chez toi? Dans quelle pièce aimes-tu passer beaucoup de temps? faire les devoirs? manger? regarder la télé?

C. Chez nous. Avec un(e) partenaire, changez la conversation entre Robert et Thomas comme indiqué.

1. Thomas lives in town on the ground floor. The university is very nearby.
2. The apartment is pretty and comfortable, but it is small and fairly expensive. The rent is $1,200 per month.
3. The conversation is between you and a classmate. Make it true for you.

NOTE *Culturelle*

Dans les hôtels et les autres immeubles au Québec et en France, faites attention! Le premier étage est l'étage au-dessus du *(above the)* rez-de-chaussée. C'est-à-dire que le rez-de-chaussée est *the first floor / ground floor* et le premier étage est *the second floor.*

Suggestion for the conversation. Go over the **Note culturelle** and point out the floors on the illustration of Thomas's building. Set the scene and have students listen, books closed, for three facts about Thomas's apartment as you play the conversation. Check their comprehension; then have them read along as you play the conversation again.

Follow-up. A. Using **deuxième** and **troisième,** have students guess other ordinal numbers. **B.** Make statements about the illustration and have students say whether they are true or false. EXEMPLE **Un monsieur travaille au sous-sol.**

Follow-up for *A. Et vous?* Complétez. 1. J'habite dans... 2. Il/Elle se trouve... 3. Il/Elle est... 4. Chez moi, il y a... pièces. Ce sont... 5. Chez moi, je passe beaucoup de temps dans... 6. Je prépare les cours dans... 7. Je regarde la télé dans... 8. Je mange dans...

---

va (aller *to go*) **mon (ma) colocataire** *my housemate, my co-renter* **un arrêt d'autobus** *a bus stop* **commode** *convenient*

1. Before which two of these numbers do you never put **un: cent, mille, million?**

2. How do you say 1,503? 12,612?

3. How do you say *first? fifth?* How do you say *on the* with a floor?

Suggestion. Review the numbers from 0 to 100 before presenting the larger numbers. Have students count by fives from 0 to 100.

Supplemental activities. A. Cut out pictures of televison sets, cars, microwaves, etc., from advertisements. Keep the price paper-clipped to the back. Have students, working in teams, guess the price, as in the television game show *The Price Is Right.* The team whose guess is closest to, without exceeding, the listed price wins the item. Finally, have students total the value of their winnings to find a grand prize winner. **B.** See who can guess the correct statistics. The answers are given in parentheses. **1.** la population de la France (60 000 000) **2.** la population de Paris (2 200 000) **3.** le nombre approximatif de francophones dans le monde (250 000 000 dont 77 000 000 ont le français comme langue maternelle). **C.** Quel étage est plus haut *(higher)?* **1.** le rez-de-chaussée ou le premier **2.** le deuxième ou le quatrième **3.** le neuvième ou le cinquième **4.** le dixième ou le vingtième **5.** le deuxième ou le douzième **D.** Questions orales. **1.** À quel étage est-ce que vous habitez? À quel étage est-ce que vous préférez habiter? **2.** Est-ce que nous sommes dans un grand immeuble? Nous sommes à quel étage maintenant? **3.** À quel étage se trouve le restaurant universitaire? le laboratoire de langues? la bibliothèque?

Giving prices and other numerical information:
Les chiffres au-dessus de 100 et les nombres ordinaux

To talk about rent and other numerical information in French, you need to know how to say numbers over 100.

100	cent	**1 000**	mille
101	cent un	**1 001**	mille un
102	cent deux	**1 352**	mille trois cent cinquante-deux
199	cent quatre-vingt-dix-neuf	**2 000**	deux mille
200	deux cents	**1 000 000**	un million
201	deux cent un	**1 234 692**	un million deux cent trente-quatre mille six cent quatre-vingt-douze
999	neuf cent quatre-vingt-dix-neuf		

Note the following about numbers:

- **Cent** means *one hundred* and **mille** means *one thousand*. Do not put **un** before them. On the other hand, you do say **un million.**
- **Cent** has an **s** in numbers like **deux cents** and **trois cents** only when no other number follows the word **cent.** For example, there is no **s** in **deux cent un.** Never add an **s** to **mille,** even in numbers like **deux mille** and **trois mille.**
- There is no hyphen between **cent, mille,** or **un million** and another number.
- In France and in Quebec, commas are used to denote decimals, and periods (or a space) are used after thousands, millions, etc. Read a decimal as **virgule (1,5 = un virgule cinq).**

USA	FRANCE / QUEBEC
1.5	1,5
1,000	1.000 *or* 1 000

Use **À quel étage?** to ask *On what floor?* To say *on the* with a floor, use **au.** When counting floors, use the ordinal numbers and remember that in a French-speaking country, you start with the ground floor **(le rez-de-chaussée).**

— **À quel étage habitez-vous?**   — *What floor do you live on?*
— **J'habite au troisième étage.**   — *I live on the fourth floor.*

In French, to convert cardinal numbers *(two, three, four . . .)* to ordinal numbers *(second, third, fourth . . .),* add the suffix **-ième.** Drop a final **-e** from cardinal numbers before adding **-ième.**

    deux → deuxième   **quatre → quatrième**   **mille → millième**

These numbers are irregular.

    premier / première   **cinquième**   **neuvième**

Follow-ups for *A. Le loyer.* A. Have students find the exchange rate for US / Canadian dollars. Discuss how to convert Canadian dollars to US dollars and have them convert the prices in *A. Le loyer,* which are in Canadian dollars, to US dollars. You might also have them convert them into euros. **B.** Dictate rent prices and have students write them. Use house purchase prices to practice larger numbers.

A. Le loyer. Quel est le loyer?

Exemple   900$ **Le loyer est de neuf cents dollars par mois.**

1. 860$	**4.** 1.100$	**7.** 1.540$	**10.** 2.435$
2. 1.325$	**5.** 675$	**8.** 750$	**11.** 3.295$
3. 410$	**6.** 885$	**9.** 660$	**12.** 1.345$

B. Et vous? Décrivez-vous en changeant les chiffres et les mots en italique.

1. La population de la ville où j'habite maintenant est de *150 000 / ???* habitants.
2. Il y a plus de *35 000 / ???* étudiants à notre *(our)* université.
3. Mon loyer est de *400$ / ???* par mois. *[Je n'ai pas de loyer.]*
4. Ma chambre est au *deuxième étage / ???*.
5. Je préfère habiter au *deuxième étage / ???*.
6. Maintenant, nous sommes au *troisième étage / ???*.

Suggestion for B. Et vous? Allow students time to prepare. When they have prepared, have them do the items in pairs.

C. Statistiques. Lisez ces statistiques sur l'université Laval, le Québec et le Canada. Devinez *(Guess)* quels chiffres correspondent à quelle description. Votre professeur dira *(will say)* **plus que ça** ou **moins que ça** jusqu'à ce que vous deviniez juste.

1. la population du Canada   **a.** 689 700
2. le nombre de francophones au Canada   **b.** 7 138 795
3. la population de la province de Québec   **c.** 31 278 097
4. la population de la ville de Québec   **d.** 218
5. la population de la ville de Montréal   **e.** 36 150
6. le nombre d'étudiants à l'université Laval   **f.** 3 480 300
7. le loyer par mois dans les résidences à   **g.** 8 920 500
    l'université Laval en dollars canadiens

Suggestion for C. Statistiques. Have students work in pairs to prepare their guesses. Then have them call out answers. Cue them with **plus que ça** or **moins que ça** until they get the right answer.

Quick-refererence answers for C. Statistiques. 1. c 2. g 3. b 4. a 5. f 6. e 7. d

D. Chez Thomas. Répondez selon l'illustration.

1. Il y a un ascenseur dans l'immeuble où habite Thomas?
2. Il y a un escalier?
3. À quel étage habite le monsieur qui travaille sur l'ordinateur?
4. À quel étage habitent Thomas et son colocataire?
5. À quel étage habite la jeune femme qui écoute de la musique?
6. Où habitent les enfants?

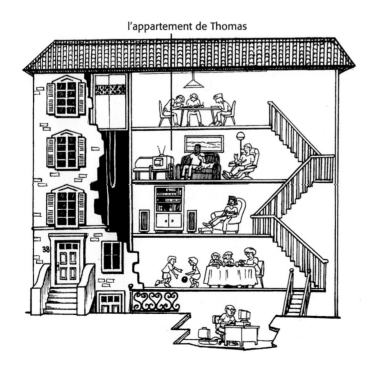

l'appartement de Thomas

Note. These readings may also be done at home. Pre-reading and post-reading activities should enable students to do this on their own.

Suggestion. Have students think of words that can have several meanings in English, such as *too* meaning *also* or *too much*.

Stratégies et lecture: *Guessing meaning from context*

You can often guess the meaning of unknown words from context. Read this passage in its entirety, then guess the meaning of the boldfaced words.

Arrivé à l'immeuble de Thomas, Robert **entre,** il **monte** l'escalier et il **sonne** à la porte de l'appartement de son ami. Une jeune femme **ouvre** la porte. Après un instant, elle commence à **refermer** la porte.

Some words may have different meanings in different contexts. For example, the word **bien** can mean *well* or it can also be used for emphasis, instead of **très** *(very)*. Read the following sentences and use the context to decide if **bien** means *well* or *very*.

Je comprends bien.
C'est bien compliqué.
Le prénom Claude est utilisé aussi bien pour une femme que pour un homme.

A. Selon le contexte. The boldfaced word in each of the following sentences can have a different meaning, depending on the context. Can you guess the different meanings?

Bravo! **Encore! Encore!**
Ça, c'est **encore** plus compliqué.
Je suis au premier étage, alors je monte **encore** un étage pour aller au deuxième?

Supplemental pre-reading activity. Have students scan the reading and make a list of the English cognates (about twenty). Then have them categorize these words in four groups: words that identify (someone, something, somewhere), words that indicate an action, words that describe, and miscellaneous.

B. Vous savez déjà... You already know the boldfaced word or words in sentence **a.** Guess the meaning of the boldfaced words in sentence **b,** using the context.

1. **a.** **Ouvrez** votre livre, **lisez** le paragraphe et **fermez** le livre.
   b. Robert **ouvre** la lettre de Thomas, **lit** les instructions et **referme** la lettre.
2. **a.** **Prenez** une feuille de papier.
   b. Elle **prend** la lettre.
3. **a.** **Donnez**-moi un café, s'il vous plaît.
   b. Thomas **donne** l'adresse de l'appartement à Robert.

Un nouvel appartement

Suggestion. Remind students not to worry about understanding every word, but to read for the gist.

Robert, un jeune Américain de Louisiane, arrive à l'immeuble où habitent Thomas et son colocataire Claude.

Robert ouvre la lettre de Thomas, consulte les instructions et vérifie l'adresse. Il lit: *«Mon appartement se trouve 38, rue Dauphine. C'est un grand immeuble avec une porte bleue. J'habite au deuxième étage.»* «Oui, c'est bien là», pense-t-il. Il descend de la voiture, entre dans l'immeuble et monte l'escalier.

Il sonne à la porte de l'appartement. Quelques instants après, une jolie jeune femme lui ouvre la porte.

—Euh... Bonjour, mademoiselle, je suis Robert. C'est bien ici que Claude et Thomas habitent?

—Claude, c'est moi. Mais...
Robert, très surpris, l'interrompt et s'exclame:
—Claude, c'est vous? Euh... Mais vous êtes une femme!
—Eh oui, monsieur, je suis bien une femme! répond la jeune femme.

—Euh... je veux dire que... C'est que, vous comprenez, en anglais, Claude, c'est un prénom masculin, dit Robert.
—En français, monsieur, le prénom Claude est utilisé aussi bien pour une femme que pour un homme, répond la jeune femme.
—Ah, je comprends! Excusez-moi, mademoiselle. Je suis confus. Alors, vous êtes Claude. Moi, je suis Robert, Robert Martin. Est-ce que Thomas est ici?
—Thomas? dit-elle d'un air surpris.
—Eh oui, Thomas, mon ami. Il habite ici avec vous, n'est-ce pas?
—Mais certainement pas, monsieur! dit-elle d'un ton énervé.
Quand elle commence à fermer la porte, Robert s'exclame:
—Un instant, s'il vous plaît, mademoiselle. Regardez! Voici l'adresse que mon ami m'a donnée.
Elle prend la lettre, lit les instructions et commence à comprendre la situation.
—Oui, monsieur, c'est bien ici le 38, rue Dauphine, mais vous êtes au premier étage et votre ami habite au deuxième étage.
—Au premier étage? Ah! Oui, je comprends maintenant. *First floor,* c'est le rez-de-chaussée et *second floor,* c'est le premier étage. Alors, je monte encore un étage pour trouver l'appartement de mon ami?
—Voilà, monsieur, c'est bien ça. Au revoir et bienvenue au Québec!
—Au revoir, mademoiselle, et merci.

Suggestion. Have students guess the meaning of **bienvenue** from context.

A. Vrai ou faux?

1. Robert arrive au 38, rue Dauphine, l'adresse de son ami Thomas.
2. Il monte directement au deuxième étage.
3. Il sonne et Claude, la jeune femme qui habite avec Thomas, ouvre la porte.
4. Claude est un prénom masculin et aussi un prénom féminin en français.
5. En France et au Québec, le *first floor,* c'est le rez-de-chaussée et le *second floor,* c'est le premier étage.

Follow-ups for *A. Vrai ou faux?* A. Have students pick out the lines from the story they think are being said in the illustrations. **B.** Have students think of English names used for both males and females: Chris, Jo(e), Alex . . .

B. Voilà pourquoi. Complétez le paragraphe pour expliquer la confusion de Robert.

Robert entre dans l'immeuble pour trouver l'appartement de _1_. Thomas habite au _2_ étage avec Claude, un ami. Robert monte au _3_ étage et sonne. Une jeune femme ouvre la porte. C'est Claude, mais elle n'habite pas avec Thomas. Robert ne comprend pas; il pense que la jeune femme habite avec _4_. Voilà le problème: Robert est au _5_ étage et Thomas et Claude habitent au _6_ étage. C'est un autre Claude, un jeune _7_, pas une jeune femme, qui habite avec Thomas.

Quick-reference answers for *B. Voilà pourquoi.* 1. Thomas (et Claude) **2.** deuxième **3.** premier **4.** Thomas **5.** premier **6.** deuxième **7.** homme

VOCABULAIRE SUPPLÉMENTAIRE
un réfrigérateur (un frigo)
une cuisinière *a stove*
un (four à) micro-ondes *a microwave (oven)*
un lave-vaisselle *a dishwasher*
une table basse *a coffee table*
une platine laser *a CD player*
un lecteur DVD *a DVD player*

Warm-up. Quelle est la réponse logique? **1.** J'habite dans une grande maison. J'habite dans un grand immeuble en ville ou j'habite en banlieue? **2.** J'habite au huitième étage. J'habite dans un immeuble ou dans une maison? **3.** J'habite dans une chambre à la résidence universitaire. J'habite avec un(e) camarade de chambre ou avec ma famille? **4.** Il y a un arrêt d'autobus tout près de mon appartement. J'habite en ville ou à la campagne? **5.** J'aime beaucoup mon appartement. Il est grand et confortable ou petit et laid? **6.** J'habite tout près d'ici. J'habite en ville ou dans une maison à la campagne?

Suggestion. Point out the difference between **une chaise** and **un fauteuil** and the difference in pronunciation between **un tableau** et **une table.** Tell students that one also says **un sofa** or **un divan** for *a couch.* In Quebec, one more commonly says **un divan.**

Les effets personnels

Qu'est-ce qu'il y a chez vous? **Avez-vous** beaucoup de **choses?**

Oui, **j'ai...**

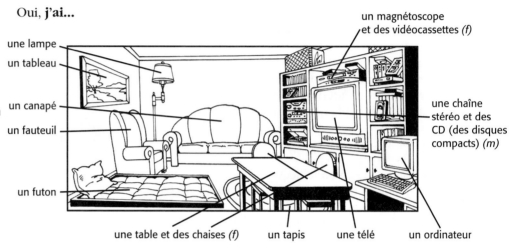

une lampe
un tableau
un canapé
un fauteuil
un futon
un magnétoscope et des vidéocassettes *(f)*
une chaîne stéréo et des CD (des disques compacts) *(m)*
une table et des chaises *(f)*   un tapis   une télé   un ordinateur

Avez-vous aussi... ?

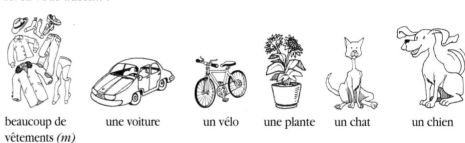

beaucoup de vêtements *(m)*   une voiture   un vélo   une plante   un chat   un chien

Chez Thomas **tout** est en ordre et bien **rangé.** Qu'est-ce qu'il y a... ?

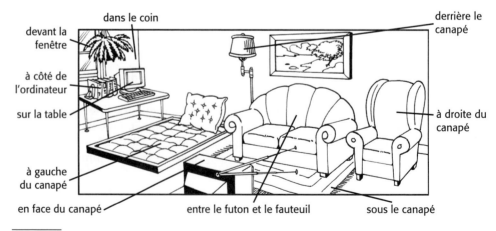

dans le coin
devant la fenêtre
à côté de l'ordinateur
sur la table
à gauche du canapé
en face du canapé
derrière le canapé
à droite du canapé
entre le futon et le fauteuil
sous le canapé

---

vous avez (avoir *to have)* **une chose** *a thing* **j'ai (avoir** *to have)* **tout** *everything, all* **rangé(e)** *arranged, put away, straightened up*

Avant d'arriver au Québec, Robert **cherche** un appartement. Il téléphone à Thomas.

THOMAS: Tu cherches un appartement ici à Québec? Écoute, tu sais, moi, je **partage** un appartement avec mon ami Claude. **Nous avons** trois chambres; tu voudrais habiter avec nous?

ROBERT: **Peut-être.** Comment est **ton** appartement?

THOMAS: Il est assez grand et confortable, mais pas trop cher. Tu aimes les animaux?

ROBERT: Oui, pourquoi? **Tu as** des animaux?

THOMAS: Non, mais **Claude a** un chien et un chat. Ils sont quelquefois **embêtants** et ils aiment dormir **partout.**

ROBERT: Pas de problème. J'aime bien les animaux. Vous **fumez?**

THOMAS: Non, je ne fume pas et Claude **non plus.**

ROBERT: Bon, moi non plus. Alors ça va.

A. Tu as... ? Demandez à votre partenaire s'il/si elle a ces choses.

Exemple
— **Tu as une voiture?**
— **Oui, j'ai une voiture. / Non, je n'ai pas de voiture.**

1.   **2.**   **3.**   **4.**

5.   **6.**   **7.**   **8.**

B. Qu'est-ce que c'est? Regardez l'illustration du salon de Thomas à la page précédente. Qu'est-ce que ces phrases décrivent?

Exemple   Ils sont sur la table.
   Les livres sont sur la table.

1. Elle est devant la fenêtre.
2. Elle est en face du canapé.
3. Elle est derrière le canapé.
4. Il est sur la table.
5. Ils sont à côté de l'ordinateur.
6. Elle est dans le coin.
7. Ils sont à gauche de l'ordinateur.
8. Il est à droite du futon.
9. Il est entre le fauteuil et le futon.
10. Il est sous le canapé.

C. Nouveaux camarades de chambre. Avec un(e) partenaire, changez la conversation entre Robert et Thomas comme indiqué.

1. Thomas lives with two housemates, Claude and Richard. There are four bedrooms. The apartment is big, pretty, and near the university.
2. The cat likes to eat on the table and the dog likes to sleep on the couch.
3. Your partner is looking for a place to live and you offer to let him/her share your place.

---

chercher to look for   **partager** to share   **Nous avons** (**avoir** to have)   **Peut-être** Maybe, Perhaps
ton, ta, tes your (familiar)   **Tu as** (**avoir** to have)   **Claude a** (**avoir** to have)   **embêtant(e)** annoying
partout everywhere   **fumer** to smoke   **non plus** neither

1. What does **avoir** mean? What are its forms? Why might one confuse the **tu** and **ils/elles** forms of **avoir** *(to have)* with those of **être** *(to be)*?
2. What does the indefinite article (**un, une, des**) change to after expressions of quantity such as **combien** or **beaucoup**? When else does this occur?
3. Which of these nouns would have a plural ending with **-x** instead of **-s**: un hôpital, un animal, un tableau, un bureau, une table, un canapé?

Supplemental activity. Prepare a set of flashcards, each with a picture of one of the possessions taught on page 108. First, distribute one (or more) of the cards to all students and have each hold up the card and say what he/she has (J'ai...). Then, divide the class into two teams. Have the teams face each other and tell students to hide their flashcards. Choose a number and have teams guess it to determine which team starts. The first person on the first team chooses any person on the other team and guesses what he/she has (– Tu as... ? – Oui, j'ai... / Non, je n'ai pas...). If the student guesses correctly, he/she gets the other student's card and the turn proceeds to the next student on the same team. The other team gets a turn as soon as someone on the first team misses. Students can only guess items that the opposite team members had originally; they cannot reclaim something the other team got from them. The team with the most cards at the end of a set time limit wins.

Script for A. Avoir ou être? EXEMPLE tu as 1. tu es 2. il est 3. il a 4. ils sont 5. ils ont.

Saying what you have: *Le verbe avoir*

To say what someone has, use the verb **avoir.** Its conjugation is irregular.

AVOIR *(to have)*	
j'**ai**	nous ᶻ**avons**
tu **as**	vous ᶻ**avez**
il/elle **a**	ils/elles ᶻ**ont**

Remember that **un, une,** and **des** change to **de (d')** in most negative sentences and after expressions of quantity, such as **beaucoup** and **assez.** This change also occurs after the word **combien** *(how much, how many).*

AFFIRMATIVE	NEGATIVE	AFTER AN EXPRESSION OF QUANTITY
J'ai **des** chats.	Je n'ai pas **de** chats.	Combien **de** chats as-tu?
J'ai **une** plante.	Je n'ai pas **de** plantes.	J'ai beaucoup **de** plantes.

Un, une, and **des** do not change after the verb **être** in negative sentences.

Ce sont **des** chats.   Ce ne sont pas **des** chats.

Although the plural of most nouns and adjectives is formed by adding **-s,** words ending in **eau, au,** or **eu** usually form their plural with **-x.** Words ending in **al** often change this ending to **-aux** in the plural.

SINGULAR	PLURAL
un tabl**eau**	des tabl**eaux**
un bur**eau**	des bur**eaux**
un anim**al**	des anim**aux**

 # Prononciation: *avoir et être*

Be careful to pronounce the forms of the verbs **avoir** and **être** distinctly. Open your mouth wide to pronounce the **a** in **tu as** and **il/elle a.** Contrast this with the vowel sound in **es** and **est.** Pronounce **ils sont** with an **s** sound, and the liaison in **ils ont** with a **z** sound.

être: Tu es professeur.   avoir: Tu as beaucoup de cours.
       Elle est professeur.   Elle a beaucoup de cours.
       Ils sont professeurs.   Ils ᶻont beaucoup de cours.

A. Avoir ou être? Entendez-vous le verbe **être,** comme dans la question **a,** ou le verbe **avoir,** comme dans la question **b?**

Exemple   **a.** Est-ce que **tu es** extraverti(e)?
                b. Est-ce que **tu as** beaucoup d'amis?
                VOUS ENTENDEZ: tu as
                VOUS RÉPONDEZ: **b**

1. a. Est-ce que **tu es** marié(e)?   **b.** Est-ce que **tu as** des animaux?
2. a. Ton appartement, **il est** comment?   **b.** **Il a** combien de chambres?
3. a. Ton immeuble, **il est** grand?   **b.** **Il a** combien d'étages?
4. a. Tes parents, **ils sont** d'ici?   **b.** **Ils ont** une grande maison?
5. a. Tes parents, **ils sont** intellectuels?   **b.** **Ils ont** beaucoup de livres?

Maintenant, posez ces questions à un(e) partenaire.

B. Qu'est-ce qu'ils ont? Complétez ces phrases selon le modèle.

Exemple   Moi, je (j')... (un chat, un chien).
              Moi, j'ai un chat. Je n'ai pas de chien.

1. Chez moi, je (j')... (une chaîne stéréo, des CD de musique française, un ordinateur, des plantes, un magnétoscope, beaucoup de vidéocassettes).
2. Mon meilleur ami (Ma meilleure amie)... (un chien, un chat, beaucoup de vêtements, une voiture, un vélo).
3. Dans le cours de français, nous... (beaucoup de devoirs, beaucoup d'examens, cours le lundi, cours le mardi, un examen aujourd'hui).
4. Généralement, les étudiants à l'université... (un vélo, une voiture, beaucoup de temps libre, 25 heures de cours par semaine)

Follow-up for *B. Qu'est-ce qu'ils ont?* **Questions orales.** Est-ce que nous avons beaucoup de devoirs? beaucoup d'examens? Combien d'examens est-ce que nous avons ce semestre? Combien de cours est-ce que vous avez? Est-ce que nous avons beaucoup de livres en français à la bibliothèque? Est-ce que nous avons des vidéocassettes françaises?

C. Chez Thomas et Claude. Robert et ses amis parlent de ce qu'ils ont dans l'appartement. Qu'est-ce que Robert dit?

Exemple   **Nous avons des vidéocassettes.**

Exemple Nous...   **1.** Thomas et Claude...   **2.** Claude...

3. Je (J')...   **4.** Thomas, est-ce que tu... ?   **5.** Claude et toi, est-ce que vous... ?

Maintenant, demandez à un(e) partenaire combien de ces choses il/elle a.

Exemple   **— Combien de vidéocassettes est-ce que tu as?**
              — J'ai beaucoup de vidéocassettes. /
                Je n'ai pas de vidéocassettes.

Follow-up for *C. Chez Thomas et Claude.* Questions orales. **1.** Est-ce que vous avez un magnétoscope? beaucoup de vidéocassettes? des vidéocassettes françaises ou canadiennes? **2.** Est-ce que vous avez une voiture? Est-ce que vous avez une voiture américaine? Elle est grande ou petite? belle ou laide? Est-ce que vous voudriez avoir une Volvo? une Mercedes? une Peugeot? **3.** Vous avez des animaux à la maison? Ils sont grands ou petits? Ils sont vieux ou jeunes? Vous préférez les chiens ou les chats? **4.** Vous avez une télé? Est-ce que vous regardez la télévision tous les jours? Quand regardez-vous la télé en général? **5.** Vous avez un vélo? Vous préférez avoir un vélo à l'université ou une voiture? **6.** Est-ce que vous avez un ordinateur? Est-ce que vous aimez travailler sur l'ordinateur?

D. Oui ou non? Vous cherchez un nouveau logement et vous parlez à d'autres étudiants qui voudraient partager leur *(their)* appartement / maison. Complétez leurs phrases avec la forme correcte du verbe **avoir**. Ensuite, dites si vous voudriez habiter avec ces personnes. Répondez **oui, non** ou **peut-être.**

1. J'_____ un très bel appartement et le loyer n'est pas trop cher.
2. Tu aimes les animaux? J'_____ trois colocataires et ils _____ neuf chats et trois petits chiens.
3. Nous _____ une grande maison près de l'université. Les chambres _____ beaucoup de fenêtres et une belle vue *(view).*
4. Mon colocataire _____ beaucoup d'amis qui fument dans l'appartement.
5. Tu _____ une voiture? Mon immeuble n'_____ pas de parking mais il est près de tout. Moi, j'_____ un vélo.
6. J'_____ un appartement. Il est au cinquième étage mais nous _____ deux nouveaux ascenseurs.
7. L'immeuble n'_____ pas assez d'eau chaude, mais le loyer est seulement *(only)* de deux cents dollars par mois et j'_____ un très joli appartement.

Saying where something is: *Quelques prépositions*

You can use the following prepositions to tell where something or someone is.

sur	*on*	**à côté (de)**	*next to, beside*
sous	*under*	**à droite (de)**	*to the right (of)*
entre	*between*	**à gauche (de)**	*to the left (of)*
dans	*in*	**en face (de)**	*across (from), facing*
devant	*in front of*	**près (de)**	*near*
derrière	*behind*	**loin (de)**	*far (from)*
		dans le coin (de)	*in the corner (of)*

When used by itself, the preposition **de** means *of, from,* or *about.* It is also used with some of the prepositions above. When **de** is followed by a definite article and a noun, it combines with the masculine singular **le** and the plural **les** to form the contractions **du** and **des.** It does not change when followed by **la** or **l'.**

CONTRACTIONS WITH DE			
de + le	→	du	J'habite près **du** centre-ville.
de + la	→	de la	La salle de classe est près **de la** bibliothèque.
de + l'	→	de l'	Mon appartement est près **de l'**université.
de + les	→	des	Il n'y a pas de parking près **des** résidences.

 Prononciation: *de, du, des*

Be careful to pronounce **de, du,** and **des** distinctly.

- As you know, the **e** in words like **de, le,** and **ne** is pronounced with the lips slightly puckered. The tongue is held firm in the lower part of the mouth.
- The **u** in **du,** as in **tu,** is pronounced with the tongue arched firmly near the roof of the mouth, as when pronouncing the French vowel **i** in **il,** but with the lips puckered.
- The vowel in **des** is a sharp sound like the **é** in **café,** pronounced with the corners of the lips spread.

Supplemental activity. Say sentences such as these and have students write only the form of the preposition **de** that they hear. **1.** L'université est loin de chez moi. **2.** L'arrêt d'autobus est en face de l'appartement. **3.** Le campus est près du centre-ville. **4.** La bibliothèque est en face des résidences. **5.** Le restaurant est près de la bibliothèque. **6.** Il y a un parking en face du restaurant. **7.** Il y a aussi un restaurant en face de chez moi. **8.** J'habite loin de l'université. **9.** Il y a un parking près des résidences. **10.** Il y a une librairie à côté de la bibliothèque.

A. Dans la salle de classe. Choisissez les mots en italique qui décrivent le mieux votre cours de français.

1. Le professeur *est / n'est pas* dans la salle de classe maintenant.
2. D'habitude, le professeur est *devant / derrière* les étudiants.
3. Le professeur *est / n'est pas* en face de moi maintenant.
4. Moi, je suis *près / loin* de la porte.
5. *Je suis / Je ne suis pas* entre le professeur et la porte.
6. *Je suis / Je ne suis pas* dans le coin de la salle de classe.
7. Le tableau est *devant les étudiants / derrière les étudiants / à côté des étudiants.*

B. C'est où?
Une amie de Thomas décrit le salon chez elle. Complétez ses phrases avec la forme convenable de la préposition **de (de, du, de la, de l', des)**. Ensuite *(Then)*, dites si les phrases sont vraies selon l'illustration.

1. Sur la table, les livres sont à gauche _____ ordinateur.
2. L'ordinateur est à côté _____ mes livres.
3. La télé est en face _____ fauteuil.
4. L'escalier est à gauche _____ table.
5. La télé est à côté _____ plantes.
6. La table est dans le coin _____ salon.
7. Le chien est dans le coin _____ salon.
8. La porte est en face _____ escalier.

C. Descriptions.
Faites des phrases pour décrire le salon dans **B. C'est où?**

Exemple les livres / la table
Les livres sont sur la table.

1. le chat / la table
2. la télé / le fauteuil
3. les plantes / la télé
4. le chien / le fauteuil et la télé
5. le chien / le fauteuil
6. la table / le salon
7. la lampe / le fauteuil
8. les livres / l'ordinateur
9. l'ordinateur / la table

D. À vendre.
Avec un(e) partenaire, préparez au moins dix phrases décrivant cette maison.

Exemple **Quand vous entrez *(enter)* dans la maison, les toilettes sont à gauche de la porte et le bureau est à droite. Derrière les toilettes il y a…**

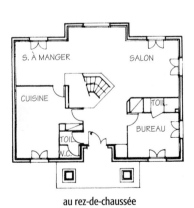

au rez-de-chaussée

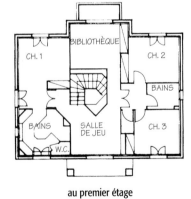

au premier étage

E. Qui est-ce?
Utilisez trois prépositions pour décrire un(e) camarade de classe. Lisez votre description et un(e) autre étudiant(e) va nommer *(is going to name)* la personne décrite.

Exemple — **Elle est près de la fenêtre. Elle est à droite de Paul et elle est derrière Catherine.**
— **C'est Julie?**
— **Oui.**

Follow-ups for C. Descriptions.
A. Follow-up questions. **Qu'est-ce qu'il y a... sur la table? sous la table? devant le fauteuil? derrière la télé? à droite de l'escalier? à gauche de l'escalier? à côté des livres? B.** Introduce the expression **par rapport à** and ask follow-up questions, such as these: **1.** Où est la lampe par rapport au fauteuil? **2.** Où sont l'ordinateur et les livres? **3.** Où est le chat? **4.** Où est la télé par rapport aux plantes? par rapport au fauteuil? **5.** Où est le chien? **C.** Have students make up sentences to describe the room in **B. C'est où?**

Supplemental activity. Using the transparency of the house on p. 102, ask the following questions. **1.** La cuisine est au rez-de-chaussée ou au premier étage? Les toilettes? La chambre? La salle de bains? Le salon? **2.** Quelle pièce est entre la salle à manger et le salon? **3.** Quelle pièce est à droite de la cuisine? à gauche? **4.** Qu'est-ce qu'il y a à droite du salon? **5.** Dans le salon, qu'est-ce qu'il y a près de la porte? derrière le canapé? devant l'escalier? Où est la lampe? **6.** Dans la salle à manger, qu'est-ce qu'il y a sous la table? Il y une plante sur la table? Il y a une chaise derrière la table? à gauche de la table? à droite de la table? devant la table? Il y a une porte entre la salle à manger et la cuisine? **7.** Il y a des vêtements dans la chambre? **8.** Qu'est-ce qu'il y a à côté de la chambre? La salle de bains est à droite ou à gauche de la chambre? **9.** Et chez vous, la cuisine est au rez-de-chaussée ou au premier étage? Quelle pièce est à droite de la cuisine? Quand vous entrez dans le salon, qu'est-ce qu'il y a en face de vous? à droite? à gauche? Quelle pièce est à côté du salon? Où est la salle à manger?

Suggestion for E. Qui est-ce? Verify that students remember one another's names before beginning.

COMPÉTENCE 3

TRANSPARENCIES: 3-3A, 3-3B

Describing your room

NOTE Culturelle

Thomas montre l'appartement à Robert parce que Robert va *(is going)* habiter avec lui *(him)*. Si *(If)* vous êtes invité(e) chez un Québécois ou un Français, ne vous attendez pas à *(don't expect to)* faire le tour de sa maison ou de son appartement. Aux USA, on montre sa maison à ses invités pour qu'ils se sentent chez eux *(so they feel at home)*. En général, dans les cultures francophones, on reste dans le salon et la salle à manger.

Suggestions. A. Point out the use of **mon, ma, mes** to say *my*, **ton, ta, tes** to say *your*, and **son, sa, ses** to say *his, her, its*. Elicit from students why there are three forms for each. The possessive adjectives are explained in the next section. B. Point out the difference between **partout** and **par terre** and that **laisser** means *to leave* in the sense of leaving something somewhere, but not in the sense of leaving a place. C. Tell students that the formal version of **ça te plaît** is **ça vous plaît**.

Note. See the **Suggestion** on the next page for presenting colors.

NOTE DE GRAMMAIRE

Like other adjectives, the words for colors must agree in gender and number with the objects they describe. **Orange** and **marron** are exceptions. They are invariable and never change form. Also notice that colors follow the noun they describe: **des chaises bleues.**

VOCABULAIRE SUPPLÉMENTAIRE

bleu clair *light blue*
bleu foncé *dark blue*
bleu vif *bright blue*
écossais(e) *plaid*
à fleurs *floral*
imprimé(e) *print*
rayé(e) *striped*
uni(e) *solid-colored*

Les meubles et les couleurs

Thomas **montre** les chambres à Robert.

Voilà ta chambre. Tu as...

une affiche
un placard
une commode
un tapis
des rideaux
un bureau
un lit
une étagère

C'est une chambre agréable. **Les murs** sont jaunes et le tapis et les rideaux sont bleus.
La couverture est bleue, rouge et verte.
J'espère que ça te plaît!

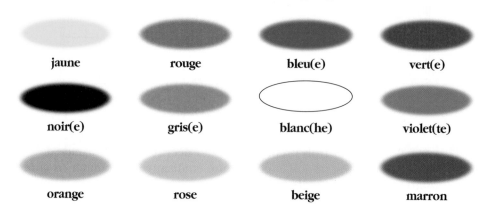

Voilà **ma** chambre.
Ma chambre est toujours **propre** et en ordre.
Tout est **à sa place.**
Mes murs sont blancs et mon tapis est jaune.

Voilà la chambre de Claude.
Sa chambre est souvent un peu **sale** et en désordre. Il **laisse** tout **par terre.**
Sa couverture est noire, marron et grise.

Et vous? Comment est votre chambre? De quelle couleur *(f)* est votre tapis? De quelle couleur sont vos murs?

Voici des adjectifs pour indiquer la couleur de quelque chose.

jaune	rouge	bleu(e)	vert(e)
noir(e)	gris(e)	blanc(he)	violet(te)
orange	rose	beige	marron

Les meubles *Furniture, Furnishings* **montrer** *to show* **un mur** *a wall* **une couverture** *a blanket, a cover* **espérer** *to hope* **ça te plaît** *you like it* **mon, ma, mes** *my* **propre** *clean* **à sa place** *in its place* **son, sa, ses** *his, her, its* **sale** *dirty* **laisser** *to leave* **par terre** *on the floor, on the ground*

Suggestion. You may wish to point out that colors do not show adjectival agreement with the noun if they are modified, as in **bleu clair.**

Suggestion for the conversation. Play the conversation and have students listen with books closed for three things about Robert's new room.

Suggestion for presenting the colors. Introduce the colors using sheets of construction paper or other masculine items of various colors. Do the following activities:
1. Point to items around the room and ask questions, giving students a choice between the correct color of the item and one other color (**Le livre est bleu et vert ou rouge et jaune?**). 2. Explain the expression **Montrez-moi...** and have students point to things of various colors (**Montrez-moi quelque chose de bleu / rouge / noir...**). 3. Ask students **Quelle couleur associez-vous aux choses suivantes: une feuille de papier? le café? un citron? une carotte? un dollar? un taxi? le jambon? les arbres? une banane? un verre de vin? un stylo? le stylo du professeur? une plante? une plante morte** (dead)? **les chaises de la salle de classe? le tableau de la salle de classe? les murs de la salle de classe? le livre de français? le cahier? notre** (our) **université? l'université de...**? (You can also use the colors of local sports teams.)

Thomas montre les chambres à Robert.

THOMAS: Voici la chambre de Claude à côté de la cuisine. Sa chambre est toujours en désordre. Il laisse ses vêtements partout.

ROBERT: C'est ta chambre en face de la chambre de Claude?

THOMAS: Oui, **comme tu vois,** je préfère avoir tout bien rangé et **chaque** chose à sa place.

ROBERT: Et ça, c'est ma chambre **au bout du couloir?**

THOMAS: Oui, **viens voir...** Tu as un lit, une commode et une grande fenêtre avec **une** belle **vue.** J'espère que ça te plaît.

ROBERT: Oui, ça me plaît beaucoup!

THOMAS: Les murs sont jaunes. Tu préfères une autre couleur?

ROBERT: Non, **justement,** ma couleur préférée, c'est le jaune.

THOMAS: Moi, je préfère le vert.

A. Chez vous? Indiquez ce qui est vrai chez vous.

(PRESQUE) TOUJOURS		souvent	quelquefois
	rarement	NE... JAMAIS	

Exemple   Ma chambre est en ordre.
**Ma chambre est presque toujours en ordre. /
Ma chambre n'est jamais en ordre.**

1. Ma chambre est propre.
2. Ma chambre est en désordre.
3. Mes livres sont sur l'étagère.
4. Ma chambre est sale.
5. Mes vêtements sont par terre.
6. Mes livres sont sur le lit.
7. Je laisse mes vêtements partout.
8. Mes livres sont sur le bureau.
9. Mes vêtements sont dans le placard ou dans la commode.

Warm-up for *A. Chez vous?* Robert range sa chambre. Où est-ce qu'il met (put) ces choses? 1. Il met ses vêtements dans... ou dans... 2. Il met sa couverture sur... 3. Il met ses livres sur... 4. Il met son ordinateur sur...

Follow-up for *A. Chez vous?* Répondez selon l'illustration de la chambre de Claude à la page précédente. 1. Qu'est-ce qu'il y a dans la chambre? 2. Est-ce qu'il y a une étagère? des livres? des plantes? 3. Qu'est-ce qu'il y a sur le lit? sous le lit? par terre? sur l'étagère? sur le bureau? 4. Où est le chien? le chat? le vélo? Où sont les vêtements? les livres? 5. De quelle couleur est la couverture? le vélo? De quelle couleur sont les rideaux?

Warm-ups for *B. Les couleurs.* A. Est-ce que vous préférez... ? 1. les voitures bleues, blanches, noires ou rouges 2. les vêtements noirs, blancs, violets ou verts 3. les murs beiges, blancs, gris ou roses 4. les meubles blancs, noirs ou bleus 5. les rideaux blancs, beiges ou jaunes 6. le vin rouge ou blanc 7. les stylos noirs ou bleus 8. les chiens noirs ou blancs B. Quelle couleur donnent... ? 1. le noir et le blanc (le gris) 2. le jaune et le bleu (le vert) 3. le jaune et le rouge (l'orange) 4. le rouge et le blanc (le rose) 5. le rouge et le bleu (le violet) C. Put these sentences on the board or on a transparency and have students complete them with the name of a color. Remind them to use the correct form of the adjective. 1. Dans la salle de classe, les chaises sont... et les murs sont... 2. Le tableau est... 3. Le livre de français est... 4. Aujourd'hui, les vêtements du professeur sont... 5. Mes vêtements sont... 6. Ma maison / Mon immeuble / Ma résidence est... 7. Les murs de ma chambre sont...

B. Les couleurs. Complétez les phrases suivantes avec le nom d'une couleur.

1. Je préfère les vêtements...
2. J'ai beaucoup de vêtements...
3. Je préfère avoir des murs...
4. Les murs de ma chambre sont...
5. Je préfère les voitures...
6. Ma voiture est...
7. Je préfère les meubles...
8. Chez moi, le canapé est...
9. Ma couleur préférée, c'est le...

C. Dans la chambre. Avec un(e) partenaire, changez la conversation entre Robert et Thomas comme indiqué.

1. Claude's room is next to the living room. Thomas's room is at the end of the hall and Robert's room is across from the bathroom.
2. Thomas points out to Robert that he has a bed, a desk, a chair, and a bookshelf in his room. The walls are yellow and Robert prefers green.
3. The conversation is between you and a classmate who is your new housemate. Create a logical conversation for you. You may wish to create an imaginary apartment or house.

comme tu vois *as you see*   **chaque** *each*   **au bout de** *at the end of*   **le couloir** *the hallway, the corridor*   **viens voir** *come see*   **une vue** *a view*   **justement** *as a matter of fact, precisely, exactly*

1. How do you say *my*? How do you say *your* (familiar)? What are the forms of each word?

2. When do you use **mon, ton,** and **son,** instead of **ma, ta,** and **sa** before a feminine noun?

3. Does French have different words for *his, her,* and *its*? How do you say *his house* and *her house* in French? How do you say *his dog* and *her dog*?

4. How do you say *John's friend* and *Mary's car* in French?

5. With which two forms of the definite article does **de** combine to form the contractions **du** and **des**?

Supplemental activities. **A.** Point out that the [e] sound indicates plurality. **Singulier ou pluriel?** un ami, des livres, mon université, mes camarades de classe, ses CD, son appartement, la cuisine, les chambres. **B.** Have students refer to the illustrations of the rooms of Thomas and Claude on page 114 and say whose room these sentences describe. 1. Sa chambre est en désordre. 2. Sa chambre est bien rangée. 3. Ses vêtements sont partout. 4. Ses vêtements sont rangés dans son placard. 5. Ses livres sont partout. 6. Son vélo est près de la porte. 7. Il y a des plantes sur son étagère. **C.** Put up a transparency of Robert's room from page 114. Point to various items and tell students to identify them as Robert would. **Robert identifie ces choses.** EXEMPLE **C'est mon lit.**

Identifying your belongings:
Les adjectifs possessifs **mon, ton** *et* **son**

In French, the possessive adjectives **mon/ma/mes** *(my)*, **ton/ta/tes** *(your [familiar])*, and **son/sa/ses** *(his, her, its)* agree in gender and number with the noun they precede. Note, however, that the masculine form is used before feminine nouns that begin with a vowel sound.

	MASCULINE SINGULAR	FEMININE SINGULAR	FEMININE SINGULAR	PLURAL
		(plus consonant sound)	*(plus vowel sound)*	
my	**mon** livre	**ma** cassette	**mon** amie	**mes** vêtements
your	**ton** livre	**ta** cassette	**ton** amie	**tes** vêtements
his/her/its	**son** livre	**sa** cassette	**son** amie	**ses** vêtements

— C'est **ton** livre?
— Oui, c'est **mon** livre et ce sont **mes** cassettes aussi.

— C'est le livre de Thomas?
— Oui, c'est **son** livre et ce sont **ses** cassettes aussi.

The use of the forms **son/sa/ses** *(his, her, its)* depends on the gender and number of the object possessed, not the person who owns it. **Son/sa/ses** can all mean *his, her,* or *its.*

C'est **son** fauteuil.

C'est **son** fauteuil aussi.

Et c'est **son** fauteuil aussi.

In English, possession and relationship can be indicated by *'s.* In French, you need to use a phrase with the word **de.**

Voilà la chambre de Thomas.   *There is Thomas's room.*
C'est le chien de Claude.   *That's Claude's dog.*

Remember that when **de** is followed by a definite article and a noun, it combines with the masculine singular **le** and the plural **les** to form the contractions **du** and **des.** It does not change when followed by **la** or **l'.**

le livre **du** professeur   les livres **des** professeurs

A. **Compliments.** Faites un compliment à un ami avec l'adjectif le plus logique.

Exemple   sœur (méchante, sympa)
          Ta sœur est sympa.

1. amis (intéressants, ennuyeux)
2. chien (bête, très intelligent)
3. vêtements (beaux, laids)
4. chaîne stéréo (vieille, excellente)
5. voiture (laide, belle)
6. appartement (grand, petit)
7. chambre (agréable, désagréable)
8. chat (sympa, embêtant)

Maintenant, décrivez vos amis et vos affaires.

Exemple   **Ma sœur est jolie et très intelligente. / Je n'ai pas de sœur.**

B. De quelle couleur? Complétez ces questions avec **ton, ta** ou **tes.** Après, posez les questions à votre partenaire.

1. De quelle couleur est _____ voiture?
2. De quelle couleur est _____ vélo?
3. De quelle couleur sont les murs de _____ chambre?
4. De quelle couleur est _____ tapis?
5. De quelle couleur sont _____ rideaux?
6. De quelle couleur est _____ couverture?
7. De quelle couleur est _____ canapé?
8. De quelle couleur est _____ fauteuil préféré?
9. De quelle couleur sont _____ vêtements aujourd'hui?
10. Quelle est _____ couleur préférée?

C. C'est à moi! Deux colocataires ne veulent plus *(no longer want)* habiter ensemble. Un locataire change d'appartement et il voudrait tout prendre avec lui *(him)* mais l'autre locataire n'est pas d'accord. Jouez les rôles avec un(e) partenaire.

Exemple la plante   —**Bon, je prends** *(I'm taking)* **ma plante.**
                          —**Ah non, ce n'est pas ta plante. C'est ma plante!**

1. le bureau   4. la table   7. les vidéocassettes
2. le canapé   5. la commode   8. les CD
3. l'ordinateur   6. l'étagère   9. les affiches

D. Chez Marieline. Voilà la chambre de Marieline, l'amie de Claude. Indiquez où se trouvent ses affaires *(things)*. Utilisez **son, sa** ou **ses.**

Exemple le bureau
Son bureau est à côté de la télé.

1. l'ordinateur   5. le magnétoscope
2. la chaise   6. les livres
3. la porte   7. les vidéocassettes
4. la télé   8. le chien

Maintenant, dites où ces choses se trouvent chez vous.

Exemple le bureau
**Mon bureau est dans ma chambre à droite de la porte. /
Je n'ai pas de bureau.**

E. La chambre de Marieline. Regardez l'illustration de la chambre de Marieline pendant une minute. Ensuite, fermez votre livre. Travaillez avec un(e) partenaire pour décrire la chambre. Le groupe avec la description la plus complète gagne.

Warm-up for C. C'est à moi! Put these three models on the board: **1.** – C'est ton livre? – Non, ce n'est pas mon livre. / Oui, c'est mon livre. **2.** – C'est ta cassette? – Non, ce n'est pas ma cassette. / Oui, c'est ma cassette. **3.** – Ce sont tes stylos? – Non, ce ne sont pas mes stylos. / Oui, ce sont mes stylos. Have students sit in rows and have the first person in each row take out a book, a cassette, and some pens. They start with the book and turn to the person behind them to ask – **C'est ton livre?** The student asked responds – **Non, ce n'est pas mon livre,** and then turns to ask the same question of the next student in the row. This continues until the last person in the row brings the book up to the first person in the row who answers – **Oui, c'est mon livre.** While this is going on, the first person in the row has started the same activity with the cassette and then follows it up with the pens.

Follow-ups for E. La chambre de Marieline. A. Ask students about one another, and have them answer using **son, sa,** or **ses. 1.** De quelle couleur est le cahier de... ? **2.** De quelle couleur sont les vêtements de... ? **3.** Où est le... de... ? **4.** Qu'est-ce qu'il y a sous la chaise de... ? à côté de la chaise de... ? **5.** Le livre de... est sur son cahier ou sous son cahier? **B.** Quelles personnes célèbres est-ce que ces phrases décrivent? **1.** J'aime bien sa musique. **2.** Je n'aime pas sa musique. **3.** J'aime ses films. **4.** Ses films sont bêtes. **5.** Ses vêtements sont toujours très élégants. **6.** Ses vêtements sont souvent laids. **7.** Je voudrais voir sa maison. **8.** Je voudrais être son colocataire.

Supplemental activity. Gather books, pens, notebooks, and other objects from students and place them in a pile in front of the class. Then give one of the objects to a student and have him/her try to remember to whom it belongs. If the wrong student is asked if the object belongs to him/her, that student should say to whom he/she thinks it belongs, and the student with the object should then go to that student. Continue until the correct owner is found. (– **C'est ton stylo, Éric?** – Non, ce n'est pas mon stylo. C'est le stylo de Chris. – **C'est ton stylo, Chris?** – Oui, c'est mon stylo.)

Indicating to whom something belongs:
Les adjectifs possessifs notre, votre et leur

You learned to use **mon/ma/mes**, **ton/ta/tes**, and **son/sa/ses** to indicate possession. The possessive adjectives for *our*, *your* (formal or plural), and *their* have only two forms, singular (**notre**, **votre**, and **leur**) and plural (**nos**, **vos**, and **leurs**).

	MASCULINE SINGULAR	FEMININE SINGULAR	FEMININE SINGULAR	PLURAL
		(plus consonant sound)	*(plus vowel sound)*	
my	**mon** lit	**ma** chambre	**mon** amie	**mes** livres
your (fam.)	**ton** lit	**ta** chambre	**ton** amie	**tes** livres
his/her/its	**son** lit	**sa** chambre	**son** amie	**ses** livres
our	**notre** lit	**notre** chambre	**notre** amie	**nos** livres
your (form./pl.)	**votre** lit	**votre** chambre	**votre** amie	**vos** livres
their	**leur** lit	**leur** chambre	**leur** amie	**leurs** livres

Prononciation:
La voyelle o de notre/votre et de nos/vos

Compare the **o** sounds in **notre/votre** and **nos/vos**. The lips are puckered to make both of these sounds and the tongue is held firm, but the **o** in **nos/vos** is pronounced with the back of the tongue arched higher in the mouth than for the **o** in **notre** and **votre**. The letter **o** is pronounced with the sound of **nos** when it is the last sound in a syllable, when it is followed by an **s**, or when it is written **ô**. Otherwise, it is pronounced with the more open sound of **notre**.

notre chien / nos chiens   votre chat / vos chats

A. Le prof.
Complétez ces questions avec **votre** ou **vos**. Après, posez les questions à votre professeur.

1. Aimez-vous _____ cours ce semestre / trimestre?
2. Est-ce que _____ étudiants sont sympas?
3. Est-ce que _____ bureau est près de la salle de classe?
4. Est-ce que _____ affaires *(things)* sont toujours en ordre?
5. Qu'est-ce qu'il y a sur _____ étagère?
6. Comment est la vue de _____ bureau?

B. Et les couleurs?
Devinez les couleurs de ces choses chez votre professeur. Utilisez **votre** ou **vos**.

Exemple   murs
Vos murs sont blancs?

> MURS   maison   **tapis**   rideaux   FAUTEUIL
> *canapé*   VÊTEMENTS PRÉFÉRÉS   voiture   **vélo**

C. Chez nous.
Deux amis voudraient persuader un troisième ami de partager leur appartement. Comment répondent-ils à ses questions? Utilisez **notre** ou **nos** dans les réponses.

1. Votre appartement est très cher?
2. Vos chiens sont méchants?
3. Votre cuisine est grande?
4. Vos parents passent beaucoup de temps à l'appartement?
5. Votre appartement a beaucoup de fenêtres?
6. Comment est la vue de votre appartement?

D. Deux universités.
Est-ce qu'il y a une autre université dans votre région? Comparez votre université avec l'autre, comme dans l'exemple.

Exemple   quartier (beau)
**Notre quartier est plus beau. / Leur quartier est plus beau. /
Notre quartier est aussi beau que leur quartier.**

1. classes (grandes)   3. université (grande)   5. cours (difficiles)
2. campus (beau)   4. étudiants (sympas)   6. professeurs (intelligents)

L'université McGill

L'université Laval

*L'université McGill et l'université Laval sont deux universités québécoises.
L'université McGill est la plus vieille université anglophone du Canada et
l'université Laval est la plus vieille université francophone.*

E. Préférences.
Aimez-vous ces choses? Utilisez **leur/leurs** ou **son/sa/ses** dans vos réponses.

Exemples   les films avec Laurel et Hardy
J'aime bien leurs films.

les films d'Alfred Hitchcock
Je n'aime pas beaucoup ses films.

1. les films de Steven Spielberg
2. les vieux films avec les Three Stooges
3. la musique des Beatles
4. la musique de Céline Dion
5. les CD de *NSYNC
6. les CD d'Enrique Iglesias

COMPÉTENCE 4

Giving your address and phone number

TRANSPARENCY: 3-4

NOTE Culturelle

Il y a deux systèmes d'éducation au Québec, tous les deux enseignés *(taught)* en français. L'un est en grande partie "protestant-anglais" et l'autre "catholique-français". Après les études secondaires, tout étudiant cherchant à entrer à l'université doit forcément faire deux ans d'études dans un *community college* avant.

NOTE DE VOCABULAIRE

In an e-mail address, say **arobase** for @ and **point** for *dot*.

TRANSPARENCY: 3-4

Warm-ups. A. Voilà les adresses de quelques sites touristiques à Québec. **Écrivez les chiffres.** (Teacher note: The sites located at these addresses are indicated in parentheses for your information.) **1.** 1, avenue Wolfe-Montcalm (musée du Québec) **2.** 16, rue Buade (basilique Notre-Dame-de-Québec) **3.** 14, rue Dauphine (chapelle des Jésuites) **4.** 31, rue des Jardins (cathédrale de la Sainte-Trinité) **5.** 25, rue St-Louis (maison Kent). **B.** Have students guess the percentage of French households that fit these descriptions. Tell them **plus que ça** or **moins que ça** until they narrow it down to the correct number. **Les Français qui... 1.** habitent dans une maison (57%) **2.** habitent dans un appartement (43%) **3.** ont le téléphone (94%) **4.** ont un réfrigérateur (99%) **5.** ont la télé (96%).

Suggestion. Point out that **américaine** is feminine with the word **nationalité**, even when describing a male's nationality. You may wish to tell students that all nouns ending in **-té** are feminine.

Suggestion. Point out the use and value of Canadian dollars. Have students listen to the conversation with books closed for three questions Robert's friend asks.

Des renseignements

Pour **s'inscrire** à l'université, Robert **doit** donner les **renseignements suivants.**

Quel est votre nom?	Martin.
Quel est votre prénom?	Robert.
Quelle est votre adresse?	C'est le 215 Ursline St.
Quelle est votre adresse e-mail?	RobMart@airmail.net
Quel est votre numéro de téléphone?	C'est le (337) 988-1284.
Dans quel pays habitez-vous?	Les États-Unis.
Quel état? (Quelle province?)	La Louisiane.
Quelle ville?	Lafayette.
Quelle est votre nationalité?	Américaine.

Robert parle de son appartement et son ami Alain lui **pose des questions.**

ALAIN: Quelle est ton adresse?
ROBERT: C'est le 38, rue Dauphine.
ALAIN: Et c'est quel appartement?
ROBERT: C'est l'appartement numéro 231.
ALAIN: Et le code postal?
ROBERT: G1K 7X2.
ALAIN: Quel est ton numéro de téléphone?
ROBERT: C'est le 692-2691.
ALAIN: Et comment est le quartier?
ROBERT: Il est agréable et près de tout.
ALAIN: L'appartement n'est pas trop cher? C'est combien, le loyer?
ROBERT: Je partage mon appartement avec deux amis, Thomas et Claude. C'est 825 dollars par mois, partagés entre nous trois. Alors pour moi, ça fait 275 dollars.

---

s'inscrire *to register*   **il doit (devoir** *must, to have to)*   **les renseignements** *(m) information*   **suivant(e)** *following*   **poser une question** *to ask a question*

A. Et Thomas? Quels renseignements est-ce que Thomas donne?

Exemple   Bertrand
C'est son nom.

1. Thomas
2. Québec
3. le Québec
4. le Canada
5. le 38, rue Dauphine
6. G1K 7X2
7. le 692-2691
8. Thomas1@homemail.com
9. 825$ par mois

B. Et vous? Répondez aux questions suivantes.

1. Quel est votre nom? Quel est votre prénom?
2. Quelle est votre adresse?
3. Vous habitez dans quelle ville?
4. Quel est votre numéro de téléphone?
5. Quelle est votre adresse e-mail?
6. Quelle est votre nationalité?

C. Un abonnement. Vous vendez des abonnements *(are selling subscriptions)* pour la revue *Brune*. Demandez les renseignements nécessaires pour compléter le formulaire d'abonnement pour un(e) camarade de classe.

Exemple
— **Quel est ton nom?**
— **Mon nom? C'est Sodji.**
— **Quel est ton prénom?...**

BULLETIN D'ABONNEMENT

Je désire m'abonner pour un an (4 numéros) à BRUNE.

TARIFS (par avion, sauf France)

7 000 F CFA . . . Afrique Zone CFA	20 € . . France	
10 000 F CFA . . Afrique Hors Zone CFA	30 € . . CEE	
40 $. . . . . USA-Canada	25 € . . Dom-Tom	

Règlement exclusivement par mandat international libellé en euros. France et Dom-Tom: paiement par chèque ou mandat-lettre à l'ordre de BRUNE.

Découper et retourner ce formulaire d'abonnement accompagné de votre règlement à:

BRUNE - SERVICE ABONNEMENTS
10, rue Charles-Divry - 75014 PARIS - FRANCE

NOM...

PRÉNOM ....

ADRESSE ....

....

CODE POSTAL ....

VILLE ....

PAYS ....

D. Renseignements. Avec un(e) partenaire, changez la conversation entre Robert et son ami comme indiqué.

1. The address is 929, rue Dauphine, apartment 245. The neighborhood is pleasant, but a little far from downtown.
2. Robert lives with Thomas only and the rent is $1,000 dollars per month.
3. The conversation is between you and a classmate. Change it to make it true for you. You may wish to create an imaginary apartment or house.

Telling which one: *Les adjectifs quel et ce*

Use **quel** to say *which* before a noun. Also use it to say *what* when:

- *what* is followed by *is* or *are*
- *what* is followed directly by a noun

Quelle est votre adresse?
Quelles sont tes villes préférées?
Dans *quel appartement* **habitez-vous?**

Quel agrees with the gender and number of the noun it modifies.

	MASCULINE	FEMININE
SINGULAR	quel	quelle
PLURAL	quels	quelles

Quel est votre numéro de téléphone?
Quelle est votre adresse?

Quels sont vos quartiers préférés?
Quelles sont vos villes préférées?

Remember to use **qu'est-ce que** or **que** to say *what* when it is the object of the verb. They are followed by a subject and verb.

Qu'est-ce que Robert aime faire?

Que voudrais-tu faire ce soir?

To point out which item or person you are talking about, use the adjective **ce** (**cet**)/**cette**/**ces** to say both *this/these* and *that/those.* Use **ces** with all plural nouns. The masculine **ce** becomes **cet** before masculine singular nouns beginning with a vowel sound.

	SINGULAR	PLURAL
MASCULINE (plus consonant sound)	ce canapé	ces canapés
MASCULINE (plus vowel sound)	cet appartement	ces appartements
FEMININE	cette maison	ces maisons

If you need to distinguish *this* from *that,* you can add the suffixes **-ci** and **-là** to the noun.

Est-ce que tu préfères **cet** appartement-**ci** ou **cet** appartement-**là**?
*Do you prefer **this** apartment or **that** apartment?*

Prononciation: *La voyelle e de ce/cet/cette/ces*

You already know that a final **e** is usually not pronounced in French, except in short words like **je.** As you notice in **ce/cet/cette/ces,** unaccented **e** has three different pronunciations, depending on what follows it.

In short words like **ce** and **que,** or when **e** is followed by a single consonant within a word, pronounce it as in:

je ne le regarde vendredi

When, as in **ces,** **e** is followed by an unpronounced consonant at the end of a word, pronounce it as in:

les mes parlez manger premier

In words like **cette** and **cet,** where **e** is followed by two consonants within a word, or a single pronounced consonant at the end of a word, pronounce it as in:

quel cher belle elle cherche

A. Renseignements.
Formez des questions pour obtenir ces renseignements d'un(e) camarade de classe.

Exemple   son numéro   — **Quel est ton numéro de téléphone?**
de téléphone   — **C'est le quatre cent quarante-quatre, vingt-deux, soixante-quinze.**

Follow-up for A. Renseignements. Have students make up a class phone list by going around the class and asking several classmates for their first and last names, phone numbers, and e-mail addresses. Remind students to spell out their e-mail addresses in French. Tell students they do not have to give out this information if they don't wish to.

> son nom   **SON PRÉNOM**   **son adresse**   SON CODE POSTAL   **???**
> *son numéro de téléphone*   LE NUMÉRO DE SON APPARTEMENT

B. Entretien.
Complétez les questions suivantes avec la forme convenable de quel ou avec qu'est-ce que. Ensuite, posez les questions à votre partenaire.

1. _____ il y a dans ta chambre?
2. Dans _____ pièce est-ce que tu passes le plus de temps?
3. _____ tu voudrais acheter pour ton salon ou pour ta chambre?
4. Dans _____ rue est-ce que tu habites?
5. Ta chambre est à _____ étage?
6. De _____ couleur sont les murs de ta chambre?
7. _____ tu voudrais changer chez toi?

C. Comparaisons.
Utilisez ce, cet, cette ou ces pour faire des comparaisons.

Exemple   cours   **Ce cours-ci est difficile, mais ce cours-là est facile.**

Exemple cours   **1.** jeune homme   **2.** jeune femme   **3.** étudiant

4. chiens   **5.** maison   **6.** appartement   **7.** vêtements

D. Préférences.
Demandez à votre partenaire quelles sont ses préférences. Après, donnez votre réaction à sa réponse en utilisant ce, cet, cette ou ces. (If you aren't familiar with what he/she names, say Je ne connais pas…)

Exemple   restaurant   — **Quel restaurant est-ce que tu aimes beaucoup?**
    — **J'aime beaucoup Pizza Nizza.**
    — **Moi aussi, j'aime beaucoup ce restaurant. /**
    Moi, je n'aime pas ce restaurant. /
    Je ne connais pas ce restaurant.

1. librairie   **3.** CD   **5.** sports
2. café   **4.** vidéocassette   **6.** voitures

Reprise: *Saying where you live and what you have*

In *Chapitre 3,* you learned to talk about your belongings and where you live.
Now you have a chance to review what you learned.

A. Quelques questions. Vous cherchez un(e) colocataire et un(e) autre étudiant(e) vous pose les questions suivantes. D'abord, complétez les questions avec **de, d', du, de la, de l'** ou **des.** Après, posez les questions à votre partenaire.

1. Est-ce que tu habites près ou loin _____ centre-ville?
2. Tu habites près _____ université?
3. Y a-t-il un arrêt d'autobus près _____ chez toi?
4. Qu'est-ce qu'il y a en face _____ chez toi?
5. Est-ce que ta chambre est près _____ cuisine?
6. Dans ta chambre, qu'est-ce qu'il y a en face _____ lit?
7. Dans le salon, qu'est-ce qu'il y a en face _____ télé?

B. Une maison. Utilisez une préposition pour décrire où les choses suivantes se trouvent l'une par rapport à l'autre *(in relationship to each other)* dans la maison. Suivez l'exemple.

Exemple le salon / les toilettes
Le salon est à gauche des toilettes.

1. le salon / la cuisine et les toilettes
2. la salle de bains / la chambre
3. le canapé / le salon
4. la lampe / le fauteuil
5. le fauteuil / l'escalier
6. la salle à manger / la cuisine
7. la table / la salle à manger
8. la table / le tapis

Maintenant, travaillez avec un(e) partenaire pour continuer la description de la maison.

Exemple **C'est une grande maison. Il y a un escalier. Le salon est au rez-de-chaussée. Dans le salon, il y a...**

C. Qu'est-ce que vous avez? Complétez les phrases suivantes avec le verbe **avoir** dans le premier blanc et un adjectif possessif dans le deuxième.

Exemple **J'ai** un téléphone portable *(cell phone).* **Mon** numéro de téléphone, c'est le 825-5479.

1. J'_____ un appartement au centre-ville. _____ adresse, c'est le 202, rue Cisneros.
2. Nous _____ beaucoup de restaurants dans _____ quartier.

3. Mes parents _____ une maison en banlieue. _____ jardin *(yard)* est très joli.
4. Mon meilleur ami (Ma meilleure amie) _____ un grand appartement très élégant. _____ loyer est de plus de mille dollars par mois.
5. J' _____ un quartier très agréable. _____ rue est très jolie.
6. Mon meilleur ami (Ma meilleure amie) _____ une belle voiture. _____ voiture est bleue.
7. À l'université, nous n' _____ pas beaucoup de parkings pour _____ voitures.

Maintenant, changez les phrases pour décrire votre situation ou celle de *(that of)* vos amis.

D. C'est combien? Vous cherchez du mobilier *(furnishings)* dans les annonces classées *(classified ads)* au Québec. Donnez le prix de chaque objet comme dans l'exemple. Utilisez **ce, cet, cette** ou **ces.**

Suggestions for *D. C'est combien?* and *E. Colocataire recherché.* **A.** You may wish to point out that classified ads are called **les petites annonces** in France and **les annonces classées** in Quebec. **B.** Remind students that they do not have to understand every word to be able to do these activities. Have the class guess unfamiliar words from context.

Exemple

> MOBILIER CUISINE:
> table, 6 chaises 450$.
> Tél: 678-2665.

> **Cette table et ces chaises coûtent** *(cost)* **quatre cent cinquante dollars.**

1.
> TABLE SALLE À MANGER, laquée noire, 6 chaises laquées noires. Très propres. 1.150$. Tél: 760-7883.

2.
> MOBILIER salon fleuri (fauteuil, canapé) 550$. Tél: 842-5835.

3.
> TÉLÉ 48", Sony, état neuf 700$. Tél: 881-9896.

4.
> LIT D'EAU "king" complet: base, lit en pin, matelas anti-vagues, éléments chauffants. Le tout en très bon état, 150$. Tél: 653-5216.

5.
> TABLE D'ORDINATEUR: blanche, 3 tiroirs, en bon état, 115$. Tél 832-7175.

6.
> FAUTEUIL en cuir noir. Excellente condition. 495$. Tél: 542-7060.

E. Colocataire recherché. Vous cherchez un nouveau logement au Québec dans les annonces classées *(classified ads)*. Pour chaque annonce, faites deux ou trois phrases décrivant l'appartement / la maison ou le/la colocataire cherché(e).

Exemple

> COLOCATAIRE RECHERCHÉ 20-35 ans, non-fumeur, pour partager grande maison de ville, secteur paisible et recherché, près de tout, 260$/mois tout compris. Tél: 472-3472

> **Il/Elle cherche un(e) colocataire qui ne fume pas. La maison est grande et près de tout. Le loyer est de 260$ par mois.**

1.
> RECHERCHE FEMME OU HOMME avec emploi entre 20 et 35 ans, pour partager maison campagne, 5 minutes de la ville, très tranquille, 200$/mois. Tél: 875-3428.

2.
> RECHERCHE PERSONNE non-fumeuse pour partager appartement, 2ᵉ étage, 2 ch. Près autobus et parc, idéal pour étudiant(e), libre 15 oct. $300, 595-9065.

3.
> 2 COLOCATAIRES RECHERCHÉS pour maison: 4 sdb / 2 salons / foyer / cuisine équipée. 450$. Tél: 680-4493.

Rue résidentielle au Québec

LECTURE ET *composition*

Note. The vocabulary in this section does not appear in the end-of-chapter vocabulary lists and is meant for recognition only. You may wish to let students know in advance whether you intend to test them on this vocabulary.

LECTURE: Les résidences de l'université Laval

You are going to read a description of the dormitories at Laval University. Before you begin, try to think of what information you might find in each of these sections of the reading: **chambre, salles communautaires, sécurité et prévention, courrier.** Then do activities *A* and *B*, which will improve your comprehension when you read. As you read, try to guess new words from context before you look them up in the glossary.

A. Familles de mots.

Recognizing words that belong to the same word family can make reading easier. Use the meaning of the first words given to guess the meaning of the boldfaced words in the sentences.

Exemple   fumer → *to smoke*
   Il y a **des détecteurs de fumée** dans chaque chambre.
   smoke detectors

1. chaque → *each*
   Dans **chacune** des résidences, il y a des salles de télévision.
2. laver → *to wash*
   Chaque chambre est équipée d'**un lavabo.**
3. colocataires → *co-renters*
   Il y a des pièces pour jouer au ping-pong à la disposition **des locataires.**
4. la poste → *the mail*
   Chaque locataire a **un casier postal** où **son courrier** est distribué tous les jours.
5. extinction → *extinguishing*
   Il y a **des extincteurs** à chaque étage.

B. Mots similaires.

In English, there is often more than one word for the same or very similar things; for example, *couch* and *sofa,* or *hallway* and *corridor.* In French, too, there is often more than one way to say the same or very similar things. Furthermore, sometimes one word is used in one region and a different word in another. This is often true of France and Quebec. Notice the two ways to say each thing listed; then translate the sentences.

1. *basic furnishings*   des meubles de base   un mobilier de base
   Chaque chambre est équipée d'un mobilier de base.
2. *a closet*   un placard   une penderie
   Il y a une penderie dans chaque chambre.
3. *a bookcase*   une étagère   une bibliothèque
   Il y a aussi une bibliothèque dans la chambre.
4. *to include*   inclure   comprendre
   L'équipement de sécurité comprend des téléphones d'urgences.
5. *a bulletin board*   un tableau d'affichage   un babillard *(québécois)*
   Le mobilier de base comprend un babillard.
6. *curtains*   des rideaux   des tentures *(québécois)*
   Le mobilier de base comprend aussi des tentures.

Suggestion for B. Mots similaires. You may also wish to point out the use of **sur chaque étage** in this article written in Quebec. In France, one would more commonly say **à chaque étage.**

DES SERVICES ET DES COMMODITÉS

Chambre
Chaque chambre est équipée d'un lavabo et d'un mobilier de base (lit, table de travail, bibliothèque, commode, penderie, chaise, fauteuil, babillard, tentures et lampe de bureau). S'y trouvent également un appareil téléphonique offrant de nombreuses options, dont la messagerie vocale, l'entrée du câble pour la télévision et une prise pour le réseau Internet.

Sanitaires
Des toilettes et des douches sont à la disposition des résidents sur chaque étage et des salles de bains sont également accessibles à différents endroits.

Salles communautaires
Dans chacune des résidences, des salles de lecture et d'étude, des salles de télévision, un service de dactylographie ainsi que des pièces à dédication socioculturelle et de loisir (billard, ping-pong...) sont à la disposition des locataires. Aux pavillons Alphonse-Marie-Parent et Agathe-Lacerte, une salle d'ordinateurs est accessible à tous les résidents du campus.

Sécurité et prévention
La sécurité des résidents est assurée par le personnel du Service de sécurité et de prévention de l'université Laval. De plus, l'accès au numéro 9-1-1 est possible en tout temps. L'équipement de sécurité comprend aussi des téléphones d'urgences et des extincteurs sur chaque étage ainsi que des détecteurs de fumée dans chaque chambre.

Courrier
Chaque locataire se voit attribuer un casier postal où le courrier est distribué chaque jour. Son adresse sera la suivante : nom du résident, numéro de chambre et nom du pavillon, Université Laval, Québec, Canada, G1K 7P4.

Suggestion. Before beginning, point out that this document is from the web page of **l'université Laval** and is designed to tell new students what to expect when they arrive in the dorm. Have students brainstorm about what type of information they would want to find on such a page and what information they would expect to find under each of the headings in the document.

Compréhension

Imaginez que vous habitez dans le pavillon Alphonse-Marie-Parent, une résidence à l'université Laval. Complétez les phrases suivantes.

1. Dans ma chambre, il y a...
2. À chaque étage de la résidence, il y a...
3. Il y a une salle pour jouer au....
4. Pour les étudiants sans ordinateur, il y a...
5. L'équipement de sécurité comprend...
6. Mon adresse, c'est...

Composition

A. Organisez-vous. Organizing your thoughts before you begin a writing assignment can greatly simplify your task. Imagine that you are responding to a roommate ad in Quebec. What would you want to know about the apartment and its occupant? Jot down as many words and phrases in French as you can under each heading, using a separate piece of paper.

location	rooms and furnishings	roommate's personality

If you have access to SYSTÈME-D software, you will find the following phrases, vocabulary, grammar, and dictionary aids there.

Phrases: Writing a letter; Introducing; Describing people; Asking for information
Vocabulary: House; Rooms; Furniture; Kitchen; Living room; Bedroom; Personality; Numbers; Direction and distance; Money
Grammar: Possessive adjectives; Demonstrative adjectives; Interrogative adjectives
Dictionary: The verb **avoir**

B. Rédaction: Une lettre. You are moving to Quebec and respond to an ad in the newspaper for a roommate. Write a letter in which you introduce yourself and tell the sort of place you are looking for. Then, write three paragraphs asking about the apartment's location, the rooms and furnishings, and what the roommate is like. Begin the letter with **Cher monsieur / Chère madame / Chère mademoiselle.** End the letter with **En attendant votre réponse,** and sign your name.

C. Une réponse. Exchange the letters you wrote in the preceding activity with a classmate and write a response describing yourself and the place where you live or an imaginary place where you would like to live.

D. Colocataires. You and the student with whom you exchanged letters in the previous activity have decided to become housemates. Choose one of your places and prepare a conversation in which the new housemate asks for information, such as the address, telephone number, rent, etc.

Le caractère unique du Québec est **en grande partie dû à** son histoire.

Voilà quelques dates importantes dans l'histoire du Québec.

1534	Jacques Cartier, explorateur français, **prend** possession du Canada (la Nouvelle France) au nom de la France et les Français commencent à **s'établir** au Canada.
1604	Beaucoup de Français s'établissent en Cadie (**plus tard** l'Acadie), aujourd'hui **la Nouvelle-Écosse,** le Nouveau-Brunswick et l'Île-du-Prince-Édouard.
1608	Samuel de Champlain **fonde** la ville de Québec.
1642	Paul de Chomedey de Maisonneuve fonde la petite colonie de Ville-Marie, aujourd'hui Montréal.
1642–1701	Les Iroquois résistent aux Français.
17ᵉ–18ᵉ siècles	Les Français et les Anglais s'opposent pour contrôler le Canada.
1755	Les Anglais, **ayant pris contrôle** de l'Acadie en 1713, commencent à **expulser** les Français de l'Acadie. **Ceux qui le peuvent, s'échappent** au Québec.
1756–1763	Les Anglais et les Français **font la guerre** pour contrôler le Canada. **À la fin de** la guerre, la France est obligée de céder tous ses territoires canadiens aux Anglais et le Québec **devient** une partie des colonies anglaises en Amérique du Nord.
1837	Après une insurrection par les francophones, **écrasée** par les Anglais, le français **cesse d'être** une langue officielle.
1867	Le Québec devient membre de la Confédération du Canada.

Jacques Cartier

Pendant 200 ans, les Québécois francophones **vivent** sous la domination de la minorité anglophone. **Réduits** à un rôle politique minoritaire, leur influence sociale, politique et culturelle est **diminuée.**

   Pendant les années 60, les Québécois francophones commencent à **lutter** pour la préservation de la francophonie face à la majorité anglophone au Canada. **Cette lutte** pour la protection de leur identité culturelle s'appelle aujourd'hui *la Révolution tranquille.* Vers la fin des années soixante émerge un mouvement séparatiste qui voudrait voir un Québec libre. Le résultat en est la formation en 1968 d'un parti politique, le Parti québécois, qui **prend la tête** du mouvement pour la protection de l'identité québécoise et pour un Québec libre.

---

en grande partie dû à *in large part due to*   **prend** *takes*   **s'établir** *to settle*   **plus tard** *later*   **la Nouvelle-Écosse** *Nova Scotia*   **fonde** *founds*   **ayant pris contrôle** *having taken control*   **expulser** *to throw out, to expel*   **Ceux qui le peuvent, s'échappent** *Those who can, escape*   **font la guerre** *make war*   **À la fin de** *At the end of*   **devient** *becomes*   **écrasé(e)** *crushed*   **cesse d'être** *ceases to be*   **Pendant 200 ans** *For 200 years*   **vivent** *live*   **Réduit(e)** *Reduced*   **diminué(e)** *diminished*   **Pendant les années 60** *During the 60s*   **lutter** *to struggle*   **Cette lutte** *This struggle*   **prend la tête** *takes the lead*

Voilà quelques **étapes** importantes dans la préservation de la langue et de la culture francophone au Québec.

1977	Au Québec, les enfants d'immigrés sont obligés d'aller dans des **écoles** francophones. L'emploi du français dans toute transaction commerciale ou gouvernementale est obligatoire.
1980	Au Québec, 40% des Québécois votent "oui" à un référendum pour un Québec indépendant.
1982	Au Canada, le bilinguisme devient obligatoire **à tous les niveaux** du gouvernement fédéral dans toutes les provinces canadiennes. Tout le Canada est considéré officiellement bilingue.
1987	Au Canada, dans les accords du lac Meech, le gouvernement canadien donne au Québec un statut de "société distincte". Ce statut donne au Québec **le droit d'**annuler toute décision du gouvernement canadien qui menace la préservation de la culture francophone.
1988	Au Québec, l'usage de l'anglais dans **l'affichage public** est **interdit**.
1990	Au Canada, les accords du lac Meech ne sont pas ratifiés.
1996	Au Québec, 49% des Québécois votent "oui" à un référendum pour un Québec indépendant.
1998	La Cour suprême du Canada affirme que le Québec **ne peut pas** procéder unilatéralement à la sécession. La sécession unilatérale est inconstitutionnelle. Mais si une majorité **se montrait** en faveur de la sécession, le reste du Canada **aurait** alors l'obligation constitutionnelle de **négocier** les conditions de la sécession.

Il n'y a pas d'action sans réaction. Certains aspects de la Révolution tranquille irritent beaucoup de Canadiens anglophones. Beaucoup d'entreprises **quittent** Montréal pour **s'installer** à Toronto. Des mouvements **pour l'interdiction de** l'usage du français **surgissent** en Ontario.

Mais à l'intérieur ou **en dehors du** Québec, les Québécois francophones **veulent** protéger leur société distincte.

À discuter

1. On appelle *(One calls)* les États-Unis un *melting pot* mais le Canada une mosaïque. Pourquoi?
2. Pensez-vous que la situation des Québécois francophones serait meilleure *(would be better)* dans un Québec indépendant?
3. Pensez-vous que ce qui se passe *(what is happening)* au Québec pourrait un jour avoir lieu *(could one day take place)* en Louisiane avec les francophones ou en Floride avec les Hispano-Américains?

---

une étape *a stage*   **une école** *a school*   **à tous les niveaux** *at all levels*   **le droit de** *the right to*   **l'affichage public** *public signs*   **interdit(e)** *forbidden*   **ne peut pas** *cannot*   **se montrait** *showed itself*   **aurait** *would have*   **négocier** *to negotiate*   **quitter** *to leave*   **s'installer** *to set up business*   **pour l'interdiction de** *to forbid*   **surgissent** *are springing up*   **en dehors de** *outside of*   **veulent** *want*

visit http://horizons.heinle.com

VOCABULAIRE

NOMS MASCULINS

un appartement	an apartment
un arrêt d'autobus	a bus stop
un ascenseur	an elevator
le centre-ville	downtown
un colocataire	a housemate, a co-renter
un dollar	a dollar
un escalier	stairs, a staircase
un étage	a floor
un immeuble	an apartment building
le logement	lodging, housing
le loyer	the rent
le rez-de-chaussée	the ground floor
un salon	a living room
le sous-sol	the basement
des W.-C.	restroom, toilet

NOMS FÉMININS

la banlieue	the suburbs
la campagne	the country
une chambre	a bedroom
une colocataire	a housemate, a co-renter
une cuisine	a kitchen
une fenêtre	a window
une maison	a house
une pièce	a room
une porte	a door
une salle à manger	a dining room
une salle de bains	a bathroom
des toilettes	restroom, toilet
une ville	a city

ADJECTIFS

cher (chère)	expensive
commode	convenient
confortable	comfortable

DIVERS

à la campagne	in the country
à la résidence universitaire	in the university dorm
À quel étage?	On what floor?
au rez-de-chaussée	on the ground floor
au premier (deuxième...) étage	on the second (third . . .) floor
au centre-ville	downtown
cent	a/one hundred
en banlieue	in the suburbs
en ville	in town
Il/Elle se trouve...	It is located . . .
Je n'ai pas de...	I don't have . . .
loin (de)	far (from)
mille	a/one thousand
un million (de)	a/one million
par mois	per month
(tout) près (de)	(very) near
trop	too (much)

Pour les nombres ordinaux, voir la page 104.

NOMS MASCULINS

un animal (pl animaux)	an animal
un canapé	a couch
un CD (un disque compact)	a CD, a compact disc
un chat	a cat
un chien	a dog
les effets personnels	personal belongings
un fauteuil	an armchair
un futon	a futon
un magnétoscope	a VCR
un ordinateur	a computer
un tableau	a painting
un tapis	a rug
un vélo	a bicycle
des vêtements	clothes

NOMS FÉMININS

une chaîne stéréo	a stereo
une chaise	a chair
une chose	a thing
une lampe	a lamp
une plante	a plant
une table	a table
une télé	a TV
une vidéocassette	a videocassette
une voiture	a car

PRÉPOSITIONS

à côté (de)	next to, beside
à droite (de)	to the right (of)
à gauche (de)	to the left (of)
dans	in
dans le coin (de)	in the corner (of)
de	of, from, about
derrière	behind
devant	in front of
en face (de)	across from, facing
entre	between
sous	under
sur	on

VERBES

arriver	to arrive
avoir	to have
chercher	to look for
fumer	to smoke
partager	to share
téléphoner (à)	to phone

DIVERS

combien (de)	how many, how much
embêtant(e)	annoying
en ordre	in order
non plus	neither
partout	everywhere
Pas de problème.	No problem.
peut-être	maybe, perhaps
rangé(e)	arranged, put away
tout	everything, all

COMPÉTENCE 3

NOMS MASCULINS

un adjectif	an adjective
un bureau	a desk
un couloir	a hall, a corridor
un lit	a bed
des meubles	furniture, furnishings
un mur	a wall
un placard	a closet
des rideaux	curtains

NOMS FÉMININS

une affiche	a poster
une commode	a dresser, a chest of drawers
une couleur	a color
une couverture	a cover, a blanket
une étagère	a bookcase, a shelf
une vue	a view

ADJECTIFS POSSESSIFS

mon/ma/mes	my
ton/ta/tes	your
son/sa/ses	his, her, its
notre/nos	our
votre/vos	your
leur/leurs	their

EXPRESSIONS VERBALES

Ça te plaît. / Ça me plaît.	You like it. / I like it.
comme tu vois	as you see
espérer	to hope
indiquer	to indicate
laisser	to leave
montrer	to show
Viens voir!	Come see!

LES COULEURS

De quelle couleur est... ?	What color is . . . ?
De quelle couleur sont... ?	What color are . . . ?
beige	beige
blanc(he)	white
bleu(e)	blue
gris(e)	gray
jaune	yellow
marron	brown
noir(e)	black
orange	orange
rose	pink
rouge	red
vert(e)	green
violet(te)	purple

DIVERS

à sa place	in its place
au bout (de)	at the end (of)
chaque	each
en désordre	in disorder
justement	as a matter of fact, precisely, exactly
par terre	on the floor, on the ground
propre	clean
sale	dirty

COMPÉTENCE 4

NOMS MASCULINS

un code postal	a zip code
un e-mail	an e-mail
un état	a state
les États-Unis	the United States
un nom	a name, a noun
un numéro de téléphone	a telephone number
un pays	a country
un prénom	a first name
des renseignements	information

NOMS FÉMININS

une adresse (e-mail)	an (e-mail) address
une nationalité	a nationality
une province	a province
une rue	a street
une ville	a city

DIVERS

ce (cet)/cette	this, that
ces	these, those
il/elle doit...	he/she must . . .
partagé(e)	shared, divided
poser une question	to ask a question
quel/quelle/quels/quelles	which, what
s'inscrire	to register
suivant(e)	following

Mardi gras

Camille Pissarro (1830–1903)
1897
© Francis G. Mayer/CORBIS

An eye condition forced Pissarro to limit the time he spent in direct sunlight and he had to paint scenes looking through windows. This work is part of a series of paintings of the same scene on a variety of occasions painted from a hotel room overlooking the boulevard Montmartre in Paris.

Suggestion. *Chapitre 4* takes place in Louisiana. Before beginning, have students locate Louisiana on a map and discuss what they already know about the French influence there. On the map on page 134, point out the 22 parishes that make up Acadiana, the Cajun area of Louisiana.

En Amérique: En Louisiane

LA LOUISIANE

SUPERFICIE: 125 674 kilomètres carrés

POPULATION: 4 372 000 (les Louisianais) (898 700 sont d'origine francophone et 261 700 parlent français, cadien ou créole à la maison)

CAPITALE: Baton Rouge

INDUSTRIES PRINCIPALES: l'agriculture, la pêche (*fishing*), le pétrole, le gaz naturel

Hanley-Gueno (*ca.* 1989–1991), Lafayette, Louisiana © Philip Gould/CORBIS
Influenced by the mysterious splendor of Mardi gras, many artists in French-speaking Louisiana use iridescent colors to create mythologies and fantasties.

En famille

COMPÉTENCE

1 **Describing your family**

Ma famille
Describing feelings and appearance
Les expressions avec **avoir**
Stratégies et compréhension auditive
Asking for clarification
  La famille de Robert

2 **Saying where you go in your free time**

Le temps libre
Saying where you are going
Le verbe **aller,** la préposition **à** et le pronom **y**
Suggesting activities
Le pronom sujet **on** et l'impératif

3 **Saying what you are going to do**

Le week-end prochain
Saying what you are going to do
Le futur immédiat
Saying when you are going to do something
Les dates

4 **Planning how to get there**

Les moyens de transport
Deciding how to get there
Le verbe **prendre** et les moyens de transport
Reprise
Talking about your family and free time

Lecture et composition

Cœur des Cajuns

Comparaisons culturelles

La Louisiane francophone et la région cadienne

Additional information. A. In Acadiana, Mardi Gras is celebrated with the **Courir du Mardi gras.** Masked and costumed riders go from house to house begging for ingredients to make a community gumbo. The day's festivities end with the gumbo and a **fais-do-do** (street dance). B. Lafayette is a modern city that respects and revels in its history. The first inhabitants were the Attakapas Indians, followed by early European settlers. The arrival of the Acadians to the region, however, was in many ways the most important cultural influence. Lafayette's strong French heritage is mixed with American, Spanish, Native American, and African influences, as well as the influence of a variety of other ethnic groups.

TRANSPARENCY: MAP-4

En Amérique: La Louisiane

À **quoi pensez-vous** quand vous pensez à la Louisiane francophone? Pensez-vous à La Nouvelle-Orléans avec son **Vieux Carré** et son célèbre Mardi gras? Pensez-vous à la tradition créole, à sa fameuse cuisine et à sa musique zydeco?

Note. Students read about the variety of ethnic origins of the francophones in Louisiana, the nature of Louisiana French, and the history of the region in the *Comparaisons culturelles* section at the end of this chapter.

Le Mardi gras à La Nouvelle-Orléans est **connu** *dans* **le monde entier.**

Suggestions. Point out that: **1.** Louisiana is divided into parishes rather than counties. **2.** Southern Louisiana is the largest French-speaking region in the U.S. **3.** New Orleans is not part of the 22-parish region that makes up Acadiana. **4.** The French Quarter is called the **Vieux Carré** (Old Square). **5. Laissez les bons temps rouler!** is an expression typical of the Louisiana region, but is not used in France.

La Nouvelle-Orléans est célèbre pour son Vieux Carré.

Lafayette est **au cœur de** *la région cadienne.*

Ou alors, pensez-vous à la culture cadienne, avec son histoire et ses traditions uniques, sa cuisine et sa musique fascinantes?

Visitez le Village Acadien pour voir comment vivaient les Acadiens dans le passé.

La région d'Acadiana **comprend** *22* **paroisses** *dans* **la partie sud de** *la Louisiane.*

À quoi pensez-vous *What do you think of* **le Vieux Carré** *the French Quarter* **connu** *known* **le monde entier** *the entire world* **cadien(ne)** *cajun* **au cœur de** *in the heart of* **comprend** *includes* **une paroisse** *a parish* (equivalent to a county) **la partie sud de** *the southern part of*

Pendant un certain temps la culture francophone de la Louisiane, entourée par la culture anglophone, **était sur le point d'être perdue. Pourtant, surtout depuis les années 1980,** cette culture **reprend vigueur.** Le folklore et les traditions francophones de la Louisiane sont très appréciés dans le monde entier, en particulier sa cuisine, sa musique et ses danses.

Aimez-vous la musique cadienne? le zydeco? le swamp-pop?

*Connaissez-vous la cuisine cadienne? la cuisine créole? Aimez-vous le boudin, l'andouille, le jambalaya, **les écrevisses?***

L'une des meilleures façons de **profiter de** la culture francophone de la Louisiane est de visiter un des **nombreux** festivals de la région. **Parmi** les festivals **les plus connus,** il y a le festival de musique acadienne et les festivals acadiens (un assemblage de plusieurs festivals qui célèbrent la musique, la cuisine et **les artisanats** cadiens). Il y a aussi le festival international de Louisiane qui, **tout en célébrant toute diversité internationale, met en valeur les liens** entre la Louisiane et les pays francophones.

Les traditions cadiennes sont très appréciées.

Laissez les bons temps rouler!

Pendant *For, During*   **était sur le point d'être perdue** *was about to be lost*   **Pourtant** *However*   **surtout depuis les années 1980** *especially since the 1980s*   **reprend vigueur** *is taking on new life*   **Connaissez-vous... ?** *Do you know . . . ?*   **les écrevisses** *crawfish*   **L'une des meilleures façons** *One of the best ways*   **profiter de** *to take advantage of*   **nombreux** *numerous*   **Parmi** *Among*   **les plus connus** *the best known*   **les artisanats** *crafts*   **tout en célébrant toute diversité internationale** *while celebrating all international diversity*   **met en valeur** *emphasizes*   **les liens** *the ties*   **Laissez les bons temps rouler!** *Let the good times roll!* (regional)

Ma famille

Robert, Thomas et Claude **ont l'intention d'**aller passer une semaine de **vacances** *(fpl)* chez **le père** de Robert à Lafayette. Robert parle de sa famille avec ses amis.

Voici ma famille.

Voilà une photo de mon père.
Il s'appelle Luke.
Il **a environ 50 ans** *(m)*.
Il **a l'air** *(m)* **encore** jeune.
Il est **de taille moyenne.**

Il **a les cheveux courts** et gris.
Il **a les yeux** *(m)* marron.
Il **a une barbe** grise et une moustache.
Il **porte des lunettes** *(f)*.

Et vous? Comment êtes-vous?

J'ai les yeux **noirs / bruns** / marron / verts / bleus / gris. J'ai les cheveux courts / **mi-longs** / longs et noirs / bruns / **châtains** / blonds / gris / blancs / **roux.**

---

avoir l'intention de *to intend to*   **des vacances** *(fpl) vacation*   **un père** *a father*   **mort(e)** *dead*   **des enfants** *children*   **un garçon** *a boy*   **une fille** *a daughter, a girl*   **un beau-frère (une belle-sœur)** *a brother-in-law (a sister-in-law)*   **un fils** *a son*   **avoir... ans** *to be . . . years old*   **environ** *about*   **avoir l'air...** *to look, to seem . . .* **encore** *still*   **de taille moyenne** *of medium height*   **avoir les cheveux...** *to have . . . hair*   **court(e)** *short* **avoir les yeux...** *to have . . . eyes*   **une barbe** *a beard*   **porter** *to wear*   **des lunettes** *(f) glasses*   **noir** *(with eyes) very dark brown*   **brun(e)** *(with hair and eyes) medium brown*   **mi-longs** *(with hair) shoulder-length*   **châtains** *(with hair) light to medium brown*   **roux (rousse)** *(refers only to hair color) red*

Robert parle de sa famille avec Thomas.

THOMAS: Vous êtes combien dans votre famille?

ROBERT: Nous sommes sept: mon père, **ma belle-mère,** ma mère, mes deux frères, ma sœur et moi. Ma sœur est mariée et elle habite à La Nouvelle-Orléans.

THOMAS: Elle est plus jeune ou **plus âgée que** toi? Quel âge a-t-elle?

ROBERT: Elle a 28 ans.

THOMAS: Comment s'appelle-t-elle?

ROBERT: Elle s'appelle Sarah.

A. La famille. Donnez l'équivalent féminin.

Exemple le frère **la sœur**

1. le père
2. l'oncle
3. le neveu
4. le beau-père
5. le fils
6. le cousin
7. le grand-père
8. le garçon
9. le mari
10. le beau-frère

B. Généalogie. Complétez les phrases.

Exemple Les parents de mon père, ce sont **mes grands-parents.**

1. Le mari de ma tante, c'est...
2. Le fils de ma sœur, c'est... Sa fille, c'est...
3. Les enfants de mon oncle, ce sont... Sa fille, c'est... et son fils, c'est... Sa femme, c'est...

C. Mon meilleur ami. Faites des phrases pour décrire votre meilleur ami.

Exemple Il s'appelle *Philippe / Chuong / ???*.
Il s'appelle Emmitt.

1. Il s'appelle *Philippe / Chuong / ???*.
2. Il est *grand / petit / de taille moyenne*.
3. Il a *18 / 25 / 38 / 45 / ???* ans.
4. Il a les cheveux *longs / mi-longs / courts* et *blonds / noirs / ???*.
5. Il a les yeux *marron / gris / ???*.
6. Il a l'air *intellectuel / sportif / jeune / bête / ???*.

D. Et vous? Refaites les phrases de *C. Mon meilleur ami* pour faire une description de vous-même *(yourself)*.

Exemple **Je m'appelle Nancy.**

E. Parlons de la famille! Avec un(e) partenaire, changez la conversation entre Robert et Thomas comme indiqué.

1. Robert has one brother and no sisters. His brother lives with Robert's mother. His name is Michel and he is 12.
2. You and a friend are talking about your family. Change the conversation to make it true for you. Then switch roles.

---

une belle-mère (un beau-père) *a stepmother, a mother-in-law (a stepfather, a father-in-law)* **plus âgé(e) que** *older than*

✓ *Pour vérifier*

1. How do you say that you are *hungry? thirsty? hot? cold? sleepy? afraid? right? wrong?*

2. Which verb do you use to say that the water is cold? That you are cold?

Describing feelings and appearance:
Les expressions avec avoir

You have been using the phrases with **avoir** in the left column to describe people. Those in the right column are also phrases with **avoir** that you can use to describe someone. Notice that most of the equivalent phrases in English are formed with *to be* and not with *to have*.

avoir... ans	*to be . . . years old*	avoir faim	*to be hungry*
avoir les cheveux...	*to have . . . hair*	avoir soif	*to be thirsty*
avoir les yeux...	*to have . . . eyes*	avoir froid	*to be cold*
avoir une barbe /	*to have a beard /*	avoir chaud	*to be hot*
une moustache /	*a moustache /*	avoir raison	*to be right*
des lunettes	*glasses*	avoir tort	*to be wrong*
avoir l'air	*to look, to seem*	avoir peur (de)	*to be afraid (of)*
		avoir sommeil	*to be sleepy*

Use **avoir** with **froid** and **chaud** to say someone *feels* hot or cold. To tell if something *is* hot or cold when you touch it, use **être**, as you would use *to be* in English. **Froid** and **chaud** agree with the noun only when they are used with **être**.

Nous **avons** chaud dans la cuisine.   BUT: La soupe **est** chaude.

In French, the equivalents of the English verbs *to need, to intend,* and *to feel like* are also expressions with **avoir**.

avoir besoin de	*to need*	J'ai besoin de la voiture. J'ai besoin d'aller voir mon frère.
		I need the car. I need to go see my brother.
avoir l'intention de	*to intend*	Mon frère a l'intention de sortir ce soir.
		My brother intends to go out tonight.
avoir envie de	*to feel like*	Tu as envie de manger? Tu as envie d'une pizza?
		You feel like eating? You feel like a pizza?

Follow-ups for *A. Comment est-il?*
A. Regardez la femme sur la couverture du magazine *Brune* à la page 121. **1.** Est-ce qu'elle est belle? **2.** A-t-elle l'air jeune ou âgée? Elle a environ quel âge? **3.** Est-ce qu'elle a les yeux bleus ou marron? A-t-elle des lunettes? **4.** De quelle couleur sont ses cheveux? A-t-elle les cheveux longs ou courts? **B.** Décrivez l'homme ou la femme de vos rêves *(dreams)*. Donnez les renseignements indiqués. (Put the cues on a transparency.) EXEMPLES son nom **Il/Elle s'appelle Terry.** la couleur de ses yeux **Il/Elle a les yeux noirs.**
1. son nom **2.** son âge **3.** la couleur de ses cheveux **4.** la couleur de ses yeux **5.** sa taille *(size)* [grand? petit? de taille moyenne?] **6.** d'autres détails [des lunettes? une barbe? une moustache?]

A. Comment est-il? Répondez aux questions pour faire une description d'un ami de Robert.

Antoine, 20 ans

1. Comment s'appelle-t-il?
2. Quel âge a-t-il?
3. A-t-il l'air content *(happy)?*
4. Il a les cheveux de quelle couleur? A-t-il les cheveux longs ou courts?
5. Il a les yeux de quelle couleur?
6. A-t-il une barbe? Porte-t-il des lunettes?

B. Les activités de Robert. Quelles sont les activités que Robert a probablement envie de faire? Quelles sont les activités qu'il a probablement besoin de faire?

Exemples   faire les devoirs   **Il a besoin de faire les devoirs.**
        regarder la télé   **Il a envie de regarder la télé.**

1. aller au cinéma   3. aller travailler   5. sortir avec des amis
2. aller prendre un verre   4. préparer les cours   6. aller en cours

C. Et toi? Demandez à votre partenaire s'il/si elle a l'intention de faire les choses de *B. Les activités de Robert* demain.

> **Exemple** faire les devoirs
> — **As-tu l'intention de faire les devoirs demain?**
> — **Non, je n'ai pas l'intention de faire les devoirs demain.**

D. Moi, j'ai... Utilisez une expression avec **avoir** selon le contexte.

> **Exemple** Je voudrais aller prendre un verre.
> **J'ai soif.**

1. Brrrr... Fermez la fenêtre.
2. Aïe! C'est un serpent!
3. Voilà. Ma réponse est correcte.
4. J'ai envie de manger quelque chose.
5. Je voudrais un coca.
6. J'ai besoin de dormir.

> SOMMEIL faim
> soif froid
> CHAUD
> tort PEUR
> raison

E. Qu'est-ce qu'ils ont? La sœur de Robert fête l'anniversaire *(is celebrating the birthday)* de sa fille. Qu'est-ce qu'elle dit? Utilisez une expression avec **avoir.**

1. Ma fille... aujourd'hui.
2. Ses amis...
3. Mon ami...
4. Mais mes autres amis...

5. Mon mari et moi, nous...
6. Moi, je (j')...
7. Le chien...
8. Tu... de faire ça au chien!

F. Entretien. Interviewez votre partenaire.

1. Vous êtes combien dans ta famille? As-tu des frères ou des sœurs? Combien de neveux as-tu? Combien de nièces?
2. Comment s'appelle ta mère? Quel âge a-t-elle?
3. As-tu des enfants? Voudrais-tu avoir des enfants un jour *(one day)*? Préfères-tu avoir une fille ou un garçon?
4. Est-ce que tu as l'intention de voir ta famille ce week-end? Qu'est-ce que tu as envie de faire ce week-end? Qu'est-ce que tu as besoin de faire? Où est-ce que tu as l'intention de dîner samedi soir? Qu'est-ce que tu as l'intention de faire dimanche soir?
5. Où aimes-tu dîner quand tu as très faim? As-tu faim maintenant? As-tu soif? Est-ce que tu as l'intention de manger quelque chose après le cours? As-tu sommeil maintenant? As-tu l'intention de dormir après le cours?

G. Ma famille. Parlez de votre famille à la classe. D'abord, dites combien vous êtes dans votre famille. Ensuite *(Next)*, décrivez un membre de votre famille.

> **Exemple** **Nous sommes six dans ma famille: mon père, ma mère, mon frère, mes deux sœurs et moi. Une de mes sœurs s'appelle Claudia. Elle a 15 ans. Elle...**

Supplemental activities. A. Have pairs of students face each other for fifteen seconds, then turn around and see how well they can guess each other's age and describe each other's hair and eye color. B. Show the class a photo/slide for a minute. Then remove the photo and have them quickly write down what they remember about the people and background: **Il y a un homme qui a les cheveux gris. Il y a une voiture noire dans la rue...**

Script for *A. Je ne comprends pas.*
SCÈNE A
– Je suis Philippe Dewailly.
– Bonjour, monsieur De... euh, Dega...
Excusez-moi, ça s'écrit comment?
– Dewailly. D-E-W-A-I-L-L-Y.
– Ah! Eh bien, bonjour, monsieur
Dewailly.
SCÈNE B
– Alors, vous êtes étudiante, non?
– Oui. Et vous, vous êtes étudiante aussi?
– Non, moi, je suis médecin ici à
Lafayette.
– Vous êtes... ? Je ne comprends pas.
Qu'est-ce que ça veut dire *médecin?*
– Oh, vous savez, je m'occupe des
malades dans un hôpital.
SCÈNE C
– Et vous, vous êtes médecin aussi?
– Non, moi, je suis pharmacien.
– Comment?
– Pharmacien. Je travaille dans une
pharmacie.
– Ah oui, je comprends maintenant.

Warm-up for *B. Comment?* How would
you ask for clarification in these
situations? **1.** You didn't quite hear what
someone said. **2.** You can't quite
recognize someone's last name and
would like to know how it is spelled.
3. You aren't certain whether a friend
said he works at the university or is a
student there. **4.** He recommends the
sandwich au jambon, but you don't
know what **jambon** means.

Script for *B. Comment?*
SCÈNE A
– Bon, un express 1 dollar 50, un coca 1
dollar et une bière ** *(cough)* dollars...
Alors, ça fait ** *(cough)* dollars.
– Euh...
SCÈNE B
– Tu voudrais aller manger avec nous?
– Ça dépend. Il est loin d'ici, le
restaurant?
– Non, il est tout près... sur le boulevard
Arnould.
– Le boulevard Ar... Arn... euh...
SCÈNE C
– Je vous recommande le jus de
pamplemousse. Il est très bon.
– Le jus de... pam... ple... mousse?
Mais... ?

Stratégies et compréhension auditive:
Asking for clarification

When you do not understand something that is key to your comprehension, it is useful to be able to ask for clarification. You already know three ways to do this: by asking for something to be repeated, or by asking what a word means or how it is spelled.

Comment? Répétez, s'il vous plaît.
Je ne comprends pas. Qu'est-ce que ça veut dire **belle-sœur?**
Ça s'écrit comment?

 A. Je ne comprends pas. Listen to three conversations. In each, which method is used to ask for clarification: **a, b,** or **c?**

a. asking for something to be repeated **(Comment? Répétez, s'il vous plaît.)**
b. asking the meaning of a word **(Qu'est-ce que ça veut dire?)**
c. asking the spelling of a word **(Ça s'écrit comment?)**

B. Comment? Listen to these three other scenes, in which one of the speakers is having difficulty understanding. In each case, what could he or she say to ask for clarification?

La famille de Robert

Robert is describing his family to a friend who is studying French. Use what you know and your ability to guess logically to help you understand what he says. The first time, listen only for the number of times his friend asks for clarification.

A. La famille de Robert. Écoutez encore une fois *(again)* la description de la famille de Robert et complétez l'arbre généalogique *(family tree)* avec les prénoms des membres de sa famille.

B. C'est qui? Écoutez encore une fois la description de la famille de Robert et répondez aux questions.

1. Qui habite à Lafayette?
2. Qui habite à Atlanta?
3. Qui habite à La Nouvelle-Orléans?
4. Qui est marié?
5. Qui est divorcé?
6. Est-ce que la mère de Robert est professeur ou pédiatre?

Script for *La famille de Robert.*
– J'ai une sœur qui s'appelle Sarah et deux frères, Paul et Yves.
– Yves? Ça s'écrit comment?
– Y-V-E-S.
– Ah, je comprends.
– Mes parents n'habitent plus ensemble. Mon père s'appelle Luke. Il habite ici à Lafayette et ma mère habite à Atlanta. Elle s'appelle Julie.
– Tes parents sont divorcés?
– Oui, depuis longtemps. Ma mère et mes deux frères habitent avec ma grand-mère à Atlanta. Ma sœur, Sarah, est mariée et elle habite à La Nouvelle-Orléans. Mon père habite ici à Lafayette. Il travaille à l'université.
– Il est professeur?
– Oui, c'est ça. Et ma mère est pédiatre.
– Pédiatre? Qu'est-ce que ça veut dire?
– Ça veut dire *pediatrician*.

Suggestion for *A. La famille de Robert.*
Before beginning, have students look over the illustrations and determine the relationships shown. Point out that not all family members are mentioned.

COMPÉTENCE 2

Saying where you go in your free time

NOTE Culturelle

Il y a beaucoup de choses à faire à Lafayette. Il y a deux musées folkloriques, le Village Acadien et Vermilionville où on peut *(one can)* voir comment vivaient les Acadiens aux 18ᵉ et 19ᵉ siècles *(how the Acadians lived in the 18th and 19th centuries).*

VOCABULAIRE SUPPLÉMENTAIRE

à la synagogue
à la mosquée
au temple to church (Protestant), to temple
à la plage to the beach

NOTES DE GRAMMAIRE

Although most adverbs expressing *how often,* such as **souvent,** are placed after the verb in the sentence, **de temps en temps,** like **quelquefois,** usually goes at the beginning or end of the clause: **Je vais au parc de temps en temps.**

Notice the accent spelling change in the conjugation of **acheter** *(to buy).*

j'achète	nous achetons
tu achètes	vous achetez
il/elle achète	ils/elles achètent

The name of a place generally follows the type of place. For example, for *Tinseltown Cinema,* you say **le cinéma Tinseltown.**

TRANSPARENCIES: 4-2A, 4-2B

Le temps libre

On s'amuse bien à Lafayette!

On aime beaucoup les activités culturelles et **de temps en temps on va...**

au musée pour voir **une exposition**

au théâtre

à un concert ou à un festival de musique

On aime aussi les activités **de plein air** et on va souvent...

au parc pour jouer

à la piscine pour **prendre un bain de soleil** et nager

Pour **retrouver** des amis, on va...

au bar

au restaurant

à l'église

Pour faire du shopping, on va...

Et pour **acheter** des livres, on va...

dans les petits magasins

au centre commercial

à la librairie

Où est-ce qu'on va pour passer son temps libre dans la ville où vous habitez?

Le temps libre *Free time* **On s'amuse bien** *One has a good time* **de temps en temps** *from time to time* **on va** *one goes* **une exposition** *an exhibit* **de plein air** *outdoor* **prendre un bain de soleil** *to sunbathe* **retrouver** *to meet* **acheter** *to buy*

Robert et Claude parlent de leurs projets pour ce soir.

CLAUDE: **On sort** ce soir?
ROBERT: D'accord. **On va** au cinéma?
CLAUDE: Ah, non, je préfère **connaître** un peu la région. **On dit que** la cuisine **cadienne** est extra! **Allons plutôt** au restaurant.
ROBERT: D'accord. Allons dîner au restaurant Préjean. C'est un très bon restaurant où **on sert** les spécialités de la région et il y a un orchestre cadien tous les soirs. **Ça te dit?**
CLAUDE: Oui, bonne idée. Allons au restaurant et après allons écouter de la musique zydeco.
ROBERT: Pas de problème. **On peut** toujours **trouver** des concerts ici!

A. On y va pour... Où est-ce qu'on va pour faire les choses suivantes?

Exemple   lire
      On va à la bibliothèque pour lire.

1. dîner
2. voir un film
3. retrouver des amis
4. prendre un verre
5. faire du shopping
6. nager
7. voir une exposition
8. prendre un bain de soleil
9. acheter des livres

> AU RESTAURANT   au café   au parc   ???   AU CINÉMA
> au musée   AU CENTRE COMMERCIAL   à la librairie
> à la piscine   à l'église

B. Entretien. Interviewez votre partenaire.

1. Dans quel restaurant aimes-tu manger? Ce restaurant est près de l'université? Il est cher?
2. Dans quel magasin aimes-tu acheter des vêtements? Ce magasin est au centre commercial? C'est un magasin cher?
3. Est-ce qu'il y a beaucoup de théâtres dans le quartier universitaire? beaucoup de musées? beaucoup de concerts? Préfères-tu aller à un concert ou au théâtre? Où aimes-tu retrouver tes amis? Où aimez-vous aller ensemble?

C. On sort? Avec un(e) partenaire, changez la conversation entre Claude et Robert comme indiqué.

1. Robert first says he would like to stay home and watch a video. Claude wants to go to a restaurant and then go hear some jazz (**du jazz**). Robert agrees.
2. A friend is visiting from out of town and you are going to go out. Change the conversation to make it true for you. Choose a type of cuisine (**mexicaine, italienne, japonaise, chinoise, française...**) and a type of music (**du rock, du pop, du hip-hop, du jazz, du country, de la musique classique...**) popular in your region.

On sort... ? *How about going out . . . ?*   **On va... ?** *How about going . . . ?*   **connaître** *to know, to get to know* **On dit que** *They say that*   **cadien(ne)** *Cajun*   **Allons...** *Let's go . . .*   **plutôt** *instead, rather*   **on sert** *they serve* (**servir** *to serve*)   **Ça te dit?** *How does that sound to you?*   **On peut** *One can* (**pouvoir** *can, may, to be able*)   **trouver** *to find*

1. What are the forms of **aller?**

2. With which forms of the definite article does **à** contract? What are the contracted forms? With which forms does it not contract? How do you say *to the café? to the library? to the university? to the students?*

3. What does the word **y** mean?

4. Where do you place **y** in a sentence when there is a verb followed by an infinitive? Where do you place it otherwise?

5. What happens to words like **je** and **ne** before **y?**

Saying where you are going:
Le verbe **aller,** la préposition **à** et le pronom **y**

To talk about going places, use the irregular verb **aller** *(to go).*

ALLER *(to go)*	
je **vais**	nous ᶻ**allons**
tu **vas**	vous ᶻ**allez**
il/elle **va**	ils/elles **vont**

Use the preposition **à** *(to, at, in)* to say where you are going. When **à** falls before **le** or **les,** the two words contract to **au** and **aux.**

CONTRACTIONS WITH À			
à + le	→	au	Je vais **au** cinéma.
à + la	→	à la	Je vais **à la** librairie.
à + l'	→	à l'	Claude va **à l'**université.
à + les	→	aux	Robert va **aux** festivals de musique de la région.

The pronoun **y** *(there)* is often used to avoid repeating the name of the place where one is going. Notice that it is treated as a vowel sound and that elision and liaison occur before it.

Je vais **au parc.**   Nous allons **au centre commercial.**
J'**y** vais avec des amis.   Nous ‿**y** allons à trois heures.

Y is generally placed *immediately* before the verb. It goes before the infinitive if there is one. If not, it goes before the conjugated verb.

— Il voudrait aller **au cinéma?**   — Ils vont **au musée?**
— Oui, il voudrait **y** aller.   — Oui, ils **y** vont.

In the negative, **y** remains *immediately* before the conjugated verb or the infinitive.

— Tu **y** vas?   — Tu voudrais **y** aller?
— Non, je n'**y** vais pas.   — Non, je ne voudrais pas **y** aller.

In French, **y** is often used where *there* is understood in English.

On y va? *Shall we go (there)?*   J'y vais. *I'm going (there).*

 Prononciation: *Les lettres a, au et ai*

Pronounce the letters **a, au,** and **ai** distinctly.

- Pronounce **a** or **à** with the mouth wide open as in the word *father,* but with the tongue slightly higher and closer to the front of the mouth.

  Ton ami va à Paris.   Tu vas à Paris avec ta camarade?

- Pronounce **au** like the **o** in **nos.**

  Laure va au restaurant?   Les autres vont aussi avec Laure?

- Pronounce the **ai** of **je vais** like the **ais** of **français.** Be sure to distinguish this sound from the **a** of **tu vas** or **il va.**

  Je vais au café.   Tu n'y vas jamais?

Supplemental activity. Have students make columns on a sheet of paper with the heads **à, à la, à l',** and **au/aux.** Read these sentences and have students mark the number of the sentence under the column of the form they hear. **1.** Thomas est **au** café. **2.** Il va **à l'**université. **3.** Il va **à la** bibliothèque pour travailler. **4.** Après, il va **au** restaurant universitaire. **5.** Il parle **aux** autres étudiants. **6.** Quand il arrive en cours, il parle **au** professeur. **7.** Il parle à ses camarades de classe aussi. (As a follow-up, give these sentences as dictation.)

A. J'aime beaucoup! Est-ce que vous aimez aller à ces endroits *(places)?*

Exemple   le cinéma
           J'aime assez aller au cinéma.

> J'aime beaucoup...   **J'aime assez....**
> **Je n'aime pas beaucoup...**   JE N'AIME PAS DU TOUT...

1. l'église
2. la bibliothèque
3. le musée
4. le centre commercial
5. la piscine
6. la librairie
7. l'université le week-end
8. les matchs de basket de notre équipe *(team)*
9. les festivals de musique de la région

B. On y va souvent? Ces personnes vont-elles souvent, quelquefois, rarement ou jamais aux endroits indiqués?

Exemple   Moi, je... (le musée)
           Moi, je vais rarement au musée. / Je ne vais jamais au musée.

1. Moi, je... (l'université, la piscine, le théâtre, le cinéma, l'opéra)
2. Mes amis et moi, nous... (les matchs de football américain de notre équipe *(team)*, la bibliothèque, le musée)
3. Mes parents... (le cinéma, Paris, le parc, le centre commercial)
4. Mon meilleur ami (Ma meilleure amie)... (l'église, la piscine, le bar, les festivals de musique de la région)

C. On sort. Robert parle de ses amis et de sa famille. Où vont-ils?

Exemple   Moi, je...   Moi, je **vais à la piscine.**

1. Thomas et moi...

2. Mes amis...

3. Thomas...

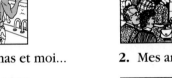

4. Claude et son frère...

5. Mon père...

6. Le chien de mon ami...

D. Et toi? Demandez à votre partenaire s'il/si elle va quelquefois à chacun des endroits *(places)* illustrés dans **C. On sort.** Votre partenaire va répondre en utilisant le pronom **y.**

Exemple   — **Est-ce que tu vas à la piscine quelquefois?**
           — **Oui, j'y vais souvent (de temps en temps, rarement...).**

E. Entretien. Interviewez votre partenaire.

1. Où aimes-tu passer ton temps libre? Préfères-tu sortir ou rester à la maison le week-end? Aimes-tu les activités culturelles? Vas-tu souvent au théâtre? au musée? Préfères-tu aller voir un concert ou aller voir une exposition?
2. Aimes-tu les activités de plein air? Tu préfères les activités culturelles ou les activités de plein air? Vas-tu souvent au parc? Vas-tu souvent à la piscine? Aimes-tu nager et prendre des bains de soleil? Tu nages bien?

Follow-ups for B. On y va souvent?
A. Questions orales. À quel restaurant est-ce que vous aimez aller? À quelle piscine? À quel musée? À quel centre commercial? B. Qui va le plus souvent au restaurant (au café, au musée, au centre commercial), votre meilleur(e) ami(e), vos parents ou vous?

Follow-up for C. On sort. Complétez les phrases avec **aller** et un endroit *(place)* logique. EXEMPLE J'aime prendre un café avec des amis. Nous **allons souvent au café. 1.** Ma mère aime faire du shopping. Elle... **2.** Mes nièces aiment lire. Elles... **3.** Mon neveu et moi aimons nager. Nous... **4.** Mon père aime faire du jogging. Il... **5.** Mon frère aime les expositions d'art. Il... **6.** J'aime acheter des livres. Je...

Supplemental oral questions. 1. Quels jours allez-vous à l'université? au cinéma? à la bibliothèque? **2.** Où allez-vous après ce cours en général? Où allez-vous aujourd'hui? Où est-ce que vous voudriez aller ce soir? Vos amis et vous, où est-ce que vous allez pour prendre un verre? Où allez-vous pour passer un après-midi tranquille?

1. What are the three possible uses of the pronoun **on?** What form of the verb do you use with **on?**

2. How do you form the imperative? What is it used for?

3. With which verbs do you drop the final **-s** in the **tu** form of the imperative?

4. Which two verbs have irregular command forms? What are the forms?

Suggesting activities: *Le pronom sujet* **on** *et l'impératif*

Use **on** as the subject of a sentence when you are referring to people in general *(one, people, they)*. **On** takes the same form of the verb as **il** and **elle**. Consider the difference between these sentences.

Tes parents? Ils parlent français?	*Your parents? Do they speak French?* (specific people)
À Paris, **on** parle français.	*In Paris, they speak French.* (general group)

The pronoun **on** is also often used instead of **nous** to say *we.*

Claude et moi, **on** aime sortir le samedi.	*Claude and I, we like to go out on Saturdays.*

You can propose doing something with someone *(How about . . .? Shall we . . .?)* by asking a question with **on.**

On va au cinéma?	*How about going to the movies?*
Qu'est-ce qu'**on** fait ce soir?	*What shall we do this evening?*

The imperative (command form) can also be used to make suggestions, as well as to tell someone else to do something. Use the imperative as follows.

- To make suggestions with *Let's . . .,* use the **nous** form of the verb, without the pronoun **nous.**

Allons au cinéma!	*Let's go to the movies!*
Ne **restons** pas à la maison!	*Let's not stay home!*

- To give instructions, or to tell someone to do something, use either the **vous** form of the verb or the **tu** form or the verb, as appropriate, without the pronoun. In **tu** form commands, drop the final **-s** of **-er** verbs and of **aller.** However, as you learn other verbs that do not end in **-er,** do not drop the **-s** in the commands.

Allez à la bibliothèque!	**Va** à la bibliothèque!	*Go to the library!*
Ne **mangez** pas ça!	Ne **mange** pas ça!	*Don't eat that!*

The verbs **être** and **avoir** have irregular command forms.

ÊTRE *(be . . .)*	
Sois sage!	*Be good!*
Soyons gentil(le)s!	*Let's be nice!*
Soyez calme(s)!	*Be calm!*

AVOIR *(have . . .)*	
Aie de la patience!	*Have patience!*
Ayons de la patience!	*Let's have patience!*
Ayez confiance!	*Have confidence!*

Note. The imperative is recycled in the next **Compétence** with the verb **prendre** and in **Chapitre 5** with the verb **faire** to provide additional practice and to remind students that the final **-s** of **tu** form commands is not dropped from verbs that do not end in **-er.** It is again recycled in **Chapitre 10** with giving directions.

Supplemental activity. Use this activity to practice using **on** meaning *one.* **Où est-ce qu'on fait les choses suivantes?** EXEMPLE On achète des vêtements **au centre commercial. 1.** On nage... **2.** On visite une exposition... **3.** On va voir un film... **4.** On achète des livres... **5.** On prend un bain de soleil... **6.** On mange avec des amis...

Supplemental activity. Remind students of the classroom commands learned on page 20. Play **Jacques a dit** *(Simon Says).* **1.** Jacques a dit: «Allez à la fenêtre.» **2.** Jacques a dit: «Regardez-moi.» **3.** Jacques a dit: «Prenez votre livre.» **4.** Ouvrez votre livre à la page 210. **5.** Jacques a dit: «Ouvrez votre livre à la page 210.» **6.** Fermez votre livre. **7.** Jacques a dit: «Fermez votre livre.» **8.** Jacques a dit: «Mettez *(Put)* vos livres sur le bureau.» **9.** Allez au tableau. **10.** Jacques a dit: «Allez au tableau.» **11.** Jacques a dit: «Écrivez la conjugaison du verbe **aller.**» **12.** Écrivez la conjugaison du verbe **avoir. 13.** Jacques a dit: «Répétez **bonjour.**» **14.** Répétez **au revoir. 15.** Jacques a dit: «Dansez le twist.»

A. Où? Est-ce qu'on fait plus souvent les choses suivantes **en Louisiane, au Québec** ou **dans les deux régions?**

Exemple   On écoute de la musique zydeco.
           On écoute plus souvent de la musique zydeco en Louisiane.

1. On parle français.
2. On fête *(celebrate)* Mardi gras.
3. On fête le 4 juillet *(July)*.
4. On écoute de la musique québécoise.
5. On mange des po-boys.
6. On va à des festivals de neige *(snow)*.
7. On va à des festivals de danse cadienne.

B. Tes amis et toi? Posez ces questions à votre partenaire. Il/Elle va répondre en utilisant le pronom **on**.

Exemple   — **Tes amis et toi, vous préférez aller à quel restaurant?**
           — **On préfère aller au restaurant Vermilionville.**

Tes amis et toi...

1. Quand aimez-vous sortir ensemble?
2. Où aimez-vous aller ensemble?
3. Mangez-vous souvent ensemble?
4. À quel restaurant allez-vous le plus souvent?
5. Où allez-vous pour retrouver des amis?
6. Allez-vous souvent au parc ensemble?
7. Jouez-vous au volley ensemble?

C. On... ? Un(e) ami(e) vous invite *(invites you)* à faire ces choses. Répondez à ses suggestions selon vos goûts *(according to your tastes)*.

Exemple   rester à la maison / aller au cinéma
           — **On reste à la maison ou on va au cinéma?**
           — **Restons à la maison. / Allons au cinéma.**

1. regarder la télé / regarder une vidéo
2. manger à la maison / dîner au restaurant
3. aller en boîte / aller au cinéma
4. visiter une exposition / aller au théâtre
5. inviter nos amis à la maison / retrouver nos amis en ville

D. Pour réussir. Donnez des conseils à un groupe de nouveaux étudiants. Utilisez l'impératif.

Exemple   habiter seuls
           Habitez seuls. / N'habitez pas seuls.

1. aller à tous les cours
2. être à l'heure *(on time)*
3. avoir confiance
4. regarder les examens des autres étudiants
5. préparer les devoirs avec d'autres étudiants
6. aller en boîte tous les soirs

Maintenant donnez les mêmes conseils à un(e) ami(e).

Exemple   habiter seul   **Habite seul(e). / N'habite pas seul(e).**

Follow-up for *A. Où?* Put these cues on the board or a transparency: **acheter des vêtements / manger / jouer au foot / regarder un film / visiter une exposition / nager / acheter des livres.** Ask students: **Qu'est-ce qu'on fait dans les endroits suivants?** EXEMPLE au centre commercial **On achète des vêtements au centre commercial. 1.** à la piscine **2.** au musée **3.** au cinéma **4.** à la librairie **5.** au parc **6.** au restaurant

Suggestions for *B. Tes amis et toi?* Remind students that: **A.** The name of a place follows the type of place it is. For example, **la librairie Book People. B.** The verb is still in the third person singular, even when **on** means *we.*

Follow-ups for *B. Tes amis et toi?* **A.** Faites une liste de choses qu'on fait souvent dans votre région et une autre liste de choses qu'on ne fait pas souvent. EXEMPLE **On nage souvent. On... B.** Have students list the following for their area: **1.** a good place to eat **2.** an interesting place to visit **3.** a good place to swim (or use another activity popular in your region) **4.** an activity they like and a place to do it. Then, have them use this information to invite a classmate to do something. EXEMPLE **Mangeons à Pizza Nizza.**

Follow-up for *D. Pour réussir.* Have students play the roles of **le diable et l'ange gardien.** Divide the class in half and assign each half one of the roles. Have them work in pairs to list things a guardian angel and the devil would tell a student to do. EXEMPLE **Travaille beaucoup. / Non, passe la journée au lit.**

COMPÉTENCE 3

Saying what you are going to do

NOTE Culturelle

Pour connaître la culture créole, visitez La Nouvelle-Orléans. Pour connaître la culture cadienne, visitez plutôt Lafayette et la région acadienne.

NOTE DE VOCABULAIRE
Use **visiter** to say that you visit a place. Use **aller voir** to say that you visit a person.

TRANSPARENCY: 4-3

Warm-ups. A. Qu'est-ce qu'ils aiment faire? **1.** Thomas et Claude aiment aller au cinéma. Ils aiment... **2.** J'aime aller au café. J'aime... **3.** Mes amis et moi, nous aimons aller à la bibliothèque. Nous aimons... **4.** Mon frère et son fils aiment aller au centre commercial. Ils aiment... **5.** Mon père aime aller au restaurant. Il aime... **6.** Mes parents et moi, nous aimons aller à la piscine. Nous aimons...
B. Quand est-ce que vous préférez faire les choses suivantes: le matin, l'après-midi ou le soir? (aller en ville, nager, jouer au tennis, préparer les cours, retrouver des amis au café, aller au cinéma, sortir avec des amis, faire du shopping)

Suggestions. Point out that the sentences on this page are talking about what someone is going to do and ask students what they notice about the verb. Discuss the difference among **quitter, partir,** and **sortir.**

Suggestions for the conversation.
A. Have students listen for the following information in the conversation with books closed: **1.** Qu'est-ce que Robert voudrait faire jeudi? **2.** Où est-ce qu'il voudrait déjeuner samedi? Then, have them listen again with books open.
B. Point out the use of **d'abord, ensuite,** and **et puis.**

Le week-end prochain

Robert va passer le week-end prochain à La Nouvelle-Orléans. Et vous? Qu'est-ce que vous allez faire?

Je vais... / Je ne vais pas...

quitter la maison **tôt**

partir pour le week-end

visiter une autre ville

faire un tour de la ville

aller **boire** quelque chose au café

rentrer **tard**

 Robert et Thomas **font des projets** pour le week-end prochain.

THOMAS: Qu'est-ce qu'on fait ce week-end?
ROBERT: J'ai beaucoup de projets pour ce week-end. Jeudi matin, on va partir très tôt pour La Nouvelle-Orléans. **D'abord,** on va visiter la ville. **Ensuite,** on va aller voir ma sœur. On va passer **la soirée** chez elle. Vendredi on va faire un tour du **Vieux Carré.** On va rentrer à Lafayette assez tard.
THOMAS: Et samedi?
ROBERT: À midi, on va déjeuner au restaurant Prudhomme. C'est un restaurant célèbre pour sa cuisine régionale. **Et puis,** le soir, on va aller à Eunice, une petite ville pas loin de Lafayette. Il y a une soirée de musique et de folklore cadiens tous les samedis.
THOMAS: **Génial!**

Le week-end prochain Next weekend   **quitter** to leave   **tôt** early   **partir** to leave   **boire** to drink   **tard** late
faire des projets to make plans   **D'abord** First   **Ensuite** Next   **la soirée** the evening   **le Vieux Carré** the French Quarter   **Et puis** And then   **Génial!** Great!

A. Le week-end prochain.
Est-ce que vous allez faire les choses suivantes samedi prochain?

Exemple   rester à la maison   **Je vais rester à la maison. / Je ne vais pas rester à la maison.**

1. quitter la maison tôt
2. partir pour la journée
3. faire un tour de la ville
4. visiter une autre ville
5. aller voir des amis
6. retrouver des amis en ville
7. aller boire quelque chose
8. dîner au restaurant
9. rentrer tard
10. inviter des amis à la maison
11. regarder une vidéo
12. passer la soirée à la maison

B. Entretien.
Interviewez votre partenaire.

1. À quelle heure est-ce que tu quittes la maison le lundi? le mardi? À quelle heure est-ce que tu rentres?
2. Quelle ville est-ce que tu aimes visiter? Qu'est-ce que tu aimes faire dans cette ville?
3. Est-ce que tu voudrais partir pour le week-end? Où est-ce que tu voudrais aller?
4. Vas-tu souvent au café? Qu'est-ce que tu aimes boire quand tu as très soif? Et quand tu as froid? Et quand tu as chaud?
5. En général, quels jours est-ce que tu passes la journée à la maison? Et la soirée? Est-ce que tu passes toute la journée chez toi de temps en temps?

C. Faisons des projets!
Avec un(e) partenaire, changez la conversation entre Robert et Thomas comme indiqué.

1. Thursday Robert and his friends are going to stay home in the morning. They are going to watch a video and eat lunch with his father. In the afternoon, they are going to go see an exhibit at the **musée de Lafayette.** In the evening, they are going to go see some friends.
2. A friend is coming to spend the weekend with you. Discuss what you are going to do during the visit. Take turns playing each role.

Supplemental activities. A. Have students look at the illustrations on the preceding page and answer these questions with one or two words. **1.** À quelle heure est-ce que Robert va quitter la maison? **2.** Est-ce que Robert a une grande voiture ou une petite voiture? **3.** Comment est Robert? A-t-il une moustache, une barbe ou des lunettes? **4.** Quelle ville est-ce que Robert, Claude et Thomas vont visiter? **5.** Où vont-ils aller pour boire quelque chose? **6.** Est-ce qu'ils vont rentrer à Lafayette tôt ou tard? **B.** Claude est très dynamique. Il n'aime pas rester à la maison. Est-ce qu'il aime faire les choses suivantes? Répondez par **oui** ou par **non: 1.** faire un tour de la ville **2.** rester au lit **3.** partir pour le week-end **4.** regarder des vidéos **5.** rester à la maison **6.** jouer au tennis **7.** regarder la télé. **C.** Est-ce que vous préférez... ? **1.** nager / prendre un bain de soleil **2.** passer le week-end seul(e) / aller voir des amis **3.** lire / regarder une vidéo **4.** partir pour le week-end / rester à la maison **5.** visiter une exposition d'art / regarder la télé **6.** regarder des vidéos / aller au cinéma **D. Questions orales.** Qu'est-ce que vous aimez faire le samedi? D'habitude, est-ce que vous quittez la maison tôt ou tard? Est-ce que vous déjeunez tôt ou tard? Est-ce que vous dînez tôt ou tard? Quand vous allez en ville avec des amis, est-ce que vous rentrez tôt ou tard?

Le Vieux Carré à La Nouvelle-Orléans

Saying what you are going to do: *Le futur immédiat*

To talk about what you *are going to do,* use a form of the verb **aller** followed by an infinitive.

— Qu'est-ce que tu **vas faire** demain?   — *What are you going to do tomorrow?*
— Je **vais travailler.**   — *I'm going to work.*

In the negative, put the **ne... pas** around the conjugated form of **aller.**

Je **ne vais pas** rester à la maison.   Ils **ne vont pas** partir demain.

Il y a becomes **il va y avoir** when you want to say *there is going to be / there are going to be.*

Il va y avoir beaucoup de choses à faire à La Nouvelle-Orléans.
Il ne va pas **y avoir** de problèmes.

Here are some expressions you can use to tell when you are going to do something.

maintenant *now*	**plus tard** *later*
aujourd'hui *today*	**demain** *tomorrow*
ce matin *this morning*	**demain matin** *tomorrow morning*
cet après-midi *this afternoon*	**demain après-midi** *tomorrow afternoon*
ce soir *tonight*	**demain soir** *tomorrow evening*
lundi *Monday*	**lundi prochain** *next Monday*
ce week-end *this weekend*	**le week-end prochain** *next weekend*
cette semaine *this week*	**la semaine prochaine** *next week*
ce mois-ci *this month*	**le mois prochain** *next month*
cette année *this year*	**l'année prochaine** *next year*

A. Qu'est-ce qu'ils vont faire? Est-ce que ces personnes vont probablement faire ces choses samedi prochain?

Exemple   Moi, je... (passer la journée à la maison, quitter la maison tôt)
Moi, je ne vais pas passer la journée à la maison. Je vais quitter la maison tôt.

1. Moi, je... (passer la journée à la maison, quitter la maison tôt, aller travailler, partir pour le week-end, rester au lit, aller voir des amis)
2. Les étudiants du cours de français... (préparer les cours ensemble, être à l'université, sortir ensemble, faire les devoirs)
3. Le professeur de français... (préparer les cours, beaucoup travailler, aller à Paris, passer le week-end à la maison)
4. Mes amis et moi... (sortir ensemble, faire un tour de la ville, visiter une autre ville, aller boire quelque chose, rentrer tard)

B. Et ensuite? Qu'est-ce que ces gens vont faire d'abord et qu'est-ce qu'ils vont faire ensuite?

Exemple   nous: manger / préparer le dîner
D'abord, nous allons préparer le dîner et ensuite, nous allons manger.

1. mon cousin et moi, nous: travailler tout l'après-midi / aller prendre un verre
2. moi, je: dormir / rentrer à la maison
3. mon frère: dîner au restaurant avec elle / retrouver sa petite amie en ville
4. ta petite amie et toi, vous: dîner au restaurant / sortir danser
5. maman, tu: rentrer du travail / jouer au tennis avec papa

C. Projets.
Demandez à un(e) camarade de classe ce qu'il/elle va faire aux moments indiqués.

Exemple   ce soir   **— David, qu'est-ce que tu vas faire ce soir?**
                                    — Je vais travailler ce soir.

1. plus tard, après les cours
2. demain matin
3. demain soir
4. le week-end prochain
5. l'année prochaine

rentrer à la maison   **???**   préparer les cours   TRAVAILLER
SORTIR   manger   *aller à l'université*   être en cours   **aller...**
partir pour le week-end   DORMIR   ALLER VOIR DES AMIS

D. Leurs projets.
De retour au (*Back in*) Québec, Thomas parle à Robert de leurs projets pour le lendemain (*the next day*). Qu'est-ce que Thomas dit?

Exemple   Moi, je **vais rester au lit.**

Follow-up for *D. Leurs projets*. Demandez à votre partenaire s'il/si elle va faire les choses illustrées dans *D. Leurs projets* demain. EXEMPLE – Est-ce que tu vas rester au lit demain? – Oui, je vais rester au lit. / Non, je ne vais pas rester au lit.

Moi, je...

1. Claude...

2. Robert, est-ce que tu... ?

3. Ta petite amie et toi, est-ce que vous... ?

4. Claude et toi, est-ce que vous... ?

5. Nos amis...

6. Nos autres amis...

7. Mes amis et moi, on...

8. Claude et son ami...

E. Entretien.
Interviewez votre partenaire.

1. Qu'est-ce que tu vas faire après le cours de français aujourd'hui? À quelle heure est-ce que tu vas rentrer à la maison? Qu'est-ce que tu vas faire ensuite?
2. À quelle heure est-ce que tu vas quitter la maison demain? Où est-ce que tu vas passer la journée? Qu'est-ce que tu vas faire?
3. Ce week-end, est-ce que tu vas partir pour le week-end? Est-ce que tu vas aller voir tes parents? Est-ce que tu vas travailler? Tu vas sortir avec des amis?

Warm-up for *E. Entretien*. Demandez à un(e) camarade de classe ce qu'il/elle va faire après les cours (ce soir / demain après-midi / vendredi soir / samedi prochain / dimanche soir).

Supplemental activity. Préparez une conversation avec un(e) partenaire dans laquelle vous parlez de ce que vous allez faire le week-end prochain. Parlez de vos activités pour vendredi soir, pour samedi et pour dimanche.

✓ *Pour vérifier*

1. Do you generally use the cardinal or ordinal numbers to give dates in French? What is the exception?

2. In what two ways can the year 1789 be expressed in French? How do you say the year 2002?

3. What are these dates in French: 15/3/1951 and 11/1/2004?

VOCABULAIRE SUPPLÉMENTAIRE

LES FÊTES

un anniversaire de mariage *a wedding anniversary*

la fête des Mères / Pères

la fête nationale *Independence Day*

Hanoukka *(f)*

le jour d'Action de Grâce *Thanksgiving*

le (réveillon du) jour de l'an *New Year's (Eve)*

Noël *(m) Christmas*

Pâques *(f) Easter*

la pâque juive *Passover*

le ramadan

la Saint-Valentin

Yom Kippour

Bon anniversaire! *Happy Birthday!*

Bonne année! *Happy New Year!*

Joyeux Noël! *Merry Christmas!*

Suggestions for practicing the dates. A. After you present the dates, ask questions such as these: **Quelle est la date du premier jour de l'année? du dernier** (last)? **Quelle est la date aujourd'hui? demain? après demain?** B. Ask students: **Quelle est la date de votre anniversaire?** As they say the date, have them line up in the front of the room in the order of their birthdate.

Warm-up for A. Dates importantes. Dictate these years and have students write them down; then identify why they are important. 1. 1776 2. 1789 3. 1867 4. 1812 5. 1492 6. 1534 7. 1755 (You may wish to add other important dates for your region.) (Quick-reference answers. 1. l'indépendance américaine 2. la Révolution française 3. Le Québec devient membre de la confédération canadienne 4. La Louisiane devient un état des États-Unis. 5. l'arrivée de Christophe Colomb en Amérique 6. l'arrivée de Jacques Cartier au Canada 7. Les premiers Acadiens sont chassés du Canada par les Anglais.)

Saying when you are going to do something: *Les dates*

You sometimes need to give dates to say when you are going to do something.

Je vais partir en vacances le 30 décembre.

To ask the date, use **Quelle est la date?** Dates in French are expressed using **le** and the cardinal numbers (**deux, trois...**), rather than the ordinal numbers (**deuxième, troisième...**), except to say it is *the first* of the month. For *the first*, use **le premier (1ᵉʳ).**

— Quelle est la date aujourd'hui?
— C'est le premier... le deux... le trois... le quatre...

— Quelle est la date de votre fête *(holiday)* préférée?

| janvier | mars | mai | juillet | septembre | novembre |
| février | avril | juin | août | octobre | décembre |

Note that the day goes before the month in French.

14/8/1957 = le quatorze août 1957

There are two ways of expressing the years 1000–1999 in French. Years starting at 2000 are only expressed using the word **mille.**

1999: mille neuf cent quatre-vingt-dix-neuf / dix-neuf cent quatre-vingt-dix-neuf
2001: deux mille un

Use **en** to say *in* what month or year.

— Ton anniversaire *(birthday)*, c'est **en** quel mois?
— C'est **en** novembre.

— **En** quelle année vas-tu finir tes études?
— **En** 2005.

A. Dates importantes. Lisez ces dates de l'histoire de la Louisiane.

1682 La France prend possession de la Louisiane.
1718 La Nouvelle-Orléans est fondée *(founded)*.
1764 Les Acadiens commencent à arriver en Louisiane.
1803 Les États-Unis achètent la Louisiane à la France pour $15 000 000.
1812 La Louisiane devient *(becomes)* un état des États-Unis.
1968 L'état établit *(establishes)* CODOFIL pour protéger *(to protect)* la langue française.
1974 Un amendement est ajouté *(added)* à la Constitution de l'état qui encourage la préservation de la culture française en Louisiane.

B. C'est en quel mois? Quel mois associez-vous avec... ?

1. le début *(beginning)* de l'année? la fin *(end)* de l'année?
2. le début de l'année scolaire? le début de ce semestre/trimestre?
3. la fin de ce semestre/trimestre?
4. la fête nationale américaine? canadienne? française?
5. Noël? le jour d'Action de Grâce *(Thanksgiving)*?
6. la Saint-Valentin? le jour de l'an *(New Year's Day)*?

C. Votre anniversaire. Vos camarades de classe devineront *(will guess)* la date de votre anniversaire. Répondez **avant** ou **après** jusqu'à ce qu'ils devinent juste *(right)*.

Suggestion for C. Votre anniversaire. Tell students to narrow down the month; then try to guess the date. Give the models: **Ton anniversaire, c'est en mars? C'est le 15 mars?**

D. C'est quelle date? Lisez ces dates.

Exemple   4/7/1776   **le quatre juillet mille sept cent soixante-seize (dix-sept cent soixante-seize)**

1. 6/6/1944
2. 11/11/1918
3. 30/4/1812
4. 1/11/1718
5. 14/7/1789
6. 18/9/1759

E. Encore des dates. Quelle est la date… ?

1. aujourd'hui
2. demain
3. du prochain cours de français
4. du prochain examen de français
5. de la fête nationale américaine / canadienne
6. de Noël
7. de *Halloween*
8. de la Saint-Valentin
9. de votre anniversaire
10. de la fête nationale française

F. À quelle date? Dites à quelle date chacun va faire les choses indiquées.

Exemple Robert / rentrer chez ses parents…
Robert va rentrer chez ses parents le 25 décembre.

1. Beaucoup d'Américains / faire un pique-nique…

2. Les Français / célébrer leur fête nationale…

3. Beaucoup de couples / dîner au restaurant…

4. On / sortir avec des amis…

5. Thomas / aller voir sa famille…

6. Moi, je / fêter *(to celebrate)* mon anniversaire…

G. Entretien. Interviewez votre partenaire.

1. Quelle est la date aujourd'hui? Quelle est la date de ton anniversaire? Qu'est-ce que tu vas probablement faire ce jour-là? Quelle est la date de l'anniversaire de ton meilleur ami (ta meilleure amie)? Est-ce que vous allez probablement faire quelque chose ensemble ce jour-là?

2. Quelle est la date du dernier *(last)* jour du cours de français? Qu'est-ce que tu vas faire après ton dernier cours ce semestre/trimestre? Vas-tu partir en vacances après la fin *(end)* du semestre/trimestre? Que vas-tu faire? Est-ce que tu vas continuer à étudier ici l'année prochaine?

Suggestion for D. C'est quelle date?
Point out that the dates in the exercise are all important historical dates and have students match the dates in the exercise with these events. **a.** le jour du débarquement en Normandie **b.** le début de la Révolution française **c.** Québec tombe aux Anglais. **d.** La Louisiane devient un état des États-Unis. **e.** la date de l'indépendance américaine **f.** le jour de l'Armistice **g.** Bienville fonde La Nouvelle-Orléans. (**Quick-reference answers.** EXEMPLE e **1.** a **2.** f **3.** d **4.** g **5.** b **6.** c)

Follow-up for D. C'est quelle date?
Present the expression **je suis né(e)**. Ask a student in the front row: **En quelle année est-ce que vous êtes né(e)**? The student answers and asks the next student in the row. Continue around the room. Write the years on the board. At the end, have students read the years; then ask: **Qui est l'étudiant le plus jeune de la classe?**

COMPÉTENCE 4

TRANSPARENCY: 4-4

Warm-up. Où est-ce que Robert et ses amis vont aller pour faire les choses suivantes? EXEMPLE Robert va voir une exposition. **Il va aller au musée.** 1. Demain matin, Robert va déjeuner avec une amie en ville. 2. Ses amis vont faire du shopping. 3. Demain après-midi, ils vont voir un film. 4. Thomas va nager. 5. Claude va jouer au volley avec des amis. 6. Après, il va dormir.

Suggestion for the conversation. Set the scene and have students listen to the conversation with books closed and answer these questions: 1. Où est-ce que Robert et ses amis vont aller? 2. Quand vont-ils partir? 3. Comment vont-ils y aller? Then have them read along as you play the conversation again.

Les moyens de transport

Robert et ses amis vont aller à La Nouvelle-Orléans en voiture. Et vous? Comment préférez-vous voyager?

Pour visiter une autre ville je préfère y aller...

en avion

en train

en bateau

en (auto)car

Je préfère aller en ville...

à pied

en vélo

en taxi

en voiture

en métro

en (auto)bus

Robert parle à Thomas du voyage à La Nouvelle-Orléans.

ROBERT: Écoute, demain matin on va partir à La Nouvelle-Orléans. Tout est **prêt**?
THOMAS: Oui. On y va en car?
ROBERT: Non, on va **louer** une voiture, c'est plus commode.
THOMAS: C'est loin? Ça **prend** combien de temps pour y aller?
ROBERT: Environ deux heures et demie en voiture, **pas plus.**

A. Moyens de transport. Répondez aux questions suivantes.

Exemple Comment allez-vous à l'université?
Je vais à l'université en autobus ou à pied.

1. Comment est-ce que vous rentrez chez vous après les cours?
2. Comment est-ce que vous allez d'un cours à l'autre?
3. En général, comment est-ce que les étudiants vont à l'université?
4. Comment est-ce que vous rentrez chez vos parents?
5. Comment est-ce que les Américains aiment voyager? Et les Français?

les moyens (m) **de transport** *means of transportation*   **prêt(e)** *ready*   **louer** *to rent*   **prend** (**prendre** *to take*)
pas plus *no more*

B. On y va comment? Dites où chacun va et comment.

Exemple   **Je vais à Paris en avion.**

Je...

1. Ils...

2. Vous...?

3. Nous...

4. Elle...

C. Entretien. Interviewez votre partenaire.

1. Préfères-tu prendre l'avion, le train ou l'autocar pour faire un long voyage?
   Est-ce que tu voyages souvent en avion? As-tu peur de prendre l'avion?
   Pour aller à l'aéroport de chez toi, ça prend combien de temps? Qu'est-ce
   que tu aimes faire pendant les longs voyages en avion? (dormir? lire?
   parler? travailler sur l'ordinateur?)
2. Est-ce que tu habites près de l'université? Est-ce qu'il y a un arrêt
   d'autobus près de chez toi? Aimes-tu prendre l'autobus?
3. Quelle autre ville est-ce que tu visites souvent? Comment est-ce que tu y
   vas? (en voiture? en train? en avion?) Ça prend combien de temps pour y
   aller?

D. Conversations. Avec un(e) partenaire, changez la conversation entre Thomas et Robert comme indiqué.

1. Thomas thinks they are going to go to New Orleans by train. Robert says
   they are going to take his father's car.
2. You and a friend are planning to visit another city. Create a conversation
   like the one between Robert and Thomas in which you discuss how to get
   there and how long it takes.

Deciding how to get there:
Le verbe prendre et les moyens de transport

The conjugation of **prendre** *(to take)* is irregular. **Prendre** can also be translated as *to have* when talking about having a drink or something to eat.

PRENDRE *(to take)*	
je **prends**	nous **prenons**
tu **prends**	vous **prenez**
il/elle/on **prend**	ils/elles **prennent**

On **prend** la voiture, n'est-ce pas?
Je **prends** une eau minérale et un sandwich.

Comprendre *(To understand)* and **apprendre** *(to learn)* are conjugated like **prendre**. When **apprendre** is followed by an infinitive, the infinitive is preceded by **à**.

Tous mes amis **apprennent** le français. Moi, j'**apprends** à parler japonais aussi. Est-ce que tu **comprends** toujours le professeur?

You can use **prendre** to say that you are *taking* a particular means of transportation, or you can say that you are *going by* a particular vehicle, using **aller** and the preposition **en**. To say you are going *on foot*, use **à pied**.

Je **prends** mon vélo. Je **prends** le métro.
J'y **vais en** vélo. J'y **vais en** métro. J'y **vais à pied**.

 Prononciation: *Le verbe prendre*

The **e** in the root of the verb **prendre** has three different pronunciations. When it is . . .

- the last sound of the word, it is nasal: **je prends / tu prends / il prend.**
- followed by a single **n** in another syllable, it rhymes with **je: vous prenez / nous prenons.**
- followed by two **n**'s, it sounds like the **è** of **mère: ils prennent / elles prennent.**

À La Nouvelle-Orléans

Suggestions. A. Remind students that they already know the expressions **Est-ce que vous comprenez?** and **Je ne comprends pas.** They can use these expressions to help them remember the conjugation of **prendre. B.** Point out that although traditionally it is considered correct to say **à vélo**, most people say **en vélo.**

Supplemental activities. A. Répétez le moyen de transport le plus rapide: le train ou l'avion, l'avion ou la voiture, la voiture ou l'autocar, la voiture ou le vélo, en autobus ou à pied, à pied ou en vélo **B.** Écoutez les phrases et déterminez si je parle d'une personne ou de plus d'une personne. **1.** Ils prennent le métro pour aller à l'université. **2.** Ils ne comprennent pas toujours. **3.** Elle n'apprend pas beaucoup. **4.** Il ne prend jamais de notes. **5.** Elles apprennent à bien prononcer. **6.** Il prend l'autobus tous les jours. **7.** Est-ce qu'ils comprennent?

A. Que faites-vous? Est-ce que ces personnes font les choses indiquées?

Exemple   Moi, je... (prendre l'autobus pour aller à l'université)
Moi, je ne prends pas l'autobus pour aller à l'université.

1. Moi, je... (prendre un café avant le cours de français, toujours comprendre en cours, prendre des notes dans mon cahier, apprendre le vocabulaire avant de commencer le chapitre, prendre mes cours au sérieux *[seriously]*, bien comprendre le français)

2. En cours, nous... (prendre beaucoup de notes, apprendre l'espagnol, apprendre le français, mieux comprendre le français tous les jours)
3. Le professeur... (prendre les devoirs tous les jours, comprendre d'autres langues que le français, apprendre une autre langue, prendre un café en cours)
4. En général ici, les étudiants... (prendre leur voiture pour aller à l'université, prendre l'autobus, comprendre une deuxième langue, apprendre beaucoup)

B. Au café. Qu'est-ce que les personnes suivantes prennent? Complétez chaque phrase de façon logique.

> *un express*   un thé   UN COCA   **un demi**
>
> *un jus de fruit*   un sandwich au jambon
>
> UN SANDWICH AU FROMAGE

Exemple   Thomas et Claude ont très froid. Ils **prennent un thé ou un express.**

1. Nous avons sommeil mais nous avons besoin d'étudier. Nous...
2. J'ai très faim, mais je n'aime pas le fromage. Je...
3. Mes amies ont faim aussi, mais elles sont végétariennes. Elles...
4. Vous avez envie d'une boisson alcoolisée? Vous... ?
5. Robert a très chaud et très soif, mais il n'aime pas les boissons alcoolisées. Il...

C. La santé. Votre ami voudrait améliorer sa santé *(to improve his health)*. Donnez-lui des conseils. Utilisez l'impératif.

Exemples   — **Je prends un coca ou un jus d'orange?**
              — **Prends un jus d'orange!**

1. Je prends une bière ou une eau minérale?
2. Je prends un café ou un jus de fruit?
3. Je prends la voiture pour aller à l'université ou je prends mon vélo?
4. Je prends une salade ou des frites?
5. Je vais au parc ou je reste à la maison?
6. Je vais au parc en voiture ou à pied?

D. Entretien. Interviewez votre partenaire.

1. Quel moyen de transport prends-tu pour aller à l'université? Ça prend combien de temps pour y aller?
2. Dans quel cours apprends-tu beaucoup de choses? Dans quels cours est-ce que tu n'apprends pas beaucoup? Est-ce que tu poses des questions quand tu ne comprends pas? Est-ce que tu prends beaucoup de notes dans tes cours?
3. Est-ce que tu comprends une autre langue étrangère? Quelles autres langues étrangères as-tu envie d'apprendre?

E. Une sortie. Avec un(e) partenaire, préparez une conversation pour présenter à la classe basée sur cette situation.

Vous demandez si un(e) ami(e) a envie de faire quelque chose avec vous. Parlez de quand vous allez y aller et de quel moyen de transport vous allez prendre.

Supplemental activities. A. Les personnes suivantes apprennent une langue étrangère pour voyager. Quelle(s) langue(s) apprennent-elles le plus probablement? **1.** Mes parents vont visiter l'Allemagne. **2.** Ma sœur va aller en France. **3.** Mon meilleur ami va passer l'été au Mexique. **4.** Mes amis vont aller voir des amis au Québec. **5.** Je vais aller en France et en Espagne. **B.** Questions orales. **1.** Combien de semaines de vacances prenez-vous chaque année? **2.** Pendant quel mois prenez-vous vos vacances généralement? **3.** Est-ce que vous apprenez le français pour voyager?

Suggestion for *C. La santé*. Before doing this exercise, review the formation and use of the imperative. Remind students that the final **-s** is dropped from **tu** form commands of verbs that end in **-er,** but not from those that do not end in **-er,** like **prendre.** Elicit the three command forms of **prendre** from students.

Reprise: *Talking about your family and free time*

In *Chapitre 4,* you learned to describe your family, say where you go and how you get there, invite or tell someone to do something, and talk about your plans for the near future. Now you have a chance to practice what you learned.

Didier Landry Anne Landry
Christine Éric

Philippe et Marie Broussard

A. Descriptions. Vous allez passer un mois chez cette famille francophone à Lafayette. La mère décrit chaque personne de la famille. Complétez ses descriptions d'une façon logique.

Mes parents habitent chez nous. Mon _____ a soixante-quinze ans. Il a une _____ mais il n'a pas de barbe. Il a besoin de _____ pour lire. Ma _____ porte des _____ aussi. Elle _____ soixante-douze _____. Les deux ont les _____ gris. Mon _____ et moi, nous _____ quarante-sept et cinquante _____. Nous _____ deux enfants, un _____ et une _____. Notre fils a les cheveux _____ comme mon mari et moi, mais notre _____ a les cheveux _____.

B. Ma famille. La famille louisianaise voudrait tout savoir sur votre famille. Ils vous demandent combien vous êtes et comment sont les membres de votre famille. Préparez une conversation avec un(e) partenaire décrivant *(describing)* votre famille.

C. Qu'est-ce qu'on fait? Vous voulez profiter au maximum de *(to make the most of)* votre visite à Lafayette. Répondez aux suggestions de la famille chez qui vous habitez. Utilisez l'impératif.

Exemple Alors, on parle anglais ou français?
Parlons français!

1. On reste à la maison aujourd'hui ou on va en ville?
2. On prend la voiture ou on prend l'autobus pour aller en ville?
3. On mange au McDonald ou on mange dans un autre restaurant?
4. On visite le musée ou on rentre à la maison?
5. On va voir un film américain ou on va voir un film français?
6. On écoute un CD de Tracy Chapman ou on écoute un CD de musique cadienne?

D. Chez les Landry. Les Landry sont à la maison. Complétez les phrases suivantes pour décrire la situation des membres de la famille.

avoir soif	**avoir peur**	avoir sommeil	AVOIR FROID
avoir faim	AVOIR ENVIE DE	*avoir besoin de*	*avoir chaud*

Exemple Les Broussard vont boire quelque chose parce qu'ils **ont soif.**

1. Madame Broussard voudrait manger quelque chose aussi parce qu'elle _____.
2. Éric voudrait mettre un pull *(to put on a sweater)* parce qu'il _____.
3. Christine voudrait enlever *(to take off)* son pull parce qu'elle _____.
4. Monsieur Broussard voudrait faire la sieste *(to take a nap)* parce qu'il _____.
5. Anne va prendre un Orangina parce qu'elle _____ boire quelque chose de sucré *(sweet).*

E. Comment vont-ils en ville? Anne Landry parle des projets de sa famille pour aujourd'hui. Complétez ces phrases avec la forme convenable du verbe **prendre.**

Exemple   Papa _____ le bus pour aller acheter des livres.
                   Papa **prend** le bus pour aller acheter des livres.

1. Didier _____ sa voiture pour aller voir un film.
2. Les enfants _____ le bus pour aller nager.
3. Moi, je _____ ma voiture pour aller faire du shopping.
4. Mes parents _____ un taxi pour aller voir une exposition.
5. Mon mari et moi _____ la voiture pour aller dîner ensemble.

Maintenant, dites où chacun va et comment il y va.

Exemple   **Papa va à la librairie. Il y va en bus.**

> *la librairie*   LE MUSÉE   **le centre commercial**
> LE RESTAURANT   le cinéma   *la piscine*

F. Visitons La Nouvelle-Orléans! Une amie des Landry va visiter La Nouvelle-Orléans. Dites-lui *(Tell her)* de faire ou de ne pas faire ces choses. Utilisez l'impératif.

1. visiter le Vieux Carré
2. manger de la cuisine créole
3. prendre un café au Café Du Monde
4. rester à l'hôtel le soir
5. visiter la rue Bourbon

G. Des projets. Didier Landry parle de ce que tous les membres de sa famille vont faire aux dates indiquées. Complétez ses phrases logiquement.

Exemple   14/2 (Anne et moi) **Le 14 février, Anne et moi allons dîner au restaurant.**

La rue Bourbon

> *passer du temps en famille / avec des amis / seul(e)...*
> SORTIR AVEC DES AMIS   **inviter des amis à la maison**
> faire une boum *(to have a party)*   DÎNER AU RESTAURANT
> aller voir un défilé *(parade)*   *aller danser*
> RESTER À LA MAISON   ???

1. 25/12 (je)
2. 1/1 (nous)
3. 4/7 (les enfants)

Maintenant, demandez à votre partenaire ce qu'il/elle va probablement faire aux dates indiquées.

Exemple   14/2   —**Qu'est-ce que tu vas probablement faire le 14 février?**
                      —**Je vais sortir avec des amis. /**
                      Je ne vais rien faire de spécial.

LECTURE ET *composition*

Note. The vocabulary in this section does not appear in the end-of-chapter vocabulary lists and is meant for recognition only. You may wish to let students know in advance whether you intend to test them on this vocabulary.

Suggestions. Point out: **1.** Since Cajun French was not primarily a written language and was preserved in oral tradition, one sees a variety of spellings for some words. **2.** In Cajun French, using **après** before a verb is the equivalent of **être en train de...** *(to be . . . ing).* For example, **aprèvalser = après valser = être en train de valser.**

LECTURE: Cœur des Cajuns

Music is an integral part of life on the bayou. You are going to read the lyrics to the song **Cœur des Cajuns** *(Heart of the Cajuns)* by Bruce Daigrepont, in which he sees Cajun music as the expression of both the **joie de vivre** *(joy of living)* and the **chagrin de cœur** *(heartache)* of the Cajun people. Before reading the lyrics, do this exercise to make your reading easier.

Familles de mots. Servez-vous des mots donnés pour déterminer le sens des mots en caractères gras.

danser: *to dance* → **une danse:** *a* _____
chanter: *to sing* → **une chanson:** *a* _____
prier: *to pray* → **une prière:** *a* _____
valser: *to waltz* → **une valse:** *a* _____
vivre: *to live* → **une vie:** *a* _____

CŒUR DES CAJUNS

La joie de vivre, c'est dans l'accordéon,
La joie de vivre, c'est dans les belles chansons.
La musique c'est une tradition
Et c'est dans les cœurs de tous les Cajuns.

Chagrin de cœur, c'est dans l'accordéon,
Chagrin de cœur, c'est dans les belles chansons.
La musique c'est une tradition
Et c'est dans les cœurs de tous les Cajuns.

Dansez ensemble les vieux et les jeunes.
Priez ensemble les vieux et les jeunes.
La tradition c'est **pour tout quelques-uns**
Et c'est dans les cœurs de tous les Cajuns.

Un **'tit** bébé dans **les bras** de sa maman,
Aprévalser dans les bras de sa maman.
Il va apprendre la tradition
Et c'est dans les cœurs de tous les Cajuns.

La joie de vivre, c'est dans l'accordéon,
La joie de vivre, c'est dans les belles chansons.
La musique c'est une tradition
Et c'est dans les cœurs de tous les Cajuns.

Chagrin de cœur, c'est dans dans l'accordéon,
Chagrin de cœur, c'est dans les belles chansons.
La musique c'est une tradition
Et c'est dans les cœurs de tous les Cajuns.

by Bruce Daigrepont
(Bayou Pon Pon, ASCAP-Happy Valley Music, BMI)
from *Cœur Des Cajuns* on Rounder Records (#6026)

---

pour tout quelques-uns *for everyone* (regional)   **'tit = petit**   **les bras** *the arms*   **Aprévalser** *Waltzing* (regional)

Cœur des Cajuns. Lisez **Cœur des Cajuns** et complétez ces phrases.

1. La musique est une expression de la joie de vivre et aussi du _____.
2. La musique est une tradition qui se trouve dans les _____ de tous les Cajuns.
3. _____ est un instrument de musique populaire.
4. Les vieux et les jeunes vont danser, valser et _____ ensemble.

Composition

A. Organisez-vous. Faites une liste de tous les membres de votre famille et écrivez tous les mots que vous associez à chacun.

> **Exemple** **mon frère (grand, beau, les yeux marron, les cheveux châtains, 26 ans, aime parler, étudiant, habite à Seattle...)**
> **ma mère (petite, les cheveux noirs...)**

B. Rédaction: La famille. Écrivez une description détaillée de votre famille. Si vous êtes marié(e) ou divorcé(e), parlez de votre mari/femme, de vos enfants et de vos animaux. Sinon *(Otherwise),* parlez de vos parents, de vos frères et sœurs et de vos animaux.

C. Questions. Échangez votre rédaction avec un(e) camarade de classe. En lisant *(While reading)* sa rédaction, préparez cinq questions sur des aspects de sa famille dont *(about which)* il/elle ne parle pas.

D. Entretien. Posez les questions préparées dans *C. Questions* à votre partenaire.

E. Sa famille. Décrivez la famille de votre partenaire à la classe.

> **Exemple** **Dans sa famille, ils sont sept: sa mère, ses deux frères et ses trois sœurs. Ses frères et sœurs habitent avec sa mère. Sa mère s'appelle...**

F. Une seconde fois. Récrivez votre rédaction en répondant aux questions posées dans *D. Entretien.*

If you have access to SYSTÈME-D software, you will find the following phrases, vocabulary, grammar, and dictionary aids there.

Phrases: Describing people; Asking for information
Vocabulary: Family members; Personality; Hair colors; Animals
Grammar: Adjective position; Contractions with **à;** Possessive adjectives
Dictionary: The verb **aller**

Note. The vocabulary in this section does not appear in the end-of-chapter vocabulary lists and is meant for recognition only. You may wish to let students know in advance whether you intend to test them on this vocabulary.

LA LOUISIANE FRANCOPHONE ET

See the *Instructor's Resource Manual* for the video script and activities.

Additional information. In the 19th century, the French nobility began to refer to the settlers from Acadia as **Acadiens** or **Cadiens.** Non-French speakers changed the term to *Cajun.* Cajun is the only modern North American language and it has undergone many changes. There are regional varieties. Some typical Cajun words are: **frêmer** (fermer), **attendre** (entendre), **mouiller** (pleuvoir), **espérer** (attendre), **un char** (une voiture), **icitte** (ici).

Additional information. In 1713, when the British took control of Acadia, the Acadians, although promising not to help the French, refused to swear loyalty to England. Although the Acadians kept their promise not to aid the French, the British decided to deport them. In 1755, they tricked 400 Acadian men into going to a meeting. There the men were arrested and their families were told to report for deportation. They were all deported and, subsequently, so were those in other Acadian communities. Those who could, fled to Quebec and other nearby areas still under French control. By 1760 about 6,000 Acadians had been deported. The British decided to disperse the Acadians among the English colonies along the Atlantic coast, a few at each colony, in order to lessen their power and influence. The deportation was disastrous. Families were separated. People were lost. Many Acadians died en route. They were not welcomed by the colonies and had no land or work. Some were sent to England to prison camps. Some became indentured servants and worked with the slaves for many years. Those who returned to France also had no way to make a living and lived in poverty. Some were lured to Saint-Domingue, now Haiti, by false promises of farmland, where again many died or lived in poverty. In 1763, Louisiana became part of Spain and small numbers of Acadians began to move there and establish farms along the Mississippi. Spain needed settlers and offered to transport Acadians to Louisiana for free. In 1785, 2,000 Acadians left France for Louisiana. Many others followed. It had taken the Acadians thirty years of hardship to find a new home!

Les francophones en Louisiane ne sont pas tous **originaires d'une seule** culture. Leurs origines sont **nombreuses et variées.**

Les Créoles sont d'origine française, d'origine africaine, d'origine européenne ou d'origine mixte.

Certains Créoles sont les descendants des **premiers colons** français et européens. Ces premiers colons **étaient souvent issus** de l'aristocratie ou de **la haute bourgeoisie.** En grande partie, ces premiers colons **se sont installés** dans la région de La Nouvelle-Orléans. D'autres sont les descendants d'immigrés français **venus** en Louisiane pour **échapper** aux campagnes militaires de Napoléon.

D'autres Créoles sont les descendants **des esclaves** ou des immigrés **des îles caraïbes, surtout** de Saint-Domingue (aujourd'hui Haïti), **la plupart d'entre eux venus pendant** la Révolte des Esclaves ou pour échapper à la révolution à Saint-Domingue.

Par contre, les Cadiens d'aujourd'hui sont les descendants des Acadiens, **expulsés** du Canada **par** les Anglais au 18e **siècle.** (Le mot *cajun* **est dérivé du mot** *acadien.)*

Les variations dans la langue française **parlée** en Louisiane sont aussi **dues à un mélange.** Le français parlé en Louisiane est dérivé du français parlé du 16e au 18e siècles par les Français, les Acadiens, les Créoles français et les Créoles africains des Antilles. **On y retrouve** aussi des mots anglais, africains et espagnols.

Grâce à l'inaccessibilité de la région, les francophones en Louisiane restent **isolés** pendant plus de 200 ans. Ils conservent leur héritage et le français reste dominant dans **le sud** de la Louisiane **jusqu'à la fin** du 19e siècle. C'est à la fin du 19e siècle que le contact avec le monde extérieur est **facilité** et **amène** plus d'anglophones dans la région. En 1916, l'état de Louisiane **exige que la scolarité soit faite** en anglais et l'anglais **devient** la langue prédominante chez les jeunes.

L'usage du français en Louisiane continue à **diminuer** jusqu'en 1968 quand l'état **crée** le Conseil pour le Développement du Français en Louisiane (CODOFIL) et un **fort** mouvement pour la préservation, le développement et la protection de la langue et de la culture françaises **surgit.**

Voici quelques dates importantes dans l'histoire de la Louisiane francophone.

1604	Les Français **fondent** l'Acadie, aujourd'hui **la Nouvelle-Écosse,** le Nouveau-Brunswick et l'Île-du-Prince-Édouard.
1682	La France prend possession de la Louisiane.
1713	Les Anglais prennent possession de l'Acadie par le traité d'Utrecht.
1718	La Nouvelle-Orléans est fondée par Jean-Baptiste Le Moyne de Bienville.
1755	Les Anglais commencent à expulser les Français de l'Acadie.

originaires d'une seule descendants of a single   **nombreuses et variées** numerous and varied   **premiers colons** first settlers   **étaient souvent issus** often came from   **la haute bourgeoisie** the upper middle class   **se sont installés** settled   **venus** who came   **échapper** to escape   **des esclaves** of slaves   **des îles des Caraïbes** from the Caribbean islands   **surtout** especially   **la plupart d'entre eux venus** the majority of whom came   **pendant** during   **Par contre** On the other hand   **expulsés par** thrown out by   **siècle** century   **est dérivé du mot** is derived from the word   **parlée** spoken   **dues à un mélange** due to a mixture   **On y retrouve** One finds in it   **Grâce à** Thanks to   **isolés** isolated   **le sud** the south   **jusqu'à** until   **la fin** the end   **facilité** facilitated   **amène** brings   **exige que la scolarité soit faite** requires that education be done   **devient** becomes   **diminuer** to diminish   **crée** creates   **fort** strong   **surgit** surges, arises   **fondent** found   **la Nouvelle-Écosse** Nova Scotia

LA RÉGION CADIENNE

1764–1785	Les Acadiens arrivent en Louisiane.
1789	**Des vagues de** Français arrivent de France pendant la Révolution française.
1791	Plus de 10 000 Créoles arrivent de Saint-Domingue (aujourd'hui Haïti) pendant la Révolte des Esclaves.
1803	Les États-Unis achètent la Louisiane à la France pour $15 000 000.
1809	5 700 Créoles **fuient** la révolution à Saint-Domingue (aujourd'hui Haïti) et **viennent s'installer** en Louisiane.
1812	La Louisiane devient un état des États-Unis.
1880–1905	Les francophones en Louisiane commencent à avoir plus de contact avec les anglophones après **l'arrivée du chemin de fer,** de l'électricité et de l'industrie pétrolière.
1916	Le Comité d'éducation de l'état exige que la scolarité soit faite en anglais.
1968	L'état **établit** CODOFIL (Conseil pour le Développement du Français en Louisiane).
1971	**L'assemblée législative crée** la région d'Acadiana, **comprenant** 22 **paroisses** francophones.
1974	Un amendement est **ajouté** à la Constitution de l'état qui encourage la préservation de la culture française en Louisiane.
1981	Les écoles commencent à établir des programmes d'immersion en Louisiane.
1999	**Tout l'état fête** trois cents ans d'héritage français en Louisiane à la Francofête.

When Louisiana became Spanish after the Treaty of Paris in 1763, the new governor welcomed colonists and many new settlers arrived, especially from the Canary Islands and Ireland. Many German and African settlers also arrived in the 19th century. The ethnic variety of the region is evident in the family names of its current residents. In addition to such names as Thibodaux, Landry, Broussard, and Boudreaux, one finds Miguez, Domingue (Dominguez), Rodrique (Rodriquez), Reed, McGee, Himel (Himmel), Oubre (Huber), Schexnayder, and Sénégal.

visit http://horizons.heinle.com

À discuter.

1. La Louisiane est le seul état aux États-Unis qui a créé une agence pour la défense de la langue et de la culture d'une minorité. Que pensez-vous de cette action?

2. L'Acadiana a une culture unique. Comment est-ce que cette région de la Louisiane diffère du reste des états du sud des États-Unis?

3. Tandis qu'un (*Whereas a*) grand nombre des habitants du sud des États-Unis ont un héritage religieux protestant fondamentaliste, les Cadiens proviennent d'une tradition catholique. Comment est-ce que cette différence de tradition religeuse se manifeste (*is reflected*) dans d'autres différences culturelles?

4. Dans certaines écoles élémentaires (*elementary schools*) en Louisiane, il y a des programmes d'immersion en français. À votre avis (*In your opinion*), à quel âge est-ce qu'on devrait (*should*) commencer à étudier une autre langue? Est-il plus important d'étudier une autre langue si on est d'une famille d'une autre tradition linguistique?

Des vagues de *Waves of* **fuient** *flee* **viennent s'installer** *come settle* **l'arrivée de** *the arrival of* **le chemin de fer** *the railroad* **établit** *establishes* **L'assemblée législative crée** *The legislature creates* **comprenant** *including* **une paroisse** *a parish* (*equivalent to a county*) **ajouté** *added* **Tout l'état** *The whole state* **fête** *celebrates*

VOCABULAIRE

COMPÉTENCE 1

Describing your family

LA FAMILLE

un beau-frère / une belle sœur	a brother-in-law / a sister-in-law
un beau-père / une belle-mère	a stepfather, a father-in-law / a stepmother, a mother-in-law
un(e) cousin(e)	a cousin
un(e) enfant	a child
un fils / une fille	a son / a daughter
un frère / une sœur	a brother / a sister
un garçon / une fille	a boy / a girl
des grands-parents / un grand-père / une grand-mère	grandparents / a grandfather / a grandmother
un mari / une femme	a husband / a wife
un neveu (pl des neveux) / une nièce	a nephew / a niece
un oncle / une tante	an uncle / an aunt
des parents / un père / une mère	parents / a father / a mother

NOMS FÉMININS

une barbe	a beard
des lunettes	glasses
une moustache	a mustache
une photo	a photo
des vacances	vacation

ADJECTIFS

âgé(e)	old
blond(e)	blonde
brun(e)	brown (with hair and eyes)
châtain	light to medium brown (with hair)
court(e)	short
long(ue)	long
mi-longs	shoulder-length (with hair)
mort(e)	dead
noir(e)	black, very dark brown (with eyes)
roux / rousse	red (with hair)

EXPRESSIONS VERBALES

avoir besoin de	to need
avoir chaud / froid	to be hot / cold
avoir envie de	to feel like, to want
avoir faim / soif	to be hungry / thirsty
avoir l'air...	to look . . . , to seem . . .
avoir les cheveux / les yeux...	to have . . . hair / eyes
avoir l'intention de	to intend to
avoir peur (de)	to be afraid (of)
avoir raison / tort	to be right / wrong
avoir sommeil	to be sleepy
Comment s'appelle-t-il/elle?	What is his/her name?
Il/Elle s'appelle...	His/Her name is . . .
porter	to wear, to carry
Quel âge a... ?	How old is . . . ?
avoir... ans	to be . . . years old
Vous êtes combien dans votre famille?	How many people are there in your family?
Nous sommes...	There are . . . of us.

DIVERS

de taille moyenne	of medium height
encore	still
environ	about
La Nouvelle-Orléans	New Orleans

COMPÉTENCE 2

Saying where you go in your free time

NOMS MASCULINS

un bar	a bar
un centre commercial	a shopping mall
un concert	a concert
un festival	a festival
un magasin	a store
un musée	a museum
un orchestre	an orchestra, a band
un parc	a park
les projets	plans
le temps libre	free time
un théâtre	a theater

NOMS FÉMININS

une activité	an activity
la confiance	confidence
la cuisine	cooking, cuisine
une église	a church
une exposition	an exhibit
une librairie	a bookstore
la musique zydeco	zydeco music
la patience	patience
une piscine	a swimming pool
une région	a region
une spécialité	a specialty

EXPRESSIONS VERBALES

acheter	to buy
aie, ayons, ayez	have, let's have, have
aller (à)	to go (to)
connaître	to know, to get to know, to be acquainted/familiar with
faire du shopping	to go shopping
pouvoir	can, may, to be able
prendre un bain de soleil	to sunbathe
retrouver	to meet
servir	to serve
sois, soyons, soyez	be, let's be, be
trouver	to find

DIVERS

bonne idée	good idea
cadien(ne)	Cajun
calme	calm
Ça te dit?	How does that sound?
culturel(le)	cultural
de plein air	outdoor
de temps en temps	from time to time
extra	great
on	one, people, they, we
On... ?	Shall we . . . ?, How about . . . ?
on dit que	they say that
on s'amuse bien	one has a good time
plutôt	rather, instead
pour	in order to
sage	good, well-behaved
tous les soirs	every evening
y	there

COMPÉTENCE 3

NOMS MASCULINS

un anniversaire	a birthday
le folklore	folklore

NOMS FÉMININS

une fête	a holiday
la soirée	the evening

EXPRESSIONS VERBALES

aller voir	to go see, to visit (a person)
boire	to drink
faire des projets	to make plans
faire un tour	to take a tour, to go for a ride
partir	to go away, to leave
quitter	to leave
rentrer	to return, to go back (home)
visiter	to visit (a place)

LES DATES

En quelle année?	In what year?
En quel mois?	In what month?
Quelle est la date?	What is the date?
C'est le premier (deux, trois...)	It's the first (second, third . . .)
janvier / février / mars / avril / mai / juin / juillet / août / septembre / octobre / novembre / décembre	January / February / March / April / May / June / July / August / September / October / November / December

EXPRESSIONS ADVERBIALES

ce matin	this morning
ce mois-ci	this month
ce soir	tonight, this evening
cet après-midi	this afternoon
cette année	this year
cette semaine	this week
ce week-end	this weekend
d'abord	first
demain matin / après-midi / soir	tomorrow morning / afternoon / evening
ensuite	then, next
l'année prochaine	next year
la semaine prochaine	next week
le mois prochain	next month
le week-end prochain	next weekend
lundi (mardi) prochain	next Monday (Tuesday)
plus tard	later
puis	then
tard	late
tôt	early

DIVERS

célèbre	famous
génial(e) (mpl geniaux)	great
régional(e) (mpl régionaux)	regional
le Vieux Carré	the French Quarter

COMPÉTENCE 4

NOMS MASCULINS

un (auto)bus	a bus
un (auto)car	a bus
un avion	a plane
un bateau	a boat
le métro	the subway
un moyen de transport	a means of transportation
un taxi	a cab, a taxi
un train	a train
un vélo	a bike
un voyage	a trip

EXPRESSIONS VERBALES

aller à pied / en vélo / en (auto)car / en (auto)bus / en avion / en bateau / en métro / en taxi / en train / en voiture	to go on foot / by bike / by bus / by bus / by plane / by boat / by subway / by taxi / by train / by car
apprendre	to learn
comprendre	to understand
louer	to rent
prendre	to take, to have (with food and drinks)

DIVERS

Ça prend combien de temps?	How long does it take?
Ça prend...	It takes . . .
pas plus	no more
prêt(e)	ready

Branchez-vous sur le français

FRENCH FOR BUSINESS

As the world economy becomes more and more competitive, the ability to speak a foreign language will help assure your success in the business world. Knowledge of French can help owners of small businesses and self-employed individuals expand their markets in Canada, Europe, and Africa. If French-speaking clients feel free to call and ask you about your product or inquire about an order in their own language, while your chief competitor requires them to struggle with their questions in English, whom do you think they will want to call? By speaking French, you make it easier for them to buy your products.

Knowing French will also increase your chances of being hired by international companies with offices in Europe, Africa, or Canada. Over 750 American companies (Mobil Oil, IBM, Newsweek Magazine, Microsoft, and Hyatt Hotels, to name a few) do business in France alone, not to mention those with offices in other francophone countries around the globe. You will have an additional advantage when seeking employment with the many companies from francophone countries with offices in the United States (Michelin, Dannon, Bic, etc.). If you wish to work with an international corporation, you should consider specializing not only in French, but also in international finance and banking, international business, international economics, international communications and journalism, or in a scientific or technical field.

Banque d'Amérique du Canada

One of the best ways to gain insight into working abroad and to get experience is to do an internship. Internships often open the door to permanent employment after graduation. Some interns are accepted on a volunteer basis, whereas others are paid a stipend. Many large American companies offer internships in foreign countries. To get information about such internships, write directly to companies related to your field of study that do business abroad. Be sure to express your career goals, explain how your goals are related to their business, and state why you are interested in working abroad.

To find a list of American businesses with offices in francophone countries, check the geographical index of the *Directory of Corporate Affiliations*, found in many libraries.

La filiale d'Union Carbide, France

DOSSIER: **Patricia Fossi**

Interviewer: *Quelle est votre profession et où est-ce que vous travaillez?*

Patricia: Je travaille dans le marketing pour **une maison d'édition** du Massachusetts.

Interviewer: *Pourquoi est-ce que le français est **utile** dans votre profession?*

Patricia: Le français est important surtout parce que la maison d'édition a plusieurs **succursales** à l'étranger et aussi en France.

Interviewer: *Y a-t-il une situation particulière où le français vous a aidée dans votre travail?*

Patricia: Il y avait un **rédacteur en chef** dans notre succursale en France qui ne parlait pas beaucoup l'anglais et **j'ai pu** travailler avec **lui** uniquement parce que je parle français. Nous avons aussi des **réunions de vente** à Montréal.

Interviewer: *Quelles recommandations **pouvez-vous** faire à un(e) étudiant(e) qui voudrait travailler au **niveau** international?*

Patricia: Au niveau international, il est très important de parler une ou même **plusieurs** langues étrangères pour **pouvoir** bien communiquer avec ses collègues ou avec les gens avec qui on **essaie** d'établir une relation. Il est aussi important d'avoir des **connaissances** de la culture du pays avec lequel **vous aurez** des relations. **Il faut** pouvoir discuter de **l'actualité**, des événements sociaux, politiques ou autres, pour ne pas **paraître** ignorant aux yeux des gens du pays.

DOSSIER: **Eric Scott**

Interviewer: *Quelle est votre profession?*

Eric: Je suis musicien. Je voudrais **devenir** musicien professionnel et **obtenir** un contrat avec une maison de disques.

Interviewer: *Pourquoi est-ce que le français est utile dans votre profession?*

Eric: Récemment, au festival South by Southwest à Austin, dans le Texas, **j'ai rencontré** la représentante d'une grande maison de disques française **lors d'**une réunion. Je me suis approché d'elle par simple curiosité parce qu'elle parlait français avec d'autres personnes. Nous avons commencé à parler français et **grâce à** cette conversation, elle a décidé de venir écouter mon groupe jouer dans un club. Quand nous avons fini de jouer, elle est venue nous parler et nous dire qu'elle avait beaucoup aimé notre musique, notre style et notre technique. Depuis, nous avons

parlé avec d'autres représentants de cette maison de disques, et nous sommes **en train de** discuter un contrat pour aller jouer de la musique dans divers pays d'Europe—en France, en Hollande et en Italie.

Interviewer: *Quelles recommandations pouvez-vous faire à un(e) étudiant(e) qui voudrait travailler au niveau international?*

Eric: Apprenez une langue étrangère! Apprenez le français! Il ne faut jamais sous-estimer l'utilité du français. Vos connaissances en français peuvent vous être utiles à tout moment!

---

une maison d'édition *a publishing company* **utile** *useful* **une succursale** *a branch office* **un rédacteur (une rédactrice) en chef** *an editor-in-chief* **j'ai pu** *I was able to* **lui** *him* **une réunion de vente** *a sales meeting* **pouvez-vous** *can you* **un niveau** *a level* **plusieurs** *several* **pouvoir** *to be able* **essaie (essayer to try)** **des connaissances** (f) *knowledge* **vous aurez** *you will have* **Il faut** *One must* **l'actualité** (f) *current events* **paraître** *to seem* **devenir** *to become* **obtenir** *to obtain* **j'ai rencontré** *I met* **lors de** *at (the time of)* **grâce à** *thanks to* **en train de** *in the process of*

La Tour Eiffel

Robert Delaunay (1885–1941)
1910–1911
Basel Kunstmuseum
Giraudon/Art Resource, New York

Between 1909 and 1911, Delaunay produced a series of thirty cubist paintings of the Eiffel Tower. To Delaunay, the Eiffel Tower symbolized modernity. It also provided him an opportunity to explore on canvas the way light distorts form and color.

À Paris

LA FRANCE (LA RÉPUBLIQUE FRANÇAISE)

SUPERFICIE: 549 000 kilomètres carrés

POPULATION: 60 186 000 (les Français)

CAPITALE: Paris

INDUSTRIES PRINCIPALES: aéronautique, agriculture, industries manufacturières, secteur des services, technologie, tourisme

Les projets

COMPÉTENCE

1 **Deciding what to wear and buying clothes**

Les vêtements
Avoiding repetition
Les pronoms **le, la, l'** et **les**
Stratégies et lecture
Using the sequence of events to make logical guesses
Qu'est-ce qu'elle fait?

2 **Discussing the weather and what to do**

Le temps et les projets
Talking about the weather and what you do
Le verbe **faire** et les expressions pour décrire le temps
Talking about activities
Les expressions avec **faire** et l'expression **ne... rien**

3 **Saying what you did**

Le week-end dernier
Saying what you did
Le passé composé avec **avoir**
Telling when you did something
Les expressions qui désignent le passé

4 **Telling where you went**

Je suis parti(e) en week-end
Telling where you went
Le passé composé avec **être**
Reprise
Talking about activities and making plans

Lecture et composition **Les week-ends des Français**

Comparaisons culturelles **Les passe-temps**

La France

TRANSPARENCY: Map-2

La France a une grande diversité géographique. Il y a...

des plaines

des montagnes

des plages de sable

des rochers escarpés

À deviner!

Est-ce que vous connaissez un peu la France? Lisez les renseignements donnés à la page 168 et regardez **la carte** de la France à **la fin** du livre. Ensuite, répondez à ces questions. (Si vous ne **savez** pas, **devinez!**)

1. La France a **à peu près** la même **superficie** que...
   a. l'Alaska   b. le Texas   c. la Louisiane
2. Regardez la carte de la France. **À cause de** sa forme, on appelle la France...
   a. le Pentagone   b. l'Octogone   c. l'Hexagone
3. Nommez les huit pays et les quatre masses d'eau qui bordent la France.
4. Nommez cinq **chaînes et massifs montagneux** qui se trouvent en France. **Lequel** ne forme pas de frontière entre la France et un autre pays?
5. Nommez sept **fleuves** ou rivières en France. Lequel **traverse** Paris?
6. Paris est la capitale de la France. Nommez deux autres villes importantes.
7. La France est un centre important de commerce, d'industrie et de technologie. L'agriculture est aussi très importante et _____ de la population française habite à la campagne.
   a. 25%   b. 50%   c. 75%

---

la carte *the map*   **la fin** *the end*   **savez (savoir** *to know)*   **deviner** *to guess*   **à peu près** *about*   **la superficie** *the area*   **À cause de** *Because of*   **chaînes et massifs montagneux** *mountain ranges*   **Lequel** *Which one*   **un fleuve** *a large river*   **traverser** *to cross*

La République française **comprend** aussi la Corse; quatre départements **d'outre-mer** (les DOM), la Guadeloupe, la Martinique, la Guyane française et la Réunion; quatre territoires d'outre-mer (les TOM), la Nouvelle-Calédonie, la Polynésie française, Wallis-et-Futuna et les Terres australes et antarctiques françaises; et deux collectivités territoriales (les CT), Mayotte et Saint-Pierre-et-Miquelon.

Regardez la carte du **monde au début du livre** pour répondre à cette question.

TRANSPARENCIES: Map-1a, Map-1b

8. Où sont ces DOM-TOM?

la Guyane française
les Antilles (la Guadeloupe et la Martinique)
la Polynésie française
Mayotte
les Terres australes et antarctiques françaises (TAAF)

a. dans la mer des Caraïbes près de l'Amérique centrale
b. en Antarctique
c. près de l'Afrique
d. dans l'océan Pacifique
e. en Amérique du sud

La Guadeloupe

La Polynésie française

comprendre *to include* **d'outre-mer** *overseas* **le monde** *the world* **au début du livre** *at the beginning of the book*

VOCABULAIRE SUPPLÉMENTAIRE

D'AUTRES VÊTEMENTS

un blouson *a windbreaker, a jacket*
une écharpe *a winter scarf*
un foulard *a dress scarf*
des gants *(m) gloves*
un gilet *a vest, a cardigan*
des hauts talons *(m) high heels*
un tailleur *a woman's suit*

DES BIJOUX *(m) JEWELRY*

une bague *a ring*
des boucles d'oreille *(f) earrings*
un bracelet
un collier *a necklace*

DES SOUS-VÊTEMENTS *UNDERWEAR*

une chemise de nuit *a nightgown*
un collant *pantyhose*
une combinaison *a slip*
un pyjama *pajamas*
un slip *briefs, panties*
un soutien-gorge *a bra*

Suggestion. Have students say what they know about French fashion or name famous designers and indicate which ones are French.

Warm-up activity. Have students describe their best friend (physical appearance, hair and eye color, personality traits) and say where he/she likes to go and what he/she likes to do.

TRANSPARENCIES: 5-1A, 5-1B

Supplemental activities. A. Name articles of clothing and have students say: **1.** whether they are usually **pour les hommes, pour les femmes,** or **pour les deux 2.** if they are wearing each one today. **B.** Name a clothing item and have students name another item they usually wear with it. EXEMPLE des chaussures **des chaussettes 1.** un jean **2.** un pantalon **3.** une jupe **4.** une cravate **5.** des sandales **6.** des bottes **7.** un parapluie **8.** un pull

Les vêtements

Paris est sans doute le centre **mondial** de **la haute couture.** Et vous? Est-ce que **la mode** est importante pour vous?

Qu'est-ce que vous **mettez** pour aller en cours? pour sortir le soir?

Je mets souvent...   Je mets rarement...

un jean   un short   un pantalon et une ceinture   une jupe

un pull   un polo ou un tee-shirt   une chemise et une cravate   un chemisier

un survêtement   une robe   un costume   des chaussures, des chaussettes, des bottes ou des sandales

un anorak   un imperméable   un manteau   un maillot de bain ou un bikini et un chapeau ou une casquette

Est-ce que vous portez aussi... ?

un parapluie   un sac ou un portefeuille   une montre   des lunettes *(f)* de soleil

---

mondial(e) *world (adj)*   **la haute couture** *designer fashion*   **la mode** *fashion*   **mettez (mettre** *to put, to put on)*

Alice Pérez, **femme d'affaires** américaine **travaillant** à Paris, cherche un nouveau maillot de bain. Elle entre dans un magasin.

LA VENDEUSE:	Bonjour, madame. **Je peux vous aider?**
ALICE:	Je cherche un maillot de bain.
LA VENDEUSE:	**Quelle taille faites-vous?**
ALICE:	**Je fais du** 42.
LA VENDEUSE:	Nous avons ces maillots-ci. Ils sont très jolis et ils sont **en solde.**
ALICE:	J'aime bien ce maillot noir. **Je peux l'essayer?**
LA VENDEUSE:	Bien sûr, madame. **La cabine d'essayage** est **par ici.**

Alice sort de la cabine d'essayage.

LA VENDEUSE:	Alors, qu'en pensez-vous?
ALICE:	**Il me plaît** beaucoup. Il **coûte** combien?
LA VENDEUSE:	**Voyons,** c'est 65 euros.
ALICE:	C'est bien. Alors, je **le** prends.

A. Et vous? Regardez les illustrations à la page précédente. Dites si vous mettez ou portez souvent chaque chose.

Exemple **Je mets souvent (rarement) un jean. /**
Je ne mets jamais de jean.

B. Préférences. Complétez les phrases suivantes pour exprimer vos préférences.

1. J'aime acheter mes vêtements *en solde / dans les meilleurs magasins / ???.*
2. Si quelque chose me plaît, je préfère l'essayer *dans le magasin / à la maison.*
3. Pour sortir le soir, je mets souvent *un jean / un pantalon / ???.*
4. Quand je voyage en voiture, je mets souvent *un jean / ???.*
5. Quand je vais à la plage *(beach),* je mets *un short / ???.*
6. Pour aller en cours, je mets *un pantalon / ???.*
7. Quand je reste à la maison, je mets souvent *un jean / ???.*
8. Je ne mets presque jamais *de short / ???.*

C. Faisons du shopping! Avec un(e) partenaire, changez la conversation entre Alice et la vendeuse comme indiqué.

1. Alice wants to buy a blouse.
2. Alice wants to buy a sweater for her husband. He wears a size 41. (Naturally, she is not going to try it on!) You will need the expressions **C'est pour mon mari. / Quelle taille fait-il? / Il fait du...**
3. You are buying a sweater for a friend or family member. Change the conversation to make it true for you.

N O T E
Culturelle

Notez que les tailles en France ne sont pas les mêmes qu'aux USA.

Robes et chemisiers

USA	FRANCE
8	38
10	40
12	42
14	44
16	46

Chemises hommes

USA	FRANCE
15	38
15 ½	39
16	40
16 ½	41
17	42

Supplemental activities. A. Bring several articles of clothing to class. Bring two of each item (i.e., two ties). Review the forms **ce, cet, cette,** and **ces** and have students say which of each pair of items they prefer. **(Je préfère cette cravate-là.)** (You may prefer to do a similar activity with pictures of clothing cut out of catalogs.) Then have students indicate their preference by color, rather than with **ce/cet/cette/ces. (Je préfère la cravate rouge et noire.) B.** Have students look around the room and pick a classmate to describe. They should jot down what he/she is wearing, then describe his/her clothing to the class, without looking. The class will guess who is being described. **(Il/Elle porte un jean noir et...)**

---

une femme d'affaires (un homme d'affaires) *a businesswoman (a businessman)* **travaillant** *working* **une vendeuse (un vendeur)** *a salesclerk* **Je peux vous aider?** *Can I help you?* **Quelle taille faites-vous?** *What size do you wear?* **Je fais du...** *I wear size . . .* **en solde** *on sale* **Je peux l'essayer? (essayer)** *Can I try it on? (to try, to try on)* **La cabine d'essayage** *The fitting room* **par ici** *this way* **Il me plaît. (plaire)** *I like it. / It pleases me. (to please)* **coûter** *to cost* **Voyons** *Let's see* **le (l')** *it*

Avoiding repetition: *Les pronoms le, la, l' et les*

Use the direct object pronouns **le, la, l'**, and **les** to replace a person, animal, or thing that is the direct object of the verb. Use **le** *(him, it)* to replace masculine singular nouns and **la** *(her, it)* to replace feminine singular nouns. **Les** *(Them)* replaces all plural nouns. **Le** and **la** become **l'** when the following word begins with a vowel sound.

	BEFORE A CONSONANT SOUND	BEFORE A VOWEL SOUND
him, it (masculine)	le	l'
her, it (feminine)	la	l'
them	les	les

— Tu prends ce maillot?   — *Are you taking this bathing suit?*
— Oui, je **le** prends.   — *Yes, I'm taking **it**.*

— Tu achètes cette chemise?   — *Are you buying this shirt?*
— Oui, je **l'**achète.   — *Yes, I'm buying **it**.*

— Tu achètes ces bottes?   — *Are you buying these boots?*
— Oui, je **les** achète.   — *Yes, I'm buying **them**.*

Like **y**, these pronouns are generally placed *immediately* before the verb. They go before the infinitive if there is one. If not, they go before the conjugated verb. In the negative, the pronoun remains *immediately* before the conjugated verb or the infinitive.

— Tu aimes cette chemise? Tu vas acheter cette chemise?
— Oui, je **l'**aime bien. Je vais **l'**acheter.

— Tu aimes ces bottes? Tu vas acheter ces bottes?
— Non, je ne **les** aime pas. Je ne vais pas **les** acheter.

Follow-up for A. Au magasin de vêtements. Avez-vous ces choses avec vous aujourd'hui? **EXEMPLE** Est-ce que vous avez votre livre de français? **Oui, je l'ai. / Non, je ne l'ai pas.** Est-ce que vous avez vos devoirs (votre cahier, vos livres pour vos autres cours, votre vélo, votre voiture, les questions du prochain examen)?

Quick-reference answers for B. À Paris. 1. la cathédrale Notre-Dame 2. le Louvre 3. le jardin des Tuileries 4. la place de la Concorde 5. la Seine

Follow-up for B. À Paris. Put these adjectives on the board or a transparency: excellent, joli, embêtant, agréable, petit, mauvais, bon, horrible, laid, sympa, ennuyeux, super. Comment trouvez-vous ces endroits (places) dans votre ville? Utilisez le pronom le, la, l' ou les. **EXEMPLE** les parcs **Je les trouve jolis.** 1. les restaurants 2. l'université 3. les théâtres 4. votre quartier 5. les activités culturelles 6. votre chambre

A. Au magasin de vêtements. Beaucoup de personnes sont au magasin de vêtements. Complétez ce que chacun dit par le pronom convenable (**le, la, l', les**).

1. J'aime ce maillot de bain. Je peux _____ essayer?
2. J'aime ces bottes. Je _____ prends.
3. Je n'aime pas ce bikini. Je ne _____ prends pas.
4. Comment trouves-tu cette robe? Voudrais-tu _____ essayer?
5. Je n'aime pas cet anorak. Je ne vais pas _____ prendre.
6. Regarde cette belle chemise! Je _____ trouve super!
7. Tu aimes ces lunettes? Tu vas _____ acheter?

B. À Paris. Dites si vous reconnaissez *(recognize)* ces sites parisiens. Utilisez **Je reconnais...** *(I recognize . . .)* et le pronom convenable (**le, la, l', les**).

Exemple   Cette avenue?
                **Oui, je la reconnais. C'est les Champs-Élysées. /
                Non, je ne la reconnais pas.**

Cette avenue?

1. Cette cathédrale?

2. Ce musée?

3. Ce parc?

4. Cette place?

5. Ce fleuve *(river)*?

C. Intentions. Un(e) ami(e) voudrait savoir ce que vous allez faire avec les choses suivantes. Répondez avec un pronom complément d'objet direct (**le, la, l', les**) et un verbe logique. Jouez les deux rôles avec un(e) partenaire.

> **Exemple**   ce disque compact
> — **Qu'est-ce que tu vas faire avec ce disque compact?**
> — **Je vais l'écouter.**

1. ces cassettes	**4.** ce vin	**7.** ces bottes
2. cette vidéo	**5.** cette chemise	**8.** cette eau minérale
3. ce sandwich	**6.** ce livre	**9.** ces frites

écouter
MANGER   acheter
regarder   *lire*
BOIRE   mettre

D. Préférences. Un ami vous pose des questions. Répondez à ses questions, en remplaçant les mots en italique par le pronom convenable.

> **Exemple**   — J'invite souvent *mes amis* à la maison. Et toi?
> — **Moi aussi, je les invite souvent à la maison. /**
> **Moi non, je ne les invite pas souvent à la maison.**

1. Je regarde souvent *la télé* le week-end. Et toi?
2. J'invite souvent *mes parents* à la maison. Et toi?
3. Je trouve *mon quartier* très agréable. Et toi?
4. Je trouve *mes cours* plutôt difficiles. Et toi?
5. Ce soir, je vais préparer *le prochain examen de français.* Et toi?
6. Ce week-end, je vais voir *mes parents.*
7. Samedi soir, je vais faire *mes devoirs.* Et toi?
8. Dimanche, je vais regarder *la télé.* Et toi?

E. Entretien. Interviewez votre partenaire. Utilisez un pronom complément d'objet direct dans vos réponses.

1. Vas-tu voir tes parents ce week-end? Invites-tu souvent tes amis chez toi? Où est-ce que tu préfères retrouver tes amis?
2. Chez toi, dans quelle pièce est-ce que tu préfères regarder la télé? écouter la chaîne stéréo? faire tes devoirs? passer ton temps libre?
3. Est-ce que tu achètes tes vêtements au centre commercial? Dans quel magasin est-ce que tu achètes tes vêtements le plus souvent?

Stratégies et lecture:
Using the sequence of events to make logical guesses

You can often guess the meaning of unfamiliar verbs in a narrative by imagining what the logical order of actions would be. For example, if you take the bus, you usually wait for the bus first, and you have to get on the bus before you get off. Learn to read a whole paragraph, rather than one word at a time. Notice that the prefix **re-** means that an action in a sequence is done again, as it can be in English *(do* and *redo, read* and *reread).*

Use the sequence of events in this passage to guess the meaning of the boldfaced words.

> Alice ouvre une enveloppe. Elle **sort** une feuille de papier de l'enveloppe. Elle **lit** les instructions sur la feuille mais elle ne comprend pas. Alors, elle **relit** les instructions et elle **remet** la feuille de papier dans l'enveloppe.
>
> Alice **attend** l'autobus devant son appartement. Quand il arrive, elle **monte** dedans, et elle **descend** quand elle arrive à sa destination. Elle entre dans un café et commande un café au lait. Elle **boit** son café, **paie l'addition** et **repart.**
>
> Elle entre dans une station de métro et elle achète un ticket **au guichet,** mais elle ne **prend** pas le métro.
>
> Elle **s'arrête** devant un magasin de vêtements où elle admire une jolie robe bleue dans **la vitrine.** Elle entre dans le magasin et demande **le prix** de la robe.

Prepositions can indicate relationships between actions. **Pour** means *in order to* when it is followed by a verb. **Sans,** meaning *without,* can also be followed by an infinitive. What do these sentences mean?

> Alice demande l'addition au serveur. Elle quitte le café **sans boire** son café. Elle entre dans le magasin de vêtements **pour demander** le prix d'une robe mais elle quitte le magasin **sans essayer** la robe.

Suggestion. You may wish to point out that you say **ticket de métro,** but **billet d'entrée** to say *ticket* for most entertainment events.

Suggestion for *A. En ordre logique.* Give students time to prepare.

A. En ordre logique.
Mettez les activités suivantes d'Alice dans l'ordre logique. La première et la dernière *(last)* sont indiquées.

— Elle va vers la porte.
— Elle lit les instructions sur la feuille de papier.
_1_ Alice voit une enveloppe sur la table.
— Elle sort une feuille de papier de l'enveloppe.
— Elle prend l'enveloppe.
— Elle ouvre l'enveloppe.
_8_ Elle ouvre la porte et elle sort.
— Elle remet la feuille dans l'enveloppe.

B. Quel verbe?
Complétez ces phrases logiquement.

1. Alice quitte l'appartement sans... (boire son café, ouvrir la porte).
2. Elle prend l'autobus pour... (rester à la maison, aller en ville).
3. Elle retrouve des amis pour... (passer le week-end seule, aller au cinéma).
4. Elle va au guichet pour... (acheter des tickets, boire une bière).
5. Après, elle va au café avec des amis pour... (boire quelque chose, danser).
6. Elle rentre à la maison sans... (quitter le café, prendre l'autobus).

Qu'est-ce qu'elle fait?

Seule dans son appartement, Alice Pérez a l'air un peu agitée. Elle prend l'enveloppe qui se trouve sur la table et en sort une feuille de papier. Elle lit les instructions et remet la feuille dans l'enveloppe. Elle met une robe, un chapeau et des lunettes de soleil. Elle met l'enveloppe dans son sac et quitte son appartement.

Alice entre dans un café où elle commande un café au lait et ensuite, demande l'addition. Quand l'addition arrive, elle la prend et paie le garçon. Elle ouvre l'enveloppe, relit les instructions, met l'addition dans l'enveloppe et quitte le café sans boire son café au lait. C'est bien bizarre! Pourquoi a-t-elle l'air si agitée?

Ensuite, Alice va à la station de métro. Elle entre dans la station et sans regarder le plan, va au guichet et demande un ticket. Quand on lui donne son ticket, elle le met dans l'enveloppe, remonte l'escalier et quitte la station de métro. Pourquoi achète-t-elle un ticket sans prendre le métro? Tout cela est fort bizarre!

Elle continue sa route jusqu'à ce qu'elle arrive devant un magasin de vêtements. Elle regarde une robe bleue qui se trouve dans la vitrine. Elle entre dans le magasin et demande le prix de la robe. Elle marque le prix de la robe sur une feuille de papier et met la feuille de papier dans l'enveloppe. Ensuite, elle sort du magasin sans même demander d'essayer la robe!

Elle va au coin de la rue pour attendre l'autobus. Quand il arrive, elle monte dans l'autobus et elle descend à l'université. Elle semble plus calme maintenant. Qu'est-ce qui se passe? Pourquoi a-t-elle fait tout ça?

A. Comprenez-vous? Est-ce qu'Alice fait ces choses?

1. Alice ouvre une enveloppe, en sort une feuille de papier et lit des instructions.
2. Elle quitte son appartement et va directement à l'université en autobus.
3. Au café, elle retrouve une amie et elles commandent un café au lait.
4. Elle achète un ticket de métro mais elle ne prend pas le métro.

B. Maintenant... c'est à vous! Est-ce que vous trouvez les actions d'Alice plutôt bizarres? Qu'est-ce qu'elle fait? Imaginez une explication.

Est-ce qu'elle...
est agent de police ou détective privé?
souffre d'amnésie?
travaille pour la CIA?

est espionne comme James Bond?
collectionne des souvenirs de Paris?
fait un exercice pour son cours de français?

Suggestion for *B. Maintenant... c'est à vous!* Have students cover up the response at the bottom of the page and vote on which explanation they think is true. Then, have one student read the correct explanation at the bottom of the page to the class.

Réponse:
Il y a une explication simple et logique! Alice suit *(is taking)* un cours de français pour étrangers à Paris. Ses devoirs, dans l'enveloppe, consistent à prouver au professeur qu'elle est capable de commander quelque chose à boire au café et d'acheter des vêtements et un ticket de métro. Elle doit rapporter *(must bring back)* l'addition, le ticket de métro et le prix de la robe dans la vitrine à son professeur.

COMPÉTENCE 2

Discussing the weather and what to do

Le temps et les projets

Quelquefois les projets **dépendent du temps qu'il fait.**

Et chez vous? **Quel temps fait-il** aujourd'hui?

Il fait froid.   Il fait frais.   Il fait chaud.   Il fait beau.   Il fait mauvais.

Il fait du soleil.   Il fait du vent.   Il pleut.   Il neige.

Quelle **saison** préférez-vous? Qu'est-ce que vous faites **pendant** cette saison?

Je préfère **l'été** *(m)*. En été...   Je préfère l'automne *(m)*. En automne...

Je vais à la plage.
Je fais du bateau et du ski nautique.

Je reste à la maison.
Je ne fais rien.

Je préfère **l'hiver** *(m)*. En hiver...   Je préfère **le printemps.** Au printemps...

Je vais à la montagne.
Je fais du ski.

Je vais au parc.
Je fais des promenades *(f)*.

 C'est vendredi après-midi et Alice Pérez et son fils, Éric, parlent de leurs projets pour le week-end.

ALICE: Demain, **s'il** fait beau, je vais faire une promenade au jardin du Luxembourg. J'ai besoin de faire de l'exercice. Et toi, qu'est-ce que tu as l'intention de faire?
ÉRIC: S'il fait beau, j'ai envie de faire du jogging.
ALICE: Et s'il fait mauvais?
ÉRIC: S'il fait mauvais, je vais rester à la maison et louer une vidéo.

―――――
dépendre de *to depend on*   **le temps qu'il fait** *what the weather is like*   **Quel temps fait-il?** *What is the weather like?*   **la saison** *the season*   **pendant** *during, for*   **l'été** *(m) summer*   **Je ne fais rien. (ne... rien)** *I do nothing. (nothing)*   **l'hiver** *(m) winter*   **le printemps** *spring*   **s'il (si)** *if it (if)*

A. Et chez vous? Chez vous, en quelle saison fait-il le temps indiqué?

Exemple   Il neige.
**Ici, il neige souvent (quelquefois) en hiver. /
Ici, il ne neige jamais.**

1. Il fait frais.
2. Il fait du vent.
3. Il fait mauvais.
4. Il fait très beau.
5. Il fait froid.
6. Il fait chaud.
7. Il fait du soleil.
8. Il pleut.
9. Il neige.

B. Quel temps fait-il? Utilisez deux expressions pour décrire le temps pour chaque saison. Dites aussi quels vêtements on met d'habitude.

Exemple   en automne
Ici, en automne, il fait frais et il fait du vent. On met souvent un jean et un pull.

1. en hiver
2. en été
3. en automne
4. au printemps

C. Et vous? Complétez les phrases.

1. Quand il fait beau, j'aime...
2. S'il fait beau ce week-end, j'ai l'intention de...
3. Quand il pleut, je préfère...
4. Quand il fait chaud, j'aime...
5. Quand il neige, j'aime...
6. Au printemps, j'aime...
7. Je ne fais rien quand...
8. À la montagne, j'aime...
9. À la plage, j'aime...
10. Aujourd'hui, il fait... et j'ai envie de...

D. Entretien. Posez ces questions à votre partenaire.

1. Aimes-tu l'été? Aimes-tu nager? faire du bateau? faire du ski nautique? aller à la plage?
2. Aimes-tu l'hiver? Aimes-tu aller à la montagne? faire des promenades? faire du ski?
3. Qu'est-ce que tu aimes faire quand il fait chaud? quand il fait froid? quand il pleut? Quand est-ce que tu ne fais rien?
4. Quelle saison préfères-tu? Qu'est-ce que tu aimes faire pendant cette saison?
5. Quel temps fait-il aujourd'hui? Qu'est-ce que tu as envie de faire? Qu'est-ce que tu vas faire après les cours?

E. Faisons des projets. Avec un(e) partenaire, changez la conversation entre Alice et Éric comme indiqué.

1. If it is nice tomorrow, Alice is going to go shopping. Éric is going to take a walk if it is nice, and go to the movies if the weather is bad.
2. It's Friday afternoon and you and a classmate are talking about your plans for the weekend. Change the conversation to make it true for you.

Suggestion for the conversation. Set the scene. Point out that the word **si** means *if* and explain that it only elides in front of **il**. Introduce the expression **faire de l'exercice.** Have students listen to the conversation with books closed for the answers to these questions. 1. Qu'est-ce qu'Alice voudrait faire demain s'il fait beau? Pourquoi? 2. Qu'est-ce qu'Éric voudrait faire s'il fait beau? Et s'il fait mauvais? Then have students read along while you play the conversation again.

Supplemental activities. A. Quelle description du temps n'est pas logique par rapport aux autres? (You may wish to put the statements on the board.) 1. Il fait chaud, il fait du soleil et il neige. 2. Il neige, il fait chaud et il fait froid. 3. Il fait du soleil, il pleut et il fait mauvais. 4. Il fait mauvais, il fait beau et il fait du soleil. 5. Il pleut, il fait du soleil et il fait beau. **B.** Quel temps fait-il si on porte ces vêtements ou ces choses? un short, un pull, des lunettes de soleil, des bottes, un parapluie, un bikini, un survêtement, un imperméable, un manteau, un maillot de bain, un anorak **C.** Qu'est-ce qu'on met quand... 1. il fait chaud? 2. il fait froid? 3. il pleut? 4. il neige? 5. il fait du soleil?

1. How do you say *to make* or *to do* in French? What are the forms of the verb **faire?** How is the **vous** form of this verb different from the usual **vous** form of a verb?
2. How do you say *What is the weather like? The weather is nice. It is raining. It is snowing.*
3. How do you say *What is the weather going to be like? It is going to be nice. It is going to rain. It is going to snow.*

Talking about the weather and what you do:
Le verbe faire et les expressions pour décrire le temps

To say *to make* or *to do*, use the irregular verb **faire.**

FAIRE (to make, to do)	
je **fais**	nous **faisons**
tu **fais**	vous **faites**
il/elle/on **fait**	ils/elles **font**

— Qu'est-ce que tu fais ce soir?
— Je reste à la maison. Je fais mes devoirs.

— Qu'est-ce que Papa fait dans la cuisine?
— Il fait des sandwichs.

Faire is also used in many, but not all, weather expressions. To tell what the weather is going to be like, you also need the infinitives **pleuvoir** *(to rain)* and **neiger** *(to snow).*

Quel temps fait-il?	Quel temps va-t-il faire?
Il fait beau / mauvais / chaud...	Il va faire beau / mauvais / chaud...
Il neige.	Il va neiger.
Il pleut.	Il va pleuvoir.

You may also want to use these words when talking about the weather.

la neige   *the snow*   la pluie   *the rain*

Warm-up for *A. Quel temps fait-il?* C'est logique? **1.** Je voudrais faire une promenade parce qu'il pleut. **2.** Mes parents font du bateau quand il neige. **3.** Je préfère jouer au tennis quand il ne fait pas très chaud. **4.** Je fais toujours du ski quand il pleut. **5.** Quand il fait mauvais, je reste à la maison et je ne fais rien. **6.** Mon ami(e) va aller au parc après les cours parce qu'il fait beau.

A. Quel temps fait-il?
Quel temps fait-il aujourd'hui dans ces régions françaises? Utilisez au moins deux expressions pour chaque photo.

Dans les Alpes

En Normandie

En Guadeloupe

Follow-ups for *A. Quel temps fait-il?* **A.** Have students guess what season it is in each photo. **B.** Have students locate the pictured places on maps. Ask students: Est-ce que vous voudriez faire un voyage dans les Alpes? en Normandie? en Guadeloupe? Est-ce qu'on va en Guadeloupe ou dans les Alpes pour faire du bateau? pour faire du ski? Qu'est-ce qu'on fait dans les Alpes? en Normandie? en Guadeloupe?

B. Quel temps va-t-il faire? Vous travaillez dans une agence de voyages. Des clients vont visiter les endroits indiqués dans l'exercice précédent et ils voudraient savoir quel temps il va faire. Jouez les rôles avec un(e) partenaire.

Exemple   — **Quel temps va-t-il faire dans les Alpes?**
                — **Il va...**

Follow-up for B. Quel temps va-t-il faire? Have students imagine that they are going to visit these places. Refer them to the vocabulary and supplemental vocabulary on pages 172 and 178. Tell them to say what the weather is going to be like, what clothing they are going to need, and what they are going to do.

C. Le prof. Complétez les questions avec la forme convenable du verbe **faire**. Ensuite, posez les questions à votre professeur.

Suggestion for C. Le prof. Have one student play the role of the professor and answer the questions as he/she thinks you would.

1. Qu'est-ce que vous _____ après le cours de français?
2. Qu'est-ce que vous _____ le week-end avec vos amis?
3. Est-ce que vous _____ souvent la cuisine ensemble?
4. Est-ce que vos amis _____ bien la cuisine française?

Maintenant, posez les mêmes questions à un(e) partenaire. Utilisez **tu**.

Exemple   — **Qu'est-ce que tu fais après le cours de français?**
                — **Je rentre chez moi.**

D. Qu'est-ce qu'on fait? Dites si ces personnes font les choses indiquées.

1. Moi, je... (faire beaucoup de choses seul[e], faire souvent des bêtises *[stupid things]*)
2. Mon meilleur ami (Ma meilleure amie)... (faire beaucoup de choses pour moi, faire beaucoup de choses le week-end)
3. En cours, nous... (faire beaucoup d'exercices oraux, faire beaucoup d'exercices ensemble)
4. Mes parents... (faire beaucoup de choses le week-end, faire beaucoup de choses avec moi)

E. Entretien. Interviewez votre partenaire.

Suggestion for E. Entretien. Point out that questions asked with **faire** are often answered with another verb.

1. Est-ce que tu fais beaucoup de choses le week-end? Qu'est-ce que tu aimes faire le vendredi soir? le samedi soir? Qu'est-ce que tu fais d'habitude le dimanche matin?
2. Quel temps va-t-il faire ce week-end? Qu'est-ce que tu as envie de faire s'il fait beau? Qu'est-ce que tu as l'intention de faire s'il fait mauvais? Qu'est-ce que tu as besoin de faire?
3. Ton meilleur ami (Ta meilleure amie) et toi, quand est-ce que vous aimez sortir ensemble? Qu'est-ce que vous faites souvent ensemble?

F. Qu'est-ce que vous allez faire?
Un(e) ami(e) passe le week-end chez vous. Vous parlez de ce que vous allez faire. Préparez la scène avec un(e) autre étudiant(e). Décidez ce que vous allez faire s'il fait beau et s'il fait mauvais.

Aimez-vous faire du snowboarding?

1. How do you say *to go camping? to ride a bike? to do housework? to do laundry?*

2. In the expressions with **faire**, which articles change to **de (d')** in a negative sentence? Which do not?

3. How do you say that you are doing *nothing*?

VOCABULAIRE SUPPLÉMENTAIRE

aller à la chasse *to go hunting*

aller à la pêche *to go fishing*

faire de l'alpinisme *to go mountain climbing*

faire de la varappe *to go rock climbing*

faire du patin (à glace) *to go (ice-) skating*

faire de la marche à pied *to go walking*

faire du cheval *to go horseback riding*

faire de la musculation *to do weight training*

faire une randonnée (des randonnées) *to go for a hike (hiking)*

faire du roller *to go rollerblading*

Supplemental activity. Quel temps fait-il quand vous faites ces choses? **1.** Je fais du ski quand... **2.** Je fais du jardinage quand... **3.** J'aime aller à la piscine quand... **4.** J'aime ne rien faire quand... **5.** Je n'aime pas rester à la maison quand... **6.** Je n'aime pas faire de sport quand...

Warm-ups for *A. On en a besoin ou envie?* A. C'est amusant ou ennuyeux? faire une promenade, faire le ménage, faire les devoirs, faire du shopping, faire la cuisine, faire du vélo, faire du jogging, faire des courses **B.** Have students write five things they do or do not intend to do this weekend. Collect the sheets of paper and read them aloud, having the class guess who wrote each one. EXEMPLE J'ai l'intention de faire la lessive. / Je n'ai pas l'intention de faire de voyage.

Talking about activities:
Les expressions avec faire et l'expression ne... rien

The verb **faire** can have a variety of meanings in idiomatic expressions.

LE SPORT ET LES DISTRACTIONS	LE MÉNAGE ET LES COURSES
faire de l'exercice	faire le ménage *(to do housework)*
faire du bateau	faire des courses *(to run errands)*
faire du camping	faire du jardinage *(to garden)*
faire du jogging	faire du shopping
faire du ski (nautique)	faire la cuisine *(to cook)*
faire du sport (du tennis, du hockey...)	faire la lessive *(to do laundry)*
faire du vélo	faire la vaisselle *(to do the dishes)*
faire une promenade	
faire un voyage *(to take a trip)*	

The **un, une, des, du, de la,** and **de l'** in the expressions with **faire** become **de (d')** when the verb is negated. The definite article (**le, la, l', les**) does not change.

Je fais **une** promenade.   Je ne fais pas **de** promenade.

BUT   Nous faisons **la** cuisine.   Nous ne faisons pas **la** cuisine.

To say *nothing*, use **ne... rien.** This expression can be the subject or object of the verb, or the object of a preposition.

Rien n'est en solde.   Je **ne** fais **rien.**   Il **ne** parle de **rien.**

When negating an infinitive, place both parts of the negative expression before the infinitive.

Je préfère **ne pas** sortir ce soir. Je voudrais **ne rien** faire.

A. On en a besoin ou envie? Commencez ces phrases logiquement par **J'ai envie de...** ou **J'ai besoin de...**

Exemples   faire des devoirs
J'ai besoin de faire des devoirs.

faire un voyage
J'ai envie de faire un voyage.

1. faire des courses
2. faire du bateau
3. faire la lessive
4. faire de l'exercice
5. faire le ménage
6. rester à la maison et ne rien faire

Avez-vous envie de faire du camping?

B. Préférences. Demandez à votre partenaire quelles sont ses préférences.

Exemple　faire des courses / faire du shopping
— **Préfères-tu faire des courses ou faire du shopping?**
— **Je préfère faire des courses / faire du shopping. /**
　J'aime les deux.

1. faire du jogging / faire des promenades
2. faire la cuisine / faire la vaisselle
3. faire du bateau / faire du camping
4. faire du sport / faire du jardinage
5. faire le ménage / faire la lessive
6. faire du ski / faire du ski nautique

C. Que font-ils? Éric parle avec sa mère des projets de la famille pour aujourd'hui. Complétez ses phrases avec une expression avec **faire**.

1. Maman, est-ce que tu... ce matin?

2. Michel et toi, vous... cet après-midi.

3. Papa...

4. Papa et toi, vous...

5. Cathy et moi, nous...

6. Moi, je...

D. Conseils. Donnez des conseils à un ami. Utilisez l'impératif.

> *faire le ménage*　louer une vidéo　FAIRE DU SHOPPING
> **???**　RESTER À LA MAISON　**faire du vélo**　FAIRE UNE PROMENADE
> **faire la cuisine**　*faire la lessive*　FAIRE TES DEVOIRS　ne rien faire

Exemple　— La vaisselle est sale.
— **Eh bien, fais la vaisselle!**

1. J'ai faim.
2. Tous mes vêtements sont sales.
3. J'ai envie de faire de l'exercice.
4. J'ai besoin d'acheter de nouveaux vêtements.
5. Mon appartement est très sale.
6. Je n'ai pas envie de sortir ce soir.
7. J'ai beaucoup de devoirs à faire ce soir!
8. Je voudrais voir un film mais je n'ai pas envie d'aller au cinéma.

Warm-up for B. Préférences. Write these activities on the board or a transparency: **faire du vélo, faire du ski, faire du sport, faire la cuisine, ne rien faire.** Tell students to list them in their order of preference. Then, give students the example and tell them to ask questions to determine the order of preference for their partner (or, if you prefer, one student may be selected for everyone to question). EXEMPLE – **Est-ce que tu préfères faire du vélo ou faire la cuisine? – Je préfère faire du vélo.**

Suggestion for B. Préférences. You may wish to supply the expression **Je n'aime ni l'un ni l'autre.**

Follow-ups for B. Préférences. A. Have students say how often they do each of the activities listed on the weekend. **(Je fais souvent des courses le week-end.)** B. Questions orales. 1. Aimez-vous faire du vélo? Faites-vous souvent du vélo? (Où? Avec qui?) 2. Est-ce que vous faites souvent du ski? (Où allez-vous pour faire du ski?) 3. Est-ce que vous aimez faire du sport? Quels sports préférez-vous? Quels sports sont très populaires ici? 4. Aimez-vous faire la cuisine? Quelle sorte de cuisine préférez-vous? Quelle cuisine est populaire ici? 5. Est-ce que vous aimez ne rien faire quelquefois? (Quand?)

Suggestion for D. Conseils. Remind students of the formation and use of the imperative and elicit the forms of the imperative of **faire** from students before beginning this activity.

Warm-up. Questions orales. **1.** Quel temps fait-il aujourd'hui? Qu'est-ce que vous aimez faire quand il fait... comme aujourd'hui? Est-ce qu'il fait souvent... ici? En quelle saison? Quelle saison préférez-vous? Pourquoi? **2.** Qu'est-ce qu'on met quand il fait... ? (Et quand il fait beau / mauvais / chaud / froid?) Qu'est-ce que vous portez aujourd'hui? Qu'est-ce que vous aimez porter pour aller en cours? **3.** Qu'est-ce que vous avez envie de faire aujourd'hui après les cours? Avez-vous besoin de faire le ménage? la lessive? la vaisselle? des courses?

COMPÉTENCE 3

Saying what you did

Note. The **passé composé** with **avoir** is taught in this *Compétence.* The **passé composé** with **être** is taught in the next *Compétence.* The expressions **je suis allé(e), je suis sorti(e), je suis resté(e),** and **je suis rentré(e)** are taught here as lexical items and as a preview for the next *Compétence,* although a brief explanation is given on p. 186.

Suggestions. A. Point out that the sentences on this page are in the past tense and ask students what they notice about the verbs. As a preview for the next *Compétence,* point out that the statements on the left have to do with going, coming, and staying, and that those on the right side tell what you did. Ask students what they notice about the structures used in the two categories. You may prefer to present the grammar on p. 186 at this time. **B.** Remind students of the use of **jusqu'à** to say *until.*

Supplemental activity. Quand est-ce qu'Alice a fait ces choses: samedi matin, samedi après-midi ou samedi soir? **1.** Elle est allée au cinéma. **2.** Elle est restée à la maison. **3.** Elle a vu un film. **4.** Elle a lu le journal. **5.** Elle a pris son petit déjeuner à la maison. **6.** Elle est allée en ville. **7.** Elle est sortie. **8.** Elle a mangé à la maison. **9.** Elle a déjeuné au restaurant. **10.** Elle a dormi jusqu'à dix heures.

Le week-end dernier

Alice parle de ses activités **samedi dernier.** Et vous?

Où est-ce que vous êtes allé(e)?   Qu'est-ce que vous avez fait?

Samedi matin...

je ne suis pas sortie, je suis restée chez moi.

J'ai dormi jusqu'à 10 heures.

J'ai **pris** mon **petit déjeuner.**

Samedi après-midi...

je suis allée en ville.

Je n'ai pas travaillé.

J'ai déjeuné au restaurant et j'ai bien mangé.

Samedi soir...

je suis sortie.

J'ai vu un film au cinéma.

J'ai retrouvé un ami au café.

je suis rentré(e).

J'ai lu le journal.

Je n'ai rien fait.

---

samedi dernier *last Saturday*   **Où est-ce que vous êtes allé(e)?** *Where did you go?*   **Qu'est-ce que vous avez fait?** *What did you do?*   **prendre son petit déjeuner** *to have breakfast*

C'est lundi et Alice parle avec un ami des activités du week-end dernier.

ALICE: Tu as passé un bon week-end?
EDGARD: Oui, génial. Samedi matin, j'ai préparé les cours et samedi après-midi, j'ai joué au foot avec des amis.
ALICE: Qu'est-ce que tu as fait samedi soir?
EDGARD: Je suis sorti. Je suis allé en boîte et j'ai beaucoup dansé.
ALICE: Et **hier**?
EDGARD: Hier matin, j'ai fait une promenade sur les Champs-Élysées où j'ai fait du shopping. Hier soir, je suis resté à la maison et j'ai regardé la télé.

Suggestion for the conversation. Set the scene and introduce the word **hier**. Have students listen to the conversation with books closed for the answers to these questions. **Vrai ou faux? 1.** Edgard a passé un bon week-end. **2.** Samedi, il est resté à la maison. **3.** Dimanche, il a préparé les cours. **4.** Dimanche soir, il a regardé la télé. Afterward, have students follow along in the book as you play the conversation again.

A. Activités logiques. Formez des phrases logiques. Complétez les phrases de la première colonne avec un choix logique de la deuxième colonne.

1. Je suis resté(e) au lit et...
2. J'ai retrouvé des amis au café où...
3. J'ai dîné au restaurant où...
4. Je suis allé(e) au cinéma où...
5. Je suis allé(e) en boîte où...
6. J'ai joué au tennis avec une amie mais...
7. Je suis allé(e) au parc où...

j'ai pris un verre.
j'ai dormi.
j'ai beaucoup dansé.
je n'ai pas gagné.
j'ai vu un film étranger.
j'ai très bien mangé.
j'ai fait une promenade.

Warm-up for A. Activités logiques. Lundi, Alice n'est pas sortie de l'appartement. Est-ce qu'elle a fait les choses suivantes? Répondez **peut-être** ou **non. 1.** Elle a passé la journée au lit. **2.** Elle a fait une promenade. **3.** Elle a parlé au téléphone. **4.** Elle a travaillé sur l'ordinateur. **5.** Elle a visité une exposition d'art. **6.** Elle a fait des courses en ville. **7.** Elle a dormi jusqu'à midi. **8.** Elle a regardé une vidéo. **9.** Elle a lu le journal. **10.** Elle a fait du vélo à la campagne.

B. Et vous? Complétez les phrases pour indiquer comment vous avez passé la journée hier.

1. J'ai dormi jusqu'à *8 heures / 10 heures / ???*.
2. J'ai pris le petit déjeuner *chez moi / au café / chez une amie / ???*. *[Je n'ai pas pris de petit déjeuner.]*
3. J'ai lu *le journal / un livre / ???*. *[Je n'ai rien lu.]*
4. *Je suis allé(e) / Je ne suis pas allé(e)* en cours.
5. J'ai déjeuné *chez moi / chez des amis / au restaurant / ???*. *[Je n'ai pas déjeuné.]*
6. *J'ai travaillé. / Je n'ai pas travaillé.*
7. J'ai dîné *chez moi / chez mes parents / dans un fast-food / ???*. *[Je n'ai pas dîné.]*
8. J'ai *beaucoup / peu* mangé. *[Je n'ai pas mangé.]*
9. Le soir, *je suis resté(e) chez moi / je suis sorti(e) / je n'ai rien fait / ???*.

C. Faisons des projets. Avec un(e) partenaire, changez la conversation entre Alice et Edgard comme indiqué.

1. Edgard asks Alice what she did last Saturday. *[Note: You know what she did by looking at the pictures on the preceding page.]*
2. It's Monday morning and you and a classmate are asking each other what you did last weekend. Change the conversation to make it true for you. *[Note: You may not know how to say everything you did. Pick two or three things that you know how to say or ask your professor for help.]*

hier *yesterday*

✓ *Pour vérifier*

1. The **passé composé** always has two parts. What are they called?
2. How do you form the past participle of most **-er** and **-ir** verbs? Which verbs that you know have irregular past participles?
3. How do you negate verbs in the **passé composé**?
4. In the **passé composé**, where do you place adverbs like **souvent** or **bien**?
5. What are the three possible English translations of **j'ai mangé**?

NOTE DE GRAMMAIRE

Some verbs expressing *going, coming,* and *staying,* such as **aller, sortir, rentrer,** and **rester,** have **être,** not **avoir,** as their auxiliary verb. You will learn about these in the next **Compétence.** For now, remember to use **je suis allé(e), je suis sorti(e), je suis resté(e),** and **je suis rentré(e)** if you want to say *I went, I went out, I stayed,* and *I returned.* (If you are female, add an extra **-e** to the past participle of these verbs, just as you did with adjectives.)

Note. There is additional practice on the **passé composé** with **avoir** in the next section (with expressions of past time), as well as in the next **Compétence,** where it is contrasted with the **passé composé** with **être.**

Suggestions. You may wish to point out that the past participles of **comprendre** (**compris**) and **apprendre** (**appris**) follow the pattern of **prendre,** and that most verbs ending in **-oir** and **-oire,** such as **voir** and **boire,** form their past participles in **-u.** Point out the pronunciation of **eu** as /y/.

Note. You may also wish to teach inversion questions in the **passé composé.**

Saying what you did: *Le passé composé avec avoir*

To say what someone did or what happened in the past, put the verb in the **passé composé.** The **passé composé** is always composed of two parts, the auxiliary verb and the past participle. The auxiliary verb, usually **avoir,** is conjugated to agree with the subject. Note how the past participle is formed for most verbs ending in **-er** or **-ir.**

PARLER → PARLÉ	
j'**ai parlé**	nous **avons parlé**
tu **as parlé**	vous **avez parlé**
il/elle/on **a parlé**	ils/elles **ont parlé**

DORMIR → DORMI	
j'**ai dormi**	nous **avons dormi**
tu **as dormi**	vous **avez dormi**
il/elle/on **a dormi**	ils/elles **ont dormi**

Many irregular verbs have irregular past participles that must be memorized.

avoir	j'ai eu, tu as eu...	être	j'ai été, tu as été...
il y a	il y a eu	faire	j'ai fait, tu as fait...
boire	j'ai bu, tu as bu...	écrire	j'ai écrit, tu as écrit...
lire	j'ai lu, tu as lu...	mettre	j'ai mis, tu as mis...
pleuvoir	il a plu	prendre	j'ai pris, tu as pris...
voir	j'ai vu, tu as vu...	apprendre	j'ai appris, tu as appris...
		comprendre	j'ai compris, tu as compris...

To talk about the weather in the past, use these expressions.

Quel temps a-t-il fait?
Il a fait beau / chaud / du soleil...
Il a plu.
Il a neigé.

In the negative, place the negative expression around the auxiliary verb.

— Est-ce que tu as travaillé hier?
— Non, je **n'**ai **pas** travaillé. Je **n'**ai **rien** fait.

Adverbs indicating how often (**toujours, souvent...**) and how well (**bien, mal, assez bien...**) are usually placed between the auxiliary verb and the past participle.

J'ai **bien** mangé. Ils ont **toujours** travaillé le week-end.

The **passé composé** can be translated in a variety of ways in English.

I took the bus.
I have taken the bus.
I did take the bus. J'ai pris l'autobus.

A. Et vous? Avez-vous fait ces choses hier?

Exemple   quitter la maison tôt
J'ai quitté la maison tôt hier. /
Je n'ai pas quitté la maison tôt hier.

1. passer la journée à la maison
2. être malade *(sick)*
3. prendre votre café au lit
4. lire le journal
5. faire des devoirs
6. mettre un jean et un tee-shirt
7. travailler
8. voir votre famille
9. préparer les cours
10. jouer au tennis

B. Devinez! Sur une feuille de papier, faites une liste de trois choses que vous avez faites samedi dernier. Les autres étudiants vont deviner *(to guess)* une des activités sur votre liste.

Suggestion for *B. Devinez!* Students may try to ask questions using verbs like **aller** and **sortir.** If so, elicit from them what the correct auxiliary verb must be and put examples on the board of questions with **aller, sortir, rester,** and **rentrer.**

???   faire les devoirs   *travailler*   JOUER AU...
PASSER LA JOURNÉE À LA MAISON   ???   louer une vidéo
danser   **dormir**   *dîner...*   lire...   ???
regarder la télé   PRENDRE UN VERRE   ???
préparer les cours   *faire une promenade*

Exemples   — **Est-ce que tu as écouté des disques compacts?**
— **Non, je n'ai pas écouté de disques compacts.**

— **Est-ce que tu as regardé la télé?**
— **Oui, j'ai regardé la télé.**

C. Entre amis. Demandez à votre partenaire s'il/si elle a fait ces choses avec son meilleur ami (sa meilleure amie) le week-end dernier.

Note for *C. Entre amis.* If you chose to teach inversion questions with the **passé composé,** you may wish to have students redo the questions in *C. Entre amis,* using inversion.

Exemple   déjeuner ensemble
— **Est-ce que vous avez déjeuné ensemble?**
— **Oui, nous avons déjeuné ensemble. /**
Non, nous n'avons pas déjeuné ensemble.

1. dîner ensemble
2. voir un film ensemble
3. faire une promenade ensemble
4. faire du sport ensemble
5. préparer les cours ensemble
6. faire du shopping ensemble
7. être ensemble toute la journée
8. louer une vidéo ensemble

Suggestion for *D. Un peu d'histoire.*
Have students prepare the sentences in groups or pairs. Encourage them to guess if they do not know the answers.

Quick-reference answers for *D. Un peu d'histoire.* **Pierre et Marie Curie** ont fait des travaux sur les effets de la radioactivité. **Les frères Lumière** ont fait le premier film. **Charles de Gaulle** a été président de la République française pendant les années cinquante et soixante. **Gustave Eiffel** a participé à la construction de la statue de la Liberté. **Simone de Beauvoir** a parlé de la situation de la femme. **Jacques Cousteau** a fait des voyages sous-marins. **Auguste Rodin et Camille Claudel** ont fait des sculptures.

Follow-up for *E. Qu'est-ce qu'ils ont fait?* Have students identify what the people in the illustrations are wearing and say what they wear in similar circumstances. (Students may need to refer to the *Vocabulaire supplémentaire* on p. 172.)

D. Un peu d'histoire. Quels Français célèbres de la colonne de gauche ont fait chacune des choses de la colonne de droite? Si vous n'êtes pas certain(e), devinez *(guess)*.

> **Exemples** **Pascal a étudié les mathématiques.**
> **Berlioz et Ravel ont composé des symphonies.**

Pascal...	participer à la construction de la statue de la Liberté
Berlioz et Ravel...	faire le premier film
Pierre et Marie Curie...	faire des sculptures
Les frères Lumière...	composer des symphonies
Charles de Gaulle...	étudier les mathématiques
Gustave Eiffel...	faire des voyages sous-marins
Simone de Beauvoir...	parler de la situation de la femme
Jacques Cousteau...	faire des travaux sur les effets de la radioactivité
Auguste Rodin et Camille Claudel...	être président de la République française pendant les années cinquante et soixante

E. Qu'est-ce qu'ils ont fait? Alice parle des activités récentes de sa famille. Complétez ses phrases.

> **Exemple** Hier, j'**ai lu.**

Hier, j'...

1. À Deauville, toute la famille...

2. Vendredi dernier, Vincent et moi...

3. À Chamonix, les enfants...

4. Hier, Vincent...

5. Ce matin, Vincent et Éric...

F. Quel temps a-t-il fait? Pour chaque dessin de l'activité précédente, dites le temps qu'il a fait ce jour-là.

> **Exemple** **Hier, il a fait mauvais. Il a plu.**

G. À Paris. Il y a beaucoup de choses à faire à Paris. Les gens sur ces photos ont visité Paris la semaine dernière. Imaginez ce qu'ils ont probablement fait.

Exemple **Ils ont visité le Quartier latin. Ils ont fait une promenade.**

Suggestion for *G. À Paris.* Have students think of as many activities as possible for each place. You may want to do this as a team competition to see which team can list the most activities.

acheter LIRE ??? REGARDER visiter

??? boire *faire une promenade* ??? *voir* PARLER

Le Quartier latin

Le musée d'Orsay

Le Forum des Halles

Les Champs-Élysées

Le bois de Boulogne

1. How do you say that you did something *yesterday? for two hours? last week? last year? three years ago? a few days ago? a long time ago?*

2. What do **déjà** and **ne... pas encore** mean? Where do you place them with a verb in the **passé composé**?

Suggestions. A. You may wish to point out the gender pattern in **un an / une année, un jour / une journée, un matin / une matinée,** and **un soir / une soirée. B.** Point out the use of **huit jours** to mean *one week* and **quinze jours** to mean *two weeks.* **C.** Point out the feminine form **dernière** and the use of the definite article with most of the expressions with **dernier (dernière).**

Supplemental activities. A. Est-ce que ces expressions évoquent **le passé** ou **le présent?** aujourd'hui, hier, hier soir, maintenant, la semaine dernière, l'année dernière **B.** Give students the following expressions in mixed order, on slips of paper or large cards. Have one student stand in front of the class and read his/her slip of paper. Form a timeline by having students read the expressions they have, one at a time, and place themselves to the left or right of the students already standing in front of the class, according to whether their expression is before or after the others. Have students hold up their cards: **il y a quelques minutes, il y a une heure, hier soir à dix heures, hier soir à six heures, hier après-midi, hier à midi, hier matin, il y a trois jours, le week-end dernier, vendredi dernier, jeudi dernier, mercredi dernier, mardi dernier, lundi dernier, le mois dernier, l'année dernière, il y a trois ans, il y a longtemps.** After the timeline is finished, have students read their slips of paper again to check that they are in order.

Telling when you did something:
Les expressions qui désignent le passé

The following expressions are useful when talking about the past.

hier (matin, après-midi)	*yesterday (morning, afternoon)*
hier soir	*last night, yesterday evening*
lundi (mardi...) dernier	*last Monday (Tuesday . . .)*
le week-end dernier	*last weekend*
la semaine dernière	*last week*
le mois dernier	*last month*
l'année dernière	*last year*
la dernière fois	*the last time*
récemment	*recently*
Pendant combien de temps?	*For how long?*
pendant deux heures (longtemps)	*for two hours (a long time)*
Il y a combien de temps?	*How long ago?*
il y a quelques secondes	*a few seconds*
(cinq minutes, trois jours, huit jours, quinze jours, cinq ans)	*(five minutes, three days, a week, two weeks, five years) ago*

Notice that you use the word **an** *(m)*, instead of **année** *(f)*, to say *year* after a number.

To talk about the past, it is also useful to know the expressions **déjà** *(already)* and **ne... pas encore** *(not yet)*. **Déjà** is placed between the auxiliary verb and the past participle. **Ne... pas encore** goes around the auxiliary verb.

Tu as **déjà** vu ce film?	*Have you **already** seen this movie?*
Non, je **n'**ai **pas encore** vu ce film.	*No, I **haven't** seen this movie **yet**.*

A. Et vous? Indiquez la dernière fois que vous avez fait les choses suivantes.

Exemple   dîner au restaurant
J'ai dîné au restaurant vendredi dernier. /
Je n'ai pas dîné au restaurant récemment.

1. voir un bon film
2. visiter un musée
3. faire du shopping
4. lire un bon livre
5. mettre une robe / un costume
6. être chez vos parents
7. jouer au volley
8. dormir toute la journée

Suggestion for A. Et vous? Ask follow-up questions after each answer. EXEMPLE **Avec qui est-ce que vous avez dîné? Est-ce que vous avez bien mangé? 1.** Quel film est-ce que vous avez vu? Quels autres films est-ce que vous avez vus récemment? **2.** Quel musée est-ce que vous avez visité? Avec qui? Vous avez vu des choses intéressantes? **3.** Qu'est-ce que vous avez acheté? Où? **4.** Quel livre est-ce que vous avez lu? Est-ce que vous avez aimé ce livre? **5.** Est-ce que vous aimez porter une robe / un costume? Est-ce que vous portez souvent une robe / un costume? Quels vêtements est-ce que vous aimez mettre? Quels vêtements est-ce que vous mettez souvent? **6.** Pendant combien de temps est-ce que vous avez été chez vos parents? Qu'est-ce que vous avez fait ensemble? **7.** Est-ce que vous avez joué au tennis récemment? Avec qui? Qui a gagné? Est-ce que vous avez nagé à la piscine récemment? **8.** Pendant combien d'heures est-ce que vous avez dormi?

B. Quand? Voilà le calendrier d'Alice. Quand est-ce qu'elle a fait les choses indiquées? Aujourd'hui, c'est le 14 novembre.

Follow-up for *B. Quand?* Vrai ou faux?
1. Nous avons eu un examen hier après-midi. **2.** Le cours a commencé il y a cinq minutes. **3.** Hier, nous avons été en cours pendant deux heures. **4.** Aujourd'hui, on a parlé français ensemble pour la première fois. **5.** Le semestre/trimestre a commencé il y a deux mois. **6.** Nous avons écouté des CD en cours la semaine dernière. **7.** Nous avons vu une vidéo le mois dernier.

il y a un mois

il y a six semaines

LE MOIS DERNIER

hier   **le week-end dernier**

mardi dernier

LA SEMAINE DERNIÈRE

il y a une semaine

Exemple   Alice a beaucoup travaillé **le mois dernier.**

1. Elle a dîné chez une amie…
2. Elle a visité le Louvre…
3. Elle a passé le week-end à Deauville…
4. Elle a fait du shopping…
5. Elle a passé *(took)* un examen…
6. Elle a préparé l'examen…

C. Entre amis. Complétez les phrases par quelque chose que vous avez fait récemment. Demandez à un(e) camarade de classe s'il/si elle a déjà fait la même chose. Il/Elle va répondre avec **déjà** ou **ne... pas encore.**

Exemple   —J'ai vu le film *Gone with the Wind* récemment. Et toi, est-ce que tu as déjà vu ce film?
                    —Oui, j'ai déjà vu ce film. /
                    Non, je n'ai pas encore vu ce film.

1. J'ai vu le film… récemment.
2. J'ai visité la ville de… récemment.
3. J'ai mangé au restaurant… récemment.
4. J'ai loué la vidéo… récemment.

D. Entretien. Interviewez votre partenaire.

1. Quel temps a-t-il fait le week-end dernier? Quels vêtements est-ce que tu as mis? Est-ce que tu as travaillé? Est-ce que tu as fait du sport? Jusqu'à quelle heure est-ce que tu as dormi samedi matin? Est-ce que tu as fait le ménage? la lessive? la vaisselle? des courses? Qu'est-ce que tu as fait dimanche?
2. Est-ce que tu as été malade *(sick)* récemment? Il y a combien de temps? Pendant combien de jours? Est-ce que tu as beaucoup dormi? Est-ce que tu as regardé la télé? Est-ce que tu as lu?
3. Quel film est-ce que tu as vu récemment? Est-ce que tu as aimé ce film? Quel film récent est-ce que tu n'as pas aimé?
4. Est-ce que tu as eu un accident de voiture récemment? Il y a combien de temps?

Follow-up for *D. Entretien.* Questions orales. **1.** Le cours a commencé il y a combien de minutes? **2.** Nous avons eu un examen il y a combien de jours (semaines)? **3.** Le semestre a commencé il y a combien de mois (semaines)? **4.** Nous avons commencé le *Chapitre 5* il y a combien de temps?

Supplemental activity. Have students write a paragraph telling what they did yesterday. Ask them to tell at least five things. To get them started, you may want to give them this sentence. **Hier, j'ai quitté la maison à… heures et je suis allé(e)…**

Je suis parti(e) en week-end

TRANSPARENCY: 5-4

La dernière fois que vous êtes parti(e) en week-end, où est-ce que vous êtes allé(e)? Qu'est-ce que vous avez fait?

Je suis allé(e)	à Denver. à New York. ???	**J'y suis allé(e)**	en avion. en train. en autocar. en voiture **(de location).**
Je suis parti(e)	le vendredi après-midi. le samedi matin. ???	**Je suis arrivé(e)**	le vendredi soir. le samedi après-midi. ???
Je suis descendu(e)	dans un hôtel. dans un camping. chez des amis. chez **des parents.**	**Je suis resté(e)**	**une nuit.** trois jours. le week-end.
Je suis allé(e)	à la plage. à un concert. dans un club.	**Je suis rentré(e)**	le dimanche soir. le lundi matin.

Alice et son amie Claire parlent d'un voyage qu'Alice a fait.

CLAIRE: Qu'est-ce que tu as fait le week-end dernier?
ALICE: J'ai pris le train pour aller à Deauville.
CLAIRE: Quand est-ce que tu es partie?
ALICE: Je suis partie samedi matin et je suis rentrée hier soir.
CLAIRE: Tu as trouvé un bon hôtel?
ALICE: Je suis descendue dans un petit hôtel confortable, pas trop loin de la plage.
CLAIRE: **Quelle chance!** Moi aussi, j'ai envie de visiter Deauville.

A. En week-end. Décrivez la dernière fois que vous êtes parti(e) en week-end.

1. Je suis allé(e) à (Chicago, ???).
2. J'y suis allé(e) (en avion, ???).
3. Je suis parti(e) (le vendredi soir, ???).
4. Je suis arrivé(e) (une heure, ???) plus tard.
5. Je suis descendu(e) (dans un hôtel, ???).
6. Je suis resté(e) (deux jours, ???).
7. Je suis allé(e) (en ville, ???).
8. Je suis rentré(e) (le lundi, ???).

de location *rental* **je suis descendu(e)** *I stayed* (**descendre [de / dans]** *to descend, to come down, to get off/out [of], to stay [at]*) **des parents** *relatives* **une nuit** *one night* **Quelle chance!** *What luck!*

B. Un tour de Paris.

Alice et sa famille adorent visiter Paris et la région parisienne. Regardez les photos et complétez les phrases avec une expression de la colonne de droite.

1. Vincent est allé à la Sainte-Chapelle pour...
2. Les enfants sont allés à Versailles pour...
3. Ils sont allés à Notre-Dame pour...
4. Ils sont allés au musée d'Orsay pour...
5. Ils sont allés au café sur les Champs-Élysées pour...
6. Alice est allée au bois de Boulogne pour...

voir une nouvelle exposition.
faire une promenade.
prendre un café.
voir son architecture gothique.
admirer les vitraux *(stained-glass windows)*.
visiter le château de Versailles.

Follow-up activities. A. Vous allez entendre une description de ce que Claire, l'amie d'Alice, a fait la semaine dernière. Pour chaque moment indiqué, dites si **elle est sortie** ou si **elle est restée à la maison. EXEMPLE** Samedi après-midi, elle est allée au cinéma. **Samedi après-midi, elle est sortie. 1.** Vendredi soir, elle a invité des amis chez elle. **2.** Samedi matin, elle a dormi jusqu'à 11 heures. **3.** Samedi à midi, elle a mangé dans un petit café du quartier. **4.** Samedi après-midi, elle a vu un film au cinéma. **5.** Samedi soir, son mari a préparé le dîner et ils ont mangé ensemble. **6.** Dimanche matin, elle est allée à l'église. **7.** Dimanche après-midi, elle a fait une promenade avec une amie. **B.** Indiquez quelle activité précède logiquement l'autre. **EXEMPLE** Les Pérez ont trouvé leur chambre. / Les Pérez sont arrivés à l'hôtel. **Les Pérez sont arrivés à l'hôtel. 1.** Ils sont allés en ville. / Ils sont rentrés à l'hôtel. **2.** Ils ont vu un bon film. / Ils sont arrivés au cinéma. **3.** Ils sont allés au parc. / Ils ont fait une promenade. **4.** Ils sont sortis. / Ils sont rentrés tard. **5.** Ils ont nagé pendant deux heures. / Ils sont allés à la piscine. **6.** Ils ont mangé. / Ils ont payé l'addition. **7.** Ils ont quitté l'hôtel. / Ils ont visité la ville.

La Sainte-Chapelle

Le château de Versailles

Le musée d'Orsay

Notre-Dame

Le bois de Boulogne

Les Champs-Élysées

C. On est parti en week-end.

Avec un(e) partenaire, changez la conversation entre Alice et Claire comme indiqué.

1. Alice went to Versailles. She left Friday morning and came back Saturday afternoon.
2. Alice took the plane to Nice. She left Monday morning and came back Friday evening. She stayed with a friend.
3. Your friend is asking about the last time you left town. Change the conversation to make it true for you.

1. What do you have to remember to do with the past participle of these verbs?

2. Where do you place the direct object pronouns and **y** in the **passé composé**?

Telling where you went: *Le passé composé avec être*

A few verbs have **être** as their auxiliary verb in the **passé composé.** The past participle of these verbs must agree with the subject in number and gender.

ALLER → ALLÉ	
je **suis allé(e)**	nous **sommes allé(e)s**
tu **es allé(e)**	vous **êtes allé(e)(s)**
il **est allé**	ils **sont allés**
elle **est allée**	elles **sont allées**
on **est allé**	

SORTIR → SORTI	
je **suis sorti(e)**	nous **sommes sorti(e)s**
tu **es sorti(e)**	vous **êtes sorti(e)(s)**
il **est sorti**	ils **sont sortis**
elle **est sortie**	elles **sont sorties**
on **est sorti**	

Here are some verbs that have **être** as their auxiliary verb.

aller	je suis allé(e)	*I went*
arriver	je suis arrivé(e)	*I arrived*
rester	je suis resté(e)	*I stayed, I remained*
entrer (dans)	je suis entré(e) (dans)	*I entered, I went in*
sortir (de)	je suis sorti(e) (de)	*I went/came out (of)*
partir (de)	je suis parti(e) (de)	*I left*
rentrer	je suis rentré(e)	*I came home, I returned*
retourner	je suis retourné(e)	*I returned, I went back*
monter (dans)	je suis monté(e) (dans)	*I went up, I got on/in*
descendre (de / dans)	je suis descendu(e) (de / dans)	*I came down, I got out/ off (of), I stayed (at)*
naître	je suis né(e)	*I was born*
mourir	il/elle est mort(e)	*he/she died*

Rentrer means *to return/go back home* (or to the place you are staying). Use **retourner** in most other cases. **Partir** means *to leave* as in *to go away.* It is the opposite of **arriver. Sortir** means *to leave* as in *to go out.* It is the opposite of **entrer** and **rentrer. Quitter** also means *to leave.* It takes **avoir** as its auxiliary verb and must have a direct object: **Elle a quitté la maison tôt.**

In the **passé composé,** the direct object pronouns and **y** are placed *immediately* before the auxiliary verb.

Je **l'**ai fait.   Je ne **l'**ai pas fait.
J'**y** suis allé(e).   Je n'**y** suis pas allé(e).

You know that the past participle agrees with the subject when the auxiliary verb is **être,** but not when it is **avoir.** When **avoir** is the auxiliary verb, the past participle agrees with the *direct object* of the verb, but only *when the object precedes the verb* in the sentence, as it does when you use the direct object pronouns **le, la, l',** and **les.**

Vincent a regardé **la télé.**   Il **l'**a regardé**e.**

 Prononciation: *Les verbes auxiliaires avoir et être*

As you practice when to use **avoir** and when to use **être** to form the **passé composé,** be careful to pronounce the forms of these auxiliary verbs distinctly.

tu as parlé / tu es parti(e)   il a parlé / il est parti   ils‿ont parlé / ils sont partis

Note. On may take the appropriate plural agreement when used to mean *we* (**on est sorti[e]s**).

Note. There is additional practice with the **passé composé** of verbs using both **avoir** and **être** as the auxiliary in the next section.

Note. In *Horizons,* emphasis is placed on the basic use and formation of the **passé composé.** Agreement of the past participle with a preceding direct object in the **passé composé** with **avoir** is presented here to give students the complete picture and to explain structures they may see later on. You may choose to give more or less emphasis to this concept, depending on the level of your students. If you want to supply additional practice with this structure, you may wish to put this exercise on the board or a transparency for students to do. **Replacez les mots en italique par le pronom convenable.** Faites attention à l'accord du participe passé. **1.** Hier matin, j'ai pris *mon petit déjeuner* à la maison. **2.** J'ai fait *mes devoirs de chimie.* **3.** Je n'ai pas lu *le journal.* **4.** L'après-midi, j'ai retrouvé *mes amis Rachid et Louise* au café. **5.** Nous avons fait *les devoirs de français* ensemble. **6.** Hier soir, j'ai regardé *la télé.* **7.** Hier, je n'ai pas fait *la lessive.*

Suggestions. A. Point out the use of **descendre dans** as *to stay at* and its past participle in **-u. B.** Remind students that most verbs ending in **-ir,** such as **sortir** and **partir,** have past participles ending in **-i.**

A. Qu'est-ce que vous avez fait? Parlez de la dernière fois que vous avez mangé au restaurant avec un(e) ami(e) ou avec des amis.

Exemple   je / sortir (avec qui?)
Je suis sorti(e) avec Thomas et Karima.

1. je / sortir (avec qui?)
2. je / partir de la maison (à quelle heure?)
3. nous / aller (à quel restaurant?)
4. nous / arriver au restaurant (vers quelle heure?)
5. nous / rester au restaurant (combien de temps?)
6. après le repas, nous / aller (où?)
7. je / rentrer (vers quelle heure?)
8. le lendemain *(the next day)* je / rester au lit (jusqu'à quelle heure?)

B. Tu es parti(e) en week-end? Parlez avec votre partenaire de la dernière fois qu'il/elle est parti(e) en week-end. Posez les questions indiquées. N'oubliez pas d'utiliser l'auxiliaire **avoir** avec les verbes **voyager** et **faire**.

Exemple   où / aller
— **Où est-ce que tu es allé(e)?**
— **Je suis allé(e) à Des Moines.**

1. quand / partir
2. avec qui / voyager
3. comment / y aller
4. quand / arriver
5. où / descendre
6. combien de temps / rester
7. que / faire
8. quand / rentrer

Follow-up for *B. Tu es parti(e) en week-end?* Demandez à votre partenaire s'il/si elle est allé(e) aux endroits *(places)* suivants récemment. Il/Elle va répondre en indiquant la dernière fois qu'il/elle y est allé(e). EXEMPLE au musée — **Tu es allé(e) au musée récemment? — Non, je n'y suis pas allé(e) récemment. / Oui, j'y suis allé(e) le mois dernier. 1.** au cinéma **2.** au théâtre **3.** à l'église **4.** chez des parents **5.** à un match de football américain

C. La journée de Cathy. Voilà les activités de Cathy, la fille d'Alice, le week-end dernier. Est-ce qu'elle a fait les choses indiquées?

Exemple   Samedi matin, Cathy...   (rester à la maison)
Samedi matin, Cathy est restée à la maison.

samedi matin

samedi après-midi

samedi soir

Samedi matin, Cathy (quitter la maison très tôt, rester au lit, aller déjeuner au café, sortir avec des amis)

Samedi après-midi, elle (rester à la maison, dormir, lire, aller à la bibliothèque, faire du ski nautique)

Samedi soir, Cathy et ses amis (sortir ensemble, aller au café, boire quelque chose, rentrer tôt)

D. Et toi? Demandez à votre partenaire s'il/si elle a fait chacune *(each)* des choses de l'exercice précédent le week-end dernier.

Exemple   — **Est-ce que tu es resté(e) à la maison samedi matin?**
— **Oui, je suis resté(e) à la maison.**

— **Samedi soir, tes amis et toi, est-ce que vous êtes sortis ensemble?**
— **Oui, nous sommes sortis ensemble.**

Après, décrivez le week-end de votre partenaire à la classe.

Exemple   **Rachel est restée à la maison samedi matin...**

Supplemental activity. Give these questions as dictation. **1.** Est-ce que vos parents sont allés à l'université? **2.** Est-ce qu'ils ont étudié le français? **3.** Est-ce qu'ils ont fait du sport? **4.** Est-ce que votre meilleur(e) ami(e) est entré(e) à l'université avec vous? **5.** Est-ce que cet(te) ami(e) a téléphoné récemment? **6.** Est-ce que cet(te) ami(e) est sorti(e) avec vous récemment?

Reprise: *Talking about activities and making plans*

In *Chapitre 5,* you practiced talking about clothing, weather, outings and activities, and saying where you went and what you did. Now you have a chance to review all that you learned.

Suggestions for A. Vos activités. Allow students time to prepare.

A. Vos activités. Comment passez-vous le temps? Répondez aux questions en remplaçant les mots en italique par le pronom convenable: **le, la, l'** ou **les.**

1. Est-ce que vous retrouvez souvent *vos camarades de classe* après les cours? Est-ce que vous faites souvent *les devoirs* ensemble? Est-ce que vous avez préparé *le cours* ensemble hier soir? Est-ce que vous allez préparer *le prochain examen de français* ensemble?
2. Est-ce que vous prenez *votre petit déjeuner* à la maison d'habitude? Est-ce que vous avez pris *le petit déjeuner* chez vous hier? Préférez-vous prendre *le petit déjeuner* chez vous, au restaurant, au café ou dans un fast-food?
3. Est-ce que vous invitez souvent *vos amis* chez vous? Est-ce que vous aimez regarder *la télé* ensemble? Est-ce que vous allez regarder *la télé* ce soir?

Suggestions for B. Quel temps fait-il? Have students use two or more expressions to describe the weather in each item. Have them name as many clothing items as possible for each picture. Have them say in what season your region's weather is like each season pictured.

Follow-up for B. Quel temps fait-il? Quels vêtements est-ce que ces personnes mettent dans les circonstances indiquées? **1.** Quand je vais à la plage, je mets... **2.** Pour aller travailler dans une banque, un homme met... et une femme met... **3.** Pour faire du jogging en décembre, on met... , mais en juin, on met... **4.** Pour sortir, mes amis et moi, nous mettons... **5.** Pour aller en cours, le professeur met...

B. Quel temps fait-il? Donnez deux expressions pour décrire le temps sur chaque illustration. Ensuite, dites quels vêtements on met ou ce qu'on porte dans ces circonstances.

Exemple **Il pleut et il fait mauvais. On met un imperméable et des bottes ou on porte un parapluie.**

1.    **2.**    **3.**

Warm-up for C. Qui fait ça? Write each **faire** expression on a slip of paper. A student pulls out a slip and has to illustrate the activity on the board for other students to identify. They may not speak or use any letters in the drawing. (You may prefer to have them mime the activities instead.)

C. Qui fait ça? Est-ce que ces gens font souvent les choses indiquées?

Exemple Mes amis **font souvent du jogging.** / Mes amis **ne font pas souvent de jogging.**

1.
Le week-end, mes parents...

2.
Mon meilleur ami (Ma meilleure amie)...

3.
Mes amis et moi...

4.

Ma mère...

5.

Moi, je...

6.

Mon père...

D. Récemment. Dites quand ces personnes ont fait les choses indiquées récemment.

Exemple   je (passer toute la journée à la maison)
**J'ai passé toute la journée à la maison il y a trois jours. /
Je n'ai pas passé toute la journée à la maison récemment. /
Je n'ai jamais passé toute la journée à la maison.**

1. je / rester au lit jusqu'à midi
2. je / travailler
3. je / rentrer tard
4. je / aller au cinéma
5. je / sortir avec des amis
6. mes amis et moi / sortir ensemble
7. nous / manger ensemble
8. nous / rentrer tard
9. mon meilleur ami (ma meilleure amie) / téléphoner
10. il (elle) / dîner avec moi
11. les autres étudiants du cours de français / préparer le cours ensemble
12. les autres étudiants du cours de français / sortir ensemble

E. Entretien. Interviewez votre partenaire.

1. Est-ce que tu es sorti(e) avec des amis récemment? Quand est-ce que tu es sorti(e) avec des amis? Quels vêtements est-ce que tu as mis? Où est-ce que vous êtes allés ensemble? Qu'est-ce que vous avez fait? Est-ce que vous êtes rentrés tard?
2. D'habitude, est-ce que tu quittes la maison tôt ou tard le matin pendant la semaine? Est-ce que tu as quitté la maison tôt ce matin? À quelle heure est-ce que tu es arrivé(e) à la fac? Jusqu'à quelle heure vas-tu rester ici? Est-ce que tu vas rentrer chez toi tôt ou tard aujourd'hui? À quelle heure est-ce que tu es rentré(e) hier?
3. Est-ce que tu es parti(e) en week-end récemment? La dernière fois que tu es parti(e) en week-end, où est-ce que tu es allé(e)? Quand est-ce que tu es parti(e)? Est-ce que tu as pris ta voiture? Où est-ce que tu es descendu(e)? Combien de temps est-ce que tu es resté(e)? Qu'est-ce que tu as fait? Quand est-ce que tu es rentré(e)?

F. En week-end. Pensez à une ville où vous avez passé un week-end magnifique. Parlez de ce week-end en donnant les renseignements suivants.

- où vous êtes allé(e)
- quand vous êtes parti(e)
- avec qui vous y êtes allé(e)
- si vous avez pris l'avion ou votre voiture
- combien de temps vous y avez passé
- où vous êtes descendu(e)
- ce que *(what)* vous y avez fait
- si vous avez l'intention d'y retourner bientôt

Suggestion for F. En week-end. You may prefer to use this exercise as a composition topic.

Supplemental activity. Have students work with a partner to prepare one of the following conversations to present to the class. **Avec un(e) camarade de classe, préparez une scène à présenter à la classe basée sur une de ces deux situations.**

- C'est lundi matin et vous parlez de ce que *(what)* vous avez fait le week-end dernier. Pour chaque chose que votre camarade vous dit, demandez plus de renseignements.
- Un(e) camarade de classe a été absent(e) pendant le dernier cours. Maintenant, il/elle vous pose des questions pour savoir ce que vous avez fait en cours.

LECTURE ET *composition*

LECTURE: Les week-ends des Français

Qu'est-ce que les Français aiment faire quand ils partent en week-end? Vous allez lire **un sondage** du magazine *Le Figaro*. Utilisez les mots que vous connaissez et le contexte pour vous aider à comprendre.

Note. The vocabulary in this section does not appear in the end-of-chapter vocabulary lists and is meant for recognition only. You may wish to let students know in advance whether you intend to test them on this vocabulary.

Selon le contexte. Utilisez le contexte pour deviner le sens des mots en italique.

— Est-ce que vous partez souvent en week-end?
— Assez souvent, mais *pas toutes les semaines.*
— Quand est-ce que vous partez d'habitude?
— Généralement, le samedi mais pas très tôt. *En fin* de matinée ou *en début* d'après-midi, vers midi.

Les week-ends des Français

*Beaucoup de Français préfèrent rester chez eux plutôt que de partir en week-end. Et 90% de ceux qui **s'évadent** utilisent leur voiture personnelle. La maison, la voiture: ce sont les refuges **rassurants** de la société du «cocooning». Voilà le principal renseignement de notre sondage «Sofres-Figaro-Magazine» sur les week-ends des Français.*

● Quand partez-vous en week-end?

Toutes les semaines	4%
Une ou deux fois par mois	13
Une ou deux fois dans l'année	26
Rarement	24
Sans réponse	33

● Le plus souvent, comment partez-vous?

Seul(e)	7%
En couple	38
En famille	50
Avec des amis	21
Sans réponse	0

● En règle générale, quel moyen de transport utilisez-vous?

Voiture personnelle	90%
Train	11
Autocar	4
Avion	3
Voiture de location	1
Sans réponse	2

● En règle générale, où allez-vous lorsque vous partez en week-end?

Dans votre résidence secondaire	10%
Chez des parents	55
Chez des amis	43
À l'hôtel	13
En camping	16
Autres réponses	4
Sans réponse	0

● Quand partez-vous en week-end?

Le vendredi après-midi	7%
Le vendredi soir	23
Le samedi matin tôt	24
Le samedi en fin de matinée ou en début d'après-midi	33
Sans réponse	13

● Combien de kilomètres faites-vous pour vous rendre sur votre lieu de séjour lorsque vous partez en week-end?

Moins de 100 kilomètres	28%
Entre 100 et 200 kilomètres	34
Entre 200 et 500 kilomètres	26
Plus de 500 kilomètres	8
Sans réponse	4

---

un sondage *a survey*   **s'évader** *to escape, to get away*   **rassurant(e)** *reassuring*

y

198 *cent quatre-vingt-dix-huit* ■ CHAPITRE 5

Ils partent. Utilisez les renseignements du sondage pour compléter ces phrases.

1. Le plus grand nombre des Français ne partent pas en week-end toutes les semaines. Ils partent...
2. Quand ils partent en week-end, ils ne partent pas très tôt le matin. La plus grande partie des Français préfèrent partir...
3. En général, ils ne partent pas seuls. Ils préfèrent partir...
4. Quand ils partent en week-end, ils ne descendent pas toujours à l'hôtel. Le plus souvent, ils vont...
5. Beaucoup de Français aiment voyager en train, mais la majorité préfère prendre...

Composition

A. Organisez-vous.
Vous allez décrire un voyage imaginaire à Paris. Regardez ces photos et les photos des pages 189, 193 et 206–207 et faites une liste des choses à faire dans trois endroits différents.

Exemple   au Quartier latin
parler avec des étudiants, faire une promenade...

If you have access to SYSTÈME-D software, you will find the following phrases, vocabulary, grammar, and dictionary aids there.

Phrases: Telling time; Linking ideas; Sequencing events
Vocabulary: Leisure; Sports; City
Grammar: Compound past tense; Locative pronoun **y**
Dictionary: The verb **faire**

SYSTÈME-D

Le musée Picasso

Le centre Georges Pompidou

B. Rédaction: Une semaine à Paris.
Vous avez passé une semaine à Paris. Écrivez une description de votre semaine. Parlez des choses suivantes:

- à quelle heure vous êtes parti(e) d'ici
- à quelle heure vous êtes arrivé(e) à Paris
- dans quelle sorte d'hôtel vous êtes descendu(e)
- combien de temps vous avez passé à l'hôtel
- ce que *(what)* vous avez fait lundi, mardi...
- ce que vous avez beaucoup aimé
- si vous avez l'intention d'y retourner et quand

C. Ressemblances.
Échangez votre description avec un(e) camarade de classe. Comparez votre semaine à Paris avec celle de votre partenaire et décrivez-les aux autres étudiants.

COMPARAISONS *culturelles*

LES PASSE-TEMPS

Note. The vocabulary in this section does not appear in the end-of-chapter vocabulary lists, and is meant for recognition only. You may wish to let students know in advance whether you intend to test them on this vocabulary.

Les Français, comme nous, aiment bien **s'amuser** et **se reposer** le week-end. Parmi leurs activités préférées du week-end, on voit quatre catégories générales: les activités culturelles, les activités domestiques, les activités sportives et les activités en famille ou entre amis.

Voilà le résultat d'**un sondage** «Sofres-Figaro-Magazine» sur les week-ends des Français. D'après ce sondage, quelles activités domestiques est-ce que les Français préfèrent? Quelles activités en famille ou entre amis? Quelles activités culturelles? Est-ce que les Français aiment mieux les activités de plein air ou les activités qu'on fait à la maison? Quelles sont les trois activités de plein air les plus populaires?

Quelles sont vos activités préférées du week-end?

Vous promener	48%	Aller voir un spectacle	13%
Voir des amis	39	Assister à une manifestation sportive	11
Voir la famille	36	Aller à la chasse ou à la pêche	11
Vous reposer	30	Aller au cinéma	10
Regarder la télévision	22	Lire des revues ou des magazines	9
Bricoler	21	Aller visiter un musée, un monument	9
Lire un livre	20	Faire des courses	7
Faire du sport	20	Sans réponse	3
Jardiner	19		
Aller au restaurant	16		

Le total des pourcentages est supérieur à 100, les personnes interrogées ayant donné plusieurs réponses.

See the *Instructor's Resource Manual* for the video script and activities.

À discuter.

1. Qu'est-ce que vous trouvez surprenant *(surprising)* dans le sondage? Qu'est-ce que vous ne trouvez pas surprenant?

2. Faites une liste des passe-temps populaires dans votre région. Comparez votre liste avec celle des Français. Est-ce que vous y trouvez les mêmes quatre catégories générales (activités domestiques, activités en famille ou entre amis, activités culturelles et activités sportives)? Sinon, quelles sont les ressemblances? les différences? Pourquoi est-ce qu'il y a des différences? Est-ce qu'il y a peut-être des différences de valeurs *(values)*, d'intérêts, de géographie ou de climat qui influencent les goûts *(tastes)* des gens?

Supplemental activity. Have students research aspects of French weekend activities (i.e., What kind of sports / TV shows / etc., are popular?).

_____

s'amuser *to have fun* **se reposer** *to rest* **un sondage** *a survey* **Assister à** *To attend* **Aller à la chasse** *To go hunting* **aller à la pêche** *to go fishing*

Les Français aiment les repas en famille.

Les promenades au parc font souvent partie des activités du dimanche.

Les Français aiment les activités culturelles.

VOCABULAIRE

COMPÉTENCE 1

Deciding what to wear and buying clothes

NOMS MASCULINS

un anorak	a ski jacket
un bikini	a bikini
un centre	a center
un chapeau	a hat
un chemisier	a blouse
un costume	a suit (for a man)
un homme d'affaires	a businessman
un imperméable	a raincoat
un jean	jeans
un maillot de bain	a swimsuit
un manteau	an overcoat
un pantalon	pants
un parapluie	an umbrella
un polo	a knit shirt
un portefeuille	a wallet
un pull	a pullover sweater
un sac	a purse, a sack
un short	shorts
un survêtement	a jogging suit
un tee-shirt	a T-shirt
un vendeur	a salesclerk

NOMS FÉMININS

une cabine d'essayage	a fitting room
une casquette	a cap
une ceinture	a belt
des chaussettes	socks
des chaussures (des bottes, des sandales)	shoes (boots, sandals)
une chemise	a shirt
une cravate	a tie
une femme d'affaires	a businesswoman
la haute couture	designer fashion
une jupe	a skirt
des lunettes (de soleil)	(sun)glasses
la mode	fashion
une montre	a watch
une robe	a dress
une vendeuse	a salesclerk

EXPRESSIONS VERBALES

coûter	to cost
entrer (dans)	to enter, to go in
essayer	to try, to try on
Il/Elle me plaît.	I like it.
mettre (je mets, vous mettez)	to put, to put on

DIVERS

Bien sûr!	Of course!
en solde	on sale
important(e)	important
Je peux vous aider?	May I help you?
le (l') / la (l')	him, it / her, it
les	them
mondial(e) (mpl mondiaux)	world (adj.)
par ici	this way
Quelle taille faites-vous?	What size do you wear?
Je fais du...	I wear size . . .
sans doute	without doubt
voyons	let's see

COMPÉTENCE 2

Discussing the weather and what to do

NOMS MASCULINS

l'automne (en automne)	autumn (in autumn)
l'été (en été)	summer (in summer)
l'hiver (en hiver)	winter (in winter)
un jardin	a garden
le printemps (au printemps)	spring (in spring)
le temps	the weather, time

NOMS FÉMININS

la neige	snow
la plage	the beach
la pluie	rain
une saison	a season

EXPRESSIONS VERBALES

aller à la montagne	to go to the mountains
dépendre (de)	to depend (on)
faire de l'exercice	to exercise
faire des courses	to run errands
faire du bateau	to go boating
faire du camping	to go camping
faire du jardinage	to garden
faire du jogging	to go jogging
faire du shopping	to go shopping
faire du ski (nautique)	to (water)ski
faire du sport (du tennis, du hockey...)	to play sports (tennis, hockey . . .)
faire du vélo	to go bike-riding
faire la cuisine	to cook
faire la lessive	to do laundry
faire la vaisselle	to do the dishes
faire le ménage	to do housework
faire une promenade	to take a walk
faire un voyage	to take a trip
neiger	to snow
pleuvoir	to rain

DIVERS

ne... rien	nothing
pendant	during, for
Quel temps fait-il?	What's the weather like?
Il fait beau/chaud/frais/ froid/mauvais/du soleil/ du vent.	It's nice/hot/cool/ cold/bad/sunny/ windy.
Il pleut.	It is raining., It rains.
il neige.	It is snowing., It snows.
Quel temps va-t-il faire?	What's the weather going to be like? It's going to be . . .
Il va faire...	
Il va pleuvoir/neiger.	It's going to rain / to snow.
si	if

COMPÉTENCE 3

NOMS MASCULINS

un an	a year
le journal	the newspaper
le petit déjeuner	breakfast

NOMS FÉMININS

une heure	an hour
une minute	a minute
une seconde	a second (in time)

EXPRESSIONS ADVERBIALES

l'année dernière	last year
déjà	already
la dernière fois	the last time
hier (matin, après-midi)	yesterday (morning, afternoon)
hier soir	last night, yesterday evening
huit / quinze jours	one / two week(s)
Il y a combien de temps?	How long ago?
il y a quelques secondes	a few seconds ago
longtemps	a long time
lundi (mardi...) dernier	last Monday (Tuesday . . .)
le mois dernier	last month
ne... pas encore	not yet
Pendant combien de temps?	For how long?
pendant deux heures	for two hours
récemment	recently
la semaine dernière	last week
le week-end dernier	last weekend

DIVERS

dernier (dernière)	last
prendre son petit déjeuner	to eat breakfast

COMPÉTENCE 4

NOMS MASCULINS

un camping	a campground
un club	a club
un hôtel	a hotel
des parents	relatives

NOMS FÉMININS

la chance	luck
une nuit	a night
une voiture de location	a rental car

EXPRESSIONS VERBALES

descendre (de / dans)	to descend, to come down, to get off/out (of), to stay (at)
monter (dans)	to go up, to get on/in
mourir (mort[e])	to die (dead)
naître (né[e])	to be born (born)
partir en week-end	to go away for the weekend
retourner	to return, to go back

DIVERS

Quelle chance!	What luck!

Notre-Dame

Henri Rousseau (1844–1910)
1909
The Phillips Collection

This painting of **Notre-Dame de Paris** was executed only a year before Rousseau's death. Many artists, including Robert Delaunay and Paul Signac, have painted **Notre-Dame** from this same spot on the **Quai Henri IV.**

À Paris

Le Baiser

Constantin Brancusi (1876–1957)
Circa 1911
Paris, Musée National d'Art Moderne
Giraudon/Art Resource
© 1998 Artists Rights Society (ARS),
New York/ADAGP, Paris

Although Brancusi was Romanian, he lived in Paris for most of his career. **Le Baiser** *(The Kiss)* is one of a series of sculptures, all bearing the same name. A full-length version of **Le Baiser** was installed in Montparnasse Cemetery in Paris.

PARIS

SUPERFICIE: 105 kilomètres carrés

POPULATION: 2 152 000 (avec la région parisienne: plus de 9 000 000) (les Parisiens)

DÉPARTEMENT: Paris

PROVINCE: Île-de-France

INDUSTRIES PRINCIPALES: activités tertiaires *(service industries),* tourisme, finance, haute-couture, industries mécaniques, technologie, transports

LIEUX D'INTÉRÊT ET MUSÉES: la tour Eiffel, l'Arc de Triomphe, la cathédrale Notre-Dame, le centre Georges Pompidou, la basilique du Sacré-Cœur, l'Opéra, la Défense, le musée du Louvre, le musée d'Orsay, le musée de l'Homme

Les sorties

Paris

Paris, la capitale de la France, est une des plus belles villes du monde. La Seine sépare la ville en deux parties, **la rive gauche** et **la rive droite**. Les deux îles situées **au milieu de** la Seine sont l'île de la Cité et l'île St-Louis. C'est sur l'île de la Cité que la ville de Paris est née il y a plus de 2.000 ans.

*La cathédrale Notre-Dame se trouve **au cœur de** Paris, sur l'île de la Cité.*

Le Louvre, l'un des plus grands musées d'art du monde, fait presque un kilomètre de longueur.

---

la rive gauche *the left bank*   **la rive droite** *the right bank*   **au milieu de** *in the middle of*   **au cœur de** *in the heart of*

La célèbre avenue des Champs-Élysées *s'étend* de la place de la Concorde à l'Arc de Triomphe.

Si vous aimez **la vie** de bohème, visitez le quartier de Montmartre.

Pour avoir une vue panoramique de la ville, on peut monter à la tour Eiffel.

Le Quartier latin est un des quartiers les plus sympathiques de Paris.

---

s'étend (s'étendre *to extend*)   **la vie** *life*

L'expression **je t'invite / je vous invite** suggère que vous allez payer.

TRANSPARENCY: 6-1

Warm-ups. A. Est-ce que vous voudriez faire les choses suivantes ce soir? **1.** sortir avec des amis **2.** aller au théâtre **3.** rentrer tard **4.** travailler **5.** aller à une boum **6.** aller voir un film **7.** aller voir des cousins **8.** visiter un musée **9.** louer des vidéos **10.** retrouver des amis au restaurant. **B.** Have students suggest a place for the following activities: EXEMPLE – **J'ai envie de jouer au tennis. – Alors, on va au parc?** **1.** J'ai envie d'aller nager. **2.** J'ai envie de voir la nouvelle exposition d'art. **3.** J'ai envie d'aller faire du shopping. **4.** J'ai envie d'aller prendre un verre. **5.** J'ai envie de voir un film. **6.** J'ai envie de manger quelque chose. **C.** Have students use **Tu voudrais... ?** or suggestions with **on** and **nous** to invite each other to go see a movie.

VOCABULAIRE SUPPLÉMENTAIRE

LES FILMS

une comédie (musicale)

un dessin animé *a cartoon*

un drame

un film d'aventures

un film de science-fiction

un film policier

Suggestion for the conversation. Review the twenty-four hour clock. Introduce the words **genre, épouvante,** and **amour.** Set the scene and play the conversation with books closed. Have students listen for the following information. **1.** Quel genre de film est-ce qu'Éric voudrait voir? Et Michèle? **2.** À quelle heure commence le film?

Les invitations

Éric Pérez **veut** inviter sa petite amie Michèle à sortir. Et vous, si **vous voulez** inviter **quelqu'un, vous pouvez dire...**

À UN(E) AMI(E)	À UNE AUTRE PERSONNE OU À UN GROUPE DE PERSONNES
Tu veux... ?	Vous voulez... ?
Tu voudrais... ?	Vous voudriez... ?
Je t'invite à...	Je voudrais vous inviter à...

Si **quelqu'un vous invite,** vous pouvez répondre...

POUR DIRE OUI	POUR DIRE NON	POUR SUGGÉRER UNE AUTRE ACTIVITÉ
Oui, je veux bien.	Je regrette mais...	Je préfère...
Quelle bonne idée!	je ne suis pas libre.	J'aime mieux...
Avec plaisir!	**je ne peux pas.**	Allons plutôt à...
	je dois travailler.	

 Éric téléphone à sa petite amie Michèle pour parler de leurs projets pour ce soir.

MICHÈLE: Allô?

ÉRIC: Salut, Michèle. C'est moi, Éric. Ça va?

MICHÈLE: Oui, très bien. Et toi?

ÉRIC: Moi, ça va. Écoute, tu es libre ce soir? Tu veux sortir?

MICHÈLE: Oui, d'accord. Je veux bien. Qu'est-ce que tu as envie de faire?

ÉRIC: Je veux voir **le film d'épouvante** qu'on **passe** au cinéma Gaumont.

MICHÈLE: Tu sais, moi, je n'aime pas **tellement** les films d'épouvante. Que penses-tu d'aller voir le nouveau film d'**amour** avec Isabelle Adjani au cinéma Rex?

ÉRIC: D'accord. À quelle heure?

MICHÈLE: Il y a **une séance** à vingt heures quarante-cinq.

ÉRIC: D'accord. Je passe chez toi vers huit heures?

MICHÈLE: D'accord. Alors, au revoir.

ÉRIC: À tout à l'heure, Michèle.

---

il veut (vouloir *to want*) **vous voulez (vouloir** *to want*) **quelqu'un** *someone* **vous pouvez (pouvoir** *can, may, to be able*) **dire** *to say* **Tu veux (vouloir** *to want*) **quelqu'un vous invite** *someone invites you* **je ne peux pas (pouvoir** *can, may, to be able*) **je dois (devoir** *must, to have to*) **un film d'épouvante** *a horror movie* **passer (un film)** *to show (a movie)* **tellement** *so much* **l'amour** *(m) love* **une séance** *a showing*

A. On sort ensemble? Acceptez ou refusez ces invitations comme indiqué. Utilisez une variété d'expressions.

ACCEPTEZ CES INVITATIONS...

1. Tu as envie de sortir ce soir? Tu veux aller au cinéma?
2. Tu voudrais sortir samedi soir? J'ai envie d'aller danser.
3. Vous êtes libre ce soir? Je voudrais vous inviter au restaurant.

REFUSEZ CES INVITATIONS...

4. Vous voulez aller au musée ce week-end? Il y a une nouvelle exposition.
5. Vous avez faim? Vous voudriez aller manger quelque chose?
6. Je t'invite au théâtre ce soir.

SUGGÉREZ UNE AUTRE ACTIVITÉ...

7. Tu veux préparer les cours ensemble ce soir?
8. Tu es libre samedi après-midi? Tu as envie de faire du jogging?
9. Vous voudriez aller voir un film ce soir?

B. Invitations. Utilisez une variété d'expressions pour faire les invitations suivantes.

INVITEZ UN(E) AMI(E) À...

1. aller danser samedi soir
2. dîner au restaurant ce soir
3. aller voir une exposition demain
4. aller prendre un verre aujourd'hui après les cours

INVITEZ UN GROUPE D'AMIS À...

5. aller voir un film d'épouvante dimanche
6. préparer les cours ensemble ce soir
7. faire du vélo au parc ce week-end
8. aller au match de football américain / de basket ce week-end

C. Sortons ensemble! Avec un(e) partenaire, changez la conversation entre Éric et Michèle comme indiqué.

1. Éric doesn't like romantic movies. He suggests a comedy **(une comédie).**
2. Michèle is not free this evening because she has to work. She prefers to go out tomorrow night.
3. You and your partner are best friends. Make plans to do something together this weekend.

1. What does **vouloir** mean? What are three meanings of **pouvoir?** What are the meanings of **devoir?**
2. The **nous** and **vous** forms have the same vowel in the stem as the infinitive. What vowels do the other forms have?
3. What auxiliary verb do you use to form the **passé composé** of these three verbs? What are their past participles?

Issuing and accepting invitations:
Les verbes vouloir, pouvoir et devoir

The verbs **vouloir** *(to want)* and **pouvoir** *(can, may, to be able)* are useful when inviting someone to do something. They have similar conjugations.

VOULOIR *(to want)*	
je **veux**	nous **voulons**
tu **veux**	vous **voulez**
il/elle/on **veut**	ils/elles **veulent**
PASSÉ COMPOSÉ: **j'ai voulu**	

POUVOIR *(can, may, to be able)*	
je **peux**	nous **pouvons**
tu **peux**	vous **pouvez**
il/elle/on **peut**	ils/elles **peuvent**
PASSÉ COMPOSÉ: **j'ai pu**	

Je **veux** sortir mais je ne **peux** pas.   *I **want** to go out, but I **can't.***

Use **devoir** followed by an infinitive to say what you *must* or *have to* do. **Devoir** also means *to owe.*

DEVOIR *(must, to have to, to owe)*	
je **dois**	nous **devons**
tu **dois**	vous **devez**
il/elle/on **doit**	ils/elles **doivent**
PASSÉ COMPOSÉ: **j'ai dû**	

Je **dois** travailler demain.   *I **have to** work tomorrow.*
Je **dois** 100 dollars à mon frère.   *I **owe** my brother 100 dollars.*

In the **passé composé, devoir** can mean that someone *had to do* something or *must have done* something. Context will clarify the meaning.

Michèle n'est pas chez elle. Elle **a dû** partir.
*Michèle isn't home. She **had to** leave. / She **must have** left.*

Ils **ont dû** aller en ville.
*They **had to** go downtown. / They **must have** gone downtown.*

Il n'a pas pu sortir parce qu'il **a dû** travailler.
*He wasn't able to go out because he **had to** work.*

Suggestions. A. Point out that the difference between third person singular and plural forms is audible in **vouloir, pouvoir,** and **devoir.** For practice, read these sentences aloud and have students indicate whether the verb forms they hear are **singulier** or **pluriel: 1.** Ils doivent travailler ce soir. **2.** Il veut aller au cinéma avec nous, mais il ne peut pas. **3.** Elles veulent rester à la maison. **4.** Elle doit rentrer tôt. **5.** Ils ne peuvent pas comprendre. You can also use these sentences for dictation. **B.** Point out the proverbs **Vouloir, c'est pouvoir** and **Ce que femme veut, Dieu le veut.**

A. Activités. Dites si ces personnes veulent ou peuvent faire chacune des choses indiquées.

Exemple   VOULOIR
Samedi, je… (rester à la maison)
Samedi, je ne veux pas rester à la maison.

VOULOIR

1. Vendredi soir, je… (travailler, rester à la maison, aller voir un film)
2. Samedi, mes amis… (aller voir un match de football américain / de basket, faire du jogging)
3. Samedi soir, mes amis et moi, nous… (sortir ensemble, aller danser, préparer les cours)
4. Dimanche, mon meilleur ami (ma meilleure amie)… (aller à l'église, aller voir sa famille, travailler)

POUVOIR

1. En cours de français, je... (toujours comprendre le professeur, boire un café)
2. En cours de français, nous... (toujours parler anglais, manger)
3. En cours de français, le prof... (toujours comprendre les étudiants, parler au téléphone)
4. En cours de français les étudiants... (dormir, souvent partir en avance *[early]*, répondre à leur portable *[cell phone]*)

B. On veut... Aujourd'hui les Pérez ne peuvent pas faire ce qu'ils veulent. Jouez le rôle d'A_____ : ce que chacun veut et doit faire.

Exemple   Moi, _____:, mais je dois faire de l'exercice.

Moi...

1. Éric...

2. Éric et Cathy...

3. Vincent...

4. Nos amis...

5. Michel...

C. Encore des explications. Plus tard, Alice dit que chacun n'a pas pu faire ce qu'il voulait *(wanted)*. Qu'est-ce qu'elle dit? Utilisez le passé composé.

Exemple   Moi, je n'ai pas pu dormir.

Maintenant, elle explique ce qu'ils ont dû faire. Qu'est-ce qu'elle dit?

Exemple   Moi, j'ai dû faire de l'exercice.

D. Entretien. Complétez les questions suivantes avec la forme convenable du verbe indiqué. Ensuite, posez les questions à votre partenaire.

1. Qu'est-ce que tu _____ (vouloir) faire après le cours? _____-tu (pouvoir) rentrer chez toi? Qu'est-ce que tu _____ (devoir) faire?
2. Qu'est-ce que tu _____ (vouloir) faire ce week-end? Est-ce que tu _____ (pouvoir) faire ce que *(what)* tu _____ (vouloir)? Qu'est-ce que tu _____ (devoir) faire?
3. Tes amis et toi, qu'est-ce que vous _____ (aimer) faire ensemble le week-end? Qu'est-ce que vous _____ (vouloir) faire ce week-end? Est-ce que vous _____ (pouvoir) sortir ensemble ce week-end?

Stratégies et compréhension auditive:
Noting the important information

When making plans, we often jot down important information for later reference. If a friend invited you to do something, what sort of information would you want to remember? Look at the following invitation and think about what information is given.

Nous vous attendons

le Samedi 18 novembre

à 19 *heures.*

Notre adresse:

85 boulevard St Michel

Téléphone 02.43.29.69.50

R.S.V.P.

Script for *A. Prenez des notes.*
INVITATION A.
— Allô, Éric? C'est Marc. Tu es libre demain? Tu veux jouer au tennis avec moi?
— Oui, je veux bien. Quand?
— Vers 14 heures. On se retrouve au parc?
— Oui, très bien.
— D'accord. À demain, alors.
— À demain.
INVITATION B.
— Allô? C'est toi, Éric? Ici Marie.
— Salut, Marie.
— Écoute, j'ai envie d'aller au musée cet après-midi. Tu m'accompagnes?
— Oui, je veux bien. On se retrouve devant le musée?
— Non, passe plutôt chez moi vers midi et demi.
— D'accord.
INVITATION C.
— Allô, Éric? C'est Jean-Luc. Michèle et toi, vous êtes libres samedi soir? Je voudrais vous inviter à dîner chez moi.
— Oui, oui, bonne idée. Vers quelle heure?
— Vers 19 heures 30.
— Très bien.

 A. Prenez des notes. Trois amis invitent Éric à faire quelque chose. Écoutez chaque invitation et prenez des notes en français.

Qu'est-ce qu'ils vont faire?   Où?   Quel jour?   À quelle heure?

B. À vous. Éric demande à Michèle de l'accompagner. Utilisez vos notes de l'exercice précédent pour jouer les rôles d'Éric et de Michèle avec un(e) partenaire.

Exemple   — **Je vais jouer au tennis avec Marc demain à... Est-ce que tu voudrais jouer avec nous?**
        — **Oui, je veux bien!**

 On va au cinéma?

Vincent demande à Alice si elle voudrait aller au cinéma. Lisez les questions de l'exercice suivant. Ensuite, écoutez la conversation et notez les détails importants.

A. Quel film?
Répondez aux questions suivantes d'après la conversation entre Alice et son mari.

1. Comment est-ce qu'Alice trouve les films avec Arnold Schwarzenegger?
2. Quel genre *(type)* de film est-ce qu'ils décident d'aller voir?
3. Où est-ce qu'on passe ce film?
4. À quelle séance est-ce qu'ils vont aller?

B. Vos notes.
Utilisez vos notes pour recréer *(to recreate)* la conversation entre Alice et Vincent avec un(e) camarade de classe.

C. Tu veux sortir?
Consultez la liste des films qui passent au cinéma Pathé Wepler. Invitez un(e) camarade de classe à aller voir un film avec vous. Choisissez une séance et décidez à quelle heure vous allez passer chez votre ami(e).

Script for *On va au cinéma?*
— On va au cinéma ce soir?
— Oui, je veux bien. Quel film est-ce que tu voudrais aller voir?
— Je ne sais pas. Il y a une comédie avec Gérard Depardieu au cinéma Gaumont. Qu'est-ce que tu en penses?
— Allons voir quelque chose d'autre. Je n'ai pas tellement envie de voir une comédie.
— Il y a le nouveau film américain de science-fiction au cinéma Rex. C'est Arnold Schwarzenegger qui joue le rôle principal. On dit que c'est un très bon film.
— Tu sais bien que je n'aime pas les films avec Arnold Schwarzenegger. Ils sont souvent bêtes ou très violents.
— Alors, qu'est-ce que tu veux aller voir?
— Allons voir le nouveau film d'amour avec Isabelle Adjani au cinéma Rex.
— Bon, si tu préfères. C'est à quelle heure?
— Il y a trois séances: une à 18h20, une à 20h45 et la dernière à 23h15.
— Allons à la séance de 18h20 et allons manger après.
— D'accord.

Follow-up for *B. Vos notes.* After students have recreated the conversation, play the tape again so students can see how well they acted it out.

SIGNIFICATION DES LETTRES PRÉCÉDANT LES TITRES DES FILMS :

AV aventure
CD comédie dramatique
CM comédie musicale
CO comédie
CT court métrage
DA dessin animé
DC documentaire
DP drame psychologique
EP film d'épouvante
ER érotique
ES espionnage
FA fantastique

FC film catastrophe
FH film historique
FM film musical
FP film politique
GC grand classique
GR guerre
GS grand spectacle
HO horreur
PO policier
SF science-fiction
WS western
© Interdits aux moins de 18 ans.

PATHÉ WEPLER 140, bd de Clichy et 8, av. de Clichy - 08.36.68.20.22 (0,3 €/mn). M° Place Clichy Pl: 8 €, TR: 6,5 €, du Lun au Ven jusqu'à 18h30 et Dim après 18h30, Étud: 6,5 € du Lun au Ven inclus; - 12 ans, + 65 ans: 4,5 €; Salles 9 à 12: 6 € (sf exception); Séance de 11h: 4 €. Carte bleue acceptée. Rens.: minitel 36 15 Pathé. 12 salles climatisées. 8 salles accessibles aux handicapés.

CO HERCULE ET SHERLOCK Son stéréo analogique. Séances: 10h45, 13h10, 15h25, 17h30, 20h10, 22h15; Sam séance suppl. à 0h25; Film 20 mn après.

DA LE BOSSU DE NOTRE DAME v. f. Son stéréo digital. Séances: Mer, Sam, Dim 11h05, 13h20, 15h30, 17h45; Film 20 mn après.

AV POURSUITE v. f. Son stéréo analogique. Séances: 10h30, 13h, 15h20, 17h40, 20h, 22h20; Sam séance suppl. à 0h40. Film 20 mn après.

CO BERNIE Int - 12 ans. Son stéréo digital. Séances: Jeu, Ven, Lun, Mar 10h55, 13h25, 15h30, 17h55, 20h15, 22h25; Sam séance suppl. à 0h30; Film 20 mn après.

DC MICROCOSMOS Son stéréo digital. Séances: 10h50, 13h30, 15h40, 17h35, 19h30, 21h30; Sam séance suppl. à 23h55; Film 20 mn après.

DP NOS FUNÉRAILLES v. o. Int - 12 ans. Son stéréo analogique. Séances: 10h35, 13h, 15h15, 17h35, 19h55, 22h15; Sam séance suppl. à 0h30; Film 20 mn après.

COMPÉTENCE 2

Talking about how you spend and used to spend your time

Suggestion. Point out that this *Compétence* introduces a new verb form that talks about how things used to be. Have students comment on what the verb form looks like. Model the pronunciation of the -ais and -ait endings.

Aujourd'hui et dans le passé

Michèle compare sa **vie** d'aujourd'hui avec sa vie quand elle était au **lycée**.

Aujourd'hui...

J'ai 21 ans.

Je suis étudiante à l'université.

J'habite avec ma famille.

J'ai cours du lundi au vendredi.

J'aime l'université.

En général, je déjeune au **restau-u**.

Le week-end, je suis souvent **fatiguée** et **je dors** beaucoup.

Le vendredi soir, **je sors** souvent avec **des copains.** On va au cinéma, en boîte ou à une boum.

Chaque samedi, je joue au tennis avec des amis et je fais aussi souvent du roller.

Quand **j'étais** au lycée...

J'avais 15 ans.

J'étais **lycéenne.**

J'habitais avec ma famille.

J'avais cours du lundi au vendredi et le samedi matin aussi.

Je n'aimais pas beaucoup **l'école** *(f)*.

Je rentrais souvent à la maison pour déjeuner.

Le week-end, j'étais toujours fatiguée et je dormais beaucoup.

Le vendredi soir, je passais du temps avec ma famille ou je sortais avec des copains. On allait au cinéma, au café ou à une boum.

Le samedi, je faisais du sport avec des amis: on jouait au foot, on faisait du roller... et on jouait au tennis.

 Michèle demande à Éric ce qu'il faisait quand il était au lycée.

MICHÈLE: Qu'est-ce que tu aimais faire quand tu étais au lycée?
ÉRIC: J'aimais passer le temps avec des copains. Le vendredi soir, on allait aux matchs de football américain ou de basket au lycée.
MICHÈLE: Et le samedi?
ÉRIC: Le samedi matin, je travaillais. Le samedi après-midi, on faisait du skateboarding. Le samedi soir, je sortais avec ma petite amie. On allait au cinéma.
MICHÈLE: Et qu'est-ce que tu faisais le dimanche?
ÉRIC: Le dimanche, je ne faisais rien de spécial. Je restais à la maison. Je regardais la télé ou je louais une vidéo.

dans le passé *in the past*   **la vie** *life*   **le lycée** *high school*   **j'étais** *I was*   **J'avais 15 ans.** *I was fifteen.*
un(e) lycéen(ne) *a high school student*   **J'habitais** *I lived, I used to live*   **J'ai cours (avoir cours** *to have class)*
J'avais *I had, I used to have*   **l'école** *(f) school*   **le restau-u** *the university cafeteria*   **fatigué(e)** *tired*   **je dors**
(dormir *to sleep)*   **je sors (sortir** *to go out)*   **un copain (une copine)** *a friend, a pal*

Warm-ups. A. Complétez ces phrases. **1.** Aujourd'hui après les cours, je veux... je dois... **2.** Vendredi soir, je veux... je dois... **3.** Samedi, je veux... je dois... **4.** Dimanche, je veux... je dois...
B. Questions orales. **1.** Qu'est-ce que vous voulez faire aujourd'hui après les cours? Pouvez-vous sortir? Devez-vous travailler? Devez-vous préparer les cours? **2.** Et ce week-end? Que voulez-vous faire s'il fait beau? Et s'il fait mauvais? Pouvez-vous sortir avec des amis? Que devez-vous faire?

TRANSPARENCY: 6-2

Suggestions. You may wish to point out that: **A.** Traditionally, many students at the **lycée** go to school Monday through Friday, except for Wednesday afternoons, and also go on Saturday mornings. **B.** Extracurricular activities are not normally part of the activities at a **lycée**. **C.** Young people in France normally go out in groups rather than in couples. **D.** It is common for college students to live with their families.

Suggestion for the conversation. Set the scene and have students listen to the conversation with books closed for the answers to these questions. **1.** Qu'est-ce qu'Éric aimait faire le vendredi soir? **2.** Qu'est-ce qu'il aimait faire le samedi? **3.** Qu'est-ce qu'il aimait faire le dimanche?

A. Maintenant ou dans le passé? Est-ce que Michèle parle de sa vie maintenant ou de quand elle avait 15 ans?

1. J'étais lycéenne.
2. J'ai cours du lundi au vendredi.
3. Je n'aimais pas beaucoup l'école.
4. D'habitude, je déjeunais à la maison.
5. Je sors beaucoup le week-end.
6. J'aime sortir avec des copains.
7. Mes copains et moi, on aimait aller au café.
8. On faisait souvent du sport ensemble.

B. Et vous? Dites si vous faites ces choses maintenant et si vous faisiez ces choses quand vous aviez 10 ans.

Exemple   Maintenant, j'habite avec ma famille.
    Maintenant, j'habite / je n'habite pas avec ma famille.

    Quand j'avais 10 ans, j'habitais avec ma famille.
    Quand j'avais 10 ans, j'habitais / je n'habitais pas avec ma famille.

1. Maintenant, je suis souvent fatigué(e).
   Quand j'avais 10 ans, j'étais souvent fatigué(e).
2. Maintenant, je dors bien.
   Quand j'avais 10 ans, je dormais bien.
3. Maintenant, je sors souvent le vendredi soir.
   Quand j'avais 10 ans, je sortais souvent le vendredi soir.
4. Maintenant, mes copains et moi, on fait souvent du sport ensemble.
   Quand j'avais 10 ans, on faisait souvent du sport ensemble.
5. Maintenant, je travaille.
   Quand j'avais 10 ans, je travaillais.

C. Au lycée. Avec un(e) partenaire, changez la conversation entre Éric et Michèle comme indiqué.

1. Friday night Éric used to stay home and watch TV. Saturday afternoons, he used to go rollerblading.
2. Éric asks Michèle what she used to like to do on weekends. Michèle used to like to go to a restaurant and a movie with her parents. Saturday, she used to like to play tennis with a girlfriend. Sundays, she stayed home with her family.
3. You and a friend are talking about what you used to do when you were in high school. Change the conversation to make it true for you. If you want to use verbs that you have not yet seen used in this *Compétence,* check with your professor on how to use them correctly.

1. What are the conjugations of **sortir**, **partir**, and **dormir**?

2. When do you use **quitter**?

3. How do you say *to go out of? to go out to? to leave from? to leave for?*

4. How do you say *to leave for the weekend? to leave on vacation? to leave on a trip?*

5. What is the difference in pronunciation between **il sort** and **ils sortent**?

Suggestion. You may wish to remind students of the use of **jusqu'à** with **dormir**.

Talking about activities:
Les verbes sortir, partir et dormir

The verbs **sortir**, **partir**, and **dormir** have similar patterns of conjugation.

SORTIR *(to go out)*	
je **sors**	nous **sortons**
tu **sors**	vous **sortez**
il/elle/on **sort**	ils/elles **sortent**
PASSÉ COMPOSÉ: **je suis sorti(e)**	

PARTIR *(to leave)*	
je **pars**	nous **partons**
tu **pars**	vous **partez**
il/elle/on **part**	ils/elles **partent**
PASSÉ COMPOSÉ: **je suis parti(e)**	

DORMIR *(to sleep)*	
je **dors**	nous **dormons**
tu **dors**	vous **dormez**
il/elle/on **dort**	ils/elles **dorment**
PASSÉ COMPOSÉ: **j'ai dormi**	

Sortir means *to go out,* both in the sense of going out with friends or going out of a place. It is the opposite of **entrer.** Notice the prepositions commonly used with **sortir.**

| *to go out of* . . . | **sortir** *de...* | Je sors **de** mon premier cours à 10 heures. |
| *to go out to* . . . | **sortir** *à...* | Je sors **au** restaurant ce soir. |

Partir means *to leave* in the sense of *to go away.* It is the opposite of **arriver.** Some common expressions with **partir** are: **partir en week-end, partir en vacances, partir en voyage.** Notice the prepositions often used with **partir.**

| *to leave from* . . . | **partir** *de...* | Je pars **de** chez moi à 9 heures. |
| *to leave for* . . . | **partir** *pour / à...* | Je pars **pour / à** Paris demain. |

Quitter means *to leave* a person or a place and is always followed by a direct object. In the **passé composé,** it is conjugated with **avoir.**

Il a quitté sa famille pour aller travailler dans une autre ville. **Il est parti** hier.

Suggestion. Ask students when they can hear the difference between the **il/elle** and **ils/elles** forms of **-er** verbs (**il arrive / ils arrivent**).

Supplemental activity. Est-ce qu'Alice parle d'**Éric** ou d'**Éric et ses amis?** 1. Il ne sort pas ce soir. 2. Il dort bien. 3. Ils sortent au restaurant demain soir. 4. Il part pour la campagne vendredi. 5. Ils dorment bien ce matin. 6. Ils partent vers 5 heures.

 Prononciation: *Les verbes sortir, partir et dormir*

You can distinguish aurally between the **il** and **ils** forms of verbs like **sortir, partir,** and **dormir.** Compare these sentences.

ALICE	ALICE ET SA FILLE
Elle dort bien.	Elles dorment bien.
Elle sort ce soir.	Elles sortent ce soir.
Elle part demain.	Elles partent demain.

When a word ends with a pronounced consonant sound in French, it must be released. Notice that when you pronounce the boldfaced consonants in the following English phrases, your tongue or lips do not have to move back and release them.

What par**t**?   What sor**t**?   In the dor**m**.

Compare how the boldfaced consonants in the following plural verb forms are released.

Ils par**t**ent.   Ils sor**t**ent.   Ils dor**m**ent.

A. Le week-end. Dites si ces personnes font souvent les choses indiquées.

Exemple je (dormir jusqu'à midi)
Je dors souvent jusqu'à midi. / Je ne dors jamais jusqu'à midi.

1. je (sortir avec des amis, partir de chez moi avant 9 heures du matin, dormir toute la journée)
2. mon meilleur ami (ma meilleure amie) (partir en vacances, sortir le vendredi soir, dormir jusqu'à 11 heures le week-end)
3. mes amis (partir en week-end, sortir le dimanche soir, dormir en cours le lendemain *[the next day]*)
4. mes amis et moi, nous (sortir ensemble, dormir en cours, partir ensemble en vacances)

B. Vos habitudes. Formez des phrases pour parler de ce que vous faites les jours du cours de français et quand vous sortez avec des amis. Demandez à votre partenaire s'il/si elle fait les mêmes choses.

Exemples Les jours du cours de français...
je / dormir jusqu'à... heures
— **Les jours du cours de français, je dors jusqu'à 7 heures. Et toi? Est-ce que tu dors jusqu'à 7 heures?**
— **Oui, je dors jusqu'à 7 heures. / Non, je dors jusqu'à 8 heures.**

Quand je sors avec des amis...
nous / sortir le plus souvent le... soir
— **Quand je sors avec des amis, nous sortons le plus souvent le samedi soir. Et vous? Est-ce que vous sortez le plus souvent le samedi soir?**
— **Oui, nous sortons le plus souvent le samedi soir. / Non, nous sortons le plus souvent le vendredi soir.**

Les jours du cours de francais...

1. je / dormir jusqu'à... heures
2. je / quitter la maison à... heures
3. je / prendre... pour aller à l'université
4. je / sortir de mon dernier cours à... heures

Quand je sors avec des amis...

5. nous / sortir le plus souvent le... soir
6. nous / quitter la maison à... heures
7. je / dormir jusqu'à... le lendemain *(the next day)*

C. Toujours des questions! Parlez avec votre partenaire de la dernière fois qu'il/elle est sorti(e) avec des amis. Posez les questions indiquées.

Exemple quel jour? / sortir ensemble
— **Quel jour est-ce que vous êtes sortis ensemble?**
— **Nous sommes sortis ensemble samedi.**

1. quand? / sortir ensemble
2. où? / aller ensemble
3. qu'est-ce que? / faire
4. à quelle heure? / quitter la maison
5. jusqu'à quelle heure? / dormir le lendemain *(the next day)*

1. Which form of the present tense do you use to create the stem for all verbs in the imperfect, except for **être?**

2. You use the **passé composé** to talk about a specific occurrence in the past. What do you use the imperfect to express?

3. Which imperfect endings are pronounced alike?

4. What single letter distinguishes the **nous** and **vous** forms of the imperfect from the present?

Note. This *Compétence* introduces the formation of the **imparfait** and focuses on its use to express continuous and repeated actions. The further uses of the **imparfait** and the contrast between the **passé composé** and the **imparfait** are presented in the next two *Compétences*.

Suggestion. Point out the **i** before the imperfect endings in the verb **étudier.**

Supplemental activity. Read sentences aloud about yourself at the age of twelve, some true and some false. Have students guess which ones are false. For example:
1. J'étais marié(e). 2. J'habitais à...
3. J'habitais seul(e). 4. J'avais un chien qui s'appelait... 5. J'avais onze chats.
6. J'étudiais le français. 7. C'était mon cours préféré. 8. J'étudiais à l'université.
9. J'aimais l'école. 10. Je jouais au basket à l'école. 11. Mon père travaillait pour...
12. Nous avions quinze chambres dans notre maison. 13. Nous n'avions pas la télévision.

Follow-ups for *Prononciation* A. Est-ce qu'on parle du présent ou du passé dans les questions suivantes? 1. Tu habitais dans un appartement? 2. Est-ce que tu jouais au basket? 3. Tes amis et toi, vous allez souvent au cinéma? 4. Où aimez-vous aller quand vous sortez ensemble? 5. Parles-tu souvent avec tes parents? 6. Est-ce que ton père joue au golf? 7. Où est-ce qu'il travaillait? 8. Où est-ce que ta mère travaille? 9. Est-ce que tu regardais la télé le samedi? 10. Qu'est-ce que tu aimais regarder à la télé? **B.** Give the same questions as dictation or have students write the answers to them.

Saying how things used to be: *L'imparfait*

You have learned to use the **passé composé** to talk about an action that took place on a specific occasion in the past. Use the **imparfait** *(imperfect)* to tell what things used to be like in general or what someone did or what happened over and over in the past.

> J'avais dix ans et j'étais très timide. *I was ten and I was very shy.*
> Je passais l'après-midi au parc. *I spent afternoons at the park.*

All verbs except **être** form this tense by dropping the **-ons** from the present tense **nous** form and adding the endings **-ais, -ais, -ait, -ions, -iez,** and **-aient.**

PARLER (nous parlóns → parl-)	FAIRE (nous faisóns → fais-)	PRENDRE (nous prenóns → pren-)
je parl**ais**	je fais**ais**	je pren**ais**
tu parl**ais**	tu fais**ais**	tu pren**ais**
il/elle/on parl**ait**	il/elle/on fais**ait**	il/elle/on pren**ait**
nous parl**ions**	nous fais**ions**	nous pren**ions**
vous parl**iez**	vous fais**iez**	vous pren**iez**
ils/elles parl**aient**	ils/elles fais**aient**	ils/elles pren**aient**

The imperfect stem of **être** is **ét-.**

ÊTRE	
j'ét**ais**	nous ét**ions**
tu ét**ais**	vous ét**iez**
il/elle/on ét**ait**	ils/elles ét**aient**

Also learn these expressions in the imperfect.

il y a	→ il y avait	Il y avait des matchs le vendredi.
il pleut	→ il pleuvait	Il pleuvait beaucoup au mois de mai.
il neige	→ il neigeait	Il neigeait souvent en hiver.

Verbs with spelling changes in the present tense **nous** form, like **manger** and **commencer,** retain the spelling change only before the imperfect endings beginning with **a.**

> nous mangeóns: je mangeais, tu mangeais, on mangeait, elles mangeaient
> BUT: nous mangions, vous mangiez
> nous commençóns: je commençais, tu commençais, on commençait, ils commençaient
> BUT: nous commencions, vous commenciez

Prononciation: *Les terminaisons de l'imparfait*

The **-ais, -ait,** and **-aient** endings of the imperfect are all pronounced alike. The **nous** and **vous** forms of the imperfect, **-ions** and **-iez,** are distinguished from the present only by the vowel **i** in the ending.

> Qu'est-ce que tu faisais? *What did you used to do?*
> Ils travaillaient pour IBM. *They worked for IBM.*
> Nous allions à la plage. *We used to go to the beach.*

A. Chez moi. Faisait-on ces choses dans votre famille quand vous aviez dix ans?

Exemple   mes parents... (travailler le week-end)
Non, mes parents ne travaillaient pas le week-end. / Ma mère travaillait le week-end mais mon père ne travaillait pas.

1. mes parents... (avoir beaucoup d'amis, être patients, prendre l'autobus pour aller au travail *[to work]*, quitter la maison tôt, rentrer tard, sortir chaque week-end)
2. mon père / ma mère... (faire du sport, partir tôt au travail, aimer lire, être à la maison le week-end, faire le ménage, faire la lessive)
3. moi, je... (dormir beaucoup, aller à l'école, aimer les maths, apprendre beaucoup de choses, avoir de bonnes notes *[good grades]*, avoir beaucoup de copains, nager bien, jouer au basket)
4. nous... (voyager souvent, aller souvent voir mes grands-parents, aller à la plage le week-end, manger dans des fast-foods, avoir un chien, habiter à...)

B. La jeunesse. Interviewez un(e) camarade de classe pour savoir ce qu'il/elle faisait quand il/elle était au lycée.

Exemple   fumer
— **Tu fumais quand tu étais au lycée?**
— **Non, je ne fumais pas.**

> *être...* ALLER TOUJOURS EN COURS ??? **travailler** *habiter...*
> AIMER... *fumer* **danser bien** AIMER SORTIR **???**
> faire... POUVOIR... *rentrer tard* VOULOIR... jouer...
> **apprendre facilement** *avoir beaucoup de copains* FAIRE DU SPORT

Maintenant, avec votre partenaire, préparez six questions pour votre professeur. Demandez ce qu'il/elle faisait quand il/elle était à l'université.

C. Entretien. Interviewez votre partenaire.

1. Est-ce que tu habitais ici quand tu étais au lycée? Avec qui habitais-tu? Est-ce que tes grands-parents habitaient près de chez vous?
2. Passais-tu beaucoup de temps avec ta famille? Partiez-vous quelquefois en week-end ensemble? Alliez-vous à la plage en été?
3. Aimais-tu ton lycée? Quels étaient tes cours préférés? Faisais-tu du sport?
4. Est-ce que tes cours étaient faciles ou difficiles? Est-ce que tes profs étaient intéressants ou ennuyeux? Avais-tu beaucoup de devoirs?
5. Avais-tu beaucoup de copains? Qu'est-ce que tu faisais avec tes copains le week-end? Sortais-tu chaque week-end? À quelle heure devais-tu rentrer chez toi? Comment s'appelait ton meilleur ami ou ta meilleure amie? Qu'est-ce que vous aimiez faire ensemble? Sortiez-vous souvent ensemble le week-end? Pouviez-vous rentrer chez vous après minuit?

D. Ma jeunesse. Préparez une conversation avec un(e) partenaire dans laquelle vous parlez de quand vous étiez au lycée. Expliquez...

- à quelle heure vos cours commençaient
- où vous déjeuniez à midi
- avec qui vous passiez beaucoup de temps
- ce que *(what)* vous faisiez après les cours et le week-end

Supplemental activities. A. Have students write a composition to describe their life at a certain age: what they looked like, where they lived, etc. Remind them not to tell about a particular incident but to describe general characteristics. You may wish to get them started with **La meilleure époque de ma vie, c'était quand... B.** Have students bring a picture from their past (their house when they were young, their room, old friends, their high school, etc.) and describe what these things or people were like. **C.** Make a transparency with pictures of you at various ages and have students work in groups to ask you about your life at each of those time periods. **D.** Have students work in groups to write lists of sentences comparing the advantages of growing up when their parents did with the advantages of growing up now. EXEMPLES **Tout était moins cher. Il n'y avait pas d'ordinateurs quand ils étaient jeunes...**

Une sortie

Cathy, la fille d'Alice, parle de la dernière fois qu'elle a dîné avec des amis. Et vous? La dernière fois que vous avez dîné avec des ami(e)s, comment était la soirée? **Qu'est-ce qui s'est passé?**

Il pleuvait quand je suis
sortie de l'appartement.

Il était sept heures et demie
quand je suis arrivée au restaurant.

On n'avait pas très faim
et on n'a pas mangé **tout de suite.**

Le repas était **délicieux**
et j'ai beaucoup mangé.

Après le repas, nous étions fatigués
et je suis partie.

Il était environ dix heures
quand je suis rentrée.

Le lendemain, c'était dimanche
et je suis restée au lit jusqu'à dix heures.

Qu'est-ce qui s'est passé? *What happened?*   **tout de suite** *right away*   **Le repas** *The meal*   **délicieux**
(délicieuse) *delicious*   **Le lendemain** *The next day*

Cathy et une amie parlent des activités du week-end dernier.

CATHY: Tu es sortie ce week-end?
MICHELINE: Oui, je suis allée au restaurant avec des copines.
CATHY: Vous êtes allées où?
MICHELINE: Au bistro Romain.
CATHY: **Ça t'a plu?**
MICHELINE: Beaucoup. C'était délicieux. On a bien mangé et on a beaucoup parlé. C'était vraiment bien!
CATHY: Et qu'est-ce que tu as fait après?
MICHELINE: **Rien du tout.** J'étais fatiguée et je suis rentrée.

Suggestion for the conversation. Have students first listen to the conversation with books closed and answer these questions. **1.** Qu'est-ce que Micheline a fait le week-end dernier? **2.** Qu'est-ce qu'elle a fait après? Pourquoi?

A. Au restaurant.

La dernière fois que vous êtes allé(e) au restaurant, qu'est-ce qui s'est passé? Changez les mots en italique pour parler de votre sortie.

1. Quand j'ai quitté *la maison*, il était *huit heures* et il *faisait froid*.
2. Quand je suis arrivé(e) au restaurant, il était *neuf heures*.
3. On *avait très faim* et on *a mangé tout de suite*.
4. Le repas était *médiocre* et j'ai *peu* mangé.
5. Après le repas, nous avions envie de *continuer la soirée* et nous *sommes allés en boîte*.
6. Quand je suis rentré(e), il était *onze heures* et j'*étais fatigué(e)*.
7. Le lendemain, c'était *dimanche* et je *suis resté(e) au lit*.

Journée d'Alice.

Décrivez la journée d'Alice vendredi dernier.

NOTE DE GRAMMAIRE
You usually answer a question in the same tense in which it is asked.

1. Est-ce qu'Alice était seule quand elle a quitté l'appartement? Quelle heure était-il?
2. Est-ce qu'elle a pris son parapluie avec elle? Est-ce qu'il pleuvait? Est-ce qu'il faisait froid? Quels vêtements est-ce qu'Alice portait?
3. Est-ce qu'Alice a pris quelque chose au café? Est-ce qu'elle était seule?
4. Quelle heure était-il quand elle est rentrée chez elle?

C. Le week-end dernier.

Avec un(e) partenaire, changez la conversation entre Cathy et Micheline comme indiqué.

1. After the restaurant, Micheline and her friends went to the movies.
2. The food was good, but Micheline and her friends did not talk much because they were very tired.
3. Talk about the last time you ate out with friends.

Ça t'a plu? *Did you like it?* **Rien du tout.** *Nothing at all.*

✓ *Pour vérifier*

If one action interrupts another one that is already in progress, which one is in the **passé composé** and which is in the **imparfait?**

Note. The overall contrast between the use of the **passé composé** and **imparfait** is presented in the next section and recycled in the next *Compétence*.

Telling what was going on when something else happened: *L'imparfait et le passé composé*

As you have seen, the **imparfait** is used to tell how things used to be or what someone did or what happened over and over in the past. You also use the **imparfait** to say what was going on when something else occurred. To say what happened, interrupting the first activity, use the **passé composé.**

> Le professeur parlait quand je suis entré(e) dans la salle de classe.
> Il pleuvait ce matin quand j'ai quitté la maison.
> J'étais très fatigué(e) quand je suis rentré(e) hier soir.

A. Quand ils sont rentrés...
Deux couples ont laissé leurs enfants avec une nouvelle baby-sitter le week-end dernier. Qui faisait les choses suivantes quand ils sont rentrés?

Exemple porter les vêtements de sa mère
Annick portait les vêtements de sa mère quand ils sont rentrés.

1. embrasser *(to kiss)* son petit ami
2. parler au téléphone
3. fumer
4. jouer dans l'escalier
5. jouer à des jeux vidéo
6. manger quelque chose sur la table

Maintenant, répondez aux questions suivantes d'après l'illustration.

1. Quelle heure était-il quand les parents sont rentrés?
2. Qui écrivait *(was writing)* sur le mur?
3. Que faisait le chien?
4. Combien d'enfants est-ce qu'il y avait dans la maison?
5. Qui était avec la baby-sitter?

B. En cours. Qu'est-ce qu'on faisait quand vous êtes arrivé(e) au cours de français aujourd'hui?

Exemple   le professeur / être dans la salle de classe
   Quand je suis arrivé(e) aujourd'hui, le professeur était dans la salle de classe / le professeur n'était pas dans la salle de classe.

Quand je suis arrivé(e) aujourd'hui...

1. des étudiants / parler
2. des étudiants / faire leurs devoirs
3. je / avoir faim
4. il / faire froid dans la salle de classe
5. je / être fatigué(e)
6. nous / aller passer un examen *(to take a test)*
7. mes devoirs / être faits *(done)*
8. la porte / être fermée *(closed)*

C. Quelques photos. Alice montre des photos de sa famille en France. Qu'est-ce qu'ils faisaient quand on a pris ces photos? Dites aussi quel temps il faisait.

Exemple   **Quand on a pris cette photo, nous faisions du bateau. Il faisait beau.**

Quand on a pris cette photo...

Exemple   nous...

1. les enfants...

2. Vincent...

3. Éric...

4. Vincent et moi...

5. Éric et Vincent...

D. Hier. Demandez à votre partenaire ce qui se passait *(what was happening)* quand il/elle est rentré(e) hier.

Follow-up for *D. Hier.* Have students report about their partners to the class.

Quand tu es rentré(e) hier...

1. quelle heure était-il?
2. quel temps faisait-il?
3. est-ce que tu étais seul(e)?
4. est-ce que tu étais fatigué(e)?
5. est-ce que tu avais envie de dormir?
6. qu'est-ce que tu avais envie de faire?
7. est-ce que tu avais des devoirs à faire?

1. Do you generally use the **passé composé** or the **imparfait** to say what happened at a specific moment? to describe how things were or used to be?

2. What are the three main uses of the **passé composé**? What are the three main uses of the **imparfait**?

3. Which would you use to talk about how you were feeling? to describe a setting? to tell what happened on a specific occasion?

Note. In this section, students are introduced to the different uses of the **passé composé** and **imparfait** and are given opportunities to practice each distinction. In the next *Compétence,* they will put paragraphs into the past, distinguishing between the two tenses.

Suggestion. Before contrasting the two past tenses, review each as follows. First, review the formation of the **passé composé.** Remind students that it is used to tell about specific events that happened. Put these sentences on the board or a transparency. Tell students that this is what happened yesterday and have them change these sentences to the **passé composé. 1.** Je vais au cinéma avec un ami. **2.** Nous prenons la voiture. **3.** Après le film nous allons au café. **4.** Je prends un chocolat et mon ami mange un sandwich. **5.** Et toi? Qu'est-ce que tu fais? **6.** Tes amis et toi, vous sortez? Then have students do **A. Hier.** Next review the formation of the **imparfait.** Remind students that the **imparfait** is used to tell how things used to be or what was going on. Tell them that this is what used to happen when you were young and have them put the same sentences you gave above into the **imparfait.** Then do **B. À dix ans.**

Telling what happened and describing the circumstances: *Le passé composé et l'imparfait*

As you have seen, you use the **passé composé** and **imparfait** to convey different meanings. In English, the use of different past tenses also changes a message. Consider these sentences. Is the message the same in each? What is the difference?

When her husband came home, they kissed.
When her husband came home, they were kissing.

You have learned to use the **imparfait** to tell how things used to be or what was going on when something else occurred. You also use the **imparfait** to:

- set the scene or describe the background (*what was*)

Il était minuit et il faisait noir.   *It was midnight and it was dark.*

- describe physical or mental states (*how someone felt*)

Elle était fatiguée et elle avait faim.   *She was tired and she was hungry.*

You have learned to use the **passé composé** to talk about what happened or what someone did at a particular moment in the past. You also use the **passé composé** to:

- relate the sequence of events (*what happened next*)

Le voleur est entré par la fenêtre   *The thief entered through the window*
et il a pris mon sac.   *and he took my purse.*

- say if a change of state occurred. (Watch for words like **tout d'un coup** *[all of a sudden]*, **soudain** *[suddenly]*, **une fois** *[once]*, and **un jour** *[one day]*.)

Tout d'un coup, elle a eu peur.   *Suddenly she got frightened.*

Consider all these uses of the **imparfait** and the **passé composé.**

USE THE IMPARFAIT TO SAY:	USE THE PASSÉ COMPOSÉ TO SAY:
1. HOW THINGS USED TO BE OR WHAT USED TO HAPPEN	**1. WHAT HAPPENED AT A PRECISE MOMENT OR FOR A SPECIFIC DURATION**
• continuous actions or states • repeated or habitual actions of an unspecified duration	• completed actions
2. WHAT WAS GOING ON	**2. WHAT HAPPENED NEXT**
• scene or setting • interrupted actions	• sequence of events • actions interrupting something in progress
3. WHAT THINGS WERE LIKE OR HOW SOMEONE FELT	**3. WHAT CHANGED**
• physical or mental states	• changes in states

Prononciation: *Le passé composé et l'imparfait*

Since the use of the **passé composé** or the **imparfait** imparts a different message, it is important that that you differentiate what you hear and that you pronounce each tense distinctly. Listen to these pairs of sentences. Where do you hear a difference?

Je travaillais.	Elle mangeait.	Tu parlais.	Il allait.
J'ai travaillé.	Elle a mangé.	Tu as parlé.	Il est allé.

A. Hier. Est-ce que vous avez fait ces choses hier? Utilisez le passé composé.

Exemple   quitter la maison avant huit heures du matin
         Oui, hier j'ai quitté la maison avant huit heures du matin.

1. prendre l'autobus pour aller à l'université
2. aller en cours
3. déjeuner avec des amis
4. rester à la maison l'après-midi
5. dîner seul(e)
6. faire vos devoirs
7. sortir avec des copains (copines)
8. rentrer tard

B. À dix ans. Est-ce que vous faisiez ces choses quand vous aviez dix ans? Utilisez l'imparfait.

Exemple   souvent parler au téléphone
         Oui, quand j'avais dix ans, je parlais souvent au téléphone.

1. aimer l'école
2. passer beaucoup de temps en famille
3. faire du sport chaque week-end
4. jouer avec des copains après l'école
5. prendre le car scolaire *(school bus)* pour aller à l'école

C. Quand? Alice parle de ce qu'elle a fait hier et aussi des choses qu'elle faisait quand elle était petite. Écoutez ce qu'elle dit et, sur une feuille de papier, écrivez le numéro de chaque phrase dans la colonne appropriée.

Exemple 1   Je jouais du piano.
Exemple 2   J'ai mangé un sandwich.

HIER	QUAND J'ÉTAIS PETITE
EXEMPLE 2	EXEMPLE 1

Suggestions for *A. Hier.* and *B. À dix ans.* A. Have students focus on pronouncing the forms of the **passé composé** and **imparfait** distinctly. **B.** Remind students that the **passé composé** is used to tell what happened for a set period of time and that the **imparfait** is used to tell how things used to be over an indefinite period of time. After students have completed the two exercises, have them translate the sentences into English to verify comprehension of the **passé composé** / **imparfait** distinction.

Script for *C. Quand?* EXEMPLE 1 Je jouais du piano. **EXEMPLE 2** J'ai mangé un sandwich. **1.** J'ai joué au tennis. **2.** Je nageais avec mes amis. **3.** Je mangeais beaucoup. **4.** Je téléphonais à ma grand-mère le dimanche. **5.** J'ai écouté un CD de jazz à la radio. **6.** J'ai dormi dix heures. **7.** Je regardais la télé après le dîner. **8.** J'ai fait du shopping.

Follow-up for *C. Quand?* Give students the same sentences as dictation. Then ask follow-up questions about each, such as: **Alice jouait du piano quand elle était petite. Et vous? Est-ce que vous jouiez du piano quand vous étiez petit(e)? Alice a mangé un sandwich hier. Et vous? Est-ce que vous avez mangé un sandwich hier?**

Passiez-vous beaucoup de temps en famille?

Follow-up for *D. On était en train de...*
Complétez les phrases suivantes avec un verbe à l'imparfait. **1.** Quand le professeur est arrivé en cours, les étudiants... **2.** Quand je suis arrivé(e) en cours, les étudiants... **3.** La dernière fois que quelqu'un a téléphoné, je... **4.** La dernière fois que je suis arrivé(e) chez un(e) ami(e), il/elle... **5.** La dernière fois que j'ai vu mon meilleur ami (ma meilleure amie), il/elle...

D. On était en train de... Expliquez ce qui s'est passé. Suivez l'exemple.

Exemple

Vincent (jouer au golf) / quand il (commencer à pleuvoir)
Vincent jouait au golf quand il a commencé à pleuvoir.

1. Cathy (parler au téléphone) / quand une amie (arriver)

2. Alice (préparer ses cours) / quand un ami (téléphoner)

3. Michèle (embrasser *[to kiss]* un copain / Éric (arriver)

4. Quand le chien (entrer) / le chat (dormir)

5. Alice (faire la cuisine) / quand le chat (voir le chien)

6. Quand Vincent (rentrer) / Alice (nettoyer *[to clean]* la cuisine)

Suggestion for *E. La journée d'Alice.*
Point out that this exercise focuses on the distinction between setting the scene and narrating events. Ask students which tense you use to do each.

E. La journée d'Alice. Alice parle de sa journée. Décidez si chaque phrase décrit la scène / la situation ou les actions. Récrivez les phrases dans chaque colonne.

Il est sept heures. Il pleut. Je quitte la maison. Il y a beaucoup de voitures sur la route. J'arrive au bureau en retard. Mon patron *(boss)* n'est pas content. Je travaille beaucoup. Je ne déjeune pas. Je rentre à cinq heures. Je suis fatiguée. Il n'y a rien à manger. Nous allons au restaurant. Nous rentrons. Je prends un bain. Il est 11 heures. Je vais au lit.

Exemple

LA SCÈNE / LA SITUATION	LES ACTIONS
Il est sept heures.	**Je quitte la maison.**

Maintenant, récrivez le paragraphe en mettant les verbes décrivant l'action **au passé composé** et les verbes décrivant la scène ou la situation **à l'imparfait**.

F. Qu'est-ce qu'ils voulaient faire?

Qu'est-ce que les Pérez et leurs amis ont fait hier? Qu'est-ce qu'ils voulaient faire?

Exemple   **Moi, j'ai fait du jogging mais je voulais dormir.**

Moi...

1. Le chien et moi, nous...

2. Éric et Cathy...

3. Vincent...

4. Nos amis...

5. Michel...

Suggestions for *F. Qu'est-ce qu'ils voulaient faire?* **and** *G. Pourquoi?* Point out that these exercises focus on the distinction between actions and mental and physical states. Ask students which tense you use to talk about each.

G. Pourquoi?

Expliquez pourquoi Alice a fait ou n'a pas fait ces choses, comme dans l'exemple.

Exemple   ne pas travailler / être malade *(sick)*
               Alice n'a pas travaillé parce qu'elle était malade.

1. faire du shopping / vouloir acheter une nouvelle robe
2. ne pas aller en cours / être malade
3. ne pas faire les devoirs / être trop fatiguée
4. ne pas sortir avec ses amis / devoir préparer un examen
5. mettre un pull / avoir froid

Suggestions for *H. Entretien.* Remind students to answer a question in the tense in which it is asked.

H. Entretien.

Interviewez votre partenaire au sujet de la dernière fois qu'il/elle est allé(e) au restaurant avec des amis.

La dernière fois que tu es allé(e) au restaurant avec des amis...

1. Quel temps faisait-il? Qu'est-ce que tu as mis pour sortir?
2. Quelle heure était-il quand tu es arrivé(e) au restaurant?
3. Avais-tu très faim? As-tu mangé tout de suite?
4. Comment était le repas?
5. Qu'est-ce que tu as fait après le repas?
6. Quelle heure était-il quand tu es rentré(e)? Étais-tu fatigué(e)? Est-ce que tu es allé(e) tout de suite au lit? As-tu bien dormi?
7. Le lendemain, jusqu'à quelle heure es-tu resté(e) au lit?

I. Une sortie.

Préparez une conversation avec un(e) camarade de classe dans laquelle vous parlez d'une sortie avec des ami(e)s. Dites ce que vous vouliez faire et pourquoi, où vous êtes allé(e)s, le jour et l'heure. Ajoutez aussi d'autres détails pour faire une bonne description.

Suggestion for *I. Une sortie.* Tell students to use their answers to the questions in *H. Entretien* and the presentation on page 220 as guides in preparing this activity.

COMPÉTENCE 4

NOTE Culturelle

Jean Cocteau (1889–1963) était poète, romancier *(novelist)*, dramaturge *(playwright)*, dessinateur *(artist)*, peintre *(painter)* et aussi cinéaste *(filmmaker)*.

TRANSPARENCY: 6-4

Warm-ups. Questions orales. *(Remind students to answer a question in the tense in which it is asked.)* **1.** Avec qui est-ce que vous avez dîné au restaurant récemment? À quel restaurant êtes-vous allé(e)s? Quelle heure était-il quand vous êtes arrivé(e)s? Est-ce que le repas était bon? Est-ce que vous avez beaucoup mangé? **2.** Combien de temps est-ce que vous êtes resté(e)s au restaurant? À quelle heure est-ce que vous êtes parti(e)s? Quel temps est-ce qu'il faisait? **3.** Qu'est-ce que vous avez fait après? Est-ce que vous étiez fatigué(e)? Est-ce que vous vouliez rentrer?

NOTE DE GRAMMAIRE

Tomber takes **être** as its auxiliary verb in the **passé composé** (Elle est tombée...).

Suggestion for the conversation. Have students first listen to the conversation with books closed and answer these questions. **1.** Qu'est-ce qu'Éric a fait le week-end dernier? **2.** Est-ce qu'il a aimé le film?

Les contes

Éric et Michèle sont allés voir le film classique *La Belle et la Bête* de Jean Cocteau. **Connaissez-vous** ce film? Connaissez-vous **le conte de fée** sur **lequel** il est basé?

Il était une fois un vieux **marchand** qui avait trois filles. Sa plus jeune fille, Belle, était très jolie, **douce** et **gracieuse.**

Un jour, la Bête a emprisonné le marchand. Belle **a promis** à la Bête de venir prendre la place de son père.

La Bête était horrible! Il était grand et laid et il avait l'air **féroce. Au début,** Belle avait très peur de **lui.** Mais elle était toujours gentille et patiente avec lui.

Petit à petit les choses ont changé. Belle et la Bête ont commencé à parler. La Bête a beaucoup changé et Belle a appris à apprécier le monstre. Finalement Belle **est tombée amoureuse de** lui! Et la Bête, lui aussi, a appris à aimer.

À suivre...

 Cathy parle à son frère de ses activités du week-end dernier.

CATHY: Tu es sorti ce week-end?
ÉRIC: Oui, je suis allé au cinéclub avec Michèle.
CATHY: Quel film est-ce que vous avez vu?
ÉRIC: Nous avons vu *La Belle et la Bête* de Cocteau.
CATHY: C'est un classique! Il t'a plu?
ÉRIC: Oui, il m'a beaucoup plu. C'était très intéressant. Les acteurs **ont bien joué. Les effets spéciaux** étaient excellents et il n'y avait pas **trop de** violence.

---

un conte *a story* ***La Belle et la Bête*** *Beauty and the Beast* **Connaissez-vous... ?** *Do you know . . . ?* **un conte de fée** *a fairy tale* **lequel (laquelle)** *which* **Il était une fois...** *Once upon a time there was . . .* **un marchand** *a merchant, a shopkeeper* **doux (douce)** *sweet, soft, gentle* **gracieux (gracieuse)** *gracious* **elle a promis (promettre** *to promise* [past participle **promis**]) **féroce** *ferocious* **Au début** *At the beginning* **lui** *him* **tomber amoureux (amoureuse) de** *to fall in love with* **À suivre** *To be continued* **bien jouer** *to act well* (in movies and theater) **Les effets spéciaux** *The special effects* **trop de** *too much*

A. Qu'est-ce qui s'est passé? Relisez l'histoire *(the story)* de *La Belle et la Bête* à la page précédente. Sur une feuille de papier, faites une liste de toutes *les actions* ou *les changements* qui ont eu lieu *(took place)* dans l'histoire. Ne mettez pas sur votre liste les phrases qui décrivent les personnages, la scène ou les circonstances.

B. C'est qui? Décidez lequel des personnages les adjectifs suivants décrivent et formez une phrase, comme dans l'exemple. N'oubliez pas d'utiliser l'imparfait pour faire une description!

LE PÈRE DE BELLE   **BELLE**   **LA BÊTE**

Exemple   douce   **Belle était douce.**

1. jolie   **2.** grande et laide   **3.** toujours gentille   **4.** vieux   **5.** gracieuse

Maintenant, formez des phrases pour dire qui a fait les choses suivantes. N'oubliez pas d'utiliser le passé composé pour raconter les actions d'un récit!

LE PÈRE DE BELLE   **BELLE**   **LA BÊTE**

Exemple   promettre de venir prendre la place de son père
Belle a promis de venir prendre la place de son père.

1. emprisonner le marchand
2. prendre la place de son père
3. commencer à parler avec la Bête
4. beaucoup changer
5. apprendre à apprécier la Bête
6. tomber amoureuse de la Bête
7. apprendre à aimer

C. Entretien. Interviewez votre partenaire.

1. Quel film est-ce que tu as vu récemment? Est-ce que tu as vu ce film au cinéma ou à la télé? Est-ce que tu as aimé le film? Est-ce que tu recommandes ce film?
2. Qui a joué dans ce film? Est-ce que les acteurs ont bien joué? Est-ce qu'il y avait beaucoup de violence? Il y avait beaucoup d'effets spéciaux?
3. Qu'est-ce que tu as fait après le film?

D. Le week-end dernier. Avec un(e) partenaire, changez la conversation entre Cathy et Éric comme indiqué.

1. Éric saw a sci-fi movie **(un film de science-fiction).** He didn't like it because it was stupid and there was too much violence, but the special effects were excellent.
2. You and a friend are talking about a movie you saw recently.

Les sorties ■ *deux cent vingt-neuf* **229**

✓ Pour vérifier

If you were describing a play that you saw, would you use **le passé composé** or **l'imparfait** to describe the setting and what was happening on stage when the curtain went up? Which tense would you use to explain the actions of the actors that advanced the story?

Narrating what happened:
Le passé composé et l'imparfait (reprise)

When recounting a story in the past, you use both the **passé composé** and the **imparfait.** Use the **imparfait** to set the scene and give background information about the characters and the setting. Use the **passé composé** to narrate the sequence of events that advance the story. For example, if you were telling the old French tale **Cendrillon** *(Cinderella),* you might begin . . .

> Il **était** une fois une belle jeune fille qui **s'appelait** Cendrillon. Son père **était** mort et elle **habitait** avec sa belle-mère et ses deux demi-sœurs. Sa belle-mère **était** cruelle et ses demi-sœurs **étaient** laides, bêtes et très gâtées *(spoiled).* C'**était** Cendrillon qui **faisait** tout le travail mais elle **était** toujours belle et gracieuse. Un jour, le prince **a décidé** de donner un bal au palais et un messager **est allé** chez Cendrillon avec une invitation.

There are only two events that occur, advancing the story in the preceding paragraph: the prince decided to give a ball and the messenger went to Cinderella's house. These two verbs are in the **passé composé.** All the rest of the paragraph is background information, setting the scene, so the verbs are in the **imparfait.**

When deciding whether to put a verb in the **passé composé** or the **imparfait,** learn to ask yourself whether you are talking about background information or something that was already in progress **(imparfait),** or the next thing that happened in the story **(passé composé).**

Suggestion for *A. Il était une fois...* and *B. Le Petit Chaperon rouge.* Encourage students to read a story in its entirety before selecting the proper tenses. You may first wish to work with them to pick out the verbs that narrate the action and those that set the scene.

A. Il était une fois... Récrivez l'histoire de *La Belle et la Bête* au passé en mettant les verbes entre parenthèses à l'imparfait ou au passé composé.

Exemple   Il y avait un marchand très riche qui **avait** (avoir) trois filles.

Il y avait un marchand très riche qui _____ (avoir) trois filles. Ils _____ (habiter) tous ensemble dans une belle maison en ville. Mais un jour, le marchand _____ (perdre *[to lose]*, past participle **perdu**) toute sa fortune et ses filles et lui _____ (devoir) aller habiter dans une petite maison à la campagne.

Ses deux filles aînées _____ (être) très malheureuses *(unhappy).* Elles _____ (parler) constamment des choses qu'elles _____ (vouloir). Belle _____ (être) la plus jeune de ses filles. Elle _____ (être) très jolie et aussi très douce. Elle _____ (accepter) sa nouvelle vie et elle _____ (être) heureuse *(happy).*

Un jour, le marchand _____ (partir) pour la ville voisine *(neighboring).* Il _____ (neiger) et il _____ (faire) très froid et en route, il ne _____ (pouvoir) rien voir dans la forêt. Le marchand _____ (penser) qu'il _____ (aller) mourir quand, soudain, il _____ (trouver) un château. La porte du château _____ (être) ouverte et il _____ (décider) d'entrer. Il _____ (remarquer *[to notice]*) une grande table couverte de plats délicieux. Il _____ (manger), puis il _____ (faire) une sieste *(nap).*

Après sa sieste, il _____ (sortir) dans le jardin où il _____ (trouver) une jolie rose qu'il _____ (vouloir) apporter *(to bring)* à Belle. À ce moment-là, un monstre horrible _____ (arriver) et _____ (commencer) à crier *(to shout)* qu'il _____ (vouloir) que Belle vienne habiter chez lui. Sinon *(Otherwise)* la Bête _____ (aller) tuer *(to kill)* le marchand.

Quand le marchand _____ (rentrer), il _____ (raconter [to recount]) ses aventures à ses filles et Belle _____ (décider) d'aller habiter chez la Bête. Quand elle _____ (arriver) au château, elle _____ (trouver) tout ce dont (that) elle _____ (avoir) besoin. Chaque jour, elle _____ (avoir) tout ce qu'elle _____ (vouloir). Mais les cinq premiers jours, elle _____ (ne pas voir) la Bête.

Un jour, elle le (l') _____ (voir) pour la première fois pendant (while) qu'elle _____ (faire) une promenade dans le jardin. Elle le (l') _____ (trouver) horrible et elle _____ (crier). Belle _____ (avoir peur) et elle _____ (ne pas pouvoir) regarder la Bête dans les yeux, mais elle _____ (aller) faire une promenade avec lui. La conversation _____ (être) agréable. Quand la Bête _____ (demander) à Belle de faire une promenade deux jours plus tard, elle _____ (accepter).

Après ce jour-là, ils _____ (faire) une promenade chaque après-midi. Ils _____ (parler) de tout. Au début, Belle _____ (avoir) très peur de la Bête mais, finalement, Belle _____ (apprendre) à avoir confiance en lui. Après un certain temps, Belle _____ (commencer) à aimer le monstre et un jour elle l'_____ (embrasser [to kiss]). Tout d'un coup, le visage (face) de la Bête _____ (changer). Ce _____ (ne plus être) une bête. C'_____ (être) un beau et jeune prince.

Supplemental activity. Have students write a short version of their favorite story.

B. Le Petit Chaperon rouge.
Racontez l'histoire du *Petit Chaperon rouge* (*Little Red Riding Hood*) en mettant les verbes entre parenthèses au passé composé ou à l'imparfait.

Une petite fille _____ (habiter) avec sa mère dans une grande forêt. Elle _____ (ne pas avoir) de père mais sa grand-mère _____ (habiter) dans une petite maison de l'autre côté de la forêt. On appelait (*called*) cette petite fille le Petit Chaperon rouge parce qu'elle _____ (porter) toujours un chaperon rouge. Un jour, sa mère _____ (demander) au Petit Chaperon rouge d'apporter (*to take*) des choses à manger chez sa grand-mère. La petite fille _____ (partir) tout de suite et elle _____ (traverser [*to cross*]) la forêt quand un grand loup (*wolf*) _____ (sortir) de derrière un arbre. Il _____ (avoir) très faim et il _____ (vouloir) savoir (*to know*) où le Petit Chaperon rouge _____ (aller) avec toutes ces choses à manger. Le Petit Chaperon rouge _____ (expliquer [*to explain*]) qu'elle les _____ (apporter) chez sa grand-mère. Le loup _____ (partir) dans la forêt et la jeune fille _____ (continuer) son chemin (*way*). Mais le loup _____ (prendre) un chemin plus court pour aller chez la grand-mère et il _____ (arriver) le premier. Comme la porte _____ (ne pas être) fermée, il _____ (entrer) dans la maison. Il _____ (manger) la grand-mère toute entière (*whole*) et _____ (prendre) sa place. Quelques minutes plus tard, le Petit Chaperon rouge _____ (entrer) dans la chambre de sa grand-mère. Il y _____ (avoir) très peu de lumière (*light*) et le Petit Chaperon rouge _____ (ne pas pouvoir) voir très bien. La petite fille _____ (commencer) à parler à sa grand-mère:
— Quels gros yeux tu as, grand-mère!
— C'est pour mieux te voir, ma petite chérie!
— Quelles grandes oreilles tu as, grand-mère!
— C'est pour mieux t'entendre, ma petite chérie!
— Quelles grandes dents tu as, grand-mère!
— C'est pour mieux te manger, ma petite chérie!
À ce moment-là, le loup _____ (sauter [*to jump*]) du lit, il _____ (manger) le Petit Chaperon rouge tout entier et il _____ (sortir) de la maison. Par hasard (*By chance*), un chasseur (*hunter*) _____ (passer) devant la maison à ce moment-là. Il _____ (voir) le loup et il le (l') _____ (tuer [*to kill*]). Quand il a ouvert le ventre (*belly*) du loup, la fille et sa grand-mère _____ (sortir) vivantes (*alive*) parce que le loup les avait mangées toutes entières.

Reprise: *Making invitations and talking about the past*

In *Chapitre 6,* you practiced issuing and accepting or declining invitations, and narrating in the past. Now you have a chance to review what you learned.

A. Invitations.
Invitez un(e) camarade de classe à faire les choses suivantes. Il/Elle va accepter une de vos invitations, refuser une de vos invitations et suggérer une autre activité pour la troisième. Utilisez une variété d'expressions.

Exemple aller au cinéma demain
— Tu voudrais aller au cinéma demain?
— Oui, je voudrais bien.

1. aller prendre un verre après les cours
2. aller danser samedi soir
3. aller voir une exposition au musée dimanche après-midi

Maintenant, refaites les trois invitations pour inviter toute la classe.

Exemple aller au cinéma demain
Vous voudriez aller au cinéma demain?

B. Non, merci.
Un ami téléphone à Éric pour l'inviter à sortir, mais Éric préfère ne rien faire et il refuse. L'ami insiste. Éric est très imaginatif dans ses excuses. Jouez les deux rôles avec un(e) partenaire.

Suggestion for C. On ne peut pas toujours faire ce qu'on veut! Allow students time to prepare.

C. On ne peut pas toujours faire ce qu'on veut!
Éric explique ce que les Pérez ont envie de faire et ce qu'ils ont besoin de faire. Refaites ses phrases en utilisant **vouloir, pouvoir** et **devoir** comme dans l'exemple.

Exemple Maman a envie de dormir, mais elle a besoin de travailler.
Maman veut dormir, mais elle ne peut pas parce qu'elle doit travailler.

1. Papa a envie de jouer au golf, mais il a besoin de faire des courses.
2. Michel a envie de faire du vélo, mais il a besoin de faire ses devoirs.
3. Michèle et moi, nous avons envie de sortir ce soir, mais nous avons besoin de préparer les cours.
4. Nos amis ont envie de sortir aussi, mais ils ont besoin de travailler.
5. Moi, j'ai envie de faire du vélo, mais j'ai besoin de faire la lessive.

D. En cours.
Dites si les personnes suivantes font les choses indiquées.

Exemple Moi, je (dormir en cours)
Moi, je ne dors pas en cours.

1. Moi, je (partir de la maison avant 8 heures pour aller à l'université, dormir en cours, sortir avec des camarades de classe le samedi soir)
2. Les meilleurs étudiants (partir de la maison tôt pour arriver en cours à l'heure *[on time]*, sortir tous les soirs, dormir dans le laboratoire de langues, faire toujours les devoirs)
3. Les autres étudiants et moi, nous (dormir en cours, faire attention *[to pay attention]* en cours, sortir du cours en avance *[early]*, sortir ensemble après les cours)
4. Quand il y a un examen, le professeur (sortir de la salle de classe, dormir pendant l'examen, sortir au café avec nous après le cours)

E. Entretien. Les questions suivantes sont au présent. Mettez-les au passé composé ou à l'imparfait pour demander à un(e) camarade de classe ce qu'il/elle a fait le dernier jour que vous étiez en cours de français.

Exemple   À quelle heure est-ce que tu quittes la maison?
   — **À quelle heure est-ce que tu as quitté la maison hier (jeudi...)?**
   — **J'ai quitté la maison à huit heures.**

1. Qu'est-ce que tu mets pour sortir?
2. Quel temps fait-il quand tu quittes la maison?
3. Est-ce que tu veux rester à la maison?
4. Est-ce que tu prends ta voiture ou l'autobus ou est-ce que tu vas à pied à l'université?
5. À quelle heure est-ce que le cours de français commence?
6. Est-ce que tu as faim quand tu sors du cours?
7. Est-ce que tu peux faire ce que tu veux après les cours?
8. Quelle heure est-il quand tu rentres?
9. Qui prépare le dîner? Est-ce que c'est bon?
10. Qu'est-ce que tu veux faire après le dîner?
11. Est-ce que tu as besoin de faire quelque chose?
12. Qu'est-ce que tu fais?

Maintenant, écrivez un paragraphe décrivant votre journée le dernier jour que vous étiez en cours de français.

F. Une aventure! Regardez l'illustration et racontez *(tell)* ce qui s'est passé chez les Fédor le week-end dernier. Dites **le voleur** pour *the thief*, **voler** pour *to steal* et **entrer par la fenêtre** pour *to come in through the window*.

Avant de commencer, réfléchissez *(think)* aux questions suivantes.

- What night was it?
- What time was it?
- What was the weather like?
- How many people were in the Fédors' living room?
- Why were they there?
- What was each person doing?
- What was in the bedroom?
- What happened?
- What happened next?

Suggestion for *E. Entretien.* Allow students time to prepare the questions and correct them together before having them interview their partners.

Follow-up for *E. Entretien.* Questions orales. **1.** Quelle heure était-il quand vous êtes arrivé(e) à l'université aujourd'hui? **2.** Quel temps faisait-il? **3.** Qu'est-ce que vous avez fait quand vous êtes arrivé(e) à la fac? **4.** Est-ce que vous avez vu d'autres étudiants? **5.** Qu'est-ce qu'ils faisaient? **6.** Qu'est-ce que vous faisiez quand je suis entré(e) dans la salle de classe?

Suggestions for *F. Une aventure!* Students may need time to prepare this activity. You may wish to have them work in groups. For the last question, you may need to supply vocabulary words such as **la police** and **arrêter.**

Options for *F. Une aventure!* The questions given are designed to help guide students in preparing their narrative. They are given in English so that students will be responsible for creating the French sentences on their own. Depending on the level of your class, you may prefer to do one of the following options: **1.** Make a transparency of the illustration without the questions. **2.** Make a transparency of the illustration with the questions in French.

TRANSPARENCY: 6-5

Follow-up for *F. Une aventure!* Ask students additional questions about the illustration, such as what various people looked like and were wearing, etc.

Supplemental activity. Have students write a paragraph about an important day in their lives, such as a marriage, the first day of college, or a first date.

le voleur

Les Dupont   Les Fédor   Simon   Pascale

LECTURE ET *composition*

Note. The vocabulary in this section does not appear in the end-of-chapter vocabulary lists and is meant for recognition only. You may wish to let students know in advance whether you intend to test them on this vocabulary.

LECTURE: Un peu d'histoire

Les domaines spécialisés (le cinéma, les affaires, la musique, les mathématiques) utilisent un vocabulaire spécialisé. Vous allez lire un article du magazine *Jeune et Jolie* dans lequel on parle de **la découverte** des techniques de projection cinématographique et des débuts difficiles du cinéma. Avant de lire l'article, faites une liste (en anglais) de mots qui **se rapportent à ce sujet.** Cette liste **vous aidera à** deviner **le sens** des mots que vous ne connaissez pas.

Devinez! Devinez le sens des mots en italique dans les contextes du cinéma et de la science.

LE CINÉMA

1. J'aime louer des vidéos, mais pour voir des films d'aventures, je préfère aller au cinéma parce que *l'écran* est plus grand.
2. Je préfère aller au cinéma l'après-midi parce que *l'entrée* est moins chère.
3. Quand le projecteur ne fonctionne pas bien, les *spectateurs* ne peuvent pas voir le film et ils ne sont pas contents.

LA SCIENCE

1. Pierre et Marie Curie ont découvert le radium. Cela a été une *découverte* importante.
2. Une *expérience* scientifique mal *réglée* peut avoir de graves conséquences.

Un peu d'histoire

En 1895, les frères Lumière, Louis et Alphonse, font une découverte sur la projection d'images. Très vite, cette découverte **devient** une curiosité scientifique... Ainsi, le cinéma est né à Paris **lors d'**une projection officielle le 28 décembre 1895, dans un sous-sol du Grand-Café, **à deux pas de** l'Opéra de Paris, 14, boulevard des Capucines. L'écran faisait un mètre **de haut** et l'entrée coûtait un franc: **il y eut** 35 spectateurs. Le cinéma quitte alors le cercle académique pour des salles toutes simples, des cafés ou des chapiteaux.

Malheureusement l'histoire commence mal! En 1897, plus de 150 personnes **meurent carbonisées** lors d'une séance, un projecteur mal réglé au Bazar de la Charité **prend feu... La classe aisée** est choquée et se réfugie vers le music-hall.

---

une découverte *a discovery*   **se rapporter à** *to be related to*   **un sujet** *a subject*   **vous aidera à** *will help you*   **le sens** *the meaning*   **devient** *becomes*   **lors de** *at the time of*   **à deux pas de** *a short distance from*   **de haut** *high*   **il y eut** *there were*   **des chapiteaux** (*m*) *tents*   **meurent carbonisées** *are burned to death*   **prendre feu** *to catch fire*   **La classe aisée** *The upper class*

A. Vrai ou faux?

1. Le cinéma est né avec une découverte des frères Lumière.
2. Il y a une première projection officielle en 1895 au sous-sol du Grand-Café à Paris.
3. Le cinéma est immédiatement populaire et on commence tout de suite à construire *(to build)* des salles de cinéma.
4. En 1897, un accident choque les spectateurs et ils décident d'abandonner le cinéma pour retourner au music-hall.

B. Un peu d'histoire.
Complétez les phrases avec un mot de la liste. Après, changez l'ordre des initiales de chacun de ces mots pour trouver un nom qu'on associe à l'histoire du cinéma. (Il est nécessaire de changer certains accents aussi!)

entrée   Lumière   écran   images   mètre   réglé   un franc

En 1895, les frères _____ font une découverte sur la projection d' _____ et voilà que le cinéma est né. La première projection officielle est le 28 décembre 1895 au sous-sol d'un café à Paris. L' _____ coûte _____ et l' _____ n'est pas grand: il mesure un _____ de haut. Pendant un certain temps, les Parisiens ont la possibilité de voir ces «projections» dans les cafés ou d'autres salles simples. En 1897, un projecteur mal _____ prend feu et 150 spectateurs meurent carbonisés. L'histoire du cinéma ne commence pas bien!

MOT TROUVÉ: ☐ ☐ ☐ ☐ ☐ ☐ ☐

Composition

A. Organisez-vous.
Vous allez décrire un film que vous avez vu. D'abord, faites une liste de dix phrases à l'imparfait dans lesquelles vous décrivez les personnages *(characters)* (personnalité, apparence physique, etc.) et la situation. Ensuite, utilisez le passé composé pour décrire dix choses qui se sont passées *(happened)* dans le film.

IMPARFAIT: DESCRIPTION DES PERSONNAGES ET DE LA SITUATION

Exemple
Une jeune Américaine et son petit ami faisaient un voyage en France. Elle était grande et très belle...

PASSÉ COMPOSÉ: CE QUI S'EST PASSÉ

Exemple
Un jour, la jeune fille a rencontré un Français.
Ils sont sortis ensemble.

B. Rédaction: Un film.
Utilisez les phrases écrites dans *A. Organisez-vous* pour écrire un résumé du film.

C. C'est quel film?
Lisez votre composition à la classe. Les autres étudiants doivent deviner de quel film vous parlez.

If you have access to SYSTÈME-D software, you will find the following phrases, vocabulary, grammar, and dictionary aids there.

Phrases: Describing people; Sequencing events; Linking ideas
Vocabulary: Personality; Hair colors
Grammar: Past imperfect; Compound past tense; Verbs with auxiliary être

COMPARAISONS *culturelles*

LE CINÉMA

See the *Instructor's Resource Manual* for the video script and activities.

Note. The vocabulary in this section does not appear in the end-of-chapter vocabulary list and is meant for recognition only. You may wish to let students know in advance whether you intend to test them on this vocabulary.

Suggestion. Have students check local video stores or the university library or media center to see what French films are available and assign groups to watch and report on different films. After each group has reported on a film, have them discuss what type of French film is popular on the local market and why this might be the case. Have them compare the content and style of French films to the content and style of those made here.

Note. Some of the movies mentioned in this section may not be appropriate for all audiences. You may wish to preview any movies before recommending them to students.

Depuis la découverte de la projection par les frères Lumière, la France joue un rôle très important dans l'histoire du cinéma. Le Français Georges Méliès a été le premier à utiliser des effets spéciaux **tels que le ralenti** et **la surimpression d'images.** Après **la Seconde Guerre mondiale, les metteurs en scène** de **la nouvelle vague** comme Claude Chabrol, Jean-Luc Godard, Éric Rohmer, Louis Malle et François Truffaut ont été les représentants les plus célèbres de **l'esprit** innovateur des **cinéastes** français. On peut trouver leurs films en vidéo avec **des sous-titres** en anglais.

Au revoir les enfants,
Louis Malle, 1987

Madame Bovary,
Claude Chabrol, 1991

Depuis la découverte *Since the discovery*   **tels que** *such as*   **le ralenti** *slow motion*   **la surimpression d'images** *double exposure*   **la Seconde Guerre mondiale** *World War II*   **un metteur en scène** *a director*   **la nouvelle vague** *new wave*   **l'esprit** *(m) spirit*   **un(e) cinéaste** *a filmmaker*   **des sous-titres** *(m) subtitles*

Comme les oscars aux États-Unis, les Français ont les césars, qui sont distribués chaque année dans les catégories des meilleurs: film, acteur, actrice, second rôle masculin, second rôle féminin, **jeune espoir masculin,** jeune espoir féminin, première **œuvre,** scénario, dialogue ou adaptation, **réalisateur,** décor, musique, photo, **son,** costumes, **montage,** film étranger et **court métrage.** Chaque année, il y a aussi un célèbre festival de films à Cannes, sur la Côte d'Azur, qui **attire** des artistes et cinéastes du monde entier.

Les films américains sont très populaires en France. Dans **un sondage** récent, les Français disent que le cinéma américain **réussit** mieux dans l'action et le suspense, **tandis que** le cinéma français est supérieur dans la réflexion, **le rire** et l'émotion. Certains films français ont eu du succès chez les Américains dont: *La Cage aux folles* (1979), *Z* (1969), *Un homme et une femme* (1966), *Emmanuelle* (1975), *Cousin, cousine* (1976), *Jean de Florette* (1987), *Manon des Sources* (1987), *Cyrano de Bergerac* (1991), *La Femme Nikita* (1991), *Le Dîner de cons* (1998). Tous ces films sont **disponibles** en vidéo avec des sous-titres en anglais.

Manon des Sources

La Femme Nikita

La Cage aux folles

À discuter.

1. Quels films français est-ce que vous connaissez? Quels genres de films les cinéastes américains font-ils le plus souvent? Et les cinéastes français?
2. À votre avis, pourquoi est-ce que les films français ne sont pas plus populaires aux États-Unis?
3. Certains Français trouvent qu'il y a trop d'influence américaine dans les salles de cinéma en France et que la culture française en est menacée. Est-ce que ce sentiment est justifié? Quel est le rôle du gouvernement dans la préservation de la culture? Est-ce qu'il doit y avoir une censure? des quotas? des subventions *(subsidies)?*
4. Est-ce que l'industrie cinématographique d'un pays est un reflet de sa culture? Si oui, quelles comparaisons culturelles peut-on faire entre les Français et les Américains?

---

jeune espoir masculin *best new actor* **une œuvre** *a work* **un réalisateur** *a producer* **le son** *sound* **le montage** *editing* **le court métrage** *short film* **attirer** *to attract* **un sondage** *a survey* **réussir** *to succeed* **tandis que** *while* **le rire** *laughter* **disponible** *available*

visit http://horizons.heinle.com

V O C A B U L A I R E

NOMS MASCULINS

l'amour	*love*
un film d'amour	*a romantic movie, a love story*
un film d'épouvante	*a horror movie*
un groupe	*a group*

NOMS FÉMININS

une idée	*an idea*
une invitation	*an invitation*
une personne	*a person*
une séance	*a showing*

EXPRESSIONS VERBALES

devoir	*must, to have to, to owe*
dire	*to say, to tell*
passer chez...	*to stop by . . . 's house*
passer un film	*to show a movie*
pouvoir	*can, may, to be able*
regretter	*to regret*
répondre (à)	*to answer, to respond (to)*
suggérer	*to suggest*
téléphoner (à)	*to phone*
vouloir	*to want*

DIVERS

allô	*hello* (on the telephone)
avec plaisir	*gladly, with pleasure*
Je t'invite...	*I'm inviting you . . .*
Je voudrais vous inviter...	*I'd like to invite you . . .*
Quelle bonne idée!	*What a good idea!*
quelqu'un	*someone, somebody*
tellement	*so much, so*
Vous voudriez... ?	*Would you like . . . ?*

NOMS MASCULINS

un copain	*a friend, a pal*
un lycée	*a high school*
un lycéen	*a high school student*
un restau-u	*a university cafeteria*

NOMS FÉMININS

une copine	*a friend, a pal*
une école	*a school*
une lycéenne	*a high school student*
la vie	*life*

EXPRESSIONS VERBALES

avoir cours	*to have class*
comparer	*to compare*
dormir	*to sleep*
faire du roller	*to rollerblade*
faire du skateboarding	*to skateboard*
partir (de / pour, à)	*to leave (from / for), to go away (from / to)*
quitter	*to leave*
sortir (de / à)	*to go out (of / to)*

DIVERS

dans le passé	*in the past*
en général	*in general*
fatigué(e)	*tired*
rien de spécial	*nothing special*

COMPÉTENCE 3

NOMS MASCULINS

un bistrot	a pub, a restaurant
le lendemain	the next day
un repas	a meal
un voleur	a thief

NOMS FÉMININS

une fois	once, one time
une sortie	an outing

EXPRESSIONS ADVERBIALES

un jour	one day
soudain	suddenly
tout de suite	right away
tout d'un coup	all of a sudden
vraiment	really, truly

DIVERS

Ça t'a plu?	Did you like it?
délicieux (délicieuse)	delicious
Il faisait noir.	It was dark.
par la fenêtre	through the window
Qu'est-ce qui s'est passé?	What happenend?
rien du tout	nothing at all

COMPÉTENCE 4

NOMS MASCULINS

un acteur	an actor
un conte	a story
un conte de fée	a fairy tale
les effets spéciaux	special effects
un marchand	a merchant, a shopkeeper
un monstre	a monster

NOMS FÉMININS

une actrice	an actress
une bête	a beast
une marchande	a merchant, a shopkeeper

EXPRESSIONS VERBALES

apprécier	to appreciate
à suivre	to be continued
changer	to change
Connaissez-vous... ?	Do you know . . . ?
emprisonner	to imprison
jouer	to act (in movies and theater)
prendre la place de	to take the place of
promettre	to promise
tomber amoureux (amoureuse) de	to fall in love with
venir	to come

ADJECTIFS

amoureux (amoureuse)	in love
basé(e) (sur)	based (on)
classique	classic
doux (douce)	sweet, soft, gentle
féroce	ferocious
gracieux (gracieuse)	gracious
horrible	horrible
patient(e)	patient

DIVERS

au début	at the beginning
finalement	finally
Il était une fois...	Once upon a time there was . . .
il / elle m'a plu	I liked it
lequel (laquelle)	which, which one
lui	him
petit à petit	little by little
trop de	too much, too many

Branchez-vous sur le français

Would you like to spend some time in France or in a French-speaking country? Would you enjoy living with a family, helping with the children? Working on an archaeological restoration? Working on a farm? There are a variety of temporary jobs available that pay only room and board, but allow you to practice your French and observe the culture.

One of the most popular ways for college-age students to spend a summer or a year in France is to work with a family as an **au pair. Au pairs** generally live with a family, where they are treated as a family member. In exchange for room and board and a small allowance, they help around the house, especially with the children, usually for five or six hours daily. They are sometimes expected to babysit at night, but they are guaranteed at least one day free each week. Many French families employ English-speaking **au pairs** to give their children contact with the English language. Lengths of stay generally range from a few months to a year.

In addition, many people are hired in France each year to work on archaeological sites or to restore old buildings. Generally you work seven or eight hours, five days per week for two or three weeks in exchange for food and accommodations. You will have to pay your own travel expenses, but if you are interested in improving your French while learning a little about history, this work can be very rewarding. The Council on International Education Exchange can arrange work at an archaeological site in France or in other francophone countries. The CIEE also arranges short jobs abroad in nature conservation or working with children and the elderly, where room and board are provided during your stay.

Traditionally, a popular late summer job among young foreigners was grape-picking. Today, with mechanization and a rising immigrant workforce from eastern Europe, farmers hire fewer and fewer inexperienced college students. Usually they prefer to hire workers on the spot during the months of September and October. However, if you are already in France visiting, and you want to practice your French for a few more weeks while learning about the wine industry, you might consider trying it. Students interested in agriculture can also find work on a variety of organic and dairy farms year round. These jobs are usually not paid, but you receive room and board.

Below are some organizations in the United States that can give you information about working in France and other French-speaking countries.

Alliances Abroad
702 West Avenue
Austin, TX 78701
(888) 622-7623
www.alliancesabroad.com

Inter-Exchange
161 Sixth Avenue
New York, NY 10013
(212) 924-0446
www.interexchange.com

Council on International
Education Exchange
633 Third Ave.
New York, NY 10017
(212) 822-2600
www.CIEE.org

Vendanges au Château Haut-Brion

DOSSIER: **Adrienne Smith**

Interviewer: *Où est-ce que vous avez travaillé en France et pendant combien de temps?*

Adrienne: La première fois que je suis allée à Paris pour travailler comme jeune fille au pair, une agence m'avait trouvé une famille qui habitait à Paris. Comme c'était pendant les vacances d'été, j'ai pu visiter **plusieurs** régions de France en voyageant avec la famille, qui **possédait** un très beau manoir dans la vallée de la Loire et une maison à Arcachon aussi. À **la fin** de l'été, mon visa était **périmé.** Donc, j'ai quitté la France, **ne sachant quoi faire d'autre.** Huit mois plus tard, j'ai décidé de retourner en France **afin de** perfectionner mon français. **J'ai appelé** une gentille famille avec qui j'avais parlé avant de partir la première fois et je suis retournée à Paris le 31 août. J'ai encore eu de la chance **puisque** cette famille avait une grande maison en Normandie, tout près de la plage, où nous sommes allés plusieurs week-ends et aussi pendant un mois d'été.

Interviewer: *Comment s'organisait une journée typique?*

Adrienne: Dans la première famille, la journée commençait vers huit heures et demie et finissait vers huit heures du soir. Une ou deux fois par semaine, je faisais du baby-sitting en plus. **Des fois,** la mère me demandait d'**étendre le linge,** de **repasser** les vêtements des trois enfants ou de **passer l'aspirateur** pendant qu'elle **faisait les courses.** J'allais chercher les deux filles à l'école, j'**emmenais** l'**aînée** à sa leçon de piano et après, j'accompagnais les trois enfants au parc. Dans la seconde famille, je travaillais beaucoup moins. Le matin et l'après-midi, j'étais libre. Trois jours par semaine, j'allais à l'Institut Parisien, où j'ai reçu un diplôme de perfectionnement, niveau III. Vers seize heures j'allais chercher les deux garçons à **la crèche** et à l'école. Je leur préparais à dîner,

leur donnais le bain et après, nous jouions dans leur chambre et nous **racontions des histoires** (c'est quelque chose qui m'a beaucoup aidée à **améliorer** mon français).

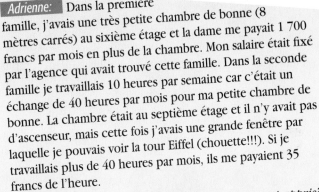

Interviewer: *Comment est-ce qu'on vous rétribuait?*

Adrienne: Dans la première famille, j'avais une très petite chambre de bonne (8 mètres carrés) au sixième étage et la dame me payait 1 700 francs par mois en plus de la chambre. Mon salaire était fixé par l'agence qui avait trouvé cette famille. Dans la seconde famille je travaillais 10 heures par semaine car c'était un échange de 40 heures par mois pour ma petite chambre de bonne. La chambre était au septième étage et il n'y avait pas d'ascenseur, mais cette fois j'avais une grande fenêtre par laquelle je pouvais voir la tour Eiffel (chouette!!!). Si je travaillais plus de 40 heures par mois, ils me payaient 35 francs de l'heure.

Interviewer: *Qu'est-ce que ces expériences vous ont appris?*

Adrienne: Mes expériences en France m'ont fait comprendre **tant de** choses dans **la vie! J'ai acquis** de la patience et le sens des responsabilités. **J'ai** aussi **découvert** une autre culture et j'ai appris une langue que **j'utilise** chaque jour. **Grâce à** ces expériences, j'ai appris **non seulement** à parler français **couramment,** ce qui est un avantage énorme **quel que soit le chemin** qu'on **choisit** dans la vie, mais j'ai appris aussi à avoir confiance en moi-même.

---

plusieurs *several*   **posséder** *to possess*   **la fin** *the end*   **périmé(e)** *expired*   **ne sachant quoi faire d'autre** *not knowing what else to do*   **afin de** *in order to*   **appeler** *to call*   **puisque** *since*   **Des fois** *At times*   **étendre le linge** *to hang out the laundry*   **repasser** *to iron*   **passer l'aspirateur** *(m) to vacuum*   **faire les courses** *to go grocery shopping*   **emmener** *to take*   **aîné(e)** *oldest*   **la crèche** *daycare*   **raconter des histoires** *(f) to tell stories*   **améliorer** *to improve*   **on vous rétribuait** *you were paid*   **tant de** *so many, so much*   **la vie** *life*   **j'ai acquis** *I acquired*   **j'ai découvert** *I discovered*   **utiliser** *to use*   **Grâce à** *Thanks to*   **non seulement** *not only*   **couramment** *fluently*   **quel que soit le chemin** *whatever path*   **choisir** *to choose*

Port de Rouen

Camille Pissarro (1830–1903)
1896
Paris, musée d'Orsay

Pissarro was born on the Caribbean island of St. Thomas. In 1841, his parents sent him to boarding school in Paris, where he was exposed to the art world. He first visited Rouen in 1883, and its bustling waterfront inspired many great paintings.

Notes. A. The next two chapters take place in Rouen. Have students locate Normandy on the map and brainstorm about what they know about it. **B.** Tell students that these chapters deal with daily life and personal relationships. Ask them what they associate with these topics.

En Normandie

LA NORMANDIE

SUPERFICIE: 30 627 kilomètres carrés

POPULATION: 3 245 000 habitants (les Normands)

INDUSTRIES PRINCIPALES: culture (céréalière et fruitière), élevage *(livestock)*, tourisme, pêche *(fishing)*, construction automobile et navale, industrie électrique et électronique

La vie quotidienne

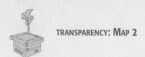

La France et sa diversité

Existe-t-il une identité française? **une seule** culture française? un caractère français? une attitude française?

Nous avons tous notre **propre** idée de ce que représente la France, mais en réalité la France n'a pas une seule identité, ou une seule culture. La France est une nation composée de régions multiples et **chacune de** ces régions est **fière** d'avoir ses propres traditions et sa propre identité.

Il est **donc** difficile de définir «la culture française». La France est un pays riche en diversité, où chaque région cherche à maintenir son héritage culturel: ses traditions, sa cuisine, sa musique, ses danses et même quelquefois sa langue.

En Bretagne, par exemple, il y a des Bretons qui parlent et écrivent non seulement le français mais aussi le breton–la seule langue d'origine celtique parlée **en dehors des** îles britanniques. En Corse, de nombreuses personnes parlent corse. Au Pays basque, le long de **la frontière** espagnole, **on entend** parler basque. Et dans toute la région du sud, on entend parfois des vestiges d'anciennes langues dérivées du latin, dont le provençal, l'occitan et le niçois sont les exemples les plus **connus**.

Une corrida dans l'arène romaine d'Arles

Des Bretons dans leurs costumes traditionnels

---

un(e) seul(e) *a single*   **propre** *own*   **chacun(e) de** *each of*   **fier (fière)** *proud*   **donc** *therefore*   **en dehors de** *outside of*   **la frontière** *the border*   **on entend** *one hears*   **connu(e)** *known*

Et pourtant, malgré cette diversité, les Français se sentent bien français! Leur identité et leur unité proviennent surtout de leur histoire, de leur patrimoine et de leurs traditions. C'est cet héritage commun qui donne à la France et aux Français une certaine unité, un certain sens de ce que c'est que d'être «français»: une histoire qui date de plus de 2.000 ans, un patrimoine riche en architecture et en culture, une tradition à la fois laïque et catholique.

Additional information.
The four principal religions in France are Catholicism (81.4%), Islam (6.9%), Protestantism (1.6%), and Judaism (1.3%). Also practiced are Buddhism (.68%), Orthodox (.34%), and other religions (8%).

France has a **Secrétariat d'État à la francophonie,** whose role is to develop and sustain a francophone identity among French speakers throughout the world.

In 1634, Richelieu created l'**Académie française** to establish and maintain linguistic and literary standards in French. Its members are known as **les Immortels.**

Un accordéoniste au Pays basque

Un restaurant de spécialités arabes à Paris

Récemment, l'immigration de gens **venus** surtout d'Asie, d'Afrique **occidentale** et d'Afrique du nord **a** aussi beaucoup **marqué** la France. Ces nouveaux immigrés cherchent à maintenir leurs langues et leurs traditions aussi. Comment est-ce qu'on peut préserver l'identité de la culture française **tout en** respectant les divers groupes ethniques qui habitent dans le pays? Est-il possible de combiner l'unité et la diversité? Ce sont des questions auxquelles la France **essaie de** trouver une réponse.

Une manifestation contre le racisme

---

pourtant *however* **malgré** *in spite of* **se sentent** *feel* **proviennent** *come from* **le patrimoine** *heritage* **à la fois** *at the same time* **laïque** *secular* **venus** *coming* **occidental(e)** *western* **a marqué** *has influenced* **tout en** *while* **essaie de** *is trying*

NOTE Culturelle

En France, on utilise souvent l'expression «métro, boulot, dodo» *("subway, work, bedtime")* pour exprimer la monotonie de la vie quotidienne.

TRANSPARENCIES: 7-1A, 7-1B

Warm-up activity. Have students complete these sentences with an appropriate time. **EXEMPLE** Le *(current day of the week),* je quitte la maison vers **huit heures et demie. 1.** J'ai mon premier cours à... **2.** Le cours de français est de... à... **3.** J'ai mon dernier cours à... **4.** Je rentre à la maison vers... **5.** Je dîne vers... **6.** Je vais au lit vers... **7.** Le *(tomorrow's day of the week),* je peux dormir jusqu'à...

Supplemental activity. Review the vocabulary for rooms of the house on page 102 and have students say where you might logically be if you are doing the following things. **1.** Je me lève. **2.** Je me lave les mains. **3.** Je m'habille. **4.** Je prépare le dîner. **5.** Je prends mon dîner. **6.** Je m'endors sur le canapé. **7.** Je me déshabille. **8.** Je prends une douche. **9.** Je me brosse les dents. **10.** Je me couche.

La vie de tous les jours

Voilà **la routine quotidienne** de Rose Richard, une jeune Américaine qui va bientôt visiter la France. Et vous? Quelle est votre routine quotidienne?

D'habitude le matin...   je **fais ma toilette.**

Je me réveille vers six heures.

Je me lève tout de suite.

Je me lave **la figure** et **les mains** *(f).*

Je prends un bain ou **une douche.**

Je me brosse les cheveux.

Je me brosse les dents.

Je me maquille.

Je m'habille.

Le soir...

Quelquefois je me repose.

Quelquefois je m'amuse avec des amis.

D'autres fois je m'ennuie.

Je me déshabille.

Je me couche et **je m'endors** facilement.

---

la routine quotidienne *daily routine*   **faire sa toilette** *to wash up*   **la figure** *the face*   **les mains** *(f) the hands*   **une douche** *a shower*   **D'autres fois** *Other times*   **je m'ennuie** *(s'ennuyer to be bored, to get bored)*   **je m'endors** *(s'endormir to fall asleep)*

Rosalie Toulouse Richard, d'origine française, habite à Atlanta **depuis** son mariage avec un Américain. **Veuve** maintenant, elle va retourner en France avec sa **petite-fille** Rose qui ne **connaît** pas du tout la France. **Comme** elles vont partager une chambre pendant leur **séjour,** elles parlent de leurs routines.

ROSALIE: Tu te lèves vers quelle heure d'habitude?

ROSE: Entre six heures et six heures et demie. Je fais **vite** ma toilette, je m'habille et puis je me maquille. Je suis prête en une demi-heure.

ROSALIE: C'est parfait. Moi, je prends quelquefois une douche le matin mais je préfère prendre mon bain le soir. Je peux très bien **attendre** jusqu'à sept heures pour faire ma toilette.

ROSE: Et moi, je ne quitte jamais la maison avant huit heures et demie. Alors si tu veux, on peut prendre le petit déjeuner ensemble tous les matins.

A. Ma routine. Complétez les phrases avec une expression de la liste.

Exemple   Je me réveille avant six heures.
Je me réveille rarement avant six heures.

TOUJOURS	tous les jours
souvent	le lundi, le mardi...
QUELQUEFOIS	le matin, l'après-midi, le soir
DE TEMPS EN TEMPS	une (deux...) fois par jour (semaine...)
rarement	
ne... jamais	

1. Je me réveille après neuf heures.
2. Je me lève tout de suite.
3. Je prends une douche ou un bain.
4. Je me lave les mains.
5. Je me lave les cheveux.
6. Je me brosse les dents.
7. Je m'habille vite.
8. Je m'ennuie.
9. Je me repose.
10. Je m'amuse bien.
11. Je me couche tard.
12. Je m'endors sur le canapé.

B. Une routine différente. Avec un(e) partenaire, changez la conversation entre Rose et sa grand-mère comme indiqué.

1. Rose wakes up at eight and gets up right away. She then takes a shower, brushes her teeth, and gets dressed.
2. Rosalie likes to bathe in the morning, then she brushes her hair and gets dressed.
3. Just like Rosalie and Rose, you are going to be visiting France with your partner. Discuss your personal daily routines.

---

depuis *since*   **Veuve (veuf)** *Widow (widower)*   **une petite-fille (un petit-fils)** *a granddaughter (a grandson)*   **elle connaît (connaître** *to know)*   **Comme** *Since, As*   **un séjour** *a stay*   **vite** *quick(ly), fast*   **attendre** *to wait (for)*

Suggestion for the conversation. Set the scene. Have students listen to the conversation with books closed for this information. **1.** Vers quelle heure est-ce que Rose se lève? **2.** Quand est-ce que Rosalie préfère prendre son bain?

Warm-up for *A. Ma routine.* Put these columns on the board or on a transparency for students to match. Trouvez la suite logique pour compléter chaque phrase. 1. Je me lève... 2. Je me brosse... 3. Je prends... 4. L'après-midi, je m'amuse... 5. Je me déshabille et puis... 6. Je me couche et... **a.** avec des amis. **b.** je me couche. **c.** vers huit heures. **d.** les dents. **e.** une douche ou un bain. **f.** je m'endors.

Suggestion for *A. Ma routine.* Point out that **toujours, souvent,** and **rarement** go right after the verb, but the other adverbial phrases listed go at the end of the sentence.

Follow-up for *A. Ma routine.* Indiquez si l'ordre des activités que vous entendez est logique. EXEMPLE D'abord, je prends mon petit déjeuner et puis je me brosse les dents. **C'est logique.** 1. D'abord, je m'habille et puis je prends un bain. 2. D'abord, je me lève et puis je me réveille. 3. D'abord, je rentre à la maison et puis je me couche. 4. D'abord, je me lève et puis je me lave. 5. D'abord, je me couche et puis je fais ma toilette. 6. D'abord, je me lève et puis je m'habille. 7. D'abord, je me réveille et puis je me lève. 8. D'abord, je me lave les mains et puis je prépare le dîner. 9. D'abord, je dîne et puis je me couche. 10. D'abord, je quitte la maison et puis je m'habille.

1. What is the difference in usage between the reflexive verb **se laver** and the non-reflexive verb **laver**?
2. What happens to the reflexive pronoun **se** when you conjugate a reflexive verb like **se laver**?
3. Where do you place **ne... pas** when negating reflexive verbs?
4. In which forms do verbs like **se lever**, **s'appeler**, and **s'ennuyer** have spelling changes? Which forms do not have spelling changes?

Describing your daily routine:
Les verbes réfléchis au présent

A verb can be used to say that you are doing something to or for yourself or that you are doing something to or for another person or thing. For example, one can dress oneself or one can dress one's children. When someone performs the action of a verb on or for himself/herself, a reflexive verb is generally used in French. Compare the differences depicted here.

REFLEXIVE   **NON-REFLEXIVE**

Je m'habille.   J'habille les enfants.

Je me lave les mains.   Je lave la voiture.

The infinitive of reflexive verbs is preceded by the reflexive pronoun **se.** When you conjugate these verbs, change the reflexive pronoun according to the subject. In the negative, place **ne** before the reflexive pronoun and **pas** after the verb.

Suggestions. A. Point out the use of the definite article with parts of the body. **B.** Have students conjugate one of the verbs listed to check comprehension.

Supplemental activities. A. Write **M. Élégant** and **M. Négligé** on the board. Ask students **Qui fait les choses suivantes, M. Élégant ou M. Négligé?** 1. Qui se lave les cheveux une fois par mois? 2. Qui se lave les cheveux tous les jours? 3. Qui ne se brosse jamais les cheveux? 4. Qui ne se rase presque jamais? 5. Qui se lève l'après-midi? 6. Qui s'habille bien? 7. Qui prend rarement un bain? 8. Qui se brosse les dents trois fois par jour? 9. Qui a les dents jaunes? 10. Qui se lave toujours les mains avant de manger? 11. Avec qui est-ce que vous préférez habiter? **B.** Distribute slips of paper with a reflexive verb on each one and have students mime the action. The rest of the class guesses which verb is being mimed.

SE LAVER *(to wash [oneself])*		NE PAS SE LAVER	
je me lave	nous nous lavons	je ne me lave pas	nous ne nous lavons pas
tu te laves	vous vous lavez	tu ne te laves pas	vous ne vous lavez pas
il/elle/on se lave	ils/elles se lavent	il/elle/on ne se lave pas	ils/elles ne se lavent pas

Note that **me, te,** and **se** change to **m', t',** and **s'** before a vowel sound: **je m'habille, tu t'habilles, elle s'habille, ils s'habillent.**

Here are some reflexive verbs you can use to talk about your daily life:

s'amuser	*to have fun*
s'appeler	*to be named*
se brosser (les cheveux, les dents)	*to brush (one's hair, one's teeth)*
se coucher / se recoucher	*to go to bed / to go back to bed*
s'endormir	*to fall asleep*
s'ennuyer	*to be bored, to get bored*
s'habiller / se déshabiller	*to get dressed / to get undressed*
se laver (les mains, la figure)	*to wash (one's hands, one's face)*
se lever	*to get up*
se maquiller	*to put on make-up*
se raser	*to shave*
se reposer	*to rest*
se réveiller	*to wake up*

The verb **s'endormir** is conjugated like **dormir.**

S'ENDORMIR *(to fall asleep)*	
je m'endors	nous nous endormons
tu t'endors	vous vous endormez
il/elle/on s'endort	ils/elles s'endorment

Notice the accent spelling change in the conjugation of **se lever.** Its conjugation is similar to that of **acheter. S'appeler** changes its spelling by doubling the final consonant of the stem in all present tense forms except those of **nous** and **vous.**

Suggestion. Review the spelling change verbs and the pronunciation of **é** and **è** from *Chapitre 2.*

SE LEVER *(to get up)*	
je me **lè**ve	nous nous levons
tu te **lè**ves	vous vous levez
il/elle/on se **lè**ve	ils/elles se **lè**vent

S'APPELER *(to be named)*	
je m'appelle	nous nous appelons
tu t'appelles	vous vous appelez
il/elle/on s'appelle	ils/elles s'appe**ll**ent

S'ennuyer and other verbs ending in **-yer,** such as **essayer** and **payer,** change **y** to **i** in all forms except those of **nous** and **vous.**

S'ENNUYER *(to be bored, to get bored)*	
je m'ennuie	nous nous ennuyons
tu t'ennuies	vous vous ennuyez
il/elle/on s'ennuie	ils/elles s'ennu**i**ent

A. Équivalents. Trouvez le verbe réfléchi correspondant à chaque définition.

1. aller au lit
2. sortir du lit
3. mettre des vêtements
4. faire quelque chose d'amusant
5. faire quelque chose d'ennuyeux
6. ne rien faire
7. commencer à dormir

a. s'endormir
b. s'ennuyer
c. se reposer
d. se lever
e. s'amuser
f. se coucher
g. s'habiller

B. D'abord... Indiquez l'ordre logique des activités données.

Exemple   se lever / prendre un bain
            D'abord, on se lève et puis on prend un bain.

1. se réveiller / se lever
2. se raser / se lever
3. se laver la figure / se maquiller
4. s'habiller / prendre un bain ou une douche
5. se brosser les dents / manger
6. quitter la maison / s'habiller
7. se reposer / rentrer du bureau
8. s'amuser / retrouver des amis
9. se déshabiller / se coucher
10. s'endormir / se coucher

Supplemental activities for practicing spelling change verbs. A. Put these questions on the board or a transparency and have students write them, completing the verbs with the correct letters. Have students ask their partners the questions, then write sentences reporting back what their partners said. **1.** Comment t'appe__es-tu? Comment s'appe__e ton/ta meilleur(e) ami(e)? Comment s'appe__ent tes parents? **2.** Est-ce que tu te l__ves tôt? Est-ce que tes parents se l__vent tôt d'habitude? **3.** Qu'est-ce que ton/ta meilleur(e) ami(e) préf__re faire le samedi matin? À quelle heure est-ce qu'il/elle se l__ve le week-end? Est-ce que vous vous ennu__ez souvent ensemble? Quand est-ce que tu t'ennu__es? Qu'est-ce que tu esp__res faire ce week-end? **B.** Give the following dictation. Have one student write each item on the board, then choose another to write the answer: **1.** Je me lève toujours facilement. Est-ce que vous vous levez facilement? **2.** Je m'appelle _____. Comment vous appelez-vous? **3.** J'espère aller au parc ce week-end. Qu'est-ce que vous espérez faire? **4.** Je m'ennuie dans mon cours de comptabilité. Est-ce que vous vous ennuyez souvent?

Warm-up for *A. Équivalents.* Quel(s) verbe(s) réfléchi(s) associez-vous... ? **aux vêtements, à une salle de bains, aux cheveux, aux dents, à un lit, à un nom, à un jeu vidéo, aux mains**

C. Un samedi typique. Voilà la routine de Rose le samedi matin. Qu'est-ce qu'elle fait?

Le samedi matin...

Exemple

... vers neuf heures.
Elle se réveille vers neuf heures.

1. ... tout de suite.

2. ... la figure et les mains.

3. ... les dents.

4. ... les cheveux.

5. ... en jean.

Le samedi soir...

6. ... avec des amis.

7. ... vers deux heures du matin et... facilement.

D. Et vous? Regardez les illustrations de *C. Un samedi typique.* Est-ce que vous faites ces mêmes choses le samedi?

Le samedi matin...

Exemple

... vers neuf heures
**Je me réveille vers neuf heures. /
Je ne me réveille pas vers neuf heures.**

E. Le week-end. Demandez à votre partenaire s'il/si elle fait les choses suivantes le week-end.

Exemple   se réveiller tôt ou tard le samedi matin
— **Est-ce que tu te réveilles tôt ou tard le samedi matin?**
— **En général, je me réveille tôt.**

1. se lever tôt ou tard le samedi matin
2. prendre un bain ou une douche
3. s'amuser ou s'ennuyer le week-end
4. se coucher tôt ou tard le samedi soir
5. s'endormir facilement

Follow-ups for E. Le week-end. A. Have students report back three things they found out about their partner. **EXEMPLE Il/Elle se réveille tôt. B.** Have students ask their partners questions based on the illustrations in **C. Un samedi typique.** EXEMPLE **Est-ce que tu te réveilles vers neuf heures le samedi matin?**

F. Questions. Avec un(e) partenaire, préparez cinq questions à poser au professeur au sujet de sa routine quotidienne. Utilisez des verbes réfléchis.

Exemple   **Est-ce que vous vous couchez tôt ou tard d'habitude?**
À quelle heure est-ce que vous vous couchez d'habitude?

Follow-up for F. Questions. Put these questions on the board or a transparency and have students answer them. Then, have them rephrase these questions using **tu** and go around the class asking them of their classmates. Tell them the object is to find one person for each question who answered the same way they did. **1.** À quelle heure est-ce que vous vous réveillez le matin pendant la semaine? **2.** Est-ce que vous vous levez tout de suite? **3.** Est-ce que vous préférez prendre un bain ou une douche? **4.** Est-ce que vous prenez votre bain ou votre douche le matin ou le soir? **5.** Pendant la semaine, est-ce que vous vous reposez le soir? **6.** Est-ce que vous vous ennuyez souvent? **7.** À quelle heure est-ce que vous vous couchez d'habitude le samedi soir? **8.** Est-ce que vous vous endormez facilement?

G. Un week-end entre amis. Demandez à votre partenaire ce qu'il/elle fait avec ses amis quand ils passent un week-end ensemble dans une autre ville.

Exemple   se réveiller tôt ou tard
— **Est-ce que vous vous réveillez tôt ou tard?**
— **Nous nous réveillons tard. /**
On se réveille tard.

1. se réveiller avant ou après dix heures
2. se lever tôt ou tard
3. se reposer ou aller en ville l'après-midi
4. sortir ou se reposer le soir
5. s'ennuyer ou s'amuser le soir
6. se coucher tôt ou tard

H. Vous faites du baby-sitting. Vous faites du baby-sitting pour les deux enfants d'un(e) ami(e). Demandez ces renseignements à votre ami(e). Votre partenaire va jouer le rôle de votre ami(e) et imaginer ses réponses.

Find out . . .

Exemple   *what time they wake up*
— **À quelle heure est-ce qu'ils se réveillent?**
— **Ils se réveillent vers huit heures.**

1. *if they get up right away*
2. *if they take a bath or a shower in the morning or the evening*
3. *if they rest in the afternoon*
4. *what time they go to bed*
5. *if they fall asleep easily*

Stratégies et lecture:
Using word families and watching out for *faux amis*

Recognizing words that belong to the same word family can make reading easier. Can you supply the missing meanings below?

la vie	vivre	l'arrêt	s'arrêter	se marier	le mariage	espérer	l'espoir
life	*to live*	*stop*	*???*	*to marry*	*marriage*	*to hope*	*???*

Using cognates and word families can make reading much easier. However, beware of **faux amis,** words that look like cognates but have different meanings. For example, you already know that **rester** does not mean *to rest,* but *to stay.* Use cognates, but if a word does not seem right in the context, look it up.

A. Familles de mots. Voilà quelques mots que vous allez voir dans l'histoire qui suit *(the story that follows)*. Servez-vous du sens des mots donnés pour déterminer le sens des autres mots.

rêver	**un rêve**	**dire**	**dit(e)**
to dream	*a dream*	*to say, to tell*	*said, told*
se souvenir de	**des souvenirs**	**connaître**	**connu(e)**
to remember	*???*	*to know*	*???*
saluer	**une salutation**	**reconnaître**	**reconnu(e)**
to greet	*???*	*to recognize*	*???*
espérer	**l'espoir**	**revenir**	**revenu(e)**
to hope	*???*	*to come back*	*???*

B. Familles de mots. Déterminez le sens des mots en caractères gras.

une rose Il adore les roses et il plante **des rosiers** partout.
un arrêt Aujourd'hui, trois filles **s'arrêtent** pour admirer son jardin et pour le saluer.
connaît Il **reconnaît** deux des filles mais il ne connaît pas la troisième.
revenir Des souvenirs lui **reviennent,** comme si c'était hier.

C. Faux amis. Donnez le sens des faux amis en caractères gras selon le contexte.

M. Dupont est dans un fauteuil au jardin quand une jolie jeune fille qui passe **attire** son attention. Il la **salue** et lui dit: «Bonjour, mademoiselle.» Cette fille ressemble à quelqu'un qu'il connaissait dans le passé et il commence à rêver. Il a de beaux **souvenirs** du temps où il était jeune. Il aimait une jeune fille et il **garde** toujours l'espoir de la revoir un jour.

Il n'est jamais trop tard!

Rosalie Toulouse Richard, qui habite à Atlanta depuis 1945, retourne à Rouen avec sa petite-fille Rose. Son vieil ami, André Dupont, ne sait pas encore que Rosalie est à Rouen.

Supplemental pre-reading activity.
Avant de lire *Il n'est jamais trop tard!*, trouvez tous les verbes dans le texte et pour chacun, décidez si on parle du présent ou du passé.

André Dupont a toujours aimé passer des heures à travailler dans son jardin. Il a toujours eu une passion pour les roses et depuis des années, il plante des rosiers de toutes les variétés et de toutes les couleurs!

Ses rosiers font l'admiration de tous les gens du quartier et beaucoup d'entre eux passent devant chez lui pour regarder son beau jardin. Aujourd'hui, ce sont trois jeunes filles qui s'arrêtent lui dire bonjour. Il reconnaît deux d'entre elles, ce sont les petites-filles de son ami Jean Toulouse, mais c'est la troisième qui attire son attention. Il ne l'a jamais vue, et pourtant il a l'impression de la connaître! Elle ressemble à quelqu'un... quelqu'un qu'il a connu il y a très longtemps.

Les souvenirs lui reviennent, comme si c'était hier. C'était en 1945, il avait dix-huit ans et il était amoureux fou d'une jolie jeune fille de son âge. Elle s'appelait Rosalie... ! Il voulait lui dire combien il l'aimait, mais il n'en avait pas le courage. Il était trop timide. Un beau jour, il s'est décidé à tout lui dire. Il a choisi des fleurs de son jardin pour en faire un bouquet, il a pris son vélo et il est allé chez Rosalie. Mais en arrivant, il a trouvé Rosalie en compagnie d'un soldat américain et elle regardait ce jeune soldat d'un regard de femme amoureuse. André, lui, est rentré chez lui sans jamais parler à Rosalie.

Quelques mois après, Rosalie s'est mariée avec l'Américain et ils sont partis vivre aux États-Unis. De temps en temps, André avait des nouvelles parce que le frère de Rosalie et lui étaient de bons amis. Il savait qu'elle habitait à Atlanta, qu'elle avait trois enfants, et il y a trois ans, il a appris que son mari était mort. Il gardait toujours l'espoir de la revoir, mais les années passaient et elle ne revenait toujours pas.

— Vos rosiers sont magnifiques, monsieur!

C'est Rosalie qui parle! En un instant, André Dupont revient au présent et ouvre les yeux. C'est la jeune fille qui parle... celle qu'il ne connaît pas.

— Rosalie???

— Moi, monsieur? Non, je m'appelle Rose. Rosalie, c'est ma grand-mère.

— Ta grand-mère?

— Oui. Vous connaissez ma grand-mère?

— Rosalie Toulouse? Oui, je la connais, mais...

— Eh bien, venez la voir, elle est chez son frère Jean! Je suis sûre qu'elle sera contente de revoir un ami d'ici! Allez, venez avec nous!

Quoi? C'est trop beau! Est-ce qu'il rêve? Rosalie, ici à Rouen! Comme la vie est à la fois belle et bizarre! Va-t-elle le reconnaître? A-t-il le courage de lui dire qu'il l'aime toujours, après toutes ces années? André Dupont choisit les plus belles roses de son jardin et en fait un magnifique bouquet. Il va enfin pouvoir les offrir à la femme pour qui il a planté tous ces rosiers au cours des années.

Qui parle?   Qui parle: André, Rosalie ou Rose?

1. J'adore les fleurs et j'aime faire du jardinage.
2. J'ai eu trois enfants, et mon mari est mort il y a trois ans.
3. Je suis passée devant une maison où il y avait des roses splendides.
4. Un monsieur m'a parlé. Il connaît ma grand-mère mais il ne l'a pas vue depuis longtemps.
5. J'ai invité ce monsieur à venir nous voir.
6. En 1945, je me suis mariée avec un Américain et je suis allée vivre aux États-Unis.
7. J'étais amoureux de Rosalie mais je n'ai jamais eu le courage de le lui dire.
8. Je garde toujours l'espoir de dire à Rosalie que je l'aime.

La vie sentimentale

À l'invitation de Rose, André va chez les Toulouse et André et Rosalie **se rencontrent** pour la première fois depuis des années. Voilà **ce qui se passe.**

André et Rosalie se regardent.

Ils s'embrassent.

Ils se parlent pendant des heures. C'est **le coup de foudre!**

Ils se quittent vers sept heures.

Pendant les semaines qui **suivent,** André et Rosalie passent beaucoup de temps ensemble. C'est **le grand amour!**

Ils se retrouvent en ville chaque après-midi.

Quelquefois ils se disputent.

Mais **la plupart du temps ils s'entendent** bien.

Enfin, André et Rosalie **prennent une décision.** Ils vont se marier et vont **s'installer** à Rouen. Ils vont être très **heureux.**

 Un soir, Rosalie parle à sa petite-fille Rose de sa relation avec André.

ROSE: Alors, **mamie,** tu as passé une bonne journée?

ROSALIE: Oui. André et moi, nous sommes allés visiter le Mont-Saint-Michel.

ROSE: Alors, vous vous entendez bien?

ROSALIE: Très bien. Nous nous retrouvons tous les jours, nous passons des heures ensemble et nous nous parlons de tout. Nous ne nous disputons presque jamais.

ROSE: Formidable! Moi, je **rêve d'une telle** relation.

ROSALIE: Et ton petit ami et toi, ça va ?

ROSE: Pas très bien. Nous nous disputons souvent et nous ne nous entendons pas très bien.

ROSALIE: **C'est dommage!**

---

se rencontrer *to meet each other (by chance), to run into each other*   **ce qui** *what*   **se passer** *to happen*   **le coup de foudre** *love at first sight*   **suivent (suivre** *to follow)*   **le grand amour** *true love*   **la plupart du temps** *most of the time*   **s'entendre** *to get along*   **Enfin** *Finally*   **prendre une décision** *to make a decision*   **s'installer (à / dans)** *to move (into), to settle (in)*   **heureux (heureuse)** *happy*   **mamie** *grandma*   **rêver (de)** *to dream (of)*   **un(e) tel(le)** *such a*   **C'est dommage!** *That's too bad!*

Suggestion for the conversation. Set the scene and have students listen to the conversation with books closed. Have them listen and make three statements about the relationship between Rosalie and André. EXEMPLE **Ils s'entendent bien.**

Le Mont-Saint-Michel

A. Meilleurs amis. Parlez de votre meilleur(e) ami(e) et vous.

1. Nous nous parlons *tous les jours / une fois par semaine / ???*.
2. Nous nous retrouvons *tous les jours / une fois par semaine / rarement / ???*.
3. Nous nous entendons *toujours bien / bien la plupart du temps / ???*.
4. Nous nous disputons *tout le temps / quelquefois / rarement / ???*.

Follow-up for *A. Meilleurs amis.* C'est un couple heureux ou un couple malheureux *(unhappy)* qui parle? **1.** On se dispute tout le temps. **2.** On se parle de tout. **3.** On ne s'entend pas bien du tout. **4.** On s'ennuie ensemble. **5.** On s'amuse ensemble. **6.** On s'embrasse tout le temps. **7.** On ne s'embrasse jamais.

B. Test. Faites ce test pour savoir si vous êtes romantique.

Êtes-vous romantique?

I. Indiquez vos opinions sur ces sujets.

1 Pensez-vous que le grand amour...
a. arrive une fois dans la vie?
b. n'existe pas?
c. est sans importance?

2 Pensez-vous qu'un couple peut s'aimer pour toujours?
a. Certainement.
b. Je ne sais pas, on peut essayer.
c. Probablement pas: la vie est trop longue.

3 Au restaurant, **vous voyez** des amoureux qui se regardent dans les yeux pendant tout le dîner. Vous trouvez ça...
a. un peu bête mais charmant.
b. ridicule.
c. adorable.

II. Comment êtes-vous en couple?

1 Vous vous rencontrez **par hasard** et c'est le coup de foudre. Que pensez-vous?
a. C'est juste un désir sexuel.
b. C'est peut-être l'amour.
c. **Attention!**

2 Vous vous disputez. Quelle est la meilleure manière de vous réconcilier?
a. Nous devons nous embrasser.
b. Nous devons essayer de parler calmement du problème.
c. Nous devons nous quitter pendant un certain temps.

3 Vous vous adorez. Vous voulez...
a. essayer de vous voir tous les jours.
b. vous téléphoner tous les jours et vous voir trois ou quatre fois par semaine.
c. vous retrouver le week-end, si vous n'avez pas d'autres projets.

SCORE: **Partie I.** 1. a–2 points 2. a–2 points, b–1 point 3. c–2 points, a–1 point
Partie II. 1. b–2 points, a–1 point 2. a–2 points, b–1 point 3. a–2 points, b–1 point

◆ Si vous avez **10–12 points,** vous êtes une personne très (peut-être même un peu trop?) romantique. Attention! **Ne perdez pas votre temps** à attendre un amour parfait. Essayez d'être un peu plus réaliste, quand même.
◆ Si vous avez **6–9 points,** vous êtes romantique, mais vous n'exagérez pas. Vous êtes prêt(e) à aimer quand le bon moment arrivera, mais vous ne perdez pas votre temps à chercher l'amour idéal partout.
◆ Si vous avez **0–5 points,** vous êtes réaliste, cynique même! Ne voulez-vous pas mettre un peu plus de poésie dans votre vie?

C. La vie sentimentale. Avec un(e) partenaire, changez la conversation entre Rosalie et Rose comme indiqué. Si vous préférez, vous pouvez imaginer que les mêmes conversations sont entre André et son petit-fils ou sa petite-fille.

1. Rosalie and André are not getting along well. They spend a lot of time together, but they don't talk to each other very much and they fight a lot.
2. Things are going fairly well between Rose and her boyfriend. They fight sometimes, but usually they get along well.
3. You and a friend are talking about your relationships. One of you is in an ideal relationship and the other is in a bad relationship.

Suggestions. A. Creating a conversation between André and his grandson may be a more comfortable option for some male students to role-play. **B.** Point out the sentences **Nous ne nous disputons presque jamais** and **Nous ne nous entendons pas très bien** in the dialogue and tell students to use them as models for their negative sentences.

---

vous voyez (voir *to see)* **par hasard** *by chance* **Attention!** *Watch out!* **perdre du temps** *to waste time*

1. When do you use a reciprocal verb?
2. What verbs can be made into reciprocal verbs? How would you say *to look at each other* or *to listen to each other*?
3. When a reflexive or reciprocal verb is used in the infinitive, does the reflexive pronoun change with the subject? How would you say *I am going to get up at 6:00*?

NOTE DE GRAMMAIRE

Note that although the verb **se marier** is reflexive, **divorcer** is not.

Suggestion. Remind students of the spelling change in verbs ending in **-cer** such as **divorcer**. You may wish to point out that some of these verbs, such as **se marier** and **s'entendre**, are used reflexively.

Follow-ups. A. Associez-vous ces mots à **se marier** ou à **divorcer**? **1.** se détester **2.** s'embrasser **3.** se disputer **4.** se quitter **5.** s'aimer **6.** s'entendre bien **B.** Indiquez le contraire: se disputer, s'aimer, divorcer, s'entendre mal, se quitter.

Saying what people do for each other:
Les verbes réciproques au présent et les verbes réfléchis et réciproques au futur immédiat

You have seen that reflexive verbs are used when someone is doing something to or for himself/herself. You use similar verbs to describe reciprocal actions; that is, to indicate that people are doing something to or for each other. Here are some reflexive and reciprocal verbs commonly used to describe relationships.

s'aimer	*to like each other, to love each other*
se détester	*to hate each other*
se disputer	*to argue*
s'embrasser	*to kiss each other, to embrace each other*
s'entendre (bien / mal)	*to get along (well / badly) with each other*
se fiancer	*to get engaged*
se marier (avec)	*to get married (to)*
se quitter	*to leave each other*
se réconcilier	*to make up*
se regarder	*to look at each other*
se rencontrer	*to meet each other* (by chance)
se retrouver	*to meet each other* (by design)
se téléphoner	*to telephone each other*

The verb **s'entendre** *(to get along)* is a regular **-re** verb. You will learn how to conjugate other **-re** verbs in the next section (page 260). The forms of **s'entendre** are:

S'ENTENDRE *(to get along)*	
je m'entends	nous nous entendons
tu t'entends	vous vous entendez
il/elle/on s'entend	ils/elles s'entendent

Notice that most verbs indicating actions done to other people can be used reciprocally.

téléphoner à quelqu'un *(to phone someone)*	Je téléphone **à Liz.**
se téléphoner *(to phone each other)*	Nous **nous** téléphonons.
regarder quelqu'un *(to look at someone)*	Je regarde **Jim.**
se regarder *(to look at each other)*	Nous **nous** regardons.

Form the immediate future of reflexive and reciprocal verbs with the verb **aller,** as always, to say what someone is going to do.

SE LEVER *(to get up)*	
je vais me lever	nous allons nous lever
tu vas te lever	vous allez vous lever
il/elle/on va se lever	ils/elles vont se lever

Whenever you use a reflexive or reciprocal verb in the infinitive, the reflexive pronoun varies with the subject. In the negative, put **ne... pas** around the conjugated verb.

Je ne vais pas **me** lever tôt.
Tu préfères **te** coucher tard.

A. Une histoire d'amour.

A. Une histoire d'amour. Isabelle, la cousine de Rose, rencontre Luc et ils tombent amoureux. Qu'est-ce qui se passe?

Warm-up for *A. Une histoire d'amour.* Dites si on fait ou on ne fait pas ces choses dans un couple idéal. EXEMPLE souvent se disputer **Dans un couple idéal, on ne se dispute pas souvent.** **1.** se retrouver tous les jours **2.** se téléphoner tous les jours **3.** s'entendre mal la plupart du temps **4.** se disputer tous les jours **5.** se réconcilier facilement **6.** s'embrasser souvent

se téléphoner	se regarder	SE MARIER	S'EMBRASSER
S'INSTALLER DANS UNE MAISON	se quitter	se fiancer	
se réconcilier	se parler	se disputer	se retrouver au parc

Exemple  **Ils se téléphonent.**

1.
2.
3.

4.
5.
6.

7.

9.

B. Questions.

B. Questions. Rose veut en savoir plus *(to know more)* sur Isabelle et Luc. Avec un(e) partenaire, imaginez ses questions et les réponses qu'Isabelle lui donne.

Exemple se disputer
— **Est-ce que vous vous disputez souvent?**
— **Non, nous ne nous disputons jamais.**

1. se téléphoner
2. se retrouver
3. s'embrasser
4. s'entendre
5. s'aimer

tous les jours	BIEN
souvent	MAL
QUELQUEFOIS	beaucoup
LA PLUPART DU TEMPS	

Warm-up for *B. Questions.* Qu'est-ce qu'on fait d'abord? **1.** On se rencontre. / On se parle. **2.** On s'aime. / On se marie. **3.** On s'embrasse. / On se rencontre. **4.** On se dispute. / On se réconcilie. **5.** On divorce. / On se marie.

Follow-up for *B. Questions.* Votre meilleur(e) ami(e) et vous... **1.** Est-ce que vous vous parlez tous les jours? Est-ce que vous vous téléphonez souvent? Est-ce que vous aimez vous voir tous les jours? Combien de fois par semaine est-ce que vous vous retrouvez? Où aimez-vous vous retrouver? Quand? **2.** Qu'est-ce que vous faites ensemble pour vous amuser? Est-ce que vous vous ennuyez quelquefois ensemble? **3.** Est-ce que vous vous entendez toujours bien? Est-ce que vous vous disputez de temps en temps?

C. Isabelle et Luc. Tout va très bien entre Isabelle et Luc. Ils se parlent et ils se retrouvent en ville tous les jours. Est-ce qu'ils vont faire les choses suivantes demain?

Exemple   se disputer
            Non, ils ne vont pas se disputer.

1. se téléphoner   **4.** bien s'entendre
2. se retrouver en ville   **5.** s'ennuyer ensemble
3. se parler de tout   **6.** s'embrasser

D. Et demain chez Rose. Dites ce que Rose va faire demain d'après les illustrations.

Demain...

Exemple

... vers neuf heures.
Elle va se réveiller vers neuf heures.

1. ... tout de suite.   **2.** ... la figure et les mains.   **3.** ... les dents.

4. ... les cheveux.   **5.** ... en jean.

Demain soir...

6. ... avec des amis.   **7.** ... vers deux heures du matin.

E. Et toi? Regardez chaque illustration de **D. Et demain chez Rose.** Demandez à un(e) partenaire s'il/si elle va faire la même chose demain.

Exemple

... vers neuf heures.

— **Est-ce que tu vas te réveiller vers neuf heures?**
— **Oui, je vais me réveiller vers neuf heures. / Non, je ne vais pas me réveiller vers neuf heures.**

F. Ce week-end. Est-ce que ces personnes vont peut-être faire ces choses ce week-end?

Exemple   Moi, je... (se lever tôt)
Moi, je vais me lever tôt. / Je ne vais pas me lever tôt.

1. Moi, je... (se réveiller tôt, se réveiller tard, se lever tout de suite, rester au lit quelques minutes, s'habiller vite, quitter la maison tôt, travailler, s'amuser samedi soir, rentrer tard samedi soir)
2. Mon meilleur ami (Ma meilleure amie)... (se lever tôt, prendre son petit déjeuner avec moi, se reposer dimanche soir)
3. Mes amis et moi, nous... (se retrouver en ville, sortir ensemble, s'amuser ensemble, s'ennuyer ensemble)

G. Partons en week-end. Vous allez faire du camping avec un groupe d'amis ce week-end. Travaillez avec un petit groupe d'étudiants et faites des projets.

Exemple   **On va se réveiller tôt.**

SE LEVER TÔT / TARD   faire un feu *(fire)*
faire des randonnées *(to go hiking)*   ???
se coucher tôt / tard   DORMIR SOUS UNE TENTE
faire du canoë *(to go canoeing)*
se laver dans la rivière *(river)*   nager
aller à la pêche *(to fish)*   s'amuser
se brosser les dents avec l'eau de la rivière

H. Entretien. Interviewez votre partenaire.

1. Est-ce que tu te réveilles facilement ou avec difficulté? Tu te lèves tôt ou tard pendant la semaine en général? Tu te lèves tout de suite? À quelle heure est-ce que tu vas te lever demain?
2. Après les cours, est-ce que tu préfères te reposer ou t'amuser avec des amis? Est-ce que tu vas te reposer ce soir après les cours? Et demain soir?
3. Est-ce que tu te couches tôt ou tard pendant la semaine d'habitude? À quelle heure vas-tu te coucher ce soir? Vas-tu te lever tôt ce week-end? À quelle heure vas-tu te lever? Est-ce que tu préfères te lever tôt ou tard?

Follow-up for *E. Et toi?* En utilisant des verbes réfléchis, faites une liste de cinq choses que vous allez ou n'allez pas faire ce week-end. EXEMPLE **Ce week-end, je vais me reposer. Je ne vais pas m'ennuyer.** Après, circulez dans la classe et trouvez quelqu'un qui va faire au moins trois des choses que vous allez faire aussi. EXEMPLE **Est-ce que tu vas te reposer?...**

Supplemental activity. Vous faites des projets pour samedi avec un(e) ami(e). Préparez une conversation dans laquelle vous dites:
- à quelle heure vous voulez vous lever
- comment vous allez passer la matinée
- ce que vous voulez faire ensemble
- quand vous avez besoin de vous coucher
- à quelle heure vous allez rentrer

Suggestion for *G. Partons en week-end.* Point out the pronunciation of **canoë** [kanɔe].

Talking about activities: *Les verbes en -re*

Many verbs that end in **-re**, like **s'entendre**, follow a regular pattern of conjugation. Study the verb **attendre** *(to wait for)* to learn this pattern.

ATTENDRE *(to wait for)*	
j'attend**s**	nous attend**ons**
tu attend**s**	vous attend**ez**
il/elle/on attend	ils/elles attend**ent**

PASSÉ COMPOSÉ: j'ai attendu
IMPARFAIT: j'attendais

Notice that you do not use **pour** after **attendre** to say *for* whom or what you are waiting.

— Vous attendez quelqu'un?
— Oui, j'attends des amis.

The following are some common **-re** verbs.

descendre	*to go down, to get off, to stay* (at a hotel)
entendre	*to hear*
s'entendre (bien / mal) avec	*to get along (well / badly) with*
perdre	*to lose, to waste*
se perdre	*to get lost*
rendre quelque chose à quelqu'un	*to return something to someone, to turn in something to someone*
rendre visite à quelqu'un	*to visit someone*
répondre (à)	*to answer, to respond*
revendre	*to sell back, to resell*
vendre	*to sell*

In the **passé composé, descendre** and the reflexive verbs are conjugated with **être** as the auxiliary verb. The other verbs in this list are all conjugated with **avoir.**

J'ai rendu visite à une amie à Paris.   Je suis descendu(e) chez elle.

A. Votre vie. Est-ce que ces personnes font les choses suivantes?

Exemple   Moi, je... (attendre l'autobus pour aller en cours)
Moi, je n'attends pas l'autobus pour aller en cours.

1. Moi, je... (attendre l'autobus pour aller en cours, rendre souvent visite à mes parents, attendre la fin du semestre/trimestre avec impatience, revendre mes livres à la fin du semestre/trimestre)
2. En cours de français, nous... (rendre nos devoirs au professeur tous les jours, répondre aux questions du prof, attendre quelquefois le professeur, perdre du temps *[to waste time]*)
3. Mes amis (descendre souvent en ville le week-end, s'entendre bien, se rendre souvent visite)
4. Mon meilleur ami (Ma meilleure amie)... (perdre quelquefois patience avec moi, s'entendre bien avec mes autres amis, perdre souvent ses choses, se perdre facilement)

Note. Students are not expected to use the verbs **se perdre** and **s'entendre** in the **passé composé** until they are taught to form the **passé composé** of reflexive/reciprocal verbs in the next section.

Suggestion. Point out the use of **à** in **répondre à** and **rendre visite à.**

Supplemental activities. A. Quel verbe en **-re** est l'antonyme de... ? **1.** trouver **2.** poser une question **3.** acheter **4.** monter **B.** À quel(s) verbe(s) en **-re** associez-vous... ? **1.** le téléphone **2.** l'autobus **3.** un magasin **4.** la patience **5.** la musique **6.** une question **7.** un hôtel **8.** des amis

Follow-up for A. Votre vie. Select appropriate cues from those in parentheses and have students ask if a classmate or you do the activity named.

Qu'est-ce qu'on vend dans ce magasin?

B. La routine de Rose.
Rose décrit *(describes)* sa routine quotidienne quand elle est chez elle. Complétez ses phrases comme indiqué.

Le matin, je (j') _____ l'autobus devant mon appartement. Quelquefois, le bus
wait for

arrive en retard *(late)* et je _____ patience. Je n'aime pas _____! Quand le
lose   *to wait*

bus arrive, je monte dedans *(inside)* et je _____ à l'université. Je n'aime pas
get off

_____ mon temps, alors je fais mes devoirs dans l'autobus. Quand je suis en
to waste

cours, je _____ toujours bien aux questions du prof. Quand il _____ mes
answer   *hears*

réponses, il est toujours content! Il y a d'autres étudiants qui ne _____ pas
answer

très bien mais le prof ne _____ jamais patience avec nous. Nous ne _____
loses   *waste*

pas notre temps en cours—nous travaillons bien! Après les cours, je vais

souvent à mon magasin préféré où on _____ des livres et des CD.
sell

Quelquefois, je _____ à mon ami Trentin. Nous _____ bien.
visit   *get along*

Rose avait plus ou moins la même routine quand elle avait 15 ans. Servez-vous des verbes donnés pour dire quatre choses que Rose faisait quand elle avait 15 ans. Utilisez l'imparfait.

Exemple (attendre) **Le matin, elle attendait l'autobus.**

1. (perdre)
2. (répondre)
3. (rendre visite à)
4. (s'entendre bien)

C. Et toi?
Choisissez le verbe logique et complétez les questions. Ensuite, posez les questions à votre partenaire. Utilisez le présent ou le passé composé comme indiqué.

AU PRÉSENT

1. À qui est-ce que tu _____ souvent visite? (perdre, rendre)
2. Est-ce que tu _____ souvent visite à tes parents? (rendre, entendre)
3. Ta famille et toi, est-ce que vous _____ bien la plupart du temps? (perdre, s'entendre)
4. Est-ce que tu _____ souvent patience avec tes parents? Est-ce qu'ils _____ souvent patience avec toi? (perdre, répondre)
5. Est-ce que tu _____ tes prochaines vacances avec impatience? (attendre, entendre)
6. Est-ce que tu _____ facilement quand tu es dans une autre ville? (se perdre, vendre)
7. Quand tu voyages avec des amis, est-ce que vous _____ dans un hôtel de luxe? (vendre, descendre)

AU PASSÉ COMPOSÉ

8. Est-ce que tu _____ visite à tes parents récemment? (revendre, rendre)
9. La dernière fois que tu as vu tes parents, est-ce qu'ils _____ patience avec toi? (perdre, vendre)
10. La dernière fois que vous êtes partis en week-end ensemble, où est-ce que vous _____? (descendre, entendre)

Follow-up for *B. La routine de Rose.*
Follow-up questions. **1.** Où est-ce que Rose attend l'autobus? **2.** Pourquoi est-ce qu'elle perd patience quelquefois? **3.** Pourquoi fait-elle ses devoirs dans l'autobus? **4.** Est-ce que le prof de Rose perd quelquefois patience? **5.** Qu'est-ce qu'on vend dans le magasin préféré de Rose? **6.** À qui est-ce que Rose aime rendre visite? Pourquoi?

Supplemental activity. Questions orales. **1.** Quand vos professeurs sont en retard *(late)*, combien de temps est-ce que vous les attendez? **2.** Est-ce que vous entendez généralement bien au laboratoire de langues? Et dans la salle de classe? **3.** Pendant quel cours est-ce que vous perdez patience de temps en temps? Dans quel cours est-ce que vous perdez beaucoup de temps? Dans quel cours est-ce que vous répondez souvent aux questions du professeur? **4.** Est-ce que vous attendez quelquefois vos amis au café après les cours?

Les activités d'hier

Rose parle de ce qu'elle a fait hier.

Le réveil a sonné et je me suis réveillée.

Je me suis levée.

J'ai pris un bain.

Je me suis peignée.

Je me suis habillée.

J'ai passé le reste de la journée avec des copains.

Nous nous sommes promenés.

Nous nous sommes arrêtés au restaurant pour manger.

Nous nous sommes bien amusés.

Nous nous sommes quittés vers 10 heures et je me suis couchée vers 11 heures.

Le réveil *The alarm clock*   **sonner** *to ring*   **s'arrêter** *to stop*

Suggestion for the conversation. Set the scene. Have students listen for the answer to the following question with books closed as you play the conversation. Then, have students read along as you play the conversation again. **Quand André et Rosalie se sont retrouvés pour la première fois après toutes ces années, est-ce qu'ils se sont bien entendus?**

 Rosalie **raconte** sa rencontre avec André à sa nièce Patricia.

PATRICIA: André et vous, vous vous êtes retrouvés après toutes ces années? Comment est-ce que ça s'est passé?

ROSALIE: Alors, André **est venu** chez mon frère et voilà... nous nous sommes vus, **nous nous sommes reconnus** bien sûr et nous nous sommes parlé. Nous avons passé tout le reste de la journée ensemble! Nous nous sommes enfin quittés vers sept heures!

PATRICIA: Vous vous êtes bien entendus, **donc?**

ROSALIE: **Parfaitement** bien. Et nous nous sommes bien amusés.

A. Récemment. Quand avez-vous fait ces choses?

ce matin	hier matin	lundi dernier	il y a deux (trois...) jours
cet après-midi	hier après-midi	le week-end dernier	(semaines, mois, ans...)
ce soir	hier soir	la semaine dernière	il y a longtemps
???	???	???	???

1. Le réveil a sonné et je me suis levé(e) tout de suite...
2. J'ai pris un bain ou une douche...
3. Je me suis brossé les cheveux ou je me suis peigné(e)...
4. Mes amis et moi, nous nous sommes bien amusés ensemble...
5. Nous nous sommes promenés en ville...
6. Je me suis arrêté(e) dans un fast-food pour manger...
7. Je me suis couché(e) après minuit...

B. Ils se sont retrouvés. Décrivez la journée où André et Rosalie se sont retrouvés en mettant ces phrases dans l'ordre logique. La première est indiquée.

_____ Ils se sont quittés.

_____ Ils se sont reconnus.

___1___ André est allé chez le frère de Rosalie.

_____ Ils se sont parlé.

_____ André et Rosalie se sont vus.

Follow-up for *B. Ils se sont retrouvés.* Qu'est-ce qui s'est passé en premier entre André et Rosalie quand ils se sont retrouvés? EXEMPLE **a.** Ils se sont parlé. **b.** Ils se sont vus. **b. Ils se sont vus.** **1. a.** Ils se sont reconnus. **b.** Ils se sont vus. **2. a.** Ils se sont quittés. **b.** Ils se sont parlé pendant des heures. **3. a.** Ils se sont reconnus. **b.** Ils se sont parlé. **4. a.** Ils se sont retrouvés. **b.** Ils passent beaucoup de temps ensemble depuis.

C. Ce jour-là. Avec un(e) partenaire, changez la conversation entre Rosalie et Patricia comme indiqué.

1. The day they saw each other again, Rosalie and André went for a walk and stopped at a fast-food restaurant to eat. They finally left each other about 10:00.
2. You and an old friend ran into each other after a long time apart. Imagine what happened and what you did and talk about it, basing your conversation on the one between Patricia and Rosalie. [If you want to say what you and your friend did not do using a reciprocal or reflexive verb, use **nous ne nous sommes pas...** For example, **nous ne nous sommes pas amusés.**]

---

raconter *to tell*   **est venu(e)** *came* (**venir** *to come*)   **nous nous sommes reconnus** (**se reconnaître** *to recognize each other*)   **donc** *then, thus, so*   **Parfaitement** *Perfectly*

✓ *Pour vérifier*

1. Do you use **être** or **avoir** as the auxiliary verb with reflexive and reciprocal verbs in the **passé composé?**

2. Where are reflexive pronouns placed with respect to the auxiliary verb? Where do you place **ne... pas** in the negative?

3. When does the past participle not agree with the subject? What are two verbs that you know that do not have agreement?

Note. On may take the appropriate plural agreement when used to mean *we* (**on** s'est levé[e][s]).

Saying what people did:

Les verbes réfléchis et réciproques au passé composé

All reflexive and reciprocal verbs use **être** as the auxiliary verb in the **passé composé.** Always place the reflexive pronoun directly before the auxiliary verb.

SE LEVER	
je me suis levé(e)	nous nous sommes levé(e)s
tu t'es levé(e)	vous vous êtes levé(e)(s)
il s'est levé	ils se sont levés
elle s'est levée	elles se sont levées
on s'est levé	

In the negative, place the negation around the auxiliary verb and include the reflexive pronoun.

NE PAS SE LEVER	
je ne me suis pas levé(e)	nous ne nous sommes pas levé(e)s
tu ne t'es pas levé(e)	vous ne vous êtes pas levé(e)(s)
il ne s'est pas levé	ils ne se sont pas levés
elle ne s'est pas levée	elles ne se sont pas levées
on ne s'est pas levé	

In the **passé composé,** the past participle agrees in gender and number with the reflexive pronoun (and the subject) when it is the direct object of the verb.

Rosalie **s'**est lev**ée** tôt.   André et Rosalie **se** sont mariés.

In this chapter, make the past participle agree except in these cases:

- It does not normally agree when the reflexive verb is followed directly by a noun that is the direct object of the verb.

Rose **s'**est lav**ée**.   BUT   Rose s'est lavé **les mains.**

- With the verbs **se parler** and **se téléphoner,** there is no agreement because the reflexive pronoun is an indirect object.

Ils se sont parlé.   Nous nous sommes téléphoné.

A. Hier chez Henri et Patricia. Patricia, la cousine de Rose, parle de ce qu'elle a fait hier. Qu'est-ce qu'elle dit?

Exemple   **Je me suis réveillée à six heures.**

Exemple   Je...   **1.** Je...   **2.** Je...

3. Je...   **4.** Je...   **5.** Henri et moi, nous...

B. Hier. Regardez les illustrations de *A. Hier chez Henri et Patricia* et expliquez ce que Patricia a fait.

Exemple

Patricia s'est réveillée à six heures.

C. Et toi? Demandez à votre partenaire s'il/si elle a fait les choses suivantes hier.

Exemple   se lever tôt
— **Est-ce que tu t'es levé(e) tôt hier?**
— **Oui, je me suis levé(e) tôt hier. /**
Non, je ne me suis pas levé(e) tôt hier.

1. se réveiller tôt
2. se lever tout de suite
3. prendre un bain ou une douche
4. se laver les cheveux
5. passer la soirée à la maison

6. s'ennuyer
7. s'amuser
8. se coucher tard
9. s'endormir facilement

D. Rose veut tout savoir. Rose voudrait savoir ce qu'André et Rosalie ont fait hier. Imaginez ses questions et les réponses de Rosalie.

Exemple   se téléphoner   — **Est-ce que vous vous êtes téléphoné hier?**
— **Oui, nous nous sommes téléphoné hier. /**
Non, nous ne nous sommes pas téléphoné hier.

> *se retrouver en ville*   ???   SE PROMENER
>
> se voir   *beaucoup se parler*   SE DISPUTER
>
> *s'embrasser*   **s'ennuyer**   S'AMUSER

E. Entretien. Posez ces questions à votre partenaire.

1. À quelle heure est-ce que tu t'es couché(e) hier soir? Est-ce que tu as bien dormi? Jusqu'à quelle heure est-ce que tu as dormi ce matin? Est-ce que tu t'es levé(e) facilement?

2. À quelle heure est-ce que tu dois te réveiller les jours du cours de français? À quelle heure est-ce que tu aimes te lever? À quelle heure est-ce que tu t'es levé(e) ce matin?

3. Avec qui est-ce que tu es sorti(e) récemment? Où est-ce que vous vous êtes retrouvé(e)s? Où est-ce que vous êtes allé(e)s ensemble? Qu'est-ce que vous avez fait? Est-ce que vous vous êtes bien amusé(e)s?

1. How do you form the **imparfait** of all verbs except **être**? What is the **imparfait** of **je m'amuse**? of **je ne m'amuse pas**?

2. Do you use the **imparfait** or the **passé composé** to say what happened on a specific occasion? to say how things used to be?

Saying what people did and used to do:

Les verbes réfléchis et réciproques à l'imparfait et reprise de l'usage du passé composé et de l'imparfait

Just as with all other verbs (except **être**), the **imparfait** of reflexive verbs is formed by dropping the **-ons** from the present tense **nous** form and adding the endings **-ais, -ais, -ait, -ions, -iez, -aient.**

SE LEVER	
je me levais	nous nous levions
tu te levais	vous vous leviez
il/elle/on se levait	ils/elles se levaient

NE PAS SE LEVER	
je ne me levais pas	nous ne nous levions pas
tu ne te levais pas	vous ne vous leviez pas
il/elle/on ne se levait pas	ils/elles ne se levaient pas

When talking about your life in the past, remember to use the **passé composé** to tell *what happened on specific occasions* and the **imparfait** to tell *what things were like in general* or *what was going on when something else happened.* Before doing the exercises in this section, review the specific uses of the **passé composé** and the **imparfait** on page 224.

Ce matin, **je me suis levé(e)** à six heures.
Quand j'étais au lycée, **je me levais** à sept heures.

Follow-up for A. À seize ans. Un couple va divorcer. Est-ce qu'ils faisaient probablement ces choses en couple? EXEMPLE s'entendre bien **Non, ils ne s'entendaient pas bien.** 1. se disputer souvent 2. s'entendre mal 3. s'amuser ensemble 4. s'embrasser souvent

Follow-ups for B. Et hier? A. Have students say when they last did these things. (You may wish to put some possible answers on the board: **hier, ce matin, la semaine dernière, en 1998, il y a cinq minutes, il y a longtemps, ne... jamais...**) 1. travailler jusqu'à minuit 2. se lever avant sept heures 3. se disputer avec un ami 4. se brosser les dents 5. se laver les cheveux 6. s'amuser 7. s'ennuyer 8. se promener au parc **B.** Put the following list on the board. Have students circulate in the class to find at least two people who did each of these things yesterday. 1. se réveiller avant sept heures 2. se laver les cheveux 3. se lever tard 4. se reposer 5. se disputer avec un(e) ami(e) 6. se coucher après minuit

A. À seize ans. Parlez de votre routine quotidienne à l'âge de 16 ans.

Exemple   se réveiller souvent tôt
À l'âge de seize ans, je me réveillais souvent tôt. /
Je ne me réveillais pas souvent tôt.

1. se réveiller souvent avant six heures
2. se lever facilement
3. prendre un bain / une douche le matin
4. se laver les cheveux tous les jours
5. prendre toujours le petit déjeuner
6. aller toujours en cours
7. s'ennuyer souvent en cours

B. Et hier? Utilisez les verbes de l'exercice précédent pour parler de ce que vous avez fait hier.

Exemple   se réveiller tôt
Hier, je me suis réveillé(e) tôt. /
Je ne me suis pas réveillé(e) tôt.

C. Et alors? Rosalie parle de ce qui s'est passé hier. Complétez ses phrases logiquement en mettant les verbes donnés au passé composé ou à l'imparfait.

Suggestion for *C. Et alors?* Review the uses of the **passé composé** and **imparfait** before doing this exercise.

Supplemental activity. Have students list five things they did last weekend. Then have them list five things they used to do on the weekend when they were in high school.

Exemple Hier matin, je (j') _____ (être) fatiguée et je _____ (rester) au lit.
Hier matin, j'**étais** fatiguée et je **suis restée** au lit.

1. Je (J') _____ (vouloir) préparer le petit déjeuner et alors, je _____ (se laver) les mains.
2. Vers midi, André et moi, nous _____ (avoir) faim et alors, nous _____ (se préparer) des sandwichs.
3. Nous _____ (boire) deux carafes d'eau minérale aussi parce que nous _____ (avoir) très soif.
4. Après, André _____ (se coucher) parce qu'il _____ (être) fatigué.
5. Vers trois heures il n'_____ (être) plus fatigué. Alors, il _____ (se lever).
6. Il _____ (faire) très beau. Alors, nous _____ (se promener).
7. Quand nous _____ (rentrer), Rose et ses copains _____ (être) à la maison.
8. Nous _____ (se quitter) assez tôt parce que nous _____ (être) fatigués.

D. La jeunesse d'Henri. Henri parle de sa jeunesse et du début de ses études universitaires. Complétez ses phrases avec le passé composé ou l'imparfait des verbes donnés.

Follow-up for *D. La jeunesse d'Henri.* Have students write about their youth and their first day at the university, using *D. La jeunesse d'Henri* as a model.

Quand je (j') *(être)* jeune, je (j') *(habiter)* près de Rouen avec ma famille. Nous *(habiter)* dans une jolie maison à la campagne. Nous *(être)* cinq dans la famille: mon père, ma mère, mes deux sœurs et moi. En général, je (j') *(être)* heureux mais je *(s'ennuyer)* quelquefois. Je (J') *(aimer)* beaucoup les études et je (j') *(aimer)* lire et sortir avec mes amis.

Quand je (j') *(avoir)* 18 ans, je (j') *(aller)* faire des études à Paris. Ma famille *(être)* contente de ma décision. Le jour de mon départ, je (j') *(partir)* tôt le matin et je (j') *(prendre)* le train pour aller à Paris. Je (J') *(dormir)* quand le train *(arriver)* à Paris mais je *(se réveiller)* tout de suite.

Le premier jour à Paris, je (j') *(trouver)* un appartement. Le soir, je *(se reposer)* un peu et alors je (j') *(décider)* d'aller manger dans un café du quartier. Il y *(avoir)* un petit café pas trop loin de l'appartement et je (j') *(décider)* d'y aller dîner. Quelle bonne surprise! Je (J') *(entrer)* dans le café et je (j') *(voir)* des amis de Rouen à une table près de la porte. Nous *(manger)* et nous *(beaucoup parler)*. Nous *(passer)* toute la soirée ensemble et nous *(bien s'amuser)*.

E. Entretien. Interviewez votre partenaire.

1. Est-ce que tu t'entendais bien avec tes parents quand tu avais quinze ans? Qu'est-ce que vous faisiez en famille? Est-ce que vous vous disputiez quelquefois? Est-ce que vous vous êtes disputés récemment?
2. À quelle heure est-ce que tu t'es réveillé(e) ce matin? Est-ce que tu t'es levé(e) tout de suite? Qu'est-ce que tu as fait ensuite? À quelle heure est-ce que tu te levais quand tu étais au lycée? Est-ce que tu te levais facilement?
3. Avec qui est-ce que tu es sorti(e) récemment? Où est-ce que vous êtes allé(e)s ensemble? Qu'est-ce que vous avez fait? Est-ce que vous vous êtes bien amusé(e)s? Avec qui aimais-tu sortir quand tu étais au lycée? Qu'est-ce que vous aimiez faire pour vous amuser?

COMPÉTENCE 4

Saying what you just did

NOTES DE VOCABULAIRE
The expression **venir de** followed by an infinitive indicates that someone *just did* something. **Il vient d'arriver.** *He just arrived.* Notice that **faire des courses** means *to run errands,* but **faire les courses** means *to go grocery shopping.*

Warm-up. Un couple commence à sortir ensemble. Où vont-ils pour faire les choses suivantes? **1.** voir un film **2.** voir une exposition d'art **3.** faire du shopping **4.** prendre un verre **5.** manger **6.** nager **7.** acheter des livres **8.** retrouver des amis

Suggestions. A. Venir de + infinitive is presented here as a lexical item. It is explained and practiced in the next section. However, you may wish to explain the expression before introducing this vocabulary section. **B.** You may wish to point out that **un guichet** is *a ticket window* and that the pronunciation of **teinturerie** is [tɛ̃tyʀʀi].

Suggestion for the conversation. Set the scene and explain the terms **un bureau de tabac, une boulangerie, une baguette,** and **des timbres.** Have students listen with books closed for the answer to the question: **Qu'est-ce qu'André a fait ce matin?** Then have students read along as you play the conversation again.

Des courses

Tout le monde a fait des courses. Qu'est-ce que **chacun vient de faire?**

André vient de **déposer de l'argent** à la banque.

Rose vient de **retirer de l'argent** du **guichet automatique.**

Henri vient d'**envoyer un colis** et une lettre au bureau de poste.

Patricia vient de laisser ses vêtements à **la teinturerie.**

Luc vient de **faire les courses** au supermarché.

Isabelle vient d'acheter des médicaments à la pharmacie.

La fille d'Henri et Patricia vient d'acheter un CD au magasin de musique.

Les fils d'Henri et Patricia viennent d'acheter des fleurs (f) chez le fleuriste.

André vient de rentrer et il parle avec Rosalie de ses activités.

ROSALIE: Ah! **Te voilà, chéri!**
ANDRÉ: Oui, je viens de finir mes courses.
ROSALIE: Où es-tu allé?
ANDRÉ: Je suis allé acheter ton livre à la librairie.
ROSALIE: Merci. Je suis impatiente de commencer à le lire.
ANDRÉ: Je suis aussi allé au **bureau de tabac** pour acheter le journal et **des timbres.**
ROSALIE: Et tu as pensé à aller à **la boulangerie** aussi?
ANDRÉ: Oui, j'ai pris **une baguette** et des croissants pour demain matin.
ROSALIE: Bon, et ici tout est prêt. Je viens de finir de préparer **le déjeuner. Passons à table!**

Tout le monde *Everyone*   **chacun(e)** *each one*   **vient de faire** *just did*   **déposer de l'argent** (m) *to deposit money*   **retirer de l'argent** *to withdraw money*   **un guichet automatique** *an automatic teller machine*   **envoyer** *to send*   **un colis** *a package*   **la teinturerie** *the dry cleaner*   **faire les courses** *to go grocery shopping*   **Te voilà!** *There you are!*   **chéri(e)** *honey, darling*   **le bureau de tabac** *a shop that sells newspapers, magazines, stamps, and tobacco products*   **un timbre** *a stamp*   **la boulangerie** *the bakery*   **une baguette** *a loaf of French bread*   **le déjeuner** *lunch*   **Passons à table!** *Let's sit down and eat!*

A. Où va-t-on... ? Où va-t-on pour... ?

1. acheter un CD
2. acheter des livres
3. envoyer un colis
4. acheter des timbres
5. faire les courses
6. déposer de l'argent
7. retirer de l'argent
8. envoyer une lettre
9. acheter des fleurs
10. acheter des médicaments
11. acheter une baguette
12. laisser des vêtements sales

> *à la librairie*
> chez le fleuriste
> **au bureau de poste**
> *à la banque*
> *au guichet automatique*
> AU BUREAU DE TABAC
> À LA TEINTURERIE
> *à la boulangerie*
> *au magasin de musique*
> **au supermarché**
> À LA PHARMACIE

Follow-ups for *A. Où va-t-on... ?*
A. Henri va faire ces choses cet après-midi. Où va-t-il aller? **EXEMPLE** acheter un CD pour Patricia **Il va aller au magasin de musique. 1.** acheter des timbres **2.** acheter un livre **3.** faire les courses pour le dîner **4.** déposer de l'argent **5.** envoyer un colis **6.** acheter du pain **B.** Où est-on si on entend ces phrases? **1.** Je voudrais deux baguettes et trois croissants, s'il vous plaît. **2.** Bonjour. Est-ce que vous avez des livres sur Picasso? **3.** Je cherche un magazine sur le cinéma. **4.** Alors, j'ai besoin de quelque chose pour le repas de ce soir. **5.** Combien d'argent voulez-vous retirer, madame? **6.** Je voudrais des cigarettes et dix timbres, s'il vous plaît.

B. Une journée chargée. Qu'est-ce que ces personnes viennent probablement de faire?

Exemple   André quitte le fleuriste.
                Il **vient d'acheter des fleurs.**

1. Henri quitte le bureau de poste. Il...
2. Rosalie sort du supermarché. Elle...
3. Luc quitte la teinturerie. Il...
4. Patricia quitte le bureau de tabac. Elle...
5. Isabelle sort de la banque. Elle...
6. Rose quitte la boulangerie. Elle...
7. André sort de la pharmacie. Il...

Chez la fleuriste

C. La journée de Rose. Avec un(e) partenaire, changez la conversation entre Rosalie et André comme indiqué.

1. André bought Rosalie's book, then went to the post office and sent a letter. He also bought some medicine at the drugstore.
2. André asks Rosalie what she did. She withdrew some money from the ATM, bought a CD, and left her clothes at the dry cleaner.
3. Create a conversation in which you and your partner discuss what errands you are going to run this weekend. Remember to use **aller** with the infinitive to say what you are going to do.

1. How is the stem of the **nous** and **vous** forms of the verb **venir** different from the stem of the other forms?
2. In French, how do you say *to become? to come back? to remember?*
3. Do you use **être** or **avoir** as the auxiliary verb for these verbs in the **passé composé?**
4. How do you use **venir** to say *I just ate? They just left? We just arrived?*

Saying what you just did:
Le verbe **venir** *et le passé immédiat*

You have seen several forms of the verb **venir** *(to come)*. Here is its conjugation.

VENIR *(to come)*	
je viens	nous venons
tu viens	vous venez
il/elle/on vient	ils/elles viennent

PASSÉ COMPOSÉ: je suis venu(e)
IMPARFAIT: je venais

Mes amis viennent chez moi ce soir.   Ils sont venus le week-end dernier aussi.

As you have seen, you can use the verb **venir** followed by **de** and an infinitive to say that something *just* happened.

Rose vient d'arriver.   *Rose just arrived.*
Henri et André viennent de partir.   *Henri and André just left.*

Devenir *(to become)*, **revenir** *(to come back)*, and **se souvenir (de)** *(to remember)* are conjugated like **venir. Venir, devenir, revenir,** and **se souvenir** all take the auxiliary verb **être** in the **passé composé.**

Le mari de Rosalie est venu en France en 1944.
Rosalie est devenue américaine en 1955.
Elle est revenue en France après la mort de son mari.
Elle s'est souvenue de son vieil ami André.

Warm-up for *A. Qu'est-ce qu'ils viennent de faire?* D'où reviennent ces personnes probablement? EXEMPLE André a acheté des fleurs. **Il revient de chez le fleuriste. 1.** Isabelle a envoyé un colis. **2.** Luc a acheté des livres. **3.** André et Rosalie ont fait les courses. **4.** Henri a déposé de l'argent. **5.** Patricia a acheté une baguette. **6.** Les enfants d'Henri et Patricia ont vu un film. **7.** Les amis de Rosalie ont vu une exposition d'art. **8.** Ses amis ont pris un verre.

Suggestion for *A. Qu'est-ce qu'ils viennent de faire?* Remind students that the reflexive pronoun must match the subject of the sentence.

A. Qu'est-ce qu'ils viennent de faire? Patricia parle de ce que chacun vient de faire. Qu'est-ce qu'elle dit?

Exemple

Henri et moi **venons de nous réveiller.**

1. Je...

2. Nous...

3. Rose, est-ce que tu... ?

4. André...

5. Luc et Isabelle, est-ce que vous... ?

6. Henri...

B. Qu'est-ce ce qu'on fait? Conjuguez les verbes entre parenthèses au présent et posez les questions à votre partenaire.

1. Est-ce que tu (venir) toujours en cours?
2. Est-ce que tu (se souvenir) toujours d'apporter *(to bring)* tes devoirs?
3. Est-ce que le professeur de français (venir) souvent en cours en retard *(late)?*
4. Est-ce qu'il/elle (devenir) impatient(e) quand les étudiants ne préparent pas bien le cours?
5. Est-ce qu'il/elle (se souvenir) toujours du nom de ses étudiants?
6. Est-ce que les autres étudiants (venir) toujours en cours?
7. Est-ce qu'ils (devenir) nerveux quand il y a un examen?
8. Tes amis et toi, est-ce que vous (revenir) quelquefois à l'université le week-end?
9. Est-ce que vous (devenir) impatients avant le week-end?

C. L'histoire de Rosalie. Racontez l'histoire de Rosalie en mettant les verbes donnés à l'imparfait ou au passé composé.

Une jeune fille qui _____ (s'appeler) Rosalie _____ (habiter) à la campagne près de Rouen. Quand elle _____ (avoir) 18 ans, Rosalie _____ (finir) ses études et elle _____ (devenir) professeur de musique.

En 1944, un jeune soldat américain _____ (venir) en France et un jour ce jeune homme et Rosalie _____ (se rencontrer). Ils _____ (se voir) et ils _____ (se parler). Ils _____ (passer) des heures ensemble. À partir de ce jour-là *(From that day on)*, Rosalie et son jeune soldat _____ (se retrouver) tous les jours. Le soldat _____ (venir) chez Rosalie ou ils _____ (se retrouver) en ville. Finalement, ils _____ (se marier) et ils _____ (aller) s'installer à Atlanta. Leur vie ensemble _____ (être) très heureuse.

Après la mort de son mari, Rosalie _____ (revenir) en France avec sa petite-fille, Rose. Un jour, Rose _____ (se promener) avec ses cousines quand elle _____ (commencer) à parler avec un monsieur. Ce monsieur, André Dupont, _____ (être) l'ancien ami de Rosalie. Il _____ (se souvenir) très bien de Rosalie parce qu'il _____ (être) amoureux d'elle quand il _____ (avoir) 18 ans.

Rosalie _____ (être) chez son frère Jean quand elle _____ (revoir) André. Ils _____ (se voir) et ils _____ (tomber) amoureux.

Reprise: *Talking about daily life and relationships*

In *Chapitre 7,* you practiced talking about your daily routine and relationships between people. Now you have a chance to review what you learned.

A. En cours de français.
D'abord, dites si ces personnes font les choses indiquées en cours de français. Ensuite, dites si ces mêmes personnes ont fait ces choses la dernière fois que vous étiez en cours.

1. les étudiants / répondre bien aux questions du professeur
2. le professeur / perdre patience avec les étudiants
3. les étudiants / s'entendre bien
4. nous / perdre du temps en cours
5. je / rendre visite au professeur dans son bureau avant le cours
6. je / rendre les devoirs au professeur

B. En cours.
Qu'est-ce qui se passe les jours du cours de français? Formez des questions et posez-les à votre partenaire.

Exemple tu / s'amuser en cours
— **Est-ce que tu t'amuses en cours?**
— **Oui, je m'amuse en cours. /**
Non, je ne m'amuse pas en cours.

Les jours du cours de français...

1. tu / se lever tôt
2. tu / s'ennuyer en cours
3. tu / s'endormir en cours
4. les autres étudiants et toi, vous / s'amuser bien en cours
5. vous / se disputer
6. vous / se retrouver après les cours
7. les autres étudiants / se parler en français en cours
8. ils / s'entendre bien
9. le prof / s'amuser en cours
10. le prof / s'endormir en cours

C. Et au dernier cours?
Demandez à votre partenaire si chacun a fait les choses indiquées dans **B. En cours** au dernier cours de français.

Au dernier cours de français...

Exemple tu / s'amuser en cours
— **Est-ce que tu t'es amusé(e) en cours?**
— **Oui, je me suis amusé(e) en cours. /**
Non, je ne me suis pas amusé(e) en cours.

D. Samedi prochain.
Dites si chacun va faire les choses indiquées samedi prochain.

Exemple je / se réveiller avant six heures
Je vais me réveiller avant six heures. /
Je ne vais pas me réveiller avant six heures.

1. je / se lever tôt
2. je / se laver les cheveux
3. mes amis et moi, nous / sortir ensemble
4. nous / s'amuser
5. je / se coucher tôt

E. Où est-ce qu'ils viennent d'aller? Dites où ces personnnes viennent d'aller et ce qu'ils ont probablement fait.

Exemple   La fille d'Henri et Patricia / au magasin de musique
La fille d'Henri et Patricia vient d'aller au magasin de musique. Elle a acheté un CD.

1. André / banque
2. Rose / guichet automatique
3. Henri / bureau de poste
4. Luc / supermarché
5. Isabelle / pharmacie
6. Les fils d'Henri et Patricia / chez le fleuriste

F. Entretien. Interviewez votre partenaire.

1. Pourquoi est-ce que tu es venu(e) à cette université? Est-ce que tes parents sont venus ici aussi? Est-ce que tu as l'intention de revenir ici l'année prochaine? Est-ce que tu voudrais devenir prof après tes études?
2. Quels jours est-ce que tu viens à l'université? Est-ce que tu es venu(e) à l'université hier? Tes amis et toi, est-ce que vous revenez quelquefois à l'université le week-end?
3. Est-ce que le cours de français devient plus difficile au deuxième semestre / trimestre? Quand est-ce que tu deviens nerveux (nerveuse) en cours?

G. Le mariage d'André et Rosalie. André et Rosalie se sont enfin mariés. Décrivez le jour de leur mariage en mettant les verbes donnés au passé composé ou à l'imparfait.

Le jour de son mariage, Rosalie _____ (se lever) tôt. André _____ (arriver) vers neuf heures mais tout de suite après, il _____ (se souvenir) d'une course qu'il _____ (devoir) faire et il _____ (repartir).

Il _____ (être) trois heures quand André _____ (revenir). La cérémonie _____ (commencer) à quatre heures. Tous les invités *(guests)* _____ (être) dans le jardin. Il _____ (faire) beau et tout le monde _____ (être) content. Rosalie _____ (porter) une jolie robe beige et André _____ (porter) un costume noir. Rosalie _____ (être) très jolie! Après la cérémonie, les amis _____ (rester) et ils _____ (manger) du gâteau *(cake)*. Ils _____ (s'amuser) bien quand tout d'un coup il _____ (commencer) à pleuvoir et alors, ils _____ (devoir) entrer dans la maison.

André _____ (partir) et il _____ (revenir) avec assez de chaises pour tout le monde. Vers huit heures les invités _____ (partir). André et Rosalie _____ (se regarder) et ils _____ (commencer) à sourire *(to smile)*. Ils _____ (être) fatigués mais très, très heureux.

Des jeunes mariés

LECTURE ET *composition*

LECTURE: Tous les matins, je me lève

Comment est-ce que vous passez votre matinée? Vous allez lire des interviews de deux Français faites par la revue *Vogue Hommes*. D'abord, faites cet exercice.

Familles de mots. Devinez le sens des mots en caractères gras.

s'endormir	Je me réveille tôt mais j'aime **me rendormir** quelques minutes.
se réveiller	L'heure du **réveil** chez nous est entre sept et huit heures.
rêver	Quand je suis d'humeur **rêveuse**, j'aime prendre un bain chaud.
la banque	Mon ami est **banquier**. Il travaille dans une banque en ville.

NICOLAS SARKOZY

Profession: député-**maire** de Neuilly-sur-Seine. Prêt en trente-cinq minutes.

Heure du réveil?

Entre 6h30 et 6h45. J'adore me lever tôt parce que j'ai l'impression de gagner du temps dans la journée.

Nombre d'heures de sommeil?

Sept heures.

Quelle est la première chose que vous faites en vous levant?

Je vais dans ma salle de bains.

La radio?

J'adore écouter la radio et **zapper**; je passe d'Europe 1 à RTL ou France Inter.

Le petit déjeuner?

Jamais de petit déjeuner à la maison. Je suis un adepte des petits déjeuners d'affaires dans les grands hôtels, mon préféré est le George V, ou dans les restaurants. J'aime **traîner** le matin dans les grands hôtels parisiens. Et puis un petit déjeuner, c'est mieux qu'un déjeuner, parce qu'en une heure on a généralement terminé. J'ai beaucoup d'appétit. J'**avale** une omelette au fromage et je bois du thé.

Vêtements?

Je choisis mes vêtements **en fonction de** mes activités du jour. On ne s'habille pas de la même manière pour une cérémonie ou pour présider un match de football.

Comment vous rendez-vous à votre travail?

De préférence à pied, **puisque la mairie n'est qu'**à dix minutes de **mon domicile**. Si je vais à un rendez-vous, c'est le chauffeur qui me **conduit**. J'écoute **volontiers** la radio, mais je suis incapable de lire en voiture.

ALAIN DE POUZHILAC

Profession: directeur d'EURO RSCG. Prêt en une heure et demie.

Heure du réveil?

6h45, et je passe trois quarts d'heure dans ma salle de bains. Je suis une véritable «**cocotte**». Deux fois par semaine, je me lève à 5h pour prendre l'avion.

Nombre d'heures de sommeil?

Entre six et sept heures par nuit. **Malheureusement,** je me réveille, je **réfléchis**, j'**angoisse**, je rêve et **je finis par** me rendormir.

Le petit déjeuner?

Tous les matins, j'ai un petit déjeuner

d'affaires avec mes collaborateurs ou des clients. Je ne mange pas, je prends juste un café. Nous nous retrouvons souvent à l'hôtel Bristol. J'adore cet **endroit** parce que je peux m'y rendre à pied; le salon et le jardin sont très agréables.

Bain ou douche?

Si j'ai l'humeur dynamique, je prends une douche; si j'ai l'humeur plutôt rêveuse, c'est un bain assez chaud.

Vêtements?

Jacques Séguéla a l'habitude de dire à mon sujet que je m'habille comme «un banquier de province». Mais, en vérité, je choisis mes vêtements selon mon instinct du matin, la couleur du temps et mon humeur.

Comment vous rendez-vous à votre travail?

Tous les matins, un chauffeur vient me chercher en **voiture de fonction** équipée d'un téléphone que je n'utilise jamais.

Le moment préféré?

Celui où je me réveille, où je **découvre** que je suis en vie, avec **des tas de** projets à **réaliser**. Je n'aime pas la solitude. J'adore m'amuser et **rire**.

■ ■ ■ ■ ■

---

le maire *the mayor*   **zapper** *to channel surf, to switch back and forth*   **traîner** *to hang around*   **avaler** *to gobble (down)*   **en fonction de** *depending on*   **puisque** *since*   **la mairie** *the town hall*   **n'est que** *is only*   **mon domicile** *my residence*   **conduire** *to drive*   **volontiers** *gladly*   **une cocotte** *a primper*   **Malheureusement** *Unfortunately*   **réfléchir** *to think*   **angoisser** *to worry*   **je finis par** *I end up*   **un endroit** *a place*   **une voiture de fonction** *a company car*   **découvrir** *to discover*   **des tas de** *lots of*   **réaliser** *to carry out*   **rire** *to laugh*

Trois interviews. Indiquez ce qui est vrai pour les trois personnes indiquées.

	NICOLAS SARKOZY	ALAIN DE POUZHILAC	VOUS
• *Profession*	_____	_____	_____
• *Prêt(e) en... minutes*	_____	_____	_____
• *Heure du réveil*	_____	_____	_____
• *Nombre d'heures de sommeil*	_____	_____	_____
• *Première activité du matin*	_____	_____	_____
• *Petit déjeuner*	_____		
• *Toilette (bain? douche?)*			
• *Vêtements*	_____	_____	_____
• *Moyen de transport pour aller travailler*	_____	_____	_____

Composition

A. Organisez-vous. Vous allez écrire une petite annonce *(ad)*. D'abord, organisez-vous en écrivant un bref profil de vous-même. Servez-vous du profil de Marie-Laure Augry, journaliste à la télévision française, comme modèle.

> NOM: *AUGRY*
> PRÉNOM: *MARIE-LAURE*
> ÂGE: *40 ANS*
> PROFESSION: *JOURNALISTE*
> ANIMAL FAVORI: *MON CHAT ARMAND*
> DÉTENTE: *LE LIT ET L'HERBE VERTE*
> MUSIQUE: *LE ROCK-AND-ROLL*
>
> LIVRE DE CHEVET: *«UNE CHAÎNE SUR LES BRAS»*
> *(HERVÉ BOURGES)*
> SPORTS: *TENNIS, RUGBY, CYCLISME*
> VACANCES: *À FONDETTES (EN TOURAINE)*
> LOISIRS: *LE TENNIS ET LA CHAISE LONGUE*
> AIME: *LA BONNE CUISINE*
> DÉTESTE: *L'INTOLÉRANCE*

B. Rédaction: Une annonce. Vous allez mettre une petite annonce dans le journal. Lisez ces annonces de *Rouen Poche* et utilisez votre autoportrait de l'exercice précédent pour écrire une annonce.

RENCONTRES

ÉVASION CLUB

RENCONTRES SÉLECTIONNÉES
HOMMES—FEMMES—COUPLES
CONTACTS IMMÉDIATS DE
QUALITÉ. TÉL. 02.35.73.52.18
Discrétion assurée

419
Homme, la trentaine, seul, recherche femme, sympa, câline, pour passer moments agréables. Écrire au journal qui transmettra.

420
Dame, souhaite rencontrer monsieur, 60 à 65 ans pour sorties et voyages. Écrire au journal qui transmettra.

422
Homme, 36 ans, sensible au charme et à l'humour, recherche femme sportive, jolie et dotée d'un heureux caractère. Écrire au journal qui transmettra.

423
Robert, 27 ans, ambitieux et sentimental, souhaite rencontrer blonde, 25 à 30 ans pour sorties + si affinités. Écrire au journal qui transmettra.

455
Cadre, 45 ans, grand, mince, souhaite rencontrer femme distinguée, vive, sensuelle, peu attachée aux valeurs matérielles, pour partager loisirs, et vivre une relation tendre et sincère. Écrire au journal qui transmettra.

456
Si vous désirez partir avec moi en Espagne du 25 août au 30 septembre, prenez dès maintenant contact avec moi. Écrire au journal qui transmettra.

C. Une lettre. Échangez votre petite annonce avec un(e) camarade de classe. Imaginez que vous êtes un homme / une femme qui répond à son annonce. Écrivez-lui une lettre dans laquelle vous vous présentez et vous lui posez des questions.

Supplemental comprehension questions. NICOLAS SARKOZY: 1. À quelle heure est-ce qu'il se réveille? Combien d'heures dort-il? 2. Qu'est-ce qu'il fait d'abord quand il se lève? 3. Écoute-t-il toujours la même station de radio? 4. Où prend-il son petit déjeuner? Que mange-t-il? 5. Est-ce qu'il porte toujours les mêmes vêtements? 6. Comment va-t-il au travail? Qu'est-ce qu'il aime faire en voiture? Qu'est-ce qu'il n'aime pas faire? ALAIN DE POUZHILAC: 1. Combien de temps passe-t-il dans la salle de bains le matin? 2. Pourquoi doit-il se lever à cinq heures deux fois par semaine? Est-ce qu'il dort bien la nuit? 3. Avec qui prend-il son petit déjeuner? Où se retrouvent-ils? Comment est-ce qu'il y va? 4. Quand préfère-t-il prendre un bain? 5. Comment s'habille-t-il? 6. Quel moment de la journée préfère-t-il? Aime-t-il passer du temps seul?

Suggestion. Have students brainstorm

If you have access to SYSTÈME-D software, you will find the following phrases, vocabulary, grammar, and dictionary aids there.

Phrases: Writing a news item; Describing people; Writing a letter; Introducing; Asking for information
Vocabulary: Trades, occupation; Professions; Animals; Leisure; Sports; People; Personality

about what kind of information one expects to find in personal ads and in ads for dating services.

Suggestions for B. Rédaction: Une annonce. A. Have students scan the ads in B. Rédaction: Une annonce and pick out cognates. B. Point out the following words and have students name another word they know with the same root and guess their meaning: des rencontres, la trentaine, rechercher, des sorties. C. Point out the faux amis, sensible and doté(e), in ad 422.

L'AMOUR ET LE COUPLE

See the *Instructor's Resource Manual* for the video script and activities.

Note. The vocabulary in this section does not appear in the end-of-chapter vocabulary lists and is meant for recognition only. You may wish to let students know in advance whether you intend to test them on this vocabulary.

Voici les résultats de **sondages** sur les opinions des Français au sujet de l'amour et du couple. Quelles sont vos opinions?

L'amour

♥ **Croyez-vous au** grand amour?

OUI 66%	NON 27%	SANS OPINION 7%

♥ Croyez-vous au coup de foudre?

OUI 70%	NON 28%	SANS OPINION 2%

♥ Peut-on aimer quelqu'un sans avoir de relations sexuelles avec lui?

OUI 71%	NON 28%	SANS OPINION 1%

♥ Si on espère rencontrer quelqu'un, que peut-on faire pour avoir la plus grande possibilité de succès?

FRÉQUENTER LES **BALS** OU LES DISCOTHÈQUES	66%
DEVENIR MEMBRE DE CLUBS OU D'ASSOCIATIONS	57%
S'ADRESSER À UNE AGENCE MATRIMONIALE	17%
PASSER **UNE PETITE ANNONCE**	16%

Le couple

❖ Est-il normal qu'un couple se dispute de temps en temps?

OUI 50%	NON 50%

❖ Pour être un couple heureux, **faut-il** partager le maximum de choses (loisirs, sorties, revenus, relations, logement) ou conserver une large autonomie?

TOUT PARTAGER 80%	CONSERVER UNE AUTONOMIE 16%	SANS OPINION 4%

❖ Pour être heureux ensemble, lesquelles de ces conditions sont les plus importantes? (Indiquez les trois conditions les plus importantes.)

> être à l'écoute de l'autre
> avoir des enfants
> la fidélité sexuelle
> l'harmonie sexuelle
> la patience
> partager **les tâches domestiques**

La liste indique l'ordre d'importance selon les réponses des Français qui ont répondu à ce sondage.

❖ Quelle est votre réaction **envers** l'infidélité? Est-ce une cause de rupture?

36% DES HOMMES / 44% DES FEMMES ONT DIT OUI

Option for *B. Chez nous.* To maintain privacy, have students write short answers to the questions of the survey with no names. Divide the class into six or seven groups. Each group collects and calculates the results for two of the questions to report to the class.

Follow-up for *C. Comparaisons.* Have students form debate teams to prepare and present a debate on one of the following issues or another of their choice: **1.** Les rôles traditionnels des femmes et des hommes (n')ont (pas) beaucoup changé depuis les années cinquante. **2.** Le sexe (n')est (pas) la chose la plus importante pour un couple. **3.** On (ne) doit (pas) cohabiter avant de s'établir comme couple permanent. **4.** La meilleure solution pour éviter le SIDA est l'abstinence.

---

un sondage *a survey*   **Croyez-vous (à)... ?** *Do you believe (in)* . . . ?   **un bal** *a dance*   **une petite annonce** *a classified ad*   **il faut** *it is necessary*   **les tâches domestiques** *(f) household chores*   **envers** *toward*

❖ Est-ce que ça peut **arriver** sans forcément **remettre** le couple **en cause?**

49% DES HOMMES / 47% DES FEMMES ONT DIT OUI

❖ Est-ce une liberté réciproque qu'on **s'accorde** dans le couple?

12% DES HOMMES / 4% DES FEMMES ONT DIT OUI

❖ À cause du **SIDA** et d'autres **MST,** doit-on:

Limiter le nombre de partenaires sexuels?			Utiliser systématiquement **un préservatif?**		
OUI 57%	NON 37%	SANS OPINION 6%	OUI 81%	NON 16%	SANS OPINION 3%

À discuter.

A. Vrai ou faux?

1. La majorité des Français croient *(believe)* au coup de foudre et au grand amour.
2. Pour les Français, le sexe n'est pas la chose la plus importante pour être heureux en couple.
3. En France, on pense qu'on a plus de chances de rencontrer quelqu'un à un bal que par une agence ou une annonce.
4. Les Français trouvent que la vie conjugale n'est pas sans difficultés. La moitié *(half)* trouve qu'il est normal de se disputer de temps en temps.
5. Selon les Français, pour être heureux en couple, il est plus important de conserver sa liberté individuelle que de partager beaucoup de choses.
6. Pour les Français, la fidélité est importante si on espère être heureux en couple.
7. Le SIDA influence la vie sexuelle des Français.

B. Chez nous. Créez un sondage similaire à celui que vous avez lu pour demander l'opinion de votre classe. Demandez aussi quelles sont les caractéristiques les plus importantes d'un couple heureux. Quels sont les plus grands problèmes pour un couple?

C. Comparaisons. Comparez les résultats du sondage de votre classe avec les opinions des Français.

1. Quelles similarités voyez-vous? Quelles différences? Pouvez-vous expliquer ces différences?
2. Dans un sondage sur ce sujet fait dans votre pays, quelles autres questions est-ce qu'on poserait *(would one ask)?* Est-ce que ça peut indiquer des attitudes différentes sur ce sujet?
3. Qu'est-ce que vous trouvez surprenant *(surprising)* dans le sondage? Qu'est-ce qui ne vous surprend pas? Pourquoi?

---

arriver *to happen*   **remettre en cause** *to call into question*   **s'accorder** *to grant each other*   **le SIDA** *AIDS*
une MST (une maladie sexuellement transmissible) *an STD (a sexually transmitted disease)*   **un préservatif**
a condom

visit http://horizons.heinle.com

COMPÉTENCE 1

Describing your daily routine

NOMS MASCULINS

le mariage	marriage
un petit-fils	a grandson
un séjour	a story
un veuf	a widower

NOMS FÉMININS

une demi-heure	a half hour
une petite-fille	a granddaughter
une routine	a routine
une veuve	a widow

EXPRESSIONS VERBALES

s'amuser	to have fun
s'appeler	to be named
attendre	to wait (for)
se brosser (les cheveux / les dents)	to brush (one's hair / one's teeth)
connaître	to be familiar / acquainted with, to know
se coucher / se recoucher	to go to bed / to go back to bed
s'endormir	to fall asleep
s'ennuyer	to be bored, to get bored
faire sa toilette	to wash up
s'habiller / se déshabiller	to get dressed / to get undressed
se laver (la figure / les mains)	to wash (one's face / one's hands)
se lever	to get up
se maquiller	to put on makeup
prendre un bain / une douche	to take a bath / a shower
se raser	to shave
se reposer	to rest
se réveiller	to wake up

DIVERS

comme	since, as
d'autres fois	other times
depuis	since, for
d'origine...	of . . . origin
facilement	easily
parfait(e)	perfect
quotidien(ne)	daily
vite	quick(ly), fast

COMPÉTENCE 2

Talking about relationships

NOMS MASCULINS

le coup de foudre	love at first sight
le grand amour	true love

NOM FÉMININ

une relation	a relationship

EXPRESSIONS VERBALES

s'aimer	to like each other, to love each other
attendre	to wait (for)
descendre	to go down, to get off, to stay (at a hotel)
se détester	to hate each other
se disputer	to argue
s'embrasser	to kiss each other, to embrace each other
entendre	to hear
s'entendre (bien / mal)	to get along (well / badly)
se fiancer	to get engaged
s'installer (à / dans)	to move (into), to settle (in)
se marier (avec)	to get married (to)
se parler	to talk to each other
se passer	to happen
perdre	to lose
se perdre	to get lost
prendre une décision	to make a decision
se quitter	to leave each other
se réconcilier	to make up with each other
se regarder	to look at each other
se rencontrer	to meet each other (by chance), to run into each other
rendre quelque chose à quelqu'un	to return something to someone
rendre visite à quelqu'un	to visit someone
répondre (à)	to answer
se retrouver	to meet each other (by design)
revendre	to sell back
rêver (de)	to dream (of, about)
suivre	to follow
se téléphoner	to phone each other
vendre	to sell

DIVERS

ce qui	what
C'est dommage!	That's too bad!
enfin	finally
formidable	great
heureux (heureuse)	happy
la plupart du temps	most of the time
mamie	grandma
sentimental(e) (mpl sentimentaux)	sentimental, emotional
un(e) tel(le)	such a

COMPÉTENCE 3

Talking about what you did and used to do

NOMS MASCULINS

le reste (de)	*the rest (of)*
un réveil	*an alarm clock*

NOM FÉMININ

une rencontre	*an encounter*

EXPRESSIONS VERBALES

s'arrêter	*to stop*
se peigner	*to comb one's hair*
se promener	*to go walking*
raconter	*to tell*
se reconnaître	*to recognize each other*
sonner	*to ring*
se voir	*to see each other*

DIVERS

donc	*then, so, thus, therefore*
parfaitement	*perfectly*

COMPÉTENCE 4

Saying what you just did

NOMS MASCULINS

l'argent	*money*
un bureau de poste	*a post office*
un bureau de tabac	*a tobacco shop*
un colis	*a package*
un croissant	*a croissant*
le déjeuner	*lunch*
un fleuriste	*a florist*
un guichet automatique	*an automatic teller machine*
un magasin de musique	*a music store*
des médicaments	*medication, medecine*
un supermarché	*a supermarket*
un timbre	*a stamp*

NOMS FÉMININS

une baguette	*a loaf of French bread*
une banque	*a bank*
une boulangerie	*a bakery*
une fleur	*a flower*
une lettre	*a letter*
une pharmacie	*a pharmacy*
une teinturerie	*a dry cleaner*

EXPRESSIONS VERBALES

déposer de l'argent	*to deposit money*
devenir	*to become*
envoyer	*to send*
faire les courses	*to go grocery shopping*
penser à	*to think about*
retirer de l'argent	*to withdraw money*
revenir	*to come back*
se souvenir de	*to remember*
venir	*to come*
venir de + infinitive	*to have just + past participle*

DIVERS

chacun(e)	*each one*
chéri(e)	*honey, darling*
impatient(e)	*impatient*
Passons à table!	*Let's sit down and eat!*
Te / Vous voilà!	*There you are!*
tout le monde	*everyone, everybody*

Les affiches à Trouville

Raoul Dufy (1877–1953)
1906
Paris, Musée National d'Art Moderne
© 1998 Artists Rights Society (ARS), New York/ADAGP, Paris

Born in Le Havre, Dufy frequently painted scenes of the coast of Normandy, including regattas and seascapes, and the resort towns of Trouville, Deauville, and Honfleur.

En Normandie

ROUEN

POPULATION: 105 470 habitants (les Rouennais)

DÉPARTEMENT: Seine-Maritime

RÉGION: Haute-Normandie

INDUSTRIES PRINCIPALES: import-export, raffineries de pétrole, métallurgie, construction, mécanique, industries chimiques, alimentaires *(food)* et textiles

La tapisserie de Bayeux

11th century
Bayeux, Musée de la Tapisserie
Erich Lessing/Art Resource

Named after the town of Bayeux in Normandy, this seventy-meter embroidered linen cloth depicts the Norman conquest of England in fifty-eight scenes.

La bonne cuisine

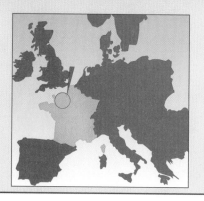

La Normandie

Comment imaginez-vous la Normandie? Imaginez-vous...

des villes au bord de la mer telles que Deauville?

d'anciennes villes historiques?

des bateaux de pêche?

des falaises isolées?

des pâturages (avec des moutons ou des vaches)?

des toits de chaume?

La Normandie, c'est tout cela! Et même plus!

_____

au bord de la mer *at the seaside*   **tel(le) que** *such as*   **de pêche** *fishing*   **une falaise** *a cliff*   **un mouton** *a sheep*   **une vache** *a cow*   **des toits** *(m)* **de chaume** *thatched roofs*

Peut-être que pour vous, la Normandie, c'est surtout le passé.

820-911: conquête de la région par les Vikings (Le nom de Normandie veut dire «Land of the Northmen».)

*1066: conquête de l'**Angleterre** par Guillaume, duc de Normandie*

1453: fin de la guerre de Cent Ans entre la France et l'Angleterre (grâce surtout aux batailles gagnées par Jeanne d'Arc)

le 6 juin 1944: le Jour J, jour du débarquement en Normandie des forces alliées (américaines, anglaises, canadiennes et françaises) commandées par le général Eisenhower

l'Angleterre *England*

TRANSPARENCIES: 8-1A, 8-1B, 8-1C

Au restaurant

Que savez-vous de la cuisine française? Avez-vous déjà mangé des plats typiquement français? En famille, entre amis ou au restaurant, les Français aiment bien les grands repas traditionnels.

On commence par une entrée (un hors-d'œuvre):

du pâté

de la salade de tomates

des crudités (f)

de la soupe à l'oignon

des œufs (m) durs

des escargots (m)

Sur la table, il y a aussi...

du pain

du sel et du poivre

Ensuite, on **sert** le plat principal:

DE LA VIANDE

DU POISSON

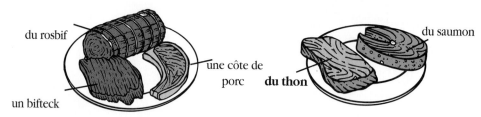

du rosbif

une côte de porc

un bifteck

du saumon

du thon

DE LA VOLAILLE

DES FRUITS (m) **DE MER**

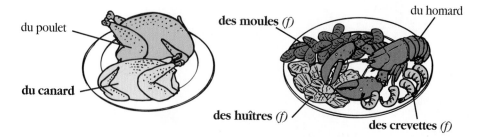

du poulet

du canard

des moules (f)

du homard

des huîtres (f)

des crevettes (f)

Que savez-vous de... ? *What do you know about . . . ?* **de la (du, de l', des)** *some* **des crudités** (f) *raw vegetables* **sert (servir** *to serve* [conjugué comme **sortir**]) **de la viande** *meat* **du poisson** *fish* **du thon** *tuna* **de la volaille** *poultry* **du canard** *duck* **des fruits** (m) **de mer** *shellfish* **des moules** (f) *mussels* **des huîtres** (f) *oysters* **des crevettes** (f) *shrimp*

Le plat principal **comprend** aussi **du riz** et des légumes *(m)*:

Pour une liste plus complète des fruits et des légumes, voir la page 295.

des pommes de terre *(f)*

des haricots verts

des petits pois

On sert la salade verte après le plat principal. On sert le fromage après la salade.

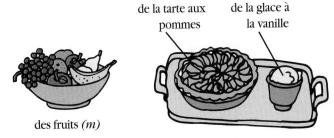

une salade

du fromage

Suggestion. Point out that in France, many use a knife and fork to eat certain fruits in a restaurant.

On finit le repas avec des fruits—ou un dessert.

de la tarte aux pommes

de la glace à la vanille

des fruits *(m)*

du gâteau au chocolat

Pour finir, on sert le café.

du café

Prenez-vous **du sucre,** du lait ou de la crème dans votre café?

Prononciation: *Le h aspiré*

In French, **h** is never pronounced and there is usually liaison and elision before it.

J'aime les‿herbes.   Il y a beaucoup **d**'huile *(oil)* dans la salade.

Before a few words beginning with **h,** there is no liaison or elision, even though the **h** is silent. These words are said to begin with **h aspiré.** In vocabulary lists, they are indicated by an asterisk (*). The following words have **h aspiré: le homard, les haricots, les hors-d'œuvre.** English words that begin with *h* often have an **h aspiré** when used in French: **les hot-dogs, les hamburgers.**

Suggestion. You may wish to point out that one hears **haricots verts** both with and without **h aspiré.** Point out that *h* is silent in some English words also *(hour, honor, honest).*

---

comprend (comprendre *to include*)   **du riz** *rice*   **du sucre** *sugar*

Suggestion for the conversation. Before playing the conversation, set the scene, then go over the menu on pp. 288–289 with students. Have them guess the meaning of unknown words and say whether they like each item, or ask which items they prefer in each category. (Tell students that they will not be tested on the vocabulary on the menu, unless it is presented elsewhere.) Have them look at the menu as they listen to the conversation to determine what André and Rosalie order. Then play the conversation again and have students read along.

NOTE *Culturelle*

Pour commander dans un restaurant français, il est bon de savoir certaines choses. On peut commander «à la carte», ce qui permet de choisir les plats qu'on préfère, ou on peut choisir un menu «à prix fixe». Dans ce cas, on a un choix plus limité mais à un prix plus raisonnable. Voir les pages 288–289.

Follow-up for the conversation.
Compréhension: **1.** Prennent-ils un apéritif? **2.** Prennent-ils le menu à 15 € ou le menu à 22 €? **3.** Que commandent-ils comme entrée? comme plat principal? **4.** Qu'est-ce qu'ils commandent comme boisson? **5.** Est-ce qu'on peut trouver de l'Évian dans les restaurants ou les supermarchés ici?

Warm-up for A. Préférences. Est-ce que les végétariens mangent les choses suivantes? **1.** du jambon **2.** de la soupe de légumes **3.** du bifteck **4.** du riz **5.** des pommes de terre **6.** du gâteau au chocolat **7.** du pâté **8.** des sandwichs au jambon **9.** des petits pois **10.** des côtes de porc

Follow-up for B. Aujourd'hui on sert... C'est une entrée, un plat principal, un dessert ou une boisson? **1.** du vin **2.** de la soupe à l'oignon **3.** de la glace **4.** du gâteau **5.** du poisson **6.** du pâté **7.** de la tarte **8.** du bifteck

André a invité Rosalie au restaurant Maraîchers. Regardez le menu aux pages 288–289.

LE SERVEUR:	Bonsoir, monsieur. Bonsoir, madame. Aimeriez-vous **un apéritif** avant de commander?
ANDRÉ:	Rosalie?
ROSALIE:	Non, merci, pas ce soir.
ANDRÉ:	Pour moi non plus.
LE SERVEUR:	Et pour dîner? Est-ce que vous avez décidé?
ANDRÉ:	Nous allons prendre le menu à 22 euros.
LE SERVEUR:	Très bien, monsieur. Et qu'est-ce que vous désirez **comme** entrée?
ANDRÉ:	Pour madame, le saumon fumé, s'il vous plaît. Et pour moi, les huîtres.
LE SERVEUR:	Et comme plat principal?
ROSALIE:	**La raie** pour moi, s'il vous plaît.
ANDRÉ:	Et pour moi, **le pavé de saumon.**
LE SERVEUR:	Bien, monsieur. Et comme boisson?
ANDRÉ:	Une carafe de vin blanc et **une bouteille d**'eau minérale.
LE SERVEUR:	De l'Évian ou du Vittel?
ROSALIE:	De l'Évian, s'il vous plaît.
LE SERVEUR:	Très bien, madame.

A. Préférences.
Demandez à votre partenaire ce qu'il/ce qu'elle aime mieux. Pour répondre *neither . . . nor . . .*, dites **ne... ni... ni...** comme dans l'exemple.

Exemple   la viande ou le poisson
— **Est-ce que tu aimes mieux la viande ou le poisson?**
— **J'aime mieux la viande. / J'aime les deux. /**
Je n'aime ni la viande ni le poisson.

1. la viande rouge ou la volaille
2. le rosbif, le bifteck ou les côtes de porc
3. le canard ou le poulet
4. les escargots ou les œufs durs
5. le poisson ou les fruits de mer
6. le thon ou le saumon
7. les crevettes ou le homard
8. les moules ou les huîtres
9. les légumes ou les fruits
10. les pommes de terre ou le riz
11. les haricots verts ou les petits pois
12. la salade verte ou la salade de tomates
13. la soupe à l'oignon ou la soupe de légumes
14. les crudités ou la salade verte
15. les desserts ou le fromage
16. la glace à la vanille ou le gâteau au chocolat

B. Aujourd'hui on sert...
Voilà ce qu'on sert aujourd'hui. Regardez la liste dans la marge *(margin)* et indiquez ce qu'il y a par catégorie.

Exemple   viande
Comme viande, il y a du rosbif...

1. entrée
2. volaille
3. viande
4. poisson
5. dessert
6. légume
7. boisson
8. fruits de mer

DU ROSBIF   du vin
de la tarte aux pommes
des petits pois   DU THON
de l'eau minérale
DES CREVETTES   des huîtres
des œufs durs   du pâté
DES HARICOTS VERTS
du bifteck   DES MOULES
du gâteau   du saumon
des côtes de porc
DES POMMES DE TERRE
du poulet   DU CANARD

un serveur (une serveuse) *a server*   **un apéritif** *a before-dinner drink*   **comme** *for, as a*   **La raie** *Skate, Rayfish*   **le pavé de saumon** *salmon steak*   **une bouteille de** *a bottle of*

C. Catégories logiques. Quel mot ne va pas logiquement avec les autres? Pourquoi?

Exemple le thé, le jus de fruit, le sel, le lait, le vin
Le sel, parce que ce n'est pas une boisson.

1. le pain, les petits pois, les pommes de terre, les haricots verts
2. le gâteau au chocolat, le poivre, la tarte aux pommes, la glace
3. la salade de tomates, le pâté, la soupe à l'oignon, le rosbif
4. le déjeuner, le dîner, le petit déjeuner, le sel
5. le homard, le rosbif, les crevettes, les huîtres, les moules
6. les pommes de terre, les petits pois, les haricots verts, le gâteau

Suggestion for *D. Les préférences.* Remind students to use the definite article to express preferences.

D. Vos préférences. Indiquez vos préférences pour chaque catégorie.

Exemple **Comme boisson, je préfère l'eau.**

> boisson   viande   POISSON   légume
> DESSERT   volaille
> hors-d'œuvre   fruits de mer

Vin d'Alsace

CONCOURS DES GRANDS VINS DE FRANCE
À MACON : MÉDAILLE D'OR 1979 et 1981
ARGENT 1979 et 1984
BRONZE 1979 et 1982
Mis en bouteille à la propriété
Charles SCHWARTZ, Propr.-Vitic. à 67650 Blienschwiller · Tél. 03 92 42 33 71

E. Un dîner. Voici ce que Rosalie a mangé hier soir. Qu'est-ce qu'elle a mangé? Dans quel ordre? Et vous? Qu'est-ce que vous avez mangé hier soir? Dans quel ordre?

F. Qu'est-ce que vous voulez? Regardez la carte à la page 289. Choisissez (*Choose*) une entrée, un plat principal et un dessert et faites le total. Comparez le prix de votre repas à la carte avec le prix des menus à prix fixe (à la page 288). Est-il moins cher de commander un menu à prix fixe ou de commander à la carte?

Warm-up for *F. Qu'est-ce que vous voulez?* Refer students back to the *Note culturelle* on page 286. Have students pick out words and phrases in the menu on pages 288–289 that illustrate the French values of balance, freshness, and attractiveness in food presentation.

G. Au restaurant. Regardez les menus à prix fixe à la page 288. Avec deux camarades de classe, changez la conversation entre André, Rosalie et le serveur comme indiqué.

1. Rosalie orders **le plateau de fruits de mer** as an appetizer and **le pavé de saumon** as the main dish.
2. André and Rosalie decide to order from the menu that costs 15 euros.
3. You and your partner are also having dinner at **le restaurant Maraîchers** tonight. Another classmate plays the role of the server and takes your orders.

37 BISTROT D'ADRIAN 37
RESTAURANT
MARAÎCHERS

Le Bistrot - 15 €.
Service 15% Compris
Adrian vous propose son petit Menu Bistrot composé uniquement de produits frais de saison

Servis Jusqu'à 23 H.

Première Assiette
9 Huîtres "Fines de Claires n°3" Sur Lit de glace
Assiette de Coquillages farcis à l'ail
Cocotte de moules marinières
Salade aux Lardons, Oeuf poché
Terrine de canard maison, au poivre vert
Plateau de fruits de mer "l'écailler" +10€

Deuxième Assiette
Brochette de poissons, beurre blanc
Moules de pays, frites
Sardines grillées aux herbes
Langue de boeuf, sauce piquante
Poêlée de Rognon de boeuf, Flambée au cognac
Bavette Poêlée à la fondue d'oignons

Troisième Assiette
Crème Caramel
Fraises au vin ou Fraises au sucre
Feuillantine aux pommes
Glace et sorbet artisanaux
Île flottante
Coupe normande

**Arrivage Journalier
de Poissons, d'Huîtres et de Fruits de Mer**

Les Maraîchers - 22 €.
Service 15% Compris
Les plus beaux produits du Terroir sélectionnés et cuisinés dans la grande tradition des Maraîchers

Première Assiette
12 Huîtres "Fines de Claires n°3" Sur Lit de glace
Saumon Fumé par nos soins, Toasts chauds
Poêlon de 12 Escargots de Bourgogne à l'ail
Beignets de Langoustines, Sauce tartare
Salade de cervelle d'agneau poêlée
Plateau de fruits de mer "l'écailler" +10€

Deuxième Assiette
Aile de Raie capucine
Daurade entière au Lard Fumé
Pavé de Saumon Rôti, beurre de moules
Filet de Canard à la Rouennaise
Andouillette à la Ficelle "du Père Tafournel"
Faux-filet grillé ou Sauce Poivre

Troisième Assiette
Salade de Saison, ou plateau de fromages

Quatrième Assiette
Tarte tatin chaude, crème fraîche
Bavarois ananas coco
Symphonie aux trois chocolats
Feuillantine aux fraises ou fraises Melba
Glace et Sorbet artisanaux
Crème Brûlée

depuis 1912

B. BEUNÈICHE

La Carte
Service 15% Compris

Nos Huîtres et Fruits de Mer (Arrivage Journalier)

12 Huîtres "Fines de Claires" Sur lit de glace n° 3 "14€" n° 2 "16€"

12 Huîtres "Spéciales St Vaast" Sur lit de glace n° 3 "15€" n° 2 "17€"

Plateau de Fruits de mer "l'écailler" 18€ "le marayeur" 30€ "le Royal" 60€ 1 ou 2 personnes avec 1 Homard frais

Fraîcheur du Marché & Préparations Maison

Soupe de poissons maison, sa rouille et ses croûtons, 6€   Assiette de coquillages farcis 6€

Moules à la crème 7€ – Salade aux lardons, œuf poché 6€   Terrine de canard maison au poivre 6€

Salade de cervelle d'agneau poêlée 8€   Beignets de langoustines, Sauce Tartare 10€

Saumon fumé par nos soins Toasts chauds 10€   Poêlon de 12 Escargots de Bourgogne à l'ail 10€

Poissons Frais d'Arrivage

– Brochette de poissons frais, beurre blanc 7,50€   Moules de pays frites 7,50€

– Sardines grillées aux herbes 7,50€   Pavé de Saumon Rôti, Beurre de Moules 10,50€

– Aile de Raie capucine 10,50€   Daurade entière au lard fumé 10,50€

– Sole Meunière ou Sole Normande 19€

Traditionnels & Spécialités

Langue de Bœuf, sauce piquante 7,50€   Tête de veau ravigote 7,50€   Bavette poêlée à la fondue d'oignons 7,50€   Poêlée de Rognon de bœuf flambée au cognac 7,50€   Faux-filet Grillé ou Sauce Poivre 10,50€   Filet de canard à la Rouennaise 10,50€   Andouillette à la ficelle 10,50€   Cœur de Filet au Poivre flambé au calvados 15€   Chateaubriand Grillé Beurre Persillé 14,50€

Desserts

Plateau de Fromages 5,50€

Île Flottante au caramel 4€   Crème au Caramel 4€   Baiser de vierge 5€   Glace et Sorbet artisanaux 5€   Fraises au vin ou sucrées 5€   After eight 5€   Coupe normande 5€   Feuillantine aux Pommes 5,50€   Tarte Tatin crème fraîche 5,50€   Crème Brûlée 5,50€   Bavarois ananas coco 5,50€   Feuillantine aux Fraises 6€   Fraises Melba 6€   Symphonie aux trois chocolats 6,50€

depuis 1912

B. BEUNEICHE

Talking about what you eat: *Le partitif*

To express the idea of *some* or *any,* use the partitive article (**du, de la, de l', des**).

Pour vérifier

1. How do you express the idea of *some* in French? What are the forms of the partitive and when do you use each? Can you drop the word for *some* or *any* in French, as you can in English?
2. In what two circumstances do you use **de** instead of the partitive?

MASCULINE SINGULAR BEGINNING WITH A CONSONANT SOUND	FEMININE SINGULAR BEGINNING WITH A CONSONANT SOUND	SINGULAR NOUNS BEGINNING WITH A VOWEL SOUND	ALL PLURAL NOUNS
du	de la	de l'	des

The words *some* or *any* may be left out in English, but the partitive article must be used in French. The partitive article becomes **de (d'):**

- after negated verbs (except after the verb **être**).

Je voudrais **du café.**   *I'd like (some) coffee.*
Tu **ne** veux **pas de café?**   *Don't you want (any) coffee?*

- after expressions of quantity like **beaucoup, combien,** and **trop.**

J'ai acheté **trop de café.**   *I bought **too much coffee.***

A. Qu'est-ce qu'on sert? Demandez à votre partenaire ce qu'on sert pour chaque plat en France.

Exemple   Comme entrée...
       de la soupe, du riz, du gâteau, des fruits, de la glace?
       — **Comme entrée, est-ce qu'on sert de la soupe, du riz, du gâteau, des fruits ou de la glace?**
       — **On sert de la soupe.**

Comme entrée...
1. des œufs durs, des petits pois, du café, du gâteau ou de la tarte?
2. de la salade verte, de la salade de tomates, des côtes de porc ou du rosbif?

Comme plat principal...
1. du pâté, de la glace, du saumon, des fruits ou de la salade verte?
2. du fromage, du gâteau, des crevettes ou des œufs durs?

Comme légume...
1. des petits pois, des huîtres, de la viande, des moules ou du rosbif?
2. du fromage, des pommes, de la volaille ou des pommes de terre?

Après le plat principal...
1. de la salade verte, du poulet, des escargots ou de la soupe?
2. de la viande, des œufs durs, des fruits de mer ou du fromage?

B. Qu'est-ce que vous prenez? Est-ce que vous prenez souvent (rarement, quelquefois...) les choses suivantes avec vos repas?

Exemple   vin
       Je prends souvent (rarement) du vin avec mes repas. /
       Je ne prends jamais de vin avec mes repas.

1. pain
2. fromage
3. fruits
4. eau minérale
5. viande rouge
6. fruits de mer
7. boissons alcoolisées
8. poisson
9. glace
10. volaille
11. soupe
12. œufs

C. Comparaisons. Indiquez si les Français prennent souvent ces choses comme entrée, comme plat principal, comme boisson, comme dessert ou comme légume. Ensuite, dites si vous faites souvent la même chose.

> **Exemple** pâté **Les Français prennent souvent du pâté comme entrée. Moi aussi, je prends souvent du pâté comme entrée. / Moi, je ne prends pas souvent de pâté comme entrée.**

1. salade de tomates   **3.** petits pois   **5.** canard   **7.** gâteau
2. eau minérale   **4.** saumon   **6.** tarte   **8.** vin

D. Qu'allez-vous servir? Vous allez préparer un grand repas traditionnel français pour des amis. Qu'allez-vous servir pour chaque catégorie?

> **Exemple** comme entrée
> **Comme entrée, je vais servir des œufs durs.**

1. comme entrée   **3.** comme légume   **5.** après le plat principal
2. comme plat principal   **4.** comme boisson   **6.** comme dessert

Suggestion for D. Qu'allez-vous servir? Give students a short time to prepare.

E. Sur la table. Rose est invitée à une boum où il y a beaucoup à manger et à boire. Voici la table de la salle à manger et la table de la cuisine. Faites des comparaisons entre les deux.

> **Exemple** **Il y a des chips dans la cuisine et dans la salle à manger. Il y a de l'eau minérale dans la salle à manger mais il n'y a pas d'eau minérale dans la cuisine.**

Warm-up for E. Sur la table. Refer students to the illustration of the tables. **Est-ce que je suis dans la salle à manger ou dans la cuisine?** 1. Mmm… j'ai faim, je vais prendre du pain, du pâté, du fromage et de l'eau minérale. 2. Je n'ai pas très faim. Je voudrais seulement du gâteau et un coca. 3. Je vais prendre du fromage, du pain, des chips et comme boisson… du vin.

Suggestion for E. Sur la table. Point out the pronunciation of **des chips** /ʃips/.

la salle à manger   la cuisine

F. Entretien. Interviewez votre partenaire.

1. Qu'est-ce que tu as mangé hier soir?
2. Qu'est-ce que tu manges souvent le soir? Qu'est-ce que tu aimes boire le soir?
3. Que préfères-tu manger à midi? (Une salade, un sandwich ou un hamburger?)
4. Est-ce que tu aimes manger dans les fast-foods? Est-ce que tu manges souvent dans un fast-food?
5. Est-ce que tu préfères boire de l'eau ou du coca avec tes repas?

G. Préparatifs. Vous allez inviter des amis chez vous pour un grand repas traditionnel à la française. Avec un(e) partenaire, faites des projets pour ce dîner. Parlez de:

- quand et où vous allez faire ce dîner et qui vous allez inviter.
- ce que vous allez servir. (Imaginez que vous n'aimez pas les mêmes choses et proposez au moins trois choses comme entrée, comme plat principal, comme dessert et comme boisson.)

Stratégies et compréhension auditive:
Planning and predicting

Since no two cultures are identical, you may sometimes find yourself lacking the cultural knowledge to understand what you hear in French. For example, if the waiter asks **De l'Évian ou du Vittel?** you will not be able to answer unless you recognize that these are brand names of French mineral waters. In such situations, try to infer what is being asked from the context. Also, when possible, prepare and predict from previous experiences what might be asked or said. For example, before ordering mineral water, glance at the menu to see what kinds are sold.

A. Pendant le repas. Vous êtes au restaurant. Est-ce qu'on vous dit les choses que vous entendez **avant le repas** ou **à la fin du repas?**

B. Questions. Faites une liste de trois questions qu'un(e) client(e) pose souvent au serveur ou à la serveuse dans un restaurant.

Au restaurant

Deux touristes se trouvent dans un restaurant français. Écoutez leur conversation. Qu'est-ce qu'ils commandent? Nommez au moins quatre choses.

A. Que demandent-ils? Écoutez encore une fois la conversation au restaurant et écrivez deux questions que les clients posent à la serveuse.

B. Qu'allez-vous choisir? Avec un(e) partenaire, jouez une scène au restaurant entre un serveur (une serveuse) et un(e) client(e). Commandez une entrée, un plat principal, un légume, un dessert et une boisson.

NOTE Culturelle

Le mot *pastries* se traduit de deux façons différentes: les **pâtisseries** (telles que les éclairs, les religieuses *[cream puffs]* et les millefeuilles) et les **viennoiseries** (telles que les croissants, les brioches et les chaussons aux pommes *[apple turnovers]).* Dans l'ordre de préférence, les Français aiment les croissants (60%), les pains au chocolat (41%), les brioches (35%) et les chaussons aux pommes (30%).

TRANSPARENCIES: 8-2A, 8-2B, 8-2C

Warm-up activities. A. Pour un repas traditionnel en France, qu'est-ce qu'on sert d'abord? **1.** le plat principal / l'entrée **2.** le rosbif / la salade **3.** le fromage / les légumes **4.** le vin / le café **5.** le poisson / le dessert **6.** la soupe / le plat principal **7.** le pâté / le gâteau **8.** le riz / la glace **B.** Do a chain activity. **Nous allons préparer un grand dîner ensemble pour toute la classe. Qu'est-ce qu'on va servir? On va servir...** Each student should list all items already named and add a new one.

Suggestions. A. Explain to students that **une boucherie** sells raw meat and that **une charcuterie** is similar to a delicatessen and sells cured meats and prepared foods, although not sandwiches, cheese, or drinks. **B.** Have students guess what is sold **à la crémerie, à la poissonnerie, à la fromagerie,** etc.

Les courses

De plus en plus de Français font leurs courses dans les supermarchés ou les hypermarchés où on vend de tout.

Mais beaucoup préfèrent aller chez les petits **commerçants** du quartier où le service est plus personnalisé.

À la boulangerie-pâtisserie, on peut acheter:

une baguette

un pain au chocolat   **un pain complet**

une tarte aux **cerises**   une tartelette aux **fraises**

À la boucherie, on achète de la viande:

du poulet

du bœuf   du porc

À la charcuterie, on achète **de la charcuterie** et des plats préparés:

du saucisson   du jambon

des saucisses *(f)*

des plats préparés

---

un(e) commerçant(e) *a shopkeeper*   **un pain complet** *a loaf of wholegrain bread*   **une cerise** *a cherry*   **une fraise** *a strawberry*   **de la charcuterie** *deli meats, cold cuts*   **un plat préparé** *a ready-to-serve dish*

On va à l'épicerie pour acheter des fruits, des légumes, **des conserves** (f) et des produits **surgelés.**

Beaucoup de Français **disent** que pour avoir un bon **choix** de légumes et de fruits vraiment **frais, il faut** aller au marché. Au marché, on peut acheter:

VOCABULAIRE SUPPLÉMENTAIRE

LÉGUMES

des asperges (f) asparagus

une aubergine an eggplant

des brocolis (m)

du céleri

des champignons (m) mushrooms

du chou cabbage

du chou-fleur cauliflower

des choux de Bruxelles (m) Brussels sprouts

un concombre a cucumber

une courgette a zucchini

des épinards (m) spinach

FRUITS

des abricots (m) apricots

un ananas a pineapple

un citron vert a lime

des framboises (f) raspberries

une mandarine a tangerine

une mangue a mango

un melon

des myrtilles (f) blueberries

une nectarine

un pamplemousse a grapefruit

une pastèque a watermelon

une prune a plum

un pruneau a prune

des raisins secs (m) raisins

Suggestions. Point out the feminine gender of nearly all fruits and vegetables ending in **-e** and the use of the singular with **du raisin.**

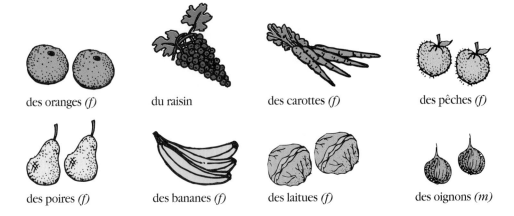

des oranges (f)　　du raisin　　des carottes (f)　　des pêches (f)

des poires (f)　　des bananes (f)　　des laitues (f)　　des oignons (m)

---

des conserves (f) canned goods　　**surgelé(e)** frozen　　**disent (dire** to say, to tell)　　**un choix** a choice　　**frais (fraîche)** fresh　　**il faut** it is necessary, one needs, one must

En France, on utilise le système métrique pour tout mesurer.

1 kilo (kg) = 1000 grammes = 2.2 *pounds*

1 litre (l) = *1.057 quarts*

Pouvez-vous trouver un équivalent approximatif pour ces quantités?

1/2 kilo = __ grammes

1 pound **= __ grammes**

2.2 pounds **= __ kilo**

1 quart **= __ litre**

1 gallon **= __ litres**

Suggestion for the conversation. Set the scene and play the conversation, having students listen for: **1.** Qu'est-ce que Rosalie achète? **2.** Combien paie-t-elle en tout?

Suggestion. Have students try at home to convert a recipe to metric measures. They can look up additional information in a dictionary.

Follow-ups for *A. De quelle couleur?*
A. Ask students if they like the foods listed, or have them ask each other.
B. C'est un fruit ou un légume? **1.** des oignons **2.** des carottes **3.** des pêches **4.** des pommes **5.** des petits pois **6.** des pommes de terre **7.** du raisin **8.** des haricots verts

Follow-up for *B. Devinettes.* En groupes, faites une liste pour chaque catégorie sur une feuille de papier. Écrivez autant de fruits ou de légumes que possible dans chacune des catégories. Le groupe avec la liste la plus longue gagne.

FRUITS	LÉGUMES
rouges:	blancs:
verts:	verts:
jaunes:	jaunes:
orange:	orange:
violets:	marron:

(This may be done with books open or closed. You may wish to give students a time limit.)

Rosalie fait ses courses au marché.

ROSALIE:	Bonjour, monsieur.
LE MARCHAND:	Bonjour, madame. **Qu'est-ce qu'il vous faut aujourd'hui?**
ROSALIE:	Euh... voyons... un kilo de pommes de terre, **une livre** de tomates... Vous avez des haricots verts?
LE MARCHAND:	Non, madame, pas aujourd'hui. Mais j'ai des petits pois. Regardez comme ils sont beaux.
ROSALIE:	Non, merci, pas de petits pois aujourd'hui.
LE MARCHAND:	Alors, qu'est-ce que je peux vous proposer d'autre?
ROSALIE:	Donnez-moi aussi 500 grammes de fraises.
LE MARCHAND:	Et voilà, 500 grammes. Et avec ça?
ROSALIE:	C'est tout, merci. Ça fait combien?
LE MARCHAND:	Voilà... Alors, un kilo de pommes de terre—1,20 €, une livre de tomates—1,36 € et 500 grammes de fraises—1,50 €. Ça fait 4,06 €.
ROSALIE:	Voici 5 euros.
LE MARCHAND:	Et voici votre monnaie. Merci, madame, et à bientôt!
ROSALIE:	Merci. Au revoir, monsieur.

A. De quelle couleur? De quelle couleur sont ces fruits et ces légumes?

1. les oranges
2. les cerises
3. les pommes
4. les bananes
5. les citrons
6. le raisin
7. les fraises
8. les carottes
9. les poires
10. les oignons
11. les petits pois
12. les pommes de terre

B. Devinettes. Qu'est-ce que c'est?

Exemple C'est un fruit rond, orange et plein de vitamine C.
C'est une orange.

1. C'est le légume préféré de Bugs Bunny.
2. C'est un fruit long et jaune que les chimpanzés adorent.
3. Beaucoup de gens pensent que c'est un légume, mais en réalité, c'est un fruit. Ce fruit est rond et rouge. On le sert souvent en salade.
4. C'est un fruit qui peut être jaune, rouge ou vert. On peut le manger cru *(raw)*, mais on peut aussi faire des gâteaux, des tartes, du jus ou du cidre avec.
5. C'est le légume vert qui est l'ingrédient principal d'une salade.
6. On utilise ce fruit pour faire du vin.
7. Ce sont de petits légumes ronds et verts.
8. Ce sont de petits fruits rouges qu'on utilise souvent pour faire une tarte.

C. Que peut-on acheter... ? Qu'est-ce qu'on peut acheter dans les magasins indiqués?

Que peut-on acheter dans une boulangerie-pâtisserie?

du pain	une baguette	du poulet	du pain complet
du bœuf	des huîtres	des éclairs	des légumes
une tarte	un gâteau	des crevettes	du poisson
du thon	du porc	des moules	des conserves

Qu'est-ce qu'il vous faut aujourd'hui? *What do you need today?* **une livre** *half a kilo (≈ a pound)*

Que peut-on acheter dans une boucherie?

du poisson	du thon	du fromage	du homard
des petits pois	du rosbif	du bœuf	des côtes de porc
des crevettes	du pâté	du saucisson	du poulet
du bifteck	du pain	de la laitue	des cerises

Que peut-on acheter dans une charcuterie?

du jambon	du rosbif	du saucisson	des légumes
du pâté	des fruits	des saucisses	des plats préparés
des tartes	du pain	du vin	des conserves
des fraises	des pommes	une baguette	des pommes de terre

D. Catégories. Identifiez la catégorie de chaque aliment.

Exemple   le rosbif
Le rosbif, c'est une viande.

1. le raisin   3. le pâté   5. la glace   7. le jambon
2. le saucisson   4. la laitue   6. le porc   8. le bœuf

> de la charcuterie   un légume
> UN PLAT PRÉPARÉ   une viande
> un fruit   un produit surgelé

E. Quel magasin? Dans quels magasins est-ce qu'on vend les produits de l'exercice précédent? (Utilisez l'article partitif!)

Exemple   le rosbif
On vend du rosbif à la boucherie.

> À LA CHARCUTERIE   au marché   à la boulangerie-pâtisserie
> à la boucherie   À L'ÉPICERIE

Suggestion for *F. Qu'est-ce qu'on vend?* Do this as a team competition. With books closed and a time limit, have students list as many items as possible for each shop.

F. Qu'est-ce qu'on vend? Nommez au moins quatre choses qu'on vend dans les endroits mentionnés dans l'exercice précédent.

Exemple   à la charcuterie
À la charcuterie, on vend du jambon...

Supplemental activity. *C'est logique?* 1. Je prépare une tarte aux pommes. J'ai besoin de pommes de terre. 2. Pour faire un gâteau au chocolat, j'ai besoin de chocolat et de sucre. 3. Pour faire une salade de fruits, j'ai besoin d'oranges, de fraises et de pommes. 4. Pour faire une omelette, j'ai besoin d'œufs, de chocolat et de sel. 5. Pour faire un sandwich au fromage, j'ai besoin de petits pois. 6. Pour faire une tarte aux fraises, j'ai besoin de pain, de jambon et de fromage.

G. Entretien. Interviewez votre partenaire.

1. Aimes-tu faire les courses? Combien de fois par semaine est-ce que tu fais les courses? Où est-ce que tu fais tes courses d'habitude? Est-ce que tu achètes quelquefois des choses chez les petits commerçants?
2. En France, où est-ce qu'on achète du pain? des plats préparés? des fruits et des légumes frais? Qu'est-ce qu'on vend à l'épicerie? à la boulangerie-pâtisserie?
3. Aimes-tu les fruits? les légumes? Préfères-tu les fruits ou les légumes?

H. Faisons les courses! Avec un(e) partenaire, changez la conversation entre Rosalie et le marchand comme indiqué.

1. Rosalie gets a kilo of carrots and 500 grams of green beans. She pays 1,36 € for the carrots and 2,20 € for the green beans.
2. You are at the **boulangerie-pâtisserie.** Buy what you would like. (Decide on a logical price in euros for each item.)

Pour vérifier

What word follows quantity expressions before nouns? Do you use **de** or **des** after a quantity expression followed by a plural noun?

Suggestion. Point out that cheese is often bought by the **morceau**, since many cheeses come in a round shape.

Saying how much: *Les expressions de quantité*

When ordering in a restaurant or shopping for food, you need to specify how much you want.

un verre de	*a glass of*	une boîte de	*a box of, a can of*
un litre de	*a liter of*	un pot de	*a jar of*
une carafe de	*a carafe of*	un paquet de	*a bag of, a sack of*
une bouteille de	*a bottle of*	une douzaine de	*a dozen*
une tranche de	*a slice of*	une livre de	*a half a kilo (≈ a pound of)*
un morceau de	*a piece of*	un kilo de	*a kilo of*
300 grammes de	*300 grams of*	un kilo et demi de	*a kilo and a half of*

Expressions of quantity are followed by **de (d')** instead of **des, du, de la,** or **de l'** when followed by any noun (masculine, feminine, singular, or plural). This is true for precise quantities (**un kilo**) or imprecise quantities such as the following:

combien de	*how much, how many*
(un) peu de	*(a) little*
assez de	*enough*
beaucoup de	*a lot of*
trop de	*too much, too many*
beaucoup trop de	*much too much, much too many*

— Tu as acheté **du** vin et **de la** viande?
— Oui, j'ai acheté une bouteille **de** vin rouge, 500 grammes **de** viande et beaucoup **de** légumes!

A. C'est assez? Est-ce que la quantité indiquée est suffisante?

Exemple   Vous prenez le petit déjeuner seul(e) le matin et il y a un verre de lait dans le réfrigérateur.
Il y a assez de lait. / Il n'y a pas assez de lait. / Il y a trop de lait.

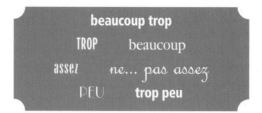

1. Vous êtes quatre au restaurant et il y a une demi-bouteille de vin.
2. Vous allez préparer une salade de tomates pour deux personnes. Vous avez un kilo de tomates.
3. Vous allez faire une omelette pour deux personnes et vous avez un œuf.
4. C'est le matin et il y a un verre de lait dans le réfrigérateur chez vous.
5. Vous dînez seul(e) au restaurant et il y a six carafes de vin.
6. Il faut préparer des carottes pour six personnes et vous avez une seule carotte.

B. Je voudrais... Précisez quelque chose de logique pour chacune des quantités proposées.

Je voudrais...

1. une bouteille de
2. un paquet de
3. une boîte de
4. une livre de
5. deux kilos de
6. un morceau de
7. un litre de
8. dix tranches de

thon   CERISES   jambon

vin   tomates   FROMAGE

jus de fruit   LAIT

sel   sucre   riz

C. Donnez-moi... Demandez au marchand de vous donner les quantités suivantes de fruits et de légumes.

1. a half a kilo of pears
2. 300 grams of grapes
3. a kilo and a half of cherries
4. a kilo of peaches
5. 800 grams of peas
6. a kilo of carrots
7. enough green beans for three people **(pour trois personnes)**

D. Les courses. Voilà ce que Rosalie a acheté aujourd'hui. Dites ce qu'elle a acheté.

Exemple   Elle a acheté une bouteille de vin rouge.

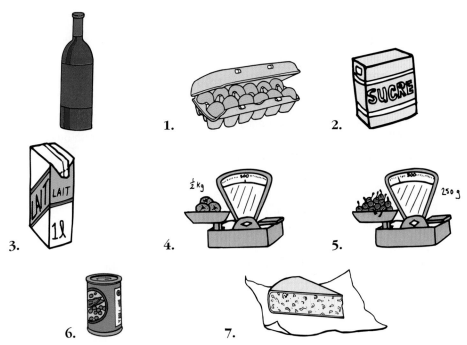

1.

2.

3.

4.

5.

6.

7.

Follow-up questions for *D. Les courses.*
(The number of each question corresponds to the number of each drawing.) **EXEMPLE** Prenez-vous un verre de vin au dîner? Achetez-vous quelquefois une bouteille de vin? Préférez-vous le vin blanc ou le vin rouge? Si vous mangez seul(e), commandez-vous un verre de vin, une bouteille de vin ou une carafe de vin? **1.** Mangez-vous des œufs tous les jours? Mangez-vous beaucoup d'omelettes? **2.** Mettez-vous du sucre dans votre café ou dans votre thé? **3.** Combien de litres de lait achetez-vous par mois? **4.** Qu'est-ce qui est le plus cher d'habitude, une livre d'oranges ou une livre de cerises? **5.** En quelle saison peut-on trouver des cerises au supermarché? Aimez-vous la tarte aux cerises? **6.** Mangez-vous beaucoup de légumes? Aimez-vous les petits pois? **7.** Aimez-vous les sandwichs au fromage?

E. Au marché. Imaginez que vous préparez un dîner pour quatre amis. Décidez ce que vous voulez servir et achetez les provisions au marché. Un(e) camarade de classe va jouer le rôle du/de la marchand(e).

Options for *E. Au marché.* A. You may prefer to let students decide to go either to the market or to any food store such as **la charcuterie** or **l'épicerie. B.** Have students use props to expand this to reflect a full cultural simulation with displays of produce, signs, money, etc.

Talking about foods: *L'usage des articles*

Each article you use with a noun conveys a different meaning. **Un** and **une** mean *a,* whereas **du, de la, de l',** and **des** mean *some* or *any.*

Vous voulez **une** tarte?
*Do you want **a** pie?*
(This refers to a whole pie.)

Vous voulez **de la** tarte?
*Do you want (**some**) pie?*
(This refers to a portion or serving.)

Remember that the indefinite article (**un, une, des**) and the partitive (**du, de la, de l'**) all change to **de (d')** in a negative sentence and after expressions of quantity, such as **trop, beaucoup, un kilo, une bouteille...**

Je ne veux pas **de** tarte.   *I don't want (**any**) pie.*
J'ai mangé trop **de** tarte!   *I ate too much pie!*

Remember to use the definite article (**le, la, l', les**) to express likes, dislikes, and preferences, to say *the,* or to make statements about entire categories. The definite article does not change to **de** after a negative or an expression of quantity.

J'aime bien **le** poisson.   *I like fish.*
Je n'aime pas beaucoup **le** poisson.   *I don't like fish very much.*
Le poisson qu'on achète ici est très bon.   *The fish you buy here is very good.*
Le poisson n'a pas beaucoup de   *Fish doesn't have a lot of calories.*
  calories.

	AFFIRMATIVE	**NEGATIVE**
PARTITIVE ARTICLE *to say some or any*	Je voudrais **du** café.	Je ne veux pas **de** café.
INDEFINITE ARTICLE *to say a; to indicate a whole or several*	Je voudrais **un** café.	Je ne veux pas **de** café.
DE WITH AN EXPRESSION OF QUANTITY	Je voudrais un kilo **de** café.	Je n'ai pas acheté beaucoup **de** café.
DEFINITE ARTICLE *to say the; to express likes; to make general statements about categories*	J'aime **le** café.	Je n'aime pas **le** café.

When using adverbs with a preference, continue to use the definitive article **le, la, l',** or **les.**

J'aime beaucoup le thé.   J'aime assez le café.   Je n'aime pas trop le coca.

A. Manges-tu bien? Demandez à votre partenaire s'il/si elle mange souvent les choses suivantes.

Exemple   fruits   — **Manges-tu souvent des fruits?**
                             — **Je mange rarement des fruits. /**
                               Je ne mange jamais de fruits.

1. escargots   **3.** légumes   **5.** poulet   **7.** glace
2. tarte   **4.** viande rouge **6.** crudités   **8.** pâté

Maintenant, demandez à votre partenaire s'il/si elle aime ces mêmes choses.

Exemple fruits — **Aimes-tu les fruits?**
— **J'aime assez les fruits. / Je n'aime pas les fruits.**

B. Vos préférences. Dites si vous achetez souvent les choses suivantes et expliquez pourquoi.

Exemple pâté **J'achète souvent du pâté parce que j'aime le pâté. / Je n'achète jamais de pâté parce que je n'aime pas le pâté.**

1. fromage
2. bananes
3. viande rouge
4. huîtres
5. raisin
6. eau minérale
7. jus
8. café

C. Vos goûts. Complétez les phrases suivantes avec le nom d'un aliment (*food*) ou d'une boisson logique. Utilisez les articles convenables.

1. Moi, j'adore...
2. J'aime bien...
3. Comme viande, je mange souvent...
4. Chez moi, il n'y a jamais...
5. Pour le déjeuner, je prends souvent...
6. La dernière fois que je suis allé(e) au restaurant, j'ai mangé...

D. Chez Rosalie. Rosalie parle du dîner qu'elle va préparer pour André ce soir. Complétez ce qu'elle dit avec l'article convenable: **un, une, du, de la, de l', des, le, la, l', les** ou **de**.

Ce soir, je vais servir ____1____ soupe de légumes, ____2____ poulet, ____3____ riz et ____4____ petits pois. Et comme dessert, je pense préparer ____5____ tarte aux cerises. Moi, je préfère ____6____ gâteau, mais André aime beaucoup ____7____ tarte! Cet après-midi, je dois aller acheter ____8____ sucre, 500 grammes ____9____ cerises et beaucoup ____10____ légumes. Il y a un marché tout près où ____11____ légumes sont toujours très frais! Mais je ne vais pas mettre ____12____ oignons dans la soupe parce qu'André n'aime pas ____13____ oignons. C'est dommage parce que ____14____ oignons sont bons pour la santé (*health*).

E. Entretien. Interviewez votre partenaire.

1. Est-ce que tu aimes mieux les fruits ou les légumes? la viande rouge ou le poisson? les fruits de mer ou le poulet? les légumes ou la viande?
2. Quels fruits de mer aimes-tu? Quelles viandes? Quelles boissons? Quels fruits préfères-tu? Quels légumes?
3. Manges-tu plus souvent des fruits ou des légumes? Quel fruit préfères-tu? Quels fruits est-ce que tu n'aimes pas? Quel légume préfères-tu? Quels légumes est-ce que tu n'aimes pas? Est-ce que tu préfères acheter des légumes surgelés, frais ou en conserve?
4. Tu aimes les desserts? Est-ce que tu préfères le gâteau ou la tarte? la glace au chocolat ou la glace à la vanille? Est-ce que tu manges souvent un dessert quand tu vas au restaurant? Quel dessert prends-tu le plus souvent?
5. À la maison, qu'est-ce que tu manges la plupart du temps? Qu'est-ce que tu ne manges jamais? Pourquoi?

Supplemental activities. A. Faites une liste des choses qui sont bonnes pour la santé (*health*) et une autre liste des choses qui sont mauvaises pour la santé. **B. Questions orales.** Est-ce que vous préférez la glace ou le gâteau (les fruits ou la glace, le jambon ou le pâté, le fromage ou la viande, les fruits ou les légumes, l'eau minérale ou le jus d'orange, le jus de pomme ou le jus d'orange, les boissons alcoolisées ou non-alcoolisées)? Quel dessert est-ce que vous préférez? Quelle viande? Quelle boisson? **C.** Have individual students think of something they do not like to eat or drink presented in this chapter. The rest of the class will try to figure out what it is by asking yes or no questions. You may wish to write these cues on the board: **C'est quelque chose à boire? C'est quelque chose à manger? C'est une boisson (non-)alcoolisée? C'est un légume vert? C'est un dessert? C'est une viande? D.** Questions orales. **1.** Est-ce que vous aimez dîner au restaurant? Quelle sorte de cuisine préférez-vous? Quel est votre restaurant préféré? Est-ce que ce restaurant est cher? **2.** Quand avez-vous dîné au restaurant la dernière fois? Dans quel restaurant? Avec qui? Qui a payé l'addition (*the bill*)? Vous êtes-vous bien amusé(e)s? Qu'est-ce que vous avez pris comme entrée? comme plat principal? comme dessert? **3.** Mangez-vous bien en général? Mangez-vous bien à midi? le soir?

Les repas

En France, le petit déjeuner est généralement un repas **léger.** On prend:

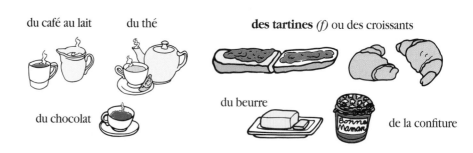

du café au lait   du thé   **des tartines** *(f)* ou des croissants

du chocolat   du beurre   de la confiture

De plus en plus de Français, **surtout** les jeunes, prennent aussi des céréales le matin.

Les Français ne prennent pas de petit déjeuner **copieux** comme les Américains et les Canadiens, qui préfèrent prendre:

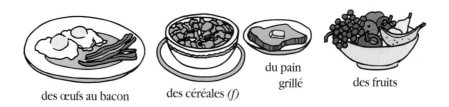

des œufs au bacon   des céréales *(f)*   du pain grillé   des fruits

À midi, certains Français prennent un repas complet. D'autres prennent un repas rapide. Dans les cafés, les fast-foods et les self-services, on peut manger:

de la soupe
une omelette
un bifteck avec des frites
de la salade
un hamburger
une pizza

Les gens qui prennent un repas rapide à midi mangent souvent un repas plus complet le soir. **Ceux** qui mangent un repas plus copieux à midi mangent **seulement** de la soupe, des légumes, des charcuteries, une salade ou des œufs comme dîner.

---

léger (légère) *light*   **une tartine** *bread with butter and jelly*   **surtout** *especially*   **copieux (copieuse)** *copious, large*   **Ceux (celles)** *Those*   **seulement** *only*

Rose et une de ses cousines préparent le petit déjeuner ensemble.

LUCIE: Tu as faim? Je peux te faire des œufs au bacon si tu veux—un vrai petit déjeuner à l'américaine.

ROSE: Merci, c'est gentil. Mais je mange très peu le matin. En plus, **j'ai grossi depuis que** je suis en France. Mais **je prendrais volontiers** des céréales et du thé.

LUCIE: Ah, je regrette... il **n'**y a **plus** de thé. Mais il y a du café. Tu **en** veux?

ROSE: Oui, je veux bien. Et toi? Qu'est-ce que tu vas prendre?

LUCIE: Le matin, **je bois** toujours du chocolat chaud et quelquefois je prends des tartines.

ROSE: Oh, regarde! **Il n'y a presque plus** de pain.

LUCIE: Mais **si!** Il y a **encore** une baguette là.

Suggestion for the conversation. Set the scene and have students listen for this information with books closed: **Qu'est-ce que Rose et sa cousine vont prendre comme petit déjeuner?** Then have students listen and read along.

A. Vrai ou faux? Corrigez les phrases fausses.

1. En France, on prend plus souvent des œufs le soir ou à midi que le matin.
2. Les Français prennent un repas copieux le matin.
3. Les Américains et les Canadiens préfèrent prendre un petit déjeuner plus léger que les Français.
4. Beaucoup de Français prennent seulement du pain et du café le matin.
5. Certains, surtout les jeunes, aiment prendre des céréales.
6. Rose a l'habitude de beaucoup manger au petit déjeuner.
7. Rose a grossi depuis qu'elle est en France.
8. Ce matin, Rose va boire du thé.
9. Il n'y a plus de café.

B. Chez nous. Aux États-Unis et au Canada, à quel repas mange-t-on le plus souvent ces choses: **au petit déjeuner, au déjeuner** ou **au dîner?**

Exemple   une omelette
    On mange une omelette au petit déjeuner.

1. des croissants
2. des céréales
3. du poisson
4. du gâteau
5. un hamburger et des frites
6. du saumon
7. des œufs au bacon
8. des légumes
9. de la soupe
10. du pain grillé avec de la confiture et du beurre

Warm-up for B. Chez nous. C'est logique de prendre les choses suivantes pour un petit déjeuner américain / canadien? 1. du bacon 2. du jambon 3. du rosbif 4. des œufs 5. des crevettes 6. du lait 7. du gâteau 8. du pain grillé 9. du jus de fruit

Supplemental activities. A. Prend-on les choses suivantes avec du sel ou avec du sucre? 1. des céréales 2. des œufs 3. du café 4. des frites 5. de la viande 6. de la soupe 7. des légumes 8. du poisson 9. du thé **B.** Introduce the words **une cuillère, une fourchette,** and **un couteau** and ask: **Est-ce que les Américains / les Canadiens mangent les choses suivantes avec les mains, avec une cuillère ou avec un couteau et une fourchette?** 1. une tartine 2. des œufs 3. des céréales 4. des fruits 5. du pain grillé 6. du bacon 7. du jambon 8. de la soupe

C. Au petit déjeuner. Avec un(e) partenaire, changez la conversation entre Rose et sa cousine comme indiqué.

1. Rose would like to have a typical American breakfast this morning. Lucie then discovers there are no more eggs, so Rose decides to have cereal and tea.
2. Lucie usually drinks tea and has croissants for breakfast.
3. Imagine you are staying with a French family for a week. Discuss what you eat for breakfast with your host and ask him/her what he/she usually has. Act out this conversation with your partner.

---

grossir to get fatter   **depuis que** since   **je prendrais volontiers** I would gladly have   **ne... plus** no more, no longer   **en** some   **je bois (boire** to drink)   **Il n'y a presque plus** There is almost no more   **si** yes (in response to a question / statement in the negative)   **encore** still, again, more

Suggestion. Point out that **en** replaces the partitive article as well as the noun, but numbers and quantity expressions remain in the sentence.

Saying what you eat and drink:
Le pronom en et le verbe boire

To avoid repetition, use the pronoun **en** to replace a noun preceded by a partitive article, an expression of quantity, **un, une,** or a number. In English, **en** is usually translated by *some, any, of it,* or *of them.* Although the equivalent expression may be omitted in English, **en** is always used in French.

En, like **y** and the direct object pronouns, is placed *immediately* before the verb. It goes before the infinitive if there is one. If not, it goes before the conjugated verb. In the **passé composé,** it is placed before the auxiliary verb.

Tu prends du gâteau?	Oui, je vais **en** prendre. Oui, j'**en** prends. Non, merci, j'**en** ai déjà pris.

Use **en** to replace:

• a noun preceded by **de, du, de la, de l'**, or **des.**

— Tu veux **du café?**	— *Do you want **some coffee?***
— Non merci, je n'**en** veux pas.	— *No thanks, I don't want **any.***

• a noun preceded by an expression of quantity. (In this case, repeat the expression of quantity in the sentence containing **en.**)

— Vous voulez un kilo **de cerises?**	— *Do you want a kilo **of cherries?***
— Oui, j'**en** veux un kilo.	— *Yes, I want a kilo **(of them).***

• a noun preceded by **un, une,** or a number. (In this case, include **un, une,** or a number in the sentence containing **en.**)

— Tu as mangé une **tartelette?**	— *You ate a **tart?***
— Oui, j'**en** ai mangé une. / J'**en** ai mangé deux!	— *Yes, I ate one **(of them).** / I ate two **(of them)!***

You have already seen some of the forms of the verb **boire** *(to drink).* Here is the full conjugation.

BOIRE *(to drink)*	
je bois	nous buvons
tu bois	vous buvez
il/elle/on boit	ils/elles boivent

PASSÉ COMPOSÉ: j'ai bu
IMPARFAIT: je buvais

Vous avez bu du vin hier soir?	Elle buvait du lait quand elle était petite.

A. À table. Un(e) ami(e) vous propose les choses suivantes au petit déjeuner. Comment répondez-vous? Utilisez le pronom **en** dans vos réponses.

Exemple du café — **Tu veux du café?**
— **Non merci, je n'en veux pas. / Oui, j'en veux bien.**

1. du café	**4.** des œufs	**7.** des tartines
2. du thé	**5.** des fruits	**8.** des céréales
3. du chocolat	**6.** du lait	**9.** de l'eau

B. Combien?
Voilà la liste de Rosalie pour les courses. Combien est-ce qu'il faut acheter de chaque chose? Utilisez des quantités logiques et le pronom **en** dans vos réponses.

Exemple du sucre
Il faut en acheter un paquet.

1. des pommes
2. du bœuf
3. du lait
4. des œufs
5. du vin rouge
6. des cerises
7. du pâté
8. des céréales

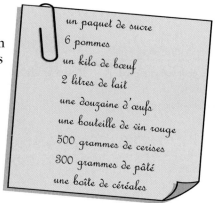

un paquet de sucre
6 pommes
un kilo de bœuf
2 litres de lait
une douzaine d'œufs
une bouteille de vin rouge
500 grammes de cerises
300 grammes de pâté
une boîte de céréales

C. Et vous?
Faites-vous attention à votre santé *(health)*? Répondez à ces questions pour dire ce que vous faites. Employez le pronom **en** avec une quantité ou une négation.

Exemple Vous mangez des desserts?
Oui, j'en mange trop. / Non, je n'en mange jamais.

Follow-up for B. Combien? Rosalie préfère faire ses courses chez les petits commerçants. Dites où elle va pour acheter chaque chose sur sa liste dans **B. Combien?** EXEMPLE du sucre **Elle va à l'épicerie pour en acheter.**

> beaucoup trop **trop** beaucoup ASSEZ (un) peu
> TROP PEU ne... jamais **ne... pas** ne... pas assez

1. Vous buvez de l'eau?
2. Vous mangez des œufs?
3. Vous faites de l'exercice?
4. Vous mangez des fruits?
5. Vous mangez du poisson?
6. Vous fumez des cigarettes?
7. Vous mangez des légumes?
8. Vous mangez de la viande?

D. Qu'est-ce qu'on boit?
Complétez les phrases logiquement en utilisant le verbe **boire.**

Exemple Le matin, je **bois du lait.**

1. Au petit déjeuner, les Français...
2. Au petit déjeuner, les Américains / Canadiens...
3. Le matin, je...
4. Quand j'étais jeune, le matin, je...
5. Ce matin, je (j')...
6. Avec un hamburger, on...
7. Dans cette région, quand il fait chaud, nous...
8. Quand j'ai très soif, je...
9. *(À un[e] camarade de classe)* À une boum, qu'est-ce que tu... ?
10. *(Au professeur)* Est-ce que vous... beaucoup de café?

E. Entretien.
Interviewez votre partenaire. Répondez à chaque question en utilisant le pronom **en.**

1. Manges-tu souvent des légumes? Est-ce que tu en as déjà mangé aujourd'hui? Manges-tu souvent de la viande rouge? En manges-tu tous les jours? Est-ce que tu vas en manger demain?
2. Fais-tu souvent de l'exercice? Combien de fois par semaine est-ce que tu en fais?
3. Est-ce que tu bois du café? En bois-tu trop? Quand est-ce que tu en bois? Et tes amis, est-ce qu'ils en boivent souvent?

1. Which forms of **-ir** verbs have **-iss-** as part of the ending?
2. What is the conjugation of **-ir** verbs in the imperfect?
3. How do you pronounce a single **s** between vowels? How do you pronounce double **ss?**

Talking about choices: *Les verbes en -ir*

Regular **-ir** verbs are conjugated as follows.

CHOISIR *(to choose)*	
je choisi**s**	nous choisi**ssons**
tu choisi**s**	vous choisi**ssez**
il/elle/on choisi**t**	ils/elles choisi**ssent**

PASSÉ COMPOSÉ: j'ai choisi
IMPARFAIT: je choisissais

All **-ir** verbs presented in this section take **avoir** as the auxiliary verb in the **passé composé**.

Many verbs that describe a change in physical appearance *(to get thinner, to turn red . . .)* end in **-ir**. Several are based on the corresponding adjective.

gros(se)	*fat*	→	grossir	*to get fatter*
grand(e)	*tall*	→	grandir	*to grow (up), to grow taller*
vieux (vieille)	*old*	→	vieillir	*to age*
maigre	*skinny*	→	maigrir	*to get thinner, to slim down*
rouge	*red*	→	rougir	*to blush, to turn red*

Here are some other common **-ir** verbs.

choisir (de faire)	*to choose (to do)*
finir (de faire)	*to finish (doing)*
obéir (à quelqu'un / à quelque chose)	*to obey (somebody / something)*
réfléchir (à)	*to think (about)*
réussir (à)	*to succeed (at), to pass* [a test]

 # Prononciation: *La lettre s et les verbes en -ir*

Sometimes it is difficult to remember whether to use one **s** or two when spelling forms of **-ir** verbs such as **choisir** or **réussir.** If you keep in mind that a single **s** between vowels is pronounced like a **z** and double **ss** is pronounced like an **s**, it will help your spelling. At the beginning of a word, **s** is always pronounced like **s**.

ils choi**s**i**ss**ent   nous réu**ss**i**ss**ons   je choi**s**i**ss**ais   je gro**ss**i**ss**ais

poi**s**on / poi**ss**on   un dé**s**ert / un de**ss**ert   vous choi**s**i**ss**ez / vous réu**ss**i**ss**ez

In the present tense, an **s** sound in the ending of **-ir** verbs indicates that you are talking about more than one person.

il rougit / ils rougissent   elle finit / elles finissent   il choisit / ils choisissent

Supplemental activity. Point out the difference in the pronunciation of the singular and plural third person endings of **-ir** verbs and do this activity: **Un ami parle de son cours de français. Est-ce qu'il parle du professeur ou des étudiants?** EXEMPLE Ils réussissent toujours à comprendre. **Il parle des étudiants. 1.** Il choisit toujours des questions faciles. **2.** D'habitude, ils finissent leurs devoirs. **3.** Il ne réfléchit pas toujours avant de parler. **4.** Ils obéissent toujours. **5.** Il rougit souvent. **6.** Il finit toujours le cours à l'heure *(on time)*.

A. C'est-à-dire... Trouvez une expression équivalente. Utilisez un verbe en **-ir**.

> **Exemple** Il devient rouge.
> **Il rougit.**

1. Il devient plus gros.
2. Il a l'air plus âgé.
3. Il pense à quelque chose.
4. Il devient plus mince.
5. L'enfant devient plus grand.
6. Il fait un choix.
7. Il termine quelque chose.
8. Il a un bon résultat à son examen.

B. Il faut bien choisir. Rosalie dit ce que chacun choisit de manger. Qu'est-ce qu'elle dit?

Exemple   Rose veut maigrir. Elle **choisit de la salade.**

> DES LÉGUMES   de la salade   **des fruits**
> du fromage   DE LA VIANDE ROUGE   *du poisson*   DES ŒUFS
> des desserts   **de la glace**   ???

1. Moi, je veux rester en bonne santé *(healthy)*. Je…
2. Rose et moi, nous voulons maigrir. Nous…
3. André veut grossir. Il…
4. Henri veut être plus fort *(strong)*. Il…
5. Et toi, Patricia, tu veux avoir plus d'énergie? Tu… ?
6. Et vous, les enfants, vous voulez grandir vite? Vous… ?
7. André et Henri veulent de la vitamine C dans leur régime *(diet)*. Ils…

C. En cours de français. Comment est votre cours de français? Dites si les personnes suivantes font les choses indiquées généralement.

Exemple   Le professeur… (choisir des questions faciles pour l'examen)
    Généralement, le professeur choisit des questions faciles pour l'examen. /
    Généralement, le professeur ne choisit pas de questions faciles pour l'examen.

1. Le professeur… (réussir à comprendre les questions des étudiants, finir le cours à l'heure *[on time]*, rougir facilement)
2. Les étudiants… (finir les devoirs, obéir au prof, réussir à bien parler français)
3. Moi, je… (finir les devoirs, réussir à comprendre la leçon, réfléchir avant de répondre)

D. Et au dernier cours? Dites si les personnes nommées ont fait les choses indiquées dans *C. En cours de français* au dernier cours.

Exemple   Le professeur (choisir des questions faciles pour l'examen)
    Au dernier cours, le professeur a choisi des questions faciles pour l'examen. /
    Au dernier cours, le professeur n'a pas choisi de questions faciles pour l'examen.

E. Au lycée. Demandez à votre partenaire s'il/si elle faisait les choses suivantes quand il/elle était au lycée.

Exemple   réfléchir toujours avant de répondre
    — Quand tu étais au lycée, est-ce que tu réfléchissais toujours avant de répondre?
    — Oui, je réfléchissais toujours avant de répondre. /
    Non, je ne réfléchissais pas toujours avant de répondre.

1. réussir à tous ses cours
2. obéir toujours à ses parents
3. finir toujours ses devoirs
4. réfléchir souvent à l'avenir *(the future)*

Supplemental activity. Qu'est-ce qui s'est passé pendant les vacances de Rose en France? Inventez une suite logique pour chaque phrase. Utilisez des verbes en **-ir** au passé composé. *(Put these verbs on the board or a transparency:* **maigir, grossir, grandir, choisir un restaurant de la région, finir ses vacances.)** **1.** Rose a beaucoup mangé. Elle… **2.** Rose et ses parents voulaient essayer des spécialités normandes. Ils… **3.** La mère de Rose a mangé seulement des salades et des fruits. Elle… **4.** Les petits frères de Rose ont bu beaucoup de lait. Ils… **5.** La mère de Rose voulait rentrer chez elle. Elle…

La bonne santé

Faites-vous attention à votre **santé?**

Aimeriez-vous devenir plus **fort(e)** ou **prendre du poids?**
    Vous pourriez...
        prendre des vitamines.
        faire de la muscu(lation).
        manger plus de protéines et de produits laitiers.

Voudriez-vous rester en forme?
    Vous devriez...
        bien manger.
        dormir assez.
        éviter l'alcool et le tabac.
        être moins stressé(e).

Avez-vous envie de maigrir?
    Vous devriez surtout...
        marcher ou faire de l'aérobic.
        manger des plats **sains** et légers.
        éviter **les matières grasses** *(f)*.14

 Rosalie invite Rose à aller prendre une glace.

ROSALIE: Tu veux aller prendre une glace?
ROSE: Je voudrais bien, mais je **suis au régime. J'aimerais** maigrir un peu.
ROSALIE: Mais pourquoi? Tu es bien comme tu es.
ROSE: J'ai grossi un peu depuis que nous sommes en France. Si je pouvais perdre deux kilos, **je serais** contente. Toi, tu es toujours en forme. **Pourrais-tu** me donner **des conseils?**
ROSALIE: Pour perdre du poids, **tu devrais** manger moins et faire plus souvent de l'exercice. En plus, tu sais, si tu mangeais plus **lentement,** tu mangerais peut-être un peu moins.

---

faire attention (à) *to pay attention (to)*   **la santé** *health*   **Vous devriez** *You should*   **éviter** *to avoid*   **fort(e)** *strong*   **prendre du poids** *to gain weight*   **Vous pourriez** *You could*   **faire de la muscu(lation)** *to do weight training, to do bodybuilding*   **marcher** *to walk*   **sain(e)** *healthy*   **les matières grasses** *(f) fats*   **être au régime** *to be on a diet*   **J'aimerais** *I would like*   **je serais** *I would be*   **tu pourrais** *you could*   **des conseils** *(m) advice*   **tu devrais** *you should*   **lentement** *slowly*

A. C'est un bon conseil? Dites si c'est un bon conseil ou un mauvais conseil pour rester en forme.

1. Il faut faire de l'exercice.
2. Vous devriez manger plus de sucre et moins de légumes.
3. Vous devriez faire de l'aérobic.
4. Il est important de boire assez d'eau.
5. Pour perdre du poids, vous devriez éviter les matières grasses.
6. Les plats sains et légers sont bons pour la santé.
7. Vous pourriez devenir plus fort(e) si vous faisiez de la muscu.
8. Vous devriez manger plus vite pour éviter de trop manger.
9. Vous devriez boire plus de vin et moins d'eau.
10. Vous devriez rester très stressé(e), ça donne de l'énergie.

B. Il faut... Complétez ces phrases.

1. Pour maigrir, on devrait (*one should*) manger...
   boire...
   éviter...
   faire...
2. Pour prendre du poids ou pour devenir plus fort, on devrait manger...
   boire...
   prendre...
   faire...
3. Pour rester en bonne santé, on devrait...

C. Entretien. Interviewez votre partenaire.

1. Fais-tu attention à ta santé? Aimerais-tu être plus fort(e)? Que fais-tu pour ta santé? Manges-tu bien?
2. Manges-tu beaucoup de fruits et de légumes? beaucoup de plats sains et légers? Est-ce que tu prends des vitamines?
3. Dors-tu assez? Combien d'heures dors-tu par nuit?
4. Est-ce que tu évites l'alcool ou est-ce que tu en bois? Est-ce que tu fumes?
5. Aimes-tu faire de l'exercice? Fais-tu de l'aérobic? de la muscu? Combien de fois par semaine fais-tu de l'exercice?

D. Conseils. Avec un(e) partenaire, changez la conversation entre Rose et Rosalie comme indiqué.

1. Rose would like to gain a little weight. She has gotten thinner and she would like to gain two kilos.
2. You would like to stay in shape and pay attention to your health. Ask your partner for advice.

Follow-up for *A. C'est un bon conseil?* Vrai ou faux? **1.** Quand on est au régime, on doit boire beaucoup de boissons alcoolisées. **2.** Si on veut grossir, il faut prendre plus de calories. **3.** Si vous voulez maigrir, vous devriez faire de l'exercice. **4.** Pour perdre du poids, il faut essayer de manger plus lentement. **5.** Les boissons alcoolisées sont excellentes pour la santé. **6.** C'est bon pour la santé de boire beaucoup d'eau. **7.** Évitez le sucre si vous voulez maigrir.

Suggestion for *C. Entretien.* Have students answer questions 2 and 5 using **en.**

Supplemental activities. A. Lequel est meilleur pour la santé? **1.** la tarte ou le riz **2.** les desserts ou les légumes **3.** les fruits ou la glace **4.** la bière ou le jus de fruit **5.** les côtes de porc ou le poisson **6.** le café ou l'eau **7.** les frites ou la salade **8.** la viande rouge ou le poisson **B.** Have students name as many healthy items as they can in each of the following categories: **la viande, les fruits, les légumes, les desserts, les boissons.**

Pour vérifier

1. What other verb tense has the same endings as the conditional? What is the stem for the conditional of most verbs?
2. When do you use the conditional?

Suggestion. Point out to students that they will always hear an **r** sound before the conditional ending.

Saying what you would do: *Le conditionnel*

To say that something *would* happen under certain circumstances, or to ask someone if they *would* do something for you, use the conditional. The conditional of most verbs is formed by adding the same endings as the **imparfait** to the infinitive of the verb. If an infinitive ends in **-e,** the **e** is dropped.

PARLER	FINIR	PERDRE
je parler**ais**	je finir**ais**	je perdr**ais**
tu parler**ais**	tu finir**ais**	tu perdr**ais**
il/elle/on parler**ait**	il/elle/on finir**ait**	il/elle/on perdr**ait**
nous parler**ions**	nous finir**ions**	nous perdr**ions**
vous parler**iez**	vous finir**iez**	vous perdr**iez**
ils/elles parler**aient**	ils/elles finir**aient**	ils/elles perdr**aient**

J'aimerais être en forme.   *I would like to be in shape.*
Aimerais-tu faire de la muscu?   *Would you like to do weight training?*

Many irregular verbs follow this same pattern.

dormir → je dormirais...   prendre → je prendrais...   boire → je boirais...

Verbs like **acheter, payer,** and **appeler** have spelling changes in the conditional stem in all the forms except **nous** and **vous** (j'achèterais, je paierais, j'appellerais). Those like **préférer** do not (**je préférerais**).

The following verbs have irregular stems in the conditional. It is easier to learn them in these three groups.

-r-		-dr- / -vr-		-rr-	
aller	ir-	vouloir	voudr-	voir	verr-
avoir	aur-	devoir	devr-	pouvoir	pourr-
être	ser-	venir	viendr-	mourir	mourr-
faire	fer-	devenir	deviendr-		
		revenir	reviendr-		

Supplemental activity. Point out the form **on devrait** and ask **Qu'est-ce qu'on devrait faire pour... ?** 1. être en bonne santé 2. être un bon parent 3. apprendre une autre langue 4. réussir à l'université 5. maigrir 6. devenir plus fort

Si j'avais le temps, **j'irais** plus souvent au club de gym.   *If I had time,* ***I would go*** *to the gym more often.*
Voudriez-vous venir?   ***Would you like*** *to come?*

You need to learn these forms too.

il y a	il y aurait	*there would be*
il pleut	il pleuvrait	*it would rain*
il faut	il faudrait	*it would be necessary*

To say *could* and *should,* use **pouvoir** and **devoir** in the conditional.

Je **devrais** manger mieux.   *I **should** eat better.*
Pourrais-tu me donner des conseils?   ***Could you*** *give me some advice?*

As you have seen, the conditional is used to say what one *would* do, *could* do, or *should* do.

Use the conditional:

- to make polite requests or offers.

Pourrais-tu me donner des conseils?   *Could you give me some advice?*
Voudriez-vous du café?   *Would you like some coffee?*

- to say what someone would do if circumstances were different.

Si je savais faire la cuisine, je mangerais mieux.
If I knew how to cook, I would eat better.

In hypothetical or contrary-to-fact statements such as the above, the **si** clause is in the imperfect and the result clause is in the conditional. Note that either clause can come first.

Si nous **avions** plus de temps libre nous **ferions plus d'exercice.**
*If we **had** more free time, we **would exercise more.***

Nous **ferions plus d'exercice,** si nous **avions** plus de temps libre.
*We **would exercise more** if we **had** more free time.*

 Prononciation: *La consonne r et le conditionnel*

The conditional stems of all verbs in French end in **-r.** To pronounce a French **r,** arch the back of the tongue firmly in the back of the mouth, as if to pronounce a *g,* and pronounce a strong English *h* sound. Practice the **r** in these words.

je pourrais   tu trouverais   nous serions   il reviendrait   ils devraient

---

A. Réactions. Quelle serait votre réaction dans les circonstances suivantes?

Je serais... / Je ne serais pas...

> CONTENT(E)   mécontent(e) *(displeased)*
>
> heureux (heureuse)   **triste (sad)**   SURPRIS(E)
>
> *furieux (furieuse)*   INDIFFÉRENT(E)   horrifié(e)   **scandalisé(e)**
>
> fatigué(e)   étonné(e) *(astonished)*   ???

1. Si le médecin me disait *(told me)* de perdre dix kilos...
2. Si je perdais deux kilos...
3. Si mon meilleur ami (ma meilleure amie) commençait un cours de muscu...
4. Si je ne pouvais plus manger de viande...
5. Si on découvrait *(discovered)* que le chocolat était très bon pour la santé...
6. Si je devais faire de l'exercice tous les jours...
7. Si mon meilleur ami (ma meilleure amie) devenait végétarien(ne)...

Follow-up for *A. Réactions.* Un(e) ami(e) veut rester en bonne santé. Donnez-lui des conseils sur ce qu'il/elle devrait ou ne devrait pas faire.
EXEMPLE Tu devrais éviter le sucre... Tu ne devrais pas... (You may wish to put these cues on the board or a transparency: **éviter... manger... boire... faire...**)

B. Scrupules. Que feriez-vous dans ces circonstances?

1. Si vous voyiez *(saw)* la fiancée de votre frère embrasser un autre garçon, est-ce que vous...
   a. le diriez *(would tell)* à votre frère?
   b. ne feriez rien?
   c. demanderiez 50 dollars à sa fiancée pour garder le silence?
2. Si vous voyiez une copie de l'examen de fin de semestre / trimestre sur le bureau du prof deux jours avant l'examen, est-ce que vous...
   a. la prendriez?
   b. ne feriez rien?
   c. liriez l'examen tout de suite?
3. Si vous trouviez un chien dans la rue, est-ce que vous...
   a. téléphoneriez à la Société protectrice des animaux?
   b. prendriez le chien et chercheriez son maître *(owner)*?
   c. ne feriez rien?
4. Si vous ne veniez pas en cours le jour d'un examen important parce que vous n'étiez pas préparé(e), est-ce que vous...
   a. expliqueriez *(explain)* la situation au professeur?
   b. diriez au professeur que vous étiez malade?
   c. choisiriez d'avoir un zéro à l'examen?
5. Si vous voyiez quelqu'un qui attaquait votre professeur de français, est-ce que vous...
   a. téléphoneriez à la police?
   b. resteriez là pour aider votre professeur?
   c. resteriez là pour aider l'agresseur?

C. Une interview. Imaginez que vous avez une interview avec Barbara Walters et elle vous pose les questions suivantes. Comment lui répondez-vous?

1. Si vous étiez une autre personne, qui voudriez-vous être?
2. Si vous habitiez dans une autre ville, où voudriez-vous habiter?
3. Si vous alliez à une autre université, où iriez-vous?
4. Si vous étiez un animal, quel animal seriez-vous: un chien, un chat, un poisson, un rat ou un oiseau *(a bird)*?
5. Si vous étiez une saison, quelle saison seriez-vous: l'hiver, l'été, le printemps ou l'automne? Pourquoi?
6. Si on écrivait *(were writing)* votre biographie, comment s'appellerait le livre?
7. Si votre vie était un morceau de musique, est-ce que ce serait de la musique populaire, de la musique classique, du rock, du blues, du jazz ou de la musique country?
8. Si votre vie était un film, est-ce que ce serait un drame, une comédie, un film d'épouvante ou un film d'aventures?

Follow-up for *D. Temps libre.* Have students name two other things they would do.

D. Temps libre. Feriez-vous les choses suivantes si vous aviez plus de temps libre?

Exemple   préparer plus de plats sains et légers
           **Oui, je préparerais plus de plats sains et légers. /
           Non, je ne préparerais pas plus de plats sains et légers.**

1. dormir plus
2. être moins stressé(e)
3. pouvoir vous reposer plus
4. apprendre une autre langue
5. aller plus souvent au parc
6. manger moins de conserves
7. faire plus d'exercice
8. voir plus souvent vos amis
9. aller plus souvent au restaurant
10. rendre plus souvent visite à votre famille

E. Situations. Qu'est-ce que ces gens feraient dans les situations suivantes?

Exemple Si nous n'avions pas cours aujourd'hui, mes amis et moi... (aller au parc)
Si nous n'avions pas cours aujourd'hui, nous irions au parc. / Si nous n'avions pas cours aujourd'hui, nous n'irions pas au parc.

1. Si nous n'avions pas cours aujourd'hui, mes amis et moi... (aller au club de gym, manger au restaurant, faire de l'aérobic, aller prendre un verre, se reposer)
2. Si Rose mangeait plus de légumes et de poisson et moins de gâteaux, elle... (devenir plus forte, perdre du poids, maigrir, grossir)
3. Si les étudiants mangeaient de la pizza et des hamburgers tous les jours pendant un mois, ils... (grossir, devoir faire un régime, devoir faire de l'exercice, être en bonne santé)
4. Si mes parents allaient en vacances en France, ils... (manger dans des restaurants français, boire du vin français, marcher beaucoup)

Warm-up for *E. Situations.* Qu'est-ce que ces gens demanderaient s'ils trouvaient la lampe d'Aladin? (You may wish to put these cues on the board or on a transparency: **un bon travail** *[job]*, **de l'argent, une maison, une voiture, des voyages...**) **1.** Mes parents... **2.** *[Au professeur]* Vous... **3.** *[À un(e) autre étudiant(e)]* Tu... **4.** Nous, la classe de français... **5.** Mon meilleur ami (Ma meilleure amie)... **6.** Moi, je...

F. Changements. Si vous pouviez transformer ces personnes, comment seraient-elles? Que feraient-elles différemment?

Exemple Mon camarade de chambre (Ma camarade de chambre)...
Mon camarade de chambre (Ma camarade de chambre) se coucherait plus tôt et il/elle ferait plus souvent le ménage. / Je ne changerais rien.

1. Mes professeurs...
2. Mon meilleur ami (Ma meilleure amie)...
3. Moi, je...
4. Nous, les étudiants...
5. Mes parents...

G. Décisions. Que feriez-vous...

1. si vous gagniez à la loterie?
2. si vous aviez des vacances *(vacation)* maintenant?
3. si vous aviez seulement un jour à vivre *(to live)*?
4. si vous pouviez faire ce que vous vouliez en ce moment?
5. si vous pouviez passer la journée avec une personne que vous admirez?

H. Par politesse. Mettez ces phrases au conditionnel pour être plus poli(e) *(polite).*

Exemple Veux-tu rester en forme?
Voudrais-tu rester en forme?

1. Tu veux faire de l'exercice?
2. Quand est-ce que tu as le temps d'aller au club de gym avec moi?
3. Peux-tu passer chez moi vers dix heures?
4. Ton amie veut venir aussi?
5. Qu'est-ce que vous voulez faire après?
6. On peut aller au restaurant végétarien?
7. Est-ce que vous voulez essayer leur nouvelle salade?

Reprise: *Talking about food and health*

In *Chapitre 8,* you practiced ordering at a restaurant, buying food, talking about meals, and deciding on a healthy lifestyle. Now you have a chance to review what you learned.

A. Chez les petits commerçants. Dites au moins quatre choses qu'on peut acheter dans les endroits suivants.

Exemple   dans un supermarché   **On peut acheter de l'eau minérale...**

1. dans une boulangerie
2. dans une charcuterie
3. dans une épicerie
4. dans une boucherie
5. au marché
6. dans une poissonnerie *(fish market)*

B. Les courses. Rose va préparer un grand dîner ce soir. Voilà la liste des choses qu'elle va acheter. Dites ce qu'elle va acheter.

Exemple   *a jar of jelly*
   Elle va acheter un pot de confiture.

Maintenant, dites où elle va aller pour acheter chacune des choses sur sa liste.

Exemple   **Elle va acheter un pot de confiture à l'épicerie.**

> *a jar of jelly*
> *a kilo of potatoes*
> *a bag of sugar*
> *6 slices of ham*
> *some ice cream*
> *an apple*
> *a chicken*

C. Des gens en bonne santé. Ces personnes font très attention à leur santé. Répondez à chaque question de façon logique pour dire ce qu'elles font. Employez le pronom **en.**

Exemple   Vous mangez beaucoup **de desserts sucrés?**
   Non, je n'en mange pas beaucoup.

1. Votre meilleur(e) ami(e) mange **de la viande rouge** tous les soirs?
2. Le professeur mange **des fruits** le matin?
3. Rosalie boit beaucoup **de vin** tous les jours?
4. Les enfants de Patricia boivent beaucoup **de coca?**
5. Vos parents font **de l'exercice** trois fois par semaine?
6. Vous prenez beaucoup **de sucre?**
7. Votre camarade de chambre fume deux paquets **de cigarettes** par jour?
8. Vous prenez toujours **un dessert** au restaurant?

D. Qu'est-ce qu'on prend? Indiquez ce qu'on prend dans chacune de ces circonstances. Ensuite, dites ce que vous prenez dans les mêmes circonstances. Nommez autant de choses que possible.

Exemple   En France, au petit déjeuner, on **prend des tartines ou des croissants avec...**
   Moi, au petit déjeuner,...

1. En France, au petit déjeuner, on...
   Moi, au petit déjeuner, je...
2. En France, pour un déjeuner dans un fast-food, on...
   Moi, pour un déjeuner dans un fast-food, je...

Warm-up for *D. Qu'est-ce qu'on prend?* A. Write these categories on the board: **C'est délicieux. C'est assez bon. Ce n'est pas bon du tout.** Call out these foods and have students categorize them: **la tarte aux pommes, la glace au chocolat, le pâté, le poisson, le saumon, les frites, les hamburgers, les escargots, le jambon, les pommes, les croissants, la bière, l'eau minérale. B.** Lequel de ces aliments a le plus de calories? **1.** le beurre / le café **2.** les frites / le poisson **3.** la salade / le fromage **4.** le poulet / le bacon **5.** le gâteau / les fruits **6.** les légumes / la viande **7.** le sucre / le sel **C.** Introduce the expressions **c'est sucré** and **c'est salé.** Review food and drink vocabulary by calling out the names of foods for students to identify as **sucré** or **salé** (le gâteau, le pâté, la glace, la tarte aux fruits, le coca, le fromage, le jambon, la confiture, le bacon). Finally, ask students: **Est-ce que vous préférez les choses sucrées ou les choses salées?**

3. En France, pour un repas traditionnel, comme entrée, on... Comme plat principal, on... Comme légume, on... Et comme dessert, on...
Moi, comme entrée, je... Comme plat principal, je... Comme légume, je... Et comme dessert, je...

4. En France, pour un dîner léger, on...
Moi, pour un dîner léger, je...

E. À table! Complétez avec la forme correcte de l'article convenable.

Ce qu'on mange varie d'une culture à l'autre. Aux États-Unis, par exemple, on prend _____1____ petit déjeuner copieux. On mange souvent _____2____ œufs au bacon et _____3____ pain grillé. On boit _____4____ jus, ____5____ lait ou ____6____ café. En France, pourtant, _____7____ petit déjeuner est un repas léger. On boit ____8____ café au lait, ____9____ thé ou ____10____ chocolat et on mange _____11____ tartines. On ne boit jamais _____12____ lait.

À midi, en France, on peut manger un repas complet ou un repas rapide. Si on mange dans un café on peut prendre _____13____ omelette, ____14____ salade ou ____15____ sandwich avec ____16____ vin ou ____17____ eau minérale. _____18____ vin français est très bon, mais ____19____ eau minérale est populaire aussi. On peut toujours finir un repas avec une tasse *(cup)* _____20____ café—peut-être avec un peu ____21____ sucre ou un peu ____22____ lait.

F. Qu'est-ce qu'ils font? Dites si logiquement ces personnes font ou ne font pas les choses indiquées. Suivez l'exemple.

Exemple   Je ne veux pas grossir. Alors, je (finir) tous mes repas avec un dessert.
   Je ne veux pas grossir. Alors, je ne finis pas tous mes repas avec un dessert.

1. Tu fais attention à ta santé. Alors, tu (choisir) des plats sains et tu (boire) beaucoup d'eau.
2. Nous mangeons beaucoup de desserts. Alors, nous (grossir).
3. Mes amis (maigrir) parce qu'ils mangent trop de matières grasses.
4. Nous ne voulons pas grossir. Alors, nous (boire) beaucoup de bière.
5. Comme nous voulons maigrir, nous (finir) tous nos repas avec un dessert.
6. Je (maigrir) parce que je marche tous les jours et je (boire) huit verres d'eau par jour.
7. Mes amis veulent rester en bonne forme. Alors, ils (boire) peu de bière.
8. Si on veut rester en forme, on (boire) du jus de fruit et on (choisir) des plats sains.
9. Tes amis et toi, vous voulez rester en forme? Alors, vous (choisir) de bien manger et vous (boire) trop de café.

G. Si... Si ces personnes avaient plus de temps libre, est-ce qu'elles feraient les choses indiquées?

Exemple   Moi, je (aller plus souvent au club de gym)
   J'irais plus souvent au club de gym. /
   Je n'irais pas plus souvent au club de gym.

1. Mon meilleur ami (Ma meilleure amie) (faire de la muscu, travailler plus)
2. Mes parents (faire plus attention à leur santé, partir souvent en voyage)
3. Moi, je (dormir plus, réussir mieux à mes cours)
4. Mes amis (réfléchir plus à leur santé, boire moins de boissons alcoolisées)
5. Mes amis et moi (se reposer, sortir plus souvent, être moins stressés)

LECTURE ET *composition*

Note. The vocabulary in this section does not appear in the end-of-chapter vocabulary lists and is meant for recognition only. You may wish to let students know in advance whether you intend to test them on this vocabulary.

LECTURE: Déjeuner du matin

Jacques Prévert (1900–1977), l'un des poètes les plus célèbres du vingtième **siècle,** aimait parler de la vie de tous les jours dans sa poésie. Avant de lire le poème qui suit, faites cet exercice.

En contexte. Devinez le sens des mots en caractères gras.

Il a pris son paquet de cigarettes qui était sur la table. Il a pris une cigarette et il l'**a allumée. La fumée** grise a rempli la pièce. Il a posé sa cigarette dans **le cendrier.** Il a laissé quelques **cendres** dans **le cendrier.** Il **a reposé** le paquet de cigarettes sur la table.

◆ Déjeuner du matin ◆

Jacques Prévert

Il a mis le café
Dans **la tasse**
Il a mis le lait
Dans la tasse de café
Il a mis le sucre
Dans le café au lait
Avec la petite **cuiller**
Il a tourné
Il a bu le café au lait
Et il a reposé la tasse
Sans me parler

Il a allumé
Une cigarette
Il a fait **des ronds**
Avec la fumée
Il a mis les cendres
Dans le cendrier
Sans me parler
Sans me regarder
Il s'est levé
Il a mis
Son chapeau sur **sa tête**

Il a mis
Son manteau de pluie
Parce qu'il pleuvait
Et il est parti
Sous la pluie
Sans **une parole**
Sans me regarder
Et moi j'ai pris
Ma tête dans mes mains
Et **j'ai pleuré**

Qu'est-ce qui s'est passé? Qu'est-ce qui s'est passé dans le poème?

1. Faites une liste des choses qu'il a faites.
2. Nommez deux choses qu'il n'a pas faites.
3. Quelle a été la réaction de l'autre personne?

---

un siècle *a century* **la tasse** *the cup* **la cuiller** *the spoon* **des ronds** *(m) smoke rings* **la tête** *the head* **une parole** *a word* **pleurer** *to cry*

Composition

A. Organisez-vous.
Vous allez imaginer ce qui s'est passé entre les personnages du poème. D'abord, organisez-vous en répondant aux questions suivantes.

1. Qui sont ces personnages? Sont-ils amis? parents? Sont-ils mariés, fiancés, divorcés... ?
2. Comment sont-ils? Faites un portrait physique (grand, petit, gros, jeune...) et psychologique (intelligent, bête, sympathique, égoïste...) des personnages.
3. Pourquoi est-ce qu'ils ne se parlent pas? Qu'est-ce qui s'est passé?

If you have access to SYSTÈME-D software, you will find the following phrases, vocabulary, grammar, and dictionary aids there.

Phrases: Describing people; Expressing an opinion; Linking ideas; Persuading
Vocabulary: Personality; Hair colors; Family members
Grammar: Past imperfect; Compound past tense

B. Rédaction: Leur vie ensemble.
Imaginez le passé des personnages du poème. Écrivez une rédaction qui explique leur passé ensemble.

C. Un scénario.
Comparez votre rédaction à celle d'un(e) camarade de classe et choisissez une explication de la situation dans le poème. Préparez une scène dans laquelle chacun des personnages explique à un troisième son point de vue sur ce qui s'est passé. Présentez la scène à la classe.

COMPARAISONS
culturelles

À TABLE!

Chaque société a ses **propres coutumes** à table, ses plats préférés, et même sa propre **façon** de manger.

Aussi, ce qui est considéré «normal» ou «**poli**» diffère souvent d'une culture à l'autre.

Regardez ces photos. Qu'est-ce que vous **remarquez?** Est-ce qu'il y a des choses qui vous **surprennent?**

_____
propre *own*   **une coutume** *a custom*   **une façon** *a way, a manner*   **poli(e)** *polite*   **remarquer** *to notice*   **surprennent (surprendre** *to surprise)*

Lisez ces phrases concernant les coutumes et les bonnes manières. Pour chacune, indiquez d'abord si c'est vrai en général dans votre région. Ensuite, devinez lesquelles sont vraies en France. Après, vérifiez vos réponses.

	CHEZ NOUS	EN FRANCE
1. Avant de manger, on dit souvent «bon appétit»!	❏	❏
2. On boit quelquefois du lait aux repas.	❏	❏
3. On mange souvent des œufs le matin.	❏	❏
4. On mange des œufs plutôt le soir ou à midi.	❏	❏
5. On mange assez souvent dans des fast-foods.	❏	❏
6. La présentation est presque aussi importante que le goût *(taste)* d'un plat.	❏	❏
7. Le pain est indispensable à tous les repas.	❏	❏
8. Le pain se mange généralement sans beurre, sauf le matin.	❏	❏
9. On fait souvent les courses chez les petits commerçants.	❏	❏
10. On mange beaucoup de choses avec les mains.	❏	❏
11. Quand on mange, on garde *(keeps)* toujours les deux mains sur la table.	❏	❏
12. On met le pain directement sur la table, pas sur l'assiette *(plate)*.	❏	❏
13. Au restaurant, on peut commander à la carte ou on peut choisir un menu à prix fixe.	❏	❏

Pour la France - Vrai: 1, 4, 5, 6, 7, 8, 9, 11, 12, 13

À discuter.

1. Quelles différences est-ce qu'il y a entre ce qu'on fait chez vous et ce qu'on fait en France? Quelles similarités?
2. Les opinions des Français ne sont pas toujours reflétées *(reflected)* dans leur vie de tous les jours. Remarquez le contraste entre les opinions et les actions qui suivent. Comment pouvez-vous expliquer ce contraste entre ce que les Français pensent et ce qu'ils font?

OPINIONS

- Pour 86% des Français les repas, c'est surtout un moment pour se retrouver en famille ou entre amis.
- Selon 85% des Français, on devrait continuer à préparer des repas traditionnels à la maison quand c'est possible.
- Pour 82% des Français, les repas déjà préparés, c'est juste pour quand on est pressé(e) *(in a hurry)*.
- Les Français préfèrent le service personnalisé qu'on retrouve chez les petits commerçants.

ACTIONS

- En France, on passe de moins en moins de temps à préparer les repas.
- Ils mangent de plus en plus souvent dans des fast-foods.
- Ils achètent de plus en plus souvent des produits surgelés ou en conserve.
- En France, on utilise de plus en plus le four à micro-ondes *(microwave oven)* pour faire la cuisine.
- Les Français font de plus en plus souvent leurs courses dans les supermarchés.

visit http://horizons.heinle.com

COMPÉTENCE 1

NOMS MASCULINS

un apéritif	a before-dinner drink
un dessert	a dessert
un fruit	a fruit
des fruits de mer	shellfish, crustaceans
*un hors-d'œuvre	an hors d'œuvre, an appetizer
du lait	milk
des légumes	vegetables
un menu à prix fixe	a set-price menu
du pain	bread
un pavé de	a thick slice of
le plat (principal)	the (main) dish
du poisson (fumé)	(smoked) fish
du poivre	pepper
un repas	a meal
du riz	rice
du sel	salt
un serveur	a server, a waiter
du sucre	sugar

NOMS FÉMININS

une bouteille (de)	a bottle (of)
une carafe (de)	a carafe (of)
la carte	the menu
de la crème	cream
une entrée	an hors d'œuvre
de la raie	rayfish, skate
une salade	a salad
une serveuse	a server, a waitress
de la viande	meat
de la volaille	poultry

DIVERS

Aimeriez-vous... ?	Would you like . . . ?
comme	for, as (a)
comprendre	to include
décider	to decide
du, de la, de l', des	some, any
finir	to finish
Que savez-vous de... ?	What do you know about . . . ?
servir	to serve
traditionnel(le)	traditional
typiquement	typically

Pour les noms des différentes sortes d'entrées, voir la page 284.
Pour les noms des différentes sortes de viandes, de volailles, de poissons et de fruits de mer, voir la page 284.
Pour les noms des différentes sortes de légumes, voir la page 285.
Pour voir les différentes possibilités pour finir un repas, voir la page 285.

COMPÉTENCE 2

NOMS MASCULINS

du bœuf	beef
un choix	a choice
un commerçant	a shopkeeper
un hypermarché	a superstore
un marché	a market
un oignon	an onion
un pain au chocolat	a chocolate-filled croissant
un pain complet	a loaf of wholegrain bread
un plat préparé	a ready-to-serve dish
du porc	pork
un produit	a product
du raisin	grapes
du saucisson	salami
le service personnalisé	personal service

NOMS FÉMININS

une banane	a banana
la boucherie	the butcher's shop
la boulangerie-pâtisserie	the bakery
une carotte	a carrot
une cerise	a cherry
la charcuterie	the deli
de la charcuterie	deli meats, cold cuts
une commerçante	a shopkeeper
des conserves	canned goods
l'épicerie	the grocery store
une fraise	a strawberry
de la laitue	lettuce
une orange	an orange
une pêche	a peach
une poire	a pear
des saucisses	sausages
une tartelette (aux fraises / aux cerises)	a (strawberry / cherry) tart

DIVERS

C'est tout.	That's all.
de plus en plus	more and more
dire	to say, to tell
frais (fraîche)	fresh
il faut	it is necessary, one needs, one must
Qu'est-ce que je peux vous proposer d'autre?	What else can I get you?
Qu'est-ce qu'il vous faut?	What do you need?
surgelé(e)	frozen

Pour les expressions de quantité, voir la page 298.

VOCABULAIRE

COMPÉTENCE 3

Talking about meals

NOMS MASCULINS

du bacon	bacon
du beurre	butter
du chocolat	chocolate
un croissant	a croissant
le dîner	dinner
un fast-food	a fast-food restaurant
***un hamburger**	a hamburger
du pain grillé	toast
un self-service	a self-service restaurant

NOMS FÉMININS

des céréales	cereal
de la confiture	jelly
une omelette	an omelet
une pizza	a pizza
une tartine	bread with butter and jelly

EXPRESSIONS VERBALES

boire	to drink
choisir (de faire)	to choose (to do)
finir (de faire)	to finish (doing)
grandir	to grow, to grow up, to get taller
grossir	to get fatter
maigrir	to get thinner, to slim down
obéir (à)	to obey
réfléchir (à)	to think (about)
réussir (à)	to succeed (at, in), to pass [a test]
rougir	to blush, to turn red
vieillir	to age

DIVERS

à l'américaine	American style
ceux (celles)	those
complet (complète)	complete
copieux (copieuse)	copious, large
depuis que	since
en	some, any, of it, of them
encore	still, again, more
en plus	furthermore
grillé(e)	toasted, grilled
je prendrais	I would have, I would take
léger (légère)	light
maigre	skinny
ne... plus	no more, no longer
rapide	rapid, fast, quick
seulement	only
si	yes (in response to a question or statement in the negative)
surtout	especially
volontiers	gladly
vrai(e)	true

COMPÉTENCE 4

Choosing a healthy lifestyle

NOMS MASCULINS

de l'alcool	alcohol
des conseils	advice
des produits laitiers	milk products
un régime	a diet
le poids	weight
du tabac	tobacco

NOMS FÉMININS

des matières grasses	fats
des protéines	protein
la santé	health
des vitamines	vitamins

EXPRESSIONS VERBALES

être au régime	to be on a diet
éviter	to avoid
faire attention (à)	to pay attention (to)
faire de l'aérobic	to do aerobics
faire de la muscu(lation)	to do weight training, to do bodybuilding
marcher	to walk
perdre du poids	to lose weight
prendre du poids	to put on weight

DIVERS

content(e)	content, happy
en forme	in shape
fort(e)	strong
lentement	slowly
sain(e)	healthy
stressé(e)	stressed out

Branchez-vous sur le français

FRENCH FOR JOBS IN THE TRAVEL INDUSTRY

Do you like to stop and daydream as you gaze at pictures of faraway places? Do you like to travel? Are you good at organizing events for your friends? Perhaps you should consider a job in the travel industry! According to the United States Labor Department, jobs in the travel industry are expected to grow at a much faster rate than average during the next several years. Knowing French will give you an advantage over your competition. Each year the French reserve about 12 million nights in American hotels and Americans spend about 19 million nights in French hotels.

À Paris

The travel industry needs the following people who are bilingual in French and English.

- **Travel agents:** If you are a travel agent, many resorts will give you trips with all expenses paid to familiarize you with their facilities. You may also get discounts of up to 75% on flights and accommodations. Knowing French will help you find a job and move more quickly to management positions within agencies.
- **Flight attendants:** French-speaking flight attendants have a better chance of being assigned to international flights, for which the pay is often better than for domestic flights. When you have a layover in Paris, Montreal, or Brussels, you can spend your time as you wish.
- **Reservation and customer service agents:** With French travelers booking 12 million nights in American hotels per year, you may have the opportunity to use your French at a hotel or airport anywhere in the 50 states.
- **Tour managers:** Many tour managers work only six to nine months per year due to a tourist season determined by weather conditions. Knowing French, you will be able to work year-round, taking people to Europe in the summer or to Tahiti in the winter. Whether you are taking a group of French speakers around the United States or you are with a group of Americans in a French-speaking country, chances are that you will stay in nice hotels and eat in some of the finest restaurants.

For information about jobs in the travel industry, you may write to:

The American Society of Travel Agents
1101 King Street
Alexandria, VA 22314
(703) 739-2782
www.astanet.com

Association of Flight Attendants
1275 K Street, NW, Suite 500
Washington, DC 20005-4090
(202) 712-9799
www.afanet.org

DOSSIER: **Constance Rudd**

Interviewer: *Où est-ce que vous travaillez?*

Constance: Je travaille une ou deux fois par an à l'étranger comme chef de groupe. J'accompagne entre 30 et 40 Américains à leur destination et je participe avec **eux** à leur programme culturel pendant trois semaines. Notre **but** n'est pas de visiter seulement les sites touristiques **tels que** la tour Eiffel, mais plutôt d'apprendre à bien connaître la culture française, le système scolaire, l'histoire, la politique. **Je sers de** liaison entre le groupe et ceux qui organisent le programme en France.

Interviewer: *Quand avez-vous besoin d'utiliser le français dans votre travail?*

Constance: J'ai souvent besoin de parler français pendant ces trois semaines en France, **soit** avec le conducteur de l'autocar, soit pour aider les voyageurs à la banque, à **la gare**, à l'hôtel, au bureau de poste, ou même à la boulangerie. On entend souvent dire aujourd'hui, «Mais **tout le monde** parle anglais!» Je trouve que ce n'est pas vrai, **même** à Paris, et **encore moins** dans les petits villages, qui sont les **endroits** les plus intéressants.

Interviewer: *Quels avantages y a-t-il à travailler dans le tourisme?*

Constance: Les **métiers** du tourisme ont plusieurs avantages: on **fait la connaissance de** toutes sortes de gens de pays différents, on apprend des choses nouvelles, on a beaucoup de possibilités de voyager, et le travail est très varié.

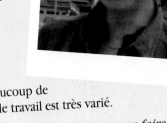

Interviewer: *Quelles recommandations pouvez-vous faire à quelqu'un qui voudrait travailler dans le tourisme?*

Constance: Je lui conseillerais de lire des livres dans tous les domaines: l'histoire, la géographie, la littérature, la politique; **autant** sur sa **propre** culture que sur celles des pays qu'il voudrait visiter. Il est aussi très important d'**améliorer** sa **connaissance** des langues étrangères.

DOSSIER: **Elisabeth Vazquez**

Interviewer: *Quelles sont vos responsabilités comme agent de voyages?*

Elisabeth: J'organise les voyages de mes clients. Je suis chargée de **la délivrance** des documents de voyages, tels que les billets d'avion, les **bons** de réservation d'hôtels, les confirmations **de location** de voitures et les documents qui concernent les **croisières.**

Interviewer: *Quels avantages y a-t-il à savoir le français quand on travaille dans le tourisme?*

Elisabeth: Il est plus facile d'éviter des **malentendus** avec des étrangers, la communication étant simplifiée. Si j'ai des doutes sur **les prestations** d'un hôtel, disons en France, j'appelle directement sur place pour avoir plus d'informations. Vous pouvez aussi **prétendre à** un meilleur salaire et à **un poste plus élevé** si vous parlez français.

Interviewer: *Quels sont les avantages des métiers du tourisme?*

Elisabeth: Le travail est agréable et varié. Les clients sont souvent sympas **car** on est là pour organiser leurs voyages, ce qui les **rend de bonne humeur.** Et puis, on a souvent des réductions très intéressantes sur le prix de nos propres voyages.

---

eux *them* **un but** *a goal* **tel(le) que** *such as* **Je sers de** *I function as* **soit** *be it* **la gare** *the train station* **tout le monde** *everyone* **même** *even* **encore moins** *still less* **un endroit** *a place* **un métier** *an occupation* **faire la connaissance de** *to meet* **autant** *as much* **propre** *own* **améliorer** *to improve* **la connaissance** *the knowledge* **la délivrance** *the delivery* **un bon** *a voucher* **de location** *rental* **une croisière** *a cruise* **un malentendu** *a misunderstanding* **une prestation** *a service* **prétendre à** *to expect* **un poste plus élevé** *a higher position* **car** *because* **rendre quelqu'un de bonne humeur** *to put someone in a good mood*

Figures carrying water

Mode Muntu (circa 1950–1986)
1973
Collection: Bogumil Jewsiewicki
© The Museum for African Art, New York

Suggestions. The next two chapters take place in **Côte-d'Ivoire.** Have students locate the francophone countries in Africa inside the back cover.

Rhythmic repetition is one aesthetic characteristic of African art, found in painting as well as in music and poetry. The paintings of Mode Muntu, an artist from the **République démocratique du Congo,** clearly display this trait; they often contain figures that are repeated in similar positions.

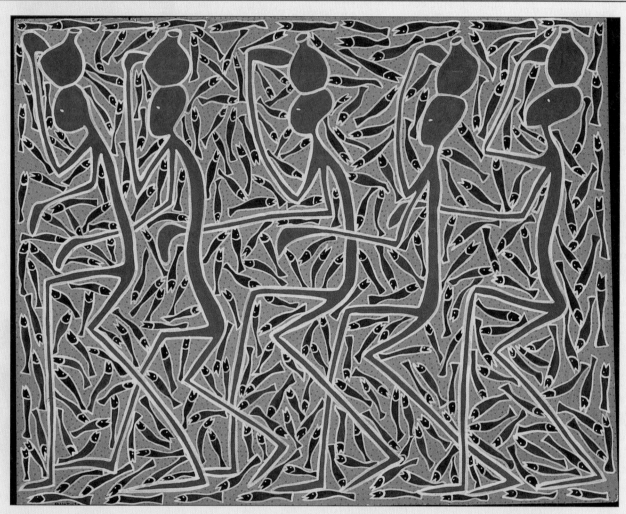

En Côte-d'Ivoire

L'AFRIQUE

SUPERFICIE: 30 259 000 kilomètres carrés

POPULATION: 805 000 000 (les Africains), dont plus de 192 000 000 habitent dans un pays où le français est la langue officielle, et 70 000 000 habitent en Algérie, au Maroc et en Tunisie, où l'arabe est la langue officielle, mais le français est largement parlé.

INDUSTRIES PRINCIPALES: agriculture (arachides *[peanuts]*, cacao, café, coton), industries manufacturières, exploitation minière (cobalt, diamant, platine, or *[gold]*, chrome, uranium, manganèse, bauxite), production de pétrole, tourisme

324

En vacances

L'Afrique francophone

La colonisation française de l'Afrique a commencé pendant la première **moitié** du 19ᵉ siècle. Les Français sont arrivés dans la région qui est aujourd'hui la Côte-d'Ivoire en 1842. La France a occupé la région jusqu'à son indépendance en 1960.

Culture notes. A. Point out that the colonization and decolonization processes led to the creation of nations in Africa without any true ethnic, linguistic, cultural, or historic unity and that this has rendered stability and democratization more difficult.
B. Students interested in colonial Africa may wish to look for the videos *Chocolat, Coup de torchon*, and *Black and White in Color*. You should preview all films for appropriateness of content for your student population, however, prior to recommending them.

Abidjan, Côte-d'Ivoire

Le Sénégal

Entre 1895 et 1958, le Sénégal a fait partie de la fédération de territoires français appelée l'Afrique-Occidentale française. Cette fédération regroupait sous un seul gouvernement toute la région **comprenant** aujourd'hui la Côte-d'Ivoire, le Sénégal, la Mauritanie, le Mali, le Burkina Faso, la Guinée, le Niger et le Bénin.

---

la moitié *half*   **un siècle** *a century*   **comprenant** *including*

Le Congo

Entre 1910 et 1958, la France a gouverné l'Afrique-Équatoriale française, une fédération comprenant le Congo, la République centrafricaine, le Gabon et le Tchad.

Le Maroc

Au nord du Sahara, la France s'est établie en Algérie, en Tunisie et au Maroc. La Tunisie et le Maroc ont obtenu leur indépendance en 1956. L'Algérie est devenue indépendante après la guerre d'Algérie, en 1962.

Devinez!

1. Combien de pays africains sont francophones? (9, 22, 68)
2. La situation linguistique du continent africain est très complexe. Les langues européennes sont souvent parlées par les classes cultivées et dans les affaires officielles, mais combien y a-t-il environ de langues diverses parlées dans les régions rurales? (50, 100, 500, 800)
3. Comment est-ce que les premiers colonisateurs européens appelaient la Côte-d'Ivoire? (la Côte-de-l'Or *[the Gold Coast]*, la Côte des Dents *[the Coast of Teeth]*, la Tour d'Ivoire)

Quick-reference answers for *Devinez!* **1.** 22 **2.** 800 **3.** la Côte des Dents (**La Côte-de-l'Or** is the former name of **le Ghana.**)

Au nord du *North of*

COMPÉTENCE 1

Talking about vacation

Les vacances

Suzanne, une jeune Parisienne, va passer ses vacances chez son frère qui habite en Côte-d'Ivoire. Et vous? Où est-ce que vous aimez passer vos vacances?

dans un pays étranger ou exotique   sur une île tropicale ou **à la mer**   dans une grande ville   à la montagne

Qu'est-ce que vous aimez mieux faire pendant les vacances?

admirer **les paysages** (m)   visiter des sites (m) historiques et touristiques   profiter des activités culturelles

bronzer   **goûter** la cuisine locale   **faire des randonnées** (f)

 Suzanne Turquin parle à une amie de ses prochaines vacances.

SUZANNE: Je vais bientôt partir en vacances.
SON AMIE: Et tu vas où?
SUZANNE: Je vais rendre visite à mon frère qui travaille en Côte-d'Ivoire.
SON AMIE: L'Afrique? Quelle chance! Ça va être génial! Tu pars quand?
SUZANNE: Je vais partir le 20 juillet et je **compte** passer cinq semaines là-bas.
SON AMIE: C'est **chouette**, ça! J'espère que **ça te plaira!**

à la mer at the coast   **les paysages** (m) scenery, landscapes   **bronzer** to tan   **goûter** to taste   **faire des randonnées** (f) to go for hikes   **compter** to plan on, to count   **chouette** great, neat   **ça te plaira** you'll like it

A. Où? Où fait-on les choses suivantes?

Exemple    **On nage à la mer.**

> *dans un pays étranger*
> *à la mer*   *à la montagne*
> **DANS UNE GRANDE VILLE**
> SUR UNE ÎLE TROPICALE

1.

2.    3.    4.

B. Entretien. Interviewez votre partenaire.

1. Est-ce que tu voyages beaucoup? Comment est-ce que tu préfères voyager? en avion? en train? en voiture? Aimes-tu voyager seul(e) quelquefois?
2. Où est-ce que tu aimerais passer tes prochaines vacances? Qu'est-ce qu'on peut faire dans cette région?
3. Où est-ce que tu as passé tes meilleures vacances? Pourquoi as-tu trouvé ces vacances agréables? Qu'est-ce que tu as fait?

C. Des vacances exotiques. Changez la conversation entre Suzanne et son amie comme indiqué.

1. Suzanne's friend asks what she is going to do in the Ivory Coast. She is going to visit some tourist sites and help her brother in his clinic **(dans sa clinique).**
2. Suzanne's brother lives on the island of Martinique **(en Martinique).** Suzanne plans on spending a lot of time at the beach, but she also wants to see the tourist sites. Suzanne's friend, who has visited **la Martinique** before, says she should **(tu devrais)** go hiking and try some of the local food specialties.
3. The conversation is between you and your partner. You are going to visit your dream city and your partner asks where you are going. You also discuss when you are taking the trip and what you are going to do there.

Warm-ups for *B. Entretien.* A. Aimez-vous mieux faire du camping ou descendre dans un hôtel de luxe (faire une randonnée ou faire du ski, visiter une île tropicale ou visiter une grande ville, visiter des musées ou aller au théâtre, faire de l'exercice ou goûter la cuisine locale, faire un pique-nique à la campagne ou faire un pique-nique à la plage, rendre visite à des amis ou rester à la maison)? **B.** Have students repeat the more active of the two activities: 1. bronzer / faire une promenade 2. faire une randonnée / dormir 3. danser / regarder la télé 4. rester au lit / faire de l'exercice 5. nager / visiter un musée 6. passer des vacances dans un hôtel de luxe / faire du camping 7. dîner au restaurant / faire un pique-nique **C.** Read the following sentences and have students say where the indicated people spent their vacations: **à l'étranger** *(abroad),* **sur une île tropicale, dans une grande ville, à la campagne, à la mer, à la montagne.** (You may wish to put the options on the board.) 1. Je suis allé(e) en Europe. J'ai visité la France, l'Italie et l'Espagne. 2. Mon frère a fait du ski dans le Colorado. Il aime les activités de plein air. 3. Ma cousine est allée à Tahiti. Elle a pris de belles photos de la mer et des plages. 4. Mes parents sont allés à New York. Ils ont vu beaucoup d'expositions et ils sont allés au théâtre tous les soirs. 5. Ma sœur et ses amis ont fait du camping pas loin d'ici. **D.** Qu'est-ce qu'on peut faire en vacances à la mer? à la campagne? dans une grande ville? à la maison?

Pour vérifier

1. What other verb form has the same stem as the future?
2. All but two of the future tense endings look like the present tense forms of the verb **avoir**. Which two are they?

Talking about how things will be: *Le futur*

You have learned to use **aller** + *infinitive* to say what someone *is going to do*. You can also use the future tense forms of the verb to say what someone *will do*. The future of most verbs is formed by adding the boldfaced endings listed below to the same stem you used for the conditional in *Chapitre 8*. The future tense endings look like the present tense forms of the verb **avoir,** except for the **nous** and **vous** forms.

PARLER	ÊTRE	VENIR
je parler**ai**	je ser**ai**	je viendr**ai**
tu parler**as**	tu ser**as**	tu viendr**as**
il/elle/on parler**a**	il/elle/on ser**a**	il/elle/on viendr**a**
nous parler**ons**	nous ser**ons**	nous viendr**ons**
vous parler**ez**	vous ser**ez**	vous viendr**ez**
ils/elles parler**ont**	ils/elles ser**ont**	ils/elles viendr**ont**

NOTE GRAMMATICALE

Do you remember these irregular future/conditional stems?

aller	ir-
avoir	aur-
être	ser-
faire	fer-
vouloir	voudr-
devoir	devr-
venir	viendr-
revenir	reviendr-
devenir	deviendr-
voir	verr-
pouvoir	pourr-
mourir	mourr-

Note these forms in the future:

il y a	il y aura
il faut	il faudra
il pleut	il pleuvra

Although the future is generally used in French as it is in English, one difference is its use in clauses with **quand** referring to the future. English has the present in such clauses.

> Quand tu **auras** ton diplôme, est-ce que tu trouveras du travail?
> *When you **have** your degree, will you find work?*

Just as in English, you also use the future tense to indicate what will happen if another event occurs first. Unlike with **quand,** you use the present tense in the clause with **si.**

> Si j'**ai** mon diplôme, je **serai** content(e)!
> *If I **get** my degree, I **will be** happy!*

A. Des prédictions. Comment sera la vie des personnes suivantes dans cinq ans? Est-ce que ces gens feront les choses indiquées?

Dans cinq ans...

Exemple   je (être riche)
   Je serai riche. / Je ne serai pas riche.

1. Moi, je... (avoir mon diplôme, travailler pour une grande société *[company]* comme IBM, voyager beaucoup, étudier à l'université, parler français, comprendre mieux la vie, habiter ici, être marié[e], avoir des enfants, être content[e], trouver un bon travail)
2. La personne de mes rêves et moi, nous (se marier, avoir des enfants, acheter une maison, faire beaucoup de voyages ensemble)
3. Mon meilleur ami (Ma meilleure amie)... (passer les vacances avec moi chaque année, habiter avec moi, être comme maintenant, travailler en France, sortir avec moi tous les week-ends, avoir un diplôme universitaire)

Maintenant, dites si vous espérez que les personnes suivantes feront ou ne feront pas les choses indiquées dans les cinq années à venir.

Exemple   mon meilleur ami (se marier, habiter loin d'ici)
   J'espère que mon meilleur ami se mariera. /
   J'espère qu'il n'habitera pas très loin d'ici.

Supplemental activities. A. Have students say who in their household will probably do these things tomorrow: 1. se lever en premier 2. se lever le plus tard 3. préparer le petit déjeuner 4. partir en premier 5. rentrer le plus tôt 6. préparer le dîner 7. regarder la télé 8. lire le journal 9. se coucher le plus tard B. Répondez aux questions suivantes. 1. S'il fait beau demain, qu'est-ce que vous ferez? 2. S'il fait mauvais demain, qu'est-ce que vous ferez? 3. Si vous avez du temps libre cette semaine, qu'est-ce que vous ferez?

4. *[Au prof de français]* vous (pouvoir prendre des vacances, aller bientôt en France, avoir beaucoup d'étudiants intelligents, devoir enseigner *[to teach]* toujours à 7h00 du matin)

5. *[À l'étudiant(e) à côté de vous]* tu (avoir une vie difficile, finir tes études, trouver un bon travail, devoir trop travailler, apprendre à bien parler le français)

B. Un voyage.
Avec un(e) partenaire, préparez un itinéraire d'un voyage que la classe de français va faire ensemble à l'un des endroits *(places)* indiqués. Quel groupe peut imaginer le meilleur voyage? Dans votre description, répondez aux questions suivantes.

1. Irez-vous en France, en Côte-d'Ivoire ou à Tahiti?
2. Quand est-ce que vous partirez et quand est-ce que vous reviendrez?
3. Comment est-ce que vous voyagerez? en avion? en train? en bateau?
4. Descendrez-vous dans des hôtels de luxe, dans des hôtels économiques ou ferez-vous du camping?
5. Qu'est-ce que vous ferez pendant le voyage? Qu'est-ce que vous verrez d'intéressant? Quels sites touristiques est-ce que vous visiterez?
6. Qu'est-ce que chacun devra apporter *(bring)*?
7. Combien est-ce que chacun devra payer pour faire le voyage?

C. Quand.
Créez des phrases logiques en utilisant un élément de chaque groupe. Écrivez au moins deux phrases pour chaque sujet.

Exemples
Je me reposerai quand je finirai mes études.
Je serai content(e) quand j'aurai mon diplôme.

1. Je...
2. Dans ma famille, nous...
3. Le professeur...
4. Les étudiants...

être content(e)(s)   être riche(s)
être nerveux (nerveuse[s])
PARLER FRANÇAIS   ÊTRE ENSEMBLE
faire un voyage   CHERCHER DU TRAVAIL
se reposer   s'amuser   bronzer
FAIRE DU SKI   ÉTUDIER   ???

quand

avoir son diplôme   aller à la plage
passer le prochain examen
VOYAGER EN FRANCE   GAGNER À LA LOTERIE
prendre des vacances   finir ses études
AVOIR PLUS DE TEMPS   sortir ce week-end
ALLER À LA MONTAGNE   ???

D. Entretien.
Demandez à votre partenaire d'imaginer sa vie dans dix ans.

1. Est-ce que tu habiteras encore ici? Où est-ce que tu habiteras?
2. Est-ce que tu seras marié(e)? Combien d'enfants est-ce que tu auras?
3. Est-ce que tu auras des cheveux gris? Tu feras de l'exercice tous les jours? Tu seras plus stressé(e) ou moins stressé(e) que maintenant?
4. Est-ce que tu iras encore à l'université? Où est-ce que tu travailleras? Est-ce que ta vie sera plus facile ou plus difficile que maintenant? Pourquoi?
5. Comment est-ce que tu passeras ton temps? Qu'est-ce que tu feras pour t'amuser? Est-ce que tu voyageras beaucoup?

4. Si vous pouvez aller en vacances cet été, où est-ce que vous irez? C. Est-ce que vous ferez les choses suivantes... ? 1. le jour de l'examen de fin de semestre / trimestre (venir en cours, dormir peu, boire beaucoup de café, être nerveux [nerveuse]) 2. le jour où vous vous marierez (aller à l'église, passer la journée seul[e], être très occupé[e] *[busy]*, manger beaucoup de gâteau, danser, partir en voyage, être nerveux [nerveuse], être content[e], être triste *[sad]*) 3. le jour de la prochaine réunion d'anciens étudiants à votre lycée (rester à la maison, voir de vieux amis, s'amuser) D. Quand vous aurez votre diplôme... 1. Est-ce que vous ferez un voyage? 2. Est-ce que vous visiterez l'Europe? 3. Est-ce que vous vous marierez? 4. Où est-ce que vous habiterez? 5. Est-ce que vous achèterez une maison? 6. Est-ce que vous trouverez du travail? 7. Comment est-ce que vous passerez votre temps? 8. Est-ce que vous serez content(e)? E. Complétez les phrases suivantes de façon logique. 1. Je serai content(e) quand... 2. Nous, les étudiants, nous réussirons aux examens quand... 3. Les étudiants étudieront plus quand... 4. Le professeur de français sera content quand... 5. Je parlerai souvent français quand... 6. J'aurai plus de temps libre quand... F. Quand ferez-vous les choses suivantes? 1. se marier 2. acheter une maison 3. aller en Europe 4. tout comprendre 5. être surpris(e) 6. être content(e) 7. avoir des enfants G. Give students the following situation on a transparency. Vous avez gagné 10 000 dollars et un billet d'avion pour le pays de votre choix en Afrique. Racontez ce que vous y ferez. Utilisez le futur. 1. Le jour de mon arrivée, je... 2. Comme activités culturelles, je... 3. Comme sports, je... 4. Mon hôtel... 5. Le soir, je... 6. Au restaurant, je... 7. Comme souvenirs, je... 8. Comme sites touristiques, je... 9. Le jour de mon départ, je... 10. À mon retour, je...

Stratégies et lecture:
Distinguishing the future and conditional tenses

Learning to distinguish verbs that indicate future and conditional actions makes reading French easier. A verb whose stem resembles the infinitive and whose endings look like the present tense form of **avoir** is in the future tense. Translate verbs in the future as *will . . .* How would you translate the last three sentences below?

Je visiterai l'Afrique.	*I will visit Africa.*
Tu trouveras les gens chaleureux.	*You will find the people warmhearted.*
On aidera beaucoup de gens.	*We will help a lot of people.*
Nous choisirons un itinéraire intéressant.	*???*
Vous aimerez ce continent.	*???*
Tu prendras l'avion.	*???*

Verbs that have the same stem as the future with the same endings as the imperfect are in the conditional. Translate them as *would . . .* How would you translate the last sentence?

J'aimerais travailler dans une clinique.	*I would like to work in a clinic.*
Nous habiterions près de la ville.	*???*

Many verbs have irregular stems in the future and the conditional. How would you translate these sentences?

Tu serais heureux ici.	*You would be happy here.*
Tu seras heureux ici.	*???*
On pourrait vivre plus simplement.	*We could live more simply.*
On pourra vivre plus simplement.	*???*
Nos connaissances en médecine seraient utiles.	*Our knowledge of medicine would be useful.*
Nos connaissances en médecine seront utiles.	*???*
On ferait quelque chose qui compte.	*We would do something that counts.*
On fera quelque chose qui compte.	*???*

A. Conditionnel ou futur? La première phrase de chaque paire est au conditionnel et la seconde est au futur. Donnez le sens de chacune en anglais.

1. Nous aurions beaucoup de travail. / Nous aurons beaucoup de travail.
2. Il y aurait beaucoup d'aventures. / Il y aura beaucoup d'aventures.
3. Tu serais fascinée par les gens. / Tu seras fascinée par les gens.
4. Tu aimerais l'Afrique. / Tu aimeras l'Afrique.
5. Notre vie serait très différente. / Notre vie sera très différente.
6. On pourrait le faire ici. / On pourra le faire ici.

B. Une liste. Regardez le texte qui suit *(Une lettre de Côte-d'Ivoire)* et faites deux listes: l'une avec tous les verbes qui sont au futur et l'autre avec tous les verbes qui sont au conditionnel.

Une lettre de Côte-d'Ivoire

Daniel Turquin, médecin français de 25 ans, travaille maintenant en Afrique avec un groupe de médecins qui sont en Côte-d'Ivoire pour aider les malades. En Afrique depuis deux mois, Daniel vient de prendre une décision qui changera le cours de sa vie. Il écrit à sa sœur qui est aussi médecin, pour lui annoncer sa décision.

> Ma chère Suzanne,
>
> J'ai téléphoné à papa et maman la semaine dernière et ils m'ont dit que tu n'étais pas satisfaite de ton travail et que tu avais des problèmes avec l'administration de la clinique. Si tu n'es pas contente là où tu es, tu devrais penser à venir travailler avec moi en Afrique. Je suis fasciné par les gens et leurs traditions. Dans chaque village que nous visitons, il y a de nouvelles choses à voir et je trouve les Ivoiriens très sympas et chaleureux.
>
> La vie ici est très simple mais pour la plupart, c'est une vie pleine de joie. Je suis venu ici pour aider, mais à beaucoup d'égards, ce sont les Africains qui m'aident. J'ai trouvé la «joie de vivre» ici. C'est pourquoi j'ai décidé de rester ici en Afrique; je vais rester au moins cinq ans... peut-être même toute ma vie. Que penses-tu de ça, ma chère Suzanne?
>
> Tu m'avais dit que tu pensais venir me voir ici en Côte-d'Ivoire. Je te demande de réfléchir à la possibilité de rester. Je te connais et je sais que tu aimeras l'Afrique et qu'une fois arrivée, tu ne voudras plus repartir. Alors, nous serons deux médecins ici au lieu d'un. Comme moi, tu as toujours voulu faire quelque chose qui compte dans le monde. Et ici, on pourra le faire!

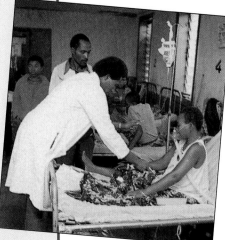

> Tu te demandes sans doute comment serait ta vie ici. Je dois t'avouer que je ne sais pas. Je sais seulement que tu serais heureuse. Il est certain que tu vivrais une vie plus simple mais certainement pleine de satisfaction. Moi-même, j'aimerais bien avoir une petite clinique dans un village. Toi, tu préférerais peut-être travailler dans l'hôpital d'une grande ville telle qu'Abidjan.
>
> De toute manière, nos connaissances en médecine seront très utiles ici et je suis certain qu'on sera tous les deux très heureux. Je te prie, ma chère Suzanne, de considérer sérieusement ce que je te propose et de m'écrire aussi vite que possible.
>
> Je t'embrasse bien fort,
> Daniel

Dans la lettre. Répondez aux questions suivantes d'après la lettre de Daniel.

1. Qui est Suzanne? Où travaille-t-elle?
2. Qu'est-ce que Daniel a décidé de faire?
3. Pourquoi est-ce qu'il aime l'Afrique? Comment trouve-t-il les Ivoiriens?
4. Que demande-t-il à sa sœur de faire? Comment serait sa vie si elle le faisait?
5. D'après Daniel, qu'est-ce qu'ils pourront faire s'ils restent en Afrique?

COMPÉTENCE 2

Buying your ticket

NOTE *Culturelle*

Pour voyager en Afrique, un visa est généralement requis *(required)* pour chaque pays que vous visitez. En Côte-d'Ivoire, il faut aussi présenter un certificat de vaccination contre la fièvre jaune. La devise *(currency)* ivoirienne est le franc C.F.A. (Communauté financière africaine). Un dollar américain vaut environ 700 francs C.F.A.

TRANSPARENCY: 9-4

Warm-up. Dites si vous ferez ou si vous ne ferez pas les choses suivantes la prochaine fois que vous partirez en voyage. **1.** visiter une île tropicale **2.** faire des randonnées **3.** aller dans un pays étranger **4.** goûter la cuisine locale **5.** bronzer **6.** admirer les paysages **7.** faire du ski **8.** prendre l'avion **9.** descendre dans un hôtel de luxe **10.** faire du camping **11.** inviter vos parents **12.** avoir besoin de votre passeport **13.** aller à la montagne

Supplemental activity. Questions orales. **1.** Est-ce que les vols sont souvent en retard *(late)* à l'aéroport ici? Généralement, quand est-ce qu'il y a des retards ici? Quand il y a un retard, comment est-ce que vous passez le temps? Est-ce que vous préférez dormir, lire, regarder la télé ou manger quelque chose? **2.** Est-ce qu'il y a des vols directs d'ici à Paris? Est-ce qu'on peut fumer sur les vols intérieurs? Et sur les vols internationaux? Généralement, est-ce qu'il y a un film? Est-ce qu'on passe des films récents ou de vieux films?

Suggestion for the conversation. Have students first listen to the conversation with books closed for the answers to these questions. **1.** À quelle date est-ce que Suzanne va partir? **2.** À quelle date est-ce qu'elle va rentrer? **3.** Combien coûte son billet?

À l'agence de voyages

Pour faire un voyage à l'étranger, il vous faut...

un passeport
des chèques *(m)* de voyage
un billet d'avion avec un itinéraire
une carte bancaire

Il faut aussi **savoir...**

le numéro de votre **vol**
l'heure de départ
l'heure d'arrivée
la porte d'**embarquement**
la porte de **débarquement**

Aimez-vous préparer vos voyages à l'avance? Il faut lire des guides touristiques pour **connaître...**

la région, l'histoire, la géographie et les sites touristiques

les gens et leur culture

les hôtels, les restaurants et le système de **transport** *(m)* **en commun,** comme le métro ou le train

Suzanne va à l'agence de voyages pour acheter son billet.

SUZANNE:	Bonjour, monsieur. Je voudrais acheter un billet Paris-Abidjan.
L'AGENT DE VOYAGES:	Très bien, madame. Vous voulez un billet aller-retour ou un aller simple?
SUZANNE:	Un billet aller-retour.
L'AGENT DE VOYAGES:	À quelle date est-ce que vous voulez partir?
SUZANNE:	Le 20 juillet.
L'AGENT DE VOYAGES:	Quand est-ce que vous voudriez rentrer?
SUZANNE:	Le 24 août.
L'AGENT DE VOYAGES:	Vous voulez un billet de première classe ou de classe touriste?
SUZANNE:	De classe touriste.
L'AGENT DE VOYAGES:	Très bien. Il y a un vol le 20 juillet, départ Paris-Charles de Gaulle à 8h45, arrivée à Abidjan à 14h50. Pour le retour, il y a un vol qui part d'Abidjan le 24 août à 10h15 et qui arrive à Paris à 16h14. **Ça vous convient?**
SUZANNE:	Oui, c'est parfait. Combien coûte le billet?
L'AGENT DE VOYAGES:	C'est 585 €.
SUZANNE:	Bon. Alors, faites ma réservation. Voilà ma carte de crédit.

savoir *to know* **un vol** *a flight* **embarquement** *departure* **débarquement** *arrival* **connaître** *to know, to be familiar with, to be acquainted with* **les transports** *(m)* **en commun** *public transportation* **Ça vous convient?** *Is that good for you?*

A. Le voyage de Suzanne. Lisez l'itinéraire de Suzanne et répondez à ces questions.

1. Est-ce que Suzanne a acheté un billet aller-retour ou un aller simple?
2. Est-ce que Suzanne voyagera en première classe ou en classe touriste?
3. Quelle est la date de son départ? de son retour? De quel aéroport partira-t-elle?
4. Elle devra arriver à l'aéroport combien d'heures avant le départ?
5. À quelle heure est son départ de Paris? À quelle heure est son arrivée à Abidjan?
6. Est-ce qu'un repas sera servi en route?
7. Quelle est la date de son retour à Paris? C'est quel jour de la semaine?

ITINÉRAIRE

À l'intention de: Turquin/Suzanne

ALLER: Mardi 20 juillet:

Départ de Paris-Charles de Gaulle	8h45
Air Afrique-Vol 189	Classe touriste
Arrivée à Abidjan	14h50

› Un repas et un petit déjeuner seront servis en vol.

RETOUR: Mardi 24 août:

Départ d'Abidjan	10h15
Air Afrique-Vol 376	Classe touriste
Arrivée à Paris-Charles de Gaulle	16h14

› Un repas et une collation seront servis en vol.

Prix du billet aller-retour: 585 €.

Prévoyez d'arriver à l'aéroport deux heures avant l'heure de départ et n'oubliez pas de reconfirmer votre retour 72 heures avant le départ.
BON VOYAGE!

B. Et vous? Choisissez la phrase qui vous décrit le mieux quand vous voyagez.

1. a. Je préfère voyager en première classe.
   b. Je préfère voyager en classe touriste.
   c. Ça dépend de qui va payer.
2. a. J'arrive à l'aéroport bien en avance.
   b. J'arrive à l'aéroport au dernier moment.
   c. Je manque (miss) quelquefois mon vol.
3. a. Si je dois attendre l'avion, je préfère lire.
   b. Si je dois attendre l'avion, je préfère manger.
   c. Si je dois attendre l'avion, je préfère visiter les petits magasins de l'aéroport.
4. a. Si on perd mes bagages, je reste calme.
   b. Je suis furieux (furieuse) si on les perd.
   c. On n'a jamais perdu mes bagages.
5. a. Dans une grande ville comme Paris, j'utilise les moyens de transport en commun.
   b. Je prends toujours un taxi ou je loue une voiture.
   c. Je ne sors pas de l'hôtel.

Suggestion. You may wish to tell students that *business class* is **classe affaires.**

C. Quelques petits changements. Changez la conversation entre Suzanne et l'employé de l'agence de voyages comme indiqué.

1. Suzanne is buying a one-way ticket. There are no seats left (**il n'y a plus de places**) on the day she wants to leave, so she decides to leave the next day instead.
2. Suzanne is buying a round-trip ticket to Montreal. She is leaving Charles de Gaulle airport next Saturday at 10:50 in the morning and she is arriving in Montreal at 12:30 in the afternoon. She is returning to Paris in six months and she will reserve (**réserver**) her flight later. The price is 872 euros.
3. You are buying a ticket for a trip you are planning. Your partner is the travel agent and asks for the pertinent information. You tell when you want to leave and return. The travel agent suggests a flight and gives a price in dollars.

Suggestion. Point out that if *to know* is followed by a word such as *who, what,* etc., you use **savoir**.

Asking what people know:
Les verbes savoir et connaître et reprise des pronoms compléments d'objet direct le, la, l' et les

You have been using **je ne sais pas** to say that you do not know an answer. Both **savoir** and **connaître** mean *to know*.

SAVOIR (to know [how])	
je **sais**	nous **savons**
tu **sais**	vous **savez**
il/elle/on **sait**	ils/elles **savent**

PASSÉ COMPOSÉ: j'**ai su**
IMPARFAIT: je **savais**
FUTUR: je **saurai**
CONDITIONNEL: je **saurais**

CONNAÎTRE (to know, to be familiar with, to be acquainted with)	
je **connais**	nous **connaissons**
tu **connais**	vous **connaissez**
il/elle/on **connaît**	ils/elles **connaissent**

PASSÉ COMPOSÉ: j'**ai connu**
IMPARFAIT: je **connaissais**
FUTUR: je **connaîtrai**
CONDITIONNEL: je **connaîtrais**

Use **savoir** to say you *know* . . .

FACTS OR INFORMATION:

Est-ce que tu **sais** mon adresse?
Nous ne **savons** pas où ils sont.

A LANGUAGE:

Je **sais** le français.
Je ne **sais** pas l'allemand.

HOW TO DO SOMETHING:

Je **sais** nager.
Je ne **sais** pas danser.

Use **connaître** to say you *know (of)* or *are familiar* or *acquainted with* . . .

PEOPLE:

Vous **connaissez** mon ami Mukala?
Je le **connais** bien.

PLACES:

Est-ce que tu **connais** bien l'Afrique?
Qui **connaît** le quartier?

THINGS:

Je ne **connais** pas bien l'histoire de l'Afrique.
Tu **connais** ce film?

Remember that if you wish to replace the object of a verb such as **connaître** or **savoir** with a pronoun, you use the direct object pronoun **le** *(him, it)*, **la** *(her, it)*, **l'** *(him, her, it)*, or **les** *(them)*. These pronouns are placed just before the verb.

— Est-ce que tu connais bien **le quartier**?
— Non, je ne **le** connais pas bien.

— *Do you know **the neighborhood** well?*
— *No, I don't know **it** well.*

Supplemental activities. A. Quelles personnes célèbres savent (bien) danser (chanter, faire de bons films, jouer au basket, jouer au base-ball, jouer au tennis)? **B.** Questions orales. **1.** Dans quel cours est-ce que vous connaissez bien les autres étudiants? **2.** Est-ce que vous connaissez d'autres professeurs de français à l'université? **3.** Est-ce que vous savez si le prochain semestre/trimestre de français va être plus difficile? **4.** Savez-vous si on va avoir le même livre? **5.** Est-ce que vous savez quand le prochain semestre/trimestre va commencer?

A. Quel pays? Suzanne vous parle des gens qu'elle connaît et des pays où ils habitent. Quels pays est-ce que ces personnes connaissent bien?

Exemple   J'habite à Paris. Je **connais bien la France.**

LA FRANCE   l'Allemagne   ???   L'ESPAGNE
les États-Unis   la Côte-d'Ivoire   LE CANADA

1. Mon amie Sophie habite à Berlin. Elle...
2. Mes cousins habitent à Barcelone. Ils...
3. Mes parents et moi habitons à Paris. Nous...
4. Mon frère habite près d'Abidjan. Il...
5. Et vous, vous habitez à *[votre ville]* Alors, vous... ?

Maintenant, elle dit quelle langue chaque personne sait parler. Qu'est-ce qu'elle dit?

Exemple J'habite à Paris. Je **sais parler français.**

B. Tu connais... ?
Demandez à un(e) camarade de classe s'il/si elle connaît bien différents endroits *(places)* de votre ville. Donnez un nom précis. Utilisez le pronom **le, la, l'** ou **les** dans la réponse.

Suggestion for B. Tu connais... ? Allow students a few minutes to think of places to name before beginning.

Exemple la rue...
— **Est-ce que tu connais la rue Canyon?**
— **Oui, je la connais. / Non, je ne la connais pas.**

1. le magasin...
2. la librairie...
3. le parc...
4. le restaurant...
5. le centre commercial...
6. la rue...
7. les appartements...
8. le cinéma...

C. Qui sait faire ça?
Dites qui sait faire les choses suivantes dans votre famille. Dites **Personne ne sait...** pour dire *No one knows how to . . .*

Exemple nager
Tout le monde sait nager dans ma famille. / Moi, je sais nager mais les autres ne savent pas nager. / Personne ne sait nager dans ma famille.

1. bien faire la cuisine
2. faire du ski
3. bien danser
4. jouer au tennis
5. bien chanter
6. parler français

Maintenant demandez aux membres de votre classe s'ils savent faire ces choses.

Exemple nager
— **Marc, tu sais nager? / Monsieur Grant, vous savez nager?**
— **Non, je ne sais pas nager.**

D. L'histoire et la géographie.
Complétez chaque question avec la forme correcte de **connaître** ou de **savoir** et posez-la à votre partenaire.

Suggestion for D. L'histoire et la géographie. Allow students time to prepare before asking the questions.

1. _____-tu une bonne agence de voyages? Est-ce que tu _____ combien coûte un billet d'ici à Paris? _____-tu combien de temps prend un vol d'ici à Paris? Est-ce que tu _____ le taux d'échange *(exchange rate)* de l'euro?
2. Combien de langues est-ce que tu _____ parler? Est-ce que tu _____ l'allemand? _____-tu un peu l'Europe? _____-tu quelle ville est la capitale de la Belgique?
3. _____-tu bien l'Afrique? Est-ce que tu _____ quels pays africains sont francophones? _____-tu bien l'histoire et la géographie de l'Afrique? _____-tu en quelle année la Côte-d'Ivoire a gagné son indépendance?

✓ *Pour vérifier*

1. What four pronouns are used for both direct and indirect objects? Where are they usually placed in a sentence with an infinitive? Where are they placed otherwise?

2. When is an unaccented **e** silent? When must you pronounce it?

Suggestions. A. Point out that with the object pronouns **nous** and **vous**, the verb form matches the subject: **Je vous parle. B.** You may wish to tell students here that in the **passé composé**, the past participle agrees with preceding direct objects, but not with indirect objects. This is explained in the next **Compétence.**

Indicating who does what to whom:
Les pronoms me, te, nous et vous

The following pronouns are used as direct or indirect objects to say *me, to me, you, to you, us,* and *to us.* **Me** and **te** become **m'** and **t'** before vowel sounds.

me, to me	me (m')	Tu ne **m'**attends pas?
you, to you (familiar)	te (t')	Nous **t'**avons attendu(e) une heure.
us, to us	nous	Tu peux venir **nous** chercher?
you, to you (plural / formal)	vous	Je **vous** téléphonerai plus tard.

Remember that object pronouns go before an infinitive in a sentence if there is one, otherwise they go before the conjugated verb. In the **passé composé,** they go before the auxiliary verb.

Je vais **te** voir demain.　　Il ne **nous** connaît pas bien.　　Je **vous** ai vu(e)(s).

The expression **il faut** followed by an infinitive generally means *it is necessary* or *one must.*

Il faut arriver une heure
à l'avance.
*It is necessary to arrive one hour in advance. /
One must arrive one hour in advance.*

Use **il faut** with indirect object pronouns such as **me, te, nous,** and **vous** to say that someone needs something or needs to do something.

Il me faut un passeport.　　*I need a passport.*
Qu'est-ce qu'il vous faut faire?　　*What do you need to do?*

 Prononciation: *Le e caduc*

Unaccented **e** is usually not pronounced if you can drop it without bringing three pronounced consonants together.

Tu m**e̸** parles?
Je n**e̸** veux pas d**e̸** vin.
Vous n**e̸** voulez pas m**e̸** donner cinq dollars?

But pronounce an unaccented **e** if dropping it would bring three pronounced consonants together.

Le professeur m<u>e</u> parle.　　Daniel t<u>e</u> cherche.　　Karim l<u>e</u> veut.

Script for A. Ça se prononce? Read aloud the sentences from the activity.

Suggestions. Point out that the **e caduc** is often dropped in the pronunciation of future tense verb forms (**j'habiterai, nous inviterons**).

A. Ça se prononce? Vous parlez à votre meilleur(e) ami(e). Lisez la phrase que vous diriez le plus probablement à votre ami(e). Ne prononcez pas les *e* en italique.

1. **a.** Tu m*e* parles trop.
   b. Tu n*e* me parles pas trop.
2. **a.** Je vais t*e* donner 100 dollars.
   b. Je ne vais pas t*e* donner 100 dollars.
3. **a.** Tu peux m*e* téléphoner demain.
   b. Tu ne peux pas me téléphoner d*e*main.
4. **a.** Tu m*e* rends souvent visite.
   b. Tu n*e* me rends pas souvent visite.
5. **a.** Tu vas v*e*nir me voir sam*e*di.
   b. Tu n*e* vas pas v*e*nir me voir sam*e*di.

B. Qu'est-ce qu'il vous faut? Dites la même chose en utilisant **il faut** avec le pronom complément d'objet indirect **me, te, nous** ou **vous**.

Exemple   J'ai besoin d'un passeport.   **Il me faut un passeport.**

1. Tu as besoin d'une carte de crédit.
2. Nous avons besoin d'un guide.
3. Vous avez besoin d'un billet.
4. J'ai besoin d'un nouveau bikini.
5. Tu as besoin d'une pièce d'identité *(identification)*.
6. Vous avez besoin d'une réservation.

Maintenant, dites pourquoi il vous faut chacune de ces choses.

Exemple   **Il me faut un passeport pour faire un voyage à l'étranger.**

CHANGER UN CHÈQUE DE VOYAGE   aller à la plage
faire un voyage à l'étranger   PAYER LE VOYAGE
monter dans l'avion   *préparer un itinéraire*   AVOIR UNE CHAMBRE D'HÔTEL

C. Je te promets! Un jeune homme dit à sa fiancée qu'il fait et qu'il va faire tout ce qu'elle veut. Elle lui pose ces questions. Comment répond-il?

Exemple   — **Tu m'aimes vraiment beaucoup?**
— **Oui, je t'aime vraiment beaucoup.**

1. Tu m'adores?
2. Tu me trouves laide?
3. Tu me comprends?
4. Tu m'écoutes quand je te parle?
5. Tu veux me voir tous les jours?
6. Tu vas me rendre visite demain?
7. Tu vas me donner des fleurs?
8. Tu vas m'aider avec mon travail?
9. Tu vas m'abandonner?
10. Tu vas m'aimer pour toujours?

D. Meilleurs amis. Demandez à votre partenaire si son meilleur ami (sa meilleure amie) fait les choses suivantes pour lui/elle.

Exemple   téléphoner souvent
— **Il/Elle te téléphone souvent?**
— **Non, il/elle ne me téléphone pas souvent.**

PARLER TOUS LES JOURS   rendre toujours visite le week-end
retrouver souvent en ville   demander beaucoup de faveurs
ÉCOUTER TOUJOURS   *donner de l'argent*   COMPRENDRE BIEN
embêter *(to annoy)* quelquefois

E. Professeurs et étudiants. Dites au professeur trois choses que les autres étudiants et vous faites pour lui et trois choses que le professeur fait pour vous. Faites deux listes sur une feuille de papier.

Exemples   **Nous vous écoutons...**   **Vous nous donnez trop de devoirs...**

F. Entretien. Interviewez votre partenaire.

1. Est-ce que tes amis t'invitent souvent à partir en voyage?
2. As-tu des amis qui te téléphonent d'un autre pays de temps en temps?
3. De tous les endroits où tu as passé les vacances, quel endroit est-ce que tu me recommandes?

Supplemental activity. Questions orales. **1.** Vous me comprenez quand je vous parle? **2.** Vous m'attendez quand je suis en retard *(late)*? **3.** Vous m'écoutez en cours? **4.** Vous me rendez les devoirs à l'avance? **5.** Je vous comprends? **6.** Vous me rendez visite dans mon bureau?

Les préparatifs

Avant de faire un voyage à l'étranger, il faut faire beaucoup de **préparatifs** *(m)*. Avant le départ, il faut...

s'informer sur des sites Web et **écrire** des e-mails pour **obtenir** des renseignements.

lire des guides touristiques.

téléphoner à l'hôtel pour réserver une chambre.

dire à un(e) ami(e) ou à vos parents où vous allez.

demander à **vos voisins** de donner à manger à votre chien.

faire vos valises *(f)*.

Pour payer le voyage, vous pouvez...

faire des économies *(f)*.

emprunter de l'argent.

payer par carte de crédit.

À votre arrivée, vous devez...

montrer votre passeport.

passer la douane.

changer de l'argent ou des chèques de voyage.

acheter **un plan** de la ville.

---

des préparatifs *(m)* preparations   **écrire** *to write*   **obtenir** *to obtain* (conjugué comme **venir,** passé composé **j'ai obtenu**)   **un(e) voisin(e)** *a neighbor*   **faire ses valises** *(f) to pack one's bags*   **emprunter (à)** *to borrow (from)*   **un plan** *a map*

Suzanne parle à une amie de ses projets de vacances.

SON AMIE: Qu'est-ce que **tu lis?**

SUZANNE: C'est une lettre que **j'ai reçue** de mon frère. Je **lui** ai écrit parce que je vais aller le voir en Côte-d'Ivoire.

SON AMIE: Et **ça lui plaît,** la Côte-d'Ivoire?

SUZANNE: Ça lui plaît beaucoup! Il dit qu'il a décidé d'y rester.

SON AMIE: L'Afrique doit être intéressante. J'aimerais faire un safari pour observer les éléphants, les hippopotames, les **singes**... et les autres animaux.

SUZANNE: Ce qui plaît surtout à Daniel, ce sont les gens et les traditions, la musique et les danses.

A. Avant le départ ou après l'arrivée? Quand on voyage, fait-on les choses suivantes **avant le départ** ou **après l'arrivée?**

Exemple   obtenir un passeport
         avant le départ

1. passer la douane
2. écrire pour des renseignements
3. s'informer sur des sites Web
4. acheter des chèques de voyage
5. changer des chèques de voyage
6. réserver une chambre
7. montrer son passeport
8. lire des guides touristiques
9. demander à un ami de donner à manger à son chien
10. faire des préparatifs

Suggestion for the conversation. Have students first listen to the conversation with books closed for the answers to these questions. **1.** Qui a écrit à Suzanne? **2.** Qu'est-ce que l'amie de Suzanne aimerait faire en Afrique? **3.** Qu'est-ce que Daniel aime en Afrique?

B. Mon dernier voyage. Dites si vous avez fait chaque chose de l'activité précédente avant ou pendant vos dernières vacances.

Exemple   obtenir un passeport
         Je n'ai pas obtenu de passeport.

Suggestion for *B. Mon dernier voyage.* Point out the past participle of **obtenir** (**obtenu**).

C. Que fait-on? Faites une liste de ce qu'on fait dans chacun des endroits (*places*) suivants.

1. à l'agence de voyages
2. à la douane
3. à la banque
4. à l'hôtel
5. sur des sites Web

D. Conversations. Changez la conversation entre Suzanne et son amie comme indiqué.

1. Suzanne received an e-mail from a cousin who is visiting Nice. Suzanne's friend says that Nice must be pleasant **(agréable)** because the weather is nice. Suzanne's cousin likes it because he can go to the beach when he wants.
2. Suzanne's brother is now in a big city that he does not like **(ça ne lui plaît pas)** and he wants to return to a small city in Ivory Coast. Suzanne's friend says she would prefer the cultural activities of a big city.
3. A friend who lives in another city sent you an e-mail about life there. You and your partner discuss why you would or would not like to live there.

---

tu lis (lire *to read*) **j'ai reçu (recevoir** *to receive*) **lui** *(to) him, (to) her* **Ça lui plaît? (plaire** *to please*) *Does he like it?* **un singe** *a monkey*

Contacting people: *Les verbes dire, lire et écrire*

You have already seen the verbs **dire** *(to say, to tell)*, **lire** *(to read)*, and **écrire** *(to write)*. Here are their full conjugations. The verb **décrire** *(to describe)* is conjugated like **écrire.**

DIRE *(to say, to tell)*	
je **dis**	nous **disons**
tu **dis**	vous **dites**
il/elle/on **dit**	ils/elles **disent**

PASSÉ COMPOSÉ: j'**ai dit**
IMPARFAIT: je **disais**
FUTUR: je **dirai**
CONDITIONNEL: je **dirais**

LIRE *(to read)*	
je **lis**	nous **lisons**
tu **lis**	vous **lisez**
il/elle/on **lit**	ils/elles **lisent**

PASSÉ COMPOSÉ: j'**ai lu**
IMPARFAIT: je **lisais**
FUTUR: je **lirai**
CONDITIONNEL: je **lirais**

ÉCRIRE *(to write)*	
j'**écris**	nous **écrivons**
tu **écris**	vous **écrivez**
il/elle/on **écrit**	ils/elles **écrivent**

PASSÉ COMPOSÉ: j'**ai écrit**
IMPARFAIT: j'**écrivais**
FUTUR: j'**écrirai**
CONDITIONNEL: j'**écrirais**

Here are some things you might want to read or write.

un article *an article*
une carte postale *a postcard*
un e-mail *an e-mail*
une histoire *a story*
un journal (pl **des journaux**) *a newspaper*

une lettre *a letter*
un magazine *a magazine*
un poème *a poem*
une rédaction *a composition*
un roman *a novel*

A. Qu'est-ce qu'ils écrivent?
Complétez ces questions avec la forme correcte du verbe **écrire**. Ensuite, posez les questions à votre partenaire.

1. Est-ce que tu _____ des cartes postales à tes amis quand tu voyages?
2. Tes amis et toi, vous vous _____ des e-mails tous les jours?
3. _____-tu beaucoup de rédactions pour tes cours ce semestre?
4. Pour quels cours est-ce que les étudiants _____ beaucoup de rédactions généralement?
5. D'après toi *(According to you)*, qui _____ des romans intéressants?

B. Qu'est-ce qu'ils lisent?
Complétez les questions suivantes avec la forme correcte du verbe **lire**. Ensuite, posez les questions à votre partenaire.

1. Est-ce que tu _____ le journal tous les jours?
2. Pour quels cours est-ce que les étudiants _____ beaucoup de livres généralement?
3. _____-tu des livres intéressants pour tes cours ce semestre?
4. Est-ce que tu _____ toujours les explications de grammaire dans le livre de français?
5. Est-ce que nous _____ quelque chose pour le prochain cours de français?

Supplemental activities. A. Est-ce que vous préférez lire... ? **1.** le journal ou un roman **2.** un roman de science-fiction ou un roman d'amour **3.** une histoire d'amour ou un article sur le sport **4.** un magazine politique ou un poème **5.** un roman historique ou un roman d'amour **B.** Have students complete the following statements: **1.** J'aime lire... **2.** Je lis souvent... **3.** Je ne lis jamais... **4.** Je n'aime pas lire... **5.** J'aime écrire... **6.** Je n'aime pas écrire... **7.** J'écris quelquefois... **8.** J'écris souvent... **9.** Je n'écris jamais... **C. Questions orales.** Est-ce que vous aimez lire le journal? Quel journal? Est-ce que vous lisez souvent des poèmes? Quels poètes est-ce que vous aimez? Quels magazines est-ce que vous lisez? Où est-ce que vous aimez lire? à la bibliothèque? au lit? Quels magazines français est-ce qu'on peut lire à la bibliothèque universitaire? à la bibliothèque municipale? Où est-ce qu'on peut acheter des magazines français? Quels magazines peut-on acheter? Est-ce que vous aimez écrire en français? Est-ce que vous préférez écrire en anglais ou en français? avec un stylo ou un crayon? une lettre ou une carte postale? un livre de poèmes ou un roman? À qui est-ce que vous écrivez souvent? Est-ce que vous écrivez à vos amis quand vous êtes en vacances? Est-ce que vous écrivez des cartes postales? des e-mails? **D.** Est-ce que vous aimez la littérature française? Qui a écrit... ? **1.** *Les Misérables* (Victor Hugo) **2.** *Le Tartuffe* (Molière) **3.** *Le Deuxième Sexe* (Simone de Beauvoir) **4.** *L'Étranger* (Albert Camus) **5.** *Cyrano de Bergerac* (Edmond Rostand) **6.** *Les Trois Mousquetaires* (Alexandre Dumas) **7.** *Le Tour du monde en quatre-vingts jours* (Jules Verne) **8.** *Madame Bovary* (Gustave Flaubert) **9.** *Candide* (Voltaire) **10.** *Rhinocéros* (Ionesco) **11.** *Le Petit Prince* (Antoine de Saint-Exupéry)

C. Qu'est-ce qu'on dit? Vous dites à un ami quand on utilise les expressions suivantes. Complétez les phrases avec la forme correcte du verbe **dire** et l'expression logique.

> Vous pouvez répéter, s'il vous plaît? **BON VOYAGE!**
>
> **Je veux bien.**   À tout à l'heure!   À DEMAIN!   *Salut!*

Exemple   Vos amis vont partir en voyage. Vous **dites «Bon voyage»**.

1. Nous n'avons pas compris le professeur. Nous...
2. Tes camarades de classe et toi allez voir le prof demain. Vous...
3. Tu vas voir tes camarades de classe plus tard, à la bibliothèque. Tu...
4. J'accepte une invitation au cinéma avec des amis. Je...
5. Mes amis retrouvent d'autres amis au cinéma. Ils...

D. En vacances. Vous faites le voyage de vos rêves avec un(e) bon(ne) ami(e). Avec un(e) partenaire, faites des phrases logiques en utilisant un élément de chaque colonne. Faites au moins deux phrases pour chaque sujet de la colonne de gauche. Le groupe qui écrit le plus grand nombre de phrases logiques gagne!

Exemple   **Je dis la date de notre départ à l'agent de voyages.**

Je... Nous... L'agent de voyages (nous)... Nos amis (nous)...	écrire lire dire	des cartes postales des e-mails des sites Web des guides touristiques «au revoir» «bon voyage» à l'hôtel les prix des billets le numéro de notre vol le nom de notre hôtel notre destination la date de notre départ	quand nous achetons le billet avant de partir à notre départ pendant le voyage pour faire une réservation pour obtenir des renseignements à des amis à nos familles à l'agent de voyages

E. Entretien. Interviewez votre partenaire.

1. Est-ce que tu écris plus de lettres ou plus d'e-mails? À qui? Est-ce que tu as écrit un e-mail ce matin? À qui? Est-ce que des personnes que tu ne connais pas t'écrivent des e-mails quelquefois? Est-ce que tu écris quelquefois des e-mails à des personnes que tu ne connais pas?
2. Lis-tu le journal tous les jours? Est-ce que tu l'as lu ce matin? Quel magazine lis-tu le plus souvent? Est-ce que tu l'as lu ce mois-ci?
3. Lis-tu beaucoup de romans? Lis-tu plus de romans d'aventures ou d'amour? Quel est le dernier roman que tu as lu? Quand est-ce que tu l'as lu?

F. Préparatifs. Vous partez en vacances avec un(e) ami(e) qui veut savoir si vous avez tout préparé. Préparez une conversation où vous dites si vous avez fait les choses suivantes.

- écrire pour réserver une chambre
- acheter les billets
- acheter des chèques de voyage
- lire des guides touristiques
- dire à un(e) ami(e) où vous allez
- faire vos valises
- demander à un(e) ami(e) de donner à manger à vos animaux

1. What types of verbs are frequently followed by indirect objects?

2. Where do you place the object pronoun when there is an infinitive in the sentence?

3. Where do you place the object pronoun in the **passé composé?**

Avoiding repetition:
Les pronoms compléments d'objet indirect

You already know how to use **le, la, l'**, and **les** to replace the direct object of the verb.

— Tu fais **ta valise** maintenant?   — Tu as acheté **ton billet?**
— Oui, je **la** fais.   — Oui, je **l'**ai acheté.

Use the indirect pronouns **lui** *(him, to him, her, to her)* and **leur** *(them, to them)* to replace a person or animal that is the indirect object of the verb. Generally, indirect objects can only be people or animals, not things. In French, you can recognize a noun that is an indirect object because it is preceded by the preposition **à (au, aux).**

Verbs indicating communication, such as **parler à, téléphoner à, dire à, écrire à, demander à,** and **rendre visite à,** and verbs indicating giving and receiving, such as **donner à, apporter à** *(to bring),* **prêter à** *(to lend),* and **emprunter à,** are often followed by indirect objects.

— Tu écris **à ta mère?**   — Tu vas rendre visite **à tes parents?**
— Oui, je **lui** écris un e-mail.   — Oui, je vais **leur** rendre visite ce week-end.

Remember that the pronouns **me, te, nous,** and **vous** function as both direct and indirect objects.

DIRECT OBJECT PRONOUNS		INDIRECT OBJECT PRONOUNS	
me (m')	nous	me (m')	nous
te (t')	vous	te (t')	vous
le, la (l')	les	lui	leur

All object pronouns are generally placed immediately before the verb. They go before the infinitive if there is one. If not, they go before the conjugated verb. In the **passé composé,** they go before the auxiliary verb.

— Elle écrit **à son frère?**   — *Is she writing **to her brother?***
— Oui, elle **lui** écrit.   — *Yes, she is writing (to) him.*
— Elle va téléphoner **à Daniel?**   — *Is she going to call **Daniel?***
— Oui, elle va **lui** téléphoner.   — *Yes, she's going to call **him.***
— Elle a parlé **à ses parents?**   — *Has she talked **to her parents?***
— Non, elle ne **leur** a pas parlé.   — *No, she hasn't talked **to them.***

When you use object pronouns in the **passé composé,** the past participle agrees with the direct object pronouns, but not with indirect objects.

Daniel a invité Suzanne.   Daniel a téléphoné à Suzanne.
Daniel **l'**a invité**e.**   Daniel **lui** a téléphoné.

A. Une excursion. Quand un groupe de touristes fait une excursion accompagné d'un guide, est-ce qu'un bon guide fait les choses suivantes pour les touristes généralement? Utilisez le pronom **leur,** comme dans l'exemple.

Exemple   parler de ses problèmes personnels
Non, il ne leur parle pas de ses problèmes personnels.

1. expliquer *(to explain)* l'itinéraire
2. parler de choses ennuyeuses
3. parler de l'histoire de la région
4. décrire la culture
5. montrer les sites historiques

6. répondre poliment *(politely)*
7. demander un pourboire *(tip)*
8. parler dans une langue qu'ils ne comprennent pas

Maintenant, dites si les touristes sympas font les choses suivantes au guide. Utilisez le pronom **lui.**

Exemple   poser des questions
Oui, ils lui posent des questions.

1. téléphoner à minuit
2. obéir
3. emprunter de l'argent

4. donner un pourboire
5. dire «merci»

B. Habitudes de voyage.
Est-ce que vous faites généralement les choses suivantes quand vous partez en vacances? Répondez en utilisant **lui** ou **leur.**

Exemple   Vous dites à vos parents où vous allez?
Oui, je leur dis où je vais. / Non, je ne leur dis pas où je vais.

1. Vous téléphonez à vos amis pendant le voyage?
2. Vous empruntez de l'argent à vos parents?
3. Vous écrivez des cartes postales à votre camarade de chambre?
4. Vous rapportez *(bring back)* un souvenir à votre meilleur(e) ami(e)?
5. Vous parlez du voyage à vos parents?
6. Vous écrivez des e-mails à votre meilleur(e) ami(e)?
7. Vous montrez des photos du voyage à votre mère?
8. Vous décrivez le voyage à vos amis?
9. Vous demandez à votre meilleur(e) ami(e) de vous accompagner?
10. Vous demandez à vos voisins de donner à manger à votre chien ou chat?

C. Et votre dernier voyage.
Posez les questions de l'exercice *B. Habitudes de voyage* à un(e) partenaire au passé composé pour décrire la dernière fois qu'il/elle est parti(e) en vacances. Votre partenaire doit répondre en utilisant **lui** ou **leur.**

Suggestion for *C. Et votre dernier voyage.* Remind students to use the **tu** form with classmates.

Exemple   Tu as dit à tes parents où tu allais?
Oui, je leur ai dit où j'allais. /
Non, je ne leur ai pas dit où j'allais.

D. À l'agence de voyages.
Vous parlez à un agent de voyages. Travaillez avec un(e) partenaire pour compléter les phrases suivantes de façon logique. Écrivez plusieurs choses pour chaque situation. Le groupe avec le plus de phrases logiques gagne.

Exemples   L'agent de voyages me demande **quand je veux partir.**
Il me demande **si je veux un billet aller retour.**

1. L'agent de voyages me demande…
2. Je lui demande…
3. L'agent de voyages me dit…
4. Je lui dis…

COMPÉTENCE 4

Deciding where to go on a trip

NOTE Culturelle

On n'est pas obligé d'aller jusqu'en Europe pour visiter la France! Dans les Antilles françaises, au sud-est *(southeast)* **d'Haïti, on peut visiter la Guadeloupe et la Martinique, deux belles îles tropicales qui sont des départements français d'outre-mer** *(overseas),* **comme Hawaii est un état des États-Unis. Qu'est-ce qu'on peut faire en vacances en Guadeloupe ou en Martinique? Voudriez-vous y aller?**

Suggestion for *Note culturelle.* You may wish to introduce the Martiniquais musical group, Kassav, and the video *Sugar Cane Alley.* Preview all such items for appropriateness for your students.

VOCABULAIRE SUPPLÉMENTAIRE

EN AFRIQUE	l'Afrique du Sud
	la Tunisie
EN ASIE	l'Inde
	l'Indochine
	l'Iran
	l'Iraq
	la Turquie
EN EUROPE	le Danemark
	la Norvège
	la Pologne
	la Suède

Suggestion. Point out to students that the word **états** is *state* spelled backward with an accent.

TRANSPARENCIES: 9-4A, 9-4B

Warm-up. Have students look at the map inside the front cover and answer these questions: **1.** Quelles sont les régions francophones aux États-Unis? **2.** Combien de régions francophones est-ce qu'il y a en Europe? en Amérique du Nord? **3.** Comment s'appelle la grande île francophone près de l'Afrique? près de l'Italie? **4.** Quels sont les noms des deux îles francophones situées dans l'océan Pacifique?

Un voyage

Suzanne va visiter la Côte-d'Ivoire.

Et vous? Quels continents et pays aimeriez-vous visiter?

Moi, j'aimerais visiter...

l'Afrique: **le Maroc,** l'Algérie, l'Égypte, le Sénégal, la Côte-d'Ivoire

l'Asie et le **Moyen-Orient:** la Chine, Israël, le Japon, le Viêtnam

l'Amérique du Nord ou l'Amérique centrale: **les Antilles,** le Canada, les États-Unis, le Mexique

l'Amérique du Sud: l'Argentine, le Brésil, le Pérou, la Colombie

l'Océanie: l'Australie, la Nouvelle-Calédonie, la Polynésie française

l'Europe: l'Allemagne, la Belgique, l'Espagne, la France, **la Grande-Bretagne,** l'Italie, la Russie, la Suisse

L'oasis Kerzaz, Algérie

La Guadeloupe

L'Arcade du Cinquantenaire, Bruxelles

---

le Maroc *Morocco*   **le Moyen-Orient** *the Middle East*   **les Antilles** *the West Indies*   **la Grande-Bretagne** *Great Britain*

Suzanne et un ami parlent des voyages qu'ils ont faits.

AHMAD: Tu vas bientôt partir pour la Côte-d'Ivoire? Tu aimes voyager à l'étranger?

SUZANNE: Oui, j'adore!

AHMAD: Quels pays étrangers as-tu visités?

SUZANNE: J'ai visité les États-Unis, la Chine et le Canada. Et toi? Tu aimes aller à l'étranger?

AHMAD: Je n'ai jamais voyagé à l'étranger mais j'aimerais bien un jour.

SUZANNE: Où aimerais-tu voyager?

AHMAD: Moi, j'aimerais visiter l'Afrique, surtout le Sénégal et le Maroc.

A. Quel continent? Indiquez sur quel continent se trouvent ces pays.

Exemple la Chine
La Chine se trouve en Asie.

> EN AFRIQUE   en Asie
> en Amérique du Nord
> en Amérique du Sud
> EN OCÉANIE   en Europe

1. les États-Unis
2. l'Algérie
3. le Japon
4. l'Australie
5. l'Allemagne
6. le Sénégal
7. le Viêtnam
8. le Maroc

B. Quels pays? Dites quels pays vous aimeriez visiter sur le continent indiqué.

Exemple en Europe
En Europe, j'aimerais visiter la France, l'Espagne...

1. en Asie et au Moyen-Orient
2. en Amérique du Nord et du Sud
3. en Océanie
4. en Afrique
5. en Europe

Marrakech, Maroc

C. Associations. Travaillez avec un(e) partenaire pour trouver l'endroit de chaque groupe qui ne va pas avec les autres.

Exemple l'Allemagne, les États-Unis, la France, la Suisse
les États-Unis: Tous les autres sont en Europe.

1. le Canada, l'Argentine, l'Espagne, le Pérou, le Mexique
2. l'Australie, la Polynésie française, la Grande-Bretagne, le Sénégal
3. la France, les États-Unis, l'Australie, la Grande-Bretagne
4. le Sénégal, l'Égypte, le Brésil, l'Algérie, le Maroc
5. la France, la Belgique, le Sénégal, la Suisse, le Mexique

D. Conversations. Changez la conversation entre Ahmad et Suzanne comme indiqué.

1. Suzanne has visited four countries bordering France. Ahmad has visited four countries in South America and the Middle East.
2. Suzanne is planning to visit four francophone countries in Africa. Ahmad knows she is going to visit Africa and asks which countries she is going to visit.
3. With a partner, talk about your upcoming travel plans, where you have traveled in the past, and which other countries and continents you would like to visit and why.

Suggestion for the conversation. First have students listen to the conversation for the answers to these questions with books closed. **Quels pays étrangers est-ce que Suzanne a visités? Quels pays est-ce que son ami aimerait visiter?** Then have them read along in their books as you play the conversation again.

Supplemental activities. A. Review large numbers by having teams of students guess the populations of the following francophone areas: la France (60 186 000), la Belgique (10 243 000), le Canada (31 278 000), la République démocratique du Congo (51 965 000), la Guadeloupe (420 943), Paris (2 152 000, metro area 9 000 000), Montréal (3 480 000). **B.** Est-ce logique? 1. Je vais aller en Grande-Bretagne, un pays où on parle anglais. 2. J'adore la plage et je vais passer mes vacances à la mer. 3. Je n'aime pas les activités de plein air, alors je vais passer mes vacances à la montagne. 4. Je préfère rester à l'hôtel mais je vais faire du camping parce que c'est moins cher. 5. Si tu aimes la mer, tu peux passer tes vacances à Las Vegas. 6. Je vais aller au Mexique parce que je voudrais visiter un pays francophone.

Quick-reference answers for C. Associations. 1. le Canada: On parle espagnol dans les autres OR l'Espagne: Tous les autres sont en Amérique. 2. le Sénégal: Tous les autres sont des îles. 3. la France: On parle anglais dans les trois autres. 4. le Brésil: Tous les autres sont en Afrique. 5. le Mexique: Tous les autres sont francophones.

✓ *Pour vérifier*

1. How do you say *to* or *in* with a city? with a feminine country? with a masculine country beginning with a consonant? with a masculine country beginning with a vowel sound? with plural countries?

2. With which one of the following do you generally not use a definite article when it is the subject or direct object of a verb: cities, states, provinces, countries, or continents?

Saying where you are going:
Les expressions géographiques

When a place name is used as the subject or object of a verb, you generally need to use the definite article with continents, countries, states, and provinces, but not with cities. Most continents, countries, states, and provinces ending in -**e** are feminine, whereas most others are masculine. Some exceptions are **le Mexique, le Nouveau-Mexique,** and **le Maine.**

J'adore l'Europe. **La** France est très belle. Nous allons visiter Londres, Paris et Nice. J'aimerais aussi voir **les** États-Unis: **la** Californie, **le** Texas, **la** Floride et **le** Maine.

To say *to* or *in* with a geographical location, the preposition you use varies.

	to / in
with cities:	**à** Paris
with feminine countries, states, provinces, and all continents:	**en** France
with masculine countries, states, or provinces beginning with a vowel:	**en** Ontario
with masculine countries, states, or provinces beginning with a consonant:	**au** Canada
with plural countries and regions:	**aux** États-Unis

Quick-reference answers for *A. C'est quelle ville?* Sénégal (Dakar), Maroc (Rabat), Québec (Québec), Belgique (Bruxelles), Haïti (Port-au-Prince), Tahiti (Papeete), Louisiane (Baton Rouge), Guyane française (Cayenne), Côte-d'Ivoire (Yamoussoukro)

Supplemental activities. A. Suggérez l'endroit (*place*) que vous préféreriez visiter de chaque paire. EXEMPLE – On va au Sénégal ou en Égypte? – Allons en Égypte! 1. On va au Maroc ou en Algérie? 2. On va aux Antilles ou en Polynésie française? 3. On va au Canada ou au Mexique? 4. On va en France ou en Suisse? 5. On va en Argentine ou au Brésil? 6. On va en Allemagne ou en Grande-Bretagne? 7. On va en Israël ou en Chine? 8. On va au Japon ou en Australie? **B.** Questions orales. 1. Aimeriez-vous mieux visiter l'Europe ou l'Asie? l'Océanie ou l'Afrique? Quel continent aimeriez-vous le plus visiter? Dans quel pays d'Europe voudriez-vous aller? Et en Asie? Et en Afrique? Et en Amérique du Nord, du Sud ou centrale? Voudriez-vous aller en Australie? 2. Avez-vous envie d'aller en France? Voudriez-vous visiter Paris? Quelles autres villes voudriez-vous visiter? Quelles provinces? Aimeriez-vous mieux visiter Paris, Québec ou Lafayette? **C.** Des avions arrivent à l'aéroport. Dans quels pays arrivent-ils? EXEMPLE Un avion arrive à Dakar. **Cet avion arrive au Sénégal.** 1. Un avion arrive à Houston. 2. Un avion arrive à Toronto. 3. Un avion arrive à Tokyo. 4. Un avion arrive à Mexico. 5. Un avion arrive à Berlin. 6. Un avion arrive au Caire. 7. Un avion arrive à Beijing.

A. C'est quelle ville? Quelle est la capitale de ces régions francophones?

Exemple   Quelle est la capitale de la France?
Paris est la capitale de la France.

Quelle est la capitale... ?
du Sénégal? du Maroc? du Québec?
de la Belgique? d'Haïti? de Tahiti?
de la Louisiane?
de la Guyane française?
de la Côte-d'Ivoire?

DAKAR Paris **Rabat**
Yamoussoukro BATON ROUGE
Papeete CAYENNE Bruxelles
Port-au-Prince Québec

B. C'est connu! D'abord, mettez la forme convenable de l'article défini devant le nom de chaque pays. Ensuite, demandez à votre partenaire quel pays est connu (*known*) pour les choses indiquées.

_____ Grande-Bretagne	_____ Égypte	_____ Suisse
_____ Colombie	_____ États-Unis	_____ France
_____ Mexique	_____ Italie	_____ Brésil

Exemple   — **Quel pays est connu pour le café?**
— **La Colombie.**

Quel pays est connu pour... ?

1. le fromage et le vin
2. le carnaval
3. le chocolat
4. le thé
5. les spaghetti
6. les pyramides
7. la musique rock
8. le sphinx

C. Leçon de géographie.

Votre ami(e) n'est pas très fort(e) en géographie et il/elle vous pose des questions. Répondez-lui. D'abord, donnez la préposition convenable pour dire *to / in* avec chaque pays. Ensuite, jouez les deux rôles avec votre partenaire.

Exemple Londres (_____ Grande-Bretagne, _____ Canada)
— **Londres se trouve <u>en</u> Grande-Bretagne ou <u>au</u> Canada?**
— **Londres se trouve en Grande-Bretagne.**

1. Tokyo (_____ Chine, _____ Japon)
2. Mexico (_____ Mexique, _____ Pérou)
3. Moscou (_____ Italie, _____ Russie)
4. Berlin (_____ Espagne, _____ Allemagne)
5. Hanoi (_____ Viêtnam, _____ Brésil)
6. Alger (_____ Algérie, _____ Maroc)
7. le Caire (_____ Maroc, _____ Égypte)
8. Dakar (_____ Sénégal, _____ Côte-d'Ivoire)
9. La Nouvelle-Orléans (_____ États-Unis, _____ France)
10. Abidjan (_____ Côte-d'Ivoire, _____ Sénégal)

D. C'est où?

Devinez où dans le monde francophone ces sites touristiques se trouvent.

1.

la Grand-Place

2.

le Château Frontenac

3.

Chambord

E. Entretien.

Interviewez votre partenaire.

1. Dans quels pays étrangers as-tu voyagé? Quels pays voudrais-tu visiter? Pourquoi?
2. Dans quelles villes as-tu habité? Quelles grandes villes aux États-Unis as-tu visitées? Est-ce que tu voudrais habiter dans ces villes? Pourquoi (pas)?
3. Qu'est-ce qu'on peut faire en vacances à Washington, D.C.? à New York? au Colorado? en Floride? De ces quatre endroits, où est-ce que tu aimerais le mieux passer tes vacances? Pourquoi?

Warm-ups. A. Play a chain game. Start off by saying **Nous allons faire le tour du monde. Nous allons en France et ensuite...** Each student lists all the places named before and adds another. Check that the correct preposition is used with each country. **B.** Quels pays ont une frontière *(border)* avec... ? **1.** les États-Unis (le Canada, le Mexique) **2.** la France (l'Espagne, l'Andorre, la Belgique, le Luxembourg, l'Allemagne, la Suisse, l'Italie, Monaco) **3.** le Canada (les États-Unis) **C.** Have students suggest a place to go based on the interests you express. EXEMPLE J'aime beaucoup les sports d'hiver. **Allons en Suisse. 1.** Je voudrais faire du ski. **2.** J'aime passer mes vacances à la plage. **3.** J'aime beaucoup les animaux exotiques. **4.** Je voudrais visiter une île où on parle français. **5.** Je voudrais pratiquer mon espagnol. **6.** J'ai envie de voir l'Asie. **D.** Combien de pays est-ce que vous pouvez nommer en Asie / en Europe / en Amérique du Nord / en Amérique du Sud / en Afrique?

Reprise: *Making travel plans and preparing for a trip*

In *Chapitre 9,* you practiced buying an airline ticket and talking about where you like to go and what you like to do on vacation. You also learned to say what people will do in the future. Now you have a chance to review what you learned.

A. Qu'est-ce qu'on fait?
À la fin de son voyage en Côte-d'Ivoire, Suzanne décide de rester quelques mois en Afrique pour visiter d'autres pays africains. Dites ce qu'elle pourrait faire dans les endroits *(places)* suivants.

> **Exemple**   dans une grande ville
> **Dans une grande ville elle pourrait profiter des activités culturelles...**

Qu'est-ce qu'elle pourrait faire dans une grande ville? à la mer? à la montagne?

B. Destinations.
Donnez l'article défini qui correspond aux pays suivants.

| ____ Pérou | ____ Égypte | ____ Sénégal | ____ Maroc |
| ____ États-Unis | ____ Japon | ____ Algérie | ____ Brésil |

Suzanne visitera tous les pays africains de la liste précédente. Quels pays visitera-t-elle?

> Elle visitera...

Maintenant, complétez les phrases suivantes avec le nom du pays logique. N'oubliez pas d'utilisez la préposition correcte: **à, en, au** ou **aux.**

> D'abord, Suzanne ira au Caire...
> Après l'Égypte, elle prendra l'avion pour Alger...
> D'Algérie, elle prendra l'autocar pour aller à Fès...
> Finalement, avant de retourner en Côte-d'Ivoire, elle prendra l'avion jusqu'à Dakar...

C. En Égypte.
Suzanne parle de son itinéraire pour le voyage de Côte-d'Ivoire en Égypte. D'abord, mettez le verbe de chaque phrase au futur. Ensuite, mettez les phrases dans l'ordre logique.

_____ On arrive au Caire.

_____ Je suis en première classe dans l'avion.

_____ Quelqu'un de l'hôtel vient me chercher à l'aéroport à mon arrivée.

_____ Le premier soir, je reste à l'hôtel et je me repose.

_____ D'abord, je pars d'Abidjan.

_____ Après mon séjour au Caire, je vais à Alexandrie où je passe trois jours.

_____ L'après-midi de mon arrivée, j'ai un guide privé pour visiter le Caire. Nous allons aux pyramides et nous visitons le sphinx aussi.

D. Un bon guide.
Quand Suzanne visite les pyramides avec un groupe de touristes, ils ont un bon guide qui est très bien informé. Complétez les phrases suivantes avec la forme convenable du verbe **savoir** ou **connaître.**

1. Le guide _____ parler arabe et plusieurs langues européennes.
2. Après cinq minutes, il _____ le nom de tous les touristes qui font l'excursion.
3. Il _____ très bien la culture égyptienne.
4. Il _____ très bien les pyramides aussi.
5. Il _____ toutes les dates importantes.
6. Il _____ répondre à toutes nos questions.

E. Qu'est-ce qu'ils ont fait?

Qu'est-ce que le guide a fait avec les touristes pendant leur visite aux pyramides? Récrivez le paragraphe suivant en remplaçant les compléments d'objets indirects en italique par le pronom **lui** ou **leur** pour éviter la répétition.

Un très bon guide a accompagné Suzanne et les autres touristes pendant l'excursion. Il a montré tous les sites historiques *aux touristes* et il a expliqué *(explained)* l'histoire de chacun *aux touristes*. Il a dit *aux touristes* qu'ils pouvaient prendre des photos mais il a demandé *aux touristes* de ne rien toucher. Le groupe a trouvé le guide très intéressant et tout le monde a posé beaucoup de questions *au guide*. À la fin de l'excursion, ils ont donné un bon pourboire *(tip) au guide*.

F. Correspondance.

Pendant son séjour *(stay)* en Afrique, Suzanne correspond par e-mail avec son fiancé en France. Son fiancé parle de leurs relations. Complétez le paragraphe suivant avec la forme correcte des verbes entre parenthèses.

Pendant que *(While)* Suzanne est en Afrique, nous _____ (s'écrire) des e-mails. Je lui _____ (écrire) tous les jours mais récemment elle m' _____ (écrire) moins. Normalement, nous _____ (se dire) tout, mais maintenant, quand je _____ (lire) ses e-mails, je suis certain qu'il y a quelque chose qu'elle ne me _____ (dire) pas. Je lui _____ (dire) que je l'aime mais elle ne me _____ (dire) jamais qu'elle m'aime.

Maintenant, le frère de Suzanne lui pose des questions sur ses relations avec son fiancé. Complétez ses questions avec la forme correcte du verbe indiqué. Ensuite, imaginez les réponses de Suzanne d'après le paragraphe précédent.

1. Est-ce que ton fiancé t' _____ (écrire) tous les jours?
2. Est-ce que tu lui _____ (écrire) aussi?
3. Est-ce qu'il te _____ (dire) qu'il t'aime?

G. Des reproches.

Le fiancé de Suzanne commence à lui faire des reproches. Il pense qu'elle va l'abandonner pour aller habiter en Afrique. Qu'est-ce qu'il dit? Utilisez le pronom **me**.

Exemple   ne pas aimer
Tu ne m'aimes pas.

1. ne pas demander mon opinion
2. ne pas écrire tous les jours
3. ne jamais téléphoner
4. ne pas parler de tes projets
5. dire très peu sur tes amis en Afrique
6. quitter pour un autre

Pour rassurer son fiancé, Suzanne dit qu'elle va ou ne va pas faire chacune de ces choses. Qu'est-ce qu'elle dit?

Exemple   Je vais t'aimer!

LECTURE ET *composition*

Note. The vocabulary in this section does not appear in the end-of-chapter vocabulary lists and is meant for recognition only. You may wish to let students know in advance whether you intend to test them on this vocabulary.

LECTURE: Les aventures de Yévi au pays des monstres

Vous allez lire la première partie de **la pièce** de théâtre *Les aventures de Yévi au pays des monstres,* par Sénouvo Agbata Zinsou, né en 1946 à Lomé, au Togo. Dans ce passage, vous allez faire la connaissance de Yévi, **une araignée,** d'**un conteur** et d'**un géant.** En lisant, pensez à deux adjectifs qui décrivent le mieux chacun de **ces personnages.** Avant de commencer, **parcourez** la pièce et faites une liste des mots et des expressions qui se répètent plusieurs fois.

LES AVENTURES DE YÉVI AU PAYS DES MONSTRES

Prologue

LE CONTEUR — Donc, vous connaissez Yévi et je n'ai pas besoin de vous le présenter. N'allez surtout pas le **confondre** avec une vulgaire petite araignée qu'on rencontre dans les coins des murs! Non! C'est un personnage très important.

Entre précipitamment Yévi.

YÉVI — Et alors? Qui a dit que je ne suis pas important? Hein? Qui a dit ça? Je suis dans tous **les contes,** moi.

LE CONTEUR — Bien sûr, calme-toi, Yévi. Calme-toi.

YÉVI — Je veux savoir qui a dit que je ne suis pas important.

LE CONTEUR — **Personne,** Seigneur Yévi, personne. Calme-toi.

YÉVI — On parle de moi partout. Oui ou non?

LE CONTEUR — Oui, Yévi, oui.

YÉVI — Le conte du soir, à la radio. J'y suis. Oui ou non?

LE CONTEUR — Oui, Yévi, oui.

YÉVI — **Les veillées** dans les villages, les villes...

LE CONTEUR — Oui, Monsieur Yévi. On vous connaît...

YÉVI — Et dans les livres? Les livres de contes. De qui parle-t-on?

LE CONTEUR — C'est de vous, Monsieur Yévi. Rien que de vous.

YÉVI — Et alors? *(Un temps)* Même la télé, la télé est venue me filmer l'autre jour dans un conte, **monté par les élèves de l'école...** En présence de **l'Inspecteur,** l'Inspecteur, vous m'entendez!

LE CONTEUR — Justement, Seigneur Yévi, c'est précisément ce conte-là que nous voulons présenter ce soir à nos aimables spectateurs. Alors, Seigneur Yévi, voulez-vous nous rappeler **le titre** de ce conte...

YÉVI — Bien sûr, il s'agit des «Dernières aventures de Yévi—c'est moi-même—donc... de Yévi au pays des monstres»!

LE CONTEUR — Oui, musique pour la parade des personnages!

Entrent tous les personnages pour la parade.

---

une pièce *a play*   **une araignée** *a spider*   **un conteur** *a storyteller*   **un géant** *giant*   **un personnage** *a character*   **parcourir** *to skim*   **confondre** *to confuse*   **un conte** *a story, a tale*   **Personne** *No one*   **Les veillées** *(f) Vigils, Communal evenings*   **monté pas les élèves de l'école** *put on by schoolchildren*   **l'Inspecteur** *(m) the school superintendent*   **le titre** *the title*

Tableau I

LE CONTEUR, *à Yévi* — Alors, mon cher ami, ce n'est pas tout de faire **de la fanfaronnade** comme ton numéro de tout à l'heure...

YÉVI — Mon numéro de tout à l'heure... **Ça a marché,** non? J'ai été **applaudi,** vivement applaudi, chaleureusement applaudi. Ovationné même.

LE CONTEUR — D'accord, mais après tout...

YÉVI — Après tout, quoi? Tu veux dire que j'ai faim?

LE CONTEUR — Ce n'est pas moi qui dis que tu as faim. Mais, c'est que tu as vraiment faim, sérieusement faim.

YÉVI — Mais quoi? La famine, **la conjoncture,** ce n'est pas moi seul que ça **frappe,** mais c'est tout le village, tout le monde, **y compris** toi.

LE CONTEUR — D'accord. Mais sais-tu ce qui fait la différence entre toi et moi? Entre tout le monde et toi?

YÉVI — Ah oui! Certainement, certainement!

LE CONTEUR — Alors, c'est quoi?

YÉVI — C'est que moi, à la différence des autres, je suis un homme important, connu, célèbre, prestigieux!

LE CONTEUR — Non! Mon cher ami, non. La différence, c'est que toi, Yévi, en plus d'être **un affamé** comme tout le monde, tu es **un con.**

YÉVI — Je suis un con, moi?

LE CONTEUR — Oui, parce que le peu d'énergie que tu as dans les muscles, le peu d'air que tu as dans **les poumons,** tu les **gaspilles** dans tes fanfaronnades.

YÉVI — Alors, là, tu m'as insulté. Je ne te pardonnerai pas. Je vais te boxer.

*Il montre **les poings, bombe le torse** et **poursuit** le conteur qui sort en fuyant. Seul, tout **essoufflé** après avoir poursuivi le conteur.*

Ah! Il m'a... Il m'a... **échappé...** échappé... Mais je l'aurai... bientôt... Ah! Je suis fatigué...

Oh! j'ai mal aux pieds... Aïe! j'ai mal aux **genoux...** aux **reins...** Ah! Je comprends: j'ai faim. J'ai encore plus faim qu'avant. Oh! mon **ventre!** Mon ventre a presque **disparu.** Vraiment, j'ai faim!

Il crie.

J'ai faim! J'ai faim!

Il voit entrer un géant de cinq mètres de haut.

LE GÉANT — Qui a crié? (*Un temps*) Qui a crié: «J'ai faim»? (*Apercevant Yévi*) C'est toi, espèce de petit insecte, qui as crié?

YÉVI, *tremblant* — Non... Non...

LE GÉANT — Si tu **mens,** je t'**écrase** du coup du **pouce.**

YÉVI — Oui... Oui...

LE GÉANT — Et pourquoi as-tu faim?

YÉVI — Je n'ai rien mangé depuis deux... trois jours...

LE GÉANT — Comment ça, tu n'as pas mangé depuis deux... trois jours? Si tu mens, je t'écrase...

YÉVI — Oh! J'ai mangé, monsieur, j'ai mangé.

LE GÉANT — Quand?

YÉVI — Euh... Tout à l'heure...

LE GÉANT — Comment ça, tu as mangé tout à l'heure et puis tu cries: «j'ai faim»? Si tu mens, je...

YÉVI — J'ai mangé... J'ai mangé...

LE GÉANT, *menaçant* — Comment mangé?

YÉVI — J'ai mangé... j'ai pas mangé. J'ai faim... j'ai pas faim. Bon, c'est comme vous voulez, monsieur.

LE GÉANT, *riant* — Ha - ha - ha! Petit insecte! Tu dis **n'importe quoi.**

YÉVI — C'est que, monsieur... quand on se trouve en face de vous... vous qui êtes... si fort... Vous qui faites trembler la terre en marchant, vous qui faites tomber les rochers en riant...

LE GÉANT — Assez! Quand on a faim, on ne parle pas.

YÉVI — Oui, monsieur.

LE GÉANT — Quand on a faim, on ne crie pas.

---

la fanfaronnade *boasting*   **Ça a marché** *That worked*   **applaudi(e)** *applauded*   **la conjoncture** *the situation*   **frapper** *to hit*   **y compris** *including*   **un(e) affamé(e)** *a starving person*   **un con** *(vulgar) a jerk*   **les poumons** *(m) the lungs*   **gaspiller** *to waste*   **les poings** *(m) the fists*   **bombe le torse** *sticks out his chest*   **poursuit (poursuivre** *to pursue)*   **essoufflé(e)** *out of breath*   **échappé (échapper** *to escape)*   **les genoux** *(m) the knees*   **les reins** *(m) the kidneys, the lower back*   **le ventre** *the belly*   **disparu (disparaître** *to disappear)*   **Apercevant** *Seeing*   **mentir** *to lie*   **écraser** *to crush*   **le pouce** *the thumb*   **riant** *laughing*   **n'importe quoi** *just about anything*

YÉVI — Oui, monsieur.

LE GÉANT — Quand on a faim, on ne **court** pas.

YÉVI — Oui, monsieur.

LE GÉANT — Quand on a faim, on ne mange pas.

YÉVI — Oui, monsieur.

LE GÉANT, *riant* — Ha - ha - ha! Au revoir, petit insecte.

Il s'en va.

YÉVI — S'il vous plaît, monsieur... s'il vous plaît, grand frère... Oncle... Cousin... Grand-père.

LE GÉANT, *menaçant, se retourne* — Quoi?

YÉVI — Rien, monsieur. Au revoir, monsieur.

LE GÉANT, *riant* — Ha - ha - ha!

YÉVI — Mais... Monsieur... Oncle...

LE GÉANT, *même jeu* — Quoi?

YÉVI — Rien, monsieur... Au revoir, monsieur...

LE GÉANT, *riant* — Ha - ha - ha!

YÉVI — Monsieur, un morceau de... **manioc.**

LE GÉANT, *même jeu* — Quoi?

YÉVI — Rien, monsieur. Au revoir, monsieur.

A. À votre avis. Lisez *Les aventures de Yévi au pays des monstres* et répondez aux questions suivantes.

1. Comment est Yévi? Qu'est-ce qu'il demande au géant?
2. Comment est le géant? Donne-t-il quelque chose à manger à Yévi?
3. À votre avis, qui est-ce que les trois personnages (Yévi, le conteur et le géant) représentent?
4. Le conteur dit que Yévi est con, mot vulgaire qui veut dire **imbécile.** Est-ce que vous êtes d'accord? Pourquoi?
5. Avez-vous de la compassion pour Yévi? Pourquoi?
6. À votre avis, est-ce que les trois personnages devraient changer? Si oui, comment?

B. Qu'est-ce qu'ils deviendront? Avec un(e) partenaire, décidez ce qui arrivera *(will happen)* à chacun des personnages dans la lecture.

Composition

If you have access to SYSTÈME-D software, you will find the following phrases, vocabulary, grammar, and dictionary aids there.

Phrases: Writing a letter (formal)
Vocabulary: Traveling; Calendar; Bedroom; Bathroom
Grammar: Future tense

A. Organisez-vous. Vous allez écrire une lettre pour réserver une chambre d'hôtel. D'abord, organisez-vous! À la page suivante, vous trouverez un formulaire d'un guide touristique. Imaginez que vous voulez faire des réservations dans un hôtel en Côte-d'Ivoire. Recopiez le formulaire sur une autre feuille de papier et complétez-le.

B. Rédaction: Une lettre de réservation. En vous basant sur le formulaire de l'activité précédente, écrivez une lettre pour réserver une chambre d'hôtel. N'oubliez pas de dire quand vous arriverez, quand vous partirez et quelle sorte de chambre vous désirez. Commencez la lettre avec **Monsieur/Madame,** et terminez-la avec **Je vous remercie de votre obligeance, et je vous prie de croire, Monsieur/Madame, à l'assurance de mes sentiments distingués.**

C. Une confirmation. Échangez votre lettre avec un(e) camarade de classe. Votre partenaire vous écrira une lettre confirmant votre réservation.

---

court (courir *to run***)   le manioc** *manioc (a foodstuff made from a plant root)*

Monsieur,

Je me propose de séjourner dans votre établissement:

DU ....

AU ....

❑ CHAMBRE AVEC PETIT DÉJEUNER

❑ DEMI-PENSION   ❑ PENSION COMPLÈTE

Je vous serais donc obligé(e) de bien vouloir me confirmer vos prix, par personne, service et taxes compris, pour:

❑ CHAMBRE 1 PERSONNE   ❑ SALLE(S) DE BAINS

❑ CHAMBRE 2 PERS.   ❑ CHAMBRE 2 PERS. (2 lits)
  (1 lit double)

❑ LIT(S) SUPPLÉMENTAIRE(S) POUR ENFANT(S)

Dès réception de vos conditions, je ne manquerai pas, si elles me conviennent, de vous confirmer ma réservation.

Je vous remercie de votre obligeance, et je vous prie de croire, Monsieur, à l'assurance de mes sentiments distingués.

Signature:

P.J. Coupon réponse international

Nom . . . .

Adresse . . . .

Ville . . . .   État . . . .

Pays . . . .

LA COLONISATION DE L'AFRIQUE

See the *Instructor's Resource Manual* for the video script and activities.

Note. The vocabulary in this section does not appear in the end-of-chapter vocabulary lists and is meant for recognition only. You may wish to let students know in advance whether you intend to test them on this vocabulary.

Quick-reference answers for the following page. The number with each country below corresponds to its number on the map. Each country is listed with its capital. Unless otherwise indicated, French is the official language. **1.** le Maroc, cap. Rabat (L'arabe est la langue officielle.) **2.** l'Algérie, cap. Alger (L'arabe est la langue officielle.) **3.** la Tunisie, cap. Tunis (L'arabe est la langue officielle.) **4.** la Mauritanie, cap. Nouakchott (L'arabe et le français sont les langues officielles.) **5.** le Mali, cap. Bamako **6.** le Niger, cap. Niamey **7.** le Tchad, cap. N'Djamena (L'arabe et le français sont les langues officielles.) **8.** le Sénégal, cap. Dakar **9.** la Guinée, cap. Conakry **10.** la Côte-d'Ivoire, cap. Yamoussoukro **11.** le Burkina Faso (s'appelait la Haute-Volta jusqu'en 1984), cap. Ouagadougou **12.** le Togo, cap. Lomé **13.** le Bénin (s'appelait le Dahomey jusqu'en 1975), cap. Porto-Novo **14.** le Cameroun, cap. Yaoundé (L'anglais et le français sont les langues officielles.) **15.** la République centrafricaine, cap. Bangui **16.** le Gabon, cap. Libreville **17.** le Congo, cap. Brazzaville **18.** la République démocratique du Congo (s'appelait le Congo belge jusqu'en 1971 et le Zaïre entre 1971–1997), cap. Kinshasa **19.** Madagascar (s'appelait la République malgache jusqu'en 1975), cap. Antananarivo (ancienne Tananarive) (Le malgache et le français sont les langues officielles.) **20.** la République de Djibouti (s'appelait la Somalie française jusqu'en 1967), cap. Djibouti (L'arabe et le français sont les langues officielles.) **21.** le Ruanda, cap. Kigali (Le français et le kinyarwanda sont les langues officielles.) **22.** le Burundi, cap. Bujumbura (Le français et le kirundi sont les langues officielles.) You may wish to refer students to the map of Africa at the end of the book and point out the francophone countries.

L'histoire africaine des deux **siècles** derniers est une histoire de colonisation et de décolonisation. À la fin du dix-neuvième siècle et au début du vingtième, les quatre coins de l'Afrique sont sous le contrôle des Européens. En partageant l'Afrique noire, les colonisateurs européens créent des frontières artificielles, regroupant des peuples divers, et souvent hostiles, sous le même gouvernement. Il y a plus de 800 langues indigènes en Afrique, mais de nos jours, la plupart des Africains parlent aussi une langue européenne.

Presque toutes les colonies africaines obtiennent leur indépendance entre 1956 et 1962. À l'exception de la rébellion malgache (1947) à Madagascar, de la révolte de l'Union des populations camerounaises (1955–1958) et de la guerre d'Algérie (1954–1962), l'évolution vers l'indépendance de l'Afrique francophone est **pacifique.** Après l'indépendance, les frontières artificielles **créées par** les colonisateurs **donnent lieu à** des oppositions et des antagonismes ethniques, **aggravés par** les problèmes économiques. Les démocraties fragiles laissées par les Européens tombent souvent sous des coups d'États et sont **remplacées par** des dictatures. Quelques pays comme la Côte-d'Ivoire et le Sénégal réussissent à maintenir la démocratie, **échappant** aux régimes autoritaires.

Le Ministère des Affaires étrangères au Sénégal

---

un siècle *a century*   **pacifique** *peaceful*   **créé(e) par** *created by*   **donner lieu à** *to give rise to*   **aggravé(e) par** *aggravated by*   **remplacé(e) par** *replaced by*   **échappant** *escaping*

Voici une liste des pays francophones en Afrique aujourd'hui avec la date d'indépendance de chacun. Regardez la carte et dites quel numéro correspond à chacun de ces pays. Vous pouvez vérifier vos réponses en utilisant **la carte** de l'Afrique **à la fin** du livre.

l'Algérie (1962)
le Bénin (1960)
le Burkina Faso (1960)
le Burundi (1962)
le Cameroun (1960)
le Congo (1960)
la Côte-d'Ivoire (1960)
le Gabon (1960)
la Guinée (1958)

Madagascar (1960)
le Mali (1960)
le Maroc (1956)
la Mauritanie (1960)
le Niger (1960)
la République centrafricaine (1960)
la République démocratique du Congo (1960)

la République de Djibouti (1977)
le Ruanda (1962)
le Sénégal (1960)
le Tchad (1960)
le Togo (1960)
la Tunisie (1956)

À discuter.

1. En quoi est-ce que la colonisation en Afrique ressemble à la colonisation en Amérique? Quelles sont les différences?
2. Quels sentiments auriez-vous si votre pays était colonisé par une autre nation? Quelles réactions pourrait avoir la population d'un pays colonisé? Pourquoi est-ce que l'évolution vers l'indépendance est relativement pacifique en Afrique?
3. Qu'est-ce que vous savez de la situation politique actuelle en Afrique? Est-ce que cela vous intéresse? Pourquoi ou pourquoi pas?

---

la carte *the map*   **à la fin** *at the end*

VOCABULAIRE

COMPÉTENCE 1

Talking about vacation

NOMS MASCULINS

un Parisien	a Parisian
le paysage	the landscape, scenery
un site	a site, a spot
du travail	work

NOMS FÉMININS

l'Afrique	Africa
la Côte-d'Ivoire	the Ivory Coast
une île	an island
la mer	the sea
une montagne	a mountain
une Parisienne	a Parisian

EXPRESSIONS VERBALES

admirer	to admire
bronzer	to tan
compter	to count, to plan on
espérer	to hope
faire une randonnée	to go for a hike
goûter	to taste
profiter de	to take advantage of

ADJECTIFS

chouette	great, neat
exotique	exotic
historique	historic
local(e) (mpl locaux)	local
touristique	touristic
tropical(e) (mpl tropicaux)	tropical

DIVERS

Ça te plaira.	You'll like it.
là-bas	over there
Quelle chance!	What luck!

COMPÉTENCE 2

Buying your ticket

NOMS MASCULINS

un agent de voyages	a travel agent
un aller simple	a one-way ticket
un billet aller-retour	a round-trip ticket
un chèque de voyage	a travelers' check
un départ	a departure
les gens	the people
un guide	a guidebook, a guide
un itinéraire	an itinerary
un passeport	a passport
le retour	the return
le système de transport en commun	the public transportation system
un vol	a flight

NOMS FÉMININS

une agence de voyages	a travel agency
une arrivée	an arrival
une carte bancaire	a bank card
une carte de crédit	a credit card
la classe touriste	tourist class, coach
la culture	the culture
la géographie	the geography
la porte de débarquement	the arrival gate
la porte d'embarquement	the departure gate
la première classe	first class
une région	a region

EXPRESSIONS VERBALES

connaître	to know, to be familiar with, to be acquainted with
faire une réservation	to make a reservation
savoir	to know

DIVERS

à l'avance	in advance
à l'étranger	abroad
Ça te/vous convient?	Does that work for you?
il me (te/nous/vous) faut	I (you/we/you) need
me	(to) me
nous	(to) us
te	(to) you
vous	(to) you

COMPÉTENCE 3

Preparing for a trip

NOMS MASCULINS

un article	an article
un éléphant	an elephant
un e-mail	an e-mail
un hippopotame	a hippopotamus
un magazine	a magazine
un plan	a map
un poème	a poem
des préparatifs	preparations
un roman	a novel
un safari	a safari
un singe	a monkey
un site Web	a Website
un voisin	a neighbor

NOMS FÉMININS

une carte postale	a postcard
une danse	a dance
la douane	customs
une histoire	a story
une lettre	a letter
une rédaction	a composition
une tradition	a tradition
une valise	a suitcase
une voisine	a neighbor

EXPRESSIONS VERBALES

apporter	to bring
changer	to change, to exchange
décrire	to describe
dire	to say, to tell
donner à manger à	to feed
écrire	to write
emprunter (à)	to borrow (from)
faire des économies	to save up (money)
faire ses valises	to pack your bags
s'informer	to find out information
lire	to read
observer	to observe
obtenir	to obtain
passer	to pass (through)
prêter	to lend
recevoir	to receive
réserver	to reserve

DIVERS

Ça lui plaît?	Does he/she like it?
leur	to them
lui	(to) him, (to) her

COMPÉTENCE 4

Deciding where to go on a trip

NOMS MASCULINS

le Brésil	Brazil
le Canada	Canada
un continent	a continent
les États-Unis	the United States
Israël	Israel
le Japon	Japan
le Maroc	Morocco
le Mexique	Mexico
le Moyen-Orient	the Middle East
le Pérou	Peru
le Sénégal	Senegal
le Viêtnam	Vietnam

NOMS FÉMININS

l'Afrique	Africa
l'Algérie	Algeria
l'Allemagne	Germany
l'Amérique centrale	Central America
l'Amérique du Nord	North America
l'Amérique du Sud	South America
les Antilles	the West Indies
l'Argentine	Argentina
l'Asie	Asia
l'Australie	Australia
la Belgique	Belgium
la Chine	China
la Colombie	Colombia
la Côte-d'Ivoire	the Ivory Coast
l'Égypte	Egypt
l'Espagne	Spain
l'Europe	Europe
la France	France
la Grande-Bretagne	Great Britain
l'Italie	Italy
la Nouvelle-Calédonie	New Caledonia
l'Océanie	Oceania
la Polynésie française	French Polynesia
la Russie	Russia
la Suisse	Switzerland

DIVERS

adorer	to adore, to love

Fresque de la région de Korhogo

In the Korhogo region, artists paint scenes inspired by local fauna and religious themes directly onto cloth.

Suggestion. This chapter deals with getting a hotel room. Highlight these aspects of French travel and hotels and get students' reactions to them: **1.** The French commonly stay in small, in-town hotels without recreational facilities and travel to beaches or other attractions. **2.** In inexpensive hotels in France, a shared bathroom is not uncommon. **3.** A centralized system regulates hotel categories and price ranges in France.

En Côte-d'Ivoire

LA CÔTE-D'IVOIRE

SUPERFICIE: 322 462 kilomètres carrés

POPULATION: 15 981 000 (les Ivoiriens)

CAPITALE: Yamoussoukro

INDUSTRIES PRINCIPALES: agriculture, métallurgie, exploitation forestière, hydroélectricité, pêche *(fishing),* textile, tourisme

Danseur traditionnel ivoirien

Like all the arts, traditional dances are tied to the religious and social life of a tribe.

À l'hôtel

La Côte-d'Ivoire

Additional information. The population of **Côte-d'Ivoire** is made up of many tribes and ethnic groups, largely due to a period of migration and colonialization by tribes from neighboring regions in precolonial times. Before French colonialization, the northern part of what is now **Côte-d'Ivoire** was part of the kingdom of Mali. According to tradition, a small native people, who are now ghosts in the forest, were the original settlers of other parts of the region. Their descendants, the Gagou, along with the Dan, are among the earliest settlers. They were later joined by the Senoufo from the area near the Niger River, who were seeking escape from Islamic influence. Around 1600, the Malinké moved in, gained control, and established a kingdom throughout the country. They converted to Islam and established a capital in Kong. A variety of other tribes also settled in the region. There are now over 60 tribal groups in the country, all with different social systems and a variety of chiefs and monarchs. However, there is a notable dominant traditional consciousness and similarity in beliefs and languages, and in recent times, particularly in cities, considerable intermarriage has occurred. There are also numerous foreign Africans, Lebanese, and Europeans living in the country. About 18% of the population practices traditional African religions, 60% Islam, and about 22% Christianity. However, the different religions are not totally separate and ideas and practices often overlap. Animism, the belief that everything shares a universal life force and is capable of helping or hurting, is at the heart of the traditional beliefs.

Although some French missionaries arrived in the early 17th century, the French did not begin serious exploration of the area until after 1830. In 1893, the region was declared a French colony and named **Côte-d'Ivoire.** In 1958, it became an autonomous republic, gaining complete independence in 1960. Félix Houphouët-Boigny was elected the first president and remained president until 1993. Politically, **Côte-d'Ivoire** is a republic with a presidential regime. There

Aimez-vous voyager? Voudriez-vous connaître une autre culture? Avez-vous envie de visiter un pays étranger ou exotique?

Que pensez-vous de visiter la Côte-d'Ivoire?

La Côte-d'Ivoire est un pays fascinant de diversité et de contrastes! Dans ce seul pays, vous pouvez découvrir des régions géographiques très variées.

*La région le long de la côte avec **ses falaises rocheuses** et ses plages bordées de **cocotiers***

La région centrale avec ses denses forêts tropicales et ses paysages de jungle

La région du Nord, une vaste savane

Il y a aussi des sites touristiques et historiques! Vous pouvez visiter des ruines de la période coloniale, des plantations et des parcs naturels.

découvrir *to discover* **une falaise rocheuse** *a rocky cliff* **un cocotier** *a coconut tree*

Aimeriez-vous connaître d'autres cultures? Il y a plus de 60 tribus différentes en Côte-d'Ivoire, chacune avec ses propres traditions.

are three branches of the government: legislative, judicial, and executive.

French is the official language throughout **Côte-d'Ivoire** and is spoken by the majority of the population. There are, in addition, numerous African dialects and languages, of which Dioula is the most important.

Côte-d'Ivoire has generally enjoyed political and ethnic stability and economic prosperity unknown to many of its neighbors. It suffers, however, from many of the problems common in the developing world: poverty, economic inequality, disease, and decimation of its native animals and forests. The country has established a large system of parks and reserves to protect the animal population and forests from further destruction.

Un séjour dans un pays du Tiers Monde, ce n'est pas pour n'importe qui! Et vous? Avez-vous l'esprit aventurier et de la patience? Si oui, une visite en Côte-d'Ivoire pourrait être une expérience unique!

_____

le Tiers Monde *the Third World* **n'importe qui** *just anybody* **l'esprit** *spirit, mind*

TRANSPARENCY: 10-1

Warm-up activities. A. Quand vous partez en vacances, est-ce que vous préférez… ? **1.** visiter un pays étranger ou rester dans votre pays **2.** réserver une chambre d'hôtel avant votre départ ou chercher une chambre après votre arrivée **3.** lire des guides touristiques et bien préparer votre voyage ou partir sans itinéraire **4.** voyager en avion ou en voiture **5.** dire à tout le monde où vous allez être ou partir sans rien dire **6.** voyager seul(e), en famille ou avec des amis **7.** avoir beaucoup de bagages ou prendre seulement une valise **8.** préparer vos repas ou manger au restaurant **B.** Questions orales. **1.** La dernière fois que vous êtes parti(e) en vacances, où est-ce que vous êtes allé(e)? **2.** Combien de temps est-ce que vous êtes resté(e)? **3.** Quand est-ce que vous êtes parti(e)? **4.** Avec qui est-ce que vous avez fait ce voyage? **5.** Qu'est-ce que vous avez fait?

Le logement

Suzanne va passer quelques jours dans un hôtel à Abidjan avant d'aller chez son frère.

Et vous, quand vous êtes en vacances, est-ce que vous aimez mieux descendre dans… ?

un hôtel pas trop cher

un hôtel de luxe

Préférez-vous avoir une chambre… ?

à deux lits ou avec un grand lit

avec ou sans salle de bains et W.-C.

avec douche

Comment préférez-vous **régler la note?**

en espèces *(f)*

en chèques de voyage

par carte de crédit

Suzanne arrive à la réception d'un hôtel.

Note. You may want to tell students that **le franc C.F.A.** is the currency used in several African countries, including **Côte-d'Ivoire** and **Sénégal.**

SUZANNE: Bonjour, monsieur.
L'HÔTELIER: Bonjour, madame.
SUZANNE: Avez-vous une chambre pour ce soir?
L'HÔTELIER: Eh bien… nous avons une chambre avec salle de bains et W.-C. privés.
SUZANNE: C'est combien la nuit?
L'HÔTELIER: 11 000 francs, madame.
SUZANNE: Vous avez quelque chose de moins cher?
L'HÔTELIER: Voyons… nous avons une chambre avec douche et **lavabo** à 9 500 francs, si vous préférez.

régler la note *to pay the bill*   **un lavabo** *a sink*

SUZANNE:	Le petit déjeuner est **compris?**
L'HÔTELIER:	Non, madame. Il y a un supplément de 2 500 francs. Il est servi entre sept heures et neuf heures dans la salle à manger.
SUZANNE:	Eh bien, je vais prendre la chambre avec douche. Vous préférez que je vous paie maintenant?
L'HÔTELIER:	Non, madame. Vous pouvez régler la note à votre départ. Voici **la clé.** C'est la chambre 210. C'est au bout du couloir.
SUZANNE:	Y a-t-il un bon restaurant dans le quartier?
L'HÔTELIER:	Il y a un bon restaurant pas loin d'ici qui sert les spécialités de la région.

6. Est-ce que vous avez envie d'y retourner? **C.** Est-ce que les choses suivantes se sont passées **avant le vol de Suzanne** ou **pendant le vol de Suzanne?** 1. Elle a téléphoné à l'agence de voyages. 2. Elle a attendu à l'aéroport pendant une heure. 3. Elle a acheté son billet. 4. Elle a fait ses valises. 5. Une hôtesse lui a donné quelque chose à lire. 6. Elle a décidé d'aller rendre visite à son frère en Afrique. 7. Le steward lui a servi du café.

Suggestion for the conversation. Have students first listen to the conversation with books closed for the answer to these questions. 1. Combien coûte la chambre avec salle de bains? 2. Combien coûte la chambre avec douche? 3. Quelle chambre est-ce que Suzanne choisit?

A. Réponses.
Votre meilleur(e) ami(e) et vous allez passer six jours dans un petit hôtel à Abidjan. Répondez aux questions de l'hôtelier selon vos besoins et vos goûts.

1. Vous voulez une chambre pour une seule personne?
2. C'est pour combien de nuits?
3. Vous voulez une chambre à deux lits ou avec un grand lit?
4. Vous préférez une chambre avec ou sans salle de bains?
5. Nous avons une chambre à 10 000 francs. Vous préférez régler la note maintenant ou à votre départ?
6. Comment voulez-vous payer?
7. C'est à quel nom?

B. Un autre hôtel.
Il n'y avait plus de chambres à l'hôtel où Suzanne est allée en premier. Elle est maintenant à la réception d'un autre hôtel dans le quartier. Complétez la conversation entre Suzanne et l'hôtelier comme indiqué.

— Bonjour, monsieur.
— Bonjour, madame.
— Avez-vous _____ *(a room)* avec _____ *(a double bed)* pour ce soir?
— Oui, nous avons une chambre avec _____ *(bathroom)* et _____ *(toilet)* privés.
— Bon, je la prends.
— Ah, attendez. Nous avons aussi une chambre avec _____ *(shower)* si vous préférez.
— Oui, je préfère ça.
— Très bien. Comment préférez-vous _____ *(to pay the bill)?*
— _____ *(In cash).*
— Alors, vous avez la chambre numéro 12, _____ *(at the end of the hallway).*
— Merci, monsieur.
— Je vous en prie.

C. À la réception.
Changez la conversation entre Suzanne et l'hôtelier comme indiqué.

1. The desk clerk asks Suzanne how she will pay the bill. Suzanne says she's going to pay with traveler's checks.
2. Suzanne asks for a room with a double bed, a bath, and a private toilet, but the only room available has a shower and two single beds. Suzanne decides to take the room.
3. You and a friend are going to stay at a hotel in Abidjan. Before you go there, you discuss what kind of room you would like to have and decide how you will pay the bill.

---

compris(e) *included* **la clé** *the key*

Suggestions. A. Point out that the past participle of the verb in the relative clause agrees with the noun that **que** represents. **B.** Point out to students that **que** changes to **qu'** before a vowel sound. **Qui** does not.

Specifying which one: *Les pronoms relatifs qui et que*

Sometimes you need to use a whole phrase to clarify which person or object you are talking about. The phrase that describes the noun is a relative clause. The word that begins the phrase, referring back to the noun described, is a relative pronoun.

La chambre **que** vous avez réservée a une salle de bains.	*The room **that** you reserved has a bathroom.*
Je préférerais la chambre **qui** a une douche.	*I would prefer the room **that** has a shower.*

The relative pronouns **qui** and **que** are both used for people and things. The choice depends on how the pronoun functions in the relative clause.

In the following examples, note how the relative pronouns are used to combine two sentences talking about the same thing. The relative clause is placed immediately after the noun it describes.

Use **qui** for people or things when they are the *subject* of the relative clause. Since **qui** is the subject, it is followed by a verb. It can mean *that, which,* or *who.*

Je connais **un restaurant ivoirien. Il** est près d'ici.
Je connais **un restaurant ivoirien qui** est près d'ici.

Le parc est très beau. **Le parc** est au coin de la rue Marchand.
Le parc qui est au coin de la rue Marchand est très beau.

Use **que (qu')** for people or things when they are the *direct object* in the relative clause. It can mean *that, which, whom,* or it may be omitted in English.

Le musée est très intéressant. Suzanne va visiter **le musée.**
Le musée que Suzanne va visiter est très intéressant.

Le Climbié est **un restaurant ivoirien.** J'aime bien **ce restaurant.**
Le Climbié est **un restaurant ivoirien que** j'aime bien.

A. Préférences. Demandez à votre partenaire ses préférences quand il/elle voyage. Utilisez le pronom **qui** avec les cinq premières phrases et **que** avec le second groupe à la page suivante.

> **Exemple**   les restaurants (servir de la grande cuisine, ne pas être chers)
> — **Est-ce que tu préfères les restaurants qui servent de la grande cuisine ou les restaurants qui ne sont pas chers?**
> — **Je préfère les restaurants qui servent de la grande cuisine.**

1. les voyages (être bien organisés, être pleins d'aventures *[full of adventure]*)
2. les hôtels (être très chers, ne pas être trop chers)
3. les voitures de location (être grosses et confortables, être plus économiques)
4. les amis (aimer sortir le soir, préférer rester à l'hôtel)
5. les chambres (avoir une salle de bains privée, être moins chères)

Exemple les sports (on pratique à la montagne, on pratique à la plage)
— **Est-ce que tu préfères les sports qu'on pratique à la montagne ou les sports qu'on pratique à la plage?**
— **Je préfère les sports qu'on pratique à la montagne.**

1. les voyages (on fait avec un ou deux amis, on fait avec un grand groupe de touristes)
2. les activités (on fait dans une grande ville, on fait à la campagne, on fait à la plage)
3. les hommes / les femmes (tu rencontres au musée, tu rencontres en boîte)
4. la cuisine (on sert dans les restaurants de la région, on sert dans un fast-food)
5. les voyages (tu fais avec tes parents, tu fais avec des amis, tu fais seul[e])

B. Devinettes. Complétez les descriptions suivantes avec **qui** ou **que** et devinez quel endroit *(place)* francophone est décrit.

Exemple VOUS COMPLÉTEZ: C'est un continent **qui** a 51 pays.
que les Européens ont colonisé au dix-neuvième siècle.

VOUS DEVINEZ: **C'est l'Afrique?**

1. C'est un pays _____ est resté neutre pendant la Seconde Guerre mondiale *(World War)*.
_____ beaucoup de gens visitent pour faire du ski.
2. C'est un pays _____ la France a colonisé en 1882.
_____ est la destination des participants à la course automobile Paris-Dakar.
3. C'est une île _____ on voit sur les tableaux de Paul Gauguin.
_____ est dans l'océan Pacifique.
4. C'est un pays _____ se trouve en Afrique du Nord.
_____ on voit dans le film *Casablanca*.
5. C'est une ville _____ a plus de trois millions d'habitants.
_____ on appelait Ville-Marie en 1642, mais son nom aujourd'hui veut dire **montagne royale**.

Option for *B. Devinettes.* You may wish to turn this into a contest, adding supplemental questions. Divide the class into teams of four or five. The first team tries to complete **1** correctly. If they use the correct relative pronouns, they get to guess to what the clues refer. If they do not use the correct pronouns, the second team gets to try. The first group to use the correct pronouns and guess what place is being described wins a point.

Quick-reference answers for *B. Devinettes.* 1. la Suisse 2. le Sénégal 3. Tahiti 4. le Maroc 5. Montréal

C. Opinions. Utilisez un élément de chaque colonne pour expliquer le genre d'homme, de femme ou d'ami(e) que vous aimez ou que vous n'aimez pas.

| J'aime...

 Je n'aime pas... | les hommes <br> les femmes <br> les ami(e)s | qui <br> que | font bien la cuisine <br> parlent beaucoup / parlent peu <br> adorent le sport / les études / ???
 mes parents préfèrent <br> fument beaucoup <br> on rencontre en boîte / à l'université / ???
 ont les yeux bruns / bleus / noirs / ???
 sont grand(e)s / romantiques / ???
 aiment les chiens / les chats / ???
 ??? |

Warm-up for *A. Dans le guide.* Have students look at the guidebook symbols and read the descriptions of the two hotels and answer these questions. **1.** Quel est le numéro de téléphone de l'hôtel Agora St-Germain? Est-ce qu'il y a un ascenseur? Est-ce qu'il y a un restaurant? Est-ce qu'on peut regarder la télévision dans les chambres? **2.** Quelle est l'adresse de l'hôtel Concorde La Fayette? Comment s'appellent les restaurants? Est-ce qu'il y a un ascenseur? Combien de chambres est-ce qu'il y a? Combien coûte la chambre la moins chère?

Script for *A. Dans le guide.* EXEMPLE Non, monsieur, le petit déjeuner n'est pas compris. Il y a un supplément de 8 euros. **1.** Notre chambre la moins chère est à 290 euros la nuit. **2.** Le bar est au trente-troisième étage. **3.** Non, madame, nous n'avons pas de restaurant. **4.** Le petit déjeuner coûte 22 euros par personne. **5.** La spécialité de notre restaurant, l'Étoile d'Or, est le dos de saumon en vessie.

Stratégies et compréhension auditive:
Anticipating a response

When you cannot understand everything you hear, use what you can understand, as well as other verbal and nonverbal cues such as circumstances, tone of voice, and appearance to guess how people will respond. Written materials such as guidebooks or signs on the wall can also help you anticipate what people will say in a particular situation.

A. Dans le guide. Il est plus facile d'anticiper ce qu'on vous dira à la réception si vous lisez un guide avant d'arriver. Familiarisez-vous avec la description de l'hôtel Concorde La Fayette et de l'hôtel Agora St-Germain dans le *Guide Michelin*. Pour chaque phrase que vous entendez, décidez dans quel hôtel se trouve la personne qui parle. Une explication des symboles se trouve ci-dessous *(below)*.

Exemple	VOUS ENTENDEZ:	Non, monsieur, le petit déjeuner n'est pas compris. Il y a un supplément de 8 euros.
	VOUS RÉPONDEZ:	**C'est l'hôtel Agora St-Germain.**

Agora St-Germain sans rest, 42 r. Bernardins (5ᵉ) ✆ 01 46 34 13 00, Fax 01 46 34 75 05 – 🛗 TV ☎ 📞 AE ⓪ GB JCB. ❊
☲ 8 – **39 ch** 100/135.　　　　　　　　　　　　　　　**K 15**

Concorde La Fayette M, 3 pl. Gén. Koenig ✆ 01 40 68 50 68, Fax 01 40 68 50 43, « Bar panoramique au 33ᵉ étage ≼ Paris » – 🛗 ✕ ☰ TV ☎ 📞 – 🕭 40 à 2 000. AE ⓪ GB JCB. ❊
voir rest. **L'Étoile d'Or** ci-après - **L'Arc-en-Ciel** ✆ 01 40 68 51 25 *(fermé août)* **Repas** 22/35 ⚘, enf. 15 – **Les Saisons** (coffee shop) ✆ 01 40 68 51 19 **Repas** 23 et carte 28/40 ⚘, enf. 10 – ☲ 22 – **966 ch** 290/400, 34 appart.　**E 6**

L'installation

30 ch	*Nombre de chambres*
🛗	*Ascenseur*
☰	*Air conditionné (dans tout ou partie de l'établissement)*
TV	*Télévision dans la chambre*
✕	*Chambres réservées aux non-fumeurs*
☎	*Téléphone dans la chambre, direct avec l'extérieur*
📞	*Prise Modem-Minitel dans la chambre*
🦽	*Chambres accessibles aux handicapés physiques*
🌳	*Repas servis au jardin ou en terrasse*
🏋	*Salle de remise en forme*
🏊	*Piscine : de plein air ou couverte*
🏖	*Plage aménagée – Jardin de repos*
🎾	*Tennis à l'hôtel*
25 à 150	*Salles de conférences : capacité des salles*
🚗	*Garage dans l'hôtel (généralement payant)*
P	*Parking réservé à la clientèle*
P	*Parking clos réservé à la clientèle*
❊	*Accès interdit aux chiens (dans tout ou partie de l'établissement)*
Fax	*Transmission de documents par télécopie*
mai-oct.	*Période d'ouverture, communiquée par l'hôtelier*
sais.	*Ouverture probable en saison mais dates non précisées. En l'absence de mention, l'établissement est ouvert toute l'année.*

Repas _____

enf. 9	*Prix du menu pour enfants*
⚘	*Établissement proposant un menu simple à moins de 12€*

Menus à prix fixe :

Repas 12,50 (déj.)	*12,50€ (déj.) servi au déjeuner uniquement*
17/23	*minimum 17€, maximum 23€*
bc	*Boisson comprise*
⚘	*Vin de table en carafe*

Repas à la carte :

Repas carte 22 à 45	*Le premier prix correspond à un repas normal comprenant : hors-d'œuvre, plat garni et dessert. Le 2ᵉ prix concerne un repas plus complet (avec spécialité) comprenant : deux plats, fromage et dessert (boisson non comprise).*

Chambres _____

ch 50/200	*Prix minimum 50€ pour une chambre d'une personne et prix maximum 200€ pour une chambre de deux personnes*
29 ch ☲ 58/205	*Prix des chambres petit déjeuner compris*
☲ 5,5	*Prix du petit déjeuner (généralement servi dans la chambre)*

B. Le ton de la voix. Des touristes arrivent dans un hôtel à Paris. Écoutez le début de leurs conversations. Pour chacune, écoutez le ton de la voix (tone of voice) pour deviner la suite (what follows), **a** ou **b**.

1. **a.** C'est bien. Nous allons prendre la chambre.
   b. Est-ce que vous avez quelque chose de moins cher?
2. **a.** Nous préférons une chambre avec salle de bains.
   b. Bon, c'est bien. Je vais prendre cette chambre.
3. **a.** Voici votre clé, monsieur. Vous avez la chambre numéro 385.
   b. Je regrette, monsieur, mais nous n'avons pas de réservation à votre nom.

À la réception

Deux touristes descendent à l'hôtel Floride Étoile. Lisez ce que le *Guide Michelin* dit de cet hôtel. Ensuite, écoutez la conversation pour déterminer le prix de leur chambre.

> **Floride Étoile** sans rest, 14, r. St-Didier ⊠ 75116 ✆ 01 47 27 23 36, Fax 01 47 27 82 87 –
> ⓘ 📺 ☎ – ♿ 40. AE ⓞ GB JCB. ✳️   **G 7**
> ☕ 7 – **60 ch** 105/150.

A. L'hôtel Floride Étoile. Écoutez la conversation une seconde fois et répondez à ces questions.

1. Est-ce que les touristes ont une réservation?
2. Pourquoi est-ce que les touristes ne veulent pas la première chambre?
3. Combien coûte le petit déjeuner? Où est-ce qu'il est servi?
4. Quel est le numéro de leur chambre?

B. À la réception. Imaginez que vous êtes à la réception de l'hôtel Agora St-Germain, de l'hôtel Concorde La Fayette ou de l'hôtel Floride Étoile. Selon les renseignements du *Guide Michelin*, préparez une conversation avec un(e) autre étudiant(e) où l'un(e) de vous demande une chambre. Ensuite, présentez votre conversation à la classe qui va deviner dans quel hôtel vous êtes.

À l'hôtel ◼ *trois cent soixante-neuf* **369**

Script for *B. Le ton de la voix.*
1. – Nous cherchons une chambre pour deux nuits.
– J'ai une chambre avec salle de bains à 123 € la nuit.
– *(Said with shock and disbelief in voice.)* 123 € la nuit!
2. – Je voudrais une chambre pour une semaine.
– Voyons... J'ai une chambre sans salle de bains pour 75 € la nuit.
– *(Said with satisfaction in voice.)* Ah... 75 € la nuit?
3. – Je m'appelle Georges Massé. J'ai réservé une chambre pour trois nuits.
– *(Said with confusion.)* Massé? Ça s'écrit comment?
– M-A-S-S-É... Voici ma carte de crédit.
– Voyons... euh... *(Said with hesitation in voice.)*

Script for *À la réception.*
– Bonjour, monsieur. Nous cherchons une chambre.
– *(With hesitation in voice.)* Euh... vous avez une réservation?
– Non, nous venons d'arriver.
– Voyons... il ne reste plus grand-chose. C'est pour combien de nuits?
– C'est pour trois nuits. Nous préférons une chambre à deux lits si possible.
– J'ai une chambre à 125 euros la nuit.
– *(With slight disappointment in voice.)* Vous n'avez pas quelque chose de moins cher?
– Euh, voyons... j'ai une chambre avec un grand lit à 105 euros la nuit.
– Le petit déjeuner est compris?
– Non, mademoiselle. Il y a un supplément de sept euros par personne. Il est servi dans votre chambre entre 7h et 9h30.
– La chambre est avec salle de bains, n'est-ce pas?
– Oui, mademoiselle.
– Bon, c'est bien. Nous allons la prendre.
– Vous payez par carte de crédit?
– Oui, vous acceptez la carte American Express?
– Oui, bien sûr... Voilà votre clé. Vous avez la chambre 38. C'est au troisième étage au bout du couloir. L'ascenseur est derrière vous à droite.
– Merci, monsieur.
– Je vous en prie, mademoiselle.
– Oh, pardon, monsieur. Il y a un restaurant dans l'hôtel?
– Non, mademoiselle, je regrette. Mais il y en a de très bons dans le quartier.

Warm-up activities. **A. 1.** Dans la classe, qui a les yeux gris (bruns, bleus, verts)? **2.** Qui a les cheveux blonds (gris, blancs, roux, noirs, bruns)? **3.** Qui a les cheveux longs? **4.** Qui a les cheve
très courts? **5.** Qui a une barbe? **6.** Qui a une moustache? **7.** Qui porte des lunettes? **8.** Est-ce que vous vous lavez les cheveux tous les jours? **9.** Est-ce que vous vous êtes lavé les cheveux ce ma
10. Combien de fois par jour est-ce que vous vous brossez les dents? **11.** Est-ce que vous vous rasez tous les jours? **12.** Est-ce que vous vous êtes rasé(e) ce matin? *(Continues on next page.)*

COMPÉTENCE 2

Going to the doctor

NOTE Culturelle

Daniel travaille en Côte-d'Ivoire pour Médecins sans frontières *(Doctors without Borders)*. Fondée en 1971 par un groupe de médecins et journalistes francophones, cette organisation humanitaire est actuellement présente dans plus de 80 pays du monde. Son objectif est d'apporter de l'aide médicale aux nécessiteux et de donner une voix *(voice)* aux victimes de violations des droits de l'homme *(human rights)*.

TRANSPARENCIES: 10-2A, 10-2B

VOCABULAIRE SUPPLÉMENTAIRE

la cheville *the ankle*
le cou *the neck*
les doigts de pied *the toes*
le dos *the back*
l'épaule *(f) the shoulder*
le genou *the knee*
la peau *the skin*
la poitrine *the chest*
les poumons *(m) the lungs*
les reins *(m) the kidneys*
avoir de la fièvre *to have a fever*
avoir le nez bouché *to have a stopped-up nose*
avoir le nez qui coule *to have a runny nose*
se brûler la main *to burn your hand*
se casser la jambe *to break your leg*
se couper le doigt *to cut your finger*
se fouler la cheville *to sprain your ankle*
faire une piqûre *to give a shot*
prendre la température *to take your temperature*

Suggestion for the conversation. First have students listen to the conversation for the answers to these questions with books closed. 1. Quels sont deux symptômes de la patiente? 2. Qu'est-ce qu'elle a?

Chez le médecin

Savez-vous communiquer avec **le médecin** si vous tombez **malade** pendant un voyage dans un pays francophone?

— Où est-ce que vous **avez mal?**
— J'ai mal à la tête et au ventre.

LE CORPS
la tête
l'œil *(m)* *(pl* les yeux)
le nez
les dents *(f)*
l'oreille *(f)*
la bouche
la gorge
la main
le bras
les doigts *(m)*
le ventre
la jambe
le pied *(m)*

— Quels autres symptômes avez-vous?

— Je tousse.

— J'éternue.

— J'ai une indigestion et j'ai envie de **vomir.**

Avez-vous **la grippe? un rhume?** un virus? des allergies? Êtes-vous **enceinte?**

 Après son arrivée, Suzanne passe la journée avec son frère à sa clinique. Son frère parle à une patiente qui est très malade.

DANIEL: Bonjour, madame. **Qu'est-ce qui ne va pas** aujourd'hui?
LA PATIENTE: Je ne sais pas exactement. **Je me sens** mal. Je tousse, j'**ai des frissons** et j'ai mal un peu partout.
DANIEL: Vous avez mal à la gorge?
LA PATIENTE: Oui, très.
DANIEL: Vous avez la grippe.
LA PATIENTE: Qu'est-ce que je devrais faire?
DANIEL: Je vais vous donner **une ordonnance.** Il faut que vous preniez ces médicaments trois fois par jour. **Il vaut mieux** que vous restiez au lit et il est important que vous buviez beaucoup de liquides. Mais **il ne faut pas que vous** buviez d'alcool.

---

un médecin *a doctor* **malade** *sick* **avoir mal (à)...** *one's... hurts* **la gorge** *the throat* **vomir** *to vomit, to throw up* **la grippe** *the flu* **un rhume** *a cold* **enceinte** *pregnant* **Qu'est-ce qui ne va pas?** *What's wrong?* **je me sens** *(se sentir to feel conjugué comme* **sortir)** **avoir des frissons** *to have the shivers* **une ordonnance** *a prescription* **il vaut mieux** *it is better* **il ne faut pas que vous...** *you must not . . .*

A. Descriptions. Décrivez le corps des personnes ou des animaux suivants.

Exemple   un vampire
           Il a les yeux rouges et de grandes dents.

1. un cyclope   **2.** un serpent   **3.** un éléphant   **4.** un extra-terrestre

B. Qu'est-ce qui ne va pas? Quels symptômes ont-ils?

Exemple   **Il a mal aux yeux.**

Exemple

1.

2.

3.

4.

5.

C. Des allergies. Vous êtes allé(e) chez le médecin parce que vous avez des allergies. Répondez aux questions suivantes.

1. Qu'est-ce qui ne va pas?
2. Est-ce que vous avez des frissons?
3. Où est-ce que vous avez mal?
4. Est-ce que vous avez d'autres symptômes?

D. Entretien. Interviewez votre partenaire.

1. La dernière fois que tu as été malade est-ce que tu avais mal à la tête? à la gorge? Est-ce que tu avais des frissons? Est-ce que tu es allé(e) chez le médecin? Qu'est-ce que tu avais? Est-ce que tu as pris des médicaments?
2. Est-ce que tu as des allergies? Pendant quels mois as-tu des symptômes? Quels symptômes as-tu? Est-ce que tu prends des médicaments? Est-ce que tu vas chez le médecin pour une ordonnance ou est-ce que tu achètes des médicaments sans ordonnance?

E. Une consultation. Changez la conversation entre Daniel et la patiente comme indiqué.

1. The patient often has indigestion and feels like throwing up. The doctor tells her he thinks she is pregnant.
2. The patient has a virus. Her stomach hurts, she is not hungry, and she feels like throwing up. The doctor gives her a prescription and tells her to stay in bed and drink a lot of liquids.
3. Imagine that you are at the doctor's office with the symptoms you had the last time you were ill.

1. What do you use as the subjunctive stem for all verb forms except **nous** and **vous?** What endings do you use?
2. For most verbs, the **nous** and **vous** forms of the subjunctive look just like what other verb tense?
3. When do you use the subjunctive?

Note. Irregular verbs in the subjunctive are presented in the next section, where there is additional practice.

Giving advice: *Les expressions impersonnelles et les verbes réguliers au subjonctif*

You can use the following impersonal expressions to give advice. When giving advice in general, rather than to someone in particular, use an infinitive after them. Although **il faut** means *it is necessary*, **il ne faut pas** means *one should not* or *one must not.* To say *it's not necessary,* use **il n'est pas nécessaire.**

Il faut	Il faut prendre des médicaments.
Il ne faut pas	Il ne faut pas boire d'alcool.
Il vaut mieux	Il vaut mieux boire du jus d'orange.
Il est nécessaire (de)	Il est nécessaire de rester à la maison.
Il n'est pas nécessaire (de)	Il n'est pas nécessaire de rester au lit.
Il est important (de)	Il est important d'écouter les conseils du médecin.
Il est bon / mauvais (de)	Il est bon de boire beaucoup de liquides.

When using these expressions to give advice to someone in particular, follow them with **que** plus a second clause.

Il faut dormir assez.   *It is necessary to sleep enough.*
(for people in general)

Il faut que tu dormes plus.   *It is necessary that you sleep more.*
(for a specific person)

In this case, the verb in the second clause is in a form called the subjunctive. You have used verbs in the indicative mode to say what happens. The subjunctive is another verb mode, which may imply either present or future actions. The subjunctive is generally used in the second clause of a sentence, when the first clause expresses an attitude or opinion about what should or might be done, rather than simply stating what is happening. These two clauses are linked by **que,** which replaces the **de** used before infinitives with the expressions on the bottom of the list at the beginning of this section.

Il faut **que vous mangiez** bien.   Il est important **que tu dormes** un peu.

For most verbs, the subjunctive is formed as follows:

- For **nous** and **vous,** the subjunctive is identical to the imperfect.
- For the other forms, find the stem of the subjunctive by dropping the **-ent** ending of the **ils/elles** form of the present indicative and use the endings: **-e, -es, -e, -ent.**

Suggestion. Point out the two **i**'s in **étudiions** and **étudiiez.**

	PARLER	FINIR	RENDRE
que je	parl**e**	finiss**e**	rend**e**
que tu	parl**es**	finiss**es**	rend**es**
qu'il/qu'elle/qu'on	parl**e**	finiss**e**	rend**e**
que nous	parl**ions**	finiss**ions**	rend**ions**
que vous	parl**iez**	finiss**iez**	rend**iez**
qu'ils/qu'elles	parl**ent**	finiss**ent**	rend**ent**

Most irregular verbs follow the same rule.

connaître	que je connaisse	que nous connaiss**ions**
dire	que je dise	que nous dis**ions**
dormir	que je dorm**e**	que nous dorm**ions**
écrire	que j'écriv**e**	que nous écriv**ions**
lire	que je lise	que nous lis**ions**
partir	que je part**e**	que nous part**ions**
sortir	que je sort**e**	que nous sort**ions**

The following verbs follow the same rule, but they have two different stems in the subjunctive.

acheter	que j'achèt**e**	que nous achet**ions**
boire	que je boive	que nous buv**ions**
devoir	que je doive	que nous dev**ions**
payer	que je pai**e**	que nous pay**ions**
prendre	que je prenn**e**	que nous pren**ions**
venir	que je vienn**e**	que nous ven**ions**

The subjunctive of **il pleut** is **qu'il pleuve.**

A. Conseils. Complétez ces phrases logiquement.

Exemple   Si on est enceinte, il faut **se reposer assez.** Il ne faut pas…

1. Si on a la grippe, il faut…   Il vaut mieux…   Il est important de…
2. Si on a un virus intestinal, il faut…   Il est bon de…   Il ne faut pas…
3. Si on veut rester en forme, il est important de…   Il est mauvais de…

B. Encore des conseils! Selon les circonstances indiquées, dites s'il faut, s'il vaut mieux, s'il n'est pas nécessaire ou s'il ne faut pas que ces personnes fassent *(do)* les choses indiquées.

il faut que   **il vaut mieux que**
il n'est pas nécessaire que
IL NE FAUT PAS QUE

Exemple   Je suis fatigué(e). Alors… je (se reposer, sortir)
Il faut que je me repose. Il ne faut pas que je sorte.

1. J'ai la grippe. Alors… je (se reposer, dormir, rendre visite à ma famille, acheter des médicaments, prendre de l'aspirine, boire beaucoup d'eau)
2. *(à votre professeur)* Vous avez la grippe aussi? Alors… vous (boire beaucoup de liquides, venir en cours, sortir, finir tous vos médicaments, fumer)
3. *(à un[e] camarade de classe)* Il y a un examen de français bientôt. Alors… tu (écrire tous les exercices dans le cahier, le dire au professeur si tu ne comprends pas, connaître bien les conjugaisons, préparer l'examen)
4. Les autres étudiants et moi voulons réussir au cours de français. Alors… nous (partir avant la fin du cours, écouter bien en cours, perdre notre temps en cours, prendre des notes, dormir en cours, sortir tous les soirs)
5. Mon meilleur ami (Ma meilleure amie) veut réussir à ses examens. Alors… il/elle (préparer bien ses cours, finir tous ses devoirs, obéir à ses professeurs, attendre ses professeurs s'ils arrivent en retard, regarder les examens des autres)
6. Mes amis s'ennuient. Alors… ils (trouver de nouveaux passe-temps, s'amuser plus, rester toujours à la maison, partir en voyage, sortir plus, apprendre quelque chose de nouveau, venir me voir)

1. What are the seven verbs that are irregular in the subjunctive?

2. Which four of these verbs have a different stem for the **nous** and **vous** forms?

3. What are ten verbs or phrases expressing feelings that are followed by a dependent clause with the verb in the subjunctive?

Expressing emotions:

Les verbes irréguliers au subjonctif et le subjonctif après les expressions d'émotion

The following seven verbs are irregular in the subjunctive. Note that **être, avoir, aller,** and **vouloir** have a different stem for the **nous** and **vous** forms. All except **être** and **avoir** have the regular subjunctive endings. The subjunctive of **il y a** is **qu'il y ait.**

	ÊTRE	AVOIR	ALLER	VOULOIR
	soi- / soy-	*ai- / ay-*	*aill- / all-*	*veuill- / voul-*
que je (j')	sois	aie	aille	veuille
que tu	sois	aies	ailles	veuilles
qu'il/qu'elle/qu'on	soit	ait	aille	veuille
que nous	soyons	ayons	allions	voulions
que vous	soyez	ayez	alliez	vouliez
qu'ils/qu'elles	soient	aient	aillent	veuillent

	FAIRE	POUVOIR	SAVOIR
	fass-	*puiss-*	*sach-*
que je	fasse	puisse	sache
que tu	fasses	puisses	saches
qu'il/qu'elle/qu'on	fasse	puisse	sache
que nous	fassions	puissions	sachions
que vous	fassiez	puissiez	sachiez
qu'ils/qu'elles	fassent	puissent	sachent

Whereas the indicative is used to say what is happening, the subjunctive is used to express someone's personal feelings about whether something should be happening. You have seen how to use it after impersonal expressions such as **il faut que.** You also use it in the second clause after verbs that express emotions, including:

être content(e) que *to be glad that*
être heureux (heureuse) que *to be happy that*
être furieux (furieuse) que *to be furious that*
être surpris(e) que *to be surprised that*
être étonné(e) que *to be amazed that*

être triste que *to be sad that*
être désolé(e) que *to be sorry that*
C'est dommage que *It's too bad that*
avoir peur que *to be afraid that*
regretter que *to regret that*

Je suis content(e) **que tu ne sois plus** malade.
Nous sommes désolé(s) **que tu aies** mal à la tête.
C'est dommage **que tu doives** rester au lit.

A. Réactions. Si votre meilleure amie vous disait les choses suivantes, quelle serait votre réaction?

> JE (NE) SUIS (PAS) CONTENT(E) QUE... *Je suis triste que...*
> Je suis surpris(e) que... *Je suis furieux (furieuse) que...*
> JE SUIS DÉSOLÉ(E) QUE... Je regrette que...

Exemple   J'ai la grippe.
           Je suis désolé(e) que tu aies la grippe.

1. Je suis enceinte.
2. Ce sont des jumeaux.
3. Je veux avoir un bébé.
4. J'ai souvent très mal au ventre.
5. Je fais de l'exercice.
6. Je vais souvent chez le médecin.
7. Je ne peux pas payer mon loyer.
8. Je veux habiter chez toi.
9. Je sais m'occuper d'un bébé *(to take care of a baby)*.

B. Quand on est enceinte.
Une femme enceinte parle avec Daniel. Est-ce qu'il lui dit qu'il est content ou qu'il regrette les choses qu'elle fait?

Exemple   Je mange bien.
           Je suis content que vous mangiez bien.

1. Je me repose assez.
2. Je ne fais pas d'exercice.
3. J'ai beaucoup de stress.
4. Je suis très fatiguée.
5. Je veux faire très attention à ma santé.
6. Je ne peux pas dormir la nuit.
7. Je prends des vitamines.
8. Je grossis beaucoup.

C. Réactions.
Posez chaque question à un(e) camarade de classe. Après, réagissez à sa réponse.

Exemple   —Tu fais du sport?
           —Non, je ne fais pas de sport.
           —Je regrette que tu ne fasses pas de sport.

1. Est-ce que tu fais attention à ta santé?
2. Est-ce que tu es souvent malade?
3. Tu dors bien, généralement?
4. Est-ce que tu veux aller au club de gym avec moi?
5. Est-ce que tu as des allergies?

D. Quel spectacle!
Imaginez la réaction de ces parents quand ils rentrent à la maison.

> ILS SONT SURPRIS QUE...   Ils sont furieux que...   Ils sont étonnés que...
> Ils ne sont pas contents que...   ILS SONT CONTENTS QUE...

Exemple   **Ils ne sont pas contents que la baby-sitter soit avec son petit ami.**

E. Camarades de chambre.
Faites une liste de cinq choses que votre camarade de chambre ou votre colocataire fait qui vous plaisent *(please you)* ou qui vous énervent *(annoy you)*.

Exemple   **Je suis content(e) qu'il/qu'elle ne soit pas souvent à la maison. Je suis furieux (furieuse) qu'il/qu'elle ne fasse jamais le ménage.**

Supplemental activities. **A.** Qu'est-ce que chacun doit ou ne doit pas faire dans ces situations? EXEMPLE Je suis très malade. (dormir beaucoup, aller danser) **Il faut que tu dormes beaucoup. Il ne faut pas que tu ailles danser! 1.** Mes collègues et moi, nous sommes très stressé(e)s. (être plus calmes, travailler plus, faire plus d'exercice, prendre des vacances) **2.** Mon frère fait une dépression. (sortir plus, penser à ses problèmes, se faire de nouveaux amis, être seul tout le temps) **3.** Mes parents grossissent. (faire de l'exercice, regarder la télé toute la journée, manger plus de légumes et moins de sucre, prendre un dessert) **4.** Ma sœur est enceinte. (manger bien, boire de l'alcool, boire beaucoup de lait, dormir assez, fumer, aller chez le médecin) **B.** Divide the class into two groups, one to play the role of **le diable** and the other **l'ange.** Each group makes a list of what you should do to be happy in life.

Warm-up activity. Using **je suis content(e) que… , je suis surpris(e) que… , c'est dommage que… ,** have students make a list of things that please, surprise, or annoy them about your university. Have several of them read their lists aloud. Afterward, read the following imaginary changes on campus and have students react: **1.** On ne peut plus fumer sur le campus. **2.** On ne peut plus avoir de voiture sur le campus. **3.** L'équipe de football américain gagne à tous les matchs. **4.** Il y a un ordinateur pour chaque étudiant. **5.** Le français devient la langue officielle pour tous les cours. **6.** Il n'y a plus de football américain ou de basket à l'université. **7.** La bibliothèque ferme à 18 heures. **8.** Il y a trois semaines de plus chaque semestre/trimestre.

COMPÉTENCE 3

Expressing your desires

NOTE Culturelle

On peut travailler dans l'enseignement *(education),* l'agriculture et la santé publique pour *le Corps de la Paix* dans plusieurs pays francophones en Afrique: le Bénin, le Burkina Faso, le Cameroun, la Côte-d'Ivoire, le Gabon, le Mali, le Maroc, la Mauritanie, le Niger, le Sénégal, le Tchad et le Togo.

TRANSPARENCY: 10-3

VOCABULAIRE SUPPLÉMENTAIRE
architecte
assistant(e) social(e) *social worker*
banquier *banker*
cadre *executive*
caissier (caissière) *cashier*
chanteur (chanteuse) *singer*
charpentier *carpenter*
coiffeur (coiffeuse) *hair stylist*
dentiste
dessinateur (dessinatrice) (de publicité) *graphic artist*
écrivain *writer*
employé(e)
fonctionnaire *government employee*
infirmier (infirmière) *nurse*
informaticien(ne) *computer scientist*
journaliste
mécanicien(ne) *mechanic*
ouvrier (ouvrière) *manual worker*
plombier *plumber*
programmeur (programmeuse)
retraité(e) *retired*
secrétaire *secretary*
serveur (serveuse) *server*
technicien(ne)
vendeur (vendeuse) *salesclerk*
vétérinaire

Des possibilités professionnelles

Suzanne et Daniel sont médecins. Et vous? Qu'est-ce que vous voulez faire **à l'avenir?** Voudriez-vous… ?

étudier la médecine pour être médecin

étudier **le droit** pour être **avocat(e)**

faire **une maîtrise** ou un doctorat

travailler pour une grande société internationale comme homme ou femme d'affaires ou **ingénieur** et gagner beaucoup d'argent

travailler à l'étranger pour une organisation **bénévole** comme *Médecins sans frontières* ou *le Corps de la Paix*

être artiste: acteur (actrice), musicien(ne) ou **peintre**

être père ou mère de famille

à l'avenir *in the future*   **le droit** *the law*   **un(e) avocat(e)** *a lawyer*   **une maîtrise** *a master's degree*   **un ingénieur** *an engineer*   **bénévole** *volunteer*   **un peintre** *a painter*

Suzanne demande des conseils à son frère sur son avenir.

DANIEL: Alors, tu vas rentrer à Paris?

SUZANNE: Je ne sais pas **quoi** faire. J'aimerais travailler ici avec toi mais mon fiancé Jean-Marc veut que je retourne à Paris.

DANIEL: L'important, c'est que tu sois heureuse. Qu'est-ce que tu veux faire?

SUZANNE: Jean-Marc veut qu'on se marie. Je l'aime beaucoup mais je ne sais pas si je veux me marier. Tu sais que ma carrière est très importante pour moi. Et papa et maman n'aiment pas Jean-Marc. Il est musicien et ils préfèrent que je me marie avec quelqu'un qui ait une situation plus stable.

DANIEL: Il faut que tu fasses ce que tu veux faire, pas ce que les autres veulent que tu fasses.

Suggestion for the conversation. First have students listen to the conversation with books closed for the answers to these questions. **1.** Qu'est-ce que Jean-Marc, le fiancé de Suzanne, veut qu'elle fasse? **2.** Pourquoi est-ce que les parents de Suzanne ne veulent pas qu'elle soit avec Jean-Marc?

A. Préférences. Si vous deviez choisir entre les possibilités données, laquelle est-ce que vous préféreriez?

Exemple   être médecin / être avocat(e)
J'aimerais mieux être avocat(e).

1. étudier la médecine / étudier le droit
2. faire un doctorat / être homme (femme) d'affaires pour une grande société internationale
3. travailler pour une grande société ici / travailler à l'étranger pour une organisation bénévole
4. être avocat(e) / être artiste
5. avoir une famille / travailler beaucoup pour gagner beaucoup d'argent

B. Entretien. Interviewez votre partenaire.

1. Travailleras-tu ou continueras-tu tes études quand tu auras ton diplôme? Aimerais-tu avoir une famille et rester à la maison?
2. Voudrais-tu étudier la médecine? le droit? Vas-tu faire une maîtrise ou un doctorat? En quoi?
3. Quelles professions sont intéressantes pour toi? Est-ce que tu gagnerais beaucoup d'argent avec ces professions? Pour toi, est-il important de gagner beaucoup d'argent? Où est-ce que tu voudrais travailler?

C. Des choix difficiles. Changez la conversation entre Daniel et Suzanne comme indiqué.

1. Suzanne's parents want her to marry Jean-Marc because he is a lawyer and makes a lot of money. Suzanne wants to get married too, but she does not know if she loves Jean-Marc.
2. Suzanne is trying to decide whether to return to her work in Paris where she is not happy, but she earns a lot of money and she has a lot of friends, or to stay in **Côte-d'Ivoire** with her brother.
3. You are talking to a friend about choosing between two different options you are thinking about pursuing when you graduate.

---

quoi *what*

Saying what you want done: *La volonté et le subjonctif*

Whereas the indicative is used to say what is happening, the subjunctive is used to talk about something that is not necessarily happening, but is being encouraged or discouraged. Use it in the second clause after the following verbs.

vouloir	Je veux **que tu sois** ici en Afrique.
préférer	Je préfère **que tu n'ailles pas** à Paris.
aimer mieux que	J'aime mieux **que tu m'aides** à la clinique.

The verb **espérer**, however, is not followed by the subjunctive.

J'espère **que tu es** heureuse ici.   Nous espérons **que tout ira** mieux.

A. Préférences. Si vous deviez choisir entre les possibilités données, qu'est-ce que vos parents aimeraient mieux que vous fassiez? Si vous ne savez pas, devinez!

Exemple   être médecin / être avocat(e)
          Ils aimeraient mieux que je sois médecin.

1. avoir une bonne carrière / avoir des enfants
2. faire un doctorat / commencer à travailler
3. travailler pour une grande société / travailler pour une organisation bénévole
4. étudier le droit / étudier la médecine / faire un doctorat
5. être médecin / ingénieur / avocat / professeur / homme (femme) d'affaires
6. gagner beaucoup d'argent / être heureux (heureuse)

Follow-up for *B. l'idéal*. Have students prepare a list of things they want changed at the university. For example: **Nous voulons que la bibliothèque soit ouverte 24 heures sur 24.** To spur their imagination, you might ask them questions such as the following: **Est-ce que les classes sont trop grandes? Est-ce que les cours coûtent trop cher? Est-ce qu'il y a assez de parkings? Est-ce qu'on est libre de faire ce qu'on veut sur le campus? Est-ce que les résidences sont agréables? Est-ce que nous avons besoin d'une nouvelle piscine? d'ordinateurs? d'un nouveau laboratoire de langues?**

B. L'idéal. Quels traits sont importants pour vous chez votre partenaire idéal(e)? Donnez votre réaction aux possibilités données.

> Je veux absolument que...   *J'aimerais que...*   JE PRÉFÈRE QUE...
> IL N'EST PAS IMPORTANT QUE...   Je ne veux pas que...

Exemple   être riche
          Je veux absolument qu'il/qu'elle soit riche. /
          Il n'est pas important qu'il/qu'elle soit riche.

1. vouloir avoir des enfants
2. avoir déjà beaucoup d'enfants
3. vouloir avoir une carrière
4. préférer rester à la maison
5. gagner beaucoup d'argent
6. aimer voyager
7. savoir parler une autre langue
8. être intelligent(e) / beau (belle) / ???
9. finir ses études universitaires
10. faire des études supérieures *(postgraduate)*

C. Quel hôtel?
Vous allez faire un voyage et vous cherchez un hôtel. Quelle sorte d'hôtel préférez-vous? Donnez votre réaction comme indiqué.

| Je veux que... | Je préfère que... | IL N'EST PAS IMPORTANT QUE... |

Exemple   l'hôtel / être près des sites touristiques
Je préfère que l'hôtel soit près des sites touristiques.

1. l'hôtel / avoir une piscine
2. la réceptionniste / savoir parler anglais
3. l'hôtel / accepter les cartes de crédit
4. la chambre / être grande
5. la chambre / avoir une douche
6. on / (ne pas) pouvoir fumer dans la chambre

D. Tu m'accompagnes?
Qu'est-ce qu'Alice veut que les autres fassent avec elle?

Exemple   **Alice veut que son mari joue au tennis avec elle.**

Exemple son mari

1. le chien

2. son amie

3. son fils

4. son mari

5. son mari

E. Pour habiter ensemble.
Vous cherchez un(e) colocataire. Comment doit-il/elle être? Complétez logiquement les phrases.

Exemple   Je veux absolument qu'il/qu'elle **range sa chambre.**

1. Je veux absolument qu'il/qu'elle...
2. J'aimerais mieux qu'il/qu'elle...
3. Je veux qu'il/qu'elle...
4. Je préfère qu'il/qu'elle...
5. Je ne veux pas qu'il/qu'elle...

F. On habite ensemble?
Votre partenaire et vous pensez peut-être habiter ensemble. Dites-lui ce qu'il faudra qu'il/qu'elle fasse s'il/si elle habite chez vous. Préparez une scène basée sur cette situation pour présenter à la classe.

 *Pour vérifier*

1. Do you use the infinitive or the subjunctive when people have feelings about what *they themselves* should or might do? When they have feelings about what *others* should or might do?

2. When do you use the infinitive after impersonal expressions such as **il faut?** When do you use the subjunctive?

Saying who you want to do something:
Le subjonctif ou l'infinitif?

You know to use the subjunctive in a second clause when the first clause expresses desires, emotions, suggestions, or opinions about what someone else is doing or should do. The subjunctive is used when there are different subjects in the main and dependent clauses. When there is no change of subject, you normally use the infinitive.

TALKING ABOUT SOMEONE ELSE	**TALKING ABOUT ONESELF**
Je veux que tu le fasses. *I want you to do it.*	Je veux le faire. *I want to do it.*
Nous préférons qu'il soit là. *We prefer that he be there.*	Nous préférons être là. *We prefer to be there.*

After the verbs **être** + *adjective* and **regretter,** use **de** before infinitives.

TALKING ABOUT SOMEONE ELSE	**TALKING ABOUT ONESELF**
Nous regrettons qu'il parte. *We're sorry he's leaving.*	Nous regrettons **de** partir. *We're sorry for leaving.*
Je suis content que tu sortes avec elle. *I'm glad you're going out with her.*	Je suis content **de** sortir avec elle. *I'm glad to go out with her.*

Remember to use an infinitive after expressions such as **il faut** or **il est important** to talk about people in general, rather than someone specific.

TALKING ABOUT SOMEONE SPECIFIC	**TALKING ABOUT PEOPLE IN GENERAL**
Il faut que nous le fassions. *We have to do it.*	Il faut le faire. *It has to be done.*
Il est important qu'il y aille. *It's important for him to go.*	Il est important **d'**y aller. *It's important to go.*

A. Volontés. Dites si vos parents veulent que vous fassiez les choses suivantes. Ensuite, dites si vous voulez les faire.

Exemple   travailler cet été
        Mes parents veulent que je travaille cet été.
        Moi, je ne veux pas travailler cet été.

1. habiter avec eux *(with them)*
2. leur téléphoner plus souvent
3. leur dire tous vos secrets
4. les accompagner en vacances
5. aller à l'université cet été
6. avoir un A en français

B. Révisons! Vous révisez pour l'examen sur ce chapitre et votre professeur dit ce qu'il faut faire. Dites s'il faut encore que vous fassiez chacune de ces choses ou si vous les avez déjà faites.

Exemple   Il faut faire *la rédaction à la page 391.*
Moi, il faut encore que je la fasse. / Moi, je l'ai déjà faite.

1. Il faut apprendre *le vocabulaire à la fin du chapitre.*
2. Il faut lire toutes *les explications (f) de grammaire du chapitre.*
3. Il faut finir *les exercices (m) du cahier.*
4. Il faut écouter *le CD* aussi.
5. Il faut étudier *les formes (f) des verbes au subjonctif.*

C. Préférences. Choisissez les mots entre parenthèses qui décrivent le mieux vos préférences quand vous voyagez. Conjuguez le verbe au subjonctif ou utilisez l'infinitif comme il convient.

1. Pour un long voyage, je préfère... (prendre l'avion, prendre le train, prendre ma voiture, ???)
2. Je préfère que mon vol... (être le matin, être l'après-midi, être le soir)
3. Pendant le vol, j'aime... (lire, voir le film, écouter de la musique, dormir, parler avec les autres passagers, ???)
4. Je n'aime pas que les autres passagers près de moi... (parler tout le temps, avoir un petit bébé, se lever tout le temps, ???)
5. Je préfère que l'hôtel... (être grand et cher, être grand mais pas trop cher)
6. Je préfère que ma chambre d'hôtel... (avoir un grand lit, avoir un petit lit)
7. Généralement, j'aime... (dîner dans ma chambre d'hôtel, manger au restaurant de l'hôtel, aller dans un autre restaurant)
8. À l'hôtel, je préfère... (payer avec un chèque de voyage, payer par carte de crédit, payer en espèces)

D. Entretien. Interviewez votre partenaire sur un voyage qu'il/elle voudrait faire.

1. Où est-ce que tu voudrais faire un voyage? Quand est-ce que tu voudrais le faire? Est-ce que tu veux que ta famille ou que tes amis voyagent avec toi?
2. Est-ce que tu préfères que ton hôtel soit un hôtel de luxe ou un hôtel économique? Est-il important qu'il y ait une piscine? Aimes-tu nager dans la piscine d'un hôtel?
3. As-tu peur de prendre l'avion? Préfères-tu qu'on puisse fumer pendant un vol ou qu'on ne puisse pas fumer? Aimes-tu parler avec les personnes à côté de toi dans l'avion ou préfères-tu ne pas parler?

E. Différences d'opinion. Faites une liste de trois choses que quelqu'un veut que vous fassiez mais que vous ne voulez pas faire.

Exemple   **Mon petit ami veut que j'aille chez ses parents ce week-end.
Moi, je ne veux pas y aller.
Mes parents veulent que j'habite avec eux *(with them)*
l'année prochaine. Moi, je veux habiter seul(e).**

Maintenant, choisissez une de ces situations et créez une conversation avec un(e) partenaire dans laquelle vous donnez plus de détails. Votre partenaire vous donnera des conseils sur ce qu'il faut faire.

COMPÉTENCE 4

TRANSPARENCIES: 10-4A, 10-4B

Les indications

Suzanne descend dans un hôtel à Abidjan. Voilà un plan du quartier de l'hôtel. Qu'est-ce qu'il y a dans le quartier?

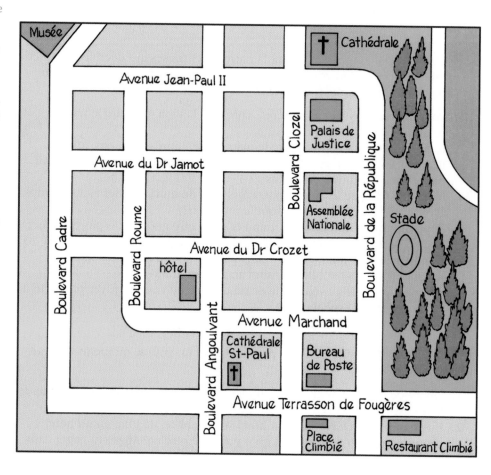

L'hôtelier va **expliquer** à Suzanne comment arriver au restaurant Climbié. Voilà quelques expressions utiles pour **indiquer le chemin.**

Prenez la rue...
Continuez **tout droit jusqu'à...**
Tournez à droite.
Tournez à gauche.
Descendez la rue...
Montez la rue...

Traversez la place...
C'est dans la rue...
   sur le boulevard...
   sur l'avenue...
   sur la place...
C'est **au coin de** la rue.

---

expliquer *to explain* **indiquer le chemin** *to give directions, to show the way* **tout droit jusqu'à...** *straight ahead until . . .* **traverser** *to cross, to go across* **la place** *the square* **au coin de** *on the corner of*

Suzanne demande à l'hôtelier de lui expliquer comment aller au restaurant Climbié.

SUZANNE: Pouvez-vous m'expliquer comment aller au restaurant Climbié?
L'HÔTELIER: Bien sûr. C'est très facile. Descendez le boulevard Angoulvant jusqu'à l'avenue Terrasson de Fougères. Là, tournez à gauche.
SUZANNE: À gauche, à l'avenue Terrasson de Fougères?
L'HÔTELIER: C'est ça. Continuez tout droit. Le restaurant Climbié est sur l'avenue Terrasson de Fougères, au coin du boulevard de la République.
SUZANNE: Je vous remercie, monsieur.
L'HÔTELIER: Je vous en prie, madame.

A. Où faut-il aller?
Vous faites un voyage avec un groupe d'étudiants. Où faut-il que les personnes suivantes aillent?

Exemple Notre vol va partir dans deux heures!
Il faut que nous **allions à l'aéroport!**

> à la banque À UN RESTAURANT à l'aéroport
> À LA PHARMACIE chez le médecin à la réception de l'hôtel

1. Vous voulez changer des chèques de voyage. Il faut que vous....
2. Vos amis ont perdu la clé de leur chambre. Il faut qu'ils...
3. Après dix heures on ne sert plus le petit déjeuner dans la chambre. Il faut qu'on...
4. Je me sens très malade depuis deux jours. Il faut que j'...
5. Tu as une ordonnance? Il faut que tu... ?

B. Où allez-vous?
Imaginez que vous êtes à l'hôtel de Suzanne. D'abord, complétez les explications suivantes en traduisant les mots entre parenthèses. Ensuite regardez le plan à la page précédente et dites où vous arrivez.

Exemple Montez le boulevard Angoulvant jusqu'à l'avenue Jean-Paul II. À l'avenue Jean-Paul II, **tournez à droite** (turn right). **Allez tout droit** (Go straight) jusqu'au boulevard Clozel. **Tournez à gauche.** (Turn left.) Elle est sur votre droite.
Nous arrivons à la cathédrale.

1. C'est tout près. _____ (Go down) le boulevard Angoulvant _____ (as far as) l'avenue Terrasson de Fougères. Elle est au coin de l'avenue Terrasson de Fougères et du boulevard Angoulvant.
2. _____ (Go up) le boulevard Angoulvant jusqu'à l'avenue du Dr Crozet. _____. (Turn right.) _____ (Continue straight) jusqu'au boulevard de la République. _____ (Cross) le boulevard. Il est en face de vous.

C. Que faire ce soir?
Avec un(e) partenaire, changez la conversation entre Suzanne et l'hôtelier comme indiqué.

1. Suzanne asks how to get to the museum.
2. Suzanne asks how to get to the **Assemblée nationale.**
3. Tell how to get to your house from campus.

Suggestion for the conversation. Have students listen to the conversation with books closed for the answers to the following questions. **1.** Est-ce que Suzanne doit tourner à droite ou à gauche sur l'avenue Terrasson de Fougères? **2.** Le restaurant Climbié est au coin de quel boulevard et de quelle avenue?

Quick-reference answers for B. Où allez-vous? **1.** la cathédrale St-Paul **2.** le stade

Follow-up for B. Où allez-vous? Looking at the map on p. 385, give oral directions from the train station (la gare) to various places for students to follow.

Suggestions for part 3 of C. Que faire ce soir? **A.** You may wish to give students phrases like **prenez l'autoroute... , prenez la sortie... vers le nord / le sud / l'est / l'ouest... B.** Have students prepare this as homework for presentation during the next class. After their presentations, ask follow-up questions such as: **Est-ce que Paul habite près de... ? Dans quelle rue est-ce qu'il habite?**

Abidjan, Côte-d'Ivoire

Une librairie à Abidjan

Un magasin à Abidjan

PLAN SCHÉMATIQUE DU CENTRE D'ABIDJAN

1 **Poste**
2 **Bloc ministériel**
3 **Hôtel de ville**
4 **Présidence de la République**
5 **Gare**
6 **Marché**
7 **Cathédrale St-Paul**
8 **Immeuble du Trésor**
9 **Assemblée nationale**
10 **Palais de Justice**
11 **Tours administratives**
12 **Stade Houphouët-Boigny**
13 **Caisse de stabilisation**
14 **Hôtel Sofitel**
15 **Agence Air Ivoire**
16 **Transcap**
17 **Globe Travel**
18 **Agence de voyages**
19 **Hôtel IBIS Plateau**
20 **Nour Al Hayat**
21 **Centre culturel français**
22 **La Pyramide**
23 **Cathédrale**
24 **Ministère de l'Information**
25 **Air Afrique (siège et agence)**
26 **BIAO**
27 **BICICI**
28 **Novotel C.I**
29 **Air Ivoire**
30 **C.I.A.M**
31 **O.I.T.H**
32 **Grand Hôtel**
33 **Tiama**

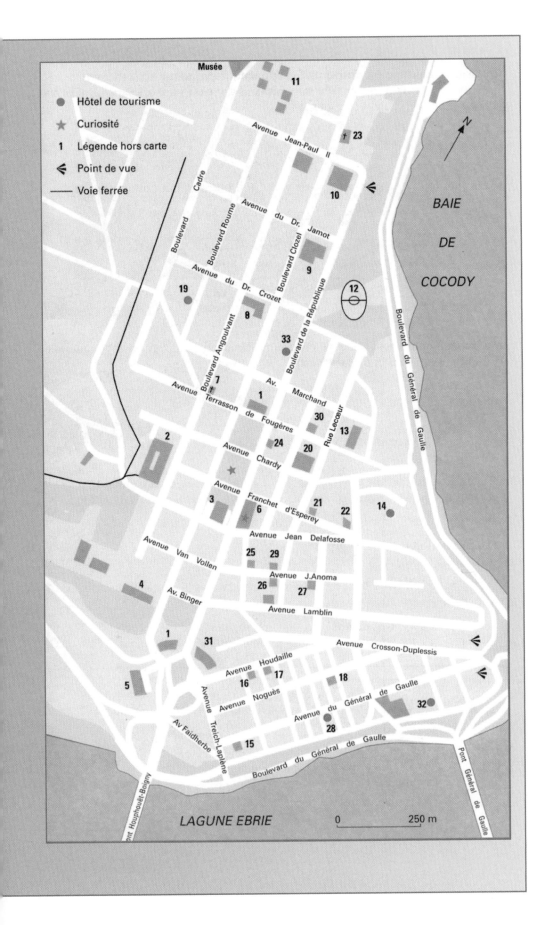

Musée

11

● Hôtel de tourisme
★ Curiosité
1 Légende hors carte
◄ Point de vue
— Voie ferrée

Avenue Jean-Paul II

† 23

10

◄

BAIE

DE

COCODY

Boulevard Cadre

Boulevard Roume

Avenue du Dr. Jamot

Boulevard Clozel

9

Avenue du Dr. Crozet

19 ●

8

12

Boulevard de la République

Boulevard Angoulvant

33 ●

7 †

Av. Marchand

1

Avenue Terrasson de Fougères

30

Rue Lecœur

13

2

24

20

Avenue Chardy

★

3

Avenue Franchet d'Esperey

6

21

22

14 ●

Avenue Jean Delafosse

Avenue Van Vollen

25 29

Avenue J.Anoma

4

Av. Binger

26

27

Avenue Lamblin

1

31

Avenue Crosson-Duplessis

◄

Avenue Houdaille

17

18

◄

5

16

Avenue Noguès

Avenue du Général de Gaulle

32 ●

Av Faidherbe

Avenue Treich-Laplene

28 ●

15

Boulevard du Général de Gaulle

Pont Général de Gaulle

Pont Houphouët-Boigny

LAGUNE EBRIE

0   250 m

Boulevard du Général de Gaulle

1. With which verbs do you drop the final **-s** in the **tu** form in the imperative?

2. Where do you place direct object, indirect object, and reflexive pronouns in affirmative commands? What happens to the pronouns **me** and **te?**

3. Where do you place object and reflexive pronouns in negative commands?

4. Which two verbs have irregular command forms? What are the forms?

Note. The **impératif** is recycled here so that students may use it to give directions. This is the first time that students use reflexive and object pronouns with commands.

Suggestions. Before beginning this section, review the forms, uses, and position of reflexive pronouns, direct and indirect object pronouns, **y**, and **en**. Then give students this warm-up activity. **A.** Vous êtes sur la plage d'une île exotique et vous rencontrez l'homme ou la femme de vos rêves. Est-ce que vous faites les choses suivantes? **1.** Est-ce que vous lui parlez? **2.** Qu'est-ce que vous lui demandez? (son numéro de téléphone? s'il/si elle est marié[e]?) **3.** Qu'est-ce que vous lui dites? (votre nom? qu'il/elle est beau/belle?) **4.** Est-ce que vous lui donnez le nom de votre hôtel? votre numéro de téléphone? **B.** Review **nous** commands and suggestions, then do this activity. **Acceptez ou refusez ces suggestions.** EXEMPLE On va à la mer pour les vacances? **Oui, allons à la mer. / Non, n'allons pas à la mer! Allons à Paris. 1.** On va à la montagne? **2.** On fait du bateau? **3.** On reste à la maison? **4.** On visite l'Europe? **5.** On descend dans un hôtel de luxe? **6.** On fait du ski? **7.** On fait une randonnée? **8.** On loue un appartement sur la plage?

Follow-up for *A. À Abidjan.* Décrivez où se trouve votre restaurant préféré, une phrase à la fois. Vos camarades de classe vont deviner le nom du restaurant. Continuez votre description jusqu'à ce que quelqu'un devine juste. EXEMPLE – **Pour aller à mon restaurant préféré, descendez la rue Lamar.** – Est-ce que c'est Casa Monterrey? – **Non. Il est à côté d'un cinéma...**

Telling how to go somewhere: *L'impératif (reprise)*

You have been using the **impératif** (command) form of the verb to give directions. As you have seen, the imperative is the **tu, vous,** or **nous** form of the verb without the subject pronoun.

Descends cette rue!	*Go down this street!*
Traversez la place!	*Cross the square!*
Allons en ville!	*Let's go to town!*

Remember to drop the final **-s** of **-er** verbs and of **aller,** but not of other verbs, in **tu** form commands.

	Tourne à gauche!	*Turn left!*
BUT:	Prend**s** un taxi!	*Take a taxi!*

Review the irregular command forms of **être** and **avoir.**

Sois calme!	*Be calm!*	Aie de la patience!	*Have patience!*
Soyons gentils!	*Let's be nice!*	Ayons confiance!	*Let's have confidence!*
Soyez à l'heure!	*Be on time!*	Ayez pitié!	*Have pity!*

In negative commands, reflexive pronouns, direct and indirect object pronouns, **y,** and **en** are placed before the verb.

Ne te perds pas!	*Don't get lost!*
Ne les prends pas!	*Don't take them!*
N'y va pas!	*Don't go there!*

In affirmative commands, these pronouns are attached to the end of the verb with a hyphen.

Invite-la au restaurant.	*Invite her to the restaurant.*
Dis-lui que nous arriverons bientôt.	*Tell her that we will arrive soon.*

When **me** and **te** follow the verb, they become **moi** and **toi.**

Attendez-moi!	*Wait for me!*
Lève-toi!	*Get up!*

When **y** or **en** follows a **tu** form command, the final **-s** is reattached to the end of the verb.

Vas-y!	*Go ahead!*	Manges-y!	*Eat there!*
Achètes-en!	*Buy some!*	Manges-en!	*Eat some!*

A. À Abidjan. Consultez le plan d'Abidjan à la page 385 et expliquez comment aller...

- de la gare *(train station)* (5) à l'hôtel de ville (3)
- de la gare (5) à la cathédrale St-Paul (7)
- de la Pyramide (22) à l'Immeuble du Trésor (8)
- du marché (6) au Palais de Justice (10)

B. E.T. chez vous. Un extra-terrestre est arrivé chez vous et il vous demande ce qu'il faut faire pour être accepté en tant qu'être humain *(as a human)*. Dites-lui ce qu'il faut ou ne faut pas faire.

Exemple   Je m'habille avant de prendre une douche?
               Non, ne t'habille pas avant de prendre une douche. Habille-toi après.

1. Je me couche par terre?
2. Je m'habille dans le jardin?
3. Je me brosse les mains?
4. Je me lève à minuit?
5. Je me couche à midi?
6. Je dors dans la cuisine?

C. La première fois. Votre frère va sortir avec une fille pour la première fois. Répondez à ses questions. Dites-lui de faire ou de ne pas faire chaque chose.

Exemple   — Est-ce que je l'invite au cinéma?
            — Oui, invite-la au cinéma. / Non, ne l'invite pas au cinéma.

1. Est-ce que je l'invite à dîner avant le film?
2. Est-ce que je lui achète des fleurs?
3. Combien de temps est-ce que je l'attends si elle est en retard?
4. Est-ce que je lui parle pendant le film?
5. Est-ce que je l'invite à la maison après?
6. Est-ce que je lui montre ma collection de cartes postales?
7. Est-ce que je l'accompagne chez elle après?
8. Est-ce que je l'embrasse avant de partir?

D. Conseils. Jean-Marc, le fiancé de Suzanne, veut qu'elle rentre à Paris. Son frère Daniel n'aime pas Jean-Marc et il veut que Suzanne reste en Afrique avec lui. Imaginez les réponses de Daniel aux questions suivantes de Suzanne. Utilisez l'impératif.

Exemple   Qu'est-ce que je dis à Jean-Marc? Je lui dis que je pense rester ici ou je ne lui dis rien?
            Dis-lui que tu penses rester ici.

1. Je voudrais visiter d'autres pays en Afrique. Je les visite ou je rentre à Paris pour être avec Jean-Marc?
2. Je me marie avec Jean-Marc ou je le quitte?
3. Je lui écris un e-mail ou je lui téléphone pour lui expliquer mes sentiments?
4. Je l'invite à venir ici ou je l'oublie *(forget)*?
5. On m'a offert un poste à l'hôpital à Abidjan. Je l'accepte ou je ne l'accepte pas?
6. Ils veulent que je commence à travailler tout de suite. Je leur dis que je peux commencer maintenant ou je leur demande un peu plus de temps?

Maintenant, Suzanne téléphone à son fiancé. Est-ce qu'il dit à Suzanne de faire ou de ne pas faire les choses suivantes?

Exemples   téléphoner plus souvent   oublier *(to forget)*
            Téléphone-moi plus souvent!   **Ne m'oublie pas!**

1. écouter
2. prendre pour un imbécile
3. envoyer des photos
4. écrire des e-mails
5. quitter
6. dire la vérité *(truth)*
7. parler de rester en Côte-d'Ivoire
8. donner une chance

Warm-ups for *B. E.T. chez vous.*
A. Dites à E.T. dans quelle pièce de la maison il doit faire les choses suivantes: **1.** se coucher **2.** préparer le petit déjeuner **3.** se laver **4.** se brosser les dents **5.** s'habiller **B.** Which would you say to do first? **1.** Levez-vous. / Habillez-vous. **2.** Habillez-vous. / Prenez un bain. **3.** Endormez-vous. / Couchez-vous. **4.** Habillez-vous. / Sortez de la maison. **5.** Prenez le petit déjeuner. / Lavez-vous les mains. **6.** Mangez. / Brossez-vous les dents. **7.** Levez-vous. / Allez travailler.

Follow-up for *B. E.T. chez vous.* Have students give commands telling a friend to do or not to do the following things on vacation: **1.** s'amuser **2.** s'ennuyer **3.** se reposer **4.** se lever tôt **5.** se coucher tard **6.** se promener **7.** se réveiller à 11 heures **8.** se disputer avec des amis

Reprise: *Going on a trip*

In *Chapitre 10*, you practiced reserving a hotel room, asking for and giving directions, talking about illnesses with a doctor, saying what you want to happen, describing feelings about what is happening, and giving advice. Now you have a chance to review what you learned.

A. Quel hôtel?

Vous faites un voyage en France avec un(e) ami(e) et vous choisissez entre les deux hôtels suivants. Indiquez l'hôtel que vous préférez en utilisant **Je préfère l'hôtel qui...** ou **Je préfère l'hôtel que...** avec les descriptions sous les photos.

Exemple   **Je préfère l'hôtel qui est loin du centre-ville. /
Je préfère l'hôtel qui est près de tout.**

Exemple Cet hôtel-ci est loin du centre-ville.	Cet hôtel-là est près de tout.
1. Cet hôtel-ci est petit et pittoresque.	Cet hôtel-là est grand.
2. Mon ami(e) n'aime pas cet hôtel-ci.	Mon ami(e) préfère cet hôtel-là.
3. Cet hôtel-ci n'a pas de restaurant.	Cet hôtel-là a deux restaurants.
4. Cet hôtel-ci est dans une rue tranquille.	Cet hôtel-là est au centre-ville.
5. Notre guide recommande cet hôtel-ci.	Le guide ne mentionne pas cet hôtel-là.
6. Cet hôtel-ci n'accepte pas les cartes de crédit.	Cet hôtel-là accepte les cartes de crédit.
7. Mon ami(e) trouve cet hôtel-ci désagréable.	Mon ami(e) trouve cet hôtel-là très bien.

B. Des préparatifs.

Vous faites les préparatifs pour votre voyage avec votre ami(e). Pour chaque paire de choses à faire, décidez ce que vous préférez faire et ce que vous préférez que votre ami(e) fasse.

Exemple   aller à la banque pour acheter des chèques de voyage / aller à l'agence de voyages pour les billets
Je préfère aller à l'agence de voyages pour les billets et je préfère que tu ailles à la banque pour acheter des chèques de voyage.

1. choisir l'hôtel / choisir le vol
2. faire les réservations d'hôtel / louer une voiture
3. lire le guide touristique / chercher des renseignements sur le Web
4. être assis(e) *(seated)* côté hublot *(window)* / être assis(e) côté couloir *(aisle)*
5. dormir dans le lit / dormir sur le canapé
6. payer le voyage / ne rien payer

C. Des préparatifs.
Votre ami(e) vous demande les choses suivantes pendant votre voyage. Répondez en utilisant l'impératif avec un pronom complément d'objet direct.

Exemple Je mets le réveil *(set the alarm)* pour six heures ou huit heures?
Mets-le pour huit heures.

1. J'apporte mon passeport avec moi ou je le laisse à l'hôtel?
2. Je paie l'hôtel avec ma carte de crédit ou avec ta carte de crédit?
3. Je fais le lit ou je le laisse pour la femme de chambre *(maid)?*
4. Je prends la clé avec moi ou je la laisse à la réception?
5. J'appelle le taxi une heure ou deux heures avant le vol?
6. J'écris ces cartes postales avant de partir ou je les écris dans l'avion?

D. Une réservation perdue.
Vous êtes dans les situations suivantes pendant votre voyage. Décrivez vos sentiments.

Exemple Votre avion est en retard *(late)*.
Je suis furieux (furieuse) que mon avion soit en retard.

> Je suis content(e) que...   Je ne suis pas content(e) que...
> C'EST DOMMAGE QUE...   JE REGRETTE QUE...   Il est bon que...
> Je suis surpris(e) que...   Je suis furieux (furieuse) que...
> Je suis étonné(e) que...   JE SUIS DÉSOLÉ(E) QUE...

1. On ne peut pas trouver votre réservation d'hôtel.
2. Il n'y a pas de chambres disponibles *(available)*.
3. Il n'y a pas de télévision dans la chambre d'hôtel.
4. L'hôtel a un grand restaurant.
5. Les repas à l'hôtel sont excellents.
6. Votre ami(e) veut passer toute la journée dans la chambre d'hôtel.
7. Il fait très mauvais et il pleut tous les jours.

E. On cherche un hôtel.
On a perdu votre réservation d'hôtel, alors vous cherchez un autre hôtel. Avec un(e) partenaire, préparez une conversation avec un(e) réceptionniste dans laquelle vous discutez les choses suivantes.

- say that you are looking for a room and for how many nights
- explain what sort of room you are looking for, including the number of beds and the sort of bathroom you need
- discuss the price, including breakfast, and ask if breakfast is served **(est servi)** in the room

F. Pourriez-vous m'indiquer le chemin?
Vous êtes à l'hôtel IBIS Plateau (numéro 19 sur le plan à la page 385) et vous désirez aller au marché (numéro 6 sur le plan). Votre partenaire va jouer le rôle de l'hôtelier (de l'hôtelière) et vous dire comment y aller. Ensuite, changez de rôles. Cette fois, votre partenaire voudrait aller de l'hôtel au Palais de Justice (numéro 10 sur le plan).

G. Chez le médecin.
Vous tombez malade pendant votre voyage. Avec un(e) partenaire, préparez la conversation suivante avec un médecin.

- The doctor greets you and asks what is wrong.
- You say that you are coughing, sneezing, and you have a sore throat.
- The doctor says you have the flu and gives you a prescription for medicine. He/She says that it is important that you take it every morning.

LECTURE ET *composition*

Note. The vocabulary in this section does not appear in the end-of-chapter vocabulary lists and is meant for recognition only. You may wish to let students know in advance whether you intend to test them on this vocabulary.

LECTURE: Si j'étais un **Dieu** nègre

L'Afrique **a produit** beaucoup de poètes d'expression française. Les thèmes préférés des poètes de l'Afrique noire sont la dignité de l'être humain, la gloire de la culture noire et **la lutte** contre **la souffrance. Parmi** les plus célèbres poètes sont Léopold Sédar Senghor, qui a été le premier président du Sénégal; Bernard Dadié, un Ivoirien; et David Diop, un Sénégalais. Lisez ce poème de Claude-Joseph M'Bafou-Zetebeg, un poète du Cameroun.

Si j'étais un Dieu nègre

Si j'étais un Dieu nègre
Je ferais **des rois** nègres
Des rois blancs
Des rois jaunes
Je **construirais** une grande maison noire
Qui **abriterait** toutes les races du monde
Je ferais une maison noire
Une maison blanche
Une maison jaune
Une maison rouge
Je ferais de l'Afrique ma capitale
Je ferais de Harlem ma résidence privée
Je ferais de l'Europe le pays des Noirs
De l'Asie le pays des Rouges
De l'Amérique le pays des Jaunes
De l'Afrique le pays des Blancs
J'aurais **autour de** moi
Des anges noirs
Des anges blancs
Des anges rouges
Des anges jaunes
Si j'étais un Dieu nègre
Il n'y aurait plus de **déluge**
Il n'y aurait plus **ni** Sodome **ni** Gomorrhe
Il y aurait **la paix**
La paix que mes frères
Prêchent depuis **des millénaires**
Je ferais un paradis noir
Un paradis blanc
Un paradis rouge
Un paradis jaune
Un paradis de l'**Amitié**
Où l'homme et la femme

Ne mangeraient plus le fruit **défendu**
J'enfanterais des nations nouvelles
Des nations d'un pour tous
Et de tous pour un
J'enverrais mes anges
Ambassadeurs sublimes
Mettre un terme aux guerres
Abattre les despotes
Bénir les pauvres
Je ferais du Kilimandjaro
Le vatican de mes frères
Si j'étais un Dieu nègre
Mes yeux **veilleraient sur le monde**
À travers les cieux
Fileraient des missiles de la paix
Finirait **la haine**
Il y aurait la joie
La joie des Noirs
La joie des Blancs
La joie des Rouges
La joie des Jaunes
La joie des peuples Unis
Si j'étais un Dieu nègre
Je marcherais de pays en pays
Invitant les masses à se laver **les cœurs**
Invitant les masses à être bonnes
Invitant les masses à **prier**
Pour ceux qui ne sont plus
Si j'étais un Dieu nègre
Un Dieu blanc
Un Dieu jaune
Un Dieu rouge
Je contribuerais à l'Union des Races.

Dieu *God* **produire** *to produce* **la lutte** *the struggle* **la souffrance** *suffering* **parmi** *among* **un roi** *a king* **construire** *to build* **abriter** *to shelter* **autour de** *around* **un ange** *an angel* **le déluge** *the flood* **ne... ni... ni...** *neither . . . nor . . .* **la paix** *peace* **prêcher** *to preach* **des millénaires** *millennia* **l'amitié (f)** *friendship* **défendu(e)** *forbidden* **j'enfanterais (enfanter** *to give birth to)* **j'enverrais (envoyer** *to send)* **mettre un terme aux guerres** *to end war* **abattre** *to strike down* **bénir** *to bless* **veiller sur le monde** *to watch over the world* **à travers** *across* **les cieux (m)** *the heavens* **filer** *to fly by* **la haine** *hatred* **le cœur** *the heart* **prier** *to pray*

130 000 000 d'Africains sont chrétiens, 150 000 000 sont musulmans et 200 000 000 pratiquent des religions indigènes.

La basilique à Yamoussoukro en Côte-d'Ivoire

Une mosquée au Mali

A. Avez-vous compris?

1. Indiquez six choses que le poète ferait s'il était Dieu.
2. Où se trouverait sa capitale? Où se trouverait le Vatican?
3. Quels vers *(lines)* du poème suggèrent que le poète est pacifiste?

B. Et vous? Que feriez-vous si vous étiez Dieu, le chef du gouvernement ou le professeur de français? Écrivez votre propre poème.

Composition

A. Organisez-vous. Vous organisez une réunion *(meeting)* dans votre ville pour une organisation bénévole, réelle ou imaginaire, et vous êtes chargé(e) d'écrire un bulletin aux participants francophones. Avant d'écrire votre bulletin, répondez d'abord aux questions suivantes.

1. Pour quelle organisation bénévole travaillez-vous?
2. Quelles sont les dates de la réunion?
3. Où dans votre ville est-ce que vous allez vous réunir *(to meet)*?
4. Où est-ce que les participants vont loger *(to lodge)*?
5. Quels moyens de transport recommandez-vous?
6. Quelles sont les indications pour aller de l'aéroport à chaque endroit *(place)*?
7. Où est-ce que les participants pourront manger?
8. Quelles autres recommandations ou conseils avez-vous pour les visiteurs?

B. Rédaction: Un bulletin. En utilisant ce que vous avez préparé dans l'exercice précédent, écrivez un bulletin donnant tous les renseignements nécessaires aux visiteurs qui viendront dans votre ville pour la réunion.

C. Un coup de téléphone. Comparez votre bulletin et celui d'un(e) partenaire. Ensuite, choisissez l'un des deux et préparez la conversation suivante.

Un(e) des participant(e)s à la réunion a perdu les renseignements que vous lui avez envoyés et il/elle téléphone pour s'informer.

If you have access to SYSTÈME-D software, you will find the following phrases, vocabulary, grammar, and dictionary aids there.

Phrases: Writing a news item; Giving directions: Advising
Vocabulary: Calendar; Telling time; City; Means of transportation; Traveling; Direction and distance; Restaurant; Meals

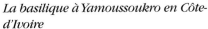

LA NÉGRITUDE

See the *Instructor's Resource Manual* for the video script and activities.

Note. The vocabulary in this section does not appear in the end-of-chapter vocabulary lists and is meant for recognition only. You may wish to let students know in advance whether you intend to test them on this vocabulary.

Pendant les années trente, **les écrivains** francophones noirs commencent à utiliser le terme de négritude pour décrire la culture noire, l'opposant à la culture imposée par les colonisateurs européens. Pour Léopold Sédar Senghor, poète et premier président sénégalais, la négritude représente «**le patrimoine** culturel, **les valeurs** et surtout **l'esprit** de la civilisation négro-africaine». Le poète et ardent anticolonialiste martiniquais Aimé Césaire la définit comme «l'acceptation et prise en charge de son destin de Noir, de son histoire, de sa culture». Alioune Diop, poète sénégalais, dit que c'est «**le génie** nègre et en même temps **la volonté** d'en révéler la dignité». En plus du désir de se libérer de la suprématie de la culture européenne, on trouve souvent aussi dans la négritude **un mépris** des problèmes apportés par le monde moderne.

Voici un poème de Claude-Emmanuel Abolo Bowole, un Camerounais, et un poème de Bernard Dadié, un Ivoirien.

Une femme et son enfant au Burkina Faso

Préférence...
de Claude-Emmanuel Abolo Bowole

Un Message
À vous qui **luttez,**
À vous qui rêvez d'un monde meilleur;
À vous qui avez le courage de dire
Ce que vous **croyez** être **la vérité...**
À vous tous
Qui écrivez...
J'adresse ce message d'**espoir.**
Le monde où nous sommes
Est un monde de **haine,**
Qui ne le sait?
Le monde où nous sommes,
Qu'en ferons-nous toi et moi?
Pouvons-nous en faire
Un monde de **paix,**
Un monde de fraternité,
Un monde d'**amitié,**
Un monde de gaieté...

---

un écrivain *a writer*   **le patrimoine** *the heritage*   **une valeur** *a value*   **l'esprit** *(m) spirit*   **le génie** *genius*   **la volonté** *the will*   **un mépris** *a disdain*   **lutter** *to struggle*   **croyez (croire** *to believe)*   **la vérité** *the truth*   **l'espoir** *(m) hope*   **la haine** *hatred*   **la paix** *peace*   **l'amitié** *(f) friendship*

Je vous remercie mon *Dieu*
de Bernard Dadié

Je vous remercie mon Dieu, de m'avoir créé Noir,
d'avoir fait de moi
la somme de toutes **les douleurs,**
mis sur ma tête,
le Monde.
J'ai **la livrée** du Centaure
Et je porte le Monde depuis le premier soir.

Je suis content
de la forme de ma tête
faite pour porter le monde,
Satisfait
de la forme de mon nez
Qui doit **humer** tout le vent du Monde,
Heureux
de la forme de mes jambes
Prêtes à **courir** toutes **les étapes** du Monde.

Je vous remercie mon Dieu, de m'avoir créé Noir,
d'avoir fait de moi
la somme de toutes les douleurs.

Trente-six **épées ont transpercé** mon **cœur**
Trente-six **brasiers** ont **brûlé** mon corps.
Et mon **sang** sur tous **les calvaires** a rougi la neige,
Et mon sang à tous **les levants** a rougi la nature.

Je suis quand même
Content de porter le Monde,
Content de mes bras courts,
  de mes bras longs,
    de **l'épaisseur** de mes **lèvres.**

Je vous remercie mon Dieu, de m'avoir créé Noir,
Je porte le Monde depuis **l'aube** des temps
Et mon **rire** sur le Monde
  dans la nuit
    crée le jour.

À discuter.

Étudie-t-on la littérature africaine et la littérature afro-américaine à l'école ici?
Devrait-on les étudier plus? Est-ce qu'il y a des mouvements pour protéger et
promouvoir *(to promote)* les cultures des divers groupes ethniques dans notre
pays?

Dieu *God* **créé(e)** *created* **la douleur** *the pain* **le monde** *the world* **la livrée** *the livery* **humer** *to breathe*
in **courir** *to run* **une étape** *a stage* (of a race) **une épée** *a sword* **transpercer** *to pierce* **le cœur** *the*
heart **un brasier** *an inferno* **brûler** *to burn* **le sang** *the blood* **un calvaire** *a Calvary* **le levant** *the*
sunrise **l'épaisseur** *(f) the thickness* **les lèvres** *(f) the lips* **l'aube** *(f) the dawn* **le rire** *the laugh, the laughter*

visit http://horizons.heinle.com

COMPÉTENCE 1

Deciding where to stay

NOMS MASCULINS

un hôtelier	a hotel manager
un lavabo	a washbasin, a sink
le logement	lodging
un supplément	an extra charge, a supplement

NOMS FÉMININS

une clé	a key
une hôtelière	a hotel manager
la réception	the front desk

ADJECTIFS

compris(e)	included
privé(e)	private
servi(e)	served

DIVERS

de luxe	deluxe
en espèces	in cash
que	that, which, whom
qui	that, which, who
régler la note	to pay the bill

COMPÉTENCE 2

Going to the doctor

NOMS MASCULINS

les frissons	the shivers
un liquide	a liquid
un médecin	a doctor
un patient	a patient
un rhume	a cold
un symptôme	a symptom
un virus	a virus

NOMS FÉMININS

une allergie	an allergy
une clinique	a clinic
la grippe	the flu
une indigestion	indigestion
une ordonnance	a prescription
une patiente	a patient

EXPRESSIONS VERBALES

avoir mal à...	one's . . . hurt(s)
communiquer	to communicate
éternuer	to sneeze
Il faut...	One must . . ., It's necessary to . . .
Il ne faut pas...	One shouldn't . . ., One must not . . .
Il vaut mieux...	It's better to . . .
regretter	to regret
se sentir	to feel
tomber malade	to get sick
tousser	to cough
vomir	to vomit, to throw up

ADJECTIFS

désolé(e)	sorry
enceinte	pregnant
étonné(e)	surprised, amazed
furieux (furieuse)	furious
malade	sick
nécessaire	necessary
surpris(e)	surprised
triste	sad

DIVERS

exactement	exactly
Qu'est-ce qui ne va pas?	What's wrong?

Pour les parties du corps, voir la page 370.

COMPÉTENCE 3

NOMS MASCULINS

un artiste	*an artist, a performer*
l'avenir	*the future*
un avocat	*a lawyer*
des conseils	*advice*
le Corps de la Paix	*the Peace Corps*
un doctorat	*a doctorate*
le droit	*(study of, field of) law*
un fiancé	*a fiancé*
un homme d'affaires	*a businessman*
un ingénieur	*an engineer*
un musicien	*a musician*
un peintre	*a painter*

NOMS FÉMININS

une artiste	*an artist, a performer*
une avocate	*a lawyer*
une carrière	*a career*
une femme d'affaires	*a businesswoman*
une fiancée	*a fiancée*
une frontière	*a border*
une maîtrise	*a master's degree*
la médecine	*(study of, field of) medicine*
une musicienne	*a musician*
une organisation	*an organization*
une possibilité	*a possibility*
une situation	*a situation*
une société	*a company*

ADJECTIFS

bénévole	*volunteer, benevolent*
international(e) (mpl **internationaux**)	*international*
professionnel(le)	*professional*
stable	*stable*

DIVERS

gagner de l'argent	*to earn money, to make money*
quoi	*what*

COMPÉTENCE 4

NOM MASCULIN

un plan	*a map*

NOMS FÉMININS

une expression	*an expression*
les indications	*directions*
une place	*a (town) square, a plaza*

EXPRESSIONS VERBALES

continuer	*to continue*
expliquer	*to explain*
indiquer le chemin	*to give directions, to show the way*
remercier	*to thank*
tourner	*to turn*
traverser	*to cross, to go across*

EXPRESSIONS PRÉPOSITIONNELLES

à droite	*to the right*
à gauche	*to the left*
au coin de	*on the corner of*
dans la rue...	*on . . . street*
jusqu'à	*until, up to, as far as*
sur l'avenue... / le boulevard... / la place...	*on . . . Avenue / . . . Boulevard / . . . Square*
tout droit	*straight (ahead)*

DIVERS

Je vous en prie.	*You're welcome.*
là	*there*
utile	*useful*

Branchez-vous sur le français

As with many jobs, the best way to get your foot in the door in diplomacy or international affairs is to do related volunteer work. Here are some organizations that place volunteers in French-speaking developing countries:

Peace Corps
1111 20th St.
Washington, D.C. 20526
(800) 424-8580 www.peacecorps.gov

International Voluntary Services
(short term) Main Office
SCI International Voluntary Service
814 NE 40th St.
Seattle, WA 98105
(206) 545-6585 sciifo@sci-ivs.org
(long term) LTV Office
SCI International Voluntary Service
205 North Plain Road
Great Barrington, MA 01230
(413) 528-1307 ltv@sci-ivs.org

Operation Crossroads Africa
475 Riverside Drive, Suite 1366
New York, NY 10015
(212) 870-2106 oca@igc.opc.org

World Teach, % Center for
International Development
Harvard University
79 JFK St.
Cambridge, MA 02138
(800) 483-2240 info@worldteach.org

For those wishing to work with international organizations such as the United Nations, it is recommended that you have fluency in English, French, and Spanish. Spanish is spoken in 19 different countries, and French, like English, is the official language of even more nations. The United Nations Offices in New York and Geneva hire French-speaking international lawyers, public information officers, demographers, secretaries, tour guides, and translators or interpreters. Translators and interpreters must be able to translate or interpret from two of the other official languages of the United Nations (French, English, Spanish, Russian, Chinese, and Arabic) into their native language. The United Nations also hires people for a variety of jobs in developing countries, working with organizations such as the United Nations Children's Fund, the World Health Organization, and the United Nations Development Program. Most employees of these organizations have a background in social work, economics, health and nutrition, teaching, technology, or languages. One way to gain valuable experience with the United Nations, which can eventually lead to a permanent job, is to volunteer. Working in a variety of fields such as education, healthcare, and agricultural and community development, volunteers are paid travel and basic living expenses. For more information, visit www.unv.org.

Knowing French can also help you obtain a job in the Foreign Service, with the United States federal government, either in Washington or in offices in over 140 different countries. In fact, persons entering the Foreign Service with no foreign language skills are put on probation until competency in a second language is demonstrated. To enter the Foreign Service, you must take a written and an oral exam that generally cover current events, history, geography, international relations, art, literature, culture, economics, and verbal expression. For more information about working for the United States State Department, visit www.state.gov/www/careers.

The State Department is not the only part of the government that hires people because they are fluent in foreign languages. Nearly all governmental departments and agencies, from the Library of Congress to the Environmental Protection Agency, need people who know French.

Les Nations unies à Genève

DOSSIER: **Dr. Joanne Leslie**

Interviewer: *Où est-ce que vous travaillez et quelles sont vos responsabilités dans cette organisation?*

Dr. Leslie: J'ai deux rôles. Je suis **enseignante** à l'école de Santé Publique à l'université de Californie à Los Angeles (UCLA). Je suis aussi une des **fondatrices** du *Pacific Institute for Women's Health,* une organisation non-gouvernementale de **recherche** et d'assistance technique. Je **gère** un des programmes de cette institution intitulé *Adolescent Health Linkages Program.*

Interviewer: *Dans quels pays francophones est-ce que votre organisation travaille et qu'est-ce que vous y faites?*

Dr. Leslie: Nous travaillons en Afrique de l'Ouest et en Afrique centrale, surtout au Cameroun, au Sénégal et au Burkina Faso. Dans ces trois régions, nous offrons une assistance technique aux **chercheurs** et **prestataires** de services dans le domaine de la santé reproductive de l'adolescent.

Interviewer: *Quels aspects de votre travail dans ces pays trouvez-vous les plus difficiles? Lesquels sont les plus satisfaisants?*

Dr. Leslie: Un des aspects les plus difficiles est **le manque** d'infrastructure et de moyens de communication. Ce que je trouve le plus satisfaisant, c'est l'enthousiasme de mes collègues africains, surtout les jeunes, face aux énormes difficultés de leurs pays comme la crise économique, **la sécheresse,** les maladies (en particulier **le paludisme** et **le SIDA**) et les effets **néfastes** du colonialisme. Ils montrent tous le désir et la capacité d'**améliorer** la vie des jeunes Africains.

Interviewer: *Quelles différences entre les États-Unis et les pays francophones où vous travaillez influencent votre travail?*

Dr. Leslie: Quand je travaille en Afrique francophone, je retrouve l'aspect humain de mon travail. En Afrique, il faut parler de la famille, et pas seulement du travail. Il faut absolument manger ensemble, discuter ensemble, **prier** et chanter ensemble si vous voulez réussir dans n'importe quel domaine.

Interviewer: *Quelles recommandations pouvez-vous faire à un(e) étudiant(e) qui voudrait travailler à l'étranger pour une organisation comme la vôtre?*

Dr. Leslie: Pour travailler à l'étranger dans le domaine de la santé publique, il est essentiel de savoir parler **couramment** une langue importante comme le français, l'espagnol, l'arabe ou le chinois. Il est **souhaitable** aussi d'habiter pendant quelque temps **hors des** États-Unis (dans un pays **du Tiers Monde**) pour développer une tolérance et un respect réels à l'égard de cultures et **de façons de vivre** et de penser qui sont différentes **des nôtres.**

---

un(e) enseignant(e) *a teacher*   **un fondateur (une fondatrice)** *a founder*   **la recherche** *research*   **gérer** *to manage*   **un chercheur (une chercheuse)** *a researcher*   **un prestataire** *a provider*   **le manque** *the lack* **la sécheresse** *drought*   **le paludisme** *malaria*   **le SIDA** *AIDS*   **néfaste** *harmful*   **améliorer** *to improve* **prier** *to pray*   **couramment** *fluently*   **souhaitable** *desirable*   **hors de** *outside of*   **du Tiers Monde** *of the Third World*   **la façon de vivre** *way of life*   **des nôtres** *from ours*

Return of the Hunters

Pieter Bruegel (Elder) (1525–1569)
1565
Künsthistorisches Museum, Gemældegalerie, Vienna
Erich Lessing/Art Resource, NY

Bruegel lived and worked in Antwerp, Belgium. This scene, depicting
the barrenness of winter, is typical of his paintings, which often portray
human activity against the backdrop of a vast landscape.

Note. This chapter contains a mystery story that incorporates review activities. Students do review activities as they solve the mystery. They are not responsible for any new vocabulary on the tests. You may wish to explain the purpose of this chapter and introduce the setting and characters before beginning.

Suggestion. This chapter is set in the Ardennes Forest in Belgium. Have students brainstorm about what they know about Belgium. Have them list all the francophone countries in Europe and tell what they know about them.

En Europe: En Belgique

LA BELGIQUE (LE ROYAUME DE BELGIQUE)

SUPERFICIE: 30 513 kilomètres carrés

POPULATION: 10 243 000 (les Belges)

CAPITALE: Bruxelles

LANGUES OFFICIELLES: le flamand *(Flemish)* (58%), le français (32%), l'allemand (1%). Neuf
  pour cent de la population est bilingue.

INDUSTRIES PRINCIPALES: industries métallurgiques, textiles et chimiques; verrerie *(glassworks);*
  agriculture; communications; commerce

Un drôle de mystère

Quelqu'un a été assassiné et c'est à vous, le détective, de trouver le criminel. En même temps, vous allez faire une révision de ce que vous avez appris dans *Horizons.* Si vous avez des difficultés en faisant un exercice, référez-vous aux pages indiquées en marge *(in the margin).*

Les personnages

Un mystère dans les Ardennes

Épilogue

Comparaisons culturelles   **L'Europe francophone**

La Belgique

Bruxelles, la capitale belge, est une ville bilingue.
Dans la Région **flamande**, dans **le nord** du pays,
on parle un dialecte **néerlandais**, le flamand.
Dans la Région wallonne, dans **le sud**, on parle français.
Dans **l'est**, un pour cent de la population parle allemand,
la troisième langue officielle en Belgique.

Anvers est la plus grande ville de la Région flamande.

La Grand-Place, Bruxelles, Belgique

La Belgique est une monarchie parlementaire.
L'opposition linguistique entre les Flamands et les
Wallons est reflétée dans une opposition
politique. Comme la majorité des Belges, le
Premier ministre est généralement flamand. Pour
certains Belges, le roi **ne** joue **aucun** rôle
important dans le gouvernement, mais pour
d'autres, sa présence assure le respect **des droits**
de la minorité wallonne.

Liège est la plus grande ville wallonne.

---

le nord *the north*   **néerlandais(e)** *Dutch*   **le sud** *the south*   **l'est** *the east*   **ne... aucun(e)** *not any, no*   **les droits** *(m) rights*

Siège de l'OTAN (Organisation du traité de l'Atlantique Nord), la Belgique a été **un champ de bataille pendant les deux guerres mondiales. Au cours de** la Première Guerre mondiale, les Allemands ont occupé le pays pendant quatre ans et près d'un million de Belges se sont réfugiés en France, en Grande-Bretagne et aux **Pays-Bas.** L'histoire s'est répétée pendant la Seconde Guerre mondiale. Occupée **à partir de 1940,** la Belgique a été libérée par les Alliés en décembre 1944, **lors de la** célèbre **bataille des Ardennes** qui a **eu lieu** près de la ville de Bastogne. **Les villageois de la région racontent** que, dans une neige **qui leur arrivait jusqu'aux genoux,** les troupes américaines ont demandé aux **citoyens** belges de leur donner leurs **draps** pour servir de camouflage. Après la guerre, ces villages **ont reçu** des paquets de draps de la part du gouvernement américain. Cette coopération entre l'Amérique et la Belgique au cours de la guerre a continué jusqu'à aujourd'hui.

Additional information. A. The North Atlantic Treaty Organization (NATO) was created on April 4, 1949, when the treaty was signed in Washington, D.C. The treaty established an organization to preserve peace and international security, and to promote stability in the North Atlantic area after World War II. It is a treaty of alliance within the framework of the United Nations charter. The twelve original signatories were: Belgium, Canada, Denmark, France, Iceland, Italy, Luxembourg, the Netherlands, Norway, Portugal, the United Kingdom, and the United States. They were later joined by Germany, Greece, Spain, Poland, Hungary, the Czech Republic, and Turkey. **B.** The Battle of the Ardennes is also called the Battle of the Bulge because the Germans forced a bulge in the Allied army's line as it advanced toward the Rhine and Germany after liberating France in late 1944. Before dawn on December 16, moving through deep snow, 200,000 German troops launched a surprise attack on American positions in an attempt to delay the Allied advance. In bad weather, some of the most bitter fighting of the Western European war continued until late January 1945, when the Germans finally retreated. Over 600,000 troops with heavy artillery were committed to that battle. The Germans suffered more than 100,000 casualties, the Americans more than 80,000.

Quick-reference answers for *À deviner!* 1. le flamand, le français et l'allemand **2.** le flamand 58%, le français 32%, l'allemand 1% (Neuf pour cent de la population est bilingue.) **3.** Liège **4.** la France, la Belgique, la Suisse, le Luxembourg, Monaco

Le musée militaire à Novion-Porcien, Ardennes

À deviner!

1. Quelles sont les trois langues officielles de la Belgique?
2. Quel pourcentage de la population belge parle chacune de ces langues?
3. Bruxelles, une ville bilingue, est la capitale du pays. Quelle est la plus grande ville francophone en Belgique après Bruxelles?
4. Quels sont les pays européens dont le français est la (ou une des) langue(s) officielle(s)?

---

le siège *the seat* **un champ de bataille** *a battlefield* **une guerre mondiale** *a world war* **au cours de** *in the course of* **les Pays-Bas** *the Netherlands* **à partir de 1940** *starting in 1940* **lors de** *at the time of* **la bataille des Ardennes** *the Battle of the Bulge* **avoir lieu** *to take place* **les villageois** *the villagers* **raconter** *to tell, to recount* **qui leur arrivait jusqu'aux genoux** *that came up to their knees* **un(e) citoyen(ne)** *a citizen* **un drap** *a bedsheet* **ont reçu** *received*

Dans ce chapitre, vous allez **résoudre** l'énigme d'un crime. C'est **un meurtre** qui **a lieu** dans un vieux château de la forêt des Ardennes, dans **le sud** de la Belgique. En résolvant le mystère, vous allez aussi réviser ce que vous avez appris dans ce livre. D'abord, faisons la connaissance des personnages du mystère.

Suggestion. Have students guess the significance of the characters' names. Point out that the use of stereotypes is typical of the mystery genre.

Regardez les personnages suivants. Comment sont-ils?

François Fédor,
millionnaire
excentrique

Laurent Lavare,
le comptable
de François Fédor

Valérie Veutoux,
l'ex-femme
de François Fédor

Bernard Boncorps,
le neveu de François Fédor

Nathalie Lanana,
la petite amie de Bernard Boncorps

Note. The instructor plays the role of the **domestique** in all activities. For any listening activity involving the **domestique,** you may play the *Text CD* or read the script aloud.

le/la domestique

le détective

Il y a encore un dernier petit détail. Le/La domestique sera joué(e) par votre professeur. Et le détective, qui est-ce? Oui, vous avez deviné juste (comme un bon détective); c'est vous!

---

résoudre *to resolve*   **un meurtre** *a murder*   **avoir lieu** *to take place*   **le sud** *the south*   **un(e) comptable** *an accountant*

A. Descriptions. Choisissez quatre adjectifs pour décrire chacun des personnages.

•Pour réviser l'accord des adjectifs, voir les pages 32, 38–39 et 46.

> *riche* ??? malhonnête *(dishonest)* **beau** ??? ÂGÉ ???
>
> snob *bête* paresseux **laid** *blond*
>
> **suspect** MÉCHANT sympathique IRRESPONSABLE ???
>
> (mal)heureux *désagréable* sexy FROID
>
> *hostile* *grand* petit INTELLIGENT ???
>
> *sportif* MATÉRIALISTE FRIVOLE sérieux INTÉRESSANT

Suggestion for **A. Description.** Point out that the final **b** in **snob** is pronounced and that you do not add an **-e** to make it feminine. Point out that **sexy** is invariable.

B. Explications. Avec un(e) partenaire, devinez qui va être la victime et qui va commettre le crime. Imaginez une explication. Utilisez un dictionnaire si nécessaire.

•Pour réviser le futur immédiat, voir les pages 38–39 et 46.

C. Stratégies. Vous avez appris plusieurs stratégies pour lire plus facilement en français. Avant de lire *Un mystère dans les Ardennes* à la page suivante, révisez les stratégies suivantes.

   a. Utilisez les mots apparentés et le contexte pour donner le sens de ces phrases.

      1. L'aptitude de François Fédor à faire fortune était sans égal. Et on pouvait dire la même chose de son aptitude à se faire des ennemis.

      2. Dans le village, où il n'allait jamais, on l'appelait le vieux Midas parce qu'on disait que tout ce qu'il touchait se transformait en or.

   b. Utilisez les mots entre parenthèses pour deviner le sens des mots en italique.

      1. (jeune) On disait que François Fédor avait fait fortune en Afrique pendant sa *jeunesse*.

      2. (attendre) Cette *attente* avait duré presque deux jours.

   c. Vous avez appris à utiliser les verbes **avoir** et **être** comme auxiliaires au passé composé. En mettant l'auxiliaire à l'imparfait, au futur ou au conditionnel, vous pouvez créer de nouveaux temps verbaux. Comparez ces phrases:

Je l'**ai** fait.	*I **have** done it.*	Il **est** parti.	*He **has** left.*
Je l'**avais** fait.	*I **had** done it.*	Il **était** parti.	*He **had** left.*
Je l'**aurai** fait.	*I **will have** done it.*	Il **sera** parti.	*He **will have** left.*
Je l'**aurais** fait.	*I **would have** done it.*	Il **serait** parti.	*He **would have** left.*

Donnez les sens des expressions en italique dans les phrases suivantes.

      1. François Fédor *avait toujours fait* ce qu'il voulait mais il *avait toujours négligé* (négliger *to neglect*) les membres de sa famille.

      2. Ils acceptaient son argent chaque mois sans poser de questions et ils *n'auraient jamais pensé* que François Fédor puisse choisir un acte de charité plus méritoire.

      3. Si M. Lavare, le comptable, *n'avait pas été* là, on *n'aurait pas dit* quatre mots durant tout le dîner.

Maintenant, utilisez ces stratégies pour lire le dossier *(file)* sur ce cas aux pages suivantes.

UN MYSTÈRE DANS LES ARDENNES

Certains l'admiraient, d'autres le détestaient. Il avait toujours fait ce qu'il voulait et **personne ne discutait** ce qu'il faisait. François Fédor habitait dans un vieux château **au fond de** la forêt des Ardennes. Dans le village, où il n'allait jamais, on l'appelait le vieux Midas parce qu'on disait que tout ce qu'il touchait se transformait en or. Personne ne savait exactement d'où venait sa fortune, mais on disait qu'il avait fait fortune en Afrique pendant sa jeunesse.

Son aptitude à faire fortune était sans égal. Et on pouvait dire la même chose de son aptitude à se faire des ennemis. François Fédor avait toujours négligé les membres de sa famille et il n'avait jamais pris le temps de se faire des amis. Quand je dis qu'il avait négligé les membres de sa famille, je ne veux pas donner l'impression qu'il ne partageait pas sa richesse avec **eux;** au contraire, ils ne **manquaient de** rien. Comme dans **un trou** noir, chaque mois, François Fédor **versait** une petite fortune sur **les comptes en banque** de son neveu Bernard Boncorps et de son ex-femme Valérie Veutoux. Il payait cet argent depuis vingt ans sans avoir **le moindre** contact avec l'un ou l'autre. En fait, il n'avait jamais rencontré son neveu, qui **vivait** une vie de play-boy à Monaco **grâce à** son vieil oncle. Et eux non plus, ils n'avaient jamais essayé de venir le voir. Ils acceptaient son argent chaque mois sans poser de questions et ils n'auraient jamais pensé que François Fédor puisse choisir un jour un acte de charité plus **méritoire.**

C'était donc avec grande surprise que son neveu et son ex-femme avaient reçu un coup de téléphone de Laurent Lavare, le comptable de François Fédor, quelques semaines **auparavant.** Ils étaient **priés de se rendre** chez le vieux Midas le dernier jour du mois **courant** avant midi. Chacun se demandait ce que le vieux Fédor pouvait bien vouloir après tout ce temps. Mais M. Lavare avait refusé de leur donner plus de détails. Quand ils étaient arrivés au grand château sombre, Valérie Veutoux, Bernard Boncorps et sa petite amie Nathalie Lanana s'étaient sentis un peu **mal à l'aise.** Après avoir passé deux journées entières dans le château sans voir leur hôte, les invités avaient senti leur **malaise** se transformer en panique. Mais que pouvaient-ils faire sinon accepter les caprices de leur **bienfaiteur** et chercher une manière de passer le temps? Quand Bernard n'était pas avec Nathalie, il jouait au billard pendant qu'elle nageait dans la piscine. Valérie Veutoux restait toute la journée dans sa chambre. Cette attente avait duré presque deux jours quand le/la domestique les avait enfin informés qu'ils verraient M. Fédor au dîner à huit heures, dans la salle à manger.

Accompagné de son comptable, François Fédor les attendait, **assis** à table, quand ils étaient descendus. Sans dire un mot, le vieil hôte leur avait indiqué d'un geste de la main où chacun devait **s'asseoir,** à l'autre bout de la table.

---

personne ne… *no one* . . . **discuter** *to question* **au fond de** *deep in* **eux** *them* **manquer de** *to lack* **un trou** *a hole* **verser** *to pour, to deposit* **un compte en banque** *a bank account* **le moindre** *the least* **vivre** *to live* **grâce à** *thanks to* **méritoire** *deserving* **auparavant** *beforehand* **prié(e) de se rendre** *requested to appear* **courant(e)** *current* **mal à l'aise** *ill at ease* **le malaise** *uneasiness* **un bienfaiteur** *a benefactor* **assis(e)** *seated* **s'asseoir** *to sit*

Le/La domestique avait servi un excellent dîner mais les invités, qui n'avaient pas l'habitude d'apprécier ce qu'on leur donnait, **n'avaient fait aucun** compliment. Ils étaient trop curieux de connaître la raison de cette réunion soudaine et **inattendue.** Si M. Lavare, le comptable, n'avait pas été là, on n'aurait pas dit quatre mots durant tout le dîner.

Le repas fini, François Fédor s'était retiré à la bibliothèque et il avait demandé au/à la domestique de faire entrer son neveu et son ex-femme l'un après l'autre pour boire un cognac avec lui... Il avait quelque chose d'important à leur dire. Ils avaient eu avec M. Fédor une conférence d'une demi-heure chacun, puis le/la domestique les avait raccompagnés à leur chambre et leur avait **souhaité** une bonne nuit. Devinaient-ils la scène qui les attendrait le lendemain matin en sortant de leur chambre? Savaient-ils qu'un détective voudrait leur parler et qu'ils seraient **soupçonnés** d'un meurtre? Au moins une personne présente cette nuit-là le savait. Mais qui était-ce?

Quand ils s'étaient levés, ils avaient appris que tôt le matin, le/la domestique avait téléphoné à la police pour dire que François Fédor avait été victime d'un meurtre au cours de la nuit. Qui avait **commis** ce crime? Quel était **le mobile** du meurtre? Pourquoi est-ce que François Fédor leur avait demandé de venir? Qu'est-ce qu'il leur avait dit dans la bibliothèque? Qu'est-ce que M. Lavare savait? Et le/la domestique? Qu'est-ce qui s'était passé ce soir-là?

C'est à vous de résoudre le mystère. Qu'est-ce que le célèbre inspecteur Maigret aurait fait à votre place? Vous allez sans doute vouloir poser beaucoup de questions et prendre des notes.

D. Détails. Lisez le texte *Un mystère dans les Ardennes* et répondez aux questions suivantes.

1. Où est-ce que François Fédor habitait?
2. D'où venait sa fortune?
3. Avait-il beaucoup d'amis?
4. Qui profitait aussi de son argent?
5. Qui a téléphoné à Bernard Boncorps et à Valérie Veutoux pour les inviter au château?
6. Combien de temps ont-ils dû attendre avant de voir François Fédor?
7. À votre avis *(opinion),* qu'est-ce que François Fédor a dit à Bernard Boncorps et à Valérie Veutoux dans la bibliothèque?

Un château de la forêt des Ardennes

---

ne... aucun(e) *no, not any*   **inattendu(e)** *unexpected*   **souhaiter** *to wish*   **soupçonné(e)** *suspected*   **commettre** *to commit*   **le mobile** *the motive*

• Pour réviser l'imparfait, voir la page 218.

• Pour réviser comment dire l'heure, voir la page 12.

E. Vous êtes le détective. Pour commencer votre enquête *(investigation)*, écoutez la déclaration de chacun des personnages qui a passé la nuit au château. En les écoutant, notez les réponses aux questions qui suivent sur une autre feuille de papier.

Bernard Boncorps   Valérie Veutoux   Laurent Lavare   le/la domestique

1. Qu'est-ce que chaque personne a fait après le dîner?
2. À quelle heure est-ce que chacun s'est couché?
3. Qu'est-ce que chacun a entendu dans le couloir pendant la nuit?

Écoutez une fois de plus les déclarations de Valérie Veutoux, de Laurent Lavare et de Bernard Boncorps et notez qui faisait chaque chose à l'heure indiquée.

Exemple   être déjà au lit
À dix heures et demie, Valérie Veutoux était déjà au lit.

1. avoir mal à la tête
   travailler sur
      l'ordinateur
   être au village

2. prendre un verre
      au café
   lire
   parler au
      téléphone

3. jouer aux cartes
   dormir

F. Il a disparu. Le corps de François Fédor a disparu *(disappeared)*. Vous devez bien examiner le lieu *(place)* du crime. Observez bien tous les indices *(clues)*. Voici la chambre de François Fédor avant le dîner et le lendemain du crime. Quelles différences y a-t-il?

• Pour réviser les prépositions, voir la page 112.

• Pour réviser les meubles, voir les pages 108 et 114.

Suggestion for *F. Il a disparu.* You may wish to supply the word **un coffre-fort.**

Follow-up for *F. Il a disparu.* Have students also tell where the cats are.

avant le dîner

le lendemain du crime

Regardez encore une fois les deux dessins. Demandez au/à la domestique si chaque chose qui se trouve dans la chambre le lendemain du crime et qui n'était pas là la nuit précédente appartenait *(belonged)* à François Fédor. Dites à qui pourraient appartenir les choses qui n'étaient pas à lui.

• Pour réviser comment exprimer la possession, voir les pages 116 et 118.

Answers. Only the men's clothing belonged to François Fédor.

Exemple — **Est-ce que c'était son ordinateur?**
— **Non, ce n'était pas l'ordinateur de M. Fédor.**
— **Alors, c'est peut-être l'ordinateur de M. Lavare.**

• Pour réviser les prépositions, voir la page 112.

G. Dans quelle chambre? Tout le monde a dormi le long du même couloir hier soir. Écoutez le/la domestique pour déterminer qui a dormi dans chaque chambre.

Exemple **Mme Veutoux était au bout du couloir, en face de la salle de bains.**

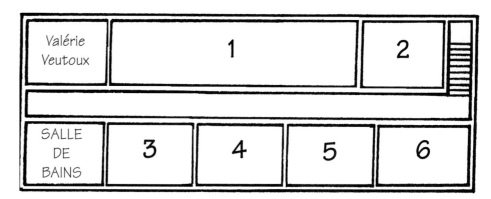

• Pour réviser les pronoms compléments d'objet direct et indirect, voir les pages 174, 338 et 344.

H. Relations. Utilisez le pronom **le** ou le pronom **lui** avec les verbes suivants à l'imparfait pour interroger le/la domestique sur ses relations avec M. Fédor. Écoutez ses réponses.

Exemple   connaître M. Fédor depuis longtemps
— **Est-ce que vous le connaissiez depuis longtemps?**
— **Je le connaissais depuis 15 ans.**

1. aimer bien M. Fédor
2. parler à M. Fédor de sa famille
3. emprunter quelquefois de l'argent à M. Fédor
4. réveiller M. Fédor à la même heure tous les jours
5. trouver M. Fédor sévère

Maintenant demandez au/à la domestique si M. Fédor faisait les choses suivantes. Écoutez ses réponses.

Exemple   vous irriter quelquefois
— **Est-ce que M. Fédor vous irritait quelquefois?**
— **Oui, il m'irritait quelquefois. Ce n'était pas un homme facile.**

1. vous dire tout
2. vous payer bien
3. vous parler de sa vie privée

I. Je ne veux pas que... Dites aux suspects ce qu'ils doivent et ne doivent pas faire.

•Pour réviser le subjonctif, voir les pages 372–373, 374 et 378.

Exemple   Je ne veux pas que vous partiez d'ici.

Il faut que... Il ne faut pas que... Je veux que... Je ne veux pas que... Il vaut mieux que...	partir d'ici dire tout ce que vous savez être calmes avoir peur toucher aux affaires *(things)* de M. Fédor faire une déposition parler à la presse m'obéir être patients ???

J. Savoir ou connaître? Votre enquête *(investigation)* progresse. Dites si vous savez ou si vous connaissez les choses ou les personnes suivantes en utilisant le verbe **savoir** ou le verbe **connaître.**

•Pour réviser **savoir** et **connaître,** voir la page 336.

1. la date du crime
2. le/la domestique de M. Fédor
3. l'heure approximative du crime
4. le château de M. Fédor
5. tous les amis de M. Fédor
6. tous les détails de la vie de M. Fédor
7. des mobiles *(motives)* possibles
8. l'identité de l'assassin

K. Il faut penser comme le/la criminel(le). Pour attraper le/la criminel(le), il faut penser comme lui/elle. Si vous étiez le/la criminel(le), est-ce que vous feriez les choses suivantes? Utilisez le conditionnel.

•Pour réviser le conditionnel, voir la page 310–311.

Si j'étais le/la criminel(le),...

Exemple   faire quelque chose d'inhabituel
Si j'étais le/la criminel(le), je ne ferais rien d'inhabituel.

1. être calme
2. parler beaucoup du crime
3. savoir tous les détails du crime
4. obéir à la police
5. s'intéresser beaucoup à l'enquête
6. dire la vérité *(truth)*
7. avoir envie de partir
8. devenir de plus en plus nerveux (nerveuse)
9. accuser quelqu'un d'autre
10. ???

• Pour réviser les verbes réfléchis, voir les pages 248–249, 256 et 264.

• Pour réviser l'imparfait, voir la page 218.

• Pour réviser comment dire l'heure, voir la page 12.

L. Une matinée typique. Voici comment François Fédor passait ses matinées. Décrivez sa journée typique. Utilisez l'imparfait.

1.

2.

3.

4.

5.

6.

(sans title)

M. Accusations. Dans le château Fédor, chacun des suspects vient vous expliquer pourquoi il/elle soupçonne *(suspects)* les autres. Complétez les paragraphes suivants en mettant les verbes entre parenthèses au passé composé ou à l'imparfait.

• Pour réviser le passé composé et l'imparfait, voir les pages 222, 224 et 230.

BERNARD BONCORPS

Je crois que c'est Laurent Lavare, le comptable de mon oncle qui le (l') _____ (assassiner). Je (J') _____ (entendre) dire récemment qu'il _____ (avoir) des problèmes financiers. Certains disent qu'il _____ (emprunter) des millions d'euros à mon oncle sans le lui dire. En fait, un ami suisse qui travaille à la banque de mon oncle me (m') _____ (dire) qu'il y _____ (avoir) très peu d'argent sur son compte. Je pense que mon oncle _____ (apprendre) ce qui _____ (se passer) et je suis certain qu'il _____ (dire) à M. Lavare qu'il _____ (aller) le dénoncer à la police.

VALÉRIE VEUTOUX

Il faut que vous sachiez que Bernard Boncorps _____ (être) furieux contre son oncle. François Fédor _____ (penser) que son neveu _____ (faire) des études de droit à l'université de Nice. En vérité, Bernard _____ (passer) tout son temps sur les plages et dans les casinos de Monaco. Quand son oncle _____ (comprendre) la situation, il _____ (se fâcher *to get angry*) et il _____ (dire) à son neveu qu'il _____ (vouloir) qu'il vienne finir ses études en Belgique, à l'université de Liège. Quand sa sœur, la mère de Bernard, _____ (mourir), elle lui _____ (demander) de se charger de l'éducation de son neveu. Bernard _____ (ne pas comprendre) pourquoi son oncle, qu'il n'avait jamais vu, _____ (s'intéresser) après tout ce temps à ce qu'il _____ (faire). Bernard _____ (ne pas vouloir) abandonner sa vie de play-boy sur la Côte d'Azur et il _____ (avoir) peur que sa petite amie, Nathalie Lanana, refuse de venir ici avec lui. Et puis, il faut ajouter aussi que Bernard _____ (avoir) des dettes énormes dans les casinos. Il _____ (ne pas pouvoir) payer ses dettes avec l'argent que son oncle lui _____ (donner) chaque mois. Bernard _____ (ne pas vouloir) attendre la mort naturelle de son oncle pour hériter de sa part de la fortune.

LAURENT LAVARE

Je suis presque certain que Valérie Veutoux _____ (assassiner) François Fédor. Récemment, elle _____ (faire) la connaissance de Jean Jigaulaux, un jeune homme de 25 ans, et elle _____ (tomber) amoureuse de lui. Ils _____ (sortir) quelques mois ensemble, puis il lui _____ (demander) de l'épouser *(to marry)*. La vieille Veutoux _____ (ne pas comprendre) qu'il ne _____ (vouloir) que *(only)* son argent et le jeune Jigaulaux _____ (ne pas savoir) qu'elle ne recevrait plus un centime de François Fédor si elle _____ (se remarier). La vaniteuse Valérie Veutoux _____ (sans doute comprendre) qu'elle n'aurait jamais le joli Jigaulaux tant que *(as long as)* François Fédor _____ (être) en vie et elle _____ (se débarrasser *to get rid*) de lui.

Répondez aux questions suivantes au sujet des suspects indiqués. Utilisez un pronom dans chaque réponse pour remplacer les mots en italique.

• Pour réviser les pronoms compléments d'objet direct et indirect, **y** et **en,** voir les pages 144, 174, 304, 338 et 344.

Note. This activity continues on the next page.

Laurent Lavare

1. Qui a accusé *Laurent Lavare* du crime?
2. D'après son accusateur, est-ce que Laurent Lavare avait *des problèmes financiers?*
3. Disait-il *à François Fédor* qu'il lui empruntait de l'argent?
4. Combien d'argent empruntait-il *à François Fédor?*
5. D'après le banquier, ami de Bernard Boncorps, combien *d'argent* y avait-il sur le compte de son oncle?

Bernard Boncorps

1. Est-ce que Bernard Boncorps rendait souvent visite *à son oncle?*
2. Combien de fois est-ce que Bernard avait vu *son oncle?*
3. Est-ce que Bernard voulait aller *à Liège* pour finir ses études?
4. Combien de temps passait-il *sur les plages et dans les casinos?*
5. Est-ce qu'il avait *des dettes?*
6. Est-ce que Bernard avait assez *d'argent* pour payer *ses dettes?*

Valérie Veutoux

1. Qui pense que Valérie Veutoux a assassiné *François Fédor?*
2. Après combien de temps est-ce que Jean Jigaulaux a demandé *à Valérie Veutoux* de l'épouser?
3. Pourquoi est-ce que le jeune Jigaulaux aimait *la vieille Veutoux?*

•Pour réviser l'usage de **c'est** et **il/elle est,** voir les pages 32 et 46.

N. Qui est-ce? Que savons-nous des suspects? Complétez les phrases suivantes avec **il est** ou **c'est.** Ensuite, dites si vous pensez que chaque phrase décrit plutôt Laurent Lavare ou Bernard Boncorps.

Exemple   **C'est** quelqu'un qui travaille beaucoup.
C'est Laurent Lavare.

1. _____ le neveu de François Fédor.
2. _____ comptable.
3. _____ suisse.
4. _____ jeune.
5. _____ un play-boy.
6. _____ malhonnête.
7. _____ sportif.
8. _____ une personne stupide.
9. _____ peut-être l'assassin.

•Pour réviser les pronoms relatifs, voir la page 366.

Suggestion for *O. Les gens du village.* Remind students that the relative pronoun **qui** is generally followed by a verb.

O. Les gens du village. Vous demandez aux gens du village ce qu'ils savaient au sujet de François Fédor. Faites des phrases en utilisant un élément de chaque colonne.

François Fédor était un homme...	qui... que (qu')...	ne parlait pas beaucoup. avait un passé mystérieux. avait une personnalité un peu bizarre. beaucoup de gens trouvaient difficile. n'avait pas beaucoup d'amis. je ne connaissais pas bien. faisait toujours ce qu'il voulait.

P. Le dîner. Complétez le paragraphe suivant avec l'article défini (**le, la, l', les**), l'article indéfini (**un, une, des**), le partitif (**du, de la, de l'**) ou **de**.

• Pour réviser les produits alimentaires, voir les pages 84, 284–285, 294–295 et 302.

• Pour réviser les articles, voir les pages 44, 50, 290 et 300.

_____ soir où M. Fédor est mort, M. Fédor et M. Lavare sont descendus vers sept heures et demie et ils ont pris _____ vin blanc avant de dîner. Pendant le repas, M. Fédor n'avait pas très faim; il a mangé _____ soupe et un peu _____ pain. Ensuite, il a pris _____ poulet et un peu _____ riz. Il n'a pas pris _____ légumes ou _____ tarte aux pommes. Il a pris un peu _____ fromage à la fin du repas. Normalement, il mangeait beaucoup. Il aimait bien _____ viande et _____ pommes de terre mais il ne prenait pas beaucoup _____ choses sucrées. Je pense qu'il n'avait pas _____ appétit ce soir-là, parce que ses problèmes le préoccupaient. Il n'a pas bu _____ vin rouge avec son repas, seulement _____ eau minérale et il a pris _____ café quand j'ai servi _____ dessert. Après _____ dîner, M. Fédor s'est retiré à _____ bibliothèque où il a bu un verre _____ cognac. Il est resté assis dans _____ fauteuil près de _____ porte pendant _____ heure après avoir parlé avec M. Boncorps et Mme Veutoux, puis il est monté se coucher.

Maintenant, dites si François Fédor a mangé ou a bu les choses suivantes le soir de son meurtre.

Exemple   **Il n'a pas mangé de pâté. Il a mangé de la soupe.**

• Pour réviser le passé composé et l'imparfait, voir les pages 222, 224 et 230.

Quick-reference answers for *Q. Valérie se marie.* Mme Veutoux est sortie de sa chambre à 8h20 du matin. Elle est descendue au rez-de-chaussée et elle a téléphoné à M. Jigaulaux à Luxembourg. Ensuite, elle a téléphoné à une agence de voyages à Bruxelles. M. Jigaulaux est arrivé ici quelques heures après. Il a retrouvé Mme Veutoux dans la forêt à midi et ils se sont embrassés passionnément. Comme M. Jigaulaux était fatigué, il a pris une chambre à l'hôtel du village, où il a passé l'après-midi. À 17h00, M. Jigaulaux et Mme Veutoux se sont retrouvés devant l'hôtel, ils sont montés dans la voiture de M. Jigaulaux et sont allés dans le village voisin où ils se sont mariés en secret à 18h20. Après la cérémonie, ils ont dîné au restaurant du village. À part le serveur, ils étaient seuls dans le restaurant. Pendant le dîner, j'ai tout observé de l'extérieur. M. Jigaulaux n'a pas beaucoup parlé mais Mme Veutoux lui a expliqué quelque chose. Ils ont quitté le restaurant à 20h50. À ce moment-là, un chien m'a attaqué dans les rosiers derrière lesquels je m'étais caché et je les ai perdus de vue.

Q. Valérie se marie. Vous avez demandé à des collègues d'observer les activités de chacun des suspects. Celui qui suit *(The one who is following)* Valérie Veutoux a rapporté ces photos prises le lendemain du crime. Vous lui demandez de vous raconter la journée de Valérie Veutoux mais ses notes sont en désordre. D'abord, remettez ses notes dans l'ordre; ensuite, racontez la journée de Valérie Veutoux en mettant les verbes au passé composé ou à l'imparfait.

Exemple **Mme Veutoux est sortie de sa chambre à 8h20 du matin. Elle est descendue...**

- M. Jigaulaux *arrive* ici quelques heures après. Il *retrouve* Mme Veutoux dans la forêt à midi et ils *s'embrassent* passionnément.
- Comme M. Jigaulaux *est* fatigué, il *prend* une chambre à l'hôtel du village, où il *passe* l'après-midi.
- Mme Veutoux *sort* de sa chambre à 8h20 du matin. Elle *descend* au rez-de-chaussée et elle *téléphone* à M. Jigaulaux à Luxembourg. Ensuite, elle *téléphone* à une agence de voyages à Bruxelles.
- Ils *quittent* le restaurant à 20h50. À ce moment-là, un chien m'*attaque* dans les rosiers derrière lesquels je m'étais caché et je les *perds* de vue.
- À 17h00, M. Jigaulaux et Mme Veutoux *se retrouvent* devant l'hôtel, ils *montent* dans la voiture de M. Jigaulaux et *vont* dans le village voisin où ils *se marient* en secret à 18h20.
- Après la cérémonie, ils *dînent* au restaurant du village. À part le serveur, ils *sont* seuls dans le restaurant.
- Pendant le dîner, *j'observe* tout de l'extérieur. M. Jigaulaux ne *parle* pas beaucoup mais Mme Veutoux lui *explique* quelque chose.

• Pour réviser le subjonctif, voir les pages 372–373, 374 et 378.

R. Réactions. Valérie Veutoux est furieuse. Imaginez sa réaction quand vous lui dites les choses suivantes.

> *Il est bon que...*   **IL EST NÉCESSAIRE QUE...**
>
> **Il est impossible que...**   IL EST IMPORTANT QUE...
>
> Il est ridicule que...   ???   *Il est essentiel que...*

Exemple Vous ne pouvez pas partir pour quelques jours.
Il est ridicule que je ne puisse pas partir.

1. Oui madame, vous êtes suspecte.
2. Nous ne savons pas où se trouve le corps de la victime.
3. M. Lavare dit que vous aviez des raisons d'assassiner M. Fédor.
4. Nous savons que vous avez retrouvé M. Jigaulaux dans la forêt.

5. Nous avons des photos de M. Jigaulaux avec vous.
6. Je veux lui parler demain.
7. Il pourra partir après l'interrogatoire.
8. Vous devez tout nous expliquer.

S. Deux billets pour Tahiti. Après une investigation, vous apprenez que François Fédor enregistrait *(recorded)* toutes les conversations téléphoniques chez lui. Vous découvrez que Valérie Veutoux a téléphoné à une agence de voyages à Bruxelles le lendemain du crime. Écoutez la conversation entre Valérie Veutoux et l'agent de voyages, et sur une autre feuille de papier, complétez les détails qui manquent sur l'itinéraire de Valérie ci-dessous.

• Pour réviser comment acheter un billet d'avion, voir la page 334.

ITINÉRAIRE

À l'intention de: *(Nom)* et de *(Nom)*

ALLER   Air France—Vol *(Numéro)*
  (Date)
Départ de Bruxelles *(Heure)*   Boeing 747
                                               Première classe/Vol direct

  (Date)
Arrivée à Tahiti *(Heure)*
                                               Prix du billet: *(Prix)*
                                               Total des deux billets: *(Prix)*

Prévoyez d'arriver à l'aéroport deux heures avant l'heure de départ.
BON VOYAGE!

Script for *S. Deux billets pour Tahiti.*
– J'aimerais deux billets pour Tahiti.
– Vous désirez des billets aller-retour?
– Non, des allers simples, s'il vous plaît.
– Et quand est-ce que vous voudriez partir?
– Jeudi, ce jeudi-ci.
– Bon, alors, deux billets pour Tahiti pour le jeudi 4 mai. Il y a un vol Air France, le vol 70, qui part à 19h35 et arrive à Tahiti le 5 mai, à 4h45.
– C'est parfait.
– Bon. Vous voulez voyager en première classe ou en classe affaires?
– En première classe, s'il vous plaît.
– Le billet le moins cher est à 3 896 euros. Pour deux, ça fait 7 792 euros. Comment est-ce que vous préférez payer?
– Je voudrais payer en espèces, à l'aéroport.
– Comment s'appellent les passagers?
– Valérie Veutoux et Jean Jigaulaux.
– Ça s'écrit comment?
– V-E-U-T-O-U-X et J-I-G-A-U-L-A-U-X.
– Bon, vous avez deux réservations aux noms de Valérie Veutoux et de Jean Jigaulaux pour Tahiti le jeudi 4 mai, vol 70, départ de Bruxelles à 19h35 et arrivée à Tahiti le 5 mai, à 4h45.
– C'est parfait! Merci, madame.
– Au revoir, madame.

On parle français à Tahiti.

• Pour réviser le futur, voir la page 330.

• Pour réviser l'impératif, voir les pages 146 et 386.

T. Une conversation téléphonique.

Voici une transcription de la conversation téléphonique entre Valérie Veutoux et son amant *(lover)*, Jean Jigaulaux, le lendemain du crime. La première partie a été effacée *(erased)* accidentellement. Complétez ce qui reste en mettant les verbes entre parenthèses au futur ou à l'impératif.

—... Après cela, François ne _____ (faire) plus obstacle à notre bonheur *(happiness)*. Nous _____ (pouvoir) nous marier quand tu _____ (vouloir).

—Je _____ (venir) aujourd'hui et nous _____ (se marier) ce soir. Je vais partir tout de suite et j' _____ (arriver) un peu avant midi.

—À deux kilomètres d'ici, il y a une vieille école abandonnée. _____ (Tourner) à gauche juste après cette école et _____ (entrer) dans la forêt. Là, personne ne nous _____ (voir). Je t' _____ (attendre) à cet endroit à midi.

—On _____ (être) heureux ensemble.

—Après-demain, nous _____ (partir) pour Tahiti et nous _____ (commencer) notre nouvelle vie ensemble.

• Pour réviser les chiffres, voir les pages 10, 86 et 104.

• Pour réviser les dates, voir la page 152.

U. Le compte en banque.

Quand vous comparez les relevés de compte *(bank statements)* de François Fédor, vous remarquez que quelqu'un avait retiré presque tout son argent ces derniers mois. Combien d'argent est-ce qu'il y avait aux dates suivantes de l'année dernière et de cette année?

Exemple   30/9   20 789 067 euros

Le 30 septembre de l'année dernière, il y avait 20 789 067 euros sur son compte.

1. 15/10   16 136 978 euros
2. 10/11   12 194 456 euros
3. 24/12   8 714 387 euros
4. 1/1   1 000 090 euros
5. 15/2   90 506 euros
6. 4/3   11 871 euros

• Pour réviser comment poser une question, voir les pages 40, 80 et 82.

V. Une vidéo révélatrice.

Vous venez de découvrir qu'une caméra de sécurité cachée dans le couloir filmait chaque personne qui entrait dans la chambre de François Fédor. Entre 20h et 8h du matin, la caméra a enregistré une seule personne qui est entrée dans la chambre de la victime. La caméra s'est arrêtée à 8h30 le lendemain matin. Préparez cinq questions que vous voudriez poser à Valérie Veutoux.

| *pourquoi* | ??? | à quelle heure | **combien de temps** | |
| comment | ??? | que | QUAND | qui | *où* |

W. La dernière volonté de François.
Vous avez interrogé Valérie Veutoux et elle a répondu que François Fédor n'était pas fâché *(upset)* qu'elle ait un amant, mais, qu'au contraire, il l'avait encouragée à l'épouser *(to marry him)*. Elle vous raconte ce que François Fédor lui a dit. Est-ce qu'il voulait qu'elle fasse les choses suivantes ou est-ce qu'il voulait les faire lui-même *(himself)*?

• Pour réviser l'usage de l'infinitif ou du subjonctif, voir les pages 372 et 380.

Exemples   se marier avec Jean Jigaulaux
            Il voulait que je me marie avec Jean Jigaulaux.

            nous offrir un cadeau de mariage
            Il voulait nous offrir un cadeau de mariage.

1. tout savoir sur Jean Jigaulaux
2. dire à Jean Jigaulaux de venir ici
3. se marier tout de suite
4. nous offrir un voyage de noces *(honeymoon trip)*
5. téléphoner pour réserver le billet pour Tahiti le lendemain
6. partir pour Tahiti cette semaine
7. être heureuse
8. venir dans sa chambre après le dîner prendre l'argent pour payer le voyage

X. Que faisait le/la domestique?
Reformulez les questions suivantes avec l'inversion et posez-les au/à la domestique. Ensuite, écoutez ses réponses.

• Pour réviser l'inversion, voir la page 82.

1. À quelle heure est-ce que vous vous êtes levé(e) le lendemain du crime?
2. Qu'est-ce que vous avez fait après?
3. Est-ce que les autres invités dormaient encore dans le château?
4. Quand est-ce que vous avez découvert (découvrir *to discover*) que François Fédor était mort?
5. Est-ce que vous avez été surpris(e)?
6. Pourquoi est-ce que vous n'avez pas crié (crier *to scream)*?
7. Est-ce que vous avez réveillé quelqu'un pour vous aider?
8. Vous avez téléphoné à la police à 8h12. À quelle heure est-ce que vous êtes entré(e) dans la chambre?
9. Combien de portes est-ce qu'il y a pour entrer dans la chambre de la victime?
10. Pourquoi est-ce que vous ne dites pas la vérité *(truth)*?
11. Ne faites pas l'innocent(e)! Comment est-ce que vous saviez que François Fédor était mort sans entrer dans sa chambre?
12. Pourquoi est-ce que vous n'êtes pas sur la vidéo de sécurité?
13. Pourquoi est-ce que la vidéo s'arrête à 8h30?
14. Alors, est-ce que vous voulez dire que François Fédor n'est pas mort?

*Script for **X. Que faisait le/la domestique?** (Although this is on the CD, so that students may prepare it at home, in class it is better to act out the role of the servant.)* **1.** Je me suis levé(e) à 6h comme d'habitude. **2.** J'ai pris une douche, comme tous les jours. **3.** Je pense que oui. Je n'ai rien entendu dans le château. **4.** Quand je suis entré(e) dans sa chambre pour le réveiller. **5.** Mais bien sûr. C'était horrible! **6.** Monsieur, on ne crie pas dans ce château! **7.** Non, je suis allé(e) directement téléphoner à la police. **8.** J'ai dû y entrer vers 8h. **9.** Il y a une seule porte. **10.** Euh... je ne comprends pas. Qu'est-ce que vous voulez dire? **11.** Mais il était mort, je l'ai vu! Il était mort! **12.** La vidéo de sécurité? La vidéo de sécurité? Non, ce n'est pas possible! **13.** Ce n'était pas mon idée, monsieur. C'était monsieur Fédor. Il m'a dit de le faire. Il m'a dit de signaler son meurtre le lendemain du dîner. Je n'avais pas le choix. C'était la seule manière, monsieur. La seule manière. **14.** C'était la seule manière. La seule manière.

• Pour réviser le passé composé et l'imparfait, voir les pages 222, 224 et 230.

Y. Une confession. Le/La domestique confesse que François Fédor n'est pas mort. En lisant sa confession, mettez les verbes entre parenthèses au passé composé ou à l'imparfait.

Je _____ (ne pas vouloir) le faire mais c'_____ (être) la seule manière! C'_____ (être) la seule manière de sauver le château. M. Fédor m'_____ (expliquer) que M. Lavare _____ (venir) de l'informer qu'il avait tout perdu. Il avait tout investi dans une société qui avait fait faillite *(had gone bankrupt)*. Il _____ (devoir) vendre le château pour payer les créanciers. «Mais, non», je lui _____ (dire). Il _____ (savoir) que je (j') _____ (adorer) ce château et que je ferais tout pour ne pas le perdre. Je _____ (naître) pas loin d'ici. Quand je (j') _____ (être) jeune, je (j') _____ (rêver) d'habiter ici un jour et je (j') _____ (inventer) des histoires fantastiques qui _____ (avoir) lieu *(to take place)* ici. Mais toutes ces histoires-là _____ (finir) toujours bien. Puis, M. Fédor _____ (suggérer) qu'il y _____ (avoir) peut-être un moyen de garder le château et que, si on _____ (réussir), il me le donnerait. Le château serait à moi pour toujours. C'est alors qu'il me (m') _____ (révéler) son plan. Il prendrait une assurance vie de 10 000 000 d'euros et j'en serais le/la bénéficiaire.

M. Fédor _____ (ne jamais le dire), mais je (j') _____ (avoir) l'impression que c'_____ (être) M. Lavare qui avait inventé ce plan. Je sais que M. Lavare avait dit à M. Fédor que Mme Veutoux avait pris ce M. Jigaulaux comme amant. Cela _____ (rendre) M. Fédor furieux. Chaque fois que M. Fédor _____ (parler) de son ex-femme avec M. Lavare, l'un _____ (devenir) tout rouge et l'autre tout pâle. La vérité, c'est que c'_____ (être) elle qui avait quitté M. Fédor il y a 15 ans et pas le contraire, comme tout le monde le disait. Il _____ (ne jamais lui pardonner) et il _____ (toujours vouloir) contrôler sa vie. Il _____ (ne pas être) obligé de lui donner cet argent depuis le divorce, mais M. Lavare l'avait persuadé de continuer à lui en donner beaucoup. Il _____ (dire) à M. Fédor que si Mme Veutoux _____ (dépendre) de lui financièrement, il pourrait contrôler sa vie. M. Fédor me (m') _____ (dire) que M. Lavare inviterait M. Boncorps et Mme Veutoux à la maison. M. Fédor expliquerait à son neveu qu'il _____ (ne plus pouvoir) lui donner d'argent. Mais il dirait à Mme Veutoux qu'il _____ (vouloir) qu'elle soit heureuse et qu'il _____ (avoir) l'intention de lui offrir un voyage à Tahiti pour sa lune de miel *(honeymoon)* si elle _____ (se marier) tout de suite.

D'après le plan, tout le monde penserait que Mme Veutoux avait assassiné M. Fédor et qu'elle était partie pour Tahiti. On la verrait sur la vidéo entrer dans sa chambre la nuit du meurtre et on penserait qu'elle l'avait assassiné pour pouvoir se marier avec son jeune amant. Mais en réalité, on assassinerait Mme Veutoux et on laisserait *(would leave)* son corps au fond de la forêt. M. Fédor s'habillerait comme elle et il partirait pour Tahiti à sa place. À l'aéroport de Bruxelles, on verrait Mme Veutoux partir pour Tahiti et personne ne saurait que c'_____ (être) elle la vraie victime. On accuserait Mme Veutoux de s'être échappée *(of having escaped)* après le meurtre de M. Fédor et on ne la reverrait plus. M. Fédor me laisserait le château et après quelques mois, je mettrais les 10 000 000 d'euros d'assurance sur un compte secret pour M. Fédor.

À ce moment-là, pendant la confession, un policier _____ (entrer) et il _____ (annoncer) que des chasseurs (hunters) *avaient trouvé le corps d'une femme morte dans la forêt et qu'ils avaient donné la description de Mme Veutoux.*

ÉPILOGUE

Vous pensez probablement avoir compris le mystère du meurtre de François Fédor. Vous pensez que le/la domestique va être **arrêté(e)** et que le vieux Midas est parti vivre sur une île tropicale. Mais êtes-vous certain(e) d'avoir trouvé les vrais criminels? Ah! Les voilà **en croisière** quelque part dans l'océan Pacifique. Écoutons un peu leur conversation.

—Quel coup! Tu es un vrai **génie,** mon chéri. Qui aurait pensé que nous pourrions réussir! Tout le monde pense que je suis morte et que François est l'assassin. Après toutes ces années, nous allons enfin pouvoir vivre ensemble sans **nous préoccuper** de ce vieux tyran. Je **me souviens de** la première fois que je t'ai vu quand tu as commencé à travailler pour lui! Quel coup de foudre! Et le pauvre François! Il n'avait aucune idée que je l'ai quitté parce que nous étions amants.

—Je trouve toujours **incroyable** qu'il ait investi toute sa fortune dans cette société qui n'existait pas. Il avait tellement confiance en moi! Ha ha ha!

—Mais pourquoi pas? Le vrai vieux Midas, c'était toi. Tu avais multiplié dix fois sa fortune. Sans toi, cet imbécile aurait perdu tout son argent longtemps avant! Mais maintenant, toute cette fortune est à nous! S'il avait su que tous ces **créanciers** que tu payais n'étaient personne d'autre que moi, son ex-femme! Ha ha ha! Qu'est-ce que tu as fait de son corps?

—Il était vraiment surpris quand, **au lieu de** l'**amener à** l'aéroport de Bruxelles, nous sommes allés au fond des Ardennes! Quand je lui ai expliqué que toi et moi, nous étions amants depuis le début, j'ai pensé pendant un moment que je n'aurais pas besoin de l'assassiner. Le pauvre, **il a failli avoir** une attaque! Et il était très comique, habillé comme toi.

—Quel dommage que nous n'ayons pas de photos! J'aurais aimé voir ça! Ha ha ha! Mais qu'est-ce qu'on dira si on trouve son corps?

—On pensera sans doute que c'est le/la domestique qui l'a assassiné pour ces 10 000 000 d'euros d'assurance!

—Mais il y a un dernier détail que je ne comprends pas. Comment est-ce que tu as persuadé ton jeune associé de jouer le rôle de Jean Jigaulaux? Il a si bien joué! Pendant un moment, j'ai vraiment eu l'impression que j'allais me marier avec lui.

—Ce jeune homme était tellement ambitieux qu'il aurait fait **n'importe quoi** pour avoir ma clientèle. Je lui ai promis de lui laisser tous mes clients, mais il ne savait pas que je n'en avais qu'un seul, et que c'était François Fédor.

—Ça, c'est trop! Tu es cruel... vicieux! C'est pour ça que je t'aime! Ha ha ha!

Naturellement Valérie Veutoux et Laurent Lavare ont dû changer de noms. Si on vous les présente aujourd'hui, vous ferez la connaissance d'Anabelle Atout et de son mari Richard!

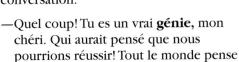

arrête(e) *arrested*   **en croisière** *on a cruise*   **un génie** *a genius*   **se préoccuper** *to worry*   **se souvenir de** *to remember*   **incroyable** *unbelievable*   **un créancier** *a creditor*   **au lieu de** *instead of*   **amener à** *to take (someone) to*   **il a failli avoir** *he almost had*   **n'importe quoi** *anything*

L'EUROPE FRANCOPHONE

TRANSPARENCY: MAP-7

*En Europe, le français est une langue officielle dans quatre pays, **une principauté** et une grande île méditerranéenne qui est un département français. En vous aidant des photos et des descriptions, essayez de déterminer quels sont **les endroits** francophones suivants.*

1 Jusqu'à son indépendance en 1830, elle a été gouvernée par Rome, la Bourgogne, la France, **l'Autriche,** l'Espagne et **les Pays-Bas.** Pendant les deux **guerres mondiales,** elle a été occupée par les Allemands. De nos jours, c'est une monarchie fondée sur une démocratie parlementaire. Dans ce pays, 58 pour cent de la population **(les Flamands)** parlent **néerlandais,** 32 pour cent (les Wallons) parlent français, neuf pour cent sont bilingues et un pour cent parle allemand. Cette division culturelle et linguistique a longtemps été une source de conflits. Pour dissiper cet antagonisme, un effort de décentralisation a donné plus de **pouvoir** aux trois régions qui forment ce pays: la Région flamande, la Région wallonne et la Région de Bruxelles-Capitale.

2 L'unique langue officielle de ce pays est le français. Il s'y trouve **quand même** plusieurs groupes ethniques ou culturels qui, voulant garder leur **propre** identité, parlent aussi une autre langue **telle que** le breton, l'occitan ou le basque. Depuis **le Moyen Âge,** ce pays a été une monarchie, un empire et une république. En 1958, Charles de Gaulle a fondé la Cinquième République dont la constitution **régit** encore aujourd'hui le pays.

---

une principauté *a principality* **un endroit** *a place* **l'Autriche** *Austria* **les Pays-Bas** *the Netherlands* **une guerre mondiale** *a world war* **les Flamands** *the Flemish* **le néerlandais** *Dutch* **le pouvoir** *power* **quand même** *even so* **propre** *own* **tel(le) que** *such as* **le Moyen Âge** *the Middle Ages* **régir** *to govern*

3 Ce petit pays (plus petit que l'état du Rhode Island) est un grand-duché. C'est une monarchie constitutionnelle **à la tête de laquelle** se trouvent le grand-duc, qui **détient** le pouvoir exécutif, et le chef du gouvernement, qui choisit les ministres. Le français est la langue officielle, mais l'allemand est **courant** dans **l'enseignement** et dans la presse. Le luxembourgeois est pourtant la langue dominante.

4 C'est une république fédérale composée de 23 cantons **liés** par la constitution fédérale de 1848. Une grande partie du pouvoir politique reste pourtant toujours **au niveau du** canton. **Siège** européen des Nations unies, ce pays continue à garder la neutralité dans les conflits internationaux depuis 1515. Ce pays a quatre langues officielles : l'allemand, le français, l'italien et le romanche.

à la tête de laquelle *at the head of which*   **détient** *holds*   **courant** *common*   **l'enseignement** *education*   **lié(e)** *linked*   **au niveau de** *at the level of*   **le siège** *the seat*

5 Cet état, dont la langue officielle est le français, est une principauté depuis plus de 300 ans. **Bien qu'elle soit devenue un protectorat** de la France en 1861, le prince y a gardé le pouvoir absolu jusqu'à l'établissement de la constitution de 1911. Aujourd'hui une monarchie constitutionnelle, cette principauté est célèbre dans **le monde** entier pour le tourisme, le luxe et **le jeu.**

6 Faisant partie de la France, cette île méditerranéenne où est né Napoléon est divisée en deux départements.

L'Europe: Un monde en formation

Dès son origine, l'histoire de l'Europe a été l'histoire de conflits, d'invasions, de conquêtes et de guerres entre les pays qui la composent. Pratiquement **détruite au niveau** politique et économique par les deux guerres mondiales, l'Europe d'aujourd'hui se tourne vers l'unification. À cause d'un climat économique en changement perpétuel et des différences culturelles et politiques entre les pays, les obstacles se révèlent nombreux et les progrès **lents.** Voici les étapes historiques vers l'unification:

Bien qu'elle soit devenue un protectorat *Although it became a protectorate*   **le monde** *the world*   **le jeu** *gambling*   **Dès son origine** *From its beginning*   **détruit(e)** *destroyed*   **au niveau** *on the level*   **lent(e)** *slow*

1949	Formation du Conseil de l'Europe. Cet organisme, dont le pouvoir est très limité, **ne peut faire que** des recommandations que les états membres sont libres d'approuver ou de rejeter. Il se prononce dans les domaines de l'éducation, de la protection de l'environnement et des **droits de l'homme.**
1951	Traité de Paris. Formation de la CECA (Communauté européenne du **charbon** et de **l'acier).** Comprenant la France, l'Allemagne Fédérale, l'Italie et les pays du Bénélux (la Belgique, le Luxembourg et les Pays-Bas), la CECA crée une zone de libre échange et **un esprit** de coopération **au cœur de** l'Europe.
1957	Le traité de Rome **donne naissance à** la CEE (Communauté économique européenne). Les principes en sont la libre circulation des **biens,** des services et des personnes **parmi** les six pays membres.
1973	L'Europe des Six (la CEE) devient l'Europe des Neuf avec l'adhésion du Danemark, de l'Irlande et du **Royaume-Uni.**
1981	La Grèce entre dans la Communauté économique européenne.
1986	Avec l'entrée du Portugal et de l'Espagne, la CEE devient l'Europe des Douze.
1991	*La CEE propose les accords de Maastricht.
1993	La CEE devient l'Union européenne (UE). Les douze pays membres ratifient les accords de Maastricht. Avec le traité de Maastricht, **le lien** entre **les citoyens** des états membres et l'Union européenne est devenu plus direct par la création d'**une citoyenneté** européenne qui a introduit une série de droits civils et politiques.
1995	*Avec l'entrée de l'Autriche, de la Finlande et de la Suède, l'Union européenne devient l'Europe des Quinze. Treize autres pays ont fait des demandes officielles pour devenir membres de l'Union européenne.
1997	*Le traité d'Amsterdam complète les droits **précisés** dans le traité de Maastricht.
1999	*Le traité d'Amsterdam précise le lien entre la citoyenneté nationale et la citoyenneté européenne. Concrètement, la citoyenneté européenne garantit quatre droits spécifiques à tout **ressortissant** d'un état membre de l'Union européenne: <ul><li>la liberté de circuler et de **séjourner** sur le territoire des états membres;</li><li>le droit de vote et d'éligibilité aux élections municipales **ainsi qu'**aux élections au Parlement européen dans l'état membre de résidence;</li><li>le droit de **bénéficier,** sur le territoire d'un pays **tiers** où l'état membre **dont** le citoyen est ressortissant n'est pas représenté, de la protection diplomatique et consulaire de tout autre état membre;</li><li>le droit de pétition devant le Parlement européen et de recours au médiateur européen.</li></ul>
1999–2002	*Le 1ᵉʳ janvier 1999, l'euro devient la monnaie officielle de onze états membres de l'Union européenne. L'Autriche, la Belgique, la Finlande, la France, l'Allemagne, l'Irlande, l'Italie, le Luxembourg, les Pays-Bas, le Portugal et l'Espagne adoptent l'euro comme monnaie officielle. Le 1ᵉʳ janvier 2001, la Grèce a rejoint la zone euro qui regroupe aujourd'hui 12 états membres. **Les billets** et **pièces** en euros font leur apparition le 1ᵉʳ janvier 2002.
	*Source: © Communautés européennes, 1995–2001, information obtained online from the Europa website: http://europa.eu.int/

Additional information. Maastricht is the name of the small Dutch town where the 1991 meeting of the EEC took place. The accords had to be ratified by all members. They specified a series of steps toward unification of political and monetary systems, immigration laws, and security measures in Europe. (As a matter of historical interest, Maastricht was also the site of an important military conference between the Allies in late 1944 to plan the final invasion of Germany.)

ne peut faire que can only make   **les droits de l'homme** human rights   **le charbon** coal   **l'acier** (m) steel   **un esprit** a spirit   **au cœur de** in the heart of   **donner naissance à** to give birth to   **les biens** (m) the goods   **parmi** among   **le Royaume-Uni** the United Kingdom   **le lien** the link   **un(e) citoyen(ne)** a citizen   **une citoyenneté** a citizenship   **précisé(e)** spelled out   **un(e) ressortissant(e)** a national   **séjourner** to stay   **ainsi que** as well as   **bénéficier** to benefit   **tiers** third   **dont** of which   **un billet** a bill (money)   **une pièce** a coin

L'évolution de l'Europe unie est à l'image de son développement historique et culturel. Politiquement, certains pays **souhaitent** aller plus loin dans l'unification **alors que** d'autres restent très attachés à l'idée de souveraineté nationale. **Par contre,** en ce qui concerne les **réseaux** de transports et de télécommunications ainsi que les relations commerciales, culturelles et sportives, les progrès sont rapides.

À discuter.

1. Pour les Français, quels sont les avantages et les inconvénients d'une Europe plus unie?
2. Si les États-Unis, le Canada et le Mexique essayaient de créer un seul système monétaire comme en Europe, quelle serait votre réaction?
3. Dans l'économie mondiale, quelles seront les conséquences d'une Europe plus unie pour d'autres pays du monde?

Monaco

Genève, Suisse

Strasbourg, France

---

souhaiter *to wish* **alors que** *whereas* **Par contre** *On the other hand* **un réseau** *a network*

Aix-en-Provence, France

Lausanne, Suisse

Monaco

Aix-en-Provence, France

APPENDICE A
L'ALPHABET PHONÉTIQUE

Voyelles

[a]	madame	[i]	qui	[œ]	sœur
[e]	thé	[o]	eau	[u]	vous
[ɛ]	être	[ɔ]	porte	[y]	sur
[ə]	que	[ø]	peu		

Semivoyelles

[j]	bien	[ɥ]	puis	[w]	oui

Voyelles nasales

[ɑ̃]	quand	[ɛ̃]	vin	[ɔ̃]	non

Consonnes

[b]	bleu	[l]	lire	[s]	sur
[d]	dormir	[m]	marron	[ʃ]	chat
[f]	faire	[n]	nouveau	[t]	triste
[g]	gris	[ɲ]	enseigner	[v]	vers
[ʒ]	jaune	[p]	parler	[z]	rose
[k]	quand	[ʀ]	rester		

TABLEAU DES VERBES

Verbes auxiliaires

VERBE INFINITIF	INDICATIF PRÉSENT	PASSÉ COMPOSÉ	IMPARFAIT	FUTUR	CONDITIONNEL PRÉSENT	SUBJONCTIF PRÉSENT	IMPÉRATIF
avoir *to have*	ai	ai eu	avais	aurai	aurais	aie	
	as	as eu	avais	auras	aurais	aies	aie
	a	a eu	avait	aura	aurait	ait	
	avons	avons eu	avions	aurons	aurions	ayons	ayons
	avez	avez eu	aviez	aurez	auriez	ayez	ayez
	ont	ont eu	avaient	auront	auraient	aient	
être *to be*	suis	ai été	étais	serai	serais	sois	
	es	as été	étais	seras	serais	sois	sois
	est	a été	était	sera	serait	soit	
	sommes	avons été	étions	serons	serions	soyons	soyons
	êtes	avez été	étiez	serez	seriez	soyez	soyez
	sont	ont été	étaient	seront	seraient	soient	

Verbes réguliers

VERBE INFINITIF	INDICATIF PRÉSENT	PASSÉ COMPOSÉ	IMPARFAIT	FUTUR	CONDITIONNEL PRÉSENT	SUBJONCTIF PRÉSENT	IMPÉRATIF
-er verbs							
parler *to talk,* *to speak*	parle	ai parlé	parlais	parlerai	parlerais	parle	
	parles	as parlé	parlais	parleras	parlerais	parles	parle
	parle	a parlé	parlait	parlera	parlerait	parle	
	parlons	avons parlé	parlions	parlerons	parlerions	parlions	parlons
	parlez	avez parlé	parliez	parlerez	parleriez	parliez	parlez
	parlent	ont parlé	parlaient	parleront	parleraient	parlent	
-ir verbs							
dormir *to sleep*	dors	ai dormi	dormais	dormirai	dormirais	dorme	
	dors	as dormi	dormais	dormiras	dormirais	dormes	dors
	dort	a dormi	dormait	dormira	dormirait	dorme	
	dormons	avons dormi	dormions	dormirons	dormirions	dormions	dormons
	dormez	avez dormi	dormiez	dormirez	dormiriez	dormiez	dormez
	dorment	ont dormi	dormaient	dormiront	dormiraient	dorment	

Verbes réguliers (suite)

VERBE INFINITIF	PRÉSENT	INDICATIF PASSÉ COMPOSÉ	IMPARFAIT	FUTUR	CONDITIONNEL PRÉSENT	SUBJONCTIF PRÉSENT	IMPÉRATIF
-ir verbs							
finir *to finish*	finis	ai fini	finissais	finirai	finirais	finisse	
	finis	as fini	finissais	finiras	finirais	finisses	finis
	finit	a fini	finissait	finira	finirait	finisse	
	finissons	avons fini	finissions	finirons	finirions	finissions	finissons
	finissez	avez fini	finissiez	finirez	finiriez	finissiez	finissez
	finissent	ont fini	finissaient	finiront	finiraient	finissent	
-re verbs							
vendre *to sell*	vends	ai vendu	vendais	vendrai	vendrais	vende	
	vends	as vendu	vendais	vendras	vendrais	vendes	vends
	vend	a vendu	vendait	vendra	vendrait	vende	
	vendons	avons vendu	vendions	vendrons	vendrions	vendions	vendons
	vendez	avez vendu	vendiez	vendrez	vendriez	vendiez	vendez
	vendent	ont vendu	vendaient	vendront	vendraient	vendent	

Verbes réfléchis

VERBE INFINITIF	PRÉSENT	INDICATIF PASSÉ COMPOSÉ	IMPARFAIT	FUTUR	CONDITIONNEL PRÉSENT	SUBJONCTIF PRÉSENT	IMPÉRATIF
se laver *to wash oneself*	me lave	me suis lavé(e)	me lavais	me laverai	me laverais	me lave	
	te laves	t'es lavé(e)	te lavais	te laveras	te laverais	te laves	lave-toi
	se lave	s'est lavé(e)	se lavait	se lavera	se laverait	se lave	
	nous lavons	nous sommes lavé(e)s	nous lavions	nous laverons	nous laverions	nous lavions	lavons-nous
	vous lavez	vous êtes lavé(e)(s)	vous laviez	vous laverez	vous laveriez	vous laviez	lavez-vous
	se lavent	se sont lavé(e)s	se lavaient	se laveront	se laveraient	se lavent	

Verbes à changements orthographiques

VERBE INFINITIF	PRÉSENT	INDICATIF PASSÉ COMPOSÉ	IMPARFAIT	FUTUR	CONDITIONNEL PRÉSENT	SUBJONCTIF PRÉSENT	IMPÉRATIF
préférer *to prefer*	préfère	ai préféré	préférais	préférerai	préférerais	préfère	
	préfères	as préféré	préférais	préféreras	préférerais	préfères	préfère
	préfère	a préféré	préférait	préférera	préférerait	préfère	
	préférons	avons préféré	préférions	préférerons	préférerions	préférions	préférons
	préférez	avez préféré	préfériez	préférerez	préféreriez	préfériez	préférez
	préfèrent	ont préféré	préféraient	préféreront	préféreraient	préfèrent	
acheter *to buy*	achète	ai acheté	achetais	achèterai	achèterais	achète	
	achètes	as acheté	achetais	achèteras	achèterais	achètes	achète
	achète	a acheté	achetait	achètera	achèterait	achète	
	achetons	avons acheté	achetions	achèterons	achèterions	achetions	achetons
	achetez	avez acheté	achetiez	achèterez	achèteriez	achetiez	achetez
	achètent	ont acheté	achetaient	achèteront	achèteraient	achètent	

Verbes à changements orthographiques (suite)

VERBE INFINITIF	PRÉSENT	PASSÉ COMPOSÉ	IMPARFAIT	FUTUR	CONDITIONNEL PRÉSENT	SUBJONCTIF PRÉSENT	IMPÉRATIF
appeler *to call*	appelle	ai appelé	appelais	appellerai	appellerais	appelle	
	appelles	as appelé	appelais	appelleras	appellerais	appelles	appelle
	appelle	a appelé	appelait	appellera	appellerait	appelle	
	appelons	avons appelé	appelions	appellerons	appellerions	appelions	appelons
	appelez	avez appelé	appeliez	appellerez	appelleriez	appeliez	appelez
	appellent	ont appelé	appelaient	appelleront	appelleraient	appellent	
essayer *to try*	essaie	ai essayé	essayais	essaierai	essaierais	essaie	
	essaies	as essayé	essayais	essaieras	essaierais	essaies	essaie
	essaie	a essayé	essayait	essaiera	essaierait	essaie	
	essayons	avons essayé	essayions	essaierons	essaierions	essayions	essayons
	essayez	avez essayé	essayiez	essaierez	essaieriez	essayiez	essayez
	essaient	ont essayé	essayaient	essaieront	essaieraient	essaient	
manger *to eat*	mange	ai mangé	mangeais	mangerai	mangerais	mange	
	manges	as mangé	mangeais	mangeras	mangerais	manges	mange
	mange	a mangé	mangeait	mangera	mangerait	mange	
	mangeons	avons mangé	mangions	mangerons	mangerions	mangions	mangeons
	mangez	avez mangé	mangiez	mangerez	mangeriez	mangiez	mangez
	mangent	ont mangé	mangeaient	mangeront	mangeraient	mangent	
commencer *to begin*	commence	ai commencé	commençais	commencerai	commencerais	commence	
	commences	as commencé	commençais	commenceras	commencerais	commences	commence
	commence	a commencé	commençait	commencera	commencerait	commence	
	commençons	avons commencé	commencions	commencerons	commencerions	commencions	commençons
	commencez	avez commencé	commenciez	commencerez	commenceriez	commenciez	commencez
	commencent	ont commencé	commençaient	commenceront	commenceraient	commencent	

Verbes irréguliers

VERBE INFINITIF	PRÉSENT	PASSÉ COMPOSÉ	IMPARFAIT	FUTUR	CONDITIONNEL PRÉSENT	SUBJONCTIF PRÉSENT	IMPÉRATIF
aller *to go*	vais	suis allé(e)	allais	irai	irais	aille	
	vas	es allé(e)	allais	iras	irais	ailles	va
	va	est allé(e)	allait	ira	irait	aille	
	allons	sommes allé(e)s	allions	irons	irions	allions	allons
	allez	êtes allé(e)(s)	alliez	irez	iriez	alliez	allez
	vont	sont allé(e)s	allaient	iront	iraient	aillent	
s'asseoir *to sit* *(down)*	m'assieds	me suis assis(e)	m'asseyais	m'assiérai	m'assiérais	m'asseye	
	t'assieds	t'es assis(e)	t'asseyais	t'assiéras	t'assiérais	t'asseyes	assieds-toi
	s'assied	s'est assis(e)	s'asseyait	s'assiéra	s'assiérait	s'asseye	
	nous asseyons	nous sommes assis(es)	nous asseyions	nous assiérons	nous assiérions	nous asseyions	asseyons-nous
	vous asseyez	vous êtes assis(es)	vous asseyiez	vous assiérez	vous assiériez	vous asseyiez	asseyez-vous
	s'asseyent	se sont assis(es)	s'asseyaient	s'assiéront	s'assiéraient	s'asseyent	
battre *to beat*	bats	ai battu	battais	battrai	battrais	batte	
	bats	as battu	battais	battras	battrais	battes	bats
	bat	a battu	battait	battra	battrait	batte	
	battons	avons battu	battions	battrons	battrions	battions	battons
	battez	avez battu	battiez	battrez	battriez	battiez	battez
	battent	ont battu	battaient	battront	battraient	battent	

Verbes irréguliers (suite)

VERBE INFINITIF	PRÉSENT	INDICATIF — PASSÉ COMPOSÉ	IMPARFAIT	FUTUR	CONDITIONNEL PRÉSENT	SUBJONCTIF PRÉSENT	IMPÉRATIF
boire *to drink*	bois	ai bu	buvais	boirai	boirais	boive	
	bois	as bu	buvais	boiras	boirais	boives	bois
	boit	a bu	buvait	boira	boirait	boive	
	buvons	avons bu	buvions	boirons	boirions	buvions	buvons
	buvez	avez bu	buviez	boirez	boiriez	buviez	buvez
	boivent	ont bu	buvaient	boiront	boiraient	boivent	
conduire *to drive*	conduis	ai conduit	conduisais	conduirai	conduirais	conduise	
	conduis	as conduit	conduisais	conduiras	conduirais	conduises	conduis
	conduit	a conduit	conduisait	conduira	conduirait	conduise	
	conduisons	avons conduit	conduisions	conduirons	conduirions	conduisions	conduisons
	conduisez	avez conduit	conduisiez	conduirez	conduiriez	conduisiez	conduisez
	conduisent	ont conduit	conduisaient	conduiront	conduiraient	conduisent	
connaître *to be acquainted with, to know*	connais	ai connu	connaissais	connaîtrai	connaîtrais	connaisse	
	connais	as connu	connaissais	connaîtras	connaîtrais	connaisses	connais
	connaît	a connu	connaissait	connaîtra	connaîtrait	connaisse	
	connaissons	avons connu	connaissions	connaîtrons	connaîtrions	connaissions	connaissons
	connaissez	avez connu	connaissiez	connaîtrez	connaîtriez	connaissiez	connaissez
	connaissent	ont connu	connaissaient	connaîtront	connaîtraient	connaissent	
courir *to run*	cours	ai couru	courais	courrai	courrais	coure	
	cours	as couru	courais	courras	courrais	coures	cours
	court	a couru	courait	courra	courrait	coure	
	courons	avons couru	courions	courrons	courrions	courions	courons
	courez	avez couru	couriez	courrez	courriez	couriez	courez
	courent	ont couru	couraient	courront	courraient	courent	
croire *to believe*	crois	ai cru	croyais	croirai	croirais	croie	
	crois	as cru	croyais	croiras	croirais	croies	crois
	croit	a cru	croyait	croira	croirait	croie	
	croyons	avons cru	croyions	croirons	croirions	croyions	croyons
	croyez	avez cru	croyiez	croirez	croiriez	croyiez	croyez
	croient	ont cru	croyaient	croiront	croiraient	croient	
devoir *must, to have to, to owe*	dois	ai dû	devais	devrai	devrais	doive	
	dois	as dû	devais	devras	devrais	doives	
	doit	a dû	devait	devra	devrait	doive	
	devons	avons dû	devions	devrons	devrions	devions	
	devez	avez dû	deviez	devrez	devriez	deviez	
	doivent	ont dû	devaient	devront	devraient	doivent	
dire *to say, to tell*	dis	ai dit	disais	dirai	dirais	dise	
	dis	as dit	disais	diras	dirais	dises	dis
	dit	a dit	disait	dira	dirait	dise	
	disons	avons dit	disions	dirons	dirions	disions	disons
	dites	avez dit	disiez	direz	diriez	disiez	dites
	disent	ont dit	disaient	diront	diraient	disent	
écrire *to write*	écris	ai écrit	écrivais	écrirai	écrirais	écrive	
	écris	as écrit	écrivais	écriras	écrirais	écrives	écris
	écrit	a écrit	écrivait	écrira	écrirait	écrive	
	écrivons	avons écrit	écrivions	écrirons	écririons	écrivions	écrivons
	écrivez	avez écrit	écriviez	écrirez	écririez	écriviez	écrivez
	écrivent	ont écrit	écrivaient	écriront	écriraient	écrivent	

Verbes irréguliers (suite)

VERBE INFINITIF	INDICATIF PRÉSENT	PASSÉ COMPOSÉ	IMPARFAIT	FUTUR	CONDITIONNEL PRÉSENT	SUBJONCTIF PRÉSENT	IMPÉRATIF
envoyer *to send*	envoie	ai envoyé	envoyais	enverrai	enverrais	envoie	
	envoies	as envoyé	envoyais	enverras	enverrais	envoies	envoie
	envoie	a envoyé	envoyait	enverra	enverrait	envoie	
	envoyons	avons envoyé	envoyions	enverrons	enverrions	envoyions	envoyons
	envoyez	avez envoyé	envoyiez	enverrez	enverriez	envoyiez	envoyez
	envoient	ont envoyé	envoyaient	enverront	enverraient	envoient	
faire *to do,* *to make*	fais	ai fait	faisais	ferai	ferais	fasse	
	fais	as fait	faisais	feras	ferais	fasses	fais
	fait	a fait	faisait	fera	ferait	fasse	
	faisons	avons fait	faisions	ferons	ferions	fassions	faisons
	faites	avez fait	faisiez	ferez	feriez	fassiez	faites
	font	ont fait	faisaient	feront	feraient	fassent	
falloir *to be* *necessary*	faut	a fallu	fallait	faudra	faudrait	faille	
lire *to read*	lis	ai lu	lisais	lirai	lirais	lise	
	lis	as lu	lisais	liras	lirais	lises	lis
	lit	a lu	lisait	lira	lirait	lise	
	lisons	avons lu	lisions	lirons	lirions	lisions	lisons
	lisez	avez lu	lisiez	lirez	liriez	lisiez	lisez
	lisent	ont lu	lisaient	liront	liraient	lisent	
mettre *to put,* *to place,* *to set*	mets	ai mis	mettais	mettrai	mettrais	mette	
	mets	as mis	mettais	mettras	mettrais	mettes	mets
	met	a mis	mettait	mettra	mettrait	mette	
	mettons	avons mis	mettions	mettrons	mettrions	mettions	mettons
	mettez	avez mis	mettiez	mettrez	mettriez	mettiez	mettez
	mettent	ont mis	mettaient	mettront	mettraient	mettent	
ouvrir *to open*	ouvre	ai ouvert	ouvrais	ouvrirai	ouvrirais	ouvre	
	ouvres	as ouvert	ouvrais	ouvriras	ouvrirais	ouvres	ouvre
	ouvre	a ouvert	ouvrait	ouvrira	ouvrirait	ouvre	
	ouvrons	avons ouvert	ouvrions	ouvrirons	ouvririons	ouvrions	ouvrons
	ouvrez	avez ouvert	ouvriez	ouvrirez	ouvririez	ouvriez	ouvrez
	ouvrent	ont ouvert	ouvraient	ouvriront	ouvriraient	ouvrent	
pleuvoir *to rain*	pleut	a plu	pleuvait	pleuvra	pleuvrait	pleuve	
pouvoir *to be able,* *can*	peux	ai pu	pouvais	pourrai	pourrais	puisse	
	peux	as pu	pouvais	pourras	pourrais	puisses	
	peut	a pu	pouvait	pourra	pourrait	puisse	
	pouvons	avons pu	pouvions	pourrons	pourrions	puissions	
	pouvez	avez pu	pouviez	pourrez	pourriez	puissiez	
	peuvent	ont pu	pouvaient	pourront	pourraient	puissent	
prendre *to take*	prends	ai pris	prenais	prendrai	prendrais	prenne	
	prends	as pris	prenais	prendras	prendrais	prennes	prends
	prend	a pris	prenait	prendra	prendrait	prenne	
	prenons	avons pris	prenions	prendrons	prendrions	prenions	prenons
	prenez	avez pris	preniez	prendrez	prendriez	preniez	prenez
	prennent	ont pris	prenaient	prendront	prendraient	prennent	

Verbes irréguliers (suite)

VERBE INFINITIF	PRÉSENT	PASSÉ COMPOSÉ	IMPARFAIT	FUTUR	CONDITIONNEL PRÉSENT	SUBJONCTIF PRÉSENT	IMPÉRATIF
recevoir *to receive*	reçois	ai reçu	recevais	recevrai	recevrais	reçoive	
	reçois	as reçu	recevais	recevras	recevrais	reçoives	reçois
	reçoit	a reçu	recevait	recevra	recevrait	reçoive	
	recevons	avons reçu	recevions	recevrons	recevrions	recevions	recevons
	recevez	avez reçu	receviez	recevrez	recevriez	receviez	recevez
	reçoivent	ont reçu	recevaient	recevront	recevraient	reçoivent	
rire *to laugh*	ris	ai ri	riais	rirai	rirais	rie	
	ris	as ri	riais	riras	rirais	ries	ris
	rit	a ri	riait	rira	rirait	rie	
	rions	avons ri	riions	rirons	ririons	riions	rions
	riez	avez ri	riiez	rirez	ririez	riiez	riez
	rient	ont ri	riaient	riront	riraient	rient	
savoir *to know*	sais	ai su	savais	saurai	saurais	sache	
	sais	as su	savais	sauras	saurais	saches	sache
	sait	a su	savait	saura	saurait	sache	
	savons	avons su	savions	saurons	saurions	sachions	sachons
	savez	avez su	saviez	saurez	sauriez	sachiez	sachez
	savent	ont su	savaient	sauront	sauraient	sachent	
suivre *to follow*	suis	ai suivi	suivais	suivrai	suivrais	suive	
	suis	as suivi	suivais	suivras	suivrais	suives	suis
	suit	a suivi	suivait	suivra	suivrait	suive	
	suivons	avons suivi	suivions	suivrons	suivrions	suivions	suivons
	suivez	avez suivi	suiviez	suivrez	suivriez	suiviez	suivez
	suivent	ont suivi	suivaient	suivront	suivraient	suivent	
venir *to come*	viens	suis venu(e)	venais	viendrai	viendrais	vienne	
	viens	es venu(e)	venais	viendras	viendrais	viennes	viens
	vient	est venu(e)	venait	viendra	viendrait	vienne	
	venons	sommes venu(e)s	venions	viendrons	viendrions	venions	venons
	venez	êtes venu(e)(s)	veniez	viendrez	viendriez	veniez	venez
	viennent	sont venu(e)s	venaient	viendront	viendraient	viennent	
vivre *to live*	vis	ai vécu	vivais	vivrai	vivrais	vive	
	vis	as vécu	vivais	vivras	vivrais	vives	vis
	vit	a vécu	vivait	vivra	vivrait	vive	
	vivons	avons vécu	vivions	vivrons	vivrions	vivions	vivons
	vivez	avez vécu	viviez	vivrez	vivriez	viviez	vivez
	vivent	ont vécu	vivaient	vivront	vivraient	vivent	
voir *to see*	vois	ai vu	voyais	verrai	verrais	voie	
	vois	as vu	voyais	verras	verrais	voies	vois
	voit	a vu	voyait	verra	verrait	voie	
	voyons	avons vu	voyions	verrons	verrions	voyions	voyons
	voyez	avez vu	voyiez	verrez	verriez	voyiez	voyez
	voient	ont vu	voyaient	verront	verraient	voient	
vouloir *to want, to wish*	veux	ai voulu	voulais	voudrai	voudrais	veuille	
	veux	as voulu	voulais	voudras	voudrais	veuilles	veuille
	veut	a voulu	voulait	voudra	voudrait	veuille	
	voulons	avons voulu	voulions	voudrons	voudrions	voulions	veuillons
	voulez	avez voulu	vouliez	voudrez	voudriez	vouliez	veuillez
	veulent	ont voulu	voulaient	voudront	voudraient	veuillent	

VOCABULAIRE FRANÇAIS-ANGLAIS

This list contains words appearing in *Horizons*, except for absolute cognates. The definitions of active vocabulary words are followed by the number of the chapter where they are first presented. A (P) refers to the *Chapitre préliminaire*. When several translations, separated by commas, are listed before a chapter number, they are all considered active. Since verbs are sometimes introduced lexically in the infinitive before the conjugation of the present indicative is presented, consult the *Index* to find out the chapter where a conjugation is introduced. An *(m)*, *(f)*, or *(pl)* following a noun indicates that it is masculine, feminine, or plural. *Inv* means that a word is invariable. An asterisk before a word beginning with an **h** indicates that the **h** is aspirate.

A

à to, at, in (P); **À bientôt.** See you soon. (P); **à cause de** due to, because of; **À ce soir.** See you tonight/this evening. (2); **à côté (de)** next to (3); **À demain.** See you tomorrow. (P); **à la campagne** in the country (3); **à la maison** at home (P); **à la page...** on page . . . (P); **à l'avance** in advance (9); **à l'étranger** abroad (9); **à l'heure** on time; **à peu près** about; **à pied** on foot (4); **À quelle heure?** At what time? (P); **à suivre** to be continued (6); **À tout à l'heure.** See you in a little while. (P); **au café** at the café (2); **au centre-ville** downtown (3); **au coin (de)** on the corner (of) (10); **au dessus de** above; **au premier étage** on the second floor (3); **Au revoir.** Good-bye. (P); **à votre avis** in your opinion; **café au lait** coffee with milk (2); **j'habite à** (+ *city*) I live in (+ *city*) (P)
abandonner to abandon, to leave
abattre to strike down
abbaye *(f)* abbey
abonnement *(m)* subscription
abonner: s'abonner à to subscribe to
abord: d'abord first (4)
abrégé(e) abbreviated
abricot *(m)* apricot
abriter to shelter
absolu(e) absolute
absolument absolutely
académique academic
Acadie *(f)* Acadia
accent *(m)* accent (P); **sans accent** without an accent (P)
acceptation *(f)* acceptance
accepter to accept
accès *(m)* access
accessoire *(m)* accessory
accidentellement accidentally
accompagner to accompany
accomplir to accomplish
accord *(m)* agreement; **D'accord!** Okay! Agreed! (2); **se mettre d'accord** to come to an agreement
accordéon *(m)* accordion
accorder: s'accorder to grant each other
accueil *(m)* welcome, reception
accueillant(e) welcoming
achat *(m)* purchase
acheter to buy (4)
acier *(m)* steel
acteur *(m)* actor (6)
Action *(f)* **de Grâce: jour** *(m)* **d'Action de Grâce** Thanksgiving Day

activité *(f)* activity (2)
actrice *(f)* actress (6)
actuellement currently
adapter: s'adapter to adapt
addition *(f)* check, bill
adepte *(mf)* one who believes in
adhésion *(f)* joining
adjectif *(m)* adjective (1)
admettre to admit
administratif(-ive): centre administratif *(m)* administration building
admirer to admire (9)
adopter to adopt
adorer to love, to adore (9)
adresse *(f)* address (3); **adresse** *(f)* **e-mail** e-mail address (3)
adresser to address; **s'adresser à** to go and see, to speak to
adulte *(mf)* adult
aérien(ne) aerial
aérobic *(m)* aerobics (8)
aéronautique aeronautical, space
aéroport *(m)* airport
affaire *(f)* thing, belonging, business; **avoir affaire à** to deal with; **femme d'affaires** businesswoman (5); **homme d'affaires** businessman (5)
affamé(e) starving
affichage: affichage public *(m)* signage; **tableau d'affichage** *(m)* bulletin board
affiche *(f)* poster (3)
affinité *(f)* affinity
africain(e) African
Afrique *(f)* Africa (9); **Afrique du Sud** *(f)* South Africa
âge *(m)* age; **Quel âge a... ?** How old is . . . ? (4)
âgé(e) old (4)
agence *(f)* **de voyages** travel agency (9)
agent *(m)* agent; **agent** *(m)* **de police** policeman; **agent** *(m)* **de voyages** travel agent (9)
aggraver to worsen
agir to act, to take action
agitation *(f)* agitation
agité(e) agitated
agneau *(m)* lamb
agréable pleasant (1)
agricole agricultural
agriculture *(f)* agriculture
aider to help (5)
aïe ouch
aigle *(m)* eagle
ail *(m)* garlic
aile *(f)* wing
ailleurs elsewhere
aimable kind, amiable
aimer to like (2), to love (7); **Aimeriez-vous... ?** Would you like. . . ? (8); **aimer mieux** to like

better, to prefer (2); **Est-ce que tu aimes / vous aimez... ?** Do you like. . . ? (1); **J'aime...** I like . . . (1); **J'aimerais...** I would like . . . ; **s'aimer** to love each other (7)
aîné(e) oldest (child)
ainsi thus; **ainsi que** as well as
air *(m)* air, look, appearance; **avoir l'air** (+ *adjective)* to look / to seem (+ *adjective)* (4); **de plein air** outdoor (4)
aise *(f)* ease; **mal à l'aise** ill at ease
aisé(e): classe aisée *(f)* upper class
ajouter to add
alcool *(m)* alcohol (8)
alcoolisé(e) alcoholic
alcoolisme *(m)* alcoholism
Algérie *(f)* Algeria (9)
algérien(ne) Algerian
aliment *(m)* food
alimentaire food
Allemagne *(f)* Germany (9)
allemand *(m)* German (1)
allemand(e) German
aller (à) to go (to) (2); **aller à la chasse** to go hunting; **aller à la pêche** to go fishing; **aller à pied** to walk, to go on foot (4); **aller très bien à quelqu'un** to look very good on someone; **Allez au tableau.** Go to the board. (P); **aller voir** to go see, to visit *(a person)* (4); **aller-retour** *(m)* round-trip ticket (9); **billet aller simple** *(m)* one-way ticket (9); **Ça va.** It's going fine. (P); **Comment allez-vous?** How are you? (P); **Comment ça va?** How's it going? (P); **Comment vas-tu?** How are you? *(informal);* **je vais** I go, I am going (1); **On va... ?** Shall we go . . . ? (2); **Qu'est-ce qui ne va pas?** What's wrong? (10); **s'en aller** to go away; **tu vas / vous allez** you go, you are going (2)
allergie *(f)* allergy (10)
allié(e) allied
allô hello *(on the telephone)* (6)
allumer to light
allumette *(f)* match
alors so, then (1)
alpinisme *(m)* mountain climbing; **faire de l'alpinisme** to go mountain climbing
amande *(f)* almond
amant(e) *(mf)* lover
ambassade *(f)* embassy
ambassadeur(-drice) *(mf)* ambassador
ambitieux(-ieuse) ambitious
améliorer to improve
aménagé(e) fitted out
amener to take, to bring
américain(e) American (P); **à l'américaine** American style (8)
amérindien(ne) Native American

Amérique *(f)* America (9); **Amérique centrale** *(f)* Central America (9); **Amérique** *(f)* **du Nord** North America (9); **Amérique** *(f)* **du Sud** South America (9)

ami(e) *(mf)* friend (P), **petit ami** *(m)* boyfriend (2); **petite amie** *(f)* girlfriend (2)

amitié *(f)* friendship

amour *(m)* love (6); **film** *(m)* **d'amour** romantic movie (6); **le grand amour** *(m)* true love (7)

amoureux(-euse) in love (6); **tomber amoureux(-euse) de** to fall in love with (6)

amovible detachable

amphithéâtre *(m)* lecture hall (1)

amusant(e) fun (1)

amuser to amuse; **On s'amuse bien.** One has a good time. (4); **s'amuser** to have fun (7)

an *(m)* year (5); **avoir... ans** to be . . . years old (4); **jour** *(m)* **de l'an** *(m)* New Year's Day

ananas *(m)* pineapple

ancêtre *(mf)* ancestor

anchois *(m)* anchovy

ancien(ne) former, old, ancient

andouille *(f)* sausage of chitterlings

ange *(m)* angel

angine *(f)* tonsillitis

anglais *(m)* English (P)

anglais(e) English

Angleterre *(f)* England; **Nouvelle-Angleterre** *(f)* New England

anglophone English-speaking

angoissé(e) anguished

angoisser to agonize, to worry

animal *(m)* *(pl animaux)* animal (3)

animé(e) animated; **dessin animé** *(m)* cartoon

année *(f)* year (4)

anniversaire *(m)* birthday (4); **anniversaire** *(m)* **de mariage** wedding anniversary

annonce *(f)* advertisement, announcement

annuaire *(m)* telephone book

annuel(le) annual

annuler to annul, to cancel; **annulé(e)** canceled

anorak *(m)* ski jacket, anorak (5)

Antarctique *(m)* Antarctica

anticiper to anticipate

antillais(e) West Indian

Antilles *(fpl)* West Indies (9)

août *(m)* August (4)

apercevoir to see, to notice

apéritif *(m)* before-dinner drink (8)

apparaître to appear

appareil *(m)* apparatus, appliance; **appareil** *(m)* **téléphonique** telephone

apparence *(f)* appearance

apparenté(e) related

appartement *(m)* apartment (3)

appartenir (à) to belong (to)

appeler to call; **Comment s'appelle... ?** What is . . .'s name? (4); **Comment t'appelles-tu?** What's your name? *(informal)*; **Comment vous appelez-vous?** What's your name? *(formal)* (P); **Il/Elle s'appelle...** His/Her name is . . . (4); **Je m'appelle...** My name is . . . (P); **s'appeler** to be named, to be called (7); **Tu t'appelles comment?** What's your name? *(informal)* (P)

appétit *(m)* appetite

applaudir to applaud

apporter to bring (9)

apprécier to appreciate (6)

apprendre to learn (4); **Apprenez...** Learn. . . (P)

approcher: s'approcher (de) to approach

approprié(e) appropriate

approuver to approve

approximatif(-ive) approximate

après after, afterward (P); **d'après** according to

après-demain the day after tomorrow

après-midi *(m)* afternoon (P); **cet après-midi** this afternoon (4); **Il est une heure de l'après-midi.** It's one o'clock in the afternoon. (P); **l'après-midi** in the afternoon, afternoons (P)

arabe *(m)* Arabic

arachide *(f)* groundnut, peanut

araignée *(f)* spider

arbre *(m)* tree (1)

arc *(m)* arch, bow; **tir** *(m)* **à l'arc** archery

archange *(m)* archangel

archéologique archeological

ardent(e) ardent, fervent

argent *(m)* money (7), silver

Argentine *(f)* Argentina (9)

aristocratie *(f)* aristocracy

armée *(f)* army

arrêt *(m)* stop; **arrêt** *(m)* **d'autobus** bus stop (3)

arrêter to stop; **s'arrêter** to stop (7)

arrivée *(f)* arrival (9)

arriver to arrive (3), to happen

arrondi(e) rounded

arrondissement *(m)* district

art *(m)* art; **les beaux-arts** the fine arts (1)

article *(m)* article (9)

artificiel(le) artificial

artisanat *(m)* crafts

artiste *(mf)* artist, performer (10)

ascenseur *(m)* elevator (3)

Asie *(f)* Asia (9)

asperge *(f)* asparagus

aspirant(e) *(mf)* candidate

assassin *(m)* murderer, assassin

assassiner to murder, to assassinate

assaut *(m)* assault, attack

assemblage *(m)* assembly, gathering

assemblée *(f)* assembly

asseoir: Asseyez-vous. Sit down.; **s'asseoir** to sit (down)

assez fairly, rather (P); **assez (de)** enough (1)

assiette *(f)* plate

assis(e) seated

assister à to attend

associer to associate

Assomption *(f)* the Assumption

assurance *(f)* insurance

assuré(e) provided, assured

astronomie *(f)* astronomy

astucieux(-euse) astute

atelier *(m)* workshop

atout *(m)* trump card

attaché(e) attached

attaque *(f)* attack; **attaque** *(f)* **d'apoplexie** stroke

attendre to wait (for) (7); **s'attendre à** to expect to

attente *(f)* waiting

attention: faire attention (à) to pay attention (to) (8)

attirant(e) attractive

attirer to attract

attraper to catch

attribuer assign, allocate

aube *(f)* dawn

auberge *(f)* inn; **auberge** *(f)* **de jeunesse** youth hostel

aubergine *(f)* eggplant

aucun(e): ne... aucun(e) no, none, not one

au-dessus above

auditif(-ive) auditory

aujourd'hui today (P)

auparavant beforehand

auquel (à laquelle, auxquels, auxquelles) to which

aussi too, also (P); **aussi... que** as . . . as (1)

aussitôt que as soon as

Australie *(f)* Australia (9)

autant (de)... (que) as much . . . (as), as many . . . (as)

authenticité *(f)* authenticity

autobus *(m)* bus (4); **arrêt** *(m)* **d'autobus** bus stop (3); **en autobus** by bus (4)

autocar *(m)* bus (4); **en autocar** by bus (4)

automatique automatic (7); **guichet automatique** *(m)* automatic teller machine (7)

automne *(m)* autumn, fall (5); **en automne** in autumn (5)

autonomie *(f)* autonomy

autoportrait *(m)* self-portrait

autoritaire authoritarian

autour de around

autre other (1); **quelquefois... d'autres fois** sometimes . . . other times (7); **Qu'est-ce que je peux vous proposer d'autre?** What else can I get you? (8)

autrefois formerly, in the past

Autriche *(f)* Austria

auxiliaire *(m)* auxiliary

avaler to swallow, to gulp

avance *(f)* advance; **à l'avance** in advance (9); **en avance** early

avancer to advance

avant before (P); **avant de partir** before leaving

avantage *(m)* advantage

avec with (P); **Avec plaisir!** With pleasure! (6)

avenir *(m)* future (10)

aventure *(f)* adventure ; **film** *(m)* **d'aventures** adventure movie

avenue *(f)* avenue (10)

avion *(m)* airplane (4); **en avion** by airplane (4)

avis *(m)* opinion

avocat(e) *(mf)* lawyer (10)

avoir to have (3); **avoir... ans** to be . . . years old (4); **avoir besoin de** to need (4); **avoir chaud** to be hot (4); **avoir cours** to have class (6); **avoir de la fièvre** to have fever; **avoir du mal à...** to have difficulty . . . , to have a hard time. . .; **avoir envie de** to feel like, to desire (4); **avoir faim** to be hungry (4); **j'ai faim** I'm hungry (2); **avoir froid** to be cold (4); **avoir *honte** to be ashamed; **avoir l'air (+ adjective)** to look / to seem (+ adjective) (4); **avoir le nez bouché** to have a stopped-up nose; **avoir le nez qui coule** to have a runny nose; **avoir les cheveux/les yeux...** to have . . . hair/eyes (4); **avoir lieu** to take place; **avoir l'intention de** to plan on, to intend to (4); **avoir mal (à)** one's. . . hurts, to ache (10); **avoir peur (de)** to be afraid (of), to fear (4); **avoir raison** to be right (4); **avoir soif** to be thirsty (4); **j'ai soif** I'm thirsty (2); **avoir sommeil** to be sleepy (4); **avoir tort** to be wrong (4); **il y a** there is, there are (1), ago (5); **Quel âge a... ?** How old is . . .? (4)

avouer to admit

avril *(m)* April (4)

ayant having

B

babillard *(m)* bulletin board
baby-sitter *(mf)* babysitter
baccalauréat (**bac**) *(m) a comprehensive examination at the end of secondary school*
bachelier(**-ière**) *(mf) someone having passed the baccalauréat*
bacon *(m)* bacon (8)
bagages *(mpl)* baggage (9)
bague *(f)* ring
baguette *(f)* loaf of French bread (7)
baie *(f)* bay
baigner: se baigner to bathe, to go swimming
bain *(m)* bath (7); **bain** *(m)* **de soleil** sunbath (4); **maillot** *(m)* **de bain** swimsuit (5); **salle** *(f)* **de bains** bathroom (3)
baiser *(m)* kiss
bal *(m)* dance
bambou *(m)* bamboo
banane *(f)* banana (8)
bancaire: carte *(f)* **bancaire** bank card (9)
banlieue *(f)* suburbs (3)
banque *(f)* bank (7)
banquette *(f)* bench, seat
banquier *(m)* banker
bar *(m)* bar (4)
barbe *(f)* beard (4)
barrer to cross out
bas *(m)* bottom
bas(**se**) low; **table basse** *(f)* coffee table
base *(f)* base; **de base** basic
base-ball *(m)* baseball (2)
basé(**e**) **sur** based on (6)
basilique *(f)* basilica
basket *(m)* basketball (1)
basque *(m)* Basque
bataille *(f)* battle
bateau *(m)* boat (4); **en bateau** by boat (4); **faire du bateau** to go boating (5)
bâtiment *(m)* building (1)
batterie *(f)* drums (2)
battre to beat
bavette *(f)* undercut
beau (**bel, belle,** *pl* **beaux, belles**) beautiful, handsome (1); **beau-frère** *(m)* brother-in-law (4); **beau-père** *(m)* father-in-law (4); **beaux-arts** *(mpl)* fine arts (1); **beaux-parents** *(mpl)* stepparents, in-laws; **belle-mère** *(f)* mother-in-law (4); **belle-sœur** *(f)* sister-in-law (4); **Il fait beau.** The weather's nice. (5)
beaucoup a lot (P); **beaucoup de** a lot of (1)
beauté *(f)* beauty
bébé *(m)* baby
beige beige (3)
beignet *(m)* fritter
belge Belgian
Belgique *(f)* Belgium (9)
bénéficiaire *(mf)* beneficiary
bénévole benefit, benevolent, voluntary (10)
bénir to bless
besoin *(m)* need; **avoir besoin de** to need (4)
bête *(f)* beast (6), animal
bête stupid, dumb (1)
beurre *(m)* butter (8)
beurré(**e**) buttered
bibliothèque *(f)* library (P), bookcase
bien well (P), very; **bien d'autres** many others; **bien que** although; **Bien sûr!** Of course! (5); **Je voudrais bien.** Sure, I'd like to. (2)

bien-être *(m)* well-being
bienfaiteur *(m)*, **bienfaitrice** *(f)* benefactor
biens *(mpl)* goods
bientôt soon (P); **À bientôt.** See you soon. (P)
bienvenu(**e**) welcome
bière *(f)* beer (2)
bifteck *(m)* steak (8); **bifteck hâché** *(m)* ground meat
bijoux *(mpl)* jewelry
bikini *(m)* bikini (5)
bilingue bilingual
billard *(m)* billiards
billet *(m)* ticket (9)
biologie *(f)* biology (1)
biscotte *(f)* melba toast
bise *(f)* kiss
bistro(**t**) *(m)* restaurant, pub (6)
bizarre bizarre, strange
blanc(**he**) white (3); **vin blanc** *(m)* white wine (2)
blanquette *(f)* stew *(usually veal)*
bleu(**e**) blue (3); **bleu clair** light blue; **bleu foncé** dark blue; **bleu vif** bright blue
blond(**e**) blond (4)
blouson *(m)* windbreaker, jacket
bœuf *(m)* beef (8)
bohème bohemian
boire to drink (4)
bois *(m)* wood, woods
boisson *(f)* drink (2)
boîte *(f)* box, can (8); **boîte** *(f)* **de nuit** nightclub (1)
bol *(m)* bowl
bombardement *(m)* bombing
bomber to stick out
bon(**ne**) good (1); **Bon anniversaire!** Happy birthday!; **Bonne année!** Happy New Year!; **Bonne idée!** Good idea! (4); **Bonne journée!** Have a good day!; **Bon séjour!** Have a nice stay!; **Bon week-end!** Have a good weekend!
bonbon *(m)* candy
bonheur *(m)* happiness
Bonjour! Hello! Good morning! (P)
bonne *(f)* maid, nanny
Bonsoir! Good evening! (P)
bord *(m)* edge; **à bord** on board; **au bord de** at the edge of; **bord** *(m)* **de la mer** seaside
bordé(**e**) bordered
bordure: en bordure de along the edge of
botte *(f)* boot (5)
bouche *(f)* mouth (10)
bouché(**e**) stopped-up; **cidre bouché** *(m)* bottled cider
boucherie *(f)* butcher's shop (8)
boucle *(f)* **d'oreille** earring
boudin *(m)* blood sausage
boue *(f)* mud
bouger to move
bouillabaisse *(f)* fish soup
bouillir to boil
boulangerie *(f)* bakery (7)
boule *(f)* ball
boulevard *(m)* boulevard (10)
boulot *(m)* work *(familiar)*
boum *(f)* party (1), bash
bourgeoisie: haute bourgeoisie *(f)* upper-middle class
bout *(m)* end (3); **au bout** (**de**) at the end (of) (3)
bouteille *(f)* bottle (8)
boutique *(f)* shop
bouton *(m)* button, pimple
boxer to box

bracelet *(m)* bracelet
branché(**e**) up with things
brancher: se brancher sur to get into
bras *(m)* arm (10)
brasier *(m)* inferno
bref(**-ève**) brief
Brésil *(m)* Brazil (9)
Bretagne *(f)* Brittany
breton *(m)* Breton
bricolage *(m)* handiwork
bricoler to do handiwork (2)
brioche *(f)* brioche *(a type of soft bread)*
briser to break
britannique British
brochette *(f)* skewer
brocolis *(mpl)* broccoli
bronchite *(f)* bronchitis
bronzer to tan (9)
brosser to brush; **se brosser** to brush (7)
brouillard *(m)* fog, mist, haze
bruit *(m)* noise
brûler to burn; **se brûler la main** to burn your hand
brun(**e**) *(with hair and eyes)* brown, brunette, dark-haired (4)
Bruxelles Brussels
bulletin *(m)* report, bulletin
bureau *(m)* desk (3), office (1); **bureau** *(m)* **de poste** post office (7); **bureau** *(m)* **de tabac** tobacco shop (7)
bus *(m)* bus (4)
but *(m)* goal

C

ça that (P); **Ça fait combien?** How much is it? (2); **Ça fait... euros.** That's . . . euros. (2); **Ça me plaît!** I like it! (3); **Ça lui plaît?** Does he like it? (9); **Ça s'écrit comment?** How is that written? (P); **Ça te/vous dit?** How does that sound to you? (4); **Ça te/vous plaît!** You like it! (3); **Ça va.** It's going fine. (P); **C'est ça!** That's right!; **comme ci comme ça** so-so (2); **Comment ça va?** How's it going? (P); **Qu'est-ce que ça veut dire?** What does that mean? (P)
cabine *(f)* **d'essayage** fitting room (5)
cacao *(m)* cocoa
cacher to hide; **se cacher** to hide oneself, to be hidden
cadien(**ne**) Cajun (4)
cadeau *(m)* gift
cadre *(m)* executive
café *(m)* café (1), coffee (2); **café** *(m)* **au lait** coffee with milk
cahier *(m)* notebook (P)
calcul *(m)* calculation
calculer to calculate
câlin(**e**) cuddly
calme calm (4)
calmement calmly
calmer: se calmer to calm down
calvaire *(m)* Calvary
camarade *(mf)* pal; **camarade** *(mf)* **de chambre** roommate (P); **camarade** *(mf)* **de classe** classmate
camerounais(**e**) Cameroonian
campagne *(f)* country (3), campaign; **à la campagne** in the country (3)
camping *(m)* camping, campground (5); **faire du camping** to go camping (5)

campus *(m)* campus (1)
Canada *(m)* Canada (9)
canadien(ne) Canadian (P)
canapé *(m)* couch (3), open-faced sandwich
canard *(m)* duck (8)
candidat(e) *(mf)* candidate, applicant
canton *(m)* canton, district
capacité *(f)* capacity, ability
capitale *(f)* capital
caprice *(m)* whim
car *(m)* bus (4)
car because
caractère *(m)* character; **en caractères gras** boldfaced
caractériser to characterize
caractéristique *(f)* characteristic
carafe *(f)* carafe *(a decanter)* (8)
caraïbe Caribbean; **mer** *(f)* **des Caraïbes** Caribbean Sea
carbonisé(e): mourir carbonisé(e) to be burned to death
carie *(f)* cavity
carotte *(f)* carrot (8)
carré(e) square; **Vieux Carré** French Quarter (4)
carrière *(f)* career (10)
carte *(f)* menu (8), card, map; **carte** *(f)* **bancaire** bank card (9); **carte** *(f)* **de crédit** credit card (9); **carte** *(f)* **d'identité** identity card; **carte** *(f)* **postale** postcard (9); **carte** *(f)* **téléphonique** telephone card
cas *(m)* case; **dans tous les cas** in any case
case *(f)* box
casier: casier postal *(m)* mailbox
casquette *(f)* cap (5)
casse-cou *(inv)* *(mf)* daredevil
casse-pieds *(inv)* *(mf)* nuisance
casser to break; **se casser la jambe** to break one's leg
cassette *(f)* cassette (P)
catastrophe *(f)* disaster
catégorie *(f)* category
cathédrale *(f)* cathedral
catholique *(mf)* Catholic
cause *(f)* cause; **à cause de** because of
causer to cause
CD *(m)* CD (P), compact disc (3)
ce (cet, cette) this, that (3); **ce que** what, that which; **ce qui** what, that which (7); **ces** these, those (3); **ce semestre** this semester (P); **ce soir** tonight, this evening (2); **ce sont** they are, those are (1); **c'est** it's (P), he is, she is, that is, this is (1); **c'est-à-dire** in other words
céder to give up
ceinture *(f)* belt (5)
cela that
célèbre famous (4)
célébrer to celebrate
célébrité *(f)* celebrity
céleri *(m)* celery
célibataire single, unmarried (1)
celte Celtic
celtique Celtic
celui (celle) the one
cendre *(f)* ash; **mercredi** *(m)* **des Cendres** Ash Wednesday
cendrier *(m)* ashtray
censure *(f)* censorship
cent *(m)* one hundred (2)
centime *(m)* centime *(one hundredth part of a euro)* (2)
central(e) *(mpl* **centraux)** central; **Amérique** *(f)* **centrale** Central America (9)

centre *(m)* center (5); **centre administratif** *(m)* administration building; **centre commercial** *(m)* shopping center, mall (4); **centre** *(m)* **d'étudiants** student center
centre-ville *(m)* downtown (3)
cercle *(m)* circle
céréales *(fpl)* cereal (8)
céréalier(-ière) cereal
cérémonie *(f)* ceremony
cerise *(f)* cherry (8)
certain(e) certain; **certains** some, certain people
certainement certainly
certes true, indeed, of course
certificat *(m)* certificate
cervelle *(f)* brain
cesser to cease
ceux (celles) those (ones) (8)
chacun(e) each one (7)
chagrin *(m)* sorrow
chaîne *(f)* chain; **chaîne stéréo** *(f)* stereo (2)
chaise *(f)* chair (3)
chaleur *(f)* warmth
chaleureux(-euse) warm-hearted
chambre *(f)* bedroom (3); **camarade** *(mf)* **de chambre** roommate (P)
champ *(m)* field; **champ** *(m)* **de bataille** battlefield
champignon *(m)* mushroom
chance *(f)* luck
changement *(m)* change
changer to change (6); **changer de l'argent** to exchange money (9)
chanson *(f)* song
chanter to sing (2)
chanteur(-euse) *(mf)* singer
chapeau *(m)* hat (5)
chapelle *(f)* chapel
chaperon: ** *(m)* hood; **le Petit Chaperon rouge Little Red Riding Hood
chapiteau *(m)* tent
chapitre *(m)* chapter
chaque each, every (3)
charbon *(m)* coal
charcuterie *(f)* delicatessen, deli meats, cold cuts (8)
charger to charge, to load; **chargé(e) (de)** busy, in charge (of); **se charger de** to take charge of
charité *(f)* charity
charmant(e) charming
chasse *(f)* hunt, hunting; **aller à la chasse** to go hunting
chasser to hunt
chasseur *(m)* hunter
chat *(m)* cat (3)
châtain *(light to medium)* brown *(hair)* (4)
château *(m)* castle
chaud(e) hot (2); **avoir chaud** to be hot (4); **chocolat chaud** *(m)* hot chocolate (2); **Il fait chaud.** It's hot. (5)
chauffant(e) heating
chauffé(e) heated
chauffeur *(m)* driver
chaume *(m)* thatch
chaussette *(f)* sock (5)
chausson *(m)* **aux pommes** apple turnover
chaussure *(f)* shoe (5)
chef *(m)* head, boss, chief
chef-d'œuvre *(m)* masterpiece
chemin *(m)* road; **chemin** *(m)* **de fer** railroad; **indiquer le chemin** to give directions, to show the way (10)
chemise *(f)* shirt (5); **chemise** *(f)* **de nuit** nightgown

chemisier *(m)* blouse (5)
chêne *(m)* oak
chèque *(m)* check (9); **chèque** *(m)* **de voyage** traveler's check (9)
cher(-ère) expensive (3), dear
chercher to look for (3), to seek; **aller / venir chercher quelqu'un** to go / to come get someone
chercheur(-euse) *(mf)* researcher
chéri(e) *(mf)* honey, darling (7)
cheval *(m)* horse; **faire du cheval** to go horseback riding
chevet: livre *(m)* **de chevet** bedside book
cheveux *(mpl)* hair (4)
cheville *(f)* ankle; **se fouler la cheville** to sprain one's ankle
chèvre *(m)* goat cheese
chez at / in / to / by . . .'s house/place (2)
chien *(m)* dog (3)
chiffre *(m)* number
chimie *(f)* chemistry (1)
chimique chemical
Chine *(f)* China (9)
chinois *(m)* Chinese
chirurgie *(f)* surgery
choc *(m)* shock, impact
chocolat *(m)* chocolate (2); **gâteau au chocolat** *(m)* chocolate cake (8); **pain au chocolat** *(m)* chocolate-filled croissant (8)
choisir (de faire) to choose (to do) (8)
choix *(m)* choice (8)
choquer to shock
chose *(f)* thing (3); **quelque chose** something (2)
chou *(m)* cabbage
chouette neat, great (9)
chou-fleur *(m)* cauliflower
choux *(mpl)* **de Bruxelles** Brussels sprouts
chrétien(ne) Christian
chrysanthème *(m)* chrysanthemum
ci: ce (cet, cette)... ci this. . . (3); **ce mois-ci** this month (4); **ces... ci** these. . . (3); **ci-dessous** below; **ci-dessus** above; **comme ci comme ça** so-so (2)
ciao bye *(informal)*
ciel *(m)* sky
cinéaste *(mf)* filmmaker
cinéclub *(m)* cinema club (2)
cinéma *(m)* cinema, movie theater (1); **aller au cinéma** to go to the movies (2)
cinématographique film
cinq five (P)
cinquante fifty (P)
cinquième fifth (3)
circonstance *(f)* circumstance
circuit *(m)* circuit, course
circulation *(f)* traffic
circuler to circulate
cité universitaire *(f)* residence halls complex
citoyen(ne) *(mf)* citizen
citoyenneté *(f)* citizenship
citron *(m)* lemon (2); **thé** *(m)* **au citron** tea with lemon (2); **citron vert** *(m)* lime
civet *(m)* stew
civil(e) civil
clair(e) light; **bleu clair** light blue
clairement clearly
classe: classe aisée *(f)* upper class; **classe** *(f)* **touriste** tourist class, coach (9); **première classe** *(f)* first class (9); **salle** *(f)* **de classe** classroom (1)
classique classical (1), classic (2)
clavier *(m)* keyboard (2)

clé *(f)* key (10)
client(e) *(mf)* customer
climat *(m)* climate
climatisé(e) air-conditioned
clinique *(f)* clinic (10)
cloche *(f)* bell
clos(e) closed
clôture *(f)* closure, closing date
club *(m)* club; **club** *(m)* **de gym** gym, fitness club (1); **club** *(m)* **de sport** sports club
coca *(m)* cola (2)
cocotier *(m)* coconut tree
cocotte *(f)* casserole, primper
code *(m)* code; **code postal** *(m)* zip code (3)
cœur *(m)* heart; **au cœur de** in the heart of
coiffure *(f)* hair style
coin *(m)* corner (3); **au coin (de)** on the corner (of) (10); **café** *(m)* **du coin** neighborhood café; **dans le coin de** in the corner of (3)
colère *(f)* anger; **en colère** angry
colis *(m)* package (7)
collaborateur(-trice) *(mf)* colleague
collant *(m)* pantyhose
collation *(f)* snack
collectionner to collect
collectivité *(f)* community
collège *(m)* secondary school
collègue *(mf)* colleague
collier *(m)* necklace
colocataire *(mf)* housemate, co-renter (3)
Colombie *(f)* Columbia (9)
colonie *(f)* colony
colonisateur(-trice) *(mf)* colonizer
coloniser to colonize
colonne *(f)* column
combattre to fight, to combat
combien (de) how much, how many (3); **Ça fait combien? / C'est combien?** How much is it? (2); **combien de** how many, how much (3); **Combien font... et... / moins... ?** How much is . . . plus . . . / minus . . . ? (P); **Pendant combien de temps?** For how long? (5); **Vous êtes combien?** How many are there (of you)? (4)
combinaison *(f)* slip
combiner to combine
comédie *(f)* comedy (6); **comédie musicale** *(f)* musical
comédien(ne) *(mf)* actor
comique comical
commander to order (2), to command
comme like (1), as (3) , since (7), for (8); **comme ci comme ça** so-so (2); **comme tu vois** as you see (3)
commencer (à) to begin (to), to start (2); **Le cours de français commence...** The French class starts . . . (P)
comment how (P); **Ça s'écrit comment?** How do you write that? (P); **Comment?** What? (P); **Comment allez-vous?** How are you? (P); **Comment ça va?** How's it going? (P); **Comment dit-on... en français?** How do you say . . . in French? (P); **Comment est (sont)... ?** What is (are) . . . like? (1); **Comment s'appelle... ?** What is . . .'s name? (4); **Comment vas-tu?** How are you? *(informal)*; **Comment vous appelez-vous?** What's your name? *(formal)* (P) **Tu t'appelles comment? / Comment t'appelles-tu?** What's your name? *(informal)* (P)
commerçant(e) *(mf)* shopkeeper, merchant (8)
commerce *(m)* business (1)

commercial: centre commercial *(m)* shopping center, mall (4)
commettre to commit
commode *(f)* dresser, chest of drawers (3)
commode convenient (3)
commodité *(f)* convenience, comfort
commun(e) common
communautaire: salles communautaires *(fpl)* community rooms, shared areas
communauté *(f)* community
communication *(f)* communication
communiquer to communicate (10)
compact: disque compact *(m)* compact disc (3)
comparaison *(f)* comparison
comparer to compare (6)
compétence *(f)* skill, competency
complément d'objet direct / indirect *(m)* direct / indirect object
complet(-ète) complete (8); **en phrases complètes** *(f)* in complete sentences (P); **pain complet** *(m)* wholegrain bread (8)
complètement completely
compléter to complete
complexe complex, complicated
compliqué(e) complicated
composer to compose; **se composer de** to be made up of
compote *(f)* stewed fruit
compotier *(m)* fruit bowl
compréhension *(f)* understanding
comprenant including
comprendre to understand (4), to include (8); **Est-ce que vous comprenez?** Do you understand? (P); **Je comprends.** I understand. (P)
compris(e) included (10)
comptabilité *(f)* accounting (1)
comptable *(mf)* accountant
compte *(m)* **en banque** bank account
compter to count (2), to plan (9); **Comptez de... à ...** Count from . . . to . . . (P)
con *(m)* *(vulgar)* jerk
concentrer: se concentrer sur to concentrate on
concerner to concern
concert *(m)* concert (1); **de concert avec** along with
concevoir to conceive
concombre *(m)* cucumber
concours *(m)* competition, competitive entrance examination
concurrent(e) *(mf)* competitor
condition *(f)* condition
conducteur(-trice) *(mf)* driver
conduire to drive
confédération *(f)* confederation
confiance *(f)* confidence (4)
confidence *(f)* secret
confier à to confide in, to entrust to
confirmer to confirm
confit *(m)* **de canard** conserve of duck
confiture *(f)* jam, jelly (8)
conflit *(m)* conflict
confondre to confuse; **confondu(e)** combined
confort *(m)* comfort
confortable comfortable (3)
confus(e) confused
conjoncture *(f)* situation
conjugal(e) *(mpl* **conjugaux)** married, conjugal
connaissance *(f)* acquaintance, knowledge; **faire connaissance** to meet (1);
connaître to know, to get to know, to be familiar / acquainted with (4); **Connaissez-vous... ?** Do you know . . . ? (6)

connu(e) known
conquérant(e) *(mf)* conqueror
conquête *(f)* conquest
conseil *(m)* a piece of advice (8), council, committee
conseiller(-ère) *(mf)* counselor, adviser
conséquence *(f)* consequence; **en conséquence** as a consequence
conservateur(-trice) conservative
conserver to keep
conserves *(fpl)* canned goods (8)
considérer to consider; **se considérer** to consider oneself
consommation *(f)* consumption, drink
consonne *(f)* consonant
constamment constantly
constituer to make up
construire to construct, to build
consulat *(m)* consulate
consulter to consult
conte *(m)* story (6); **conte** *(m)* **de fée** fairy tale (6)
contemporain(e) contemporary
contenir to contain
content(e) happy, glad (8)
conteur(-euse) *(mf)* storyteller
contexte *(m)* context
continent *(m)* continent (9)
continuer to continue (10)
contraire *(m)* contrary; **au contraire** on the contrary
contraste *(m)* contrast
contrat *(m)* contract
contre against; **par contre** on the other hand
contribuer to contribute
contrôle *(m)* control
contrôler to control
convenable appropriate, suitable
convenir to be suitable; **Ça vous convient?** Does that work for you? (9)
convoité(e) coveted
copain *(m)* (male) friend, pal (6); **copain** *(m)* **de chambre** roommate
copieux(-euse) copious, large (8)
copine *(f)* (female) friend, pal (6); **copine** *(f)* **de chambre** roommate
coquillage *(m)* shellfish
coquilles St-Jacques *(fpl)* scallops
corps *(m)* body (10); **Corps** *(m)* **de la Paix** Peace Corps (10)
correspondant(e) corresponding
correspondre (à) to correspond (to)
Corse *(f)* Corsica
corse *(m)* Corsican *(language)*
costume *(m)* man's suit (5)
côte *(f)* coast; **côte** *(f)* **de porc** pork chop (8)
côté *(m)* side (3); **à côté (de)** next to (3); **de l'autre côté (de)** on the other side (of) (3)
Côte-d'Ivoire *(f)* Ivory Coast (9)
coton *(m)* cotton
cou *(m)* neck
coucher: se coucher to go to bed (7)
coulée *(f)* flow
couler to run *(liquids)*
couleur *(f)* color (3); **De quelle couleur est/sont... ?** What color is/are . . . ? (3)
coulis *(m)* purée
couloir *(m)* hall, corridor (3)
coup *(m)* stroke, blow; **coup** *(m)* **de foudre** love at first sight (7); **coup** *(m)* **d'état** coup; **coup** *(m)* **de téléphone** telephone call; **tout d'un coup** all of a sudden (6)
coupe *(f)* dessert dish

couper to cut; **se couper le doigt** to cut one's finger

couramment fluently

courant(e) present, current, common

courgette *(f)* zucchini

courir to run

courrier *(m)* mail; **courrier électronique** *(m)* e-mail

cours *(m)* class (P), course; **au cours de** in the course of; **avoir cours** to have class (6); **suivre un cours** to take a course

course *(f)* errand (5), race; **faire des courses** to run errands (5); **faire les courses** to go grocery shopping (7)

court *(m)* **de tennis** tennis court

court(e) short (4); **court métrage** *(m)* short film

cousin(e) *(mf)* cousin (4)

coûter to cost (5)

coutume *(f)* custom

couture *(f)* sewing, dressmaking; **haute couture* *(f)* designer fashion (5)

couverture *(f)* blanket, cover (3)

couvrir to cover

cravate *(f)* tie (5)

crayon *(m)* pencil (P)

créancier(-ière) *(mf)* creditor

créateur(-trice) *(mf)* creator

crèche *(f)* (government-sponsored) day care

crédit: carte *(f)* **de crédit** credit card (9)

créer to create

crème *(f)* cream (8)

créole Creole

crevette *(f)* shrimp (8)

crier to shout

criminel(le) *(mf)* criminal

crise *(f)* crisis; **crise cardiaque** *(f)* heart attack

critique *(f)* criticism

croc *(m)* fang

croire (à) (que) to believe (in) (that) (10); **je crois** I think

croissant *(m)* croissant (7)

croque-madame *(m)* toasted ham-and-cheese sandwich with an egg on top

croque-monsieur *(m)* toasted ham-and-cheese sandwich

cru(e) raw

crudités *(fpl)* raw vegetables (8)

cuiller *(f)* spoon

cuillerée *(f)* spoonful

cuir *(m)* leather

cuire to cook

cuisine *(f)* kitchen (3); cuisine, cooking (4); **faire de la cuisine** to cook (5)

cuisinière *(f)* stove

cuisson *(f)* cooking

cuivre *(m)* copper

cultiver to cultivate

culture *(f)* culture (9), cultivation

culturel(le) cultural (4)

curieux(-euse) curious, odd

curiosité *(f)* curiosity

cursus *(m)* degree course

cyclisme *(m)* cycling

cycliste *(mf)* cyclist

D

dactylographie *(f)* typing

dame *(f)* lady; **messieurs-dames** gentlemen-ladies (2)

Danemark *(m)* Denmark

danger *(m)* danger

dangereux(-euse) dangerous

dans in (P); **dans la rue...** on . . . street (10)

danse *(f)* dance (9)

danser to dance (2)

danseur(-euse) *(mf)* dancer

date *(f)* date (4); **Quelle est la date aujourd'hui?** What is the date today? (4)

dater de to date from

daurade *(f)* sea bream

davantage more

de from, of (P), about (1); **de la, de l'** some (8); **de luxe** deluxe (10); **parler de** to talk about

débarquement *(m)* landing; **porte** *(f)* **de débarquement** arrival gate (9)

débrouiller: se débrouiller to get by

début *(m)* beginning (6)

débutant(e) *(mf)* beginner

décembre *(m)* December (4)

décennie *(f)* decade

déchets *(mpl)* trash, rubbish

décidément decidedly, for sure

décider to decide (8); **se décider** to make up one's mind

décision *(f)* decision (7); **prendre une décision** to make a decision (7)

découper to cut out

découverte *(f)* discovery

découvrir to discover

décrire to describe (9)

décrocher to to unhook, to get, to land

défaire: défaire ses valises to unpack

défendu(e) forbidden

défi *(m)* challenge

défilé *(m)* parade

défini(e) definite

définir to define

degré *(m)* degree

dégustation *(f)* sampling

dehors outside

déjà already (5)

déjeuner *(m)* lunch (7); **petit déjeuner** *(m)* breakfast (5)

déjeuner to have lunch (2)

délicieux(-euse) delicious (6)

délivrance *(f)* issue, delivery

déluge *(m)* flood

demain tomorrow (P); **À demain!** See you tomorrow! (P)

demande *(f)* request

demander to ask (for) (2); **se demander** to wonder

demi *(m)* draft beer (2)

demi(e) half (P); **demi-heure** *(f)* half hour (7); **Il est deux heures et demie.** It's half past two. (P); **un kilo et demi** a kilo and a half (8)

démocratie *(f)* democracy

démocratique democratic

dénoncer to denounce, to turn in

dent *(f)* tooth (7)

dentaire dental

départ *(m)* departure (9)

département *(m)* department *(a French administrative region)*

dépêcher: se dépêcher to hurry

dépendre (de) to depend (on) (5); **Ça dépend.** That depends.

déplier to unfold

déposer to deposit (7)

déprime *(f)* depression

déprimé(e) depressed

depuis since, for (7), from; **depuis que** since (8)

député *(m)* deputy

dérivé(e) derived

dernier(-ère) last (5)

derrière behind (3)

des some (1)

dés *(mpl)* dice

dès since, right after; **dès que** as soon as

désagréable unpleasant (1)

descendre (de) to go down, to get off (5); **descendre dans** to stay at *(a hotel)* (5)

déshabiller to undress; **se déshabiller** to get undressed (7)

désir *(m)* desire

désirer to desire; **Vous désirez?** What would you like?, May I help you? (2)

désolé(e) sorry (10)

désordre: en désordre in disorder (3)

désormais henceforth, from now on

dessert *(m)* dessert (8)

dessin *(m)* drawing; **dessin animé** *(m)* cartoon

dessinateur *(m)* artist

dessiner to draw

dessous: ci-dessous below

dessus: au dessus de above

destin *(m)* destiny

détaillé(e) detailed

détecteur: détecteur *(m)* **de fumée** smoke detector

détenir to hold, to possess

détente *(f)* relaxation

détenteur(-trice) *(mf)* holder

déterminer to determine

détester to hate (7); **se détester** to hate each other (7)

détruit(e) destroyed

dette *(f)* debt

deux two (P); **deux-tiers** two-thirds

deuxième second (3)

devant in front of (3)

développement *(m)* development

développer to develop

devenir to become (7)

deviner to guess

devinette *(f)* riddle

devise *(f)* currency

devoir must, to have to, to owe (6); **il/elle doit** he/she must (3)

devoirs *(mpl)* homework (P)

diabète *(m)* diabetes

diable *(m)* devil

diamant *(m)* diamond

diarrhée *(f)* diarrhea

dictature *(f)* dictatorship

dictée *(f)* dictation

dictionnaire *(m)* dictionary

dieu *(m)* god

différemment differently

différent(e) different

difficile difficult (P)

difficulté *(f)* difficulty

digérer to digest

dignité *(f)* dignity

digue *(f)* causeway

dimanche *(m)* Sunday (P)

diminuer to diminish

dinde *(f)* turkey

dîner *(m)* dinner (8)

dîner to have dinner, to dine (2)

diplôme *(m)* diploma, degree

diplômé(e) *(mf)* graduate
dire to say, to tell (6); **Ça te/vous dit?** How does that sound to you? (4); **Comment dit-on... en français?** How do you say . . . in French? (P); **On dit que...** They say that . . . (4); **Qu'est-ce que ça veut dire?** What does that mean? (P)
direct(e) direct
directement directly
directeur(-trice) *(mf)* director
diriger to direct, to conduct
discothèque *(f)* dance club
discuter to discuss
disparaître to disappear; **disparu(e)** having disappeared
disponible available
disposer de to have available
disposition: à la disposition de available to
disputer to dispute; **se disputer (avec)** to argue (with) (7)
disque *(m)* record; **disque compact** *(m)* compact disc (3)
dissiper to dissipate
distingué(e) distinguished
distraction *(f)* fun activity
distribué(e) distributed
divers(e) diverse, different
diversité *(f)* diversity
diviser to divide; **se diviser (en)** to divide (into)
divorcé(e) divorced (1)
divorcer to divorce
dix ten (P); **dix-huit** eighteen (P); **dix-huitième** eighteenth; **dix-neuf** nineteen (P); **dix-sept** seventeen (P)
dixième tenth (3)
doctorat *(m)* doctorate (10)
documentaire *(m)* documentary
dodo *(m)* bedtime *(familiar)*
doigt *(m)* finger (10); **doigt** *(m)* **de pied** toe
dollar *(m)* dollar (3)
dolmen *(m)* dolmen *(an ancient megalithic structure)*
domaine *(m)* domain, field
domestique *(mf)* servant
domestique domestic, household; **tâche domestique** *(f)* household chore
domicile *(m)* place of residence
dominer to dominate
dommage: C'est dommage! It's a shame! It's a pity! (7)
donc so, therefore, thus, then (7)
donner to give (2); **donner à manger à** to feed (9); **donner lieu à** to give rise to; **Donnez-moi...** Give me . . . (P)
dont of which, among which, whose
dormir to sleep (2)
dos *(m)* back (10)
dossier *(m)* file
doté(e) endowed
douane *(f)* customs (9)
douanier(-ière) customs
douche *(f)* shower (7)
douleur *(f)* pain, ache
douloureux(-euse) painful
doute *(m)* doubt; **sans doute** without doubt (5)
doux (douce) sweet, soft, gentle (6)
douzaine *(f)* dozen (8)
douze twelve (P)
dramatique dramatic
dramaturge *(m)* playwright
drame *(m)* drama
drap *(m)* sheet

dresser to set up
droit *(m)* law *(field of study)* (10), right *(legal)*; **droits** *(mpl)* **de l'homme** human rights; **tout droit** straight (10)
droite *(f)* right *(direction)*: **à droite (de)** to the right (of) (3)
du (de la, de l', des) some (8)
dû (due, dus, dues) à due to
duc *(m)* duke
duché *(m)* dukedom, duchy
dur(e) hard; **œuf dur** *(m)* hard-boiled egg (8)
durant during
durée *(f)* duration
durer to last
dynamique active (1)

E

eau *(f)* water (2)
écailler to open *(shellfish)*
échange *(m)* exchange
échanger to exchange
échapper to escape; **s'échapper** to escape
écharpe *(f)* winter scarf
échelle *(f)* ladder
éclair *(m)* éclair *(a pastry)*
éclairage *(m)* lighting
éclaircie *(f)* sunny spell
éclairé(e) lighted
école *(f)* school (6)
écolo(giste) *(mf)* environmentalist
économie *(f)* economy; **faire des économies** to save money (9)
économique economic; **sciences économiques** *(fpl)* economics
écossais(e) plaid
écossé(e) shelled
écoute: être à l'écoute de to be listening to
écouter to listen (to) (2); **Écoutez...** Listen to . . . (P)
écran *(m)* screen
écraser to crush
écrevisse *(f)* crawfish
écrire to write (9); **Ça s'écrit comment?** How do you write that? (P); **écrit(e)** written; **Écrivez...** Write . . . (P)
écrivain *(m)* writer
édition: maison *(f)* **d'édition** publishing company
éduquer to educate
effectuer to carry out
effet *(m)* effect; **effets personnels** personal belongings (10); **effets spéciaux** special effects (6)
efforcer: s'efforcer (de) to endeavor
égal(e) *(mpl* **égaux)** equal; **Ça m'est égal.** It's all the same to me.
également also, as well
égalité *(f)* equality
égard *(m)* respect
église *(f)* church (4)
égoïste selfish
Égypte *(f)* Egypt (9)
élection *(f)* election
électricité *(f)* electricity
électrique electrical
électronique electronic; **courrier électronique** *(m)* e-mail
élément *(m)* element
éléphant *(m)* elephant (9)

élevage *(m)* raising livestock
élève *(mf)* pupil, student
élevé(e) high, elevated
elle she, it (1), her; **elles** they (1), them; **elle-même** herself
e-mail *(m)* e-mail (3)
embarquement *(m)* boarding; **porte** *(f)* **d'embarquement** departure gate (9)
embêtant(e) annoying (3)
embrasser to kiss (7); **s'embrasser** to kiss each other, to embrace each other (7)
émincé(e) thinly sliced
emmener to take
emploi *(m)* employment, use; **emploi** *(m)* **du temps** schedule (P)
employé(e) *(mf)* employee
employer to use
emprisonner to imprison (6)
emporter to carry away
emprunter (à) to borrow (from) (9)
en in (P); **de temps en temps** from time to time (4); **en avance** early; **en avion** by plane (4); **en désordre** in disorder (3); **en face (de)** across from, facing (3); **en ordre** in order (3); **en plus** furthermore (8); **en retard** late; **en solde** on sale (5); **en tout temps** at all times; **en vacances** on vacation; **être en train de...** to be in the process of . . . ; **partir en week-end** to go away for the weekend (5); **payer en espèces** to pay cash (10)
en some, any, about it/them, of it/them (8); **Je vous / t'en prie.** You're welcome. (10); **s'en aller** to go away
enceinte pregnant (10)
enchaîné(e) chained up
Enchanté(e). Delighted to meet you.
encore still (4), again, more (8); **ne... pas encore** not yet (5)
encourager to encourage
endormir: s'endormir to fall asleep (7)
endroit *(m)* place
énergie *(f)* energy
énerver to irritate
enfance *(f)* childhood
enfant *(mf)* child (4)
enfanter to give birth to
enfer *(m)* hell
enfin finally (7)
enflé(e) swollen
engager to hire
ennemi(e) *(mf)* enemy
ennui *(m)* trouble
ennuyer to bore; **s'ennuyer (de)** to get bored (with), to be bored (with) (7)
ennuyeux(-euse) boring (1)
énorme enormous
enquête *(f)* investigation
enregistrer to record
enrichir to enrich
enseignement *(m)* teaching, education; **enseignement supérieur** higher education
enseigner to teach
ensemble together (2)
ensuite next, then (4)
entendre to hear (7); **s'entendre bien/mal (avec)** to get along well/badly (with) (7)
enthousiasme *(m)* enthusiasm
entier(-ère) entire, whole
entouré(e) (de) surrounded (by)
entre between (3), among
entrée *(f)* hors d'œuvre (8), entry ticket, entrance, entry

entreprise (f) firm, enterprise
entrée (f) entrance
entrer (**dans**) to enter, to go in (5)
entretien (m) conversation, interview
envahir to invade
enveloppe (f) envelope
envers towards
envie: avoir envie de to feel like, to desire (4)
environ around, about (4)
environnement (m) environment
environs (mpl) surrounding area
envoyer to send (7)
épaisseur (f) thickness
épanouir: s'épanouir to flourish
épaule (f) shoulder
épée (f) sword
épicerie (f) grocer's shop (8)
épicier(-ière) (mf) grocer
épinards (mpl) spinach
époque (f) time period; **à cette époque-là** at that time, in those days
épouser to marry; **s'épouser** to get married
épouvante: film (m) **d'épouvante** horror movie (6)
époux (épouse) (mf) spouse
épreuve (f) test
épuisé(e) exhausted
équilibré(e) balanced
équipe (f) team
équipé(e) equipped
équipée (f) venture
équipement (m) equipment
érotique erotic
escalade (f) (rock-)climbing
escale (f) stopover
escalier (m) stairs, staircase (3)
escargot (m) snail (8)
escarpé(e) steep
esclave (mf) slave
espace (m) space
Espagne (f) Spain (9)
espagnol (m) Spanish (P)
espagnol(e) Spanish
espèce (f) species; **Espèce de... !** You . . . !; **payer en espèces** to pay cash (10)
espérer to hope (3)
espiègle mischevious
espion(ne) (mf) spy
espionnage (m) spying
espoir (m) hope; **meilleur jeune espoir** (m) best new actor
esprit (m) mind, spirit
essayage (m) fitting; **cabine** (f) **d'essayage** fitting room (5)
essayer to try on (5); **essayer (de faire)** to try (to do)
essentiel(le) essential
essoufflé(e) to be out of breath
est (m) east
est-ce que (question marker) (1); **Est-ce que vous comprenez?** Do you understand? (P)
et and (P)
établir to establish; **s'établir** to establish oneself, to settle
établissement (m) establishment
étage (m) floor (3); **à l'étage** on the same floor, down the hall; **À quel étage?** On what floor? (3); **au premier étage** on the second floor (3)
étagère (f) shelf, bookcase (3)

étain (m) tin
étape (f) stopping place, step
état (m) state (3), condition
États-Unis (mpl) United States (3)
été (m) summer (5); **en été** in summer (5)
étendre: s'étendre to extend
éternuer to sneeze (10)
ethnique ethnic
étoile (f) star
étonné(e) surprised, amazed (10)
étonner to surprise, to amaze
étranger(-ère) foreign (1); **à l'étranger** abroad (9)
être to be (1); **c'est** it's (P), he is, she is this is, that is (1); **C'est quel jour aujourd'hui?** What day is today? (P); **Comment est/sont... ?** What is/are . . . like? (1); **être à** to belong to; **je suis** I'm (P); **le français est...** French is . . . (P); **Nous sommes six.** There are six of us. (4); **Quelle est la date aujourd'hui?** What is the date today? (4); **tu es, vous êtes** you are (P)
être humain (m) human being
étroit(e) tight
étude: études (fpl) studies (1), **salle** (f) **d'étude** study room
étudiant(e) (mf) student (P)
étudier to study (1)
euro (m) euro (2)
Europe (f) Europe (9)
européen(ne) European
eux them, they
évader: s'évader to escape
évasion (f) escape
événement (m) event
évidemment of course, obviously
éviter to avoid (8)
exact(e) exact
exactement exactly (10)
examen (m) test, exam (P)
excentrique eccentric
exception (f) exception
exclamer: s'exclamer to exclaim, to cry out
excuser to excuse, to forgive; **s'excuser** to apologize
exécutif(-ive) executive
exemple (m) example; **par exemple** for example (2)
exercer to exert
exercice (m) exercise (P); **faire de l'exercice** to exercise (5)
exiger to require
exister to exist
exotique exotic (9)
expérience (f) experience, experiment
explication (f) explanation
expliquer to explain (10)
explorateur(-trice) (mf) explorer
exploser to explode
exposition (f) exhibit (4)
express (m) espresso (2)
expression (f) expression (10)
exprimer to express
expulser to throw out
extérieur (m) outside, exterior
extincteur (m) fire extinguisher
extinction (f) extinguishing
extra great, terrific (4); **extra-scolaire** extracurricular
extrait (m) excerpt
extraverti(e) outgoing, extroverted (1)

F

fac (f) university, campus (2)
face: en face (de) across from, facing (3); **face à** across from, confronted with; **faire face à** to face
facile easy (P)
facilement easily (7)
faciliter to facilitate, to make easy
façon (f) way
faculté (fac) (f) university, campus (2)
faillir: j'ai failli tomber I almost fell
faim (f) hunger; **avoir faim** to be hungry (4); **j'ai faim** I'm hungry (2)
faire to do, to make (2); **Ça fait... euros.** That's . . . euros. (2); **Ça ne se fait pas!** That is not done!; **faire attention (à)** to pay attention (to) (8); **faire connaissance** to meet (1); **faire de l'aérobic** to do aerobics (8); **faire de l'alpinisme** to go mountain climbing; **faire de la marche à pied** to go walking; **faire de la musculation** to do weight training, to do bodybuilding (8); **faire de la musique** to play music (2); **faire de la planche à voile** to go windsurfing; **faire de la plongée sous-marine** to go scuba diving; **faire de la varappe** to go rock climbing; **faire de l'exercice** to exercise (5); **faire des courses** to run errands (5); **faire des économies** to save up (money) (9); **faire des projets** to make plans (4); **faire du bateau** to go boating (5); **faire du camping** to go camping (5); **faire du cheval** to go horseback riding; **faire du jardinage** to garden (5); **faire du jogging** to jog (2); **faire du patin (à glace)** to go (ice-)skating; **faire du roller** to go rollerblading (6); **faire du shopping** to go shopping (2); **faire du skateboarding** to skateboard (6); **faire du ski (nautique)** to go (water-)skiing (5); **faire du sport** to play sports (2); **faire du tuba** to go snorkeling; **faire du vélo** to go bike-riding (5); **faire face à** to face; **faire la cuisine** to cook (5); **faire la lessive** to do laundry (5); **faire la vaisselle** to do the dishes (5); **faire le ménage** to do housework (5); **faire les courses** to go grocery shopping (7); **faire mal** to hurt; **faire noir** to be dark (6); **faire sa toilette** to wash up (7); **faire ses valises** to pack one's bags (9); **faire une promenade** to go for a walk (5); **faire une randonnée** to go for a hike (9); **faire une réservation** to make a reservation (9); **faire un tour** to take a tour, to go for a ride (4); **faire un voyage** to take a trip (5); **Faites les devoirs dans le cahier.** Do the homework in the workbook. (P); **Faites l'exercice A à la page 21.** Do exercise A on page 21. (P); **Il fait beau / chaud / du soleil / du vent / frais / froid / mauvais.** It's nice / hot / sunny / windy / cool / cold / bad. (5); **Il fait bon / du brouillard.** It's nice / foggy.; **Il va faire beau...** It's going to be nice. . . (5); **Je fais du 42.** I wear a 42. (5); **Je ne fais pas de musique / de sport.** I don't play music / sports. (2); **Quelle taille faites-vous?** What size do you need? (5); **Quel temps fait-il?** What's the weather like? (5); **Quel temps va-t-il faire?** What's the weather going to be like? (5); **Qu'est-ce que vous faites / tu fais?** What are you doing? What do you do? (2)

faisan *(m)* pheasant
falaise *(f)* cliff
falloir: il faut... it is necessary . . . , one must . . . , one needs . . . (8); **il me/te/nous/vous faut** I/you/we/you need (9); **il ne faut pas** one shouldn't, one must not . . . (10)
fameux(-euse) famous
familial(e) *(mpl* **familiaux)** family
familiariser: se familiariser (avec) to get to know
familier(-ère) familiar, informal
familièrement colloquially
famille *(f)* family (P)
famine *(f)* famine, starvation
fanfaronnade *(f)* boasting
fantastique fantastic; **film fantastique** *(m)* fantasy movie
farci(e) stuffed
farine *(f)* flour
fascinant(e) fascinating
fasciner to fascinate
fast-food *(m)* fast-food restaurant (1)
fatigant(e) tiring
fatigué(e) tired (6)
faut *See* **falloir.**
faute *(f)* lack, mistake, fault
fauteuil *(m)* armchair (3)
faux (fausse) false
favoriser to favor, to further
fédéral(e) *(mpl* **fédéraux)** federal
fée *(f)* fairy; **conte** *(m)* **de fée** fairy tale (6)
femme *(f)* woman (1), wife (2); **femme** *(f)* **d'affaires** businesswoman (5); **ex-femme** *(f)* ex-wife
fenêtre *(f)* window (3)
fenouil *(m)* fennel
fer *(m)* iron; **chemin** *(m)* **de fer** railroad
férié(e): jour férié *(m)* holiday
fermer to close (2); **Fermez votre livre.** Close your book. (P); **La bibliothèque ferme à...** The library closes at . . . (P)
féroce ferocious (6)
festival *(m)* festival (4)
fête *(f)* holiday, celebration (4), party; **fête des mères** *(f)* Mother's Day; **fête des pères** *(f)* Father's Day; **fête du travail** *(f)* Labor Day; **fête nationale** *(f)* national holiday
fêter to celebrate
feu *(m)* fire; **prendre feu** to catch fire
feuille *(f)* **de papier** sheet of paper (P)
feuilleté(e) flaky *(pastry)*
février *(m)* February (4)
fiancé *(m)* fiancé (10)
fiancée *(f)* fiancée (10)
fiancé(e) engaged (1)
fiancer: se fiancer to get engaged (7)
ficelle *(f)* string
fiche *(f)* form
fidélité *(f)* faithfulness
fier(-ère) proud
fièvre *(m)* fever; **avoir de la fièvre** to have fever; **fièvre jaune** *(f)* yellow fever
figure *(f)* face (7)
filière *(f)* career path
fille *(f)* girl; daughter (4); **fille unique** *(f)* only child
film *(m)* movie (1)
filmer to film
fils *(m)* son (4); **fils unique** *(m)* only child
fin *(f)* end
fin(e) fine

finalement finally (6)
financier(-ère) financial
financièrement financially
finir (de faire) to finish (doing) (8); **finir par faire** to end up doing; **Le cours de français finit...** The French class ends . . . (P)
fixe fixed (8)
fixer to set, to fix
flamand *(m)* Flemish *(language)*
fleur *(f)* flower (7)
fleuri(e) with a floral pattern
fleuriste *(mf)* florist (7)
fleuve *(m)* river
foie *(m)* liver
fois *(f)* time, occasion (5); **à la fois** at the same time; **d'autres fois** other times (7); **Il était une fois...** Once upon a time . . . (6)
folk *(m)* folk music
folklore *(m)* folklore (4)
foncé(e) dark; **bleu foncé** dark blue
fonction *(f)* function; **en fonction de** according to; **voiture** *(f)* **de fonction** company car
fonctionner to function, to work
fond *(m)* bottom, back
fonder to found
fonderie *(f)* foundry
fondre to melt
fontaine *(f)* fountain
football *(m)* soccer (1); **football américain** football (1)
force *(f)* force, strength
forcément necessarily, inevitably
forestier(-ère): exploitation forestière *(f)* forestry
forêt *(f)* forest
formation *(f)* education
forme *(f)* shape, **en forme** in shape (8)
former to form, to educate
formidable great (7)
formulaire *(m)* form
formule *(f)* formula, expression
fort(e) strong (8)
fort very
fortifié(e) fortified
fou (folle) crazy
foudre: coup *(m)* **de foudre** love at first sight (7)
foulard *(m)* dress scarf
fouler: se fouler la cheville to sprain your ankle
four (à micro-ondes) *(m)* (microwave) oven
fournir to furnish
foyer *(m)* **des étudiants** student center
fragile fragile
fragmenté(e) fragmented
frais (fraîche) fresh (8); **Il fait frais.** It's cool. (5)
fraise *(f)* strawberry (8)
framboise *(f)* raspberry
franc *(m)* franc (2)
français *(m)* French (P)
français(e) French (1)
France *(f)* France (1)
franchir to cross
francophone French-speaking
frapper to strike
fraternité *(f)* brotherhood
frénésie *(f)* frenzy
fréquemment frequently
fréquenter to frequent, to hang out at
frère *(m)* brother (1); **beau-frère** *(m)* brother-in-law (4); **demi-frère** *(m)* stepbrother, half-brother
frigo *(m)* refrigerator

frire to fry
frisé(e) curly
frisée *(f)* curly endive
frisson *(m)* shiver (10)
frites *(fpl)* French fries (2)
frivole frivolous
froid(e) cold (4); **avoir froid** to be cold (4); **Il fait froid.** It's cold. (5)
fromage *(m)* cheese (2)
frontière *(f)* border (10)
fruit *(m)* fruit (8); **fruits** *(mpl)* **de mer** shellfish (8); **jus** *(m)* **de fruit** fruit juice (2)
fruitier(-ère) fruit
fuir to flee, to run away
fumé(e) smoked (8)
fumée *(f)* smoke; **détecteur** *(m)* **de fumée** smoke detector
fumer to smoke (3)
fumeur(-euse) *(mf)* smoker; **section (non-) fumeur** *(f)* (non-)smoking section
funérailles *(fpl)* funeral
furieux(-euse) furious (10)
futon *(m)* futon (3)
futur *(m)* future *(tense)*

G

gagner to win (2), to gain; **gagner de l'argent** to earn money, to make money (10)
gai(e) gay, lively
gaieté *(f)* cheerfulness
gant *(m)* glove
garage *(m)* garage
garantir to guarantee
garçon *(m)* boy (4), waiter (2)
garder to keep
gare *(f)* train station
garni(e) served with vegetables
garniture *(f)* garnish
gaspiller to waste
gâteau *(m)* cake (8)
gauche *(f)* left; **à gauche (de)** to the left (of) (3)
gaulois(e) from Gaul *(ancient name for the region of modern France)*
gaz: gaz naturel *(m)* natural gas
géant *(m)* giant
gêné(e) embarrassed
généalogie *(f)* genealogy
général(e) *(mpl* **généraux)** general; **en général** in general (6)
généralement generally (7)
généraliste *(mf)* generalist
génial(e) *(mpl* **géniaux)** great (4)
genou *(m)* knee
genre *(m)* gender, kind, type, genre
gens *(mpl)* people (1)
gentil(le) nice (1)
géographie *(f)* geography (9)
géographique geographical
géographiquement geographically
géologie *(f)* geology
gestion *(f)* management
gilet *(m)* vest
glace *(f)* ice cream (8), ice; **glace à la vanille** vanilla ice cream (8)
glacier *(m)* ice cream shop
global(e) *(mpl* **globaux)** global
gloire *(f)* glory
goéland *(m)* seagull

golf *(m)* golf (2)
gommage *(m)* rubbing out
gorge *(f)* throat (10); **soutien-gorge** *(m)* bra
gorille *(m)* gorilla
gosse *(mf)* kid
goulu(e) gluttonous
gousse *(f)* clove
goût *(m)* taste
goûter to taste (9)
goutte *(f)* drop
gouvernement *(m)* government
gouverner to govern
grâce *(f)* grace; **le jour** *(m)* **d'Action de grâce** Thanksgiving
grâce à thanks to, because of
gracieux(-euse) gracious (6)
grammaire *(f)* grammar
gramme *(m)* gram (8)
grand(e) big, large, tall (1); **le grand amour** *(m)* true love (7)
grand-chose: ne... pas grand-chose not much, not a lot
Grande-Bretagne *(f)* Great Britain (9)
grandir to grow up, to grow, to get taller (8)
grand-mère *(f)* grandmother (4)
grand-père *(m)* grandfather (4)
grands-parents *(mpl)* grandparents (4)
gras(se) *(f)* fatty; **en caractères gras** boldfaced; **matière grasse** *(f)* fat (8)
gratuit(e) free *(of charge)*
gratuitement without charge
grave serious, grave
Grèce *(f)* Greece
grenade *(f)* pomegranate
grillé(e) grilled (8); **pain grillé(e)** toast (8)
grippe *(f)* flu (10)
gris(e) gray (3)
gros(se) big, fat (1)
grossir to get fatter (8)
groupe *(m)* group (6); **en groupe** in a group
grouper to group
gruyère *(m)* Swiss cheese
guérir to cure, to heal
guerre *(f)* war
guichet *(m)* ticket window; **guichet automatique** *(m)* automatic teller machine (7)
guide *(m)* guide, guidebook (9)
guitare *(f)* guitar (2)
Guyane *(f)* Guiana
gym: club *(m)* **de gym** gym, fitness club (1)
gymnase *(m)* gym

H

habiller to dress; **s'habiller** to get dressed (7)
habitant(e) *(mf)* inhabitant
habiter to live (2); **j'habite à** (+ *city*) I live in (+ *city*) (P); **Vous habitez... ?** Do you live. . .? (P)
habitude *(f)* habit; **d'habitude** usually (2)
habitué(e) à used to, accustomed to
habituel(le) customary, usual
***haché(e)** chopped (up)
*****haine** *(f)* hatred
Haïti *(m)* Haiti
*****hamburger** *(m)* hamburger (8)
*****handicapé(e)** handicapped
*****Hanoukka** *(f)* Hanukkah
*****haricots verts** *(mpl)* green beans (8)
harmonie *(f)* harmony
*****hasard: par hasard** by chance

*****haut: dans les hauts** high above; **(tout) en haut** at the (very) top
*****haut(e)** high; **haute couture** *(f)* high fashion (5); **haut talon** *(m)* high heel
hébergement *(m)* accommodation
hébreu *(m)* Hebrew
*****hein?** huh?
hépatite *(f)* hepatitis
herbe *(f)* grass
héritage *(m)* inheritance, heritage
hériter to inherit
hésiter to hesitate
heure *(f)* hour (5); **à l'heure** on time; **À tout à l'heure.** See you in a little while. (P); **Il est... heure(s).** It's . . . o'clock. (P); **Quelle heure est-il?** What time is it? (P); **tout à l'heure** in a little while (P), a little while ago
heureusement luckily
heureux(-euse) happy (7)
hier yesterday (5)
hippopotame *(m)* hippopotamus (9)
histoire *(f)* history (1); story (9)
historique historical (9)
historiquement historically
hiver *(m)* winter (5); **en hiver** in winter (5)
*****hockey** *(m)* hockey (2)
*****homard** *(m)* lobster (8)
homme *(m)* man (1); **homme** *(m)* **d'affaires** businessman (5)
homogène homogeneous
honnête honest
honneur *(f)* honor
hôpital *(m)* hospital
horaire *(m)* schedule
horreur *(f)* horror
horrible horrible (6)
*****hors** outside of; *****hors-d'œuvre** *(m)* *(inv)* hors d'oeuvre, appetizer (8)
hôte *(m)* host
hôtel *(m)* hotel (5)
hôtelier(-ère) *(mf)* hotel manager (10)
hôtesse *(f)* hostess
huile *(f)* oil
*****huit** eight (P); **huit jours** one week (5)
*****huitième** eighth (3)
huître *(f)* oyster (8)
humain(e) human; **sciences humaines** *(f)* social sciences (1)
humanité *(f)* humanity
humer to breathe in
humeur *(f)* mood; **de bonne humeur** in a good mood
humour *(m)* humor
hypermarché *(m)* superstore (8)
hypertension *(f)* high blood pressure

I

ici here (P); **par ici** this way (5)
idéaliste idealistic (1)
idée *(f)* idea (4)
identifier to identify
identité *(f)* identity; **carte** *(f)* **/ pièce** *(f)* **d'identité** identity card
igname *(f)* yam
il he (1), it (P); **il faut...** it is necessary . . . , one must . . . (8); **il ne faut pas** one should not, one must not (10); **ils** they (1); **il y a** there is, there are (1), ago (5); **Qu'est-ce qu'il y a?** What's the matter?; **s'il vous plaît** please (P)

île *(f)* island (9)
imaginaire imaginary
imaginer to imagine
immédiatement immediately
immeuble *(m)* apartment building (3)
immigré(e) *(mf)* immigrant
immobilier(-ère) real estate
imparfait *(m)* imperfect
impatient(e) impatient (7)
impératif *(m)* imperative
imperméable *(m)* raincoat (5)
impoli(e) impolite
important(e) important (5)
importer to be important; **n'importe où** (just) anywhere; **n'importe quel(le)** (just) any; **n'importe qui** (just) anyone; **n'importe quoi** (just) anything
imposer to impose, to lay down
impressionnant(e) impressive
imprimé(e) printed
inaccessibilité *(f)* inaccessibility
inattendu(e) unexpected
inclure to include
inclus(e) included
inconvénient *(m)* disadvantage
incroyable incredible
Inde *(f)* India
indéfini indefinite
indépendant(e) independent
indicatif régional *(m)* area code
indications *(fpl)* directions (10)
indigène native
indigestion *(f)* indigestion (10)
indiquer to show, to indicate (3); **indiqué(e)** indicated; **indiquer le chemin** to give directions, to show the way (10)
indispensable essential
Indochine *(f)* Indochina
industrie *(f)* industry
inégalité *(f)* inequality
infidélité *(f)* unfaithfulness
infinitif *(m)* infinitive
infirmier(-ère) *(mf)* nurse
influencer to influence; **s'influencer** to influence each other
informatique *(f)* computer science (1)
informer to inform; **s'informer** to find out information (9)
infusion *(f)* herbal tea
ingénieur *(m)* engineer (10)
innover to innovate
inquiétant(e) disturbing
inscription *(f)* registration
inscrire to register; **s'inscrire** to register (3)
insecte *(m)* insect
insister to insist
inspecteur(-trice) *(mf)* inspector
instabilité *(f)* instability
installation *(f)* arrangements
installer: s'installer (à/dans) to settle (in), to move (into) (7), to set up business
instant *(m)* instant; **Un instant!** Just a moment!
institut *(m)* institute
instituteur(-trice) *(mf)* elementary school teacher
institution *(f)* institution
instructions *(fpl)* instructions
instrument *(m)* instrument; **instrument** *(m)* **de musique** musical instrument
insulter to insult
insupportable unbearable, intolerable
intellectuel(le) intellectual (1)

intelligent(e) intelligent (1)

intention: avoir l'intention de to plan on, to intend to (4)

interdire to forbid

interdit(e) forbidden

intéressant(e) interesting (P)

intéresser to interest; **s'intéresser à** to be interested in

intérêt *(m)* interest

intérieur *(m)* inside

intermédiaire intermediate

international(e) *(mpl* **internationaux)** international (10)

interprète *(mf)* interpreter

interrogatif(-ive) interrogative, question

interroger to question

interrompre to interrupt

intitulé(e) titled, called

introduire to introduce

introverti(e) introverted

investir to invest

invitation *(f)* invitation (6)

invité(e) *(mf)* guest

inviter (à) to invite (to) (2)

irresponsable irresponsible

irriter to irritate

isolé(e) isolated

Israël *(m)* Israel (9)

issu(e): être issu(e) de to come from

Italie *(f)* Italy (9)

italien(ne) Italian

italique: en italique in italics

itinéraire *(m)* itinerary (9)

ivoirien(ne) from the Ivory Coast

J

jadis formerly

jamais: ne... jamais never (2)

jambe *(f)* leg (10); **se casser la jambe** to break your leg

jambon *(m)* ham (2); **sandwich** *(m)* **au jambon** ham sandwich (2)

janvier *(m)* January (4)

Japon *(m)* Japan (9)

japonais *(m)* Japanese

jardin *(m)* garden (5), yard

jardinage *(m)* gardening; **faire du jardinage** to garden (5)

jardiner to garden

jaune yellow (3)

jazz *(m)* jazz (1)

je (j') I (P)

jean *(m)* jeans (5)

jet *(m)* stream

jeu *(m)* game; **jeu** *(m)* **de société** board game; **jeu** *(m)* **vidéo** video game (2)

jeudi *(m)* Thursday (P)

jeune young (1); **jeunes** *(pl)* young people

jeunesse *(f)* youth

jogging: faire du jogging to jog (2)

joie *(f)* joy

joindre: se joindre à to join

joli(e) pretty (1)

jouer to act *(in movies and theater)* (6); **jouer à** to play *(a sport or game)* (2); **jouer de** to play *(an instrument)* (2)

jour *(m)* day (P); **C'est quel jour, aujourd'hui?** What day is today? (P); **huit jours** one week (5); **jour** *(m)* **de l'an** New Year's Day; **jour J**

(m) D-day; **quinze jours** two weeks (5); **tous les jours** every day (2)

journal *(m)* newspaper (5), journal

journaliste *(mf)* journalist

journée *(f)* day, daytime (2); **Bonne journée!** Have a good day!; **journée continue** nine-to-five schedule; **toute la journée** the whole day (2)

joyeux(-euse) happy; **Joyeux Noël!** Merry Christmas!

juif(-ive) *(mf)* Jew

juillet *(m)* July (4)

juin *(m)* June (4)

jumeau (jumelle) twin (1)

jupe *(f)* skirt (5)

jus (de fruit) *(m)* (fruit) juice (2)

jusqu'à until, up to (2)

jusque until

juste just, fair; **juste là** right there

justement precisely, exactly; as a matter of fact (3)

justifier to justify

K

kilo *(m)* kilo(gram) *(2.2 pounds)* (8)

kilomètre *(m)* kilometer *(.6 miles)*

L

la the (1), her, it (5)

là there (10); **ce... là** that. . . (3); **à ce moment-là** at that time; **là-bas** over there (8)

laboratoire: laboratoire *(m)* **de langues / d'informatique** language / computer laboratory (1)

lac *(m)* lake

laid(e) ugly (1)

laïque lay, secular, civil

laisser to leave (behind) (3), to let; **laisser tomber** to drop

lait *(m)* milk (8); **café au lait** coffee with milk (2)

laitier(-ère) milk, dairy (8)

laitue *(f)* lettuce (8)

lampe *(f)* lamp (3); **lampe** *(f)* **de poche** flashlight

langouste *(f)* spiny lobster

langoustines *(fpl)* scampi

langue *(f)* language (1); tongue

lapin *(m)* rabbit

laqué(e) lacquered, with a gloss finish

lardon *(m)* piece of bacon

large wide

largement widely

laser: platine laser *(f)* CD player

lavabo *(m)* washbasin, sink (10)

laver to wash; **se laver** to wash (up) (7)

lave-vaisselle *(m)* dishwasher

le the (1), him, it (5); **le lundi** on Mondays (P); **le matin** in the morning, mornings (P); **le week-end** on the weekend, weekends (P)

leçon *(f)* lesson

lecture *(f)* reading

légende *(f)* legend

léger(-ère) light (8)

légume *(m)* vegetable (8)

lendemain *(m)* the next day (6)

lentement slowly (8)

lequel (laquelle, lesquels, lesquelles) which, which one(s) (6)

les the (1); them (5);

lessive *(f)* laundry (5)

lettre *(f)* letter (7); **lettres** *(fpl)* study of literature

leur (to, for) them (9)

leur their (3)

levant *(m)* east, sunrise

lever: se lever to get up (7)

lèvre *(f)* lip

liaison *(f)* linking, link

libéral(e) *(mpl* **libéraux)** liberal

libérer: se libérer to free oneself

liberté *(f)* freedom

librairie *(f)* bookstore (1)

libre free (2); **temps libre** *(m)* free time (4)

licence *(f)* *three-year university degree*

licencié(e) *(mf)* *someone with the* **licence** *degree*

lien *(m)* link

lier to connect, to link

lieu *(m)* place; **avoir lieu** to take place

ligne *(f)* figure; line

limande *(f)* dab

limiter to limit, to border; **se limiter à** to limit oneself to

linguistique linguistic

liquide *(m)* liquid (10)

lire to read (2); **Lisez...** Read . . . (P)

liste *(f)* list

lit *(m)* bed (3); **rester au lit** to stay in bed (2)

litre *(m)* liter *(approximately one quart)* (8)

littéraire literary

littérature *(f)* literature (1)

living *(m)* living room

livre *(m)* book (P)

livre *(f)* pound, half-kilo (8)

livrer: se livrer à to participate in

local(e) *(mpl* **locaux)** local (9)

locataire *(mf)* renter

location *(f)* rental; **voiture** *(f)* **de location** rental car (5)

logement *(m)* lodging (3)

loger to lodge

logique logical

logiquement logically

loi *(f)* law

loin (de) far (from) (3)

loisir *(m)* leisure activity

Londres London

long: le long de along

long(ue) long (4)

longtemps a long time (5)

longueur *(f)* length

lors de at the time of

lorsque when

loterie *(f)* lottery

loto *(m)* lotto, bingo

louer to rent (4)

Louisiane *(f)* Louisiana

loup *(m)* wolf

loyer *(m)* rent (3)

lui him (6), (to, for) him (9); **lui-même** himself

lundi *(m)* Monday (P)

lune *(f)* moon; **lune** *(f)* **de miel** honeymoon

lunettes *(fpl)* glasses (4); **lunettes** *(fpl)* **de soleil** sunglasses (5)

lutte *(f)* struggle, fight

lutter to struggle, to fight

luxe *(m)* luxury; **de luxe** deluxe (10)

luxembourgeois *(m)* Luxemburgian *(native language of Luxembourg)*

luxembourgeois(e) from Luxembourg

lycée *(m)* *French secondary school* (6)

lycéen(ne) *(mf)* high school student (6)

M

macérer to soak
madame (Mme) *(f)* madam (Mrs.) (P)
mademoiselle (Mlle) *(f)* miss (P)
magasin *(m)* store, shop (4)
magazine *(m)* magazine (9)
magnétoscope *(m)* video cassette recorder (3)
magnifique magnificent
mai *(m)* May (P)
maigre skinny (8)
maigrir to get thinner, to slim down (8)
maillot *(m)* **de bain** swimsuit (5)
main *(f)* hand (7)
maintenant now (P)
maintenir to maintain
maire *(m)* mayor
mairie *(f)* town hall
mais but (P)
maïs *(m)* corn
maison *(f)* house (1); **à la maison** (at) home (P); **maison** *(f)* **d'édition** publishing company
maître *(m)* master
maîtrise *(f)* master's degree (10)
majoré(e) with a surcharge
majorité *(f)* majority
mal *(m)* bad, evil; **avoir mal à...** one's... hurts; **faire mal (à)** to hurt
mal badly (P); **mal à l'aise** ill at ease; **pas mal** not bad(ly) (P)
malade *(mf)* sick person
malade ill, sick (10)
maladie *(f)* illness; **maladie** *(f)* **des nerfs** nervous disorder
malaise *(f)* discomfort
malgache Madagascan
malgré in spite of
malheureusement unfortunately
malheureux(-euse) unhappy
malhonnête dishonest
maman *(f)* mama, mom
mamie *(f)* granny, grandma (7)
Manche *(f)* English Channel
mandarine *(f)* tangerine
mandat *(m)* money order
manger to eat (2); **donner à manger à** to feed (9); **salle** *(f)* **à manger** dining room (3)
mangue *(f)* mango
manière *(f)* manner, way
manifestation *(f)* demonstration; **manifestation sportive** *(f)* sports event
manifester: se manifester to be reflected
manioc *(m)* manioc, cassava
manoir *(m)* manor, country house
manquer to miss, to lack
manteau *(m)* overcoat (5)
manufacturier(-ère) manufacturing
manuscrit *(m)* manuscript
maquillage *(m)* make-up
maquiller: se maquiller to put on make-up (7)
marais *(m)* swamp
marchand(e) *(mf)* merchant, shopkeeper (6)
marche à pied *(f)* walking; **faire de la marche à pied** to go walking
marché *(m)* market (8)
marcher to walk (8), to work
mardi *(m)* Tuesday (P); **Mardi gras** *(m)* Fat Tuesday
maréchal *(m)* marshall
marée *(f)* tide

marge *(f)* margin
mari *(m)* husband (2); **ex-mari** *(m)* ex-husband
mariage *(m)* marriage (7)
marié(e) married (1)
marier: se marier (avec) to get married (to) (7)
marinier(-ère): moules marinières *(f)* mussels cooked with onions and white wine
marketing *(m)* marketing (1)
Maroc *(m)* Morocco (9)
marquer to mark
marron *(inv)* brown (3)
mars *(m)* March (4)
martiniquais(e) from Martinique
masse *(f)* **d'eau** body of water
massif *(m)* group of mountains, clump
match *(m)* match, game (1)
matelas *(m)* mattress
matérialiste materialistic
matériel(le) material
maternel(le) maternal; **école maternelle** *(f)* kindergarten
mathématiques *(fpl)* mathematics (1)
matière *(f)* matter; **matières grasses** fat (8)
matin *(m)* morning (P); **À huit heures du matin.** At eight o'clock in the morning. (P); **le matin** mornings, in the morning (P)
matinée *(f)* morning (2)
matrimonial(e) *(mpl* **matrimoniaux)** marriage
mauvais(e) bad (1); **Il fait mauvais.** The weather's bad. (5)
me (to, for) me (9), myself (7); **Ça me plaît!** I like it! (3); **il me faut...** I need... (9)
méchant(e) mean (1)
médaille *(f)* medal
médecin *(m)* doctor, physician (10)
médecine *(f)* medicine (10)
médicament *(m)* medication, medicine, drugs (7)
médiocre mediocre (6)
Méditerranée: (mer) Méditerranée *(f)* Mediterranean (Sea)
méditerranéen(ne) Mediterranean
méfiance *(f)* mistrust
meilleur(e) best (1), better
mélange *(m)* mixture
membre *(m)* member
même same (1), even; **moi-même** myself; **quand même** all the same
menacer to threaten
ménage *(m)* housework (5), household
ménager(-ère) household
mener to lead
menhir *(m)* menhir *(an ancient megalithic structure)*
menthe *(f)* mint
mentionner to mention
mentir to lie
menu *(m)* menu (8)
mépris *(m)* scorn
mer *(f)* sea (9); **bord** *(m)* **de la mer** seaside; **fruits** *(mpl)* **de mer** shellfish (8)
merci thank you (P)
mercredi *(m)* Wednesday (P)
mère *(f)* mother (4)
méritoire deserving
merveille *(f)* marvel, wonder
merveilleux(-euse) marvelous
messager(-ère) *(mf)* messenger
messagerie vocale *(f)* voice mail
messieurs (MM.) gentlemen, sirs (2)
mesurer to measure
métier *(m)* occupation
métrage: court métrage *(m)* short film

mètre *(m)* meter
métrique metric
métro *(m)* subway (4); **en métro** by subway (4)
metteur *(m)* **en scène** director
mettre to put (on), to place (5); **mettre en valeur** to emphasize; **mettre la table** to set the table; **se mettre d'accord** to come to an agreement
meubles *(mpl)* furniture, furnishings (3)
meublé(e) furnished
meurtre *(m)* murder
meurtrier *(m)* murderer
meurtrière *(f)* murderess
Mexico Mexico City
Mexique *(m)* Mexico (9)
mi- mid-, half-; **cheveux mi-longs** *(mpl)* shoulder-length hair (4)
micro-ondes *(m)* microwave oven
midi *(m)* noon (P)
mie: pain *(m)* **de mie** soft sandwich bread
mieux (que) better (than) (2); **aimer mieux** to prefer (2); **il vaut mieux** it's better (10); **le mieux** the best
milieu *(m)* middle; **au milieu (de)** in the middle (of)
militaire military
mille one thousand (3)
mille-feuille *(f)* mille-feuille *(a layered pastry)*
millénaire *(m)* millennium
million: un million (de) *(m)* one million (3)
millionnaire *(mf)* millionaire
mince thin (1)
minéral(e) *(mpl* **minéraux): eau minérale** *(f)* mineral water (2)
minier(-ère): exploitation minière *(f)* mining
ministère *(m)* ministry, department
ministre *(m)* minister, secretary
minoritaire minority
minorité *(f)* minority
minuit *(m)* midnight (P)
minute *(f)* minute (5)
miroir *(m)* mirror
mise *(f)* putting; **mise** *(f)* **à niveau** achievement of standard; **mise** *(f)* **en bouteille** bottling; **mise** *(f)* **en place** establishment; **mise** *(f)* **en relief** highlighting, accentuating
mobile *(m)* motive
mobilier *(m)* furnishings
mode *(f)* fashion (5)
modèle *(m)* model
moderne modern (1)
moi me (P); **chez moi** at my house (2); **Donnez-moi...** Give me... (P); **moi-même** myself
moindre: le moindre the least
moins minus (P); **au moins** at least; **de moins en moins** fewer and fewer, less and less; **Il est trois heures moins le quart.** It's a quarter to three. (P); **le moins** the least; **moins... que** less... than (1); **moins de... que** fewer... than
mois *(m)* month (3); **ce mois-ci** this month (4); **par mois** per month (3)
moitié *(f)* half
moment *(m)* moment; **à ce moment-là** at that time; **au dernier moment** at the last minute
mon (ma, mes) my (3); **ma famille** my family (P); **mes amis** my friends (1)
monarchie *(f)* monarchy
monde *(m)* world, crowd; **faire le tour du monde** to take a trip around the world; **Tiers Monde** *(m)* Third World; **tout le monde** everybody, everyone (7)

mondial(e) *(mpl* **mondiaux)** world(-wide) (5)
monétaire monetary
monnaie *(f)* change (2), currency
monoparental(e) *(mpl* **monoparentaux)** single-parent
monotonie *(f)* monotony
monsieur (M.) *(m)* mister (Mr.), sir (P), man
monstre *(m)* monster (6)
montagne *(f)* mountain (5); **aller à la montagne** to go to the mountains (5)
montagneux(-euse) mountainous
monter (dans) to go up; to get on/in (5), to set up, to climb
montre *(f)* watch (5)
montrer to show (3)
morceau *(m)* piece (8)
mort *(f)* death
mort(e) dead (4)
mosaïque *(f)* mosaic
mosquée *(f)* mosque
mot *(m)* word (P)
moule *(f)* mussel (8)
moulin *(m)* mill
mourant(e) dying
mourir to die (5)
moustache *(f)* mustache (4)
moutarde *(f)* mustard
mouton *(m)* sheep
mouvement *(m)* movement
moyen *(m)* means; **moyen** *(m)* **de transport** means of transportation (4)
moyen(ne) medium; **de taille moyenne** medium-sized (4); **Moyen-Orient** *(m)* Middle East (9)
moyenne *(f)* average
MST *(f)* STD
muet(te) silent
multiplier to multiply
mur *(m)* wall (3)
musculation: faire de la musculation to do weight training, to do bodybuilding (8)
musée *(m)* museum (4)
musical(e) *(mpl* **musicaux): comédie musicale** *(f)* musical
musicien(ne) *(mf)* musician (10)
musicien(ne) musical
musique *(f)* music (1); **musique zydeco** zydeco music (4)
musulman(e) Muslim
myrtille *(f)* blueberry
mystère *(m)* mystery

N

nager to swim (2)
naissance *(f)* birth
naître to be born (5); **être né(e)** to be born (5)
natal(e) native
nationalité *(f)* nationality (3)
nature *(f)* nature; **grandeur nature** *(f)* life-sized; **nature morte** *(f)* still life; **omelette nature** *(f)* plain omelet
naturel(le) natural
naturellement naturally
nausée *(f)* nausea
nautique: ski nautique *(m)* water-skiing (5)
ne: je ne travaille pas I don't work (P); **ne... aucun(e)** none, not one; **ne... jamais** never (2); **ne... ni... ni...** neither . . . nor; **ne... nulle part** nowhere; **ne... pas (du tout)** not (at all) (1); **ne... pas encore** not yet (5); **ne... personne** nobody, no one; **ne... plus** no more, no longer (8); **ne... que** only; **ne... rien** nothing (5); **ne... rien que** nothing but; **n'est-ce pas?** right? (1); **n'importe où** (just) anywhere

né(e): être né(e) to be born (5)
nécessaire necessary (10)
nécessiteux *(mpl)* needy
néerlandais(e) Dutch
néfaste harmful
négliger to neglect
nègre negro
négritude *(f)* negritude
neige *(f)* snow (5)
neiger to snow (5)
nerf *(m)* nerve; **maladie** *(f)* **des nerfs** nervous disorder; **nerfs à vif** nerves on edge
nerveux(-euse) nervous
n'est-ce pas? right? (1)
Net: surfer le Net to surf the Net (2)
neuf nine (P)
neuf (neuve) brand-new
neutralité *(f)* neutrality
neutre neutral
neuvième ninth (3)
neveu *(m)* *(pl* **neveux)** nephew (4)
nez *(m)* nose (10); **avoir le nez bouché** to have a stopped-up nose
ni: ne... ni... ni... neither . . . nor
niçois(e) from Nice
nièce *(f)* niece (4)
niveau *(m)* level
Noël *(m)* Christmas
noir(e) black (3); **Il faisait noir.** It was dark. (6)
nom *(m)* name (3); **au nom de** in the name of
nombre *(m)* number
nombreux(-euse) numerous
nommer to name
non no (P); **non?** right? (1); **non plus** neither (3)
non-pratiquant(e) *(mf)* non-churchgoer
nord *(m)* north; **Amérique** *(f)* **du Nord** North America (9)
normal(e) *(mpl* **normaux)** normal
normalement normally
Norvège *(f)* Norway
note *(f)* grade, note; **régler la note** to pay the bill (10)
noter to note, to notice
notre *(pl* **nos)** our (3)
nourriture *(f)* food, nourishment
nous we (1); (to, for) us (9), ourselves (7); **avec nous** with us (2); **Nous sommes six.** There are six of us. (4)
nouveau (nouvel, nouvelle) new (1); **de nouveau** again, anew; **Nouvelle-Angleterre** *(f)* New England; **Nouvelle-Calédonie** *(f)* New Caledonia (9); **La Nouvelle-Orléans** *(f)* New Orleans (4)
novembre *(m)* November (4)
noyau *(m)* pit
nu(e) naked
nuage *(m)* cloud
nuageux(-euse) cloudy
nucléaire nuclear
nuisible harmful
nuit *(f)* night (5); **boîte** *(f)* **de nuit** nightclub (1)
nul(le) **(en)** no good (at), really bad (at); **ne... nulle part** nowhere
numéro *(m)* number (3), issue
numéroté(e) numbered

O

obéir (à) to obey (8)
objectif *(m)* objective
objet *(m)* object
obligatoire obligatory, required
obligé(e) obliged, forced
obligeance *(f)* kindness
observer to observe (9)
obtenir to get, to obtain (9)
occasion: d'occasion second-hand
occidental(e) *(mpl* **occidentaux)** western
occitan *(m)* Occitan
occupé(e) busy
occuper to occupy
océan *(m)* ocean
Océanie *(f)* Oceania (9)
octobre *(m)* October (4)
œil *(pl* **yeux)** *(m)* eye (10); **avoir les yeux...** to have . . . eyes (4)
œuf *(m)* egg (8); **œuf dur** *(m)* hard-boiled egg (8)
œuvre *(f)* work
office *(m)* **de tourisme** tourist office
officiel(le) official
officiellement officially
offrir to offer; **offrant** offering
oignon *(m)* onion (8); **soupe** *(f)* **à l'oignon** onion soupe (8)
oiseau *(m)* bird
ombre *(f)* shadow, shade
omelette *(f)* omelet (8)
on one, they, we, people, you (4); **Comment dit-on... en français?** How do you say . . . in French? (P); **On... ?** Shall we . . . ?, How about. . . ? (4); **On va... ?** Shall we go. . . ? (2); **On dit que...** They say that . . . (4)
oncle *(m)* uncle (4)
onze eleven (P)
opposer to oppose; **s'opposer** to confront each other
optimiste optimistic (1)
or *(m)* gold
orage *(m)* storm
orange *(f)* orange (8); **jus** *(m)* **d'orange** orange juice (2)
orange *(inv)* orange (3)
Orangina *(m)* Orangina *(an orange drink)* (2)
oratoire *(m)* oratory, small chapel
orchestre *(m)* orchestra, band (4)
ordonnance *(f)* prescription (10)
ordinateur *(m)* computer (2)
ordre *(m)* order; **en ordre** in order (3)
oreille *(f)* ear (10)
oreillons *(mpl)* mumps
organisation *(f)* organization (10)
organiser to organize; **s'organiser** to get organized
organisme *(m)* organism, body
originaire de coming from
origine *(f)* origin; **d'origine...** of. . . origin (7)
orner to decorate
orthographique spelling
os *(m)* bone
ou or (P)
où where (1); **d'où** from where (1); **n'importe où** (just) anywhere
oublier to forget
ouest *(m)* west
oui yes (P)

outre-mer overseas
ouvert(e) open
ouverture *(f)* opening
ouvrir to open; **La bibliothèque ouvre à...** The library opens at . . . (P); **Ouvrez...** Open . . . (P)
ovationner to give an ovation

P

pacifique pacific, peaceful
page *(f)* page (P)
paiement *(m)* payment
pain *(m)* bread (8); **pain au chocolat** *(m)* croissant with chocolate filling (8); **pain complet** *(m)* wholegrain bread (8); **pain grillé** *(m)* toast (8)
pair: jeune fille au pair au pair, nanny
paisible peaceful, calm
paix *(f)* peace; **Corps** *(m)* **de la Paix** Peace Corps (10)
palais *(m)* palace
pâle pale
palme *(f)* palm leaf
paludisme *(m)* paludism, malaria
pamplemousse *(m)* grapefruit
panique *(f)* panic
panoramique panoramic
pantalon *(m)* pants (5)
papa *(m)* dad, papa
papier *(m)* paper; **feuille** *(f)* **de papier** sheet of paper (P)
pâque juive *(f)* Passover
Pâques *(fpl)* Easter
paquet *(m)* package, bag (8)
par per (3), by; **par contre** on the other hand; **par exemple** for example (2); **par *hasard** by chance; **par ici** this way (5); **par la fenêtre** through the window (6); **par mois** per month (3); **par terre** on the ground / floor (3)
paradis *(m)* paradise, heaven
paraître to appear
parapluie *(m)* umbrella (5)
parc *(m)* park (1); **parc naturel** natural park, nature reserve
parce que because (P)
parcourir to skim, to glance through
pardonner to forgive, to pardon
parent *(m)* parent (4), relative (5)
parenthèses *(fpl)* parentheses
paresseux(-euse) lazy (1)
parfait(e) perfect (7)
parfaitement perfectly (7)
parfois sometimes
Parisien(ne) *(mf)* Parisian (9)
parking *(m)* parking lot (1), parking garage
parlementaire parlementary
parler to talk, to speak (2); **je parle** I speak (P); **se parler** to talk to each other (7); **Vous parlez... ?** Do you speak. . . ? (P)
parmi among
paroisse *(f)* parish
parole *(f)* word, lyric
part: à part... besides . . . ; **ne... nulle part** nowhere; **quelque part** somewhere
partagé(e) shared, divided (3)
partager to share (3), to divide up
partenaire *(mf)* partner
parti (politique) *(m)* (political) party

participer (à) to participate (in)
particulier(-ère) particular; **en particulier** especially
partie part *(f)*; **en grande partie** mostly, in large part; **en partie** partially; **faire partie de** to be a part of
partir (de... pour) to leave (from . . . for), to go away (4); **à partir de** starting from
partout everywhere (3)
pas not (P); **je ne comprends pas** I don't understand (P); **ne... pas (du tout)** not (at all) (1); **ne... pas encore** not yet (5); **Pas de problème!** No problem! (3); **pas plus** no more (4)
passant(e) *(mf)* passerby
passé *(m)* past (6)
passeport *(m)* passport (9)
passer to spend, to pass (2); **passer chez** to go by . . .'s house (2); **passer le temps / la matinée** to spend one's time / the morning (2); **passer un film** to show a movie (6); **Passons à table!** Let's sit down and eat! (7); **Qu'est-ce qui s'est passé?** What happened? (6); **se passer** to happen (7)
passe-temps *(m)* pastime (2)
pastèque *(f)* watermelon
pâte *(f)* paste, dough
pâté *(m)* pâté, pâté spread (8)
patience *(f)* patience (4)
patient(e) *(mf)* patient (10)
patient(e) patient (6)
patin *(m)* skate; **patin** *(m)* **à glace** ice-skate, ice-skating; **patin** *(m)* **à roulettes** roller skate, roller skating
pâtisserie *(f)* pastry shop (8), pastry
patrimoine *(m)* patrimony, heritage
patron(ne) *(mf)* owner, boss
pâturage *(m)* pasture
pauvre poor
pavé *(m)* thick slice (8)
pavé(e) paved
pavillon *(m)* hall
payant(e) not free
payer to pay (2)
pays *(m)* country (3)
paysage *(m)* landscape (9)
Pays-Bas *(mpl)* Netherlands
peau *(f)* skin
pêche *(f)* peach (8), fishing; **aller à la pêche** to go fishing
peigner: se peigner to comb one's hair (7)
peintre *(m)* painter (10)
peinture *(f)* painting
pèlerin *(m)* pilgrim
pendant during, for (5); **pendant que** while
penderie *(f)* closet
penser to think (2); **penser à** think about (7); **je pense que** I think that (P)
pension *(f)* room and board
perdre to lose, to waste *(time)* (7); **se perdre** to get lost (7)
perdu(e) lost
père *(m)* father (4); **le père Noël** Santa Claus
perfectionnement *(m)* perfecting
perfectionner to perfect
période *(f)* period
permettre (de) to permit, to allow; **permis(e)** permitted, allowed
permission *(f)* permission
Pérou *(m)* Peru (9)
perpétuel(le) perpetual
personnage *(m)* character

personnalisé(e) personalized (8)
personnalité *(f)* personality (1)
personne *(f)* person (6); **ne... personne** nobody, no one
personnel(le) personal; **effets personnels** *(mpl)* personal belongings (3)
persuader to persuade
pessimiste pessimistic (1)
petit(e) small, little, short (1); **petit ami** *(m)* boyfriend (2); **petit à petit** little by little (6); **petit déjeuner** *(m)* breakfast (5); **petite amie** *(f)* girlfriend (2); **petite annonce** *(f)* classified ad; **petits pois** *(mpl)* peas (8)
petite-fille *(f)* granddaughter (7)
petit-fils *(m)* grandson (7)
petits-enfants *(mpl)* grandchildren
pétrole *(m)* oil
pétrolier(-ière): industries pétrolières *(f)* oil industry
peu little (P); **à peu près** approximately, about
peuple *(m)* people
peur: avoir peur (de) to be afraid (of), to fear (4)
peut-être perhaps, maybe (3)
pharmacie *(f)* pharmacy (7)
pharmacien(ne) *(mf)* pharmacist
philosophe *(mf)* philosopher
philosophie *(f)* philosophy (1)
photo *(f)* photo (4)
phrase *(f)* sentence (P)
physique *(f)* physics (1)
physique physical
piano *(m)* piano (2)
pièce *(f)* room (3); **pièce** *(f)* **de théâtre** play; **pièce** *(f)* **d'identité** identity card
pied *(m)* foot (10); **aller à pied** to walk, to go on foot (4)
pin *(m)* pine
pique-nique *(m)* picnic
piscine *(f)* swimming pool (4)
piste *(f)* trail, lead
pitié *(f)* pity
pizza *(f)* pizza (8)
placard *(m)* closet (3)
place *(f)* square, place, plaza (10); **à sa place** in its place (3)
plage *(f)* beach (5)
plaine *(f)* plain
plaire to please (9); **Ça me plaît!** I like it! (3); **Ça te plaît!** You like it! (3); **Ça t'a plu?** Did you like it? (6); **Ça te plaira!** You'll like it! (9); **s'il vous plaît** please (P)
plaisant(e) pleasant
plaisir *(m)* pleasure; **Avec plaisir!** It would be a pleasure! (6); **faire plaisir à** to please
plan *(m)* map (9), level; **plan** *(m)* **d'eau** stretch of water
planche *(f)* **à voile** windsurfing; **faire de la planche à voile** to windsurf
plante *(f)* plant (3)
planter to plant
plastique *(m)* plastic; **sac** *(m)* **en plastique** plastic bag
plat *(m)* dish (8); **plat préparé** *(m)* ready-to-serve dish (8)
plat(e) flat; **œuf au plat** *(m)* fried egg
plateau *(m)* tray
platine *(m)* platinum
platine laser *(f)* CD player
plein(e) full (4); **de plein air** outdoor (4); **plein de** full of, a lot of
pleur *(m)* sobbing

pleurer to cry
pleuvoir to rain (5)
plongée sous-marine *(f)* scuba diving
plonger to dive, to plunge
pluie *(f)* rain (5)
plupart: la plupart *(f)* the most part; **la plupart de** *(f)* the majority of (7); **la plupart du temps** most of the time (7)
plus plus; **de plus** in addition; **de plus en plus** more and more (8); **en plus** besides, furthermore (8); **ne... plus** no more, no longer (8); **non plus** neither (3); **pas plus** no more (4); **plus... que** more . . . than (1); **plus tard** later (4)
plusieurs several
plutôt rather (1); instead (4); **plutôt que** rather than
pneumonie *(f)* pneumonia
poche *(f)* pocket; **lampe** *(f)* **de poche** flashlight
poêle *(f)* frying pan
poêlée (de) *(f)* frying pan full (of)
poème *(m)* poem (9)
poésie *(f)* poetry
poète *(m)* poet
poids *(m)* weight (8)
poing *(m)* fist
point *(m)* point; **au point de** to be about to; **point** *(m)* **de vue** viewpoint
poire *(f)* pear (8)
poireau *(m)* leek
pois: petits pois *(mpl)* peas (8)
poisson *(m)* fish (8); **poissons** *(mpl)* **d'avril** April Fool's Day
poissonnerie *(f)* fish shop
poitrine *(f)* chest
poivre *(m)* pepper (8)
poivron *(m)* (bell) pepper
poli(e) polite
police *(f)* police, policy
policier(-ère) detective, police
politesse *(f)* politeness
politique *(f)* policy, politics
politique political; **homme politique** *(m)* politician
polo *(m)* knit shirt (5)
Pologne *(f)* Poland
Polynésie française *(f)* French Polynesia (9)
pomme *(f)* apple (8); **pomme** *(f)* **de terre** potato (8)
pommier *(m)* apple tree
populaire popular, pop (1)
porc *(m)* pork (8); **côte** *(f)* **de porc** pork chop (8)
porte *(f)* door (3); **porte** *(f)* **d'embarquement** departure gate (9); **porte** *(f)* **de débarquement** arrival gate (9)
portefeuille *(m)* wallet (5)
porter to wear, to carry (4)
portugais *(m)* Portuguese
poser to place; **poser une question** to ask a question (3)
posséder to possess, to own
possibilité *(f)* possibility (10)
postal(e) *(mpl* **postaux)**: **carte postale** *(f)* postcard (9); **casier postal** *(m)* mailbox; **code postal** *(m)* zip code (3)
poste *(f)* post office; **bureau** *(m)* **de poste** post office (7)
poste *(m)* position
pot *(m)* jar (8)
poubelle *(f)* trash can
pouce *(m)* thumb
poudre *(f)* powder

poulet *(m)* chicken (8)
poumon *(m)* lung
pour for (P), in order to (1); **pour cent** percent; **pour que** so that
pourcentage *(m)* percentage
pourquoi why (2)
poursuite *(f)* pursuit, chase
poursuivre to pursue
pourtant however
poussière *(f)* dust
pouvoir *(m)* power
pouvoir to be able, can, may (6); **Je peux vous aider?** Can I help you? (5); **on peut** one can (4)
pratique *(f)* practice
pratique practical
pratiquement practically
pratiquer to practice, to play *(a sport)*
préavis *(m)* (previous) notice
précédent(e) preceding
prêcher to preach
précipitamment hurriedly
préciser to specify
préféré(e) favorite (2)
préférence *(f)* preference; **de préférence** preferably
préférer to prefer (2); **je préfère** I prefer (1)
premier(-ère) first (1); **premier ministre** prime minister
prendre to take (4); **prendre contact** to get in touch; **prendre du poids** to put on weight (8); **prendre feu** to catch fire; **prendre possession de** to take possession of; **prendre son petit déjeuner** to have breakfast (5); **prendre un bain** to take a bath (7); **prendre un bain de soleil** to sunbathe (4); **prendre une décision** to make a decision (7); **prendre une douche** to take a shower (7); **prendre un verre** to have a drink (2); **Prenez une feuille de papier et un crayon ou un stylo.** Take out a piece of paper and a pencil or a pen. (P)
prénom *(m)* first name (3)
préoccuper to worry; **se préoccuper (de)** to worry (about)
préparatifs *(mpl)* preparations (9)
préparer to prepare (2); **plat préparé** ready-to-serve dish (8); **préparer les cours** to prepare for class, to study (2); **Préparez l'examen.** Prepare / Study for the exam. (P)
près (de) near (1); **près de** nearly; **à peu près** approximately, about
présentation *(f)* introduction
présenter to introduce, to present; **Je vous/te présente...** I would like to introduce . . . to you.; **se présenter** to arise, to introduce oneself
préservatif *(m)* condom
préserver to preserve
présider (à) to preside
presque almost, nearly (2)
presse *(f)* press
pressé(e) hurried
pression *(f)* pressure
prestigieux(-euse) prestigious
prêt(e) ready (4)
prétendre to claim
prêter to loan, to lend (9)
preuve *(f)* proof
prévisions météo *(fpl)* weather forecast
prier to beg, to request, to pray; **Je vous en prie.** You're welcome. (10)
prière *(f)* prayer

primaire: école primaire *(f)* elementary school
primeur *(m)* produce
principal(e) *(mpl* **principaux)** main (8)
principauté *(f)* principality
principe *(m)* principle
printemps *(m)* spring (5); **au printemps** in spring (5)
prise *(f)* electrical outlet
prise en charge *(f)* taking up
privé(e) private (10)
prix *(m)* price; **à prix fixe** with a set price (8)
probablement probably
problème *(m)* problem; **pas de problème** no problem (3)
prochain(e) next (4); **le prochain cours** the next class (P)
proche (de) near (to)
produire to produce
produit *(m)* product (8)
professeur *(m)* professor (P)
professionnel(le) professional (10)
profil *(m)* profile
profiter de to take advantage of (9)
profond(e) deep
programme *(m)* program
programmeur(-euse) *(mf)* computer programmer
progrès *(m)* progress
projecteur *(m)* projector
projet *(m)* plan (4); **faire des projets** to make plans (4)
promenade *(f)* walk (5); **faire une promenade** to take a walk (5)
promener: se promener to go walking (7)
promettre (de) to promise (6)
promouvoir to promote
promulguer (des lois) to create laws
pronom *(m)* pronoun
prononcer to pronounce
prononciation *(f)* pronunciation
proposer to offer, to suggest, to propose; **Qu'est-ce que je peux vous proposer d'autre?** What else can I get you? (8); **se proposer de** to intend
propre clean (3), own
propriétaire *(mf)* owner
propriété *(f)* property
prospérité *(f)* prosperity
protectorat *(m)* protectorate
protéger to protect
protéines *(fpl)* protein (8)
protestant(e) *(mf)* Protestant
provençal *(m)* Provençal
provenir de to come from
province *(f)* province (3)
provisions *(fpl)* supplies, groceries
proximité: à proximité de in the vicinity of
prune *(f)* plum
pruneau *(m)* prune
psychologie *(f)* psychology (1)
psychologique psychological
publicité *(f)* advertising, advertisement
public(-que) public; **santé publique** *(f)* public health
publier to publish
puis then (4)
puisque since
puissant(e) powerful
pull *(m)* pullover sweater (5)
punir to punish
purée *(f)* mashed potatoes
pyjama *(m)* pajamas

Q

quai *(m)* quay, wharf
qualité *(f)* quality
quand when (2); **quand même** all the same
quantité *(f)* quantity
quarante forty (P)
quart *(m)* quarter; **Il est deux heures et quart.** It's a quarter past two. (P)
quartier *(m)* neighborhood (1)
quatorze fourteen (P)
quatre four (P)
quatre-vingt-dix ninety (2)
quatre-vingts eighty (2)
quatrième fourth (3)
que that (P), than, as (1), what (2), which, whom (10); **ce que** what, that which; **ne... que** only; **ne... rien que** nothing but; **qu'est-ce que** what (1); **Qu'est-ce que ça veut dire?** What does that mean? (P)
quel(le) which, what (3); **À quelle heure?** At what time? (P); **C'est quel jour aujourd'hui?** What day is today? (P); **n'importe quel(le)...** (just) any . . . ; **Quel âge a... ?** How old is . . . ? (4)
quelconque any
quelque some; **quelque chose** something (2); **quelque part** somewhere; **quelques** a few, several (1); **quelqu'un** someone, somebody (6)
quelquefois sometimes (2)
quelques-un(e)s *(mf)* a few
question *(f)* question (P)
qui who (2), that, which, who (10); **ce qui** what (7); **Qu'est-ce qui s'est passé?** What happened? (6); **Qu'est-ce qui ne va pas?** What's wrong? (10)
quinze fifteen (P); **quinze jours** two weeks (5)
quinzième fifteenth
quitter to leave (4); **se quitter** to leave each other (7)
quoi what (10); **n'importe quoi** (just) anything
quoique although
quotidien(ne) daily (7)

R

raccompagner to (re)accompany
raccrocher to hang up
racisme *(m)* racism
raconter to tell, to recount (7)
radio *(f)* radio (2), X-ray
rafale *(f)* blast, gust
raffinerie *(f)* refinery
raie *(f)* skate *(fish)*, rayfish (8)
raisin *(m)* grape(s) (8); **raisins secs** *(mpl)* raisins
raison *(f)* reason; **avoir raison** to be right (4)
raisonnable reasonable
ralenti *(m)* slow motion
ramadan *(m)* Ramadan
randonnée *(f)* hike (9); **faire une randonnée** to go for a hike (9)
rangé(e) straightened up, arranged, put away (3)
rapide rapid (8)
rappeler to remind
rapport *(m)* relationship, report
rapporter to bring back; **se rapporter à** to be related to

rapprochement *(m)* coming closer together
rarement rarely (2)
raser: se raser to shave (7)
rasoir *(m)* razor
rassis(e) stale
rassurant(e) reassuring
rater to miss
ratifier to ratify
ravigote *(f)* vinaigrette
rayé(e) striped
réagir (à) to react (to)
réalisateur *(m)* producer
réalisation *(f)* carrying out
réaliser to accomplish
réaliste realistic (1)
réalité *(f)* reality
réapparaître to reappear
récemment recently (5)
réception *(f)* front desk (10), receiving
recette *(f)* recipe
recevoir to receive (9)
recherche *(f)* research
recherché(e) sought
réciproque reciprocal
recommander to recommend
récompenser to recompense
réconcilier: se réconcilier to make up with each other (7)
reconfirmer to reconfirm
reconnaître to recognize; **se reconnaître** to recognize each other (7)
reconstruire to reconstruct
recopier to copy
recoucher: se recoucher to go back to bed (7)
recouvert(e) covered
recréer to recreate
récrire to rewrite
rédacteur (-trice) *(mf)* **en chef** editor-in-chief
rédaction *(f)* composition (9)
redéfinir to redefine
réduire to reduce
réel(le) real
référer: se référer à to refer to
refermer to close back up
réfléchi(e) reflexive
réfléchir (à) to think (about), to reflect (on) (8)
reflet *(m)* reflection
refléter to reflect
réflexion *(f)* reflection, thought
réfrigérateur *(m)* refrigerator
réfugier: se réfugier to take refuge
regagner to regain
regard *(m)* look
regarder to look at, to watch (2); **se regarder** to look at each other (7)
régime *(m)* diet (8); regime; **être au régime** to be on a diet (8)
région *(f)* region (4)
régional(e) *(mpl* **régionaux)** regional (4)
régir to govern
règle *(f)* rule
règlement *(m)* payment
réglementé(e) regulated
régler to adjust; **régler la note** to pay the bill (10)
regretter to regret (6)
regrouper to regroup
régulier(-ière) regular
régulièrement regularly
rein *(m)* kidney; **reins** *(mpl)* lower back
reine *(f)* queen
rejeter to reject
rejoindre to join

relais *(m)* inn
relation *(f)* relationship (7)
relativement relatively
relier to connect
religieuse *(f)* cream puff
religieux(-euse) religious
relire to reread
remarquer to notice
remède *(m)* remedy, cure
remercier (de) to thank (for) (10)
remettre to put back; **remettre en cause** to call into question
remonter to go back (up)
remplacer to replace
remporter to win
rencontre *(f)* meeting, encounter (7)
rencontrer to meet, to run into (7); **se rencontrer** to run into each other (7)
rendez-vous *(m)* date, appointment; **Rendez-vous à...** Let's meet at . . .
rendormir: se rendormir to fall back asleep
rendre (quelque chose à quelqu'un) to return, to give something back to someone (7); **rendre (+ *adjective*)** to make (+ *adjective*); **rendre visite à** to visit *(someone)* (7); **se rendre (à / chez)** to go (to)
renommée *(f)* fame
rénové(e) renovated
renseignement *(m)* a piece of information (3)
renseigner to inform
rentrée *(f)* return
rentrer to return, to come / go back (home) (2)
repartir to start again, to leave again
repas *(m)* meal (6)
répéter to repeat (2); **Répétez, s'il vous plaît.** Repeat, please. (P); **se répéter** to be repeated
répondre (à) to answer (6); **Répondez à la question.** Answer the question. (P)
réponse *(f)* answer (P)
reposant(e) restful
reposer to set down; **se reposer** to rest (7)
représentant(e) *(mf)* representative
représenter to represent
reproche *(m)* reproach
république *(f)* republic
requis(e) required
réseau *(m)* network
réservation *(f)* reservation (9); **faire une réservation** to make a reservation (9)
réserve: sous réserve de subject to
réserver to reserve (9)
résidence *(f)* dormitory, residence hall (1); **résidence secondaire** *(f)* second home
résultat *(m)* result
résoudre to solve
respecter to respect
respirer to breathe
responsabilité *(f)* responsiblity
ressemblance *(f)* similarity
ressembler à to look like, to resemble
ressentir to feel
restaurant *(m)* restaurant (1); **dîner au restaurant** to dine out (2); **restau-u** *(m)* university cafeteria (6)
reste *(m)* rest (7); **le reste (de)** the rest (of) (7)
rester to stay (2); **rester au lit** to stay in bed (2)
résultat *(m)* result
résumé *(m)* summary
retard *(m)* delay; **en retard** late
retirer to take out, to withdraw (7)
retour *(m)* return (9); **(billet) aller-retour** *(m)* round-trip ticket (9)

retourner to return (5); **se retourner** to turn around

retravailler to rework

rétrécir to shrink

retrouver to meet (4), to find (again); **se retrouver** to meet (each other), to find each other again (7)

réunion (f) meeting

réunir: se réunir to meet

réussir (à) to succeed (in) (8)

rêve (m) dream

réveil (m) alarm clock (7), awakening

réveiller to wake up; **se réveiller** to wake up (7)

réveillon (m) **du jour de l'an** New Year's Eve

révélateur(-trice) revealing

révéler to reveal; **se révéler** to turn out to be

revendre to resell, to sell back (7)

revenir to come back (7)

revenu (m) income; **Revenu National Brut (R.N.B)** (m) gross national product (GNP)

rêver (de) to dream (about) (7)

rêveur(-euse) dreamy

réviser to review

révision (f) review

revoir to see again; **Au revoir.** Good-bye. (P)

révolte (f) revolt

revue (f) magazine

rez-de-chaussée (m) ground floor (3)

rhum (m) rum

rhume (m) cold (10)

riche rich (2)

richesse (f) wealth

ride (f) wrinkle

rideau (m) curtain (3)

ridicule ridiculous

rien: ne... rien nothing (5); **ne... rien que** nothing but; **rien de spécial** nothing special (6); **rien du tout** nothing at all (6)

rigoureux(-euse) rigorous, harsh

rillettes (fpl) potted pork or goose

rire (m) laugh, laughter,

rire to laugh

rive (f) bank

rivière (f) river

riz (m) rice (8)

robe (f) dress (5)

rocher (m) rock, boulder

rocheux(-euse) rocky

rock (m) rock music (1)

roi (m) king

rôle (m) role

roller: faire du roller to go rollerblading (6)

romain(e) Roman

roman (m) novel (9)

romanche (m) Romansh

romancier (m) novelist

romantique romantic

rond (m) circle

rosbif (m) roast beef (8)

rose pink (3)

rosier (m) rosebush

rôti(e) roasted; **rôti** (m) **de porc** pork roast

roue (f) wheel

rouge red (3); **vin rouge** (m) red wine (2)

rougeole (f) measles

rougir to turn red, to blush (8)

roulette: patin (m) **à roulettes** roller skate

route (f) route, way

routine (f) routine (7)

roux (rousse) red (hair) (4)

royaume (m) kingdom; **Royaume-Uni** (m) United Kingdom

rue (f) street (3); **dans la rue...** on . . . street (10)

ruine (f) ruin

ruminer to ponder

rupture (f) breaking up

rural(e) (mpl **ruraux**) rural

russe (m) Russian

Russie (f) Russia (9)

S

sable (m) sand

sac (m) purse (5)

safari (m) safari (9)

sage good, well-behaved (4)

sain(e) healthy (8)

Saint-Valentin (f) Valentine's Day

saison (f) season (5)

salade (f) salad (8); **salade** (f) **de tomates** tomato salad (8)

salaire (m) salary

sale dirty (3)

salé(e) salted

salle (f) room; **salle** (f) **à manger** dining room (3); **salle communautaire** (f) shared area; **salle** (f) **de bains** bathroom (3); **salle** (f) **de classe** classroom (1)

salon (m) living room (3)

saluer to greet

Salut! Hi! (P), Bye!

salutation (f) greeting

samedi (m) Saturday (P)

sandale (f) sandal (5)

sandwich (m) sandwich (2)

sang (m) blood

sanglier (m) wild boar

sanitaires (mpl) bathroom

sans without (P)

santé (f) health (8); **santé publique** (f) public health

satisfaisant(e) satisfying

satisfait(e) satisfied

sauce (f) sauce, gravy, dip

saucière (f) sauceboat

saucisse (f) sausage (8)

saucisson (m) salami (8)

sauf except (2)

saumon (m) salmon (8)

sauvage wild

sauver to save; **sauvé(e)** saved

savane (f) savanna

savoir to know (how) (9); **Je ne sais pas.** I don't know. (P); **Que savez-vous de... ?** What do you know about. . . ? (8)

savon (m) soap

saxophone (m) saxophone (2)

scénario (m) screenplay

scène (f) stage, scene, skit

sceptique sceptical

science (f) science (1); **film** (m) **de science-fiction** science fiction movie; **sciences économiques** (fpl) economics; **sciences humaines** (fpl) social sciences (1); **sciences politiques** (fpl) political science, government (1)

scientifique scientific

scolaire school; **extra-scolaire** extracurricular

sculpteur (m) sculptor

se herself, himself, itself, oneself, themselves (7); **Il/Elle se trouve...** It is located. . . (3)

séance (f) showing (6)

sec (sèche) dry

second(e) second

secondaire secondary

seconde (f) second (5)

secrétaire (mf) secretary

secteur (m) sector, area

section: section (non-)fumeur (f) (non-)smoking section

sécurité (f) security, safety

séduisant(e) seductive

sein (m) breast

seize sixteen (P)

seizième sixteenth

séjour (m) stay (7)

séjourner to stay

sel (m) salt (8)

self-service (m) self-service restaurant (8)

selon according to

semaine (f) week (P); **en semaine** weekdays

semblable similar

sembler to seem

semestre (m) semester (P)

Sénégal (m) Senegal (9)

sénégalais(e) Senegalese

sens (m) meaning, sense

sensible sensitive

sensuel(le) sensual

sentiment (m) feeling

sentimental(e) (mpl **sentimentaux**) sentimental, emotional (7)

sentir: se sentir to feel (10)

séparé(e) separated

sept seven (P)

septième seventh (3)

septembre (m) September (4)

série (f) series, category

sérieusement seriously

sérieux(-euse) serious

serveur (m) waiter (8)

serveuse (f) waitress (8)

service (m) service (8)

serviette (f) towel

servir to serve (4); **servi(e)** served (10); **se servir de** to use

seul(e) alone (P), single, lonely, only

seulement only (8)

sévère strict

sexuel(le) sexual

sexy (inv) sexy (2)

shopping: faire du shopping to go shopping (2)

short (m) shorts (5)

si if (5), yes (8); **s'il vous plaît** please (P)

SIDA (m) AIDS

siècle (m) century

siège (m) seat

sieste (f) nap

sigle (m) set of initials

signaler to draw attention to

similaire (à) similar (to)

similarité (f) similarity

simple simple; **billet aller simple** (m) one-way ticket (9)

singe (m) monkey (9)

sinon if not, otherwise

sinusite (f) sinusitis

site (m) site (9)

situation (f) situation (10)

situer: se situer to be situated

six six (P)

sixième sixth (3)

skateboarding: faire du skateboarding to skateboard (6)

ski (nautique) *(m)* (water-)skiing (5); **faire du ski (nautique)** to go (water-)skiing (5)
skier to ski
slip *(m)* briefs, panties
social(e) *(mpl* **sociaux)** social
société *(f)* company (10), society; **jeu** *(m)* **de société** board game
socioculturel(le): à dédication socioculturelle for social activities
sociologie *(f)* sociology
sœur *(f)* sister (1); **belle-sœur** *(f)* sister-in-law (4); **demi-sœur** *(f)* stepsister, half-sister
soi oneself
soif: avoir soif to be thirsty (4); **j'ai soif** I'm thirsty (2)
soin *(m)* care
soir *(m)* evening (P); **à huit heures du soir** at eight in the evening (P); **ce soir** tonight, this evening (2); **le soir** evenings, in the evening (P)
soirée *(f)* evening (4)
soixante sixty (2)
soixante-dix seventy (2)
soja *(m)* soya
sol *(m)* ground
soldat *(m)* soldier
solde: en solde on sale (5)
sole *(f)* sole *(fish)*
soleil *(m)* sun; **Il fait du soleil.** It's sunny. (5); **lunettes** *(fpl)* **de soleil** sunglasses (5); **prendre un bain de soleil** to sunbathe (4)
solitaire lonely
solitude *(f)* loneliness
sombre dark, gloomy
somme *(f)* sum
sommeil *(m)* sleep; **avoir sommeil** to be sleepy (4)
son *(m)* sound
son (sa, ses) her, his, its (3)
sondage *(m)* poll
sonner to ring (7)
sorcière *(f)* witch
sorte *(f)* kind, sort
sortie *(f)* outing (6), exit
sortir (de) to go out (2); to leave (6); to take out
soudain suddenly (6)
soudain(e) sudden
soudainement suddenly
souffrance *(f)* suffering
souffrir to suffer
souhait *(m)* wish
souhaiter to wish
soumettre: se soumettre à to submit to
soupçonner to suspect
soupe *(f)* soup (8); **soupe** *(f)* **à l'oignon** onion soup (8)
souper to have supper
sous under (3); **sous réserve de** subject to
sous-estimer to underestimate
sous-marin(e) underwater; **plongée sous-marine** *(f)* scuba diving
sous-sol *(m)* basement (3)
sous-titres *(mpl)* subtitles
sous-vêtements *(mpl)* underwear
soutenu(e) supported
soutien-gorge *(m)* bra
souvenir *(m)* memory
souvenir: se souvenir (de) to remember (7)
souvent often (1)
souveraineté *(f)* sovereignty

spécial(e) *(mpl* **spéciaux)** special; **effets spéciaux** *(mpl)* special effects (6); **rien de spécial** nothing special (6)
spécialisation *(f)* specialization, major
spécialisé(e) specialized
spécialité *(f)* specialty (4)
spectacle *(m)* show
spectaculaire spectacular
spectateur(-trice) *(mf)* spectator, viewer
sport *(m)* sport (1); **faire du sport** to play sports (5)
sportif(-ive) athletic (1)
stabilité *(f)* stability
stable stable (10)
stade *(m)* stadium (1)
stage *(m)* internship
standard *(m)* switchboard
station *(f)* station; **station-service** *(f)* service station
statut *(m)* statute, status
stéréo: chaîne stéréo *(f)* stereo (2)
stratégie *(f)* strategy
stress *(m)* stress
stressé(e) stressed (out) (8)
style *(m)* style
stylo *(m)* pen (P)
subventions *(fpl)* subsidies
succursale *(f)* branch office
sucer to suck
sucre *(m)* sugar (8)
sucré(e) sweet, sugary
sud *(m)* south; **Amérique** *(f)* **du Sud** South America (9)
Suède *(f)* Sweden
suffire: il suffit de… it's enough to . . .
suffisant(e) sufficient
suggérer to suggest (6)
Suisse *(f)* Switzerland (9)
suisse Swiss
suite: toute de suite right away (6)
suivant(e) following (3)
suivre to follow (7); **à suivre** to be continued (6); **suivre un cours** to take a course
sujet *(m)* subject
super great (P)
superficie *(f)* area
supérieur(e) superior, higher
supermarché *(m)* supermarket (7)
supplément *(m)* extra charge (10)
supplémentaire supplementary
suprématie *(f)* supremacy
sur on (1); **sept jours sur sept** seven days out of seven
sûr(e) sure; **Bien sûr!** Of course! (5)
sûrement surely
surfer: surfer le Net to surf the Net (2)
surgelé(e) frozen (8)
surgir to arise, to come up; to appear suddenly, to surge, to begin to grow
surimpression *(f)* **d'images** double exposure
surpasser to surpass
surprenant(e) surprising
surprendre to surprise
surpris(e) surprised (10)
surtout especially, above all (8)
survêtement *(m)* jogging suit (5)
sympathique (sympa) nice (1)
symptôme *(m)* symptom (10)
synagogue *(f)* synagogue
systématiquement systematically

système *(m)* system (9); **système** *(m)* **de transports en commun** public transportation system (9)

T

tabac *(m)* tobacco (8); **bureau** *(m)* **de tabac** tobacco shop (7)
table *(f)* table (3); **table basse** *(f)* coffee table
tableau *(m)* board (P); painting, picture (3), act, scene; **tableau** *(m)* **d'affichage** bulletin board
tâche *(f)* task; **tâche domestique** household chore
taille *(f)* size (4); **de taille moyenne** medium-sized, of medium height (4); **Quelle taille faites-vous?** What size do you wear? (5)
tailleur *(m)* woman's suit
taire: se taire to be silent
talon *(m)* heel; ***haut talon** *(m)* high heel
tandis que whereas, while
tant (de) so much, so many; **tant que** as long as
tante *(f)* aunt (4)
tapis *(m)* rug (3)
tapisserie *(f)* tapestry
tard late (4); **plus tard** later (4)
tarte *(f)* pie (8); **tarte** *(f)* **aux pommes** apple pie (8)
tartelette *(f)* **(aux fraises)** (strawberry) tart (8)
tartine *(f)* bread and butter (with jam) (8)
tas *(m)* pile; **un tas de** a bunch of
tasse *(f)* cup
taxi *(m)* taxi (4); **en taxi** by taxi (4)
te (to, for) you (9), yourself (7); **Ça te dit?** How does that sound to you? (4); **Ça te plaît?** Do you like it? (3); **Je te présente…** I would like to introduce . . . to you.; **s'il te plaît** please; **Te voilà!** There you are! (7)
technique technical (1)
technologie *(f)* technology
tee-shirt *(m)* T-shirt (5)
teinturerie *(f)* dry cleaner's (7)
tel(le): tel(le) que such as; **un(e) tel(le)** such a (7)
télé *(f)* TV (2)
télécopie *(f)* fax
téléphone *(m)* telephone (2); **au téléphone** on the telephone (2); **numéro** *(m)* **de téléphone** telephone number (3)
téléphoner (à) to phone (3); **se téléphoner** to telephone each other (7)
téléphonique: appareil *(m)* **téléphonique** telephone
télévision (télé) *(f)* television (2)
tellement so much, so (6)
témoignage *(m)* testimony, evidence
température *(f)* temperature
temple *(m)* temple, Protestant church
temps *(m)* time (2), weather (5); **de temps en temps** from time to time (4); **emploi** *(m)* **du temps** schedule (P); **en tout temps** at all times; **Pendant combien de temps?** For how long? (5); **Quel temps fait-il?** What's the weather like? (5); **temps libre** *(m)* free time (4); **temps verbal** *(m)* tense
tendance *(f)* tendency
tendre tender
tenir to hold; **Ah tiens!** Hey!; **tenir à** to value
tennis *(m)* tennis (1); **court** *(m)* **de tennis** tennis court
tentation *(f)* temptation

tenter to attempt
tenture (f) curtain
terme: mettre terme à to put an end to
terminaison (f) ending
terminer to finish
terrain: sur le terrain on site
terre (f) earth; **par terre** on the ground / floor (3); **pomme** (f) **de terre** potato (8)
territoire (m) territory
tertiaire: activités tertiaires (fpl) service industries
tête (f) head (10); **prendre la tête** to take charge
thé (m) tea (2)
théâtre (m) theater (1), drama (1)
thon (m) tuna (8)
tiers (m) third; **Tiers Monde** (m) Third World
timbre (m) stamp (7)
timide shy, timid (1)
tiroir (m) drawer
titre (m) title
titulaire (mf) holder
toi you (P); **chez toi** at your house (2)
toilettes (fpl) toilet, restroom (3); **faire sa toilette** to wash up (7)
toit (m) roof
tomate (f) tomato (8)
tombe (f) grave
tomber to fall; **tomber amoureux(-euse) (de)** to fall in love (with) (6); **tomber malade** to get sick (10)
ton (m) tone
ton (**ta, tes**) your (3); **tes amis** your friends (1); **ton université** your university (1)
torse (m) torso
tort: avoir tort to be wrong (4)
tôt early (4)
toucher to touch
toujours always (2), still
tour (m) tour, ride (4); **faire un tour** to take a tour, to go for a ride (4)
tour (f) tower
touriste (mf) tourist; **classe touriste** (f) tourist class, coach (9)
touristique tourist (9)
tournée (f) tour
tourner to turn (10), to stir; **se tourner** (**vers**) to turn (toward)
tourte (f) pie
Toussaint (f) All Saints' Day
tousser to cough (10)
tout (**toute, tous, toutes**) everything, all (3), whole; **ne... pas du tout** not at all (1); **rien du tout** nothing at all (6); **tous** (**toutes**) **les deux** both; **tous les jours** every day (2); **tous les soirs** every evening (4); **tout à fait** completely; **tout à l'heure** in a little while (P), a while ago; **tout de suite** right away (6); **tout droit** straight (10); **tout d'un coup** all of a sudden (6); **toute la journée** the whole day (2); **tout en** while; **toutes sortes de...** all kinds of . . . ; **tout le monde** everybody, everyone (7); **tout près (de)** right by, very near (3)
tradition (f) tradition (9)
traditionnel(le) traditional (8)
traditionnellement traditionally
traducteur(-trice) (mf) translator
traduire to translate
train (m) train (4); **en train** by train (4); **être en train de...** to be in the process of. . .

traîner to hang around
traité (m) treaty
traitement (m) treatment
tranche (f) slice (8)
tranquille tranquil, calm
transformer: se transformer en to change into
transmettre to transmit; to pass on
transpercer to pierce
transport (m) transportation; **moyen** (m) **de transport** means of transportation (4); **système** (m) **de transports en commun** public transportation system (9)
travail (m) work (9); **fête du travail** (f) Labor Day
travailler to work, to study (2); **je travaille** I work (P); **Tu travailles? / Vous travaillez?** Do you work? (P)
travailleur(-euse) (mf) worker
travers: à travers across
traversée (f) crossing
traverser to cross, to go across (10)
treize thirteen (P)
trembler to tremble
trentaine (f) thirties
trente thirty (P)
très very (P)
tribu (f) tribe
triste sad (10)
trois three (P)
troisième third (3); **troisième âge** (m) age of retirement
trompette (f) trumpet (2)
tronc commun (m) common-core syllabus
trop too, too much (3); **trop de** too much, too many (6)
tropical(e) (mpl **tropicaux**) tropical (9)
trou (m) hole
trouver to find (4); **Il/Elle se trouve...** It is located. . . (3)
truc (m) thing (1); **Ce n'est pas mon truc.** That's not my thing. (1)
truite (f) trout
tu you (P)
tuba: faire du tuba to go snorkeling
tuberculose (f) tuberculosis
tuer to kill
Tunisie (f) Tunisia
Turquie (f) Turkey
typique typical
typiquement typically (2)
tyran (m) tyrant

U

un(e) one, a (1)
uni(e) (à) close (to), united, solid-colored; **Nations unies** (fpl) United Nations
unique only, single, unique
uniquement only
unité (f) unity, unit
universitaire university (1)
université (f) university (P)
urgence (f) emergency
usage (m) use
usine (f) factory
utile useful (10)
utiliser to use, to utilize

V

vacances (fpl) vacation (4); **en vacances** on vacation (4)
vacancier (m) vacationer
vaccination (f) vaccination; **certificat** (m) **de vaccination** vaccination certificate
vache (f) cow
vague (f) wave
vaincu(e) defeated
vaisselle (f) dishes; **faire la vaisselle** to wash dishes (5); **lave-vaisselle** (m) dishwasher
valeur (f) value; **mettre en valeur** to emphasize
valise (f) suitcase (9); **faire ses valises** to pack one's bags (9)
vallée (f) valley
valoir to be worth; **il vaut mieux (que)...** it's better (that) . . . (10)
valse (f) waltz
valser to waltz
vanille (f) vanilla (8)
vaniteux(-euse) vain
varappe (f) rock climbing; **faire de la varappe** to go rock climbing
varicelle (f) chicken pox
varié(e) varied
variété (f) variety
vaste vast
vaut See valoir.
veau (m) veal
végétarien(ne) vegetarian
véhicule (m) vehicle
veillée (f) evening together
veiller to watch over
vélo (m) bicycle (3); **en vélo** by bike (4); **faire du vélo** to go bike-riding (5)
vendeur(-euse) (mf) salesperson (5)
vendre to sell (7)
vendredi (m) Friday (P)
venir to come (6); **venir de** (+ infinitive) to have just (+ past participle) (7); **Viens voir...** Come see . . . (3)
vent (m) wind; **Il fait du vent.** It's windy. (5)
vente (f) sale
ventre (m) stomach, belly (10)
verbe (m) verb
verglaçant(e) icy
verglas: Il y a du verglas. It's icy.
vérifier to check
véritable true, real
vérité (f) truth
verre (m) glass (2); **prendre un verre** to have a drink (2)
vers (m) verse
vers toward(s), about, around (2)
vert(e) green (3)
vestige (m) remnant
vêtements (mpl) clothes (3); **sous-vêtements** (mpl) underwear
vétérinaire (m) veterinarian
veuf (m) widower (7)
veuve (f) widow (7)
vexer to vex, to upset
viande (f) meat (8)
vicieux(-euse) vicious
victime (f) victim

vidéo *(f)* video (2); **vidéocassette** *(f)* video cassette (3); **jeu vidéo** *(m)* video game (2)

vie *(f)* life (6)

vieillir to age, to get old (8)

viennoiserie *(f) baked goods sold at a bakery*

Viêtnam *(m)* Vietnam (9)

vieux / vieil (vieille) old (1); **Vieux Carré** *(m)* French Quarter (4)

vif(-ive) lively, bright; **bleu vif** bright blue

vigueur: en vigueur in effect; **reprendre vigueur** to take on a new life

village *(m)* village, town

villageois(e) *(mf)* villager

ville *(f)* city (3); **en ville** in town (3)

vin *(m)* wine (2)

vinaigre *(m)* vinegar

vingt twenty (P)

vingtième twentieth

violence *(f)* violence

violet(te) violet (3)

virus *(m)* virus (10)

visa *(m)* visa

visage *(m)* face

visé(e) stamped, approved

vigueur: en vigueur in effect

visite: rendre visite à to visit *(a person)* (7)

visiter to visit (1)

visiteur(-esue) *(mf)* visitor

vitamine *(f)* vitamin (8)

vite quickly, fast (7)

vitesse *(f)* speed

vivant(e) alive

vivement greatly

vivier *(m)* fish reservoir

vivoir *(m)* living room

vivre to live

vocabulaire *(m)* vocabulary (P)

voici here is, here are (2)

voilà there is, there are (2); **Te / Vous voilà!** There you are! (7)

voile *(f)* sailing; **faire de la planche à voile** *(f)* to go windsurfing

voir to see (1); **aller voir** to go see, to visit (4); **comme tu vois** as you see (3); **se voir** to see each other (7), to find oneself; **Voyons!** Let's see! (5)

voisin(e) *(mf)* neighbor (9)

voiture *(f)* car (3); **en voiture** by car (4); **voiture** *(f)* **de location** rental car (5)

voix *(f)* voice

vol *(m)* flight (9)

volaille *(f)* poultry (8)

volcan *(m)* volcano

voleur *(m)* thief (6)

volley *(m)* volleyball (2)

volonté *(f)* will, wish

volontiers gladly, willingly (8)

vomir to vomit (10)

voter to vote

vôtre: le/la vôtre yours

votre *(pl* **vos)** your (3); **Ouvrez votre livre.** Open your book. (P)

vouloir to want (6); **Je voudrais (bien)…** I would like . . . (2); **Qu'est-ce que ça veut dire?** What does that mean? (P); **Qu'est-ce que vous voudriez faire?** What would you like to do? (2); **Tu voudrais… ?** Would you like . . . ? (2)

vous you (P), (to, for) you (9), yourself(-selves) (7); **Je vous présente…** I would like to introduce . . . to you.; **s'il vous plaît** please (P); **vous-même** yourself; **Vous voilà!** There you are! (7)

voyage *(m)* trip (4); **agence** *(f)* **de voyages** travel agency (9); **agent** *(m)* **de voyages** travel agent (9); **chèque** *(m)* **de voyage** traveler's check (9); **faire un voyage** to take a trip (5); **voyage** *(m)* **de noces** honeymoon

voyager to travel (2)

voyelle *(f)* vowel

vrai(e) true

vraiment really, truly (6)

vue *(f)* view (3); **point** *(m)* **de vue** viewpoint

vulgaire vulgar, crude

W

wallon(ne) Walloon

W.-C. *(mpl)* toilet, restroom (3)

Web: site *(m)* **Web** Website (9)

week-end *(m)* weekend (P); **Bon week-end!** Have a good weekend!; **le week-end** on weekends (P)

Y

y there (4); **il y a** there is, there are (1), ago (5)

yaourt *(m)* yogurt

yeux *(mpl) (sing* **œil)** eyes (4)

Yom Kippour *(m)* Yom Kippur

Z

zapper to channel surf, to switch back and forth

zéro *(m)* zero (P)

zydeco: musique *(f)* **zydeco** zydeco music (4)

VOCABULAIRE ANGLAIS-FRANÇAIS

The *Vocabulaire anglais–français* includes all words presented in *Horizons* for active use, as well as others that students may need for more personalized expression. The definitions of active vocabulary words are followed by the number of the chapter where they are first presented. A (P) refers to the *Chapitre préliminaire*. When several translations, separated by commas, are listed before a chapter number, they are all considered active. Since verbs are sometimes introduced lexically in the infinitive before the conjugation of the present indicative is presented, consult the *Index* to find out the chapter where a conjugation is introduced. An (m), (f), or (pl) following a noun indicates that it is masculine, feminine, or plural. *Inv* means that a word is invariable. An asterisk before a word beginning with an **h** indicates that the **h** is aspirate.

A

a un(e) (P); **a few** quelques (1); **a lot** beaucoup (P)
able: be able pouvoir (4)
about vers (2), environ (4), de (1); **about it/them** en (8); **About what?** À propos de quoi?; **think about** penser à (7)
above au-dessus de; **above all** surtout (8)
abroad à l'étranger (9)
absolutely absolument
Acadia Acadie (f)
accent accent (m) (P); **without an accent** sans accent (P)
accept accepter
accident accident (m)
accompany accompagner
according to selon
account compte (m)
accountant comptable (mf)
accounting comptabilité (f) (1)
accustomed to habitué(e) à
ache douleur (f)
ache avoir mal (à) (10)
acquaintance: make the acquaintance of faire la connaissance de
acquainted: be/get acquainted with connaître (4)
across (from) en face (de) (3); **go across** traverser (10)
act jouer (in movies and theater) (6); agir
active dynamique (1)
activity activité (f) (2)
actor acteur (m) (6)
actress actrice (f) (6)
actually effectivement, réellement
adapt s'adapter
add ajouter
address adresse (f) (3); **e-mail address** adresse (f) e-mail (3)
adjective adjectif (m) (1)
administration building centre administratif (m)
admire admirer (9)
adopted adopté(e)
adore adorer
adult adulte (mf)
advance avance (f); **in advance** à l'avance (9)
advantage avantage (m); **take advantage of** profiter de
adventure aventure (f); **adventure movie** film (m) d'aventures
advertisement publicité (f); **classified ad** petite annonce (f)

advertising publicité (f)
advice conseils (mpl) (10); **give a piece of advice** donner un conseil
aerobics: do aerobics faire de l'aérobic (8)
afraid: be afraid (of) avoir peur (de) (4)
Africa Afrique (f) (9)
African africain(e)
after après (P); **after having done . . .** après avoir fait... ; **day after tomorrow** après-demain
afternoon après-midi (m) (P); **in the afternoon, afternoons** l'après-midi (P); **It's one o'clock in the afternoon.** Il est une heure de l'après-midi. (P); **this afternoon** cet après-midi (4)
afterward(s) après (P), ensuite (4)
again encore (8), de nouveau
against contre (10)
age âge (m)
age vieillir (8)
agency: travel agency agence (f) de voyages (9)
agent agent (m); **travel agent** agent (m) de voyages (9)
ago il y a (5); **How long ago?** Il y a combien de temps? (5)
agree être d'accord; **Agreed!** D'accord! (2)
agricultural agricole
ahead: straight ahead tout droit (10)
AIDS SIDA (m)
air air (m)
airplane avion (m) (4); **by airplane** en avion (4)
airport aéroport (m)
alarm: alarm clock réveil (m) (7)
alcohol alcool (m) (8)
alcoholic drink boisson alcoolisée (f)
algebra algèbre (f)
Algeria Algérie (f) (9)
alive vivant(e)
all tout (toute, tous, toutes) (3); **above all** surtout (8); **all day** toute la journée (2); **all of a sudden** tout d'un coup (6); **all of the time** tout le temps; **all sorts of** toutes sortes de; **all the better** tant mieux; **not at all** ne... pas du tout (1); **nothing at all** rien du tout (6); **That's all.** C'est tout. (8)
allergy allergie (f) (10)
allow permettre (de); **allowed** permis(e)
almost presque (2)
alone seul(e) (P)
along le long de (9); **get along well/badly** s'entendre bien/mal (7)
already déjà (5)
also aussi (P)
although bien que, quoique
always toujours (2)
A.M. du matin (P)
amaze étonner; **amazed** étonné(e) (10)
America Amérique (f) (9)

American américain(e) (P); **American style** à l'américaine (8)
among parmi
amusing amusant(e) (1)
an un(e) (1)
ancestor ancêtre (mf)
and et (P)
angry fâché(e); **get angry** se fâcher
animal animal (m) (pl animaux) (3)
animated animé(e)
ankle cheville (f)
anniversary (wedding) anniversaire (m) de mariage
annoying embêtant(e) (3)
another un(e) autre (1); **another glass of...** encore un verre de... ; **another thing** autre chose; **one another** se, nous, vous (7)
answer réponse (f) (P)
answer répondre (à) (6); **Answer the question.** Répondez à la question. (P)
anthropology anthropologie (f)
any du, de la, de l', de, des, en (8)
anymore: not anymore ne... plus (8)
anyone quelqu'un (6); **(just) anyone** n'importe qui; **not . . . anyone** ne... personne
anything quelque chose (2); **(just) anything** n'importe quoi; **not . . . anything** ne... rien (5)
anyway quand même
anywhere: (just) anywhere n'importe où; **not . . . anywhere** nulle part
apartment appartement (m) (3); **apartment building** immeuble (m) (3)
appear paraître
appetite appétit (m)
appetizer *hors-d'œuvre (m) (8)
apple pomme (f) (8); **apple pie** tarte (f) aux pommes (8)
appointment rendez-vous (m) (6)
appreciate apprécier (6)
appropriate approprié(e), convenable
apricot abricot (m)
April avril (m) (4); **April Fool's Day** les poissons (mpl) d'avril
Arabic arabe (m)
architect architecte (mf)
architecture architecture (f)
Argentina Argentine (f) (9)
argue (with) se disputer (avec) (7)
arm bras (m) (10)
armchair fauteuil (m) (3)
around vers (2), environ (4) autour de
arranged rangé(e) (3)
arrival arrivée (f) (9); **arrival gate** porte (f) de débarquement
arrive arriver (3)

art art *(m);* **fine arts** beaux-arts *(mpl)* (1)
article article *(m)* (9)
artist artiste *(mf)* (10); **graphic artist**
   dessinateur(-trice) *(mf)* (de publicité)
as comme (3); **as . . . as** aussi... que (1); **as long
   as** tant que; **as many . . . (as)** autant de...
   (que); **as much . . . (as)** autant de... (que);
   as soon as aussitôt que; **as you see** comme
   tu vois (3)
ash cendre *(f);* **Ash Wednesday** mercredi *(m)*
   des Cendres
ashamed: be ashamed avoir *honte
Asia Asie *(f)* (9)
ask (for) demander (2); **ask a question** poser
   une question (3)
asleep: fall asleep s'endormir (7)
asparagus asperges *(fpl)*
aspirin aspirine *(f)*
assembly assemblage *(m)*
associate associer
astronomy astronomie *(f)*
at à (P); **at home** à la maison (P); **at . . . 's
   house/place** chez... (2)
athletic sportif(-ive) (1)
attend assister à
attention attention *(f);* **pay attention (to)** faire
   attention (à) (8)
attract attirer
August août *(m)* (4)
aunt tante *(f)* (4)
Australia Australie *(f)* (9)
automatic: automatic teller machine guichet
   automatique *(m)* (7)
autumn automne *(m)* (5); **in autumn** en
   automne (5)
available disponible
avenue avenue *(f)* (10)
average moyen(ne)
avoid éviter (8)
awaken se réveiller (7)
awakening réveil *(m)*
away: go away partir (4), s'en aller; **put away**
   rangé(e) (3); **right away** tout de suite (6)

B

baby bébé *(m)*
babysitter baby-sitter *(mf)*
back dos *(m)*
back: bring back rapporter; **come back** revenir
   (7); **give back** rendre (7); **go back** rentrer
   (2), retourner (5); **go back to bed** se
   recoucher (7); **in the back of** au fond de; **sell
   back** revendre (7)
bacon bacon *(m)* (8)
bad mauvais(e) (1); **It's too bad!** C'est dommage!
   (7); **really bad** nul(le); **The weather's bad.** Il
   fait mauvais. (5)
badly mal (P); **not badly** pas mal (P)
bag sac *(m)* (5), paquet *(m)* (8); **pack one's bags**
   faire ses valises (9)
baggage bagages *(mpl)* (9)
bakery boulangerie *(f)* (7), pâtisserie *(f)* (8)
balcony balcon *(m)*
bald chauve
ball balle *(f),* (inflated) ballon *(m)*
banana banane *(f)* (8)
band orchestre *(m)* (4)
bank banque *(f)* (7); **bank card** carte bancaire
   (f) (9)

banker banquier *(m)*
bar bar *(m)* (4)
baseball base-ball *(m)* (2)
based: based on basé(e) sur (6)
basement sous-sol *(m)* (3)
basketball basket *(m)* (1)
bath bain *(m)* (7)
bathe prendre un bain (7), se baigner
bathroom salle *(f)* de bains (3)
be être (1); **be able** pouvoir (4); **be afraid (of)**
   avoir peur (de) (4); **be ashamed** avoir
   *honte; **be bored** s'ennuyer (7); **be born**
   naître, être né(e) (5); **be cold** avoir froid (4);
   be familiar with connaître (4); **be hot** avoir
   chaud (4); **be hungry** avoir faim (4); **I'm
   hungry.** J'ai faim. (2); **be interested in**
   s'intéresser à; **be named** s'appeler (7); **be
   right** avoir raison (4); **be sleepy** avoir
   sommeil (4); **be thirsty** avoir soif (4); **I'm
   thirsty.** J'ai soif.(2); **be wrong** avoir tort (4);
   be . . . years old avoir... ans (4); **here is/are**
   voici (2); **How are you?** Comment allez-
   vous? (P); **How is it going?** Comment ça va?
   (P); **I am . . .** Je suis... (P); **isn't it?** n'est-ce
   pas?, non? (1); **It is located...** Il/Elle se
   trouve... (3); **It's Monday.** C'est lundi. (P); **My
   name is . . .** Je m'appelle... (P); **That's . . .
   euros.** Ça fait... euros. (2); **There are six of
   us.** Nous sommes six. (4); **there is/are** il y a
   (1), voilà (2); **The weather's nice / bad /
   cold / cool / hot / sunny / windy.** Il fait beau
   / mauvais / froid / frais / chaud / du soleil /
   du vent. (5); **to be continued** à suivre (6);
   you are tu es, vous êtes (P)
beach plage *(f)* (4)
beans: green beans *haricots verts *(mpl)* (8)
bear supporter
beard barbe *(f)* (4)
beast animal *(m)* (6)
beat battre
beautiful beau (bel, belle, *pl* beaux, belles) (1)
because parce que (P); **because of** à cause de
become devenir (7)
bed lit *(m)* (2); **go back to bed** se recoucher (7);
   go to bed se coucher (7); **stay in bed** rester
   au lit (2)
bedroom chambre *(f)* (3)
bedspread couverture *(f)* (3)
beef bœuf *(m)* (8); **roast beef** rosbif *(m)* (8)
beer bière *(f)* (2); **draft beer** demi *(m)* (2)
before avant (P); **before (doing)** avant de
   (faire); **before-dinner drink** apéritif *(m)* (8)
beforehand auparavant
begin commencer (2); **Le cours de français
   commence à...** The French class begins
   at. . . (P)
beginning début *(m); au début* at the beginning
   (6)
behaved: well-behaved sage (4)
behind derrière (3)
beige beige (3)
Belgium Belgique *(f)* (9)
believe (in) croire (à)
bell cloche *(f)*
belly ventre *(m)* (10)
belong to appartenir à, être à
belongings effets personnels *(mpl)* (3), affaires
   (fpl)
belt ceinture *(f)* (5)
benefit *(work)* bénévole (10)
benevolent bénévole (10)
beside à côté de (3)

besides de plus, d'ailleurs
best (le/la) meilleur(e) *(adjective);* (le) mieux
   (adverb)
better meilleur(e) *(adjective)* (1), mieux
   (adverb) (2); **do better to . . .** faire mieux
   de...; **it's better, you had better** il vaut mieux
   (10)
between entre (3)
beverage boisson *(f)* (2)
bicycle vélo *(m)* (3)
bicycle-riding: go bicycle-riding faire du vélo
   (5)
big grand(e) (1), gros(se) (1)
bike vélo *(m)* (3); **by bike** en vélo (4)
bikini bikini *(m)* (5)
bilingual bilingue
bill *(restaurant)* addition *(f),* (utilities) facture
   (f); **pay the bill** *(at a hotel)* régler la note
   (10)
billiards billard *(m)*
biology biologie *(f)* (1)
bird oiseau *(m)*
birth naissance *(f);* **date of birth** date *(f)* de
   naissance
birthday anniversaire *(m)* (4)
bizarre bizarre
black noir(e) (3)
blackboard tableau *(m)* (P)
blanket couverture *(f)* (3)
bless bénir
blond blond(e) (4)
blood sang *(m)*
blouse chemisier *(m)* (5)
blue bleu(e) (3)
blueberry myrtille *(f)*
blues *(music)* blues *(m)*
blush rougir (8)
board tableau *(m)* (P)
boat bateau *(m)* (4); **by boat** en bateau (4)
boating: go boating faire du bateau (5)
body corps *(m)* (10)
bodybuilding: to do bodybuilding faire de la
   musculation (8)
book livre *(m)* (P)
bookcase étagère *(f)* (3)
bookstore librairie *(f)* (1)
boot botte *(f)* (5)
border frontière *(f)* (10)
bored: be/get bored s'ennuyer (7)
boring ennuyeux(-euse) (1)
born né(e) (5); **be born** naître (5), He/She was
   born . . . Il/Elle est né(e)... (5)
borrow emprunter (9)
boss patron(ne) *(mf)*
both les deux
bottle bouteille *(f)* (8)
boulevard boulevard *(m)* (10)
bowl bol *(m)*
box boîte *(f)* (8), paquet *(m)*
boy garçon *(m)* (4)
boyfriend petit ami *(m)* (2)
bra soutien-gorge *(m)*
bracelet bracelet *(m)*
brave courageux(-euse)
Brazil Brésil *(m)* (9)
bread pain *(m)* (8); **bread-and-butter** tartine *(f)*
   (8); **loaf of French bread** baguette *(f)* (7);
   wholegrain bread pain complet *(m)* (8)
break casser; **break down** *(machine)* tomber en
   panne; **break one's arm** se casser le bras
breakfast petit déjeuner *(m)* (5); **to have/eat
   breakfast** prendre son petit déjeuner (5)

breathe respirer (10)
brief bref (brève)
briefly brièvement
briefs slip (m)
bright (colors) vif(-ive)
bring (a thing) apporter (9), (a person) amener;
   bring back rapporter
Britain: Great Britain Grande-Bretagne (f) (9)
Brittany Bretagne (f)
broccoli brocolis (mpl)
brother frère (m) (1); **brother-in-law** beau-frère
   (m) (4)
brown marron (3), brun(e) (4), (hair) châtain (4)
brunette brun(e)
brush (one's teeth) (se) brosser (les dents) (7)
Brussels sprouts choux (mpl) de Bruxelles
build construire
building bâtiment (m) (1); **administration
   building** centre administratif (m);
   apartment building immeuble (m) (3)
burn (oneself) (se) brûler
bus (in city) autobus (m) (3), (between cities)
   autocar (m) (4); **bus stop** arrêt (m)
   d'autobus (3)
business affaires (fpl); **business course** cours
   (m) de commerce (1)
businessman homme (m) d'affaires (5)
businesswoman femme (f) d'affaires (5)
busy chargé(e), occupé(e)
but mais (P); **nothing but** ne... rien que
butcher's shop boucherie (f) (8)
butter beurre (m) (8); **bread-and-butter** tartine
   (f) (8)
buy acheter (4)
by par; **by bike / boat / bus / car / plane / taxi**
   en vélo / bateau / autobus (autocar) / voiture
   / avion / taxi (4); **by chance** par *hasard; **by
   the way** à propos; **go by. . .'s house** passer
   chez... (2); **right by** tout près (de) (3)
Bye! Salut!, Ciao!

C

cab taxi (m) (4)
cabbage chou (m)
café café (m) (1)
cafeteria cafétéria (f); **university cafeteria**
   restau-u (m) (6)
Cajun cadien(ne) (4)
cake gâteau (m) (8); **chocolate cake** gâteau au
   chocolat (8)
calculator calculatrice (f)
Caledonia: New Caledonia Nouvelle-Calédonie
   (f) (9)
call communication (f); appel (m)
call téléphoner (3), appeler; **Who's calling?** Qui
   est à l'appareil?
calm calme (4), tranquille
calm down se calmer
camera appareil photo (m)
campground camping (m) (5)
camping camping (m) (5); **go camping** faire du
   camping (5)
campus campus (m) (1), fac(ulté) (f) (2)
can boîte (f) (8)
can (be able) pouvoir (4)
Canada Canada (m) (9)
Canadian canadien(ne) (P)
canceled annulé(e)

candy bonbon (m)
canned goods conserves (fpl) (8)
cap casquette (f) (5)
capital capitale (f)
car voiture (f) (3); **by car** en voiture (4); **rental
   car** voiture (f) de location (5)
carafe carafe (f) (8)
card carte (f); **bank card** carte bancaire (f) (9);
   credit card carte (f) de crédit (9); **identity
   card** carte (f) d'identité
care: I don't care. Ça m'est égal.; **take care of**
   s'occuper de, (health) (se) soigner
career carrière (f) (10)
careful soigneux(-euse); **be careful** faire
   attention (à)
carefully soigneusement
carpenter charpentier (m)
carrot carotte (f) (8)
carry porter (4); **carry away** emporter
cartoon dessin animé (m)
cash: pay cash payer en espèces (10)
cashier caissier(-ère) (mf)
cassette cassette (f) (P); **video cassette**
   vidéocassette (f) (3); **video cassette player**
   magnétoscope (m) (3)
castle château (m)
cat chat (m) (3)
cathedral cathédrale (f)
cauliflower chou-fleur (m)
cause cause (f)
cause causer
CD CD (m) (P), disque compact (m) (3); **CD
   player** platine laser (f)
celebrate célébrer (6), fêter
celebration fête (f) (4)
celery céleri (m)
cent centime (m) (2)
center centre (m); **shopping center** centre
   commercial (m) (4)
centime centime (m) (2)
central central(e) (mpl centraux)
Central America Amérique centrale (f) (9)
century siècle (m)
cereal céréales (fpl) (8)
certain certain(e), sûr(e)
certainly certainement
certificate certificat (m)
chair chaise (f) (3)
chance: by chance par *hasard; **have the
   chance to** avoir l'occasion de
change monnaie (f) (2); **Here's your change.**
   Voici votre monnaie. (2)
change changer (de) (6); **change one's mind**
   changer d'avis
character (disposition) caractère (m), (from a
   story) personnage (m)
charge: extra charge supplément (m) (10); **in
   charge of** chargé(e) de, responsable de
charge charger
cheap bon marché
check chèque (m) (9), (restaurant) addition (f);
   traveler's check chèque (m) de voyage (9)
cheese fromage (m) (2); **cheese sandwich**
   sandwich (m) au fromage (2)
chemistry chimie (f) (1)
cherry cerise (f) (8)
chest poitrine (f); **chest of drawers** commode (f)
   (3)
chicken poulet (m) (8)
child enfant (mf) (4)
childhood enfance (f)
chill frisson (m) (10)

China Chine (f) (9)
Chinese chinois (m)
chips chips (mpl)
chocolate chocolat (m) (2); **chocolate cake**
   gâteau (m) au chocolat (8); **chocolate-filled
   croissant** pain au chocolat (8)
choice choix (m) (8)
choose (to do) choisir (de faire) (8)
chop: pork chop côte (f) de porc (8)
chore: household chore tâche domestique (f)
Christian chrétien(ne)
Christmas Noël (m); **Merry Christmas!** Joyeux
   Noël!
church église (f) (4), (Protestant) temple (m)
cinema cinéma (m) (1); **cinema club** cinéclub
   (m) (2)
circumstance circonstance (f)
city ville (f) (3)
class cours (m) (P); **avoir cours** have class (6);
   first class première classe (f) (9); **tourist
   class** classe touriste (f) (9); **What is the
   homework for the next class?** Quels sont les
   devoirs pour le prochain cours?
classic classique (2)
classical classique (1)
classmate camarade (mf) de classe
classroom salle (f) de classe (1)
clean propre (3)
cleaner: dry cleaner teinturerie (f) (7)
climb (tree) grimper, (rocks) escalader
climbing: go mountain climbing faire de
   l'alpinisme; **go rock climbing** faire de la
   varappe
clinic clinique (f) (10)
clock horloge (f), **alarm clock** réveil (m) (7)
close fermer (2); **Close your book.** Fermez votre
   livre. (P); **The library closes . . .** La
   bibliothèque ferme... (P)
close to (location) près de (1); (a friend) uni(e),
   proche
closet placard (m) (3)
clothes vêtements (mpl) (3)
cloud nuage (m)
cloudy nuageux(-euse); **It's cloudy.** Il y a des
   nuages.
club club (m) (5); **cinema club** cinéclub (2);
   fitness club club (m) de gym (1); **nightclub**
   boîte (f) de nuit (1)
coach classe touriste (f) (9)
coast côte (f)
coat manteau (m) (5), pardessus (m)
code: zip code code postal (m) (3)
coffee café (m) (2); **coffee table** table basse (f)
coin pièce (f) de monnaie
Coke coca (m) (2)
cola coca (m) (2)
cold froid(e); **be cold** avoir froid (4); **cold cuts**
   charcuterie (f) (8); **It's cold.** Il fait froid. (5)
cold rhume (m) (10)
colleague collègue (mf)
collect collectionner
college: go to college étudier à l'université
Colombia Colombie (f) (9)
color couleur (f) (3); **What color is/are . . . ?** De
   quelle couleur est/sont... ? (3)
comb one's hair se peigner (7)
come venir (6); **come back** revenir (7); **come
   down (from)** descendre (de) (5); **come get
   someone** venir chercher quelqu'un; **Come
   see!** Viens voir! (3)
comedy comédie (f)
comfortable confortable (3)

commercial publicité *(f)*
communicate communiquer (10)
communication communication *(f)*
compact disc disque compact *(m)* (3)
company société *(f)* (10), compagnie *(f)*, entreprise *(f)*
compare comparer (6)
complain se plaindre
complete complet(-ète) (8); **in complete sentences** en phrases complètes (P)
completely tout à fait
complicated compliqué(e)
composition rédaction *(f)* (9), composition *(f)*
computer ordinateur *(m)* (2); **computer science** informatique *(f)* (1); **computer scientist** informaticien(ne) *(mf)*
concern concerner
concert concert *(m)* (1)
condition condition *(f)*
confidence confiance *(f)* (4)
confused confus(e)
congratulations félicitations *(fpl)*
connection *(telephone)* communication *(f)*
conservative conservateur(-trice)
conserve conserver
constantly constamment
consulate consulat *(m)*
contact contact *(m)*; **contact lenses** lentilles *(fpl)*
content content(e) (8)
continent continent *(m)* (9)
continue continuer (10)
continued: to be continued à suivre (6)
contrary: on the contrary par contre; au contraire
convenient commode (3)
cook faire la cuisine (5); (faire) cuire
cooking cuisine *(f)* (4)
cool frais (fraîche); **The weather's cool.** Il fait frais. (5)
copious copieux(-euse) (8)
co-renter colocataire *(mf)* (3)
corn maïs *(m)*
corner coin *(m)* (3); **on the corner (of)** au coin (de) (3)
corps: Peace Corps Corps *(m)* de la Paix (10)
corridor couloir *(m)* (3)
cost coûter (5)
cotton coton *(m)*
couch canapé *(m)* (3)
cough tousser (10)
count compter (2); **Count from . . . to . . .** Comptez de... à... (P)
country campagne *(f)* (3), pays *(m)* (3); **country music** musique country *(f)*; **in the country** à la campagne (3)
couple couple *(m)*
course cours *(m)* (1); **first course** *(of a meal)* entrée *(f)* (8); **Of course!** Bien sûr! (5), Évidemment!; **take a course** suivre un cours
court: tennis court court *(m)* de tennis
cousin cousin(e) *(mf)* (4)
cover couverture *(f)* (3)
cover couvrir
crab crabe *(m)*
crazy fou (folle)
cream crème *(f)* (8); **ice cream** glace *(f)* (8)
create créer
credit card carte *(f)* de crédit (9)
crime crime *(m)*, criminalité *(f)*
criminal criminel(le) *(mf)*

criticize critiquer
croissant croissant *(m)* (7); **chocolate-filled croissant** pain *(m)* au chocloat (8)
cross traverser (10)
crustaceans fruits *(mpl)* de mer 8
cry pleurer
cucumber concombre *(m)*
cuisine cuisine *(f)* (4)
cultural culturel(le) (4)
culture culture *(f)* (9)
cup tasse *(f)*
cure guérir
curly frisé(e)
current actuel(le)
currently actuellement, réellement
curtains rideaux *(mpl)* (3)
custom coutume *(f)*
customs *(border)* douane *(f)* (9)
cut: cold cuts charcuterie *(f)* (8)
cut (one's finger) (se) couper (le doigt); **cut class** sécher un cours
cycling cyclisme *(m)*

D

dad(dy) papa *(m)*
daily quotidien(ne) (7)
dairy laitier(-ère) (8)
dance danse *(f)* (9)
dance danser (2)
dancer danseur(-euse) *(mf)*
danger danger *(m)*
dangerous dangereux(-euse)
dark foncé(e); **dark-haired** brun(e) (4); **be dark** faire noir (6)
darling chéri(e) (7)
date date *(f)* (4); rendez-vous *(m)*; **What is the date?** Quelle est la date? (4)
date sortir avec
daughter fille *(f)* (4)
day jour *(m)* (P), journée *(f)* (2); **day after tomorrow** après-demain; **day before yesterday** avant-hier; **every day** tous les jours (2); **Father's Day** fête *(f)* des Pères; **Have a good day!** Bonne journée!; **Mother's Day** fête *(f)* des Mères; **the next day** le lendemain *(m)* (6); **the whole day** toute la journée (2); **What day is today?** C'est quel jour, aujourd'hui? (P)
daycare crèche *(f)*
daytime journée *(f)*
dead mort(e) (4)
death mort *(f)*
December décembre *(m)* (4)
decide décider (de) (8)
decision décision *(f)*; **make a decision** prendre une décision (7)
degree *(temperature)* degré *(m)*, *(university)* diplôme *(m)*
delay retard *(m)*
delicatessen charcuterie *(f)* (8); **deli meats** charcuterie *(f)* (8)
delicious délicieux(-euse) (6)
delighted ravi(e); **Delighted to meet you.** Enchanté(e).
deluxe de luxe (10)
demand exiger
democracy démocratie *(f)*
democratic démocratique
Denmark Danemark *(m)*

dentist dentiste *(mf)*
department département *(m)*; **department store** grand magasin *(m)*
departure départ *(m)* (9); **departure gate** porte *(f)* d'embarquement (9)
depend (on) dépendre (de) (5); **That depends.** Ça dépend.
deposit déposer (7)
depressed déprimé(e)
depressing déprimant(e)
depression déprime *(f)*
descend descendre (5)
describe décrire (9)
description description *(f)*
designer fashion *haute couture *(f)* (5)
desire avoir envie de (4), désirer
desk bureau *(m)* (3); **front desk** réception *(f)* (10)
despite malgré
dessert dessert *(m)* (8)
destroy détruire
detest (each other) (se) détester (7)
develop (se) développer
dictatorship dictature *(f)*
dictionary dictionnaire *(m)*
die mourir (5)
diet régime *(m)* (8); **be on a diet** être au régime (8)
different différent(e)
differently différemment
difficult difficile (P)
difficulty difficulté *(f)*
digest digérer
dine (out) dîner (au restaurant) (2)
dining: dining hall restaurant universitaire, restau-u *(m)* (6); **dining room** salle à manger *(f)* (3)
dinner dîner *(m)* (8); **before-dinner drink** apéritif *(m)* (10); **have dinner** dîner (2)
diploma diplôme *(m)*
direct diriger
direct direct(e)
directions indications *(fpl)* (10); **give directions** indiquer le chemin (10)
directly directement
dirty sale (3)
disadvantage inconvénient *(m)*
disappointed déçu(e)
disc: compact disc disque compact *(m)* (3); **compact disc player** platine *(f)* laser
discover découvrir
discuss discuter (de)
disguise (oneself) (se) déguiser
dish plat *(m)* (8); **do the dishes** faire la vaisselle (5); **ready-to serve dish** plat préparé *(m)* (8)
dishwasher lave-vaisselle *(m)*
disorder désordre *(m)*; **en désordre** in disorder (3)
diversity diversité *(f)*
divided partagé(e) (3)
diving: scuba diving plongée sous-marine *(f)*
divorce divorcer
divorced divorcé(e) (1)
do faire (2); **do aerobics** faire de l'aérobic (8); **do handiwork** bricoler (2); **Do the homework.** Faites les devoirs. (P); **do weight training** faire de la musculation (8); **Do you . . . ?** Est-ce que vous... ? (1); **I do not. . .** je ne... pas (p)
doctor médecin *(m)* (10)
doctorate doctorat *(m)* (10)

dog chien *(m)* (3)
dollar dollar *(m)* (3)
domestic domestique
door porte *(f)* (3); **next door** d'à côté
dormitory résidence universitaire *(f)* (1)
doubt doute *(m)*; **without doubt** sans doute (5)
doubt douter
down: go/come down descendre (5)
downtown (au) centre-ville *(m)* (3)
dozen douzaine *(f)* (8)
draft beer demi *(m)* (2)
drama drame *(m)*; **drama course** cours *(m)* de théâtre
dramatic dramatique
draw dessiner
drawer tiroir *(m)*; **chest of drawers** commode *(f)* (3)
drawing dessin *(m)*
dream rêve *(m)*
dream (about) rêver (de) (7)
dress robe *(f)* (4)
dress habiller; **get dressed** s'habiller (7)
dresser commode *(f)* (3)
drink boisson *(f)* (2); **before-dinner drink** apéritif *(m)* (8); **have a drink** prendre un verre (2)
drink boire (4)
drive conduire; **go for a drive** faire un tour en voiture
drop laisser tomber
drums batterie *(f)* (2)
dry sécher; **dry cleaner** teinturerie *(f)* (7)
duck canard *(m)* (8)
due to à cause de
dumb bête (1)
during pendant (5)
DVD player lecteur DVD *(m)*

E

each chaque (3); **each one** chacun(e) (7); **each other** se, vous, nous (7), l'un(e) l'autre
ear oreille *(f)* (10)
early tôt (4), en avance
earn gagner (10)
earring boucle *(f)* d'oreille
earth terre *(f)*
easily facilement (7)
east est *(m)*; **Middle East** Moyen-Orient *(m)* (9)
Easter Pâques *(fpl)*
easy facile (P)
eat manger (2); **eat breakfast** prendre son petit déjeuner (5); **eat dinner** dîner (2); **eat dinner out** dîner au restaurant (2); **eat lunch** déjeuner (2); **Let's sit down and eat!** Passons à table! (7)
eccentric excentrique
ecological écologique
economics sciences économiques *(fpl)*
economy économie *(f)*
editor rédacteur(-trice) *(mf)*
educate éduquer
education éducation *(f)*
effect effet *(m)* (6); **special effects** effets spéciaux *(mpl)* (6)
egg œuf *(m)* (8); **hard-boiled egg** œuf dur *(m)* (8)
eggplant aubergine *(f)*
Egypt Égypte *(f)* (9)
eight *huit (P)

eighteen dix-huit (P)
eighty quatre-vingts (2)
eighth *huitième (3)
either . . . or . . . soit... soit...
elect élire
election élection *(f)*
element élément *(m)*
elementary school école primaire/élémentaire *(f)*
elephant éléphant *(m)* (9)
elevated élevé(e)
elevator ascenseur *(m)* (3)
eleven onze (P)
else: What else? Quoi d'autre?; **What else can I get you?** Qu'est-ce que je peux vous proposer d'autre? (8)
elsewhere ailleurs
e-mail e-mail *(m)* (3), courrier électronique *(m)*; **e-mail address** adresse *(f)* e-mail (3)
embarrassed gêné(e)
embassy ambassade *(f)*
embrace (each other) (s')embrasser (7)
emotional sentimental(e) *(mpl* sentimentaux) (7)
employee employé(e) *(mf)*; **government employee** fonctionnaire *(mf)*
encounter rencontre *(f)* (7)
end fin *(f)*; **at the end (of)** au bout (de) (3)
end finir (8), (se) terminer; **end up doing** finir par faire; **French class ends . . .** Le cours de français finit... (P)
energy énergie *(f)*
engaged fiancé(e) (1); **get engaged** se fiancer (7)
engineer ingénieur *(m)* (10)
engineering études *(fpl)* d'ingénieur, génie *(m)*
English anglais *(m)* (P)
English anglais(e)
enough assez (de) (1)
enter entrer (dans) (5)
enterprise entreprise *(f)*
enthusiastic enthousiaste
entire entier(-ère)
environment environnement *(m)*
equality égalité *(f)*
equals: . . . plus . . . equals . . . ... et... font... (P)
errand course *(f)* (5); **run errands** faire des courses (5)
especially surtout (8)
espresso express *(m)* (2)
essential essentiel(le)
establish établir
euro euro *(m)* (2)
Europe Europe *(f)* (9)
European européen(ne)
eve: New Year's Eve party le réveillon *(m)* du jour de l'an
even même; **even though** bien que
evening soir *(m)* (P), soirée *(f)* (4); **At ten o'clock in the evening.** À dix heures du soir. (P); **Good evening.** Bonsoir. (P); **in the evening, evenings** le soir (P); **See you this evening.** À ce soir. (2)
every tout (toute, tous, toutes) (3), chaque (3); **every day** tous les jours (2); **every evening** tous les soirs (4)
everybody tout le monde (7)
everyone tout le monde (7)
everything tout (3)
everywhere partout (3)
exactly justement (3), exactement (10)
exam examen *(m)* (P)

example exemple *(m)*; **for example** par exemple (2)
except sauf (2)
exception exception *(f)*; **with the exception of** à l'exception de
exchange money changer de l'argent (9)
exciting passionnant(e)
excuse excuser
executive cadre *(m)*
exercise exercice *(m)* (P)
exercise faire de l'exercice (5)
exhausted épuisé(e)
exhibit exposition *(f)* (4)
ex-husband ex-mari *(m)*
exotic exotique (9)
expensive cher (chère) (3)
experience expérience *(f)*
explain expliquer (10)
express exprimer
expression expression *(f)* (10)
extra charge supplément *(m)* (10)
extracurricular extra-scolaire
extroverted extraverti(e) (1)
ex-wife ex-femme *(f)*
eye œil *(m)* *(pl* yeux) (10); **have . . . eyes** avoir les yeux... (4)

F

face figure *(f)* (7), visage *(m)*
facing en face (de) (3)
fact fait *(m)*; **in fact** en fait
fail (at) échouer (à)
fair juste
fairly assez (P)
fairy tale conte *(m)* de fée (6)
fall automne *(m)* (5); **in the fall** en automne (5)
fall tomber; **fall asleep** s'endormir (7); **fall in love (with)** tomber amoureux(-euse) (de) (6)
false faux (fausse)
fame renommée *(f)*
familiar: be familiar with connaître (4)
family famille *(f)* (P)
famous célèbre (4), fameux(-euse)
far (from) loin (de) (3); **as far as** jusqu'à (10)
farm ferme *(f)*
fashion mode *(f)* (5); **designer fashion** *haute couture *(f)* (5)
fast vite (7), rapide (8)
fast-food restaurant fast-food *(m)* (1)
fat matières grasses *(fpl)* (8)
fat gros(se) (1); **get fatter** grossir (8)
father père *(m)* (4); **father-in-law** beau-père *(m)* (4); **Father's Day** fête *(f)* des Pères
fatty gras(se)
favorite préféré(e) (2)
fear avoir peur (de) (4)
February février *(m)* (4)
feed donner à manger à (9)
feel (se) sentir (10); **feel like** avoir envie de (4)
ferocious féroce (6)
festival festival *(m)* (4)
fever fièvre *(f)*; **have fever** avoir de la fièvre
few: a few quelques (1), quelques-un(e)s
fewer . . . than moins... que
fiancé fiancé *(m)* (10)
fiancée fiancée *(f)* (10)
field champ *(m)*: **battlefield** champ *(m)* de bataille

fifteen quinze (P)
fifth cinquième (3)
fifty cinquante (P)
fight combattre, se battre; **fight (against)** lutter (contre)
fill (in) remplir
film film *(m)* (1)
finally finalement (6), enfin (7)
find trouver (4); **find out information** s'informer (9)
fine arts beaux-arts *(mpl)* (1); **It's going fine.** Ça va. (P)
finger doigt *(m)* (10)
finish (doing) finir (de faire) (8), terminer
firm entreprise *(f)*
first premier(-ère) (1); **at first** au début; **first course** *(of a meal)* entrée *(f)* (8); **first floor** rez-de-chaussée *(m)* (3); **first name** prénom *(m)* (3); **first (of all)** d'abord (4); **in first class** en première classe (9); **love at first sight** coup *(m)* de foudre (7)
fish poisson *(m)* (8); **fish shop** poissonnerie *(f)*
fishing pêche *(f)*; **go fishing** aller à la pêche
fist poing *(m)*
fitness club club *(m)* de gym (1)
fitting room cabine *(f)* d'essayage (5)
five cinq (P)
fixed: at a fixed price à prix fixe (8)
flashlight lampe *(f)* de poche
flight vol *(m)* (9)
floor étage *(m)* (3); **ground floor** rez-de-chaussée *(m)* (3); **on the floor** par terre (3); **on the second floor** au premier étage (3)
floral à fleurs
florist fleuriste *(mf)* (7)
flower fleur *(f)* (7)
flu grippe *(f)* (10)
fluently couramment
foggy: It's foggy. Il fait du brouillard.
folk music folk *(m)*
folklore folklore *(m)* (4)
follow suivre (7)
following suivant(e) (3)
food aliments *(mpl)*, nourriture *(f)*
foot pied *(m)* (10); **go on foot** aller à pied (4)
football football américain *(m)* (1)
for pour (P), pendant (5), depuis (7), comme (8); **for example** par exemple (2); **For how long?** Pendant combien de temps? (5); **for the last three days** depuis les trois derniers jours; **go away for the weekend** partir en week-end (5); **look for** chercher (3)
forbidden: It's forbidden to . . . Il est inderdit de... (10)
foreign étranger(-ère) (1)
forest forêt *(f)*
forget oublier
forgive pardonner
fork fourchette *(f)*
former ancien(ne)
formerly autrefois, jadis
forty quarante (P)
fountain fontaine *(f)*
four quatre (P)
fourteen quatorze (P)
fourth quatrième (4)
franc franc *(m)* (2)
France France *(f)* (1)
frankly franchement
free libre (2), *(price)* gratuit(e); **free time** temps libre *(m)* (4)
freedom liberté *(f)*

French français *(m)* (P); **French class** cours *(m)* de français (P); **How do you say . . . in French?** Comment dit-on... en français? (P)
French français(e) (1); **French fries** frites *(fpl)* (8); **French Polynesia** Polynésie française *(f)* (9); **French Quarter** Vieux Carré *(m)* (4); **French West Indies** Antilles *(fpl)* (9); **loaf of French bread** baguette *(f)* (7)
French-speaking francophone
frequently fréquemment
fresh frais (fraîche) (8)
Friday vendredi *(m)* (P)
friend ami(e) *(mf)* (P), copain *(m)*, copine *(f)* (6)
friendly amical(e) *(mpl* amicaux)
fries: French fries frites *(fpl)* (2)
from de (P), depuis
front: front desk réception *(f)* (10); **in front of** devant (3)
frozen surgelé(e) (8)
fruit fruit *(m)* (8); **fruit juice** jus *(m)* de fruit (2)
full plein(e)
fun amusant(e) (1); **Does that sound like fun?** Ça te dit? (4); **have fun (doing)** s'amuser (à faire) (7); **make fun of** se moquer de
funny drôle
furious furieux(-euse) (10)
furnishings meubles *(mpl)* (3)
furniture meubles *(mpl)* (3)
furthermore en plus (8)
future avenir *(m)* (10)

G

gain gagner; **gain weight** grossir (8)
game match *(m)* (1), jeu *(m)* (2); **video game** jeu vidéo *(m)* (2)
garage garage *(m)*
garden jardin *(m)* (5)
garden faire du jardinage (5), jardiner
gardening jardinage *(m)*
gate: arrival gate porte *(f)* de débarquement (9); **departure gate** porte *(f)* d'embarquement (9)
general: in general en général (6)
generally généralement
generous généreux(-euse)
gentle doux(-ce) (6)
gentleman monsieur *(m)*; **ladies-gentlemen** messieurs-dames (2)
geography géographie *(f)* (9)
geology géologie *(f)*
German allemand *(m)* (1)
German allemand(e)
Germany Allemagne *(f)* (9)
get obtenir (9), recevoir; **get along** s'entendre (7); **get bored** s'ennuyer (7); **get dressed** s'habiller (7); **get engaged** se fiancer (7); **get fatter** grossir (8); **get lost** se perdre (7); **get married (to)** se marier (avec) (7); **get off** descendre (de) (5); **get older** vieillir (8); **get on** monter (dans) (5); **get ready** se préparer; **get sick** tomber malade (10); **get taller** grandir (8); **get thinner** maigrir (8), **get to know** connaître (4); **get undressed** se déshabiller (7); **get up** se lever (7); **get well** guérir; **go/come get someone** aller/venir chercher quelqu'un; **What else can I get you?** Qu'est-ce que je peux vous proposer d'autre? (8)
gift cadeau *(m)*
girl (jeune) fille *(f)* (4)

girlfriend petite amie *(f)* (2)
give donner (2); **give (something) back (to someone)** rendre (quelque chose à quelqu'un) (7); **give directions** indiquer le chemin (10); **Give me your sheet of paper.** Donnez-moi votre feuille de papier. (P)
glad content(e)
gladly avec plaisir (6), volontiers (8)
glass verre *(m)* (2); **a glass of** un verre de (2)
glasses lunettes *(fpl)* (4)
global global(e) *(mpl* globaux)
glove gant *(f)*
go aller (2), se rendre (à / chez); **go across** traverser (10); **go away** partir (4), s'en aller; **go back** rentrer (2), retourner (5); **go bike-riding** faire du vélo (5); **go boating** faire du bateau (5); **go by/past** passer (2); **go camping** faire du camping (5); **go down** descendre (5); **go for a hike** faire une randonnée (9); **go for a ride** faire un tour (5); **go for a walk** faire une promenade (5); **go get someone** aller chercher quelqu'un; **go grocery shopping** faire les courses (7); **go in** entrer (dans) (5); **go home** rentrer (2); **go jogging** faire du jogging (2); **go on foot** aller à pied (4); **go out** sortir (2); **go rollerblading** faire du roller (6); **go scuba diving** faire de la plongée sous-marine; **go see** *(a person)* aller voir (4); **go shopping** faire du shopping (2); **go (water-)skiing** faire du ski (nautique) (5); **go to bed** se coucher (7); **Go to the board!** Allez au tableau! (P); **go to the movies** aller au cinéma (2); **go up** monter (5); **go walking** se promener (7), faire de la marche à pied; **go windsurfing** faire de la planche à voile; **How's it going?** Comment ça va? (P); **It's going fine.** Ça va. (P)
goal but *(m)*
god dieu *(m)*
golf golf *(m)* (2)
good: canned goods conserves *(fpl)* (8)
good bon(ne) (1), sage (4); **Good evening.** Bonsoir. (P); **Good idea!** Bonne idée! (4); **good in/at** fort(e) en; **Good morning.** Bonjour. (P); **Have a good day!** Bonne journée!; **Have a good weekend!** Bon week-end!; **One has a good time.** On s'amuse bien. (4)
good-bye au revoir (P)
government gouvernement *(m)*; **government worker** fonctionnaire *(mf)*
gracious gracieux(-euse) (6)
grade note *(f)*
gram gramme *(m)* (8)
grammar grammaire *(f)*
grandchildren petits-enfants *(mpl)*
granddaughter petite-fille *(f)* (7)
grandfather grand-père *(m)* (4)
grandma mamie *(f)* (7)
grandmother grand-mère *(f)* (4)
grandparents grands-parents *(mpl)* (4)
grandson petit-fils *(m)* (7)
granny mamie *(f)* (7)
grape(s) raisin *(m)* (8)
grapefruit pamplemousse *(m)*
graphic artist dessinateur(-trice) *(mf)* (de publicité)
gray gris(e) (3)
great super (P), extra, génial(e) *(mpl* géniaux) (4), formidable (7), chouette (9), magnifique
Great Britain Grande-Bretagne *(f)* (9)
green vert(e) (4); **green beans** *haricots verts *(mpl)* (8)
greet saluer

grilled grillé(e) (8)

grocery: go grocery shopping faire les courses (7); **grocery store** épicerie *(f)* (8)

ground terre *(f)*; **ground floor** rez-de-chaussée *(m)* (3); **on the ground** par terre (3)

ground: ground meat bifteck *haché (m)*

group groupe *(m)* (6)

grow (up) grandir (8)

guess deviner

guide guide *(m)* (9)

guidebook guide *(m)* (9)

guilty coupable

guitar guitare *(f)* (2)

gym club *(m)* de gym (1), gymnase *(m)*

H

hair cheveux *(mpl)* (4); **comb one's hair** se peigner (7); **hair stylist** coiffeur(-euse) *(mf)*

Haiti Haïti *(m)*

half moitié *(f)*

half demi(e) (P); **half-brother** demi-frère *(m)*; **half hour** demi-heure *(f)* (7); **half-sister** demi-sœur *(f)*; **It's half past two.** Il est deux heures et demie. (P); **a kilo and a half** un kilo et demi (8)

hall couloir *(m)* (3); **dining hall** restaurant universitaire, restau-u *(m)* (6); **lecture hall** amphithéâtre *(m)* (1); **residence hall** résidence universitaire *(f)* (1)

ham jambon *(m)* (2); **ham sandwich** sandwich au jambon *(m)* (2)

hamburger *hamburger (m)* (8)

hand main *(f)* (7); **on the other hand** par contre

handiwork: do handiwork bricoler (2)

handsome beau/bel (belle) (1)

hang up raccrocher

Hanukkah *Hanoukka (f)*

happen se passer (7), arriver; **What happened?** Qu'est-ce qui s'est passé? (6)

happiness bonheur *(m)*

happy content(e) (8), heureux(-euse) (7); **Happy Birthday!** Bon anniversaire!

hard dur(e); **have a hard time** avoir du mal à

hard-boiled egg œuf dur *(m)* (8)

hardly ne... guère

hard-working travailleur(-euse)

hat chapeau *(m)* (5)

hate (each other) (se) détester (7)

hatred *haine (f)*

have avoir (3); **have a drink** prendre un verre (2); **have breakfast** prendre son petit déjeuner (5); **have class** avoir cours (6); **have difficulty doing** avoir du mal à faire; **have dinner** dîner (2); **have fun (doing)** s'amuser (à faire) (7); **have just (done)** venir de (faire) (7); **have lunch** déjeuner (2); **have to** devoir (6)

hazel eyes yeux couleur noisette *(mpl)*

he il (1); **he is . . .** c'est... il est... (1)

head tête *(f)* (10)

health santé *(f)* (8); **health center** infirmerie *(f)*

healthy sain(e) (8)

hear entendre (7)

heart cœur *(m)*

heavy lourd(e)

Hebrew hébreu *(m)*

heels: high heels *hauts talons (mpl)*

height *hauteur (f)*, taille *(f)*; **of medium height** de taille moyenne (4)

hello bonjour (P), *(on the telephone)* allô (6)

help aider (5); **May I help you?** Je peux vous aider? (5)

henceforth désormais

her la (5); **to her** lui (9); **with her** avec elle

her son (sa, ses) (3)

here ici (P); **here is/are** voici (2)

herself se (7), elle-même

Hi! Salut! (P)

high élevé(e), *haut(e)*; **high fashion** *haute couture (f)* (5); **high heels** *hauts talons (mpl)*; **high school** lycée *(m)* (6); **high school student** lycéen(ne) *(mf)* (6)

hike: go for a hike faire une randonnée (9)

him le (5); **to him** lui (9); **with him** avec lui (6)

himself se (7), lui-même

hippopotamus hippopotame *(m)* (9)

his son (sa, ses) (3)

historic historique (9)

history histoire *(f)* (1)

hobby passe-temps *(m)* (2)

hockey *hockey (m)* (2)

hold tenir

holiday fête *(f)* (4); **national holiday** fête nationale *(f)*

home: at home à la maison (P); **come/go home** rentrer (2)

homework devoirs *(mpl)* (P); **Do the homework.** Faites les devoirs. (P)

honest honnête

honey chéri(e) (7), miel *(m)*

honeymoon lune *(f)* de miel, voyage *(m)* de noces

hope espérer (3)

horrible horrible (6), affreux(-euse)

horror movie film *(m)* d'épouvante (6)

hors d'oeuvre *hors-d'œuvre (m) (inv)*, entrée *(f)* (8)

horse cheval *(m)* *(pl* chevaux); **ride a horse** monter à cheval

horseback: go horseback riding faire du cheval

hose: pantyhose collant *(m)*

hospital hôpital *(m)*

hostel: youth hostel auberge *(f)* de jeunesse

hot chaud(e) (2); **be hot** avoir chaud (4); **hot chocolate** chocolat chaud (2); **The weather's hot.** Il fait chaud. (5)

hotel hôtel *(m)* (5); **hotel manager** hôtelier(-ère) *(mf)* (10)

hour heure *(f)* (5); **half hour** demi-heure *(f)* (7)

house maison *(f)* (1); **at/to/in my house** chez moi (2); **pass by the house of . . .** passer chez... (2)

household ménage *(m)*; **household chore** tâche domestique *(f)*

housemate colocataire *(mf)* (3)

housework ménage *(m)* (5)

housing logement *(m)* (3)

how comment (P); **How are you?** Comment allez-vous? (P); **How does that sound to you?** Ça te dit? (4); **How do you say . . . ?** Comment dit-on... ? (P); **how many** combien (de) (3); **How many are there of you?** Vous êtes combien? (4); **how much** combien (de) (3); **How much is it?** C'est combien?, Ça fait combien? (2); **How much is . . . plus / minus . . . ?** Combien font... et / moins... ? (P); **How old is . . . ?** Quel âge a... ? (4); **How's it going?** Comment ça va? (P); **How's the weather?** Quel temps fait-il? (5); **That takes how long?** Ça prend combien de temps? (4)

however pourtant

human humain(e)

hundred: one hundred cent (2)

hunger faim *(f)*

hungry: be hungry avoir faim (4); **I'm hungry.** J'ai faim, (2)

hunter chasseur *(m)*

hunting chasse *(f)*; **go hunting** aller à la chasse

hurry se dépêcher (de); **hurried** pressé(e)

hurt: one's. . . hurt(s) avoir mal (à)... (10); **hurt (someone)** faire mal (à quelqu'un)

husband mari *(m)* (2)

I

I je, j' (P)

ice glace *(f)*; **ice cream** glace *(f)* (8)

ice-skating patin *(m)* à glace; **go ice-skating** faire du patin à glace

icy: It's icy. Il y a du verglas.

idea idée *(f)* (4)

idealistic idéaliste (1)

identify identifier

identity card carte *(f)* d'identité

if si (5)

ill malade (10)

illness maladie *(f)*

image image *(f)*

immediately immédiatement, tout de suite

impatient impatient(e) (7)

important important(e) (5)

imprison emprisonner (6)

improve améliorer

impulsive impulsif(-ive)

in dans (P), en (P); **go in** entrer (dans) (5); **I live in (+ city)** j'habite à (+ city) (P); **in advance** à l'avance (9); **in bed** au lit (2); **in front of** devant (3); **in love** amoureux(-euse); **in order to** pour (1); **in the country** à la campagne (3); **in the morning** le matin (P); **in your opinion** à votre avis

include comprendre (8); **included** compris(e) (10)

indefinite indéfini *(m)*

independent indépendant(e)

India Inde *(f)*

Indies: West Indies Antilles *(fpl)* (9)

indigestion indigestion *(f)* (10)

Indochina Indochine *(f)*

industry industrie *(f)*

inequality inégalité *(f)*

inexpensive pas cher(-ère)

influence each other s'influencer

inform (oneself) (s')informer (9)

information renseignements *(mpl)* (3); **find out information** s'informer (9)

inherit hériter

in-laws beaux-parents *(mpl)*

inside à l'intérieur

insist insister

instant instant *(m)*

instead plutôt (4)

institution institution *(f)*

instructions instructions *(fpl)*

intellectual intellectuel(le) (1)

intelligent intelligent(e) (1)

intend avoir l'intention de (4)

interested: be interested in s'intéresser à

interesting intéressant(e) (P)

international international(e) *(mpl* internationaux) (10)
interpret interpreter
interpreter interprète *(mf)*
introduce présenter; **Let me introduce . . . to you.** Je vous/te présente...
introverted introverti(e)
investigation enquête *(f)*
invitation invitation *(f)* (6)
invite inviter (à) (2)
Irak Iraq *(m)*
Iran Iran *(m)*
island île *(f)* (9)
Israel Israël *(m)* (9)
it ce (P), il (P), elle (1), le, la (5); **How's it going?** Comment ça va? (P); **isn't it?** n'est-ce pas?, non? (1); **it's . . .** c'est... (P); **It's going fine.** Ça va. (P); **of it** en (8)
Italian italien *(m)*
Italian italien(ne)
Italy Italie *(f)* (9)
itinerary itinéraire *(m)* (9)
its son (sa, ses) (3)
Ivory Coast Côte-d'Ivoire *(f)* (9); **from the Ivory Coast** ivoirien(ne)

J

jacket veste *(f)*, blouson *(m);* **ski jacket** anorak *(m)* (5); **windbreaker jacket** blouson *(m)*
jam confiture *(f)* (8)
January janvier *(m)* (4)
Japan Japon *(m)* (9)
Japanese japonais *(m)*
Japanese japonais(e)
jar pot *(m)* (8)
jazz jazz *(m)* (1)
jeans jean *(m)* (5)
jelly confiture *(f)* (8)
jewelry bijoux *(mpl)*
job poste *(m)*, travail *(m)*
jog faire du jogging (2)
jogging jogging *(m)* (2); **go jogging** faire du jogging (2); **jogging suit** survêtement *(m)* (5)
join rejoindre
journal journal *(m)*
journalism journalisme *(m)*
journalist journaliste *(mf)*
judge juge *(m)*
juice jus *(m)* (2)
July juillet *(m)* (4)
June juin *(m)* (4)
just seulement (8); **have just (done)** venir de (faire) (7); **just anything** n'importe quoi

K

keep garder
key clé *(f)* (10)
keyboard clavier *(m)* (2)
kidney rein *(m)*
kilo kilo *(m)* (8)
kilometer kilomètre *(m)*
kind genre *(m);* **all kinds of . . .** toutes sortes de...
kindergarten école maternelle *(f)*
kiss baiser *(m)*, bise *(f)*
kiss (each other) (s')embrasser (7)

kitchen cuisine *(f)* (3)
knee genou *(m)*
knife couteau *(m)*
knit shirt polo *(m)* (5)
know *(person, place)* connaître (4), *(how, answers)* savoir (9); **get to know** connaître (4); **I don't know.** Je ne sais pas. (P); **known** connu(e); **What do you know about. . .?** Que savez-vous de... ? (8)
knowledge connaissance *(f)*

L

Labor Day fête du travail *(f)*
laboratory: computer lab laboratoire *(m)* d'informatique (1); **language lab** laboratoire *(m)* de langues (1)
lack of manque de *(m)*
lady dame *(f);* **lady's suit** tailleur *(m)*
lake lac *(m)*
lamb agneau *(m)*
lamp lampe *(f)* (3)
landscape paysage *(m)* (9)
language langue *(f)* (1); **language lab** laboratoire *(m)* de langues (1)
large grand(e) (1); copieux(-euse) (8)
last durer
last dernier(-ère) (5)
late tard (4), en retard; **later** plus tard (4); **See you later.** À tout à l'heure. (P)
laugh rire
laundry linge *(m);* **do laundry** faire la lessive (5)
law *(field)* droit *(m)* (10), loi *(f)*
lawyer avocat(e) *(mf)* (10)
lazy paresseux(-euse) (1)
learn apprendre (à) (4); **Learn...** Apprenez... (P)
leave quitter (4), partir (de) (4), sortir (de) (6), *(something behind)* laisser (3), s'en aller; **leave each other** se quitter (7)
lecture hall amphithéâtre *(m)* (1)
left gauche *(f)* (3); **to the left (of)** à gauche (de) (3)
leg jambe *(f)* (10)
leisure activity loisir *(m)*
lemon citron *(m)* (2); **tea with lemon** thé au citron *(m)* (2)
lend prêter (9)
lense: contact lenses lentilles *(fpl)*
less . . . than moins... que (1)
let laisser; **Let's see!** Voyons! (5); **Let's sit down and eat!** Passons à table! (8)
letter lettre *(f)* (7)
lettuce laitue *(f)* (8)
level niveau *(m)*
liberal libéral(e) *(mpl* libéraux)
library bibliothèque *(f)* (P)
life vie *(f)* (6)
lift weights faire de la musculation (8); faire des haltères
light *(weight)* léger(-ère) (8), *(color)* clair(e)
like aimer (2); **Did you like it?** Ça t'a plu? (6); **Does he like it?** Ça lui plaît? (9); **Do you like. . .?** Est-ce que vous aimez... ? (1); **I like . . .** J'aime... (1); **I like it.** Il/Elle me plaît. (5); **I would like . . .** Je voudrais (bien)... (2); **like each other** s'aimer bien (7); **What would you like?** Vous désirez? (2); **You'll like it!** Ça te/vous plaira! (9); **You would like . . .** Tu voudrais... , Vous voudriez... (2)

like comme (1); **What is/are . . . like?** Comment est/sont... ? (1)
lime citron vert *(m)*
lip lèvre *(f)*
liquid liquide *(m)* (10)
listen (to) écouter (2); **Listen to the cassettes.** Écoutez les cassettes. (P)
liter litre *(m)* (8)
literature littérature *(f)* (1)
little peu (de) (8); **a little** un peu (P); **little by little** petit à petit (6)
little petit(e) (1)
live habiter (2); **Do you live. . .?** Vous habitez... ? (P); **I live in . . .** (+ *city*) J'habite à... (+ *city*) (P)
liver foie *(m)*
living room salon *(m)* (3)
loaf of French bread baguette *(f)* (7)
loafers mocassins *(mpl)*
loan prêter (9)
lobster *homard *(m)* (8)
local local(e) *(mpl* locaux) (9)
located situé(e); **It is located. . .** Il/Elle se trouve... (3)
lock fermer à clé
lodge: ski lodge chalet *(m)* de ski
lodging logement *(m)* (3)
lonely seul(e)
long long(ue) (4); **a long time** longtemps (5); **as long as** tant que; **How long?** Combien de temps? (4); **no longer** ne... plus (8)
look (at) regarder (2); **look (+ *adjective*)** avoir l'air (+ *adjective*) (4); **look at each other** se regarder (7); **look for** chercher (3); **look like** ressembler à; **look very good on someone** aller très bien à quelqu'un
lose perdre (7); **get lost** se perdre (7); **lose weight** maigrir, perdre du poids (8)
lot: a lot beaucoup (P), **a lot of** beaucoup de (1); **not a lot** pas grand-chose
love amour *(m)* (6); **fall in love (with)** tomber amoureux(-euse) (de) (6); **love at first sight** coup *(m)* de foudre (7); **love story** film *(m)* d'amour (6); **true love** le grand amour (7)
love aimer (7), adorer; **love each other** s'aimer (7)
luck chance *(f)* (5)
lucky: be lucky avoir de la chance (9)
luggage bagages *(mpl)*
lunch déjeuner *(m)* (2); **have lunch** déjeuner (2)
lung poumon *(m)*
luxury luxe *(m)*
lyrics paroles *(fpl)*

M

machine machine *(f);* **automatic teller machine** guichet automatique *(m)* (7)
madam (Mrs.) madame (Mme) (P)
magazine magazine *(m)* (9)
magnificent magnifique
mail courrier *(m);* **e-mail** e-mail *(m)* (3), courrier électronique *(m);* **mail carrier** facteur *(m)*, factrice *(f)*
main principal(e) *(mpl* principaux) (8)
major in se spécialiser en
majority: the majority of the time la plupart du temps (7)
make faire (2); **make (+ *adjective*)** rendre (+ *adjective*); **make a decision** prendre une décision (7); **make money** gagner de l'argent

(10); **make up with each other** se réconcilier (7); **made up of** composé(e) de

make-up maquillage *(m)*; **put on make-up** se maquiller (7)

mall centre commercial *(m)* (4)

mama maman *(f)*

man homme *(m)* (1); monsieur *(m)*

management gestion *(f)*

mango mangue *(f)*

manual worker ouvrier(-ière) *(mf)*

many beaucoup (de) (1); **how many** combien (de) (3); **How many are there of you?** Vous êtes combien? (4); **so many** tant (de); **too many** trop (de) (6)

map plan *(m)* (9), carte *(f)*

March mars *(m)* (4)

market marché *(m)* (8)

marketing marketing *(m)* (1)

marriage mariage *(m)* (7)

married marié(e) (1); **get married (to)** se marier (avec) (7)

marvelous merveilleux(-euse)

Master's degree maîtrise *(f)* (10)

mathematics mathématiques (maths) *(fpl)* (1)

matter: It doesn't matter to me. Ça m'est égal.; **What's the matter?** Qu'est-ce qu'il y a?

May mai *(m)* (3)

may pouvoir (4); **May I help you?** Je peux vous aider? (5)

maybe peut-être (3)

me moi (P), me (9); **Give me . . .** Donnez-moi... (P)

meal repas *(m)* (6)

mean: What does that mean? Qu'est-ce que ça veut dire? (P)

mean méchant(e) (1)

means moyen *(m)*; **means of transportation** moyen *(m)* de transport (4)

meat viande *(f)* (8); **ground meat** bifteck *haché *(m)*; **meat spread** pâté *(m)* (8)

mechanic mécanicien(ne) *(mf)*

medical médical(e) *(mpl* médicaux)

medication médicament *(m)* (7)

medicine *(studies)* médecine *(f)*, *(medication)* médicaments *(mpl)* (7)

medium moyen(ne); **medium-sized** de taille moyenne (4)

meet *(by design)* retrouver (4), *(by chance)* rencontrer (7), faire connaissance (1), se réunir; **Let's meet at . . .** Rendez-vous à...; **meet each other** se rencontrer, se retrouver (7)

meeting réunion *(f)*

melon melon *(m)*

member membre *(m)*

memory souvenir *(m)*, mémoire *(f)*

menu *(fixed price)* menu *(m)* (a prix fixe), carte *(f)* (8)

merchant marchand(e) *(mf)* (6)

Merry Christmas! Joyeux Noël!

message message *(m)*

Mexico Mexique *(m)* (9)

microwave oven four *(m)* à micro-ondes

middle milieu *(m)*; **in the middle of** au milieu de

Middle East Moyen-Orient *(m)* (9)

midnight minuit *(m)* (P)

milk lait *(m)* (8); **coffee with milk** café *(m)* au lait (2)

milk laitier(-ère) (8)

million: one million un million (de) (3)

millionaire millionnaire *(m)*

mine le mien (la mienne, les miens, les miennes)

mineral water eau minérale *(f)* (2)

minus: How much is . . . minus . . . ? Combien font... moins... ? (P)

minute minute *(f)* (5); **at the last minute** au dernier moment

mirror miroir *(m)*

mischievous espiègle

miss mademoiselle (Mlle) (P)

mistake erreur *(f)*; **make a mistake** se tromper

mister (Mr.) monsieur (M.) (P)

mistrust se méfier de

modern moderne (1)

mom maman *(f)*

moment instant *(m)*, moment *(m)*

Monday lundi *(m)* (P)

money argent *(m)* (7); **save up money** faire des économies (9)

monkey singe *(m)* (9)

monster monstre *(m)* (6)

month mois *(m)* (3); **per month** par mois (3); **this month** ce mois-ci (4)

mood; in a good/bad mood de bonne/mauvaise humeur

more plus (1), encore (8): **more and more** de plus en plus (8); **more or less** environ (4); **more . . . than** plus... que (1); **no more** ne... plus (8), pas plus (4)

morning matin *(m)* (P); **at eight o'clock in the morning** à huit heures du matin (P); **Good morning.** Bonjour. (P); **in the morning, mornings** le matin (P); **morning hours** matinée *(f)* (2)

Morocco Maroc *(m)* (9)

mosque mosquée *(f)*

most: most of la plupart de (7), **the most** le (la) plus

mother mère *(f)* (4); **mother-in-law** belle-mère *(f)* (4); **Mother's Day** fête *(f)* des Mères

mountain montagne *(f)* (5); **go mountain climbing** faire de l'alpinisme; **go to the mountains** aller à la montagne (5)

mouth bouche *(f)* (10)

move (into) s'installer (à/dans) (7)

movement mouvement *(m)*

movie film *(m)* (1); **go to the movies** aller au cinéma (2); **movie theater** cinéma *(m)* (1); **romantic movie** film *(m)* d'amour (6); **show a movie** passer un film (6)

Mr. monsieur (M.) (P)

Mrs. madame (Mme) (P)

much beaucoup (de) (1); **as much . . . (as)** autant de... (que) (3); **how much** combien de (3); **How much is it?** C'est combien?, Ça fait combien? (2); **not much** ne... pas grand-chose; **so much** tellement (6), tant; **too much** trop (3)

muscular musclé(e)

museum musée *(m)* (4)

mushroom champignon *(m)*

music musique *(f)* (1); **music store** magasin *(m)* de musique (7); **listen to music** écouter de la musique (2)

musical *(movie)* comédie musicale *(f)*

musical musicien(ne)

musician musicien(ne) *(mf)* (10)

mussel moule *(f)* (8)

must devoir (6); **he/she must** il/elle doit (3); **one/you must . . .** il faut... (8)

mustache moustache *(f)* (4)

my mon (ma, mes) (3); **at/in/to my house** chez moi (2); **my best friend** mon meilleur ami *(m)*, ma meilleure amie *(f)* (1); **my friends** mes amis (1); **My name is . . .** Je m'appelle... (P); **with my family** avec ma famille (P)

myself me (7), moi-même

N

naive naïf(-ïve)

name nom *(m)* (3); **first name** prénom *(m)* (3); **His/Her name is . . .** Il/Elle s'appelle... (4); **My name is . . .** Je m'appelle... (P); **What is . . . 's name?** Comment s'appelle... ? (4); **What's your name?** Tu t'appelles comment? *(familiar)* (P), Comment vous appelez-vous? *(formal)* (P)

named: be named s'appeler (7)

nap sieste *(f)*; **take a nap** faire la sieste

nationality nationalité *(f)* (3)

native natal(e)

natural naturel(le)

nature nature *(f)*; **nature reserve** parc naturel *(m)*

near près (de) (1)

nearly presque (2)

Neat! Chouette! (9)

necessary nécessaire (10); **it is necessary to . . .** il faut... (8), il est nécessaire (de)... (10); **it will be necessary to . . .** il faudra...

neck cou *(m)*

necklace collier *(m)*

necktie cravate *(f)* (5)

nectarine nectarine *(f)*

need avoir besoin de (4); **I/you/we/you need** il me/te/nous/vous faut (9); **one needs...** il faut... (8); **What size do you need?** Quelle taille faites-vous? (5)

needy nécessiteux *(mpl)*

neighbor voisin(e) *(mf)* (9)

neighborhood quartier *(m)* (1)

neither non plus (3); **neither . . . nor** ne... ni... ni...

nephew neveu *(pl* neveux) *(m)* (4)

nervous nerveux(-euse); **feel nervous** se sentir mal à l'aise

never ne... jamais (2)

new nouveau (nouvel, nouvelle) (1); neuf (neuve); **Happy New Year!** Bonne année!; **New Caledonia** Nouvelle-Calédonie *(f)* (9); **New Orleans** La Nouvelle-Orléans (4); **New Year's Eve party** le réveillon *(m)* du jour de l'an

news nouvelles *(fpl)*, *(television program)* informations *(fpl)*

newspaper journal *(m)* (5)

next prochain(e) (4), ensuite (4); **next to** à côté (de) (3); **the next class** le prochain cours (P); **the next day** le lendemain (4)

nice sympathique (sympa) (1), gentil(le) (1); **The weather's nice.** Il fait beau. (5)

niece nièce *(f)* (4)

night nuit *(f)* (5); **night stand** table *(f)* de chevet

nightclub boîte *(f)* de nuit (1); **to go to a nightclub** aller en boîte (2)

nightgown chemise *(f)* de nuit

nine neuf (P)

nineteen dix-neuf (P)

ninety quatre-vingt-dix (2)

ninth neuvième (3)

no non (P); **no longer** ne... plus (8); **no more** ne... plus (8), pas plus (4); **no one** ne... personne; **No problem!** Pas de problème! (3)

nobody ne... personne

noise bruit *(m)*

none ne... aucun(e)

non-smoking section section non-fumeur *(f)*

noon midi *(m)* (P)

nor: neither . . . nor ne... ni... ni

normal normal(e) *(mpl* normaux)

normally normalement

north nord *(m);* **North America** Amérique *(f)* du Nord (9)

Norway Norvège *(f)*

nose nez *(m)* (10)

not ne... pas (P); **I do not work.** Je ne travaille pas. (P); **not. . . anymore** ne...plus (8); **not at all** ne... pas du tout (1); **not bad** pas mal (P); **not one** ne... aucun(e); **not yet** ne... pas encore (5); **Why not?** Pourquoi pas? (2)

notebook cahier *(m)* (P)

nothing ne... rien (5); **nothing at all** rien du tout (6); **nothing but** ne... rien que; **nothing special** rien de spécial (6)

notice remarquer

noun nom (3)

nourishment nourriture *(f)*

novel roman *(m)* (9)

now maintenant (P)

nowadays de nos jours

nowhere nulle part

number numéro *(m)* (3), nombre *(m)*, chiffre *(m);* **telephone number** numéro *(m)* de téléphone (3)

numerous nombreux(-euse)

nurse infirmier(-ière) *(mf)*

O

obey obéir (à) (8)

object objet *(m)*

observe observer (9)

obtain obtenir (9)

obvious évident(e)

obviously évidemment

ocean océan *(m)*

Oceania Océanie *(f)* (9)

o'clock: It's . . . o'clock. Il est... heure(s). (P)

October octobre *(m)* (4)

of de (1); **Of course!** Bien sûr! (5), Évidemment!; **of it/them** en (8)

off: get off descendre (de) (5)

offer proposer (8), offrir

office bureau *(m)* (1); **post office** bureau *(m)* de poste (7); **tourist office** office *(m)* de tourisme

often souvent (1)

oil huile *(f)*

okay d'accord (2); **It's going okay.** Ça va.

old vieux/vieil (vieille) (1), âgé(e) (4); **be . . . years old** avoir... ans (4); **get older** vieillir (8); **How old is . . .?** Quel âge a... ? (4); **oldest** aîné(e)

omelet omelette *(f)* (8)

on sur (1); **get on** monter dans (5); **on foot** à pied (4); **on Mondays** le lundi (P); **on page . . .** à la page... (P); **on sale** en solde (5); **on . . . street** dans la rue... (10); **on the corner (of)** au coin (de) (10); **on the ground/floor** par terre (3); **on the weekend** le week-end (P); **on time** à l'heure; **On what floor?** À quel étage? (3); **put on** mettre (5); **try on** essayer (5)

once une fois (6); **all at once** tout d'un coup (6); **once more** encore une fois; **once upon a time** il était une fois (6)

one un(e) (P); on (4); **no one** ne... personne; **not one** ne... aucun(e); **one another** se, nous, vous (7)

oneself se (7)

one-way ticket aller simple *(m)* (9)

onion oignon *(m)* (8); **onion soup** soupe *(f)* à l'oignon (8)

only seulement (8), ne... que; **only child** fille unique *(f),* fils unique *(m)*

open ouvrir; **Open your book.** Ouvrez votre livre. (P); **The library opens . . .** La bibliothèque ouvre... (P)

opinion avis *(m);* **in your opinion** à votre avis

opportunity: have the opportunity to avoir l'occasion de

opposite contraire *(m)*

optimistic optimiste (1)

or ou (P)

orange orange *(f)* (8); **orange juice** jus *(m)* d'orange (2)

orange orange (3)

Orangina Orangina (2)

orchestra orchestre *(m)* (4)

order commander (2)

order ordre *(m);* **in order** en ordre (3); **in order to** pour (1)

organization organisation *(f)* (10)

origin origine *(f);* **of. . . origin** d'origine... (7)

Orleans: New Orleans La Nouvelle-Orléans (4)

other autre (1); **each other** se, nous, vous (7); **on the other hand** par contre; **on the other side (of)** de l'autre côté (de); **sometimes. . . other times** quelquefois... d'autres fois (7)

ought to devoir (6)

our notre (nos) (3)

ourselves nous (7); nous-mêmes

out: dine out dîner au restaurant (2); **go out** sortir (2); **Take out a sheet of paper.** Prenez une feuille de papier. (P)

outdoor de plein air (4)

outdoors en plein air

outgoing extraverti(e) (1)

outing sortie *(f)* (6)

outside à l'extérieur, dehors, en plein air; **outside of** *hors de

oven four *(m);* **microwave oven** four *(m)* à micro-ondes

over (par-)dessus; **invite friends over** inviter des amis à la maison (2); **over there** là-bas (8)

overcast: The sky is overcast. Le ciel est couvert.

overcoat manteau *(m)* (5), pardessus *(m)*

owe devoir (6)

own propre

oyster huître *(f)* (8)

P

pack one's bags faire ses valises *(f)* (9)

package paquet *(m)* (8), colis *(m)* (7)

page page *(f)* (P)

pain douleur *(f)*

paint peindre

painter peintre *(mf)* (10)

painting tableau *(m)* (3), peinture *(f)*

pajamas pyjama *(m)*

pal copain *(m),* copine *(f)* (6)

pale pâle

panties slip *(m);* **panty hose** collant *(m)*

pants pantalon *(m)* (5)

papa papa *(m)*

paper papier *(m);* **sheet of paper** feuille *(f)* de papier (P)

parade défilé *(m)*

pardon me pardon

parents parents *(mpl)* (4)

Parisian Parisien(ne) *(mf)* (9)

park parc *(m)* (1)

parking lot parking *(m)* (1)

part partie *(f)*

participate (in) participer (à)

particular: in particular en particulier

partner partenaire *(mf)*

part-time à temps partiel

party *(social)* boum *(f)* (1), fête *(f); (political)* parti *(m)*

pass passer (2), *(exam)* réussir à (8); **pass by the house of . . .** passer chez... (2)

passenger passager(-ère) *(mf)*

passerby passant(e) *(mf)*

passion passion *(f)*

Passover la pâque juive *(f)*

passport passeport *(m)* (9)

past passé *(m);* **in the past** au passé, autrefois

past passé(e) (6); **It's a quarter past two.** Il est deux heures et quart. (P)

pasta pâtes *(fpl)*

pastime passe-temps *(m)* (2)

pastry pâtisserie *(f);* **pastry shop** pâtisserie *(f)* (8)

pâté pâté *(m)* (8)

patience patience *(f)* (4)

patient patient(e) *(mf)* (10)

patient patient(e) (6)

pay (for) payer (2); **pay attention (to)** faire attention (à) (8); **pay the bill** régler la note (10)

peace paix *(f);* **Peace Corps** Corps *(m)* de la Paix (10)

peaceful tranquille

peach pêche *(f)* (8)

peanut cacahouète *(f)*

pear poire *(f)* (8)

peas petits pois *(mpl)* (8)

pen stylo *(m)* (P)

pencil crayon *(m)* (P)

people gens *(mpl)* (1), on (4); **poor people** les pauvres *(mpl);* **some people** certains *(mpl);* **young people** les jeunes *(mpl)*

pepper poivre *(m)* (8)

per par (3)

percent pour cent

perfect perfectionner

perfect parfait(e) (7)

perfectly parfaitement (7)

performer artiste *(mf)* (10)

perhaps peut-être (3)

period période *(f),* époque *(f)*

permit permettre (de); **permitted** permis(e)

person personne *(f)* (6)

personal personnel(le) (3); **personal service** service personnalisé *(m)* (8)

personality personnalité *(f)* (1)

personally personnellement

Peru Pérou *(m)* (9)

pessimistic pessimiste (1)

pharmacist pharmacien(ne) *(mf)*

pharmacy pharmacie *(f)* (7)

philosophy philosophie *(f)* (1)

phone téléphone *(m)* (2); **on the phone** au téléphone (2)

phone téléphoner à (3); **phone each other** se téléphoner (7)

photo photo (f) (4)

physical physique

physics physique (f) (1)

piano piano (m) (2)

picnic pique-nique (m)

picture tableau (m) (3)

pie tarte (f) (8); **apple pie** tarte (f) aux pommes (8)

piece morceau (m) (8); **piece of advice** conseil (m) (8)

pierced percé(e)

pineapple ananas (m)

pink rose (3)

pity pitié (f); **what a pity** c'est dommage (7)

pizza pizza (f) (8)

place place (f) (3), endroit (m); **at/to/in . . .'s place** chez (2); **in its place** à sa place (3); **take place** avoir lieu

place mettre

plaid écossais(e)

plan projet (m) (4); **make plans** faire des projets (4)

plan organiser; **plan on doing** avoir l'intention de faire (4), compter faire (9)

plane avion (m) (4); **by plane** en avion (4)

plant plante (f) (3)

plastic plastique (m); **plastic bag** sac (m) en plastique

plate assiette (f)

play (theater) pièce (f)

play (a sport) jouer (à un sport) (2), faire (du sport) (5); **play music** faire de la musique (2); **play (the piano)** jouer (du piano) (2)

player: CD player platine laser (f); **DVD player** lecteur DVD (m)

plaza place (f) (10)

pleasant agréable (1)

please plaire à

please s'il vous plaît (formal) (P), s'il te plaît (familiar)

pleased content(e)

pleasure plaisir (m); **It would be a pleasure!** Avec plaisir! (6)

plum prune (f)

plumber plombier (m)

plus: How much is . . . plus . . . ? Combien font... et... ? (P)

P.M. de l'après-midi, du soir (P)

poem poème (m) (9)

point out signaler

Poland Pologne (f)

police police (f)

policeman agent (m) de police

polite poli(e)

political politique (1); **political science** sciences politiques (fpl) (1)

politics politique (f)

poll sondage (m)

pollution pollution (f)

Polynesia: French Polynesia Polynésie française (f) (9)

pool billard (m); **swimming pool** piscine (f) (4)

poor pauvre

pop music musique populaire (f) (1)

popular populaire (1)

population population (f)

pork porc (m) (8); **pork chop** côte (f) de porc (8); **pork roast** rôti (m) de porc

Portuguese portugais (m)

possibility possibilité (f) (10)

possible possible

post office bureau (m) de poste (7)

postcard carte postale (f) (9)

poster affiche (f) (3)

potato pomme (f) de terre (8)

poultry volaille (f) (8)

pound livre (f) (8)

poverty pauvreté (f)

powerful puissant(e)

preach prêcher

precisely justement (3)

prefer préférer (2), aimer mieux (2); **I prefer . . .** Je préfère... (1)

preferable préférable

pregnant enceinte (10)

preparations préparatifs (mpl) (9)

prepare préparer (2); **Prepare for the exam.** Préparez l'examen. (P)

prepared: prepared dish plat préparé (m) (8)

preschool école maternelle (f)

prescription ordonnance (f) (10)

pretty joli(e); **beau (belle)** (1)

prevent empêcher

price prix (m); **at a set price** à prix fixe (8)

print imprimé(e)

private privé(e) (10)

probable probable

probably probablement

problem problème (m); **No problem!** Pas de problème! (3)

process: be in the process of doing être en train de faire

product produit (m) (8)

profession profession (f), métier (m)

professional professionnel(le) (10)

professor professeur (m) (P)

program programme (m)

programmer programmeur(-euse) (mf)

progress progrès (m); **make progress** faire des progrès

promise promettre (de) (6)

pronunciation prononciation (f)

protect (oneself) (against) (se) protéger (contre)

protein protéines (fpl) (8)

proud fier(-ère)

province province (f) (3)

prune pruneau (m)

psychology psychologie (f) (1)

public: public transportation transports en commun (mpl) (9)

publish: publishing company maison (f) d'édition

pullover (sweater) pull (m) (5)

punish punir

purple violet(te) (3)

purpose: on purpose exprès

purse sac (m) (5)

put (on) mettre (5); **put away** rangé(e) (3); **put on make-up** se maquiller (7); **put on weight** prendre du poids (8)

Q

qualify qualifier

quarter quart (m) (P); **It's a quarter past two.** Il est deux heures et quart. (P)

question question (f) (P); **ask a question** poser une question (3)

quick rapide (8)

quickly vite (7)

quiet tranquille; **be quiet** se taire

quite assez, plutôt; **quite a bit** pas mal de

R

rabbit lapin (m)

radio radio (f) (2)

rain pluie (f) (5)

rain pleuvoir (5); **It's raining. It rains.** Il pleut. (5)

raincoat imperméable (m) (5)

raisin raisin sec (m)

Ramadan ramadan (m)

rapid rapide (8)

rarely rarement (2)

raspberry framboise (f)

rather plutôt (1), assez (1)

raw vegetables crudités (fpl) (8)

rayfish raie (f) (8)

reach atteindre

react (to) réagir (à)

read lire (2); **Read . . .** Lisez... (P)

ready (to) prêt(e) (à) (4); **get ready** se préparer; **ready-to-serve dish** plat préparé (m) (8)

real réel(le), véritable

realistic réaliste (1)

realize se rendre compte

really vraiment (6)

reason raison (f); **the reason why I . . .** la raison pour laquelle je...

reasonable raisonnable

receive recevoir (9)

recent récent(e)

recently récemment (5)

recognize (each other) (se) reconnaître (7)

recommend recommander

reconfirm reconfirmer

record disque (m), (sports) record (m)

record enregistrer

recorder: video cassette recorder magnétoscope (m) (3)

recount raconter (7)

recycle recycler

red rouge (3), (hair) roux (rousse) (4); **red wine** vin rouge (m) (2); **turn red** rougir (8)

reflect (on) réfléchir (à) (8)

refrigerator réfrigérateur (m)

refuse refuser (de)

region région (f) (4)

regional régional(e) (mpl régionaux) (4)

register s'inscrire (3)

regret regretter (6)

regularly régulièrement

relationship relation (f) (7), rapport (m)

relatives parents (mpl) (5)

relax se reposer (7), se détendre; **relaxed** décontracté(e)

religious religieux(-euse)

remain rester

remarried remarié(e)

remember se souvenir (de) (7)

rent loyer (m) (3)

rent louer (4)

rental car voiture (f) de location (5)

repeat répéter (2); **Please repeat.** Répétez, s'il vous plaît. (P)

replace remplacer

require exiger, demander; **required** requis(e), obligatoire

research recherche (f); **do research** faire des recherches

resell revendre

resemble ressembler à

reservation réservation (f) (9); **make a reservation** faire une réservation (9)

reserve: nature reserve parc naturel (m)

reserve réserver (9)

residence hall résidence universitaire (f) (1)

resources ressources (fpl)

respond répondre (6)

rest: the rest (of) le reste (de) (7)

rest se reposer (7); **rested** reposé(e)

restaurant restaurant (m) (1); **fast-food restaurant** fast-food (m) (1); **university restaurant** restau-u (m) (6)

restful reposant(e)

restroom toilettes (fpl) (3); W.-C. (mpl) (3)

retired retraité(e)

return retour (m) (9)

return rentrer (2), retourner (5); **return something to someone** rendre quelque chose à quelqu'un (7)

review (for a test) réviser

rice riz (m) (8)

rich riche (2)

ride: go for a ride faire un tour en voiture (en vélo) (4)

right (direction) droite (f), (legal) droit (m); **to the right of** à droite de (3)

right correct(e); **be right** avoir raison (4); **right away** tout de suite (6); **right by** tout près (de) (3); **right there** juste là; **right?** n'est-ce pas?, non? (1)

ring bague (f)

ring sonner (7)

river fleuve (m), rivière (f)

road chemin (m), route (f)

roast: roast beef rosbif (m) (8); **pork roast** rôti (m) de porc

rock: rock music rock (m) (1); **go rock climbing** faire de la varappe; **hard rock** *hard rock (m)

rollerblade faire du roller (6)

rollerblading roller (m); **go rollerblading** faire du roller (6)

romantic romantique; **romantic movie** film (m) d'amour (3)

room pièce (f) (3), salle (f); **classroom** salle (f) de classe (1); **dining room** salle à manger (f) (3); **fitting room** cabine (f) d'essayage (5); **living room** salon (m) (3)

roommate camarade (mf) de chambre (P)

round-trip ticket (billet) aller-retour (m) (9)

routine routine (f) (7)

row rang (m)

rug tapis (m) (3)

run courir; **run errands** faire des courses (5); **run into (each other)** se rencontrer (7)

Russia Russie (f) (9)

Russian russe (m)

S

sack sac (m) (5), paquet (8) (m)

sad triste

safari safari (m) (9)

safety sécurité (f)

sailing: go sailing faire de la voile

salad salade (f) (8)

salami saucisson (m) (8)

sale: on sale en solde (5)

salesclerk vendeur(-euse) (mf) (5)

salmon saumon (m) (8)

salt sel (m) (8)

same même (1); **all the same** quand même

sandal sandale (f) (5)

sandwich sandwich (m) (2); **bread-and-butter sandwich** tartine (f) (8); **cheese sandwich** sandwich au fromage (m) (2)

Santa Claus le père Noël

satisfied satisfait(e)

Saturday samedi (m) (P)

sauce sauce (f)

sausage saucisse (f) (8)

save sauver; **save up money** faire des économies (9)

saxophone saxophone (m) (2)

say dire (6); **How do you say . . . in French?** Comment dit-on... en français? (P); **They say that . . .** On dit que... (4)

scallops coquilles St-Jacques (fpl)

scarf (winter) écharpe (f), (dressy) foulard (m)

scenery paysage (9)

sceptical sceptique

schedule (classes) emploi (m) du temps (P), (train) horaire (m)

school école (f) (6); **high school** lycée (m) (6)

science science (f) (1); **computer science** informatique (f) (1); **political science** sciences politiques (fpl) (1); **science fiction** science-fiction (f); **social sciences** sciences humaines (fpl) (1)

scientist scientifique (mf); **computer scientist** informaticien(ne) (mf)

scuba diving plongée sous-marine (f)

sculpture sculpture (f)

sea mer (f) (9)

season saison (f) (5)

seat place (f), siège (m)

seated assis(e)

second seconde (f) (5)

second deuxième (3); second(e); **in second class** en classe touriste (9)

secretary secrétaire (mf)

section section (f)

security sécurité (f)

see voir (1); **as you see** comme tu vois (3); **Let's see!** Voyons! (5); **see each other** se voir (7); **See you in a little while.** À tout à l'heure. (P); **See you soon.** À bientôt. (P); **See you tomorrow.** À demain. (P)

seem avoir l'air... (4), sembler; **It seems to me that . . .** Il me semble que...

self-service restaurant self-service (m) (8)

sell vendre (7); **sell back** revendre (7)

semester semestre (m) (P)

send envoyer (7)

Senegal Sénégal (m) (9)

sensitive sensible

sentence phrase (f) (P); **in complete sentences** en phrases complètes (P)

sentimental sentimental(e) (mpl sentimentaux) (7)

separate séparer; **separated** séparé(e)

separately séparément

September septembre (m) (4)

serious sérieux(-euse), grave

serve servir (4); **served** servi(e) (10)

server serveur (m), serveuse (f) (8)

service service (m) (8); **service station** station-service (f)

set mettre (8); **set the table** mettre la table; **with a set price** à prix fixe (8)

settle (in) s'installer (à/dans) (7)

seven sept (P)

seventeen dix-sept (P)

seventh septième (3)

seventy soixante-dix (2)

several plusieurs

sexy sexy (2)

shall: Shall we go . . . ? On va... ? (2); **What shall we do?** Qu'est-ce qu'on fait?

shame *honte (f); **It's a shame!** C'est dommage! (7)

shape forme (f); **in shape** en forme (8)

share partager (3)

shared partagé(e) (3)

shave se raser (7)

she elle (1); **she is . . .** c'est... , elle est... (1)

sheet of paper feuille (f) de papier (P)

shelf étagère (f) (3)

shellfish fruits (mpl) de mer (8)

shirt chemise (f) (5); **knit shirt** polo (5)

shiver frisson (m) (10)

shock choquer

shoe chaussure (f) (5)

shop magasin (m) (4); **butcher's shop** boucherie (f) (8); **fish shop** poissonnerie (f); **pastry shop** pâtisserie (f) (8); **tobacco shop** bureau (m) de tabac (7)

shopkeeper marchand(e) (mf) (6), commerçant(e) (mf) (8)

shopping: go grocery shopping faire les courses (7); **go shopping** faire du shopping (2); **shopping center** centre commercial (m) (4)

short petit(e) (1), court(e) (4)

shorts short (m) (5)

shot piqûre (f); **give a shot** faire une piqûre

should devoir (6); **one shouldn't . . .** il ne faut pas (10)

shoulder épaule (f); **shoulder-length hair** cheveux mi-longs (mpl) (4)

show montrer (3), indiquer (3); **show a movie** passer un film (6)

show time séance (f) (6)

shower douche (f) (7)

shrimp crevette (f) (8)

shy timide (1)

sick malade (10); **get sick** tomber malade (10)

side côté (m); **on the other side (of)** de l'autre côté (de)

sight vue (f); **love at first sight** coup (m) de foudre (7)

similar to semblable à, pareil(le) à

simply simplement

since depuis, comme (7), depuis que (8)

sincere sincère

sing chanter (2)

singer chanteur(-euse) (mf)

single célibataire (1), seul(e)

sink (bathroom) lavabo (m) (10), (kitchen) évier (m)

sir monsieur (M.) (P)

sister sœur (f) (1); **sister-in-law** belle-sœur (f) (4)

sit (down) s'asseoir; **Let's sit down and eat!** Passons à table! (7); **Sit down!** Asseyez-vous!

site site (m) (9)

situation situation (f) (10)

six six (P)

sixteen seize (P)

sixth sixième (3)

sixty soixante (2)

size taille (f) (4); **medium-sized** de taille moyenne (4)

skate (fish) raie (f) (8); patin (m)

skateboard faire du skateboarding (6)

skating patin (m); **go (ice-)skating** faire du patin (à glace)

ski ski (m); **ski jacket** anorak (m) (5); **ski lodge** chalet (m) de ski

ski faire du ski (5); **water-ski** faire du ski nautique (5)

skiing ski (m) (5); **water-skiing** ski nautique (m) (5)

skin peau (f)

skinny maigre (8)

skirt jupe *(f)* (5)
sleep dormir (2)
sleepy: be sleepy avoir sommeil (4)
slice tranche *(f)*, pavé *(m)* (8)
slightly légèrement
slim down maigrir (8)
slip combinaison *(f)*
slow lent(e); **slow motion** ralenti *(m)*
slowly lentement (8)
small petit(e) (1)
smell sentir
smoke fumée *(f)*
smoke fumer (3); **smoked** fumé(e) (8)
smoking section section fumeur *(f)*
snack collation *(f)*
snail escargot *(m)* (8)
sneeze éternuer (10)
snob snob
snorkeling: go snorkeling faire du tuba
snow neige *(f)* (5)
snow neiger (5)
so alors (1), tellement (6), donc (7); **so many, so much** tant (de), tellement (de); **so-so** comme ci comme ça (2); **so that** afin que
soap savon *(m)*
soccer football *(m)* (1)
social social(e) *(mpl* sociaux); **social sciences** sciences humaines *(fpl)* (1); **social worker** assistant(e) social(e) *(mf)*
society société *(f)*
sociology sociologie *(f)*
sock chaussette *(f)* (5)
sofa canapé *(m)* (3)
soft doux(-ce) (6)
software logiciel *(m)*
sole sole *(f)*
solid-colored uni(e)
solution solution *(f)*
some des (1), du, de la, de l', en (8), certain(e)s
somebody quelqu'un (6)
someone quelqu'un (6)
something quelque chose (2)
sometimes quelquefois (2), parfois
somewhere quelque part
son fils *(m)* (4)
song chanson *(f)*
soon bientôt (P); **as soon as** aussitôt que; **See you soon.** À bientôt.
sorry désolé(e) (10); **be sorry** être désolé(e) (10), regretter (6)
sort: all sorts of toutes sortes de
sound: How does that sound to you? Ça te dit? (4)
soup soupe *(f)* (8); **onion soup** soupe *(f)* à l'oignon (8)
south sud *(m)*; **South Africa** Afrique *(f)* du Sud; **South America** Amérique du Sud *(f)* (9)
space espace *(m)*
Spain Espagne *(f)* (9)
Spanish espagnol *(m)* (P)
Spanish espagnol(e)
speak parler (2); **Do you speak. . . ?** Vous parlez... ? (P); **I speak . . .** Je parle... (P); **speak to each other** se parler (7)
special spécial(e) *(mpl* spéciaux) (6)
specialty spécialité *(f)* (4)
speech discours *(m)*
speed vitesse *(f)*
spend *(time)* passer (2), *(money)* dépenser
spider araignée *(f)*
spinach épinards *(mpl)*
spite: in spite of malgré
split partagé(e) (3)

spoon cuillère *(f)*
sports sport *(m)* (1); **play sports** faire du sport (2); **sports club** club *(m)* de gym (1)
spot site (9)
sprain: sprain one's ankle se fouler la cheville
spring printemps *(m)* (5); **in spring** au printemps (5)
square *(town)* place *(f)* (10)
stable stable (10)
stadium stade *(m)* (1)
staircase escalier *(m)* (3)
stairs escalier *(m)* (3)
stamp timbre *(m)* (7)
stand: I can't stand . . . J'ai horreur de...
star étoile *(f)*
start commencer (2); **Le cours de français commnce ...** French class starts. . . (P)
state état *(m)* (3); **United States** États-Unis (3) *(mpl)*
station: radio station station *(f)* de radio; **service station** station-service *(f)*; **subway station** station *(f)* de métro; **train station** gare *(f)*
stay séjour *(m)* (7); **Have a nice stay!** Bon séjour!
stay rester (2), *(at a hotel)* descendre (dans) (5)
steak bifteck *(m)* (8)
steal voler
stepbrother demi-frère *(m)*
stepfather beau-père *(m)* (4)
stepmother belle-mère *(f)* (4)
stepparents beaux-parents *(mpl)*
stepsister demi-sœur *(f)*
stereo chaîne stéréo *(f)* (3)
still encore (4), toujours
stomach ventre *(m)* (10)
stop: bus stop arrêt *(m)* d'autobus (3)
stop (s')arrêter (7); **stop by the house of . . .** passer chez... (2); **stopped up** bouché(e)
store magasin *(m)* (4); **bookstore** librairie *(f)* (1)
storm orage *(m)*
story histoire *(f)* (9), conte *(m)* (6)
stove cuisinière *(f)*
straight tout droit (10)
straightened up rangé(e) (3)
strange bizarre
strawberry fraise *(f)* (8)
street rue *(f)* (3); **on . . . street** dans la rue... (10)
strength force *(f)*
stressed (out) stressé(e) (8)
strict sévère
striped rayé(e)
strong fort(e) (8)
struggle (against) lutter (contre)
student étudiant(e) *(mf)* (P); **high school student** lycéen(ne) *(mf)* (6); **student center** centre *(m)* d'étudiants
studies études *(fpl)* (1)
study étudier (1), préparer les cours (2); **I study . . .** J'étudie... (1); **Study for the exam.** Préparez l'examen. (P); **What are you studying?** Qu'est-ce que vous étudiez? (1)
stupid bête (1), stupide
style style *(m)*; **American style** à l'américaine (8)
stylist: hair stylist coiffeur(-euse) *(mf)*
suburbs banlieue *(f)* (3); **in the suburbs** en banlieue (3)
subway métro *(m)* (4); **by subway** en métro (4)
succeed (in) réussir (à) (8)
such as tel(le) que (7)
sudden: all of a sudden tout d'un coup (6)

suddenly soudain, tout d'un coup (6), soudainement
suffer souffrir
sufficiently suffisamment
sugar sucre *(m)* (8)
suggest suggérer (6)
suggestion suggestion *(f)*
suit *(man's)* costume *(m)* (5), *(woman's)* tailleur *(m)*; **jogging suit** survêtement *(m)* (5)
suitcase valise *(f)* (9)
summer été *(m)* (5); **in summer** en été (5)
sun soleil *(m)*
sunbathe prendre un bain de soleil (4)
Sunday dimanche *(m)* (P)
sunglasses lunettes *(f)* de soleil (5)
sunny: It's sunny. Il fait du soleil. (5)
superior supérieur(e)
supermarket supermarché *(m)* (7)
superstore hypermarché *(m)* (8)
supplement supplément *(m)* (10)
supplies provisions *(fpl)*
sure sûr(e), certain(e)
surely sûrement
surf surfer; **surf the Net** surfer le Net (2)
surprise étonner, surprendre; **surprised** étonné(e), surpris(e) (10)
surrounded (by) entouré(e) (de)
swallow avaler
sweater: pullover sweater pull *(m)* (5)
sweatshirt sweat *(m)*
sweatsuit survêtement *(m)* (5)
Sweden Suède *(f)*
sweet doux(-ce) (6)
sweets bonbons *(mpl)*
swim nager (4), se baigner
swimming pool piscine *(f)* (4)
swimsuit maillot *(m)* de bain (5)
Switzerland Suisse *(f)* (9)
swollen enflé(e)
sword épée *(f)*
symptom symptôme *(m)* (10)
synagogue synagogue *(f)*
system: public transportation system système *(m)* de transports en commun (9)

T

table table *(f)* (3)
take prendre (4), *(something along)* apporter (9), *(a person)* emmener; **take a course** suivre un cours; **take advantage of** profiter de (9); **take a tour** faire un tour (4); **take a trip** faire un voyage (5); **take a walk** faire une promenade (5); **take out** retirer (7); **Take out a sheet of paper.** Prenez une feuille de papier. (P); **take place** avoir lieu
tale: fairy tale conte *(m)* de fée (6)
talent talent *(m)*
talented doué(e)
talk parler (2); **talk to each other** se parler (7)
tall grand(e) (1)
tan bronzer (9); **tanned** bronzé(e)
tangerine mandarine *(f)*
tart tartelette *(f)* (8)
taste goûter (9)
taxi taxi *(m)* (4); **by taxi** en taxi (4)
tea (with lemon) thé (au citron) *(m)* (2)
teacher *(elementary school)* instituteur(-trice) *(mf)*; *(secondary school)* professeur *(m)*
team équipe *(f)*
technical technique (1)

technician technicien(ne) *(mf)*
technology technologie *(f)*
tee shirt tee-shirt *(m)* (5)
telephone téléphone *(m)* (2); **talk on the telephone** parler au téléphone (2); **telephone number** numéro *(m)* de téléphone (3)
telephone téléphoner (à) (3); **telephone each other** se téléphoner (7)
television télévision (télé) *(f)* (2)
tell dire (6), raconter (7)
teller: automatic teller machine guichet automatique *(m)* (7)
temperature température *(f)*
temple temple *(m)*
ten dix (P)
tennis tennis *(m)* (1); **tennis court** court *(m)* de tennis; **tennis shoes** tennis *(mpl)*
tenth dixième (3)
test examen *(m)* (P), contrôle *(m)*
than: more . . . than plus... que (1)
thank (for) remercier (de) (10); **thank you** merci (P)
Thanksgiving jour *(m)* d'Action de grâce
that ça (P), ce (cet, cette) (...-là) (3), que (P), qui (10), cela; **I think that . . .** je pense que... (P); **that is . . .** c'est... (1)
the le (la, l', les) (1)
theater théâtre *(for live performances)* *(m)* (1); **movie theater** cinéma *(m)* (1)
theft vol *(m)*
their leur(s) (3)
them les (5); **of them** en (8); **to them** leur (9); **with them** avec eux, avec elles
themselves se (7), eux-mêmes *(mpl)*, elles-mêmes *(fpl)*
then alors (1), ensuite, puis (4), donc (7)
there là (10), y (4); **over there** là-bas (8); **right there** juste là; **there is, there are** il y a (1), voilà (2); **There are six of us.** Nous sommes six. (4); **There you are!** Te / Vous voilà! (7)
therefore donc (7)
these ces (...-ci) (3); **these are . . .** ce sont... (1)
they ils, elles, ce (1), on (4)
thick gros(se)
thickness épaisseur *(f)*
thief voleur *(m)* (6)
thin mince (1); **get thinner** maigrir (8)
thing(s) truc (1), chose(s) *(f)* (3), affaires *(fpl)*; **That's not my thing.** Ce n'est pas mon truc. (1)
think (about) penser (à) (7), réfléchir (à) (8); **I think that . . .** Je pense que... (P); **What do you think (about it)?** Qu'en penses-tu?, Qu'en pensez-vous?
third troisième (3); **Third World** Tiers Monde *(m)*
thirsty: be thirsty avoir soif (4); **I'm thirsty.** J'ai soif. (2)
thirteen treize (P)
thirty trente (P)
this ce (cet, cette) (...-ci) (3); **this evening** ce soir (2); **this is . . .** c'est... (1); **this month** ce mois-ci (4); **this semester** ce semestre (P); **this way** par ici (5)
those ces (...-là) (3); **those are . . .** ce sont... (1); **those (ones)** ceux (celles) (8)
thousand: one thousand mille (3)
three trois (P)
throat gorge *(f)* (10); **have a sore throat** avoir mal à la gorge
through par; **through the window** par la fenêtre (6)

throw jeter; **throw up** vomir (10)
thumb pouce *(m)*
Thursday jeudi *(m)* (P)
thus donc (7)
ticket billet *(m)* (9), ticket *(m)*; **one-way ticket** aller simple *(m)* (9); **round-trip ticket** billet aller-retour *(m)* (9); **ticket window** guichet *(m)*
tide marée *(f)*
tie cravate *(f)* (5)
tight étroit(e)
till: a quarter till moins le quart (P)
time *(clock)* heure *(f)* (P), temps *(m)* (2), *(occasion)* fois *(f)* (5); **a long time** longtemps (5); **at that time** à ce moment-là; **At what time?** À quelle heure? (P); **free time** temps libre *(m)* (4); **from time to time** de temps en temps (4); **have a hard time** avoir du mal à; **most of the time** la plupart du temps (7); **Once upon a time. . .** Il était une fois... (6); **one has a good time** on s'amuse bien (4); **on time** à l'heure; **show time** séance *(f)* (6); **sometimes . . . other times** quelquefois... d'autres fois (7); **time period** époque *(f)*; **What time is it?** Quelle heure est-il? (P)
timid timide (1)
tip pourboire *(m)*
tired fatigué(e) (6)
tiring fatiguant(e)
title titre *(m)*
to à (P); **go to a club** aller en boîte (2); **to . . .'s house/place** chez... (2)
toast pain grillé *(m)* (8)
toasted grillé(e) (8)
tobacco tabac *(m)* (7); **tobacco shop** bureau *(m)* de tabac (7)
today aujourd'hui (P)
toe doigt *(m)* de pied
together ensemble (2)
toilet toilettes *(fpl)* (3); W.-C. *(mpl)* (3)
tomato tomate *(f)* (8)
tomorrow demain (P); **the day after tomorrow** après-demain; **tomorrow morning** demain matin (4)
tonight ce soir (2); **See you tonight.** À ce soir. (2)
too aussi (P), trop *(much)* (3); **That's too bad!** C'est dommage! (7); **too many** trop (de) (8); **too much** trop (de) (6)
tooth dent *(f)* (7)
tour tour *(m)*; **take a tour** faire un tour (4)
tourism tourisme *(m)*
tourist touriste *(mf)*; **tourist class** classe touriste *(f)* (9); **tourist office** office *(m)* de tourisme (9)
touristic touristique (9)
toward(s) vers (2)
towel serviette *(f)*
town ville *(f)* (3); **in town** en ville (3)
toy jouet *(m)*
tradition tradition *(f)* (9)
traditional traditionnel(le) (8)
traffic circulation *(f)*
train train *(m)* (4); **by train** en train (4); **train station** gare *(f)*
training: to do weight training faire de la muscu(lation) (8), faire des haltères
translate traduire
translation traduction *(f)*
transmit transmettre
transportation transport; **means of transportation** moyen *(m)* de transport (4); **public transportation** transports *(mpl)* en commun (9)

travel: travel agency agence *(f)* de voyages (9); **travel agent** agent *(m)* de voyages (9)
travel voyager (2)
traveler's check chèque *(m)* de voyage (9)
treatment traitement *(m)*
tree arbre (1) *(m)*
trimester trimestre *(m)*
trip voyage *(m)* (4); **take a trip** faire un voyage (5)
tropical tropical(e) *(mpl* tropicaux) (9)
trouble difficulté *(f)*; **have trouble** avoir des difficultés, avoir du mal (à)
trout truite *(f)*
truck camion *(m)*, *(pick-up)* camionnette *(f)*
true vrai(e) (8); **true love** le grand amour (7)
truly vraiment (6)
trumpet trompette *(f)* (2)
truth vérité *(f)*
try (on) essayer (5)
T-shirt tee-shirt *(m)* (5)
Tuesday mardi *(m)* (P)
tuna thon *(m)* (8)
Tunisia Tunisie *(f)*
Turkey Turquie *(f)*
turkey dinde *(f)*
turn tourner (10); **turn in (something to someone)** rendre (quelque chose à quelqu'un) (7); **turn on** mettre; **turn red** rougir (8)
turnover: apple turnover chausson aux pommes *(m)*
TV télé (2)
twelve douze (P)
twenty vingt (P)
twin jumeau (jumelle) (1)
two deux (P)
type genre *(m)*
typical typique
typically typiquement (2)

U

ugly laid(e) (1)
umbrella parapluie *(m)* (5)
unbearable insupportable
unbelievable incroyable
uncle oncle *(m)* (4)
under sous (3)
understand comprendre (4); **Do you understand?** Est-ce que vous comprenez? (P); **I understand.** Je comprends. (P); **No, I don't understand.** Non, je ne comprends pas. (P)
understanding compréhension *(f)*
underwear sous-vêtements *(mpl)*
undressed: get undressed se déshabiller (7)
unfortunately malheureusement
unhappy malheureux(-euse)
United States États-Unis *(mpl)* (3)
university université *(f)* (P); fac(ulté) *(f)* (2); **university restaurant** restau-u *(m)* (6)
university universitaire (1)
unless à moins que
unlikely peu probable
unmarried célibataire (1)
unpack défaire ses valises
unpleasant désagréable (1)
until jusqu'à (2)
up: get up se lever (7); **go up** monter (5); **straightened up** rangé(e) (3); **up to** jusqu'à (2); **wake up** se réveiller (7); **wash up** faire sa toilette (7)

us nous (9)
use utiliser, employer
used to habitué(e) à
useful utile (10)
usually d'habitude (2)

V

vacation vacances *(fpl)* (4); **on vacation** en vacances
vaccination vaccination *(f)*
Valentine's Day Saint-Valentin *(f)*
vanilla ice cream glace à la vanille *(f)* (8)
variety variété *(f)*
VCR magnétoscope *(m)* (3)
veal veau *(m)*
vegetable légume *(m)* (8); **raw vegetables** crudités *(fpl)* (8); **vegetable soup** soupe *(f)* de légumes
vegetarian végétarien(ne)
very très (P); **very near** tout près (de) (3)
vest gilet *(m)*
veterinarian vétérinaire *(mf)*
video vidéo *(f)* (2); **video cassette** vidéocassette *(f)* (3); **video cassette recorder** magnétoscope *(m)* (3); **video game** jeu vidéo *(m)* (2)
Vietnam Viêtnam *(m)* (9)
view vue *(f)* (3)
vinegar vinaigre *(m)*
violence violence *(f)*
violent violent(e)
violet violet(te) (3)
virus virus *(m)* (10)
visa visa *(m)*
visit visite *(f)*; **medical visit** consultation *(f)*
visit *(place)* visiter (1), *(someone)* rendre visite à (7); **go visit** *(a person)* aller voir (4)
vitamin vitamine *(f)* (8)
vocabulary vocabulaire *(m)* (P)
voice voix *(f)*
volleyball volley *(m)* (2)
volunteer *(work)* bénévole (10)
vomit vomir (10)
vote voter

W

wait **(for)** attendre (7)
waiter garçon *(m)* (2), serveur *(m)* (8)
waitress serveuse *(f)* (8)
wake up (se) réveiller (7)
walk promenade *(f)* (5); **go for / take a walk** faire une promenade (5)
walk aller à pied (4), marcher (8)
walking marche *(f)* à pied; **go walking** se promener (7), faire de la marche à pied
wall mur *(m)* (3)
wallet portefeuille *(m)* (5)
want vouloir (6), avoir envie de (4)
war guerre *(f)*
warmth chaleur *(f)*
wash (se) laver (7); **wash clothes** faire la lessive (5); **wash up** faire sa toilette (7)
washbasin lavabo *(m)* (10)
waste gaspiller; **waste time** perdre du temps
watch montre *(f)* (5)
watch regarder (2); **watch over** veiller

water eau *(f)* (2)
watermelon pastèque *(f)*
water-skiing ski nautique *(m)* (5)
way: show the way indiquer le chemin (10); **this way** par ici (5)
we nous (1), on (4); **Shall we go . . . ?** On va... ? (2); **What shall we do?** Qu'est-ce qu'on fait?
weak faible
weakness faiblesse *(f)*
wear porter (4); **I wear a 42.** Je fais du 42. (5); **What size do you wear?** Quelle taille faites-vous? (5)
weather temps *(m)* (5); **The weather's bad / cold / cool / hot / nice / sunny / windy.** Il fait mauvais / froid / frais / chaud / beau / du soleil / du vent. (5); **What's the weather like?** Quel temps fait-il? (5)
Website site *(m)* Web (9)
wedding mariage *(m)*; **wedding anniversary** anniversaire *(m)* de mariage
Wednesday mercredi *(m)* (P)
week semaine *(f)* (P); **in one/two week(s)** dans huit/quinze jours (5)
weekend week-end *(m)* (P); **Have a good weekend!** Bon week-end!; **on weekends** le week-end (P)
weigh peser
weight poids *(m)* (8); **do weight training** faire de la musculation (8), faire des haltères; **gain weight** grossir (8); **lose weight** maigrir, perdre du poids (8); **put on weight** prendre du poids (8)
welcome bienvenue *(f)*; **You're welcome.** Je vous en prie. (10), Je t'en prie., De rien.
well bien (P); **get well** guérir; **well-behaved** sage (4)
west ouest *(m)*; **West Indies** Antilles *(fpl)* (9)
what qu'est-ce que (1), que (2), comment (P), quel(le) (3), ce que (5), ce qui (7), quoi (10); **What day is today?** C'est quel jour, aujourd'hui? (P); **What does that mean in English?** Qu'est-ce que ça veut dire en anglais? (P); **What is/are . . . like?** Comment est/sont... ? (1); **What is . . . 's name?** Comment s'appelle... ? (4); **What is your name?** Tu t'appelles comment? *(familiar)* (P), Comment vous appelez-vous? *(formal)* (P); **What luck!** Quelle chance! (5); **What's the weather like?** Quel temps fait-il? (5); **What time is it?** Quelle heure est-il? (P)
when quand (2)
where où (1); **from where** d'où (1)
whereas tandis que
which quel(le) (3), que, qui (10); **about/of which** dont; **which ones** lequel (laquelle) (6)
while tandis que, pendant que; **See you in a little while.** À tout à l'heure. (P)
white blanc(he) (3); **white wine** vin blanc *(m)* (2)
who qui (2)
whom qui (2), que (10)
whole tout (toute); **the whole day** toute la journée (2)
whose dont
why pourquoi (2)
widespread répandu(e)
widow veuve *(f)* (7)
widower veuf *(m)* (7)
wife femme *(f)* (2)
win gagner (2)
wind vent *(m)*

windbreaker blouson *(m)*
window fenêtre *(f)* (3); **ticket window** guichet *(m)*
windsurfing: go windsurfing faire de la planche à voile
windy: It's windy. Il fait du vent. (5)
wine vin *(m)* (2)
winter hiver *(m)* (5); **in winter** en hiver (5)
with avec (P); **coffee with milk** café au lait *(m)* (2)
withdraw retirer (7)
without sans (P); **without doing it** sans le faire
woman femme *(f)* (1); **woman's suit** tailleur *(m)*
wonder se demander
wonderful merveilleux(-euse)
word mot *(m)* (P); *(lyrics)* parole *(f)*
work travail *(m)* (9)
work travailler (2); **Does that work for you?** Ça te/vous convient? (9); **Do you work?** Tu travailles? / Vous travaillez? (P); **I work . . .** Je travaille... (P)
workbook cahier *(m)* (P)
worker *(manual)* ouvrier(-ère) *(mf)*
world monde *(m)*; **Third World** Tiers Monde *(m)*
world-(wide) mondial(e) *(mpl* mondiaux) (5)
worry (about) (se) préoccuper (de)
worse pire
would: I would like to . . . Je voudrais (bien)... (2); **What would you like to do?** Qu'est-ce que vous voudriez faire... (2); **You would like . . .** Tu voudrais... (2)
write écrire (9); **How is that written?** Ça s'écrit comment? (P); **Write the answer.** Écrivez la réponse. (P)
writer écrivain *(m)*
wrong: be wrong avoir tort (4); **What's wrong?** Qu'est-ce qui ne va pas? (10)

Y

yard jardin *(m)*
year année *(f)* (4), an *(m)* (5); **be . . . years old** avoir... ans (4); **Happy New Year!** Bonne année!; **New Year's Eve** le réveillon *(m)* du jour de l'an
yellow jaune (3)
yes oui (P), si (8)
yesterday hier (5)
yet pourtant, déjà; **not yet** ne... pas encore (5)
yogurt yaourt *(m)*
you tu, vous (P), te (9); **And you?** Et toi?, Et vous? (P); **See you tomorrow!** À demain! (P); **Thank you!** Merci! (P); **There you are!** Te / Vous voilà! (7); **with you** avec toi, avec vous
young jeune (P)
your ton (ta, tes) (3); votre (vos) (3); **Open your book.** Ouvrez votre livre. (P); **What is your name?** Tu t'appelles comment? *(familiar)* (P), Comment vous appelez-vous? *(formal)* (P); **your friends** tes amis (1)
yourself te, vous (7); toi-même, vous-même(s)
youth jeunesse *(f)*

Z

zero zéro (P), nul(le)
zip code code postal *(m)* (3)
zucchini courgette *(f)*
zydeco: musique zydeco musique *(f)* zydeco (4)

INDICE

TEXT CREDITS

p. 15 Document France Télécom —Les pages jaunes — édition 1991; **p. 54** *L'Étudiant* (la couverture), avril 1996 (No. 173), reprinted by permission; **p. 54** IPAG; **p. 54** SPLEF; **p. 79** Le Trapèze; **p. 89** L'heure du thé; **p. 90** Aux Trois Obus; **p. 120** Université Laval; **p. 121** *Brune*, n° 5, 1992; **p. 160** "Cœur des Cajuns," by Bruce Daigrepont, Bayou Pon Pon, ASCAP-Happy Valley Music, BMI from *Cœur des Cajuns* on Rounder Records (#6026); **p. 198** "Les week-ends des Français" *Figaro Magazine*, copyright Figaro Magazine/SOFRES, n° 13960, 1989; **p. 200** "Les Passe-temps," *Figaro Magazine*, copyright Figaro Magazine/SOFRES, n° 13960, 1989; **p. 213** *Pariscope*, 4–11 décembre 1996; **p. 237** *Première*, n° 245, août 1997; **p. 274** "Tous les matins, je me lève," vu dans *Vogue Hommes*, n° 152, septembre 1992; **p. 275** *Rouen Poche*, n° 92, du 15 au 21 juillet 1987; **p. 292** Maraîchers; **p. 293** Maraîchers; **p. 316** "Déjeuner du matin," Jacques Prévert, *Paroles,* 1942, © Éditions Gallimard; **p. 352** "La tortue qui chante" de *Les aventures de Yévi au pays des monstres,* Hatier 1987; **p. 359** *Selected hotels of France,* French Government Tourist Office; **p. 361** Deville & Georges, *Les départements d'outre-mer,* © Découvertes Gallimard, 1996; **pp. 368, 369** Excerpts from Michelin Guide, *France Hôtels et Restaurants,* édition 1997, Pneu Michelin, Services de Tourisme: © MICHELIN, d'après Guide FRANCE (1997). Autorisation No. 9711527; **pp. 384, 385** Extrait de la Côte d'Ivoire d'aujourd'hui" de Mylène Rémy, Editions du Jaguar, Paris; **p. 390** "Si j'étais un Dieu nègre," par A. Martin Honoré Zeufack, vu dans le livre *Poèmes de demain,* Éditions Nouvelles du Sud, 1980; **p. 392** "Préférence," par Claude-Emmanuel Abolo Bowole, vu dans le livre *Poèmes de demain,* Éditions Nouvelles du Sud, 1980; **p. 393** "Je vous remercie mon Dieu," par Bernard Dadié, Éditions Seghers

PHOTO CREDITS

Unless specified below, all the photos in this text were selected from the Heinle & Heinle Image Resource Bank.

Photos from Corbis Images:
p. 28 (bottom) © Charles and Josette Lenars/CORBIS; **p. 29** (top left) © Marc Garanger/CORBIS; **p. 52** (left) © Reuters New Media Inc./CORBIS; **p. 62** (top right) © Jim Zuckerman/CORBIS; **p. 83** © Temp Sport/CORBIS; **p. 132** (top) © Frances G. Mayer/CORBIS, (bottom) © Philip Gould/CORBIS; **p. 134** (top left) © Neil Rabinowitz/CORBIS, (top center) © Reuters New Media Inc./CORBIS, (top right, bottom left) © Philip Gould/CORBIS; **p. 135** (top left) © Nathan Benn/CORBIS, (top right) © Philp Gould/CORBIS, (left, bottom) © Owen Franken/CORBIS (bottom right) © Philip Gould/CORBIS; **p. 149** © Robert Holmes/CORBIS; **p. 156** © Philip Gould/CORBIS; **p. 159** Danny Lehman/CORBIS; **p. 166** (bottom) © Philip Gould/CORBIS; **p. 168** (bottom) © Philippe Gould/CORBIS; **p. 180** (left) © Sandro Vannini/CORBIS; **p. 189** (top left) © Bill Ross/CORBIS, (top right, bottom) © Robert Holmes/CORBIS; **p. 193** (top left) Hugh Rooney, Eye Ubiquitous/CORBIS, (center) Macduff Everton/CORBIS; **p. 207** (bottom) © Yann Arthus-Bertand/CORBIS; **p. 241** © Reuters New Media Inc./CORBIS; p. 244 © (top) Catherine Kamow/CORBIS, (bottom left) © Marc Garanger/CORBIS; **p. 259** © Owen Franken/CORBIS; **p. 326** (top) © Albrecht G. Schaefer/CORBIS, (bottom) © Sabdro Vannini/CORBIS; **p. 327** (top) © Paul Almasy/CORBIS; **p. 346** (top) © Tiziana and Gianni Baldizzone/CORBIS; **p. 374** © Lawrence Manning/CORBIS; **p. 349** (top left) © Michael Freeman/CORBIS; **p. 363** (center) © Charles and Josette Lenars/CORBIS; **p. 376** (top left) © R. W. Jones/CORBIS, (top center) © leng/CORBIS, (middle left) © AFP/CORBIS, (middle right) Charles D. Winters/Stock Boston; **p. 384** (top) Daniel Lainé/CORBIS; **p. 391** (top right) Brian Vikander/CORBIS; **p. 392** Richard List/CORBIS;

Photos from other sources
p. 2 Evergreen House Foundation/The Johns Hopkins University; **p. 5** (top right) Beryl Goldberg, (top left) Bonnie Kamin/Photo Edit, (bottom right) Gontier/The Image Works; **p. 26 Giraudon/Art Resource, New York** © 1998 Estate of Pablo Picasso/Artists Rights Society (ARS), New York; **p. 29** (bottom left) R. Sidney/The Image Works, (bottom right) D. Bretzfolder/Photo Edit; **p. 56** (top) Beryl Goldberg; **p. 57** Philippe Caron; **p. 60** (left) Beryl Goldberge, (right) Giraudon/Art Resource, New York © 1998 Succession H. Matisse/Artists Rights Society (ARS), New York; **p. 62** (top left) Beryl Goldberg; **p. 63** (top) © Thierry Prat/Sygma, (center left) Tophan/The Image Works, (center right, bottom left, bottom right) Beryl Goldberg; **p. 92** Comstock; **p. 93** (top left) © IPA/The Image Works, (top right) Nicholas Raducanu; **p. 96** (top) Gerard Goron/Sygma, (bottom) Ulrike Welsch; **p. 98** The National Gallery of Canada, Vincent Massey Bequest, 1968; **p. 100** David G. Houser; **p. 101** (top) Alain Errard/ Liaison International, (bottom) Lee Snider/The Image Works; **p. 119** (left) Jeff Greenberg/Photo Edit, (right) Ulrike Welsch; **p. 128** FPG International; **p. 166** (top) © David Simson/Stock Boston; **p. 168** Giraudon/Art Resource, New York; **p. 170** (top left) Ulrike Welsch, (bottom right) Rhoda Sidney/Photo Edit;

France

MER DU NORD

Pays-Bas

Angleterre

Allemagne

Dunkerque
Calais
Belgique

NORD-PAS-
DE-CALAIS
Lille
Valenciennes

Luxembourg

LA MANCHE

Cherbourg
HAUTE-
NORMANDIE
Amiens
PICARDIE

Le Havre
Rouen
Reims
Metz
LORRAINE
ALSACE

Caen
Seine
Nancy
Strasbourg

Saint-Malo
BASSE-
NORMANDIE
Versailles
☆Paris
CHAMPAGNE-
ARDENNE
ÎLE-DE-
FRANCE
Troyes
Moselle
Mulhouse

Brest
BRETAGNE
Fougères
Rennes
Le Mans
Orléans
Seine
Saône
Besançon

PAYS DE LA LOIRE
Angers
Blois
Chambord
BOURGOGNE
Dijon
FRANCHE-
COMTÉ

St-Nazaire
Tours
Chenonceaux
Chalon-sur-
Saône
Suisse

Nantes
Chinon
Azay-le-
Rideau
Bourges
Nevers
Loire

CENTRE
Loire

Poitiers

La Rochelle
LIMOUSIN
Vichy
Rhône
Annecy

OCÉAN
POITOU-
CHARENTES
Limoges
Clermont-
Ferrand
Lyon
Italie

ATLANTIQUE
Saint Étienne
RHÔNE-ALPES
Grenoble

Périgueux
AUVERGNE

Bordeaux
MASSIF CENTRAL
Rodez
PROVENCE-
ALPES-
CÔTE-
D'AZUR

AQUITAINE
Garonne
MIDI-PYRÉNÉES
Rhône
Avignon
Monte-
Carlo
Monaco

Biarritz
Bayonne
Nîmes
Tarascon
Grasse
Aix-en-
Provence
Nice

Pau
PYRÉNÉES
Toulouse
Montpellier
Béziers
Toulon
Cannes

Carcassonne
Narbonne
Marseille

Espagne
LANGUEDOC-
ROUSSILLON

Andorre
Perpignan

MER MÉDITERRANÉE

0   75 km

©1993 Magellan Geographix℠Santa Barbara CA

CORSE
Ajaccio

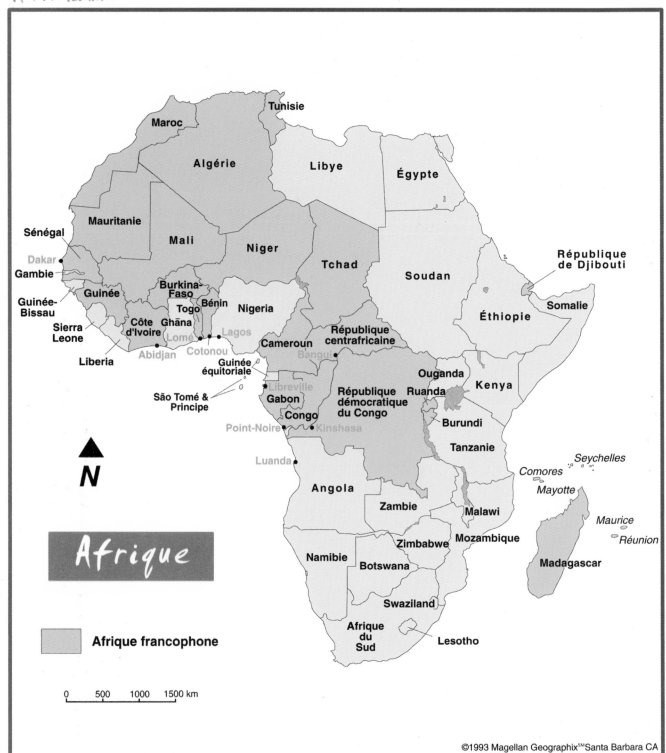

Afrique